ALSO BY SUSAN BRAUDY

Between Marriage and Divorce

Who Killed Sal Mineo?

What the Movies Made Me Do

THIS CRAZY THING
CALLED LOVE

THIS CRAZY THING CALLED LOVE

The Golden World and Fatal Marriage
of Ann and Billy Woodward

Susan Braudy

Alfred A. Knopf

NEW YORK

1992

THIS IS A BORZOI BOOK
PUBLISHED BY ALFRED A. KNOPF, INC.

Library of Congress Cataloging-in-Publication Data

Braudy, Susan.
This crazy thing called love / Susan Braudy. — 1st ed.
  p. cm.
Includes bibliographical references and index.
ISBN 0-394-53247-3
1. Murder—New York (State)—Case studies. 2. Woodward, Ann, d. 1975. 3. Woodward, William, d. 1955. I. Title.
HV6533.N5B73 1992
364.1′523′09747245—dc20   91-35738
                                                              CIP

Manufactured in the United States of America

First Edition

To Edward Patterson, Charles Allen, Jr.,
Cynthia and Edward Lasker, Victoria Wilson,
and the memory of Bill Sudduth

"What is this thing called love?
This funny thing called love?
Just who can solve its mystery?"

—COLE PORTER,
"What Is This Thing Called Love"
from *Wake Up and Dream,* 1939

"In the real world, no hatred is totally without
justification, no love totally innocent."

—W. H. AUDEN

CONTENTS

INTRODUCTION

I met Ann Woodward's sons in the early 1970s. Soon afterward, a mutual friend told me a piece of gossip: it seemed their mother, Ann, "a common chorus girl and a former prostitute," had murdered their father because he had been having "an affair with Marilyn Monroe." It reminded me of high and low fiction—Greek tragedy and bad movies. Most amazing was the possibility that it could be true. It turned out to be one of many Woodward "myths"—containing a distorted truth.

The Woodward boys had the diffident manners of rich European princes in 1950s movies. They kissed my hand warmly in greeting; in dungarees they were dressing down.

In the *New York Times* morgue file on the family there is a front-page article on the shooting of America's outstanding sportsman William Woodward, Jr., by his beautiful wife, Ann—formerly Angeline Crowell. The *Times* identified Ann as a former Copacabana dancer—another skewed fact.

The ten-page *Life* magazine article from November 1955 was entitled "The Shooting of the Century." It was clear from the clippings that most Americans believed Ann Woodward was guilty of murder, despite the fact that she had been cleared by a Nassau County grand jury three weeks after the shooting occurred. What was unclear was why the story and the Woodwards people had merited so much publicity.

What struck me most was the October 31, 1955, wire service interview with Ann Woodward's father, a retired Detroit trolley-car conductor who had not seen his daughter in fifteen years. Jesse Claude Crowell had been under the mistaken impression that his daughter had gone to Hollywood and changed her name from Angeline ("Angie") Crowell to Eve Arden. Jesse Claude went to every one of Eve Arden's movies, including *Mildred Pierce,* several times over to stare proudly at what he thought was his daughter's image. Eve Arden reminded him of his first wife, Ethel Smiley Crowell Jordan, Ann's mother.

The confusion of Ann's father suggested a lifetime of guilty secrets and seemed to indict Ann Woodward, at the very least, of disloyalty.

Shortly thereafter I went to a party given by Libby Woodward Pratt, who greeted me at the door of her cottage, Price's Neck, on the beach at Newport. I had just sailed up to her dock on her nephew's boat, the *Albacore.* Mrs. Pratt said, upon learning that I was a journalist, "You work, my dear? Isn't it wonderful that my nephews are so democratic?"

I met Ann Woodward only once, after having dinner with her younger son, Jimmy.

Jimmy announced he had to retrieve a letter from his mama's apartment. (He and his brother said "m'mah" as though they were English.) Ann was on a three-week trip to Australia. He avoided the lobby of his mother's Fifth Avenue building, letting himself into her duplex maisonette from the street entrance.

His mother had unexpectedly returned from the South Pacific; neither she nor Jimmy seemed pleased to see the other. As Ann Woodward glanced at my bare knees, I realized that I was dressed improperly—and it mattered. It took me years to understand that Ann was treating me in the Woodward manner. This was the way her husband's family had treated her.

I stared at the woman with the uneasy blue-green eyes. Jimmy brushed past his mother, mumbling about retrieving a postcard. I was invited to the drawing room, where a Louis Vuitton trunk was opened to neat piles of clothing and a framed photograph of Ann posed with a rifle next to a dead tiger.

Ann Woodward sat on the edge of a silk couch by the fireplace. The room resembled an unused Broadway stage set. The bibelots, pictures, and chairs were placed in unfamiliar patterns. A curved mirror suggested the 1940s and France. The fragile silk carpet gleamed.

Ann Woodward's conversation began with a complaint about closing houses in Sardinia. The coil of her hair was pulled back from her high brow into a bun, without any attempt to flatter the features of her face. Her only jewelry was a wedding band and a pair of small gold earrings. Her manners were aggressive and genteel. There was an English sound to some of her vowels, but they were not clipped. Nothing about her suggested the immaculate socialite could have murdered the father of her sons.

I could see in her eyes and around her mouth that my staring had begun to bother her. Her face became a sullen mask.

Moments later Jimmy joined us, sitting hunched over and staring at the carpet. I realized that Ann Woodward excused him from the points of decorum I was straining to comprehend. She smiled when I recognized the Modigliani painting above the fireplace. I began to relax and was soon excited to find myself in the company of such elegant people with a shocking and public secret.

During my last few moments in her company, Ann Woodward told me she had written down details of a visit in 1955 to the Duchess of Windsor's home in Paris. She murmured the name Nashua. I recognized the name of the Woodward horse that had won two legs of the Triple Crown in 1955, the year she killed her husband. Ann also said that someday she planned to write a book about her life. We both stared at Jimmy after he said under his breath, "Who'd believe it?"

I asked Ann what the Duchess had served for dinner. As she recited the menu, down to the hors d'oeuvres, her manner seemed less imposing and I realized that the Duchess seemed as exotic a figure to Ann as she did to me. "The meal ended with Camembert ice cream," Ann said. "It is called a savory."

Ann Woodward did not look or talk like anybody I knew, but she did remind me of the woman in coral lipstick and a floral chiffon gown who had greeted Ann's older son, Woody Woodward, and myself at a Museum of Modern Art benefit. (I had met Woody before meeting his brother, Jimmy. Woody and I were both working on a journalism review called *More.*) While Peter Duchin's band played on in the sculpture garden, the woman spoke in the same transatlantic accent as Ann about horse races in the Bois de Boulogne.

"And your mother?" she asked Woody.

"Off hunting tigers."

"Hunting? Good God!"

"My mother is a dangerous woman," said Woody, drawing out the word "dangerous" in an amused tone.

The woman had laughed.

I wondered if this was the closest Woody would come to mentioning the sad incident.

In 1975, I read Ann Woodward's obituary in *The New York Times*, and a week after that, I read Truman Capote's thinly disguised fictional description of her in a section of his then forthcoming novel, *Answered Prayers*, in *Esquire* magazine. In the piece, Capote had characterized "Ann

Hopkins'' as a bigamist and cold-blooded murderess. I began to make notes on my own impressions of Ann Woodward.

Several society people told me with intimidating authority that the Capote tale was "positively factual." During the five years before I began to research this book, I was convinced that Capote had discovered the secrets of Ann Woodward.

"Once upon a time," Capote began, "a jazzy little carrot-top killer rolled into town." He wrote that she looked like "a malicious Betty Grable," an eighteen-year-old who had been brought up "in some country-slum way."

In Capote's version, "Ann Cutler" quickly became a Manhattan call girl who broke into café society because she had been "the favorite lay of one of Frank Costello's shysters" and was often photographed against the zebra-striped banquettes of Costello's famous El Morocco nightclub. It was at El Morocco, according to Capote, that Ann Cutler captured "David Hopkins." David was a rich young society boy who, like his wealthy father, was "an anal-oriented Episcopalian." "She knew she'd hooked a biggie, even if he was only a kid, so she quit what she was doing and got a job in lingerie at Saks. In fact she had already been knocked up and it was his kid."

Through clever machinations, including a phony proclamation that she did not want to marry him, but just wanted the child to know his grandparents, Ann got David to marry her and began to transform herself: "She learned to ride, and became the horsiest horse-nag in Newport. She studied French and had a French butler and campaigned for the Best Dressed List by lunching with Eleanor Lambert and inviting her for weekends. She learned about furniture and fabrics from Sister Parish and Billy Baldwin; and little Henry Geldzahler was pleased to come to tea (Tea! Ann Cutler! My God!) and to talk about modern paintings."

Capote claimed that Ann Hopkins had attached herself to the Duchess of Windsor, although Ann was particularly transparent to the Duchess: "after all, the Duchess is too much of a con artist not to twig another one; but the idea amused her of taking this cool-eyed card player and lacquering her with a little real style, launching her on the circuit, and the young Mrs. Hopkins became quite notorious—though without the style."

In Capote's fantasy, David's wife, Ann, soon gained a "reputation up and down the French Riviera for what she did to men's organs with her mouth and some marmalade." Her exasperated husband finally threatened to expose Ann's "shabby birthplace" and her "bigamy"—a first husband (from her rural hometown) whom she had never bothered to divorce.

By now David saw her as a youthful error; he had fallen in love with a dull distant cousin, the sort of woman his family had hoped he would marry from the start.

According to Capote, Ann then concocted her own scheme. She began by burglarizing several neighboring estates to establish the existence of a prowler. Finally, Capote's Ann shoots down her husband—claiming she thought she was shooting "the prowler." Truman Capote had satisfied himself and such society friends as Babe Paley and C. Z. Guest by establishing a motive for the killing of Billy Woodward.

In 1981, when Ann's mother-in-law, Elsie Woodward, grande dame of New York society, died, I set out to prove Capote's fiction had foundation in fact. I was enthralled by the myth of Elsie Woodward's social power. I wanted my research to support the myth that Elsie Woodward had covered up the murder of her only son for the sake of her grandsons. She was powerful enough to keep Ann from being punished—I believed—in the criminal justice system.

I have come to see that my own and Truman Capote's predisposition to believe that Ann Woodward was a murderess is part of the Woodward story.

With the help of Ann Woodward's journals, her three aunts, her late friend Bill Sudduth, and many other people, who included Eugene De-Gruson, the special projects coordinator at Pittsburg State University, Mary Sanford, Dorothy Schiff, Mrs. Charles Schwartz, Lady Sarah Churchill, Edward Patterson, Jean Murray Vanderbilt, Irene Selznick, Lydia Smiley Wasson, Ina Claire, Joan Fontaine, Deputy Nassau County Police Commissioner Charles Spahr, Paul Wirths, and Charles Allen, Jr., I was able to reconstruct the lives and milieu of Elsie Woodward and her husband, William Sr., Billy, Ann, and their sons.

I came to see that Ann Woodward was innocent of the murder of her husband, Billy, and that Capote had invented Ann's motive for murder.

From reading hundreds of pages of police documents and interviewing police officers and over 1,100 people in Palm Beach; Malibu; Newport; Bar Harbor; Cambridge; Marbella; Pittsburg, Kansas; Wichita; Kansas City; London; Paris; Geneva; Santa Barbara; Fishers Island; Oyster Bay; Locust Valley; Huntington; Mineola; Manhattan; Washington, D.C.; Hobe Sound; Saratoga Springs; Hamburg and Föhr Island, Germany; Madrid; Sardinia; and Williamsburg, it became clear to me that Ann Woodward had killed her husband, Billy, by mistake.

Unlike the Ann Hopkins of Capote's tale, Ann Woodward had no first husband. Capote had invented her bigamy. As Ann Woodward's few supporters, such as the late Edith Baker Schiff, said at the time of the shooting, Billy was worth more to Ann alive than dead. (She would be far richer divorced from Billy than as his widow.)

Unlike Capote's fictional prowler, Ann Hopkins, there was a real prowler, Paul Wirths, who had terrorized the Woodwards' Oyster Bay Cove neighbors—such as the Schiffs—by sleeping in their pool cabanas and taking items from their kitchens, gun closets, bedrooms, and pool houses. Wirths was arrested a few days after Ann shot Billy, and confessed to having walked across the roof of Ann's bedroom and entered their home seconds before the shooting. Wirths was convicted and sentenced to six years in Ossining prison.

Many people told me that Elsie had undoubtedly bribed the "prowler" in order to support Ann's story. Subsequent blackmail letters from Paul Wirths to Ann Woodward that were revealed to me indicate that no such bribe took place.

In spite of the judicial outcome, Ann Crowell Woodward was found guilty of murder at society dinner tables, charity balls, and thorough-bred racing meetings. People—such as society hostess Liz Fondaras—claim to have had close friends who saw the Woodwards fighting at Mrs. George F. Baker's house party for the Duchess of Windsor on the night of the murder, but the "witnesses" were not on the Baker party guest list.

To Elsie Woodward and her circle, Ann's guilt was an affirmation of their superiority. To the rest of us, if Ann was a murderer, it proved our lack of social standing to be a sign of virtue.

Who were the Woodwards?

By 1920 the parents of William Woodward had achieved the exalted status their families had been striving for since the end of the nineteenth century. After graduating from Choate (1898) and Harvard (1902), William Woodward, Sr., became secretary to Ambassador Joseph H. Choate at the Court of St. James's, where he honed a lifelong practice of "acting British."

In 1910, after returning from England and marrying, he inherited Hanover Bank from his uncle and father. The bank's assets at that time were about $200 million. At the same time, William also inherited Belair Farm, newly purchased by his uncle James. Belair was the oldest thorough-bred stud and tenant farm in America, founded in the eighteenth century by the first governor of Maryland. From this point until his death, William

Woodward devoted himself with increasing obsessiveness to enlarging the farm's thousand acres and breeding and racing thoroughbred horses. He had extraordinary success in America, though he was disappointed in his lifelong dream of winning the English Derby. Even more than his wealth, his success in racing proved an expedient route to elite social position.

His wife, Elsie Cryder Woodward—one of the poor but famous Cryder triplets—capitalized on her husband's somewhat flashy public persona. She had upstaged her rival hostess, Grace Vanderbilt, who once reproached Elsie for smoking in public. Despite Grace and the handful of women with husbands richer than William, Elsie succeeded in crashing Old Guard society. By the 1920s, hers became the reigning salon in New York. The Iselins, Goelets, Astors, and Vanderbilts forgot that the Woodwards had not been on Ward McAllister's highly publicized list of the New York Four Hundred in 1892.

It had taken the Woodwards thirty years to become visible leaders of what Joseph Alsop remembers as the "WASP ascendancy," whose great family houses in Manhattan, Newport, Maryland, and on Long Island's North Shore had staffs of twelve or more servants and an aroma of beeswax furniture polish and cut roses and chrysanthemums from their gardens.

Although by 1955 widowed grande dame Elsie Woodward still controlled approximately $20 million worth of Central Hanover Bank stock, her son, Billy, had already inherited major pieces of his father's empire. His personal fortune was over $10 million, and he was the inexperienced owner of what was arguably the most successful racing stable in America and England. His big bay colt Nashua, the result of his father's fifty years of genealogical engineering, had won two legs of the Triple Crown and become one of the largest money winners in thoroughbred history.

In the fifties, women had eagerly returned to their place in the family, thankful that their men had come back alive from war. The motto of the fifties was "A family that prays together stays together." And a woman's crowning achievement was a marriage to a rich man—a "playboy" who had inherited money and an aristocratic English style.

On October 29, 1955, the night of the Woodward shooting, the evening's television entertainment included Jackie Gleason's "The Honeymooners," the Perry Como show, the Jimmy Durante variety show with guest Peter Lawford, and, of course, "Gunsmoke." The country was relieved to hear from his doctor Paul Dudley White that President Eisenhower was recovering from his heart attack. The Yankees, under manager

Casey Stengel, won their twenty-first pennant. Two white men were acquitted by a jury of twelve white neighbors of the murder of a black fourteen-year-old from Chicago named Emmett Louis Till.

Rebel Without a Cause had been released that week, making James Dean a posthumous superstar (he had died on September 30, 1955, in a car accident at age twenty-four). Next to the front-page story and picture headlined "Wife Kills Woodward, Owner of Nashua; Says She Shot Thinking He Was a Prowler," *The New York Times* reported that Governor Adlai Stevenson had been invited to enter the Minnesota presidential primary.

As with most ambitious people, Ann's career followed the trends of her era. In the late 1930s, she had thrown herself into Manhattan life as a Powers magazine model and radio actress. Her life resembled a Joan Crawford movie, in which, typically, a poor shopgirl married a rich man for love.

This book traces Angeline Luceil Crowell's path from an impoverished rural Kansas background to international café society. Ann was a self-made woman in every sense of the word. She fashioned herself to the specifications of the class myths. Her will and powers of self-creation were impressive, but she could never be as good as she had to be.

Ann's nemesis was Elsie Woodward—her mother-in-law—who decreed that her daughter-in-law lacked style—and that meant class.

By the 1950s Ann was flailing. Even though she had become a familiar sight on television, in the winner's circle with her husband and the champion thoroughbred horse Nashua, her marriage was in trouble. Like most Americans of the era, Ann seemed satisfied to appear successful and affluent. But the lengths to which she had to go in order to keep appearances intact—and hold on to her man—would eventually destroy her and perhaps even the Woodward dynasty.

This book is the result of eight years of research. I am sure I have left out people whom I should acknowledge, and I ask their forbearance and express my appreciation. I take full responsibility for any errors and, of course, for all interpretations and judgments.

ACKNOWLEDGMENTS

Thanks to Victoria Wilson for her brilliant editing and publishing.

I would also like to thank Slim Aarons, George Abbott, Wayne Adams, Count Vassili Adlerberg, Constantin Alajalav, Richard Allen, Oliver Ames, Angelo (El Morocco), Patrick Ashton, Whitney Bourne Atwood, Lily Auchincloss, Louis Auchincloss, Dubose Ausley, Mrs. Robert Bach, Mary B. Baer, George Baker III, Shirley Vlasak Baltz, Mel Barkan, Charles Baskerville, Dr. Kenneth Bateman, Chuck Bates, Julie Baumgold, Anson Beard, Peter Beard, Count Henri de Beaumont, Noel Behn, Arthur Bell, Dr. Howard Bellin, Teddy Bemberg, Philip Benkard, Mrs. Edgar Bering (Harriet Aldridge), Bernard Berkowitz, Eleanor Lambert Berkson, Mrs. Charles S. Bird, Stephen Birmingham, Barbara Bishop, David Black, Reverend Wayne Black, Earl Blackwell, Joseph Blankenship, Bill Blass, Norman Block, Patricia Bloomer, Stella Blum, Bruno Bock, Cynthia Boissevain, Peter Bond, Mitchell Booth, Patricia Bosworth, Lester Bowman, Sergeant Kenneth Boyd, Elizabeth Ingalls Boykin, Sam Boykin, Irma Bradbury, Marlin Brenner, Clarence Brent, Jimmy Breslin, Frederika Brillembourg, Florence Britton, Delores Brosshard, Eric Brotherson, Jo Hartford Bryce, Mrs. Jules Buck, Lester Buck, Jack Buckley, Amanda Burden, Mr. and Mrs. I. Townsend Burden, James Burt, Michael Butler, Mrs. Marie Sullivan Byrd, Jim Calio, Kim Kendall Baker Campbell, Michael Canaloso, Truman Capote, Judith Caputo, Nancy Cardozo, David Carlson, Jim Carroll, L. M. Kit Carson, Gianmarco Casellini, Constance Dudley Casey, Oleg Cassini, Sergeant Fred Catapano, Edith Cates, Gene Cavallero, Mrs. William (Mary) Carpenter, John Chapin, Joseph Chaprionière, Paul Chase, Penny Chenerey, Dr. Lee Christiansen, Sarah Churchill, Ina Claire, David Clark, Olga Clark, Gerald Clarke, Martha Clarke, Mrs. Robin Clarke, Stewart Clement, Carlyle Coash, Shelby Coates, Edna Cobb, Roy Cohn, Joyce Coit, Roz Cole, Ann Coleman, Bob Collacello, Governor LeRoy Collins, Leslie Combs, Eugene Condon, Edwin B. Constant, Henry Cormier, Rod Coupe, Mona Cowan, Countess Consuelo Crespi, Count Rudi Crespi, Vivienne Crowell, Wendy Cryan, Nassau County Homicide Squad Commander Edward Curran, Phoebe Curry, Charlotte Curtis, Libby Woodward Cushing, Mary Catherine Cuthbertson, Dr. Robert Cuthbertson, William Cuthbertson, Ann Cutler, Augusta Dabney, Ken Daley, Jean Dalrymple, Judith Daniels, Martha Darnell, Jimmy Darrow, Dorothy Davies, Monica Davis, Dorothy Davison, Count Henri de Beaumont, Eugene DeGruson, John DeJeju, Jane DelAmo, Gioia DeLiberta, Peter DePalma, Prince Phillip De Masterangelo, Dominique DeMenil, Anna DeNerciat, Carmine DeSapio, Brigite Desausseure, Alfred de Liagre, Mrs. Palmer Dixon, Guerita Donnelly, Sandy Dorr, Bill Draper, Dorothy Draper, Mrs. Andre (Ruth) Dubonnet, Peter Duchin, Mrs. Walter Dunnington, Frederick Eberstadt, Detective Richard Ebright, Hubert L. Edey, Hal Edgar, Diane Edkins, Dr. Burton Einspruck, Susan Elias, John Elois Elston, Mrs. Lincoln Ellsworth, Rex Ellsworth, Robert Ellsworth, Squad Commander George Erdoty, Don Erickson, Maria Estaban, Raphael Falco, Frank Farrell, James Fayek, Robert Fellner, Jerry Finklestein, Hamilton Fish, Wentworth Fling, Paul Flower, Liz Fondaras, Joan Fontaine, Evelyn Ford, Karen Foster, Larry Foster, Arlene Francis and Martin Gabel, Otto Fredrich, Pauline French, Donald Fresne, Larry Freundlich, Leon Friedman, Otto Friedrich, Mr. and Mrs. Winston Frost, Mrs. Andrew Fuller, Irene Galitzine, Gertrude Gallagher, Gladys Gallagher, Larry Gang, Helen Ganz, Dorothy Gary, Thelma Brady Gasch, Jackie Gebhardt, Albert Gelardin, Henry Geldzahler, Elbridge Gerry, Telde Getz, Princess Giacci, Fern Tailor Gimbel, Jane Goard, William W. Good, Jr., Clark Goodchild, Bob Gottlieb, Umberto Goyen, Joseph Lewis Grant, Mary Grant, Bob Greene, Mary Ruth Greenwood, Douglas Griffin, Frank Gulotta, Murray Gurfein, Leyla Hadley, Fernanda Hafers, Russell Haff, Mrs. Phyllis Havenstrite Hall, Mrs. John Hammond, Arthur "Bull" Hancock, Mrs. Arthur Hancock, Mary Hancock, Tom Hanley, Pauline Hardrodt, Nell Harmon, Jones Harris, Bernard Harrison, Huntington Hartford, Detective Andy Heberer, Lore Heinen, Abby Gurfein Hellworth, John H. Heminway, Sr., Marty Henley, Betty Jane Henry, Reinaldo Herrera, Lenore Hershey, Grant B. Hill, Mildred Hillson, MaryAnn Hinton, Odette O'Higgins Hinton, Margaret Holbrooke, Princess Honeychile Hohenlohe, W. D. Hopkins, Horst, Mrs. Joanne Horton,

Katherine Hourigan, Eleanor Howard, Josephine Hughes, Henry Hyde, Howard Imoff, Sally Iselin, Joseph Iseman, Nancy Ittleson, William Harding Jackson, Eva James, Jack James, Mrs. Martin Jensen, Bernard Jolis, Mrs. Carl Jones, Netta Jordan, Chester M. Jozwiak, Adele Jurgens, Joyce Jurnovoy, Sheila Kaelon, Bill Kahn, Evelyn Kaiser, Lawrence Kaiser, Linda Sudduth Karin, Edith Kates, Marcia Kaufman, Suzanne Kaufman, Dr. Ben Kean, Barbara D. Kelley, Ambassador Francis Kellogg, Mr. and Mrs. Peter Kent, Jimmy Kilroe, Chayan Kim, Mrs. Arthur Lee Kinsolving, John Kobal, Jesse Kornbluth, Mrs. Edmonde Labbe, Chief Daniel Lambertson (Oyster Bay Cove), Kenneth Lane, Gaston Lanneau, Joseph Lapatin, Mary Lasker, Valentine Lawford, Gaby Leff, Jac Lewis, Robert Leylan, Bill Lieberman, Renee Link, Kent Linnet, Bert Lippincott, Gordon Lish, John Loeb, Nedda Logan, Bernard Long, Thelma Longthowsky, Elaine Lorillard, Dr. Leslie Lukash, Betty Secri Lussier, Larry Luther, Edmund Lynch, Charles MacLean, Nick Madigan, Norman Mailer, Brian Mark, Dr. Mary Markham, Tony Marro, Hunter Marston, Mrs. Glen Martin, Detective Tom Martin, Florence Martinau, Eileen Masline, June Mather, John McAward, Mrs. Bill McCandless, Guy R. McComb, Thierry McCormick, Jane McCornell, Eleanor Whitney McCullom, Dorothy McGee, Tom McQuire, Ahlene Mehle, Suzy Menkes, Sylvia Miles, Devereau Millburn, Andrea Miller, Alverda Milligan, George Milligan, James A. Milligan, Mrs. Minot Milliken, Joseph Minish, Jim Mitchell, Alice Leone Moats, Olga Mohr, Harry Monroe, John Monroe, Claire Moore, Dr. Francis Moore, Paloma Mora, Judge L. L. Morgan, Willard Morgan, Mrs. Judith Morrel, Henry Mortimer, Stanley Mortimer, Michael Mosher, Robert Mosher, Harold Moss, Rudy Muelner, Dr. Brian Muldoon, John J. Mullin, Jackie Tierney Muneman, Sidney Mutum, Victor Navasky, George Neary, Tom Nieport, Maggie McNellis Newhouse, Mrs. Florence Norris, Herbert Oakes, Prince Ivan Obolensky, Mrs. Serge Obolensky, Dr. Jane Oldden, Jim O'Neill, Jody O'Neill, Jack Orhit, Sally Parsons Oriel, Principesa Gerarda Orleans y Borbon, Mrs. Helen Osterlin, Maurice Page, Reever Smith Paige, Eustice Paine, Bill Paley, Kate Paley, Frederico Pallavecino, Hurley Papock, Tony Parente, Ted Peckham, Senator Claiborne Pell, Peter Pels, Patrick Pettigrew, Chuck Pfeiffer, Eleanor Phillips, Mary Phipps, Mrs. Walter Pidgeon, George Plimpton, S. Lee Pogostin, Barron Polan, Richard Pollack, Michel Porges, Tony Potochniak, Robert Potter, Mrs. Frederick Prince, Livio Principe, Len Puccinelli, George Putman, Jr., Charles Putnam, Conrad Rafield, Monica Randall, Dennis Rano, Mary Louise Rasmussen, Mrs. Geraldyn Redmond, Harold Reeves, Victor Resnevics, Sarah Etta Reynolds, John Richardson, Frank Roach, Eddie Robinson, Jr., Mrs.

Edward Robinson, Mrs. Winthrop (Barbara) Rockefeller, Franklin Roosevelt, Jr., Norton Rosenbaum, Julian Rosenthal, Joseph Rottenberg, Mimi Russell, Richard Russell, Victor Samrock, Mrs. Stafford Sands, Mary Sanford, Gene Scanlon, Marty Schenck, Natalie Sherman, Prince and Princess Kyril Scherbatow, Princess Nedija Scherbatov, Dorothy Schiff, John Schiff, Rudolf Schirmer, Mrs. Charles Schwartz, Irene Selznick, Saul Shames, Allen Shaw, Virginia Swain Shepard, Virginia Sheward, Frank Shields, Jr., William Shields, Mort Sheinman, Bobby Short, Ida Shriver, Charles Sibre, Jay Sicre, Marvin Siegel, John Siffert, John Simpson, Mrs. George Sims, Ann Slater, Edward Slater, Ellen Slocum, Earl Smith, Meredith Etherington Smith, W. P. Smith, Dr. Allen Snart, Detective Ray Soper, Mrs. Margaret Soper, Toni Sorrel, Deputy Police Commissioner Charles Spahr, Saun Spillane, Detective Dan Stark, Pamela Stebbins, Detective Frank Steiner, Caron Steingarten, Henry Root Stern, Jr., Joanne Stern, Pam Stevens, Oliver Stone, Oscar Streuber, Jeanie Strouse, Tracey Swope, Herbert Swope, Jr., Julius Tadsen, Mrs. William Talbert, Sam Taylor, Merle Thomason, Barbara Thompson, Regina Tierney, Elizabeth Whitney Tippett, Whitney Tower, Mr. and Mrs. Peter Townend, Margie Slocum Trevor, Herbert Sears Tuckerman, Jocelyn Kress Turner, Webb Turner, Craig Unger, Sue Vallenstein, Teresa Van Dyke, Alfred Gwynn Vanderbilt, Jeanne Murray Vanderbilt, Frank Vargata, Gore Vidal, Ellen Violet, Claus Von Bülow, Prince Egon von Furstenberg, Maxeeda von Hesse, Baron Hubert von Pantz, Baroness Terry von Pantz, Diana Vreeland, Charles Wacker, Jr., Sam Wagstaff, David Walters, Frank Wangeman, Henry Wangeman, Andy Warhol, Jack Warner, John Wasson, Lydia Smiley Wasson, Bessie Mae Watson, David Webb, Cassy Sands Weeks, Ferdinand Wendt, Allen Tarwater West, Dr. Charles Wheeler, Floyd Whiddon, Antoinette White, Sam White, Betsey Cushing Whitney, Herschel Williams, Louise Hagney Wilson, Oleta Wilson, Thornton Wilson, Mrs. John Winslow, Morris Wirths, Paul Wirths, Mrs. Robert Wolcott, David Wolkowsky, Dana Woodward, Richard Yates, Dan Yergin, Gavin Young, Frank Zachary, Jerome Zerbe, Jo Zimmerman, and Richard Zoerink.

I would also like to express my gratitude to the librarians and the staffs of the following libraries and special collections: the Missouri Valley Room, Kansas City Public Library; the New York Public Library—Main Library, the Genealogy Room at the Main Library, and the Billy Rose Library of the Arts at Lincoln Center; the New-York Historical Society; the Crawford County Genealogical Society; the Bel Air Museum; Pittsburg State University, Special Collections; the Buckley School; the Groton School; Le Rosey; Widener Library, Harvard University; the John Kobal Collection of Photographs; the Museum of Racing, Saratoga, New York.

I would like to add the names of some friends, a sterling and sturdy bunch, who over the years have seen me through all sorts of things: Rick Angres, Helen and Tony Berlant, Susan Brownmiller, Ruth Charny, Bob Conte, Michael Douglas, Edward Jay Epstein, David Freeman and Judy Gingold, Barry Gewen, Albert Goldman, Julia Judge, Dick and Bob Kalich, Martha Kaplan, Joe Kennedy, Larry Lasker, Owen Laster, Harriet Lyons, Michael Mason, Dr. Donna Mildvan, Jeannine Oppewal, Blanche Orr (my mother), Janet Orr Newman (my sister), Leonard Orr and Elizabeth Buckner Orr (my brother and sister-in-law), Claudia Cohen Perelman and family, Gloria Steinem, Ron Replogle, Ron Rosenbaum, Edythe Roth, Paul Schrader, Hugh Seidman and Jayne Holsinger, Marvin Siegel, Robert Singer and Angela Poggioni, Lynn Povich and Steve Shepard, Erica Spellman, Harvey Shapiro, Raphael Falco, Robin Reisig, Tom Pollock, Tom Powers, and Helen Wilson.

THIS CRAZY THING
CALLED LOVE

1

KANSAS POOR

*The wind blows so hard in Kansas it would blow a
chicken up against the side of a barn and hold it there
for twenty-four hours.*

—EARLY SETTLER, 1855

I n 1918 Ethel Smiley Crowell was twenty-three and strong-willed. Her
husband, Jesse Claude, had let a hobo sleep in the barn, until Ethel
became convinced he was stealing grain. Ethel's mind was never still;
nor were her hands. She separated milk for butter, peeled potatoes, collected eggs. Ethel enjoyed hatching baby chickens in the pantry and hoeing
green onions. But the worst was milking the cow: its tail would sting her
face and neck. She took care of her husband and his parents, as well as her
children, two-year old Angeline and Jesse Jr., who was almost four.

Ethel had inherited her mother's desire for self-improvement through
education. She had just finished a course in teaching methods at the State
Manual Training Normal School in nearby Pittsburg. Ethel and her mother
prided themselves on being different from most southeastern Kansas farm
women. They polished their shoes every night and were "proud as all get-
out" that they were trained as schoolteachers at Pittsburg Normal School.
Ethel had been trained to teach at a "white children's" school. Her sisters and
she refused work in the local Indian school—just as they bragged that their
parents painted their house white, unlike foreign miners, who painted houses
yellow and pink. The Smiley women spoke more carefully than many of their
neighbors but used the same slow vowels. The word "ranch," for instance,
was pronounced as though it were spelled "ray-unch" and "school" was
"skew-well." In the first few years of the century, their parents had driven
to southeastern Kansas in a covered wagon from a failed farm in Mexico,
Missouri. Their father, William Smiley, had high hopes for a surface min-

3

ing job in Frontenac, Kansas, near Pittsburg. He had heard about a new invention used there, the steam shovel. His wife, Laura Smith Smiley, disliked Frontenac because the miners were "foreigners" and "colored." At first William was reduced to hauling wood in his wagon from the train depot. When he finally got a job, he was picked up by a steam shovel in a grotesque accident and squeezed until his back was broken. From that time on he had been unable to work more than half a day. Laura Smiley vowed her daughters would be teachers. She temporarily separated from her husband and moved the girls to Pittsburg to be near the Normal School. She advised them to marry men who worked in offices or in trade.

Laura told her children that she was a Daughter of the American Revolution, descended from Edmund Terrell, a captain in the revolutionary army whose coat of arms pictured an animal that appeared to be a cross between a griffin and a pig. She was proud that her father and all her brothers were ministers and church elders.

Born in 1895, her daughter Ethel had at first seemed blessed. The Reverend Sam I. Smith once told the whole congregation that Ethel Smiley was the prettiest girl in Crawford County. It was obvious. The Smileys spent a lot of time at the First Christian Church at Fifth and Pine—like the Baptist Church, it had grown up on the frontier in the last half of the nineteenth century.

The flourishing church had been shaped by the millionaire novelist Harold Bell Wright, an eccentric, unordained minister. Wright believed one did not have to be a member of the congregation to receive the church's bounty. He abolished pie suppers that benefited only church members. He sheltered the homeless and set up a twenty-four-hour-a-day soup kitchen. His exciting short sermons were about current events, not biblical lore.

Ethel and her sisters had been "willing hands": women who made quilts and sold them to support the church's good works. They went to extra prayers on Wednesday night and to the Sunday-night Endeavor Services for young people, held in the basement. One night Ethel, who was known for her rhetorical skills, delivered a ringing sermon about teaching as a holy art.

Ethel was the ringleader of the Smiley girls. She made up secret "church" games using the juice of crushed cherries and a piece of bread for holy communion, once preaching a eulogy for a large rat that had rotted in a wood wagon. She was a leading light of the Russonian Society, the high school dramatic club. Her evening recitals of Tennyson's poems were always applauded by her sisters. Her father favored Ethel, but she was also the most difficult. One summer afternoon when she was fourteen, she borrowed a neighbor's songbook to sing what was considered a racy song, "The Girl in the Bowery," the first verse of which closed with the words "and a man was the cause of it all." The windows were open and her mother hushed her, fearing the neighbors would get a bad impression. "They already have their impression," Ethel said, "and I don't give a hoot what it is."

In 1913, and just eighteen, Ethel proudly received her provisional three-year teaching certificate from the Training Normal School. But unbeknownst to her family, she had set her cap for Jesse Claude Crowell, whose family owned their own farm. Ethel proposed to him, put on her Copenhagen blue brocade dress, and, in a secret ceremony, married him.

She married without telling a soul. In many states at that time, women teachers were not permitted to marry. The headstrong girl thought the rule "silly." She made Jesse Claude swear to tell no one about their wedding.

From June to December 1913 was a time of giddy adventure for Ethel. The young elementary school teacher and Jesse Claude Crowell enjoyed conjugal visits, although Ethel was careful to sleep only at her mother's rented house in Pittsburg. It was a serious rebellion for that place and time and it might have continued indefinitely had Ethel not become pregnant. Disappointed and angry, she realized she had to stop teaching at the Smelter School. Thus, it felt like a scandal that Christmas when the families gathered for a double wedding ceremony that included the couple and the bride's brother, Hugh. The Reverend Sam I. Smith announced that Ethel's wedding had taken place six months earlier and that Ethel was already three months pregnant. Ethel's mother cried when she heard the news. For years, she wondered whether Ethel had cleverly persuaded the minister to pretend he had already performed the first ceremony.

But the Pittsburg *Headlight* ran a news item backing Ethel's story on December 27, 1913: "That a married woman may teach school without having to face objections from the members of the board and the patrons has been demonstrated by Mrs. Claude Crowell, teacher at the Smelter district, east of Pittsburg. Mrs. Crowell taught the entire first half of the term without a single kick being raised as to her being married. The way she accomplished the feat was by not letting it be known in the district that she was married."

Early in 1914, while she was pregnant with little Jesse Claude, Ethel moved in with her husband and his parents. She did her best to live within the tight family circle, tending to her bedridden, dying mother-in-law, Angeline Wright Crowell. But she was not eager to raise sons to work the unproductive Crowell farm. "Kansas is just a desert," said Ethel.

Sometimes it made Jesse Claude nervous to find Ethel quoting scriptures over Jesse Jr. when he had coughing spells at night. "Membrase croup," said the doctor, sadly. Ethel wondered if she should take a bank loan and bring her son to a big city hospital. Angeline Luceil Crowell had been delivered by a doctor on December 12, 1915. She had been born in "the black box," the shack near the Crowell barn where animals were slaughtered and in which Angie's namesake, grandmother Angeline Wright Crowell, had given birth to Angie's father, Jesse Claude.

Grandma Angeline "Ana" told of the Crowells' history of bad luck. They traced the name back to two brothers named Cromwell. When the brothers left England in the eighteenth century, the family myth went, they dropped the *m*. During the Civil War Jesse Claude's grandparents lost a small plantation and slaves to Sherman on his bloody march. Afterward, they joined a stream of poverty-stricken southerners migrating west. But in the years that followed, the long days of farming in Oklahoma and eastern Kansas never paid off.

In 1917, two years after Angie was born, Ethel urged her husband to go to school to study the new science of automobile mechanics. He had always enjoyed fixing farm machines with bailing wire. "Where's Daddy?" Angie would ask. "He's off bettering himself," her mother would reply. When Jesse Claude's friends formed the Square Deal garage in nearby Mulberry, it was Ethel who urged Jesse Claude to invest in a share. Meanwhile, Ethel had embarrassed her husband by going back to school, as a correspondence student. She was tired of farm work and welcomed the escape into studies.

One afternoon, after Ethel's twenty-third birthday party, her sister Lydia was taking care of Angie and her brother. A photographer knocked on the kitchen door. For twenty cents he offered to photograph the Crowell children. Lydia invited him in. She tied one of Angie's ribbons around her niece's top curl and washed Jesse Jr.'s face. It started drizzling while Jesse and Angie stood by the square vegetable plot, dotted with green spring spikes. "You better smile," Angie said, as the rain poured on them. Little Jesse Claude complained of the cold. The child burned with fever for two weeks. Ethel kept him in her bed and gave him cough medicine, but in the middle of the night he choked to death "on his own fluids." The doctor came and wrapped the little boy in wool quilts.

Laura Smiley and her three other daughters stood around Ethel's bed for days. But no one could console her. Laura straightened the sheets and prayed over her most promising daughter. Her father told Ethel she had another child to worry about, but Ethel turned away. They sent Angie to stay in town with Grandma Laura. After a day Angie climbed up onto a kitchen chair and started banging a wooden spoon. "Where is brother?" she demanded. "He'll be an angel in heaven," said Grandma Laura. "What about me? Can I go soon?" "You are staying with us."

At Mount Olive Cemetery, Ethel's aunts, cousin, and grandparents huddled together, listening to her sobs as the raindrops pelted the coffin of Jesse Jr. They lowered the small casket into a puddle of water. Suddenly Ethel said, "He can't go to heaven all muddy and wet." Ethel shook off her mother's arm and ran toward the coffin. "I want to dry him off," she said calmly. "That box won't keep out the rain." Angie started to cry.

That summer, the doctor paid regular visits to Ethel. By the end of July, he told Jesse Claude she couldn't continue to live on the farm. Grandma Laura sent for Reverend Smith, but Ethel did not pray as he thanked God for her daughter, Angie. Ethel told her mother that she should have taken her advice and never married a farmer. The marriage had brought her only bad luck and a sick child. When her mother left, Ethel told Jesse Claude and Angie that she had decided to go back to the Normal school. Jesse Claude had never heard of a mother with a husband, a daughter, and farm chores going to college in eastern Kansas. But he agreed that a change of scene might mend Ethel's nerves. The death of their son had driven a wedge between Ethel and Jesse Claude. She convinced herself that if only they had the money, she could have taken little Jesse Jr. to a good hospital in Kansas City. Now she had to escape the poverty to save her only child. Ethel began to devise ways to flee from the debt-ridden farm and her marriage. By the time she turned fourteen, Angie would have lived in at least eight different homes with her mother, father, and grandmother.

By the age of three, she had learned to recognize short words and numbers. She was an unusually bright little girl whose IQ tests at school measured at 139. Angie drew a hopscotch court with a stick in the dirt and jumped from box to box. Late afternoons she would sit in front of the house and wait for the grinding sound of her mother shifting the gears of her two-door, two-seater Ford. She held imaginary conversations with her mother about new words in her picture books. These quiet times at dusk, when she was hungry for supper and lonely for her parents and her brother, were what Angie would remember most vividly of her childhood.

When the Ford finally pulled up, motor running, Angie would throw herself at her mother in an explosion of love.

Sunday dinner at the Crowell farm was a grim affair. Angie watched her mother turning pages of her books on teaching methods. Her father ate quickly. After dinner when he invited Angie to walk out in the corn with him, Angie would refuse. But a few minutes later, he would see her running behind him. Angie would grab his hand and pull him into a run.

The summer of 1919, a year before Ethel was to graduate with a bachelor of science degree, the family's fortunes worsened. One weekday, when Angie and her mother were in town, a midday stillness alerted Jesse Claude to a tornado coming from the Dakotas. It sounded faint at first, like a distant train. Jesse Claude prayed the disaster would not strike his farm. But the hellish wind broke his cornstalks. Jesse Claude hid in the basement. He was lucky: most farmhouses did not have basements. The storm sucked the windows out. Silt piled into the house. Later that night, one of the neighbors told of a farmer who had shot his cow and killed himself.

Jesse Claude told his wife that the bank was repossessing the farm, but he was not in a panic. He showed Ethel a government flier offering homesteads in the western Kansas prairie, where he had worked as a teenager on a cattle ranch. If he planted spruce and cottonwood trees and tilled a piece of land, in six years the homestead would be his property. But Ethel did not want another failing farm in the middle of nowhere.

Jesse Claude took the new Santa Fe train to the prairie town of Hugoton, near the Oklahoma border. It was Indian territory and the last bastion of homesteaders. The prairie had been ignored by farmers because it was too sandy and dry. Jesse Claude filed for a single quarter section of 160 acres near the dry Cimarron River bed. The land was dotted with blue-stemmed prairie grass and included a small one-story shack and shed, aban-doned by the last man who had gone broke living there.

Ethel told Angie that they were the wretched of the earth and would never be able to eke out a living. But Ethel did her duty as a wife. She carried drinking water from the well in buckets and got sun blisters helping Jesse Claude plant maize, feed (broom) corn, and wheat. Although her depression was often overwhelming, she still managed to teach Angie to read, to snap beans, and to gather eggs. She kept Angie's shoes polished and continued her teaching courses by mail. She was still determined to make something of herself. Ethel's parents joined her in Hugoton that July to help harvest the wheat. Ethel and Jesse drove a header barge and the sweating horses. The dusty wheat stalks made Angie's skin itch. Grandma Laura was worried over a change she noticed in Angie. The child had developed a quiet watchfulness, and would lie in bed at night wondering why her parents had brought her there.

Ethel completed her correspondence course and graduated on June 20, 1920, with a bachelor of science degree in social science, and accepted a new job as principal of a one-room schoolhouse in the next county. Five-year-old Angie stood silent and terrified when Ethel kissed her good-bye. Ethel wrote letters to her from the rented room where she boarded with a family in Seward County. She had told county officials that she was a widow, since married women were still not allowed to teach. Angie worried that her mother would get sick and go to heaven. A year later, in the summer of 1921, Ethel came home for a week and left again to begin work on a master's degree at the University of Kansas in Lawrence, some 400 miles away.

Angie hunted arrowheads in the sand hills, put grasshoppers in tin cans, and filled her apron with wild asters for the kitchen table. Before meals with her father, she said grace. But she missed her mother, even though her grandmother picked the sandburs out of her hair. She cried when she was alone.

Ethel came home that fall. She soon took a new job, driving thirty-two miles each way by car to teach at a normal school in the rough frontier town of Liberal, Kansas, where the blizzards were so formidable that she and the other teachers actually tied students together with ropes and scarves to prevent them from getting lost going home. Jesse Claude resented her absences. But her salary helped them survive. At school, she was paid $100 a month her first year and $150 a month the second.

While Ethel was at Liberal, Jesse Claude sent Angie, then five years old, to live temporarily with her mother's sister Lydia, who was teaching near Pittsburg in a one-room elementary school. On Friday night Lydia and Angie rode a horse the three miles to Little Union elementary school for a box supper evening. In an auction, local boys bid quarters to buy the girls' boxes, which were decorated with crepe paper.

In late 1921, Jesse Claude asked Ethel to come home again to help out on the farm, but Ethel responded that the hard sand hills would never support them. Her parents had given up and returned to eastern Kansas. Jesse Claude claimed that he needed two or three more years to make the homestead work. This time Ethel left her husband, taking Angie with her. Angie was thrilled to join her mother on a great adventure, the first of many escapes they would make together. They moved to an unpainted log cabin in the primitive frontier town of Johnson, Kansas, with a population of less than 300. The cabin had no porch, only a slab of cement at the front door.

The town was filled with rough cowboys and had no paved roads—only cowpaths. It also lacked running water and indoor toilets. Ethel taught at the three-room high school above the post office. For six months, Ethel and Angie lived in Johnson and attended a tiny Methodist church with a broken coal stove. Ethel sent Jesse Claude half of her monthly paycheck and visited with him one weekend every few months. Angie saw little of her mother, and there was no one to care for her during the day. The little girl held imaginary conversations with her father about living with him in the future.

In order to teach, Ethel had again described herself as a widow—but everyone soon heard about Ethel's stormy marriage. Her students admired her independence and her struggle to inspire them to think. Ethel did a great deal of reading in order to teach arithmetic, spelling, history, and geography—as well as social studies. She held the teenage girls spellbound as she lectured on the new women's suffragism. She told the boys to think ahead and not to go into farming only because their fathers had.

On visits to her father, Angie heard her parents argue over Jesse Claude's friendship with a widow in Hugoton. Angie cried in the next room the night Ethel confronted Jesse Claude and called off a party for Jesse Claude's and Angie's birthdays. Angie assumed that fights were the way married people talked. She spent hours devising ways to protect each parent from the other. She wished her father would suddenly make her mother happy. She made Ethel laugh by telling her that Jesse Claude had found buried treasure in the fields.

Suddenly, one summer day, Ethel told her daughter that the two of them were moving to a more distant school back near Pittsburg. Angie did not want to be that far from her father. "Don't shout at me, Angie," said Ethel, striking her daughter. Then she hugged her, begging her for forgiveness. "Don't worry, things are going to be much better for us."

That semester, Ethel and six-year-old Angie were living in Cherokee, Kansas, in a rooming house with real neighbors, running water, and a front porch. Angie made few friends—it was too hard leaving them when her mother moved. Before falling asleep she combed her hair and neatly arranged her nightgown, just in case her father might come back to see her during the night.

Jesse Claude soon asked Ethel for a divorce on grounds of incompatibility. He had felt like a fool, always waiting for his wife to make up her mind whether she was coming back to him. He was awarded most of the livestock, farm machinery, and household furnishings. He tried to obtain custody of Angie, claiming Ethel was an unfit mother because she worked. But the little girl had become the emotional center of Ethel's life, and after a few months of negotiations, Jesse Claude gave up. He wanted to get on with his life. He and Ethel divorced, in November 1923, agreeing to respect a fence on their homesteading parcel.

In the meantime, Ethel was seeking yet another change in her life. In 1923, she accepted a post at the Pittsburg Senior High School. She told Angie that moving back to Pittsburg, where Ethel's parents and sisters lived, would be the answer. And, indeed, the next three years in Pittsburg turned out to be the most settled of Angie's solitary childhood. Ethel sold her share of the homestead to the Santa Fe Mining Company in Hugoton. She was delighted that she received much more than Jesse Claude had paid for the wretched farm, and in 1924, she bought a house next to the Malle filling station in Pittsburg.

The reunion with her family in Pittsburg was not the happy one Ethel had anticipated. The Smileys were humiliated by her divorce—the first in the family's history. Her mother took pride in another of her other daughters, Fannie, who had been hired as the local church librarian.

Angie was enrolled in Lakeside Elementary School, where her fellow students were farm children and Italian children whose parents worked in the mines. Angie's grades were fine—"excellent"'s with only an occasional "good." There were three movie theaters in town, and the cashier at the Cozy sometimes allowed Angie to slip in without paying. She loved watching the same movies again and again. Her favorite star was Lillian Gish. When she was eleven, Angie made her mother laugh by seductively gyrating a shoulder and announcing that she was going to Hollywood. "Absolutely not," said Ethel. Angie had read in a newspaper that Clara Bow had been poor until the age of seventeen, when she won a beauty contest and was whisked off to Hollywood. "Clara Bow would never do it," Angie once told her mother when she was asked to clean up the kitchen. Ethel flew into a rage and hit her. She also forbade Angie to swing her hips like Clara Bow and she disapproved of Angie's wearing her slip and playing dress-up.

The little girl had few friends. She would put on her mother's shoes to recite poems Ethel had taught her. Occasionally, she was allowed to attend the girls' basketball games—one of the major events in Pittsburg. Local people rode horseback or drove to these games from twenty miles away. Angie sat proudly by her mother, aware of the admiring stares of

Ethel's students. Ethel was not popular with local matrons: she was a divorced, unattached woman. "Jealous women are my problem," she said repeatedly.

In 1926, Angie was left in Pittsburg with Ethel's mother and sisters while Ethel made frequent trips to use the library in Lawrence, Kansas. When Angie asked to move in with Jesse Claude, her aunts told her that he did not have the money, and Angie felt betrayed by her father.

During Ethel's third year in Pittsburg, less than three years after she had sold her share of the homestead to the Santa Fe Mining Company, it became the site of a major well. When the first gas drill was brought to Hugoton, the former Crowell property produced one of the richest deposits of natural gas in the state of Kansas. For the rest of her life, Ethel would say in a sad voice, "Oh my, but things would be so different if we'd only hung on to that land." Jesse Claude was more philosophical about the well. He had sold his half of the land fair and square. To him, the disappointment was not being able to support his family on his farm.

Jesse Claude had set off alone for Detroit, where he worked as a streetcar conductor. He had little money to spare for Ethel, who told Angie that he had refused them money for food. Since Ethel lived in terror that Jesse Claude would take Angie away from her, she intercepted his letters to Angie. When he showed up in Pittsburg, Ethel forbade him to see Angie.

Sometime in 1926, a tall white-haired man almost seventeen years older than Ethel attended a lecture she gave on the lessons of history at the First Christian Church. Ethel wore a dark floor-length dress and a cardigan sweater. Afterward, Percy Victor Jordan waited his turn in the crowd to meet the popular thirty-year old teacher. "P.V." was a recent widower, the son of a Missouri bank teller, and Ethel was pleased he was not a farmer. P.V. was proud of his corner office at the telephone company, where he accepted customers' payments of their bills. His salary was equal to Ethel's, $150 a month. He and his seventeen-year-old son, Charles, boarded with a widow.

As he began his courtship of Ethel, Angie kept her distance from him; she feared losing her mother. She dogged Ethel's heels when she washed her hair and stockings. Her mother sought to minimize Angie's fears and recited Bible passages about suffering. Angie hated the way Ethel jumped up from the table to serve P.V. a second helping of Sunday dinner. She ignored P.V. when he cautioned her to chew her food more. Ethel slapped her. She and her daughter were now fighting more frequently, and Ethel felt guilty. Weeping and hugging Angie, she would beg for her daughter's forgiveness. One night Angie dreamed that Jesse Claude was in their house. She woke up expecting to see him kneeling by the incubator at the old farm, trying to put broken eggshells back together.

Despite her feelings, Angie smiled a big movie smile at P. V. Jordan like a good little girl. It was something she had practiced in front of the mirror. As time went by, she began, at difficult moments, to imitate the gestures of her favorite actresses.

It was Ethel's idea to elope with P.V. to Kansas City, which they did on September 12, 1926. When Angie, then almost twelve, woke up that morning, it was several minutes before she realized that her mother was not there. She called her name, crying, believing she had finally been abandoned. When she found her mother's note explaining what had happened, she still did not believe Ethel would return. She stayed home from school, shivering in bed.

Angie soon felt invaded by P.V. and his son, but she tried to accommodate her mother's quest for a new life. As an openly married woman, Ethel had to stop teaching school, and she felt poor, even though P.V. contributed his income to run the household. For six weeks she tried to busy herself by sewing curtains and cleaning. Angie was secretly pleased to see how soon Ethel tired of her new husband. P.V. and she seemed to agree on very little, although he did leave the Methodist Church his first wife had joined and attended Wednesday prayer nights at the First Christian Church with Ethel and Angie.

Ethel was devastated when P.V. demanded that she stop giving her popular evening church lectures on the lessons of history. Nor did he want her to continue her University of Kansas master's degree courses by mail. He accused her of being "morbidly fascinated" by new courses in socio-pathology and criminology and complained of her long monologues on his unconscious motivations. Ethel soon developed insomnia and slept late into the mornings. In the middle of October, Ethel chased her husband down the street brandishing a pot and accusing him of being a "darned tyrant." Angie followed her, frightened for her mother's safety and hoping P.V. would never return. The neighbors never forgot the way P.V. ran from his "hellcat wife."

After six weeks of marriage, Ethel filled her suitcases with clothes and schoolbooks and drove 145 miles without stopping to Lawrence, Kansas, to continue to work for her master's degree. In the car, she talked in a long monologue of her plans for her future. Someday she would teach college students at Lawrence. It was one of the most euphoric nights of Angie's young life. She had won, she was Ethel's true ally: it was P.V.—and not Angie—whom Ethel had abandoned.

In Lawrence, Ethel enrolled her daughter in school, tutored her at home, and worked long hours—attending classes and selling encyclopedias door-to-door. Although she was left in a dormitory room alone during the day, Angie was ecstatic to have her mother to herself again. Ethel wrote to her own mother to say that she was busy taking graduate teaching courses, but asked her not to tell P.V.

After five weeks, she and Angie awoke one morning to a rapping on their door. Ethel closed the door quickly and told Angie to get dressed and go out for a walk. Filled with dread, Angie could not stay away. Ten minutes later, she returned. Ethel was packing; P.V. was standing over her.

Once in Pittsburg, unbeknownst to her husband, Ethel continued to take graduate courses by correspondence. When he caught her studying for a final exam that May, P.V. threatened to leave her unless she withdrew from school. Ethel rushed at her husband, pummeling him. But she eventually backed down, since she did not want to face the community with a second divorce. Although Angie was frightened by the fights between her mother and P.V., she was no longer as worried about herself. Ethel needed her again. Ethel was given full blame by P.V.'s friends for the calamitous relationship.

During the summer of 1927, despite her pleas, P.V. again refused to let Ethel enroll in teaching courses, nor did he permit her to return to graduate school that fall. By the time Angie was twelve, her mother struck her as being two people—a disciplined teacher and an explosively angry woman. After a particularly grim fight with P.V., Ethel once again packed her belongings. In a now familiar routine, she dragged Angie to Lawrence, where she finished the courses for her master's degree. She began to call herself Ethel Smiley Crowell in an effort to expunge P.V. from her life.

In Lawrence, Angie again entered the eighth grade, but she stayed in her mother's rented room most of the time, reading her schoolbooks and taking care of the kitten she hid from the landlady. It was too confusing to try to make friends.

Ethel was a whirlwind of energy; besides selling encyclopedias door-to-door, she helped raise funds for the building of a college stadium, for which she was awarded a gold pen and pencil set. She also became pregnant, although she was separated from her husband. When she finally triumphed by graduating that June with high grades, Ethel resolved to seek wider horizons. She dedicated her thesis, "The Status of Social Sciences in

Kansas High Schools," "To Angie, with love." It was filled with charts that illustrated the range of social studies courses taught in Kansas high schools.

Ethel would not return to Pittsburg and face the gossip about her pregnancy. There was also the strong possibility that two divorces would be unacceptable to the school authorities. Ethel Crowell decided instead to gamble on herself and her considerable skills. That summer, despite her pregnancy, she added a finishing touch to her academic record. She took a full load of education courses at Kansas State University.

She began preparing her daughter for what she said would be their greatest adventure. Ethel was convinced that her destiny was to escape rural Kansas and teach high school social studies in the bustling, sophisticated metropolis of Kansas City. She drove to Pittsburg in July to consult Dr. Charles Dudley about her pregnancy and to file for divorce on the grounds of mental cruelty. She promised to pay her gynecologist's bill soon after her appointment, but in a pattern that was to emerge with increasing frequency, she failed to pay it at all. The physician obtained a civil summons that was issued for the $50, but it was returned, stamped "unable to locate in county." Ethel was becoming a mixture of personal rules and lawless behavior. If Angie was raised by the book, Ethel took liberties with her own behavior. Ethel had moved back into her mother's house and did not go out by day except to drive the car. She was at the end of her pregnancy and she did not want gossip. Her mother was against Ethel's plan to escape to Kansas City and wanted her to return to P.V. Ethel told her mother that she had left him because he had given her a venereal disease.

Ethel's baby, whom she named Mary Elizabeth Jordan, was born dead. Her death seemed to revive Angie's and her mother's memories of little Jesse Claude. In the preliminary divorce hearings in Pittsburg, however, Ethel's lawyer swore that there was no issue from her union with P.V. In the final divorce decree, Ethel was awarded the Diana automobile that P.V. had claimed and other property that she had owned when she entered the marriage, including her share of Jesse Claude's Square Deal garage. P.V. asked for the property he had owned when he entered the two-year marriage, as well as his trunks of clothing and a large photograph of himself.

Ethel and Angie crammed crates of their possessions into the back of the Diana. Ethel wrote a list of the contents on each box in her neat handwriting. She had lists and hour-by-hour plans for her departure. This was to be the most ambitious exit of her life.

Angie loved the excitement she felt whenever Ethel threw the pieces

of her life into new patterns. Her mother recited descriptions of historic
Indian battles as she drove through Fort Scott. They stopped at the military
cemetery while Ethel said a prayer for the soldiers who had fought in the
Indian wars. Like many teachers, Ethel tended to deliver long discourses
rather than engage in two-way conversations. Angie was desperate to please
her mother and took these lectures as Ethel's way of showing affection.
Ethel drove nonstop through the first night of the trip. At sundown the
next night, she parked in the stubble of a harvested cornfield. She and
Angie slept in the locked car a safe distance from a nearby farmhouse until
the sun woke them. Ethel talked at length about her plan to teach at
Westport High School, the most progressive high school in the state. She
was convinced that the letters of recommendation from her university
teachers would open the necessary doors. She told Angie that they would
soon be living in the fashionable new neighborhood of Westport, near
elegant stores. Ethel had already contacted a Westport woman who took
in boarders. Angie would be one of the best honor students to graduate
Westport High. Ethel was sure of it.

It was the second week in September of 1928. Ahead chimneys puffed
trails of smoke into the morning sky. Angie marveled at the new sights of
stockyards, department stores, and trains filled with coal and farm produce.

2

ANN IN KANSAS CITY

Angie and Ethel had been living in Kansas City for more than two years. Angie was skinny by Kansas farm standards; she was not yet the extraordinary beauty she would become, but already there was something beyond her pale coloring and straight-as-a-string posture. It was more than her sensual habit of stroking her soft arms. It was her unabashed delight in getting a boy's attention.

Ethel had opened a storefront taxi office at 813 West Thirty-ninth Street. A penciled sign hung from the side of the old wood desk: WESTPORT TAXI AND LIVERY SERVICE: 50 cents an hour, $1.50 a night. The taxi shack's back door opened into the men's room of the Roanoke Movie Theatre.

One afternoon Ethel answered the telephone. It was Ed Mayes, Ethel's second-favorite taxi driver. Ethel needed to talk to him privately. Unfortunately, Ed was always just one step ahead of the mob. He was a taciturn man who, like fifteen-year-old Eugene Condon, would do almost anything for Ethel, like change a fan belt or a battery. The problem was that Ed was always dirty from repairing taxi engines. As Ethel whispered into the telephone, Angie looked frightened. She and Eugene knew that the day before Ed Mayes had run over an elderly Jewish man. The old man was in the hospital and had no relatives.

The police had come around that morning. Somebody had seen a hack run the old man over. "Hit and run," said the police. Ethel had lied to the police to cover up the fact that her taxicab had been involved. Frightened of insurance problems, lawsuits, and even criminal charges, she had insisted on a vow of silence from all her cabdrivers. Since Ethel liked poor Ed Mayes, she always sent him and Eugene Condon on the best trips.

They called her "Ma" and took turns taking Miss Irma West, a counselor at the YWCA, and her girls on picnics across the Missouri. Ed's brother-in-law Dave Finklestein was a hired mob goon who sold funeral statuary.

In the taxi shack, Ethel told Ed Mayes to stay on the telephone line. It seemed that the victim had died. Although Ethel spent hours talking to Ed, trying to cover up the hit-and-run accident, when it looked as though she herself might be blamed, she had Ed turn himself in. The police realized the accident had not been his fault, and he was let off. The drivers admired the way that Ethel arranged matters so that the taxi company never received any publicity about it.

From the moment she had arrived, euphoric, in Kansas City, Ethel had been knocked back on her heels. Her hopes soaring, she had taken her sealed letters of recommendation to Westport High School. Of course, she had realized she was late in applying for the fall term. But she was a teacher with an outstanding three-year record in Crawford County, a summer teaching stint at the State University, and a brand-new master's degree. She assumed she could find substitute teaching until a full-time position became available. But she expected too much from Kansas City. Teaching jobs came through political connections—not because of good credentials. A year after she arrived in Kansas City, the stock market crashed. Unemployed men stood on street corners, and women waited for free food on breadlines. Hoarding the last dollars of her divorce settlement, she moved with Angie into the tiny second-floor front apartment of the Ruxton, a five-story yellow brick apartment building. Angie was thrilled that the parlor had two china closets built into the wall and a Murphy bed.

When Ethel was denied a teaching job again in 1929, she met with her ward leader at the local Democratic headquarters. Then she spoke to a man in the office of Johnny Lazia, the handsome Italian gangster who ran the local liquor business and other criminal activities for Boss Pendergast.* Angie asked Ethel why she was compromising her principles. Ethel shouted, "I'm not going to let you starve." But still no teaching job came of it.

*From the 1890s to 1939 Jim Pendergast and his younger brother, Tom, built and ran the notorious political machine of Kansas City. Amid struggle, scandal, and gangsterism, the Pendergasts manufactured judges, police, governors, and congressmen. The machine's gear work eventually produced a president of the United States: Harry S. Truman. The construction, engineering, and collapse of the Pendergast machine have become a classic case of American urban bossism.

*   *   *

Ethel soon began to talk to Angie about buying two bus tickets to New York. Angie was thrilled to be included in another escape. Ethel had been working sporadically as a clerk in a meat store and was the manager of her apartment building in exchange for reduced rent. Then one cold day, while Ethel was buying tomatoes at the busy Trabon Fruit Market, Louis Trabon, the owner's son and himself the owner of the Colonial Cab fleet, asked her out to dinner at the Sportsmen's Lounge.

To Ethel, it was a ray of hope. It was her first social invitation from a man in Kansas City. Relieved to see Ethel less anxious, Angie held a little silver hand mirror high while Ethel fixed her red curls. Angie helped her pin on a little pearl brooch. After her mother left with Louis Trabon in his dapper three-piece suit, Angie read her civics book and crawled under the bedcovers, trying to picture herself at the Sportsmen's Lounge, sitting next to her mother under a crystal chandelier while Louis Trabon lit Ethel's Lucky Strike cigarette. (Ethel smoked whenever she could find the pennies for a pack.) In Angie's fantasy, Louis Trabon looked like the actor Ronald Colman.

An hour later, Ethel followed Louis Trabon up a flight of outside stairs to the fashionable Prohibition speakeasy. The Sportsmen's Lounge was owned by a local gangster named Jimmy Needles, the hit man for Johnny Lazia. Ethel was nervous to be in an illegal place, but Trabon told her Lazia had put the Lounge "on ice"—meaning that the police would not raid it. Ethel squeezed into a booth with two of Louis's brothers, who were both policemen. A third was a local boxer. While she pretended to sip the warm gin, Ethel relaxed. Nobody knew about her and her divorces here. Kansas City was more fun than small-town gossip and failing farms. Ethel's temper flared when one of Louis's brothers tried to get her to drink more gin. Louis Trabon saw Ethel's passions as similar to those of the Italian women of his family. They both knew that his invitation to dinner concerned a possible marriage, but Ethel could not easily forget her mother's disdain for foreign miners in Pittsburg. She asked Trabon about starting a cab company. In 1928, she did not even need a cab license, only a sign, a telephone listing of her numbers, and some cabs. A finance company bought the cabs—the owner paid a mortgage and shared the profits.

Two nights later, Ethel seemed preoccupied as she dressed for her second date with Trabon. Angie felt abandoned. Kansas City was supposed to be their great adventure together. Suppose Louis Trabon was really a gangster. She feared Ethel would die in a gunfight. When Ethel returned hours later, she awakened Angie to discuss Trabon's proposal of marriage. Angie became hysterical. Grandmother Laura would not leave her at night like this. "I don't want another father," she said. "Not Mr. Trabon." Ethel became frightened for her daughter. She did not want anything else to go wrong. Ethel swore to Angie on her Bible that she would not marry Trabon. She told Angie that she had decided to open up a taxi company of her own. Angie promised that she would be Ethel's partner and work hard.

Living in small towns without a husband, Ethel had seen herself as a kind of adventurous outsider. The semilawless streets of Kansas City looked manageable to her. So, at the end of 1929, one of the worst moments in American history to open a business, Ethel took the big plunge. She invested the remaining cash from her divorce settlement in big mortgages on four used eight-cylinder De Sotos. Louis Trabon was amused. No woman had ever dispatched cabs in Kansas City before. He helped her rent an office at the Roanoke Theatre. It was clear that he expected her to marry him, and he assumed they would merge their two companies. Ethel etched the letters of her sign: WESTPORT TAXI. She pushed her first set of drivers around the clock. They were mostly tough men who could not get work anywhere else. Several carried guns and metal jack-handles in their boots. They drank and brawled and stole fares from her. They were supposed to split their ten-dollar-average daily take with Ethel. They kept kickbacks from madams and bootleggers for bringing in customers.

Ethel hung on to her marginal cab business by tricks and eighteen-hour workdays. "Ma Crowell" or "the old lady," as Ethel was known on the street, lived on the edge. She never opened a bank account, but carried her money in five-dollar bills in a little tobacco sack pinned inside her blouse. Sleep became precious to Ethel. She had a cold all the time. Although Ethel felt guilty asking her daughter to do it, Angie started sleeping on the office cot, waking up to relieve her mother for short periods during the night. Angie listened intently as her mother warned her about the cabdrivers. It flattered Angie, who was pleased at being treated as her mother's dearest possession. But sometimes Angie wanted to take risks and live a little. The drivers were the only people she talked to in Kansas City other than her mother.

Angie sat in the taxi shack with young Eugene Condon day after day. He was the only driver Ethel trusted with Angie. Angie showed him her articles from the school newspaper, the Westport *Crier*, pasted into a lined composition book. Throughout her life, she would treasure scrapbooks of her press clippings. It was as though she needed objective proof that she had been at a party or won an award. She showed Eugene an article she'd written about Prohibition. She had polled teachers and school custodians about whether the law should remain on the books. Angie had written, "The beer mug lagged far behind. Sixty voted for prohibition, 15 against, 5 noncommittal." The article had been Ethel's idea.

Angie told Eugene that many movie stars had come from Kansas City. William Powell and Ginger Rogers were two. She said she made her mother take her to Union Station to see Joan Crawford and her new husband, Douglas Fairbanks, Jr. When they changed trains there Angie had thought she had seen Joan Crawford's big black hat when she jumped up above the crowd. Angie told Eugene that she and Joan Crawford had the same name—Lucille.

Angie begged her mother to let her go on a Saturday night date to a picture show, a Joan Crawford movie. It was playing downtown next to a dance hall. Angie had read in a magazine that young Joan Crawford had lived for a few months at the corner of Armour and Wyandotte. She and Eugene rang a doorbell until a woman came out and said Joan Crawford had been a crazy slut and always came home in broad daylight with different men. Her name had been Lucille LeSueur, and she had always put on more makeup instead of washing her face. Angie told Eugene that the woman was jealous. She told Eugene to shake the woman's hand; she had actually known Joan Crawford.

Angie was beginning to dread the future. She and her mother seemed to have less and less. Ethel tried to reassure them both. She had fallen in love with Phil Kellet. The Kellets were important people in their working-class neighborhood. Phil's sister had married into the Pendergast family. Since Kansas City was a town in which political favors meant everything, a connection to Boss Pendergast was an important tie. Eugene often heard Ethel musing about how she could use Phil to get political favors from Pendergast. A few years later she had a love affair with his brother, Mike Kellet, the handsome one, but he was not very taken with her. Neither Kellet brother had wanted to marry Ethel. They both feared her temper.

Ethel was like a runner on a last sprint. She'd get excited after a night of work. At dawn, Angie would listen to her mother's fantasies of buying more taxicabs. Then Ethel would go to the Rosedale Bathhouse, where she would relax in a hot sulfur tub until she was able to fall asleep. One morning when Angie awoke in the taxi shack, Ethel was gone. Angie refused to leave for school. She asked one of the drivers to call the police. It turned out that Ethel had fainted in the steam of the bathhouse tub and had almost drowned. She was rescued by the woman who gave salt rubs.

Ethel had had a continuing dispute with the manager of the Roanoke Theatre, George Wilcox, because of the stench of the men's room adjoining the taxi shack. The smell seeped through the locked door into their little office. One night it was snowing and the chilly movie rows were empty. The last show had ended and the ladies' room was locked. Ethel left Angie asleep on the cot, unbolted the rear door of her office, and went into the men's room. When Angie woke up alone in the taxi shack she tried the door to the men's room. In a stall, she discovered that her mother had fainted. She dressed her, washed her face, and checked to make certain that Ethel's little tobacco sack of five-dollar bills was still pinned inside her blouse. The following day, Ethel refused to stay home and rest, muttering about how the mortgage company owned her cabs.

Her drivers resented Ethel's domination and made dirty jokes about Ethel's misadventure in the men's room. Eugene was sorry he told them about her fainting there, after a couple of them joked that Ethel had not fainted: they said she had just been waiting to surprise a man walking into the bathroom with his pants down and had fallen asleep. Angie heard their jokes, and she hated and pitied her mother. Angie was becoming her mother's caretaker.

Throughout her adolescence, Angie's favorite escape was to go to the movies. She adored Lillian Gish, Joan Crawford, and Ann Harding, who had a blond Ivy League look and a real life as tumultuous as Joan Crawford's. In the summer of 1929, *The Wind,* starring Lillian Gish, opened at the Roanoke Theatre. Angie slipped out of the Westport Taxi office and sneaked in through the men's room. She sat in the dark theater, velvet curtains on all sides smelling of mildew and popcorn, and watched her favorite scene at the end, where Lillian Gish cowers, trapped by a fierce windstorm inside her desolate prairie cabin. It had dawned on Ethel that Angie was curling her hair in a messy aureole around her face, with a bit of it pinned up in back, like Miss Gish.

The following December, Ethel decided to let Angie see the birthday card Jesse Claude had sent with a dollar bill in it. Angie's response jolted her mother. "Didn't he love me?" asked Angie.

Ethel nodded, despite herself.

"Was he worse than Mr. Jordan?" Angie asked.

"Don't ask me," Ethel said, her temper flaring. "He never sent you financial support, the way he promised the judge. Thank the Lord, you're nothing like him."

Angie wrote her father a secret letter. She mailed it in care of his cousin, Paul Crowell. She was angry that he had abandoned them as her mother said. But she missed him, particularly when she saw a man in the street with clumpy yellow hair.

Kansas City defeated Ethel in a series of small skirmishes. The first came early in 1931, when a new law required taxi companies to buy state licenses. Then three of her drivers stole the name of her company. The driver known as "Handsome Harry" Higgins had been jailed for murder and then changed his name to start a new life. His former wife managed a run-down hotel, the Berkeley. Higgins used to get drunk and beat her up. He flirted with Ethel, whose drivers thought she had wanted their romance to go further. One afternoon, Higgins and another driver drove one of Ethel's cabs to the State Capitol in Jefferson City to register the name Westport Livery and Ethel's telephone numbers as their own. In a rage, Ethel jumped into her Diana and drove to Jefferson City. She registered herself and her cabs under a new name—Westport Taxi and Livery. When she returned, she came down with bronchitis.

After this incident Ethel recruited some of Eugene Condon's friends who were also high school dropouts. The young boys were easier to handle. Unlike her first batch of drivers, they had no criminal records. Within a year she had the satisfaction of seeing the new owners of Westport Taxi bankrupt. When her old drivers tried to get work with her old suitor, Louis Trabon, she told him so many horror stories that he refused to hire them.

Ethel's health deteriorated as she sought to live by her wits. Her cough became so serious that on winter nights it made her retch. In spite of her many troubles, during the winter of 1931 Ethel became engaged to a wealthy rancher from Nebraska named August C. Brennemann. She told him that the five-story Ruxton apartment building where she lived was for sale. He advanced her $4,750 to buy it so that they could "put down roots." It also turned out to be a good investment. Angie liked Brennemann. He had a hearty laugh and always wanted to have a good time when he visited Kansas City. But Ethel lost patience when he kept postponing the day on which he would introduce her to his family, and she canceled their wedding date. When he asked for his money back, she refused to return it, saying she had spent it to make the down payment, as they had agreed. His lawyer sent her several letters and ultimately filed a civil suit on the grounds that the money had only been given with the understanding that the marriage would take place. Ethel pleaded with Brennemann to relent and promised she would marry him after all.

He dropped the suit a day later. But the relationship quickly deteriorated. On July 13, 1931, the Pittsburg *Headlight* published a story on the front page that the former Pittsburg schoolteacher was being prosecuted for embezzlement in Kansas City on criminal charges brought by her disappointed fiancé. The newspaper reported that Ethel had spent one night in the county jail, after which she raised the $9,000 bond and was released.

When two detectives came to take her mother to jail, Angie said in a loud voice, "Ma, don't go, I'll think of something." "Go along, Angeline," said Ethel, weeping. "Eugene, stay close to Angie and keep the office going." Ethel also instructed Eugene to ask the Kellet brothers to borrow money for bail. Angie spent the night answering the telephone and despaired of ever being a normal girl with a normal life. The charges against Ethel were eventually dismissed.

Since the taxi business made little profit, Ethel added a second venture that grew out of her connections to organized crime. The new business was a speakeasy; it was known as a "joint." Ethel unhappily joked that being a schoolteacher had taught her enough to keep drinking men in line. She decided to arrange a meeting with the gangster Johnny Lazia, to ask him to sell her bootleg liquor. For several months, Ethel had been trying to convince the Kellet brothers to introduce her to Lazia. Then one evening in late 1931, taking matters into her own hands, Ethel walked into the Sunset Lounge. Lazia, his wife, and bodyguard were in the front booth. He was wearing a conservative business suit and rimless eyeglasses. While a waiter followed her, saying, "But, ma'am," Ethel ignored the bodyguard and extended her hand to Lazia's startled wife. "Ethel Crowell," she said firmly. She had never stood so close to a woman wearing so many diamonds. Lazia stood to greet Ethel.

"I want to sell beer and gin," Ethel said in her most forceful classroom manner. "Will you sell to me?"

"To a lovely lady?" Lazia asked, smiling. Ethel liked his looks. She told him she knew the Kellet brothers. Lazia promised to consider it. He gave her a telephone number to call. "Good evening, Ethel Crowell," his wife said.

Angie and Ethel moved to a two-story house big enough for a speakeasy, with side sun porches and a two-car garage. It was more expensive than the last place, but Ethel considered it an investment. She bought a large used icebox. Angie was embarrassed that her mother was going into an illegal business. But Ethel was committed. She not only made light of her daughter's concerns, she went so far as to put Angie in charge of the joint. At the age of fifteen, Angie became a cocktail waitress in her own home. While her mother dispatched taxicabs three blocks away, Angie arranged the chairs each night in their long brown living room. Ethel had hidden Johnny Lazia's flat liquor bottles with their plain white labels behind three empty milk bottles in the icebox. Each night Angie would iron her Sunday dress. Then she stood by the tin sink pouring liquor into jelly jars. She dreamed of finding her true love, as Clara Bow had, among her customers.

By seven-thirty Angie was sitting in the yellow dining booth, doing her homework sums in her notebook. Eugene Condon sat nearby her as her bodyguard. He was becoming smitten with Angie. He liked watching her run with her expectant smile when the door chimed. Every night was a new party. Years later, in the role of society hostess, she would repeat the pattern. She always liked dressing up, and she enjoyed playing the woman of the house. She particularly liked not knowing who would show up.

Although Eugene was only eighteen, Ethel had been right to select him as her bouncer. For one thing, he was strong for his age. For another, he was fascinated by Ethel and half in love with Angie. He gladly ran errands for them. He thought Ethel Crowell the most brilliant woman he had ever met, but he viewed her as a warrior who never laughed. He found her soured by men and by life.

In the evenings, the last man to ring the doorbell was always a courtly old Irish police captain. John Gleason felt very protective of Ethel. He stopped in to make sure the women were all right. Ethel would sometimes sit with him on the porch. The younger police on the force knew he would object if they dared to harass her.

A girl in her home economics class had once told Angie that she must be the twin of Ann Harding. Angie clipped magazine articles about the actress. Ann Harding had a patrician face with a wide forehead, high-bridged, prominent nose, and enormous eyes—softened by full cheeks, baby-blond hair, and a small truculent mouth. She was said to have taken her last name from President Harding. When a Kansas businessman bought Ann Harding's monoplane, Angie went to see it at the airport.

By now dinners at home were filled with unresolved fights between mother and daughter. Angie wanted to be a normal teenager. She wanted pocket money to buy hair ribbons, movie tickets, and movie magazines. Johnny Elston, a student at nearby Kemper Military Academy, was now her official boyfriend, and she saw him on school vacations. Johnny's parents were also divorced, and there was no place in either of their lives for him. Ethel was still a domestic creature at heart. Angie helped bake cakes for Johnny's birthdays. She knit him Christmas gloves that she put under their tree, crocheted him socks, and made Ethel's special roast chicken. Johnny was impressed with Angie's cooking. On the rare evenings that Angie did not work, she turned on Ethel's radio in the living room for Johnny while she washed dinner plates. Then she would sit next to him on the davenport while they listened to music and radio dramas. Angie laughed and cried at the vicissitudes of the soap opera heroines' lives.

In her senior year at Westport, Angie became the pet of her speech arts teacher and helped judge other students' auditions. She won a starring role in the spring graduation play, Oscar Wilde's *The Importance of Being Earnest*. Ethel was impressed, but she did not want to spare Angie for rehearsals. "Then I'll just go to Hollywood now," said Angie, raising her voice. "I don't need to graduate." She had tried out for the play because Ann Harding always credited her high school plays with having been an important part of her training.

Ethel tried to temper Angie's enthusiasms and dreams. But Angie was burning to escape Ethel's world. Ethel was enraged when she saw Angie's Westport High yearbook picture. Angie looked boldly over her raised left shoulder at the camera. Her dress looked backless. It was a daring glamour pose. The caption read: "Ann Harding is with us." The yearbook also suggested that Angie had turned the yearbook staff office into an experimental beauty salon.

By now Angie was responsible for cooking and doing light housekeeping for two boarders. With the applause of her classmates and their parents still ringing in her ears, she started in earnest to plan her getaway. Her fantasies of the future included dancing in Busby Berkeley chorus lines and dazzling rich men. She silently debated her mother's precepts. Good marks in school had not helped Ethel scrape together a living in Kansas City.

As graduation approached, Angie daydreamed of marrying Johnny Elston. He was determined to see the good in everyone. She liked him more than any other boy, and he did not boss her around. Angie was not attracted to Wilson Armour, a good, plodding boy who had been her only suitor from Westport High. Wilson drove her home in his rag-top green convertible Chevrolet fitted with an exhaust pipe that exuded its own special sound. After graduating, he worked for the next forty years as the office manager of Greenlease Cadillac showrooms in Kansas City. Angie began to worry that lack of sleep was ruining her looks. She never knew when her mother was going to awaken her to sit by the phone in the taxi shack in the middle of the night while she went out to rescue a driver.

One Saturday afternoon, Johnny asked Angie out to an evening show. Angie squeezed her big eyes closed with exaggerated pleasure. She asked him to go to see *Holiday* (1930), a movie that Angie had already seen twice. The star was Ann Harding.

That evening, the Westport cabdrivers could hear Angie and her mother shouting at each other, using words no ladies ever used. Angie tried to throw the telephone at her mother. Alarmed, Ethel stopped short, her jaw shaking. She agreed to make time for Angie to go on a date with Johnny. Angie knew Ethel was worried about the mortgage company taking the cabs away. She burst into tears and hugged Ethel.

During their nearly nine years together in Kansas City, Ethel and Angie moved at least three times in the middle of the night when they were unable to pay rent. In one instance Ethel stalled for several months by prolonging a fight with her landlord over leaking pipes. Finally, she and Angie closed the taxi shack early, went home, and removed all their possessions in cartons. This became a routine. Eventually, landlords gave up trying to collect their back rent. At neighborhood shops, some merchants refused to do business with Angie and Ethel. Ethel refused to pay bills, claiming goods had been damaged before she bought them. Once, Angie was humiliated when the local druggist refused to take her money for cough drops. Ethel was becoming increasingly bitter. Her young drivers would tell one another that Ethel sought friendships only to gain something.

Angie was beginning to realize that her mother was in over her head. "You should go back to Pittsburg," Angie said. "I'd rather die," said Ethel, who could envision herself as the town pariah. Instead, she continued scrambling to make $4.50 a day on her fleet of cabs. She closed the saloon at the end of Prohibition in 1934.

Angie was admitted to Kansas City Junior College and to Rockford in Illinois, but she had no way to pay the tuition. She was a year out of high school and depressed by the taxi shack. She forced herself to keep cleaning up after her mother's boarders. She read newspaper notices of road companies doing plays. She knew that theatrical auditions were the first step to a movie career. In Hollywood, she would be recognized for what she dreamed she was.

A vicious gangster massacre in Kansas City during the summer of 1933 made Angie more eager than ever to escape. On July 17 Frank "Jelly" Nash, a bank robber, and one of the nation's most wanted criminals, was being transported to the federal penitentiary at Leavenworth through Union Station in Kansas City. (Nash had begun his criminal life by shooting a close friend in the back.) The authorities had to move him from a train to a police car.

At seven that morning, Angie was walking home from the taxi shack. At the same time, in Union Station, two policemen sat waiting inside an armored car for the train bearing Frank Nash. The two undoubtedly thought it strange that someone had ordered the submachine guns removed from their squad car. They also may have wondered why they were the only police at the station. Around them, cabs and cars pulled into the station, discharging and picking up their customers. The two policemen did not notice the three hoodlums slouched in a Chevrolet sedan in the parking lot. They, too, were waiting for Frank Nash, but unlike the Kansas City policemen, they had submachine guns.

Suddenly, when the manacled Nash and his FBI guards arrived, bullets sprayed the walls of Union Station. People ran screaming from the parking lot, cabdrivers hit the floors of their cars, and three nuns picked up their habits and ran for the station entrance. It took the hoodlums only ninety seconds to kill the Oklahoma police chief, an FBI agent, and the two Kansas City policemen. Nash also lay bleeding to death from a bullet wound. The three gangsters drove away. No Kansas City newspaper published what every citizen knew. Johnny Lazia, who always protected hit men in Kansas City and the surrounding Midwest, had arranged the massacre, which would mark the beginning of J. Edgar Hoover's war on crime.

Hours after the bloodbath, FBI agents poured into Kansas City. Unwilling to share information with the police, they searched for the hoodlums, bursting into the jazz clubs, crap joints, gambling houses, and houses of prostitution owned by Lazia.

Peering out of her kitchen window, Ethel's neighbor saw a strange car parked next to Ethel's. It looked like Pretty Boy Floyd's Chevrolet, described in emergency radio broadcasts as the getaway car used by the hoodlums at Union Station. The woman called the FBI and told agents that she'd once also seen Charles Carrollo, Lazia's bodyguard, pull up to Ethel's house.

Angie was completely unaware of the massacre. Outside her house,

The graduating class of the Kansas State Manual Training Normal School, 1912. Ann Woodward's mother, Ethel Smiley, age nineteen, second row, far left.

Ethel, now Mrs. Jesse Claude Crowell, age twenty-one, living on the Crowell farm, Pittsburg, Kansas.

Angeline Luceil Crowell, later Ann
Eden Woodward, 1932. From her
Westport, Kansas, high school
yearbook.

The Westport, Kansas, high school dramatic society, with Angeline at center (her
idol was the Broadway actress Ann Harding). Angeline was about to appear as
Gwendolyn in *The Importance of Being Earnest*.

two carloads of FBI agents pulled up on the curb and surrounded the house. Angie awoke to the slamming of car doors. She had been planning to dress and return to the taxi office. Suddenly, the front door came flying in and broke into pieces. Three men in blue suits jumped over the slivers of wood, two pointing shotguns. "Where are they?" asked a third man, brandishing an ax. More men came in. "Stay put, lady." She did not move while she listened to footsteps and shotgun butts crashing into her mother's bedroom door. Angie was frightened that something terrible had happened to her mother. In the basement, doors slammed. A man slid and fell on her mother's old brown rug.

The agents formed a tight circle around her in the hallway. "You hear of Frank Nash?" asked a man in a Stetson hat.

Angie could not speak.

"FBI," he said.

"Come on, she doesn't know anything," another man said.

"I know Mr. Nash's son Melvin." She started to cry. "He lives near here in an orphanage." Angie's teeth started to chatter. "What's wrong?" she asked. "Where's my ma?"

The agents did not reply. As they left, two of them picked up the front door and leaned it in place. Angie changed into a sundress and raced out into the hot sun. She found the taxi shack door wide open. She was relieved to find her mother in one piece and not in jail.

Angie slept fitfully for weeks. She awoke with a start whenever a car turned the corner. Despite the heat, she locked the first-floor windows. Ethel paid Eugene to drive around the house several times a night in his Model A. Angie was plagued by nightmares of FBI agents shooting guns while she hid behind the icebox in the pantry.

At twenty, Angie was suddenly in bloom. When she laughed, throwing her head back, the taxi drivers looked hypnotized. She had been a skinny little girl with a pale white face. Now she had a proud bosom and glowing skin. She practiced playing with a loose strand of hair and folding her hands in her lap. Like Ann Harding, she lightened her hair with peroxide, doing it as well as any hairdresser in Kansas City. Sometimes she wore a low bun on her neck. She tanned herself until her hair and skin looked pale gold. Johnny Elston felt threatened by her transformation. She alarmed him by announcing that she preferred to be called "Ann." She had read a biography of Queen Anne of Austria, who had married a king of France.

"What in hell is going on?" Ethel asked. "You're acting like a

stranger." Angie had begun putting on airs. She flounced. She fluttered her
hand over her mouth to convey surprise. Ethel could see that Angie had
filled out and reluctantly agreed to let her take modeling courses at Kansas
City Junior College. She blamed herself for giving her daughter so little
stability in life. She was immensely relieved when, in the summer of 1936,
Angie told her that Johnny had suggested marriage. But Angie was still
talking about Hollywood and New York. To Ethel that meant one thing—
danger from deceitful men. Ethel knew she had to give ground. She sent
Angie to work as a volunteer at the local society thrift shop run by the
Junior League. There Angie would meet a better class of people. Angie
loved trying on expensive dresses at the shop. Ethel gave her money for
thrift-shop silks and lace. Angie developed a sense of style and began to
look even better than the wealthy society ladies who came in to donate
their clothes. Ethel suggested she try to get an invitation to meet a rich
brother or friend of one of the other volunteers.

On her twenty-first birthday, December 12, 1936, Johnny presented
Angie with a small Tiffany cut diamond ring. Ethel clasped her hands in
approval. She had been campaigning for this moment for six years. Smiling,
Angie ran to the mirror to look at her left hand with a diamond on it.

Angie told Johnny she wanted to work at the Junior League shop
until he finished college. He objected. The shop filled her head with big
ideas. The night of her engagement, Angie could not stop talking of her
passing acquaintance with the powerful city manager's daughter, Mary
McElroy. The wealthy girl's stylish clothes and her nervous confidences
intrigued Angie, who collected news clippings of Mary's social appearances.
A year earlier, Mary had been in the headlines when she had been kidnapped at gunpoint from her father's mansion.

One day, Mary handed Angie a big green-and-white-striped box from
Harzfelds, the leading department store in Kansas City, saying, "The blouse
is for you, not for the shop, if you like it. I never wore it." Angie called
Mary a few times on the telephone, but their friendship did not develop.*

Johnny Elston broke his engagement to Angie on the first day of his
summer vacation in June 1937. He arrived at Ethel's house in high spirits
at four in the afternoon. Angie greeted him warmly. They had not seen
each other in several months. She eagerly told Johnny she was taking
modeling lessons and had auditioned for a touring theater company. She
said that Joan Crawford had escaped Kansas City in a touring company.

*Six years later, Ann would read a New York newspaper account of Mary McElroy's
suicide, a shooting after a solitary dinner.

Angie fixed Johnny a cool drink. Johnny had little to say about Joan Craw-ford. He almost told Angie that she wanted a lot more out of life than he could ever give her. But instead he stood up, saying, "I've got to get back to the hotel."

"Why can't I come?" Angie followed him out of the darkened living room, and they stood on her front porch.

Johnny was tired of this fight. "No girls come," he said finally. "The guys blow off steam."

"Don't go, let's do something, you and me, tonight."

"I want to go," Johnny said, feeling pushed. He'd been looking for-ward to getting drunk with his graduating buddies. This was the last time in his life he would see most of them.

"Then please take me."

"I can't."

Angie's voice rose. "Then I never want to see you again. Never come back," she said.

Johnny felt more angry than he knew was possible. "That's okay by me." He walked down the porch steps.

"Well, are you coming back tonight or not?" she asked, expecting him to turn around. Her voice rising again, she said, "Please, don't leave," but he quickened his step.

There was something frightening to Johnny about Angie's demands. He felt her loneliness jump out at him and start to choke him.

When she wrote him a polite letter in Omaha a few weeks later, he never answered it. She called three times and asked if she could come and visit him, but he told her it was not a good idea. She wrote him two more letters. He did not answer.

Angie told Ethel that she wanted to get into something where she could make money of her own. She was twenty-one years old and an old maid. To divert her unhappy daughter, Ethel wrote to her sister, Edna Smiley Cobb, in Dodge City. Although it was a financial sacrifice for Ethel, she gave Angie a vacation. She bought her a train ticket to Dodge City to meet her aunt and two preschool nieces and accompany them on a summer sightseeing drive through the Colorado Rockies. Ann loved the wide streets of Denver and the fresh clean air in Rocky Mountain National Park. Later in life, when she was depressed, she would visit the Swiss and Bavarian Alps, hoping to be happier amid the high, clean peaks. But in the car driving home to Kansas, she felt doomed to be a second-class member of her own family—poor and unmarried. When she returned to Kansas City, tanner than ever, Ann called Johnny Elston again. "You said we were finished," he said, and quietly hung up.

Ann swore she was going to leave Kansas City and all her memories of Johnny Elston forever. Instead, she called Mary McElroy. Mary agreed to ask around about local modeling jobs. Two days later, dressed in her thrift-shop finest, Ann took a taxi to Petticoat Lane and Main Street. She met with Johnny Harzfeld, the son of the owner of the department store. The wealthiest women in the Midwest shopped at Harzfelds. Ann was soon working as a salesgirl and model in the millinery department. Her new job touched off yet another argument with her mother: now Ann wanted to move into her own apartment. They agreed to a compromise; she took an apartment next door on Belleview Avenue.

Hats were all the rage in 1936; the hat department was the major focal point of the store. Its small dressing tables with mirrors stretched out for an entire floor—half a city block. In the summer, large floor fans would create a breeze over the artificial red cherries and the chiffon streamers. Hats on display were also decorated with buckles, flowers, and floor-length patterned scarves. Twelve saleswomen sold the promise of glamour, mystery, and beauty.

A great favorite of her well-to-do customers, Ann placed the hats on women's heads as if she were crowning them in beauty pageants. It was a reminder of her childhood games of dressing up. It did not escape Ann's notice that many of the other millinery saleswomen were older, unmarried ladies.

Ann was thrilled to be photographed for brochures and newspaper advertisements. The John-Frederics hats were bright, brimless, and dainty. Under them, Ann wore her blond hair short with curls at the nape of her neck. An evening hat was decorated with big daisies. She looked plump-faced and wholesome. Mr. John himself came from Manhattan to mount the millinery fashion show for his fifty best customers. Ann asked to model. She had, she told him, professional training. He looked her over and decided she had the looks and the audacity to be the main millinery model.

Ann was a great success, smiling at each face in the audience. She had learned how to make entrances on stage, but this was even better. She asked Mr. John to give her his business card—John-Frederics Co., 29 East Forty-eighth Street, New York—and he told her to come see him if she ever got to Manhattan. Ann saved every penny of her Harzfelds salary except for her rent. After pestering Mr. John for a recommendation by telephone, she took the big step. She sent glossy pictures to his colleague

John Robert Powers, who owned a big New York modeling agency. When she called long distance, the woman said, "It looks like your nose is wrong. Better to show up here in person, honey."

"Angeline, I forbid it," said Ethel.

Ann withdrew her savings and bought a used car. "I reckon I know what I'm doing, Ma, I got to go."

"I need you here," said Ethel, breaking down in front of Eugene. "I'd never leave you, Angie."

Ann did not mention how frequently Ethel had left her. Instead, she said, "I'll send you more money in six months than we made in our whole lives."

Her mother's tears hurt Ann. She often felt guilty for abandoning Ethel. "I'll send you a ticket to come to New York when I get money." But Ann also liked to picture herself hopping a freight train to New York, like Barbara Stanwyck in *Baby Face*.

Slowly, Ethel's concern about her daughter's safety became more important to her than her own hurt feelings. "Never talk to strange men," she told her one day. "Never look at them past daylight in the street. Make friends with your landlord. Write to me if there's any problem. Find a cheap restaurant to eat at regularly. They'll worry if they don't see you."

The day Ann left, her mother gave her a little sack of five-dollar bills. It contained $400. The girl hugged her mother. "I'm sorry to leave you," she said.

3

SCANDAL

"I'm not Old Guard. We were poor and we weren't pretty. But my mother was very publicity-conscious and dressed us all alike and things like that, so we were pretty well known. Of course, in those days there wasn't any press the way there is today—just Town Topics—*but there was a real Old Guard and they really had power."*

—ELSIE WOODWARD

The first scandal in the long life of Elsie Woodward erupted in 1891. Elsie and the other two triplets were only eight years old when their uncle W. Wetmore Cryder was indicted for perjury and for embezzling $39,000 from Madison Square Bank, of which he was president. He was a pillar of the New York social and financial community, a member of the Knickerbocker Club who lived in a big stone house in the new suburb of Tuxedo Park, New York.

Elsie Cryder's father, Duncan, had his own problems. His trips to China for his tea-importing business had been a financial embarrassment. But thanks to his brother Wetmore, life in Duncan's household on West Ninth Street had a way of looking far more prosperous than it was.

The "freakish" birth of three tiny identical baby girls on December 1, 1882 (although not officially recorded), had precedent in both of their parents' families. Duncan Cryder himself had twin siblings who had died at birth. His wife's sister would give birth to twins Henry and John Adams.

Duncan Cryder's favorite was Elizabeth, whom everyone called "Elsie." "Stuck-up," she seemed eerily grown-up; neither of her sisters understood their father's jokes. The importance of the Ogden family pedigree was impressed upon the little girls early and often. Elsie Ogden Cryder was named for her mother and for Elizabethtown, New Jersey, founded in the mid-seventeenth century by her illustrious Ogden ancestors. In 1670, John Ogden had abandoned hundreds of acres in Shinnecock, Long Island, because he did not like the way the Indians were being treated there, to become the leader of Elizabethtown—and later governor of New Jersey. The family had been pillars of the community, many of them governors and supreme court justices since that time.

The banking scandal made Duncan Cryder stop smiling for the first time in years. Reporters were turned away from his door. His wife, Elizabeth, wept continually. His own past business failures now seemed minor. Embarrassment was only part of Duncan Cryder's problem. He was ruined. Without his brother's backing, Duncan Cryder was without prospects. He had no credit. He had no way to finance his next trip to China. He instructed his daughters to play only indoors and not to accept invitations. Matters grew worse when *The New York Times* revealed on its front page that Uncle Wetmore had been accused of exaggerating the bank's capital in a quarterly report. Gambling debts were rumored to be the cause.

Three years before, a far less damaging front-page *New York Times* article had embarrassed Duncan's wife. That article had implied that the pedigreed young society matron had no important jewelry. The *Times* had reported a robbery of the family's five-story home. A dishonest butler (borrowed from Wetmore's household) had substituted paste stones for diamonds in her best earrings. The newspaper hypothesized that the earrings were made of such tiny stones that the counterfeiter could not make small enough paste copies. Thus, the switch was easily discovered. Despite her handsome husband's amusement over the newspaper revelation, Elizabeth had privately wept. These were times that might have crushed the spirit of a less audacious man. But Duncan Cryder soothed his wife's worries, laughing at poverty. "Make do and mend, let's add it to our family crest," he said.

Elizabeth Ogden Cryder had lowered her standards only once in her life, when she married for love. She was too polite ever to say that her main problem in life was her husband. She undoubtedly envied her sister Caroline's marriage to the eminent statesman and scholar Charles Francis Adams, scion of the presidential Adamses.

In yet another front-page story, a few weeks after Wetmore's indictment, the *Times* remarked on the still-burgeoning scandal. "Clubroom gossip concerning the financial affairs of W. Wetmore Cryder, former president of Madison Square Bank, was given a new turn yesterday. . . ." Wetmore had forged his wife's signature on notes, borrowed heavily against their house, and then deserted her. Duncan Cryder realized he had to do something. His own debts were growing. They might soon be forced to sell their house. Duncan Cryder joked that the triplets were his "most stable asset."

Elsie Cryder's mother told her she was descended from Robert Bruce, the ancient King of Scotland. The prosperous Callenders, on her own mother's side, were high Hudson River society. When Franklin Roosevelt proposed to Eleanor, it was in the garden behind the Callenders' eighteenth-century Hudson River mansion. The Callenders' fortune came from the steamboat invented by their business partner Robert Fulton. Duncan Cryder had married a woman with a place in society, but there was no money. Nonetheless, Elizabeth Cryder was invited to tea dances, cotillions, and salons in the wealthiest homes of Manhattan, Boston, and Newport. She was a prim Victorian woman. At the beach, her skirt almost touched the ground, her enormous hats were veiled, and a corset pinched her waist. It would have been easier for Elizabeth if Duncan Cryder had simply been a failure whom she could dislike. Instead, he was dashing, cosmopolitan, with intense brown eyes, a sweeping mustache, and great wit. Raised in Europe, he was entirely at his ease carrying a sun umbrella (similar to a lady's parasol) as he strolled through the Bois de Boulogne.

His daughter Elsie Cryder would always favor men who danced well. Duncan Cryder was very popular in Paris and waltzed as well as any man in the world. He was at home in London, where he had been raised by his Philadelphia-born father, who was also an importer. He took the waters at Europe's finest spas and gambled the nights away at casinos. Duncan Cryder made ladies smile. He seemed destined to adorn parties the world over. A generation later, Elsie would mold her son, Billy Woodward, in his grandfather's image.

After his brother's indictment, Duncan Cryder was often depressed because he could barely afford a summer carriage, not to mention a winter sleigh. Midwinter sleigh rides took the place of the spring and summer coaching parades in Central Park, where there was intense rivalry for the smartest "equipage." In the afternoons the air was full of ringing sleigh bells. Crowds gathered to watch Mrs. Cornelius Vanderbilt as she flashed by on the clean white snow, pulled by her horses in a blaze of red livery, crimson plumes, and gilt tassels.

Elsie would one day tell Billy that his grandfather brought the game of golf from Scotland to America. He went on to help found the Shinnecock Golf Club, which had turned Southampton into a fashionable resort. But the three successes of Duncan Cryder's life had all occurred, alas, in his youth—the founding of the Shinnecock Golf Club, the winning of the hand of the illustrious Elizabeth Callender Ogden as his wife on June 17, 1879, and the birth of his triplet daughters in 1882, the same year that Oscar Wilde made his first trip to America, telling the great robber barons that "art" was all that mattered in life. Duncan Cryder cited the quotation more than once as he avoided going to his office, dedicating himself instead to the "art of living" and earning less and less each year. Duncan Cryder sought to save money in odd ways. Elsie later told friends how the three little girls shared only two dress-up dresses, which meant that all three triplets never appeared together in public.

The banking scandal intensified when W. Wetmore Cryder deserted his wife. A *New York Times* article, published on April 20, 1892, appeared under the headline "Mr. Cryder's Unpaid Note"; it told how Wetmore had reneged on a promissory note of $160.94 and then ducked a summons to appear before a judge.

A few days later, Duncan Cryder told his wife he wanted to take his family abroad. A decade of European exile would give New York society time to forget his brother's disgrace. His son and daughters would be far away from school gossip. In Europe, he could raise cash and do business with merchants who did not know of his brother's ruin.

He then declared a new goal in life: he would marry his triplet daughters to men "who did not have to go to business every day." His goals for his daughters were neither spiritual nor intellectual. He wanted to make sure that Elsie, Edith, and Ethel Cryder acquired the right social connections and polish. Duncan Cryder asked his daughters if they preferred being rich to being healthy. "I prefer being rich," he said, smiling.

It would be more than half a century before Elsie Cryder Woodward could bring herself to speak of her father's financial ruin. Even as a grande dame of Manhattan in the 1950s and 1960s, Elsie would discreetly maintain that she and her sisters had taken their seven-year European tour for "educational reasons." When pressed, the eighty-nine-year-old Elsie dismissed her father's bankruptcy as having come about through the machinations of a dishonest partner who had absconded with his money.

In the last years of the nineteenth century, European exile was a genteel solution to scandal, and indefinite travel on the continent would be fun for Duncan Cryder. Even when scandal did not motivate the journey, it was all the rage for young American socialites to emulate Europeans.

In Paris, at age ten, the Cryder triplets learned French and invented a secret language. Uncomfortable listening to strangers, they created their own mixture of French and English words. *"C'est* finished." *"Tout va bien,* as always."

Elsie did not resent her father's pressure; she adored his amusing attentions. They played tricks on each other. She put off his acquaintances, saying, *"Je m'appelle* Edith." Her audacity was meant to please him—and it always did. Her sisters assumed she would be the most successful in carrying out her father's ambitions.

From earliest childhood, Elsie was taught to develop the mask that became her personality. Already the triplets appeared smugly calm. They had rules for descent from a carriage and for shaking hands. The girls had been taught to pronounce the word "shirt" as "shut"; the "r" strongly implied, never stated. True members of their class would not drop the "r" at the end of the word, like a theatrical Englishman. The Cryder girls would have the best manners in New York. In fact, the word "best" was crucial to their sense of themselves. Elsie and her sisters believed, like Edith Wharton, that the true hallmarks of the upper classes could never be learned by outsiders. The triplets never raised their voices, or ran, or showed anger. They were congenial but never intimate with outsiders. They were taught how to seem helpless. Elsie, who was always on guard against being thought intellectual, firmly believed that girls who went to Bryn Mawr ended up as spinster teachers. She and her sisters learned the same songs on the harpsichord. They were also taught a smattering of English grammar, Latin, mathematics, and science in two hours of daily lessons. Elsie was told to say she had a bosom, not breasts, and below the waist to mention only her frilly petticoats. She knew little of sex.

It was in Paris that Elsie made up her mind to be a great hostess with a salon. She acquired the French passion for conversation. The Cryder triplets were superb listeners; they always seemed about to be amused. They also perfected the art of delivering casual sentences as though they were punch lines to jokes. Unlike most Americans in Paris, the girls were not ostentatiously dressed in fur, tulle roses, tassels, silk fringes, and lace bodices. Elsie usually wore a plain high-necked peach-colored blouse over a midcalf navy skirt. Her bonnets were simple, with one yellow ribbon and a real yellow rose. (Her distinguishing color was yellow; her yellow hair ribbon was the only way anyone but the triplets' most intimate friends could tell Elsie from her sisters.)

In the spring, Paris seemed like a carnival, with street singers and parades of trumpet players on horseback. Rich and social Americans flocked to the racetrack at Longchamp to shop or simply to enjoy the "season." But as Elsie later said, the Cryders did not have the money to keep up. As children, however, the triplets established social ties that extended into their adult lives. They met Conseulo Vanderbilt, who became Ethel's best friend. (Consuelo's ambitious mother would make social history by forcing her into an illustrious and unhappy marriage to the Duke of Marlborough.)

In Baden-Baden, Duncan Cryder taught the girls to curtsy. In St. Moritz, he taught them how to behave with footmen. The sisters smoked cigarettes on the sly. But otherwise—particularly in public—they were perfect examples of *jeunes filles bien élevées*. When Duncan had luck at Longchamp or at the Paris gambling tables, he celebrated by taking his girls— with second-class tickets—to the most fashionable watering spots of the Continent. He blithely maintained that Elsie, Edith, and Ethel must become familiar with these resorts. Duncan saved money by making these "educational" jaunts during the off-season.

In January, Baden-Baden, the playground of Edward VII, was damp, murky, mysterious—and fun for three adolescent girls playing "rich and grown-up." The treetops hid in an unfriendly mist, but a delighted Fraulein Elsie strolled the empty rose and jasmine gardens. There was no hunting in the Black Forest, but happily for Duncan Cryder the casino had not yet closed.

Summers, when the low mountains surrounding St. Moritz shed snowcaps, Elsie did not mind in the least dining with her sisters in an empty teahouse. The triplets in their best muslin dresses looked surreal in this formal setting surrounded by flickering candles and potted palms. Their mother, however, yearned for what she deemed "proper" people. The local Swiss caretakers were not up to her standards. *"Tiens, tiens, tiens,"* laughed Elsie, sipping her tea. Widening her eyes, Elsie whispered to her sisters in mock horror, *"pas devant les domestiques."*

Most of all, Elsie never forgot visiting Biarritz when snow fell. The girls laughed as their father filled the empty avenues with characters drawn from his vivid memories. No matter that the triplets were training on a bare winter stage; the true Cryder extravaganza was still far in the future. The girls sang French Christmas carols, teeth chattering as they paced the striped beach tent, trying to ignore the sea wind. In the 1920s Elsie would visit Biarritz again, but in triumph. As the impressive young Mrs. William Woodward, Elsie regaled newcomers such as Henry Ford and Lillian Gish with her girlhood memories of the place.

After several years in Paris, Duncan Cryder had succeeded in turning the triplets into famous young ladies. They were pointed out on the streets by admiring Parisians. But he was still not finished with their training. Through his adroit cultivation of an old French scientist who gambled with him, the sixteen-year-old triplets were honored by an invitation from the Empress Eugénie, widow of the last Emperor of France, Louis-Napoléon.

It was 1897, and the Empress was living in exile in rural England under the loving auspices of Queen Victoria. Empress Eugénie's imperial court was incongruous at Farnborough Hill, a Tudor mansion set amidst pastures of hay. Empress Eugénie had survived the loss of her empire and her husband. But she was brokenhearted over the recent death of her young son, Louis-Napoléon, in South Africa, where he had been fighting under the British flag.

One damp and green afternoon the Empress received the famous triplets in her grand salon. Willowy and identically dressed, except for their hair ribbons, the three girls made a startling entrance. They coordinated their gestures, walking slowly toward the black-robed Eugénie and her servingwomen. The triplets wore neither lace nor jewelry. Their bosoms were tightly wrapped to appear flat, as was the style of the day. Their hair was rolled up into a Gibson-like twist on the tops of their heads—which emphasized their strong chins. They appeared as austere as their mother's Pilgrim ancestors, by Duncan Cryder's design. They were to be presented as prime examples of pristine American gentility. Like her sisters, Elsie carried a few white stephanotis stems in one hand.

Despite their excitement, the girls had no trouble remaining serene. But it was difficult for Elsie to keep her eyes on the Empress's almond-shaped eyes and wrinkled face. She glanced quickly at the huge Rousseau and David oil paintings and at the wittily painted walls and ceiling. Overlooking the wide room was a trompe l'oeil balcony painted with climbing roses under a blue clouded sky. The girls were in high spirits. They had memorized the protocol they had to follow: they knew they must not leave the audience room before the Empress.

Reciting flawless French greetings, Elsie and her sisters dropped into an extravagant curtsy. They silently counted the beats. Each held her long skirt with one hand. Finally, the sisters ducked their heads in unison, looking down past the folds of the Empress's black rustling skirts. But when Elsie looked down to the floor, she was aghast to see that the Empress was not wearing proper black silk hose. Instead, she wore white anklets under her stiff hem. "*Très sportive,*" Elsie whispered.

Her sister Ethel gasped. It was very bad form to make fun of the Empress's sensible white socks. When she straightened up, Elsie knew she had nothing to fear from this old lady. To the surprise of her ladies-in-waiting, Eugénie sat down on a little stool. She rarely sat during these afternoon audiences because she did not wish to encourage her guests to stay. Elsie suddenly realized the old Empress was staring too intently at her and her sisters. Something had struck Empress Eugénie. Perhaps she imagined an air of religious purity in the three adolescents. Suddenly, Eugénie rose and led them down a twenty-foot-wide hall filled with priceless gold and porcelain palace furnishings.

They found themselves in the back of the castle in the sealed-off "*cabinet du Prince.*" Unopened letters addressed to the Prince Imperial were neatly stacked on a desk. A glass cabinet held his bloodied shirt, his sketchbooks, and the sword he had inherited from his father. The Empress showed them the silver bassinet that had been given to her son by the city of Paris. A gold tea service had been a gift from the Prince of Wales. Eugénie crossed herself and murmured prayers. A worried Frenchwoman signaled the Empress that it was time to lead her afternoon rosary for the Prince's soul. The Empress blessed the three girls. Elsie Cryder took the blessing to heart.

Her son Billy Woodward would ask in particular to hear the story of his mother's presentation at court on the rare occasions that Elsie visited his nursery. Billy loved the story, and it always made his mother smile to tell it.

In 1899 the return of the Cryder triplets took Manhattan society by storm. After a seven-year absence, the three thin, haughty, tall—nearly five feet seven—young socialites became instant news. Reporters accosted the startled girls in the streets of Greenwich Village. The triplets found themselves celebrities. The city's newspapers fed on news of society. The stars of sports and silent cinema—Jack Dempsey, Babe Ruth, and Mary Pickford—did not start competing with socialites for newspapers and magazine covers until the 1920s. One hundred years after the revolutionary war threw off an oppressive English aristocracy, many "democratic" Americans felt the need for fantasies about homegrown imitations.

The girls were overjoyed to be back at 43 West Ninth Street. They decorated their parlor with inexpensive French clutter; small flower prints covered the horsehair chairs. The carved oak mantel was laden with souvenirs of their European travels. In the parlor, the tinny new gramophone emitted strains of popular songs from the current Broadway musical theater. The triplets especially liked singing a popular song from the play *Florodora* that began, "Tell me pretty maiden, are there any more at home like you?"

In their ten-year absence, the Cryders had missed the furor over the Four Hundred that had erupted in 1892. The list of New York's 400 most socially impeccable (and socially desirable) persons was said to have been dreamed up by the society fop and "extra man" Ward McAllister. (An "extra man" was a bachelor who liked nothing better than to don formal attire and take a partnerless lady to dinner at the house of a grande dame.)

Neither the Cryders nor the Woodwards were on the list. Nonetheless, decades later, Elsie Woodward would be cited by society watchers as an "original member of the New York Four Hundred." So great was her aura of power that it was simply assumed that she had been an early peer of the Vanderbilts, Schuylers, Cuttings, Goelets, Rhinelanders, Burdens, Iselins, and Cushings.

The Cryder girls' debut in mid-December 1900 at a "too crowded and fearfully mixed ball" was the evening's highlight, "the most novel feature of that event." Dorothy Davison of Oyster Bay Cove remembers them: "They were plain, not really pretty, but slim, and graceful. They were a novelty and eye-catching. Three of anything is interesting to look at."

The following appeared on the front page of the society gossip sheet *Town Topics:* "The novel feature of the ball was the presence of the now famous Cryder triplets, the Misses Edith, Elsie, and Ethel Cryder. There has been much nonsense published regarding these girls, and not only themselves but their parents have been subjected to great annoyance by the daily journals, which endeavored to obtain pictures of them and their belongings. . . . They are pleasant, well-mannered, but not really pretty girls, tall and slight in figure and graceful in movement."

Fashionable people went to these balls to see the gowns and jewels. The three girls wore extravagant dresses whose folds and fabric and cut were more opulent than most contemporary window drapes. It was only a matter of time before the wealthy suitors would appear at West Ninth Street.

In August 1903, the hot air stood still at Saratoga Springs, where 50,000 racing fans had flocked. Saratoga was the archetypical resort of the Gilded Age. Society people and gamblers such as "Bet-You-a-Million" Gates rented houses for $15,000 a month or rooms at the United States Hotel, where placards announced: "No dogs or jews [sic] allowed." At the gaming tables, the well-dressed socialites sometimes placed bets that totaled $2 million a day. Diamond Jim Brady was the flashiest gambler. He traveled with twenty-seven Japanese houseboys and thirty complete sets of jewels, one for each day of the month, including underwear buttons.

On the morning of the day she first met William Woodward, Elsie laced her heavy corset under a flounced silk floor-length dress, rolled her hair, put on a heavy picture hat and long kid gloves, and took her parasol. Her father, Duncan Cryder, had just left the all-night roulette wheel up-stairs at Canfields with substantial winnings. He was still wearing his stove-pipe hat, light trousers, black patent leather shoes, and black frock coat. Although her father could hardly bear to tear himself away from the private gambling party, he never permitted Elsie to set foot inside a casino.

At breakfast by the paddock, Elsie and her father watched the horses gallop through the morning mist. They had Duncan Cryder's favorite meal, frogs' legs and champagne. Saratoga was a man's town, but as a girl Elsie loved visiting it with her father and listening to his tales of people like Lillian Russell, Diamond Jim Brady's mistress who flaunted his money by riding a gold-plated bicycle with her initials in diamonds and emeralds on the handlebars.

The Cryders strolled to the finish line, where the privileged few sat in boxes. There, perspiring in her silk dress and corset, Elsie, indifferent to horses, twirled her yellow parasol, adjusted her skirts, and helped her father pick a winner.

One box away and a few rows down, a handsome young banker named William Woodward jumped to his feet to watch the horses finish. He turned to glimpse Elsie's strong chin and graceful, swanlike neck. Her long fingers smoothed her kid gloves and stroked the ivory fan hanging from her wrist. When Elsie asked her father the young man's name, she was pleased to hear that young Woodward was heir to one of the greatest new banking fortunes in America. Woodward had just returned from two years in London as secretary to the American ambassador. He had been a racing intimate of the new king, Edward VII, and the vice president of the important Central Hanover Bank. Banks were more powerful and free-wheeling in an era of no government regulation. William Woodward's uncle, as president of Hanover Bank, had the power to issue letters of credit, which were considered as good as money.

The Woodwards were trying to become members of New York so-ciety. The rather recent family fortune was based on selling cotton for uniforms to the Confederate Army during the Civil War. William's mother was a Rodman, whose forbears had settled in Rhode Island in 1675. His uncle had recently bought a seventy-five-room red-stone Victorian "cottage" in Newport. William Woodward was considered by the society columnists to be an "almost-member" of the Astor set there.

Duncan Cryder turned to catch the young man's stare. Cryder knew his wife would call the Woodwards "war profiteers"; her brother had died fighting the Confederates in Virginia, but such matters had to be overlooked. Their other daughter, Edith, was now married to Frederick Lothrop Ames, whose family had sold picks and shovels to the Yankees to bury the dead. At least their money had been made in business with the North.

In his box, the young Woodward heir inquired about the imperious young woman. To his annoyance, she caught him in the act, and she smiled with just the corners of her mouth. He was told it was "either Miss Edith, Miss Elsie, or Miss Ethel Cryder—one of the famous Cryder triplets." Woodward was impressed; he had been back in New York long enough to read the society columns. He was also told that the famous sisters were models for a set of "Gibson Girls." Examples of glorious American beauty and refinement, the triplets had been sketched by Charles Dana Gibson in the pages of *Life*, the elegant society humor magazine.

Woodward walked casually to the Cryders' box. He bowed low in the extravagant Edwardian court manner. "Mr. Woodward," Elsie said at last as though she were telling a joke. It was by that name that she would address him often in public. Woodward began their conversation by talking about horse breeding. He wanted to impress Elsie with the fact that his uncle James had just purchased a "new" ancestral home, the oldest horse farm in America, called Belair, built by the first governor of Maryland. The Georgian manor house was surrounded by nearly 1,000 acres of pasture. Benjamin Franklin had visited Belair. Six fawns from its deer park had been presented to George Washington at Mount Vernon.

Meanwhile, Elsie inwardly flinched. A seam had opened at the back of her flounced lace and organza dress. It was not entirely unexpected. A year before, her mother had bought the small piece of lace at a bargain rate. There had been enough money for only one afternoon dress. Elsie and her sister Edith had taken turns wearing it. Unfortunately, at a tea dance, Edith had already torn the seam. Their mother repaired it many times, but soon the lace barely met in the back. With a nod in Woodward's direction, Elsie turned away and pressed the ripping seam firmly against the back of the wooden chair.

As is the case with many rich people who were once poor, Elsie would in later years profess to remember poverty as a few droll incidents such as this one—rather than as real hardship. In her memory, she transcended the awkward moment and managed to give William Woodward the impression that she was worth his courtship. She also remembered the meeting as "love at first sight." Although her life with him would quickly become a matter of duty fulfilled, Elsie never questioned her choice.

William Woodward's courtship did not begin immediately. He was nursing a bruised ego, if not a broken heart. Until recently, he had been unofficially engaged to the dark-haired Mary Goelet, whose Dutch ancestors and extensive Manhattan real estate holdings made her the prize catch of two continents. Her father showed his disdain for relatively new English settlers by naming one of his favorite steam yachts the *Mayflower.* In wealth and pedigree, the Goelets far outdid the Vanderbilts and, of course, the Woodwards. King Edward VII liked to tease Mary when he invited her to visit the royal yacht. "Miss Goelet, she must marry," he said.

But her mother had more ambitious notions than William Woodward and pushed Miss Mary into a match with the Duke of Roxburghe. Mary Goelet dressed in black the day before she married. Woodward accepted Mrs. Ogden Goelet's invitation to usher at her daughter's wedding. His morose presence attracted more attention than the groom himself. Elsie's rival was several years younger than she and had far more money and a more impressive social background; the two girls were, in fact, distant cousins. Mary Goelet's great-grandfather, who had founded Chemical Bank, had married Sarah Ogden, a great-great-aunt of Elsie Cryder's. But Elsie Cryder was an inspired choice for newly rich William Woodward. Like Miss Goelet's her background was superb. For their part, dashing William Woodward was everything Elsie's parents wanted. Elsie had enough illustrious relatives. What the Cryders dreamed of was freedom from debt. William Woodward could choose to go to his office at the bank every day, but thank God he did not have to.

In the mid-1750s the first William Woodward, a poor goldsmith, arrived in Maryland from England. By the twentieth century, the newly wealthy Woodwards had begun taking some license with their family tree. They added an extra century to their American ancestry, claiming the goldsmith arrived in 1650. The Woodwards made little money before the Civil War. Born poor near Baltimore in the first half of the nineteenth century, the first two successful Woodward brothers forswore college and the Confederate Army. In later years, their father, Henry, would be described in press releases from Hanover Bank as a wealthy farmer, although in reality Henry Woodward had died in debt in his thirties in 1841.

The Civil War gave Henry Woodward's two sons the opportunity to broker cotton to the Confederate Army. Within two decades the family fortunes were made, thanks to younger brother James Woodward's merchant skills and William's dogged collection of funds owed them by the Confederacy. James and William Woodward then bought a controlling interest in the Hanover National Bank.

The reclusive bachelor James became president of the bank. Known for his charmless manner, he was excused because of his financial genius. He had taken the lead in the banking community by helping to rehabilitate the postbellum South—in particular, merchants and planters. He made so much money that people stopped complaining that the Woodwards were carpetbaggers or "bouncers"—newly rich from the Civil War. In 1877, Hanover National's deposits totaled $6 million. By the time Elsie Cryder met her husband-to-be in 1903, the deposits were close to $100 million.

When William Woodward died in 1889, his son, who was thirteen, had inherited half a banking dynasty and was informally adopted by his bachelor uncle James. James Woodward pledged to teach his nephew everything he knew about banking and money. By 1905, James Woodward was portrayed as one of the top eighty-five Americans in social and political life in a curious thick green and gold morocco leather book called *Fads and Fancies*.

James relaxed his obsessive work habits enough to begin enjoying his nephew's sporting style. He encouraged the young man to ride to the hounds and attend thoroughbred races. He also sent him to Groton, a new boarding school modeled on the public schools to which English gentlemen sent their sons. At Groton, William rowed in the slow cold waters of the Nashua River (which would provide the name of the horse raced by his son, Billy, more than half a century later). William Woodward remained unaffected by Rector Endicott Peabody's plea that the boys not grow up into snobs but rather believe in "Democracy." Woodward joined the missionary society that founded a camp for poor local boys.

In a rowdy school play the following year, the six-foot Woodward impressed his fellow Grotonians by playing Martha, the landlady of a French inn. According to the review in *The Grotonian*, "Woodward was the prettiest landlady on record. . . . Dressed simply in the style of the Alsatian peasant, in a black bodice and red skirt. . . . During the progress of the play, he received two handsome bouquets from the audience."

After Groton, William attended Harvard and Harvard Law School. He played varsity football, from which he emerged with cracked shins and a broken nose. In 1901 James Woodward arranged the finishing touch for his nephew. He secured for William the prestigious post of secretary to Joseph H. Choate, the American ambassador to the Court of St. James's. Former President Grover Cleveland, James Woodward's close friend, had helped negotiate the appointment.

James Woodward knew that during two years in England at the new King's court, young Woodward could acquire polish. There was no point in William Woodward's imitating American aristocrats imitating the British when he could learn at first hand. James also hoped the boy would sow his wild oats at a proper distance from home.

James's plan worked almost too well. In London, the dashing twenty-three-year-old became part of King Edward VII's inner circle, visiting thoroughbred racing courses with him, attired in formal breeches and black stockings. William remembered the remark that the King made when a courtier appeared underdressed for court. "I presume," His Majesty said caustically, "that you have come in the suite [as a guest] of the American ambassador." William vowed that the King would never be able to make such a remark about him.

Woodward's frequent attendance at the Newmarket races with the King made his employer sound almost envious. Ambassador Choate wrote a letter to his wife on October 14, 1902: "The King and W. Woodward . . . have gone to Newmarket. How anybody can stand such frequent races quite passes my comprehension."

Woodward soon noticed that he was more welcome at the Royal Box in the Jockey Club than at some tables in New York society. In England, he described himself as a "Victorian through and through." He spent the rest of his life emulating King Edward, who had been spoiled by years of frivolity as the Prince of Wales, while he waited through the decades for the end of the reign of his mother, Queen Victoria.

In 1901, Woodward watched an American, William Cornelius Whitney, win the English Derby with a horse called Volodyovski. It was the beginning of Woodward's lifelong and obsessive determination to breed a horse that would win the English Derby.

Like the King, Woodward would also fear the disapproval of his associates, who felt an interest in horses was unseemly. As a young prince in 1861, Edward had disguised himself and ridden in many steeplechase races under the assumed name of Captain Melville. William Woodward would follow this example when he began his breeding career under the name A. N. Clarke to avoid the disapproval of fellow directors at Central Hanover, who suspected he was far more interested in racing than in banking.

Soon Woodward began a ten-year thorough study of the earliest race-horses known to man, their records, and their breeding and inbreeding patterns, until he was finally ready to select his own outstanding brood mares. Their colts would capture nearly every important stake in America and win over $2 million.

Even more gratifying to his uncle than young Woodward's friendship with the King was the fact that the banking heir was also meeting socially prominent Americans. Woodward dined at stately Embassy dinners with King Edward, his beautiful Danish Queen, and their daughter Princess Victoria, along with Pierpont Morgan, Lord and Lady Derby, and the Bishop of London. It was at one of these dinners that he met Mary Goelet and her father.

In London, on April 28, 1902, Woodward organized a large "at home" formal reception for the inauguration of President Theodore Roosevelt. He supervised the tendering of 700 correct invitations.

Besides the frivolity, Woodward also sat in on crucial sessions for diplomats like Lord Pauncefote, then negotiating to build the Panama Canal.

That Christmas, he learned that Mary Goelet and her mother would be at the King's estate at Sandringham for the annual bird hunt. Woodward joined the party. The first night he danced with several young ladies in order to confuse Mary Goelet's mother.

The next morning, the guests, in hunters' tweed jackets and rifles, assembled with the King in a wood two miles from the house. The sight of hundreds of pheasants, seafowl, and gamecocks rising above the guns thrilled Woodward. He promised himself to add more ceremony to his uncle's Belair shoots. The ladies, including the Queen and the Princess of Wales, joined the shooting party at a lunch of Irish stew, roast beef, and Yorkshire pudding. Hundreds of dead game birds were lined up on the ground outside the luncheon tent.

Mary Goelet's rejection of Woodward only served to fuel his ambitions. He was now determined to improve his place in Anglo-American society. He would, he swore, return triumphant one day to London as the outstanding American breeder to win the Derby race.

In London, at the turn of the century, William Woodward discovered what would become a guiding principle of his social life: the arrogant display of his own superiority. He would translate the manners, dress, and formality of Edwardian England to conservative boardrooms of America.

In his banker's gray flannels in years to come, Woodward looked as though he were a leading figure of the British stage, accidentally assigned to play an American banker. In his private as well as his professional life, he sought to emulate the English aristocracy. Aristocratic English children played with nannies and gamekeepers. William would raise Billy in the country, and, like English children, the boy would have a pony. English country life would be the model on which William would base his son's upbringing.

The year of expectation preceding her brilliant marriage was the happiest of Elsie's life. The tall banker who talked so intensely about horses in his English accent was to be her destiny. William did not go often to the bank office that year; instead he visited with Elsie in her parlor, escorted her to dances, and took her to see the yearlings at Belair and at Saratoga. Elsie dreamed of presiding at Belair, selecting wines, silverware, meats, and, above all, leading conversations. The empty teahouses at Baden-Baden, the mended frocks, her past life paled; it had all been but a series of rehearsals.

On October 24, 1904, the young couple was married. Newspapers called it the most brilliant society wedding of the year. The sidewalks outside Grace Church were crowded with onlookers hoping for a glimpse of the famous bride. Elsie had become even more imperious. She wore a flowing white chiffon gown and train trimmed with heavy lace and a long tulle veil. Her waistline measured seventeen inches, tight-laced by her new French lady's maid. She carried a bouquet of delicate lilies of the valley as though they were fine jewels. She already looked rich. Around her long neck was a new large rivière of diamonds, a lavish gift from her husband's uncle James.

Inside, Grace Church was decorated with hundreds of fresh chrysanthemums and autumn leaves. The pews were filled with Cryder, Adams, Gihon, Wetmore, and Ogden family members. Elsie's maid of honor, her sister Ethel, wore a blue hat and a white appliquéd lace dress.* The bridesmaids wore immense plumed hats and carried pink roses tied with blue ribbons. Among the ushers was Elsie's cousin from the illustrious Adams family who was himself a twin, the future writer Henry Adams.

The Cryder house on West Ninth Street was filled with autumn leaves and palms and was the setting for the pouring of much French

---

*The New York Times misreported the wedding, mixing up the identities of the triplets. It named Edith as Elsie's maid of honor. In fact, Edith was a guest, already married to Frederick Lothrop Ames.

champagne at an afternoon party. The guests were members of the East Coast elite and wealthy southern planters who came to celebrate the nuptials of their future banker. The Cryders released the guest list to the Newport *News* and *The New York Times*. Many who had been invited did not come, preferring to enjoy the fine autumnal weather in places such as Tuxedo Park and Newport. The New York gossip sheet *Town Topics* listed a number of old American names as not showing up, among them the Astors, Iselins, Gerrys, and Goelets, Mrs. Cornelius Vanderbilt, Alice Roosevelt—"and that set."

Elsie's proud wedding day smile undoubtedly faded during her honeymoon in London. It was not only the sexual demands of marriage. Nor was it only Woodward's clear indication that the courtship was over and that Elsie must now learn to serve him from a respectful distance. The pall had been cast by a snide article about her wedding in *Town Topics*, which named another girl as "prettier than the bride." Worse, it also named her rival Mary Goelet as the more opportune marriage for her husband to have made.

However, Elsie Ogden Cryder had scored a public success at the altar, a success that she would wear like a proud mantle for the next seventy years.

When they returned from their honeymoon in 1905, Elsie's new husband took her to live with his widowed mother in the family brownstone on West Fifty-first Street. William Woodward, vice president at Central Hanover, buried himself in banking affairs by day. Now that his courtship of Elsie Cryder was over, he felt free to ignore her as he faced his new responsibilities. At dinner, he lectured his wife and mother about thoroughbred lineage from the beginning of written history. Perhaps Elsie was a bit jealous of the passion Woodward spent on racing. By night he planned barns, paddocks, breeding schemes, and new wings for Belair. Even with his breeding friends, good conversation was a ticklish business. It was up to Elsie to divert a monologue by directing a pointed question to the exhausted listener.

Elsie chafed in the household of her mother-in-law. Her greatest problem was—as she saw it—that she wanted to entertain. Her overwhelming goal was to join "the Old Guard" of the New York society. The Vanderbilts and Iselins had not come to her wedding, but, armed with the Woodward millions, she would show them she was more than their social equal.

Mrs. Sara Woodward reproved her daughter-in-law, Elsie, about the

James T. Woodward in 1890. He was one of the leading financial geniuses of his day; from a number of small banks, he built the Hanover National Bank empire and was its president from 1877 to 1910. An austere bachelor, he helped to raise his nephew William after the boy's father died. Through James Woodward's influence, William attended Choate, Harvard, and Harvard Law School, and was later appointed secretary to the Ambassador to the Court of Saint James's.

James Woodward's 2,300-acre Belair stud farm. It was the first horse farm in America and was built in 1740 by the Governor of Maryland. When James Woodward died, his nephew William Woodward inherited the Belair stud farm as well as the Hanover Bank.

The "famous" Cryder triplets, New York, 1902. Left to right: Ethel, Elsie (considered the most imperious by those who knew her, and soon to be Mrs. William Woodward), and Edith. The Cryders had just returned from a seven-year exile in Europe, the result of a banking scandal. After their debut the triplets became the talk of New York and appeared on the covers of many magazines, such as *Town Topics*.

William Woodward, 1910, the new president of Central Hanover Bank.

divorce of Elsie's sister Ethel, who had married on December 2, 1906, the triplets' birthday. Cecil Higgins, an impoverished Englishman, had quickly proved to be a bad penny. He abandoned Ethel in a London garret when she became ill with pneumonia. Ethel consoled herself by strolling the terraced gardens of roses, peaches, and phlox surrounding the ancient Tudor cottage, Cowhurst, home of her best friend, Consuelo Vanderbilt, Duchess of Marlborough. It was a very warm friendship that also served Ethel well in society.

Elsie soon gave birth to the Woodwards' first child, a girl she named after her sister Edith. At her mother-in-law's home, Elsie began her practice of long afternoon napping. She developed headaches. Her chief domestic chore was making sure the nurses kept Edie out of the way when William Woodward was home. The family bank was an increased source of pride to Elsie since in 1903, William's uncle had erected a handsome twenty-two-story building on Nassau and Pine streets in Manhattan's financial district as its headquarters. The building was called the city's first bank skyscraper.

Elsie's life was run by her husband and her mother-in-law. Her friends describe her as having to play "the brown wren" to Woodward's "peacock." She had dreamed of leading brilliant conversation at her own salon, of assembling her own party list. "It was rather defeating for me," she told an interviewer in 1974, "because whenever we gave a dinner party, there was my mother-in-law receiving instead of me, and always in formal black velvet dresses and pearls. There was never any question about who ruled the roost, so our social life was really restricted."

She asked her husband if she could invite her sister Ethel to America to take the soothing waters with her at White Sulphur Springs Spa in West Virginia. She wanted to throw brilliant parties in Ethel's honor to introduce her to amusing men. But at first William firmly forbade such an "escapade." A divorced sister would not reflect well on the Woodwards, and Elsie's duty as a young mother was to tend to her domestic life. Elsie's afternoon naps grew longer.

Much to Elsie's relief, when their second daughter, Elizabeth, or "Libby," was born, her husband moved the family to a house of their own, at 9 East Fifty-sixth Street, where two more daughters, Sara and Ethel, were born. After the birth of the couple's fourth daughter, William began his practice of leaving his bank and domestic duties to travel to England to see horses race. Elsie did not particularly like to be touched or to have sex. Unfortunately, her marital duty would not be fulfilled until she gave birth to a boy. She was aware that on these trips her husband did not avoid the company of pretty young ladies.

In her marriage, Elsie had exchanged the good-humored authority of her father for Woodward's tyranny. Her strong code of denial and public masks carried her. When he was in residence, William Woodward watched her every action. His reasoning was clear: she reflected on him, and his presentation must be beyond reproach. The other Cryder triplets did not fare as well. Elsie's was the only first marriage made by any of them that lasted.* During the half century that she was William Woodward's wife, she devoted herself to duty. It was her pride in being Mrs. William Woodward that kept her marriage together.

Elsie and her husband had few tastes in common, save their desire to associate with the "best" families. As much as Elsie liked wit and drawing rooms, Woodward liked horse talk and male clubs. But Woodward admired Elsie's graces and her pedigree. Elsie Ogden Cryder, the descendant of the venerable Governor John Ogden of New Jersey, was proof of Woodward's membership in the highest social class and was his second-favorite trophy— after his seventeenth-century stud farm. It made Woodward feel secure to have Elsie in charge of his homes. Her closest friends came to understand that she and William were not congenial, but they feared asking direct personal questions. It was accepted that Woodward was unfaithful: he was a sporting gentleman. Elsie was respected for holding her head high at parties which she attended in his absence and for refusing to complain.

In 1908, after four years of marriage, Woodward and his wife were photographed on Fifth Avenue in their open horse and carriage for *Town & Country* magazine. Woodward wore a tall hat and held the reins. Four matched horses pulled Woodward's high open coach. The streets were lined with curious people pleased to watch the famous Mrs. Elsie Cryder Woodward. It was proper that Mrs. Vanderbilt pass the Woodwards. The serious faux pas was overtaking or passing a coach of greater social importance.

Years later Elsie recalled the slights of Grace Vanderbilt: "Imagine a society where one woman's invitation to dinner defines society."

Tough old Grace Vanderbilt had sensed a rival in the young Elsie Woodward and wrote to a friend from Paris: "Yesterday I sat next to Rodin at a luncheon at our embassy. . . . Charles Carroll told me Elsie (Mrs.

---

*Her sisters each remarried. The union of Edith Cryder Ames ended with her husband's death at age forty-four, and Edith's second husband was the much younger, handsome—and, many felt, inappropriate—Roger Cutler, a good-humored playboy who kept a prize herd of cattle at their farm in Easton, Massachusetts. After her unfortunate first marriage, Ethel Cryder Higgins married Arthur Fowler—a widower whose first wife had been wealthy in her own right. Fowler bequeathed to Ethel his first wife's fortune. At his death, she moved to Washington, where she developed a reputation like her sister Elsie's as a great hostess in a small house in Georgetown. Ethel was a Washington hostess second only to her close friend Alice Roosevelt Longworth.

William Woodward) went to a prize fight the other night. Rather a vulgar taste, don't you think? He seemed quite shocked and surprised by it and said New York society would shun her parties from now on. I also heard she has 'taken up smoking.' Isn't that too crude for words!"

When William Woodward's Uncle James died in April 1909, the flags on Wall Street flew at half-mast. William's obsession with horses became a serious problem at the Hanover Bank. Having observed him for five years, the directors unanimously refused to accept him as president on the grounds that he was a playboy, more interested in horses than in banking. William cut too grand a figure with his short tailored coats, flourishing mustaches, and cigarette in a little ivory holder. The conservative directors tried to ignore the fact that William now owned his late father's and his late uncle's majority shares of the bank. Instead, the Hanover Bank board voted that the rightful successor to the position was a senior vice president of the bank named James M. Donald, a self-made businessman who had worked his way up from the bottom. *The Wall Street Journal* credited him with having been in large part responsible for the growth of the bank.

Woodward made light of the board of directors' vote. He thought it a clear case of envy. He later alluded to his fellow bankers' rigidity: "When I was a young bank officer, I smoked a great many cigarettes. Then one morning one of my superiors suggested a banker should smoke cigars. It's not so hard to learn banking, but those cigars made me sick."

Woodward fought the hostile directors by announcing that since he had been rejected as bank president, he would take his majority shares elsewhere. This was a time when banks were starting to be regulated by the federal government and were in a state of flux. Hanover Bank would fail without the Woodward family shares. Within hours of his threat, William Woodward was voted president.

Although their styles differed, the bank's board of directors had no cause to complain about Woodward's banking performance: he was president of the Central Hanover for nineteen years. He was also a director of the new Federal Reserve Board. He was at the top of the American mercantile class—one of the 150 wealthiest men in the country. He lived a baronial existence—at times in as many as five homes—and was driven in a silver Rolls-Royce whose hood ornament had been replaced by a sterling-silver prancing horse.

Meanwhile, Elsie had started to create a new society in her salon. Unconventional theater people reminded her of her father. She began to invite Cole Porter to pretheater suppers. William Woodward was a problem. He acted his most haughty and soon stopped attending altogether. He was glimpsed by her guests only as he ducked out the front door in his trademark double-breasted short coat. Woodward was uncomfortable when Elsie's friends discussed artists and plays. He collected paintings, but they were of horses, principally by the English painter John Frederick Herring.

"Father did adore mother, and he'd give her anything," said their daughter, Libby. "But he wasn't going to lead a frivolous life or what he considered frivolous—people of the theater or the arts."

If he was less than a hit at dinner, Woodward was a big favorite at Harvard reunions, where he drank tankards of ale and champagne and cooked up pranks. For instance, in the softball tournament in 1918, at his twentieth reunion, he threw his Yale opponents into havoc by dressing his Harvard teammates in blue Yale jerseys.

James Woodward had left Belair to his nephew. Woodward bought 2,000 more surrounding acres, added herds of sheep, and built stone and brick stables for the eleven carriages and the mares, sucklings, and weanlings. In 1912, a tragic death occurred on the Belair estate. William Woodward's domination of the local police provided a model for his wife forty-three years later when their son was killed by his wife in Oyster Bay. The Belair accident involved the boating death of a neighboring child who was visiting the children of the Belair estate manager. The estate manager's son rescued his sister when the boat overturned, but not their guest. William Woodward took charge. He told the coroner that the death was accidental. His word was law. The coroner issued a death certificate attributing the tragedy to accidental drowning and ruled that there would be no inquiry. Woodward visited the dead child's family to offer his formal condolences.

In 1916, William Woodward bought two building lots on Eighty-sixth Street in Manhattan and commissioned a grand eighty-two-foot-wide gray-stone palace. His house would be only steps away from Millionaires' Row on Fifth Avenue. At the height of his banking career, Woodward wanted an opulent but dignified monument to his success. He hired William Adams Delano, a prestigious and conservative architect of the era. Delano, who had built much of West Point and Woodward's own Knickerbocker Club, designed the Woodward house on eighteenth-century French proportions. The six-story house was more elegant than the gaudy French Renaissance palace built by the Vanderbilts. The plain street façade was Indiana lime-stone and Huntsville marble, the mansard roof green slate. The floor-to-ceiling windows were simply decorated with handmade iron grille. An imposing first-floor reception area with magnificent height and openness was lined with black-and-white diamond-patterned marble floors that were an impressive setting for green-black marble columns. At Woodward's request the intimate library was lined in rare butternut wood. The total cost of the house was $150,000.

Elsie knew that the Woodward houses—the Cloisters in Newport, their Manhattan residence, and Belair—operated flawlessly under the watchful eye of her very formal English butler Arthur "Bertie" Putz, who wore white tie and patent leather evening shoes and whom Elsie saw more often than her husband. In her employ for almost fifty years, Putz was like a favored cousin. He adored Elsie. When Putz's son went bankrupt, Elsie bought him a restaurant in Baltimore.

Putz had the air of a diplomat as he greeted guests in the entrance gallery surrounded by dark green marble pillars. He always remembered everyone's name and their favorite drinks. Behind him on the staircase, he sometimes orchestrated a line of as many as fifteen white-gloved footmen holding candelabra. He wrote the evening's menu on Mrs. Woodward's yellow-bordered vellum cards and placed them in silver holders on the table.

At dinner parties, a footman, Joseph Chaprionière, would stand behind a guest and serve at table, while Putz stood behind his mistress and signaled the other servants by lowering his chin or raising a white-gloved finger. Putz commanded footmen, gardeners, parlormaids, and upstairs maids. His rule was that the second butler and footman must polish Mr. Woodward's silver horse trophies until the metal burned their skin. He made certain that guests' suitcases were always unpacked. At Belair, he filled every room in the house with fresh violets, wild daisies and mustard, and camellias—and, in Elsie's bedroom alone, roses. Putz belonged to a private club in New York for butlers, where he played backgammon. As the years went by, Elsie seemed to treat him as the host when her husband was absent.

He also commanded the twenty in staff who kept up the dark, gloomy Victorian eighty-five-room "cottage" on Ruggles Avenue in Newport, the Cloisters, where six gardeners trimmed the honeysuckle, flowerbeds, and rose gardens on the ample lawns sloping down to the ocean. Afternoons he made sure Mrs. Woodward had her carriage to drive her in her loose-fitting black bathing costume a short distance to the private Bailey's Beach Club. If William Woodward was in residence, after dinner Putz passed out goblets of Woodward's special stock of brandy and chartreuse.

Every August, Elsie Woodward reluctantly sent Putz to Saratoga Springs to help William entertain in his rented yellow house next to the Reading Room. Then she traveled with her lady's maid, Pauline, to meet her sisters at White Sulphur Springs. Pauline looked down her nose at the hotel servants. She ironed Elsie's private linens, replacing hotel towels as well as bed linens. Elsie had two ladies' maids in her lifetime—and they both revered her. They touched her more than any family member. Besides treating them with impeccable if distant good manners, she bought them perfumes and Hermès scarves from Paris and gave them generous bonuses.

By 1916, William Woodward felt secure enough at Hanover Bank to flaunt his thoroughbred horses. He organized an old-fashioned four-day coaching trip from Manhattan to Belair. The night before, he slept only a few hours at the Knickerbocker Club in order to be up before sunrise. This was not unusual; he was now sleeping at the club with increasing frequency. Upon returning from a trip to buy mares in France, he would often check into the club instead of returning to Eighty-sixth Street.

On October 11, a team of handsome horses was harnessed to the gilt and wood Pioneer coach in front of the Knickerbocker Club. Woodward in his brown high hat supervised the loading of trunks into the coach for himself and his five guests. A club porter served mugs of tea. The party would travel by coach for four days, switching teams of horses that would also be transported by railroad car. Woodward hired a photographer for the trip. The results were donated to the Belair Museum by Elsie Woodward after her husband's death.

Woodward drove his horses at high speeds over loose and sandy lanes up the final lap—the mile-long driveway of Belair, lined with great tulip poplars. His colleagues toured Belair's pastures and stables, while Woodward lectured his guests about his plans to create a thoroughbred racing empire and win the English Derby.

While her husband was becoming more open with his banking colleagues about his love of racehorses, Elsie embarked on a friendship— rare among upper-class women—with an actress and soprano, Ann Swinburne, who had been born Ann Ditchburn in Oregon and had come to New York at eighteen to study music. A girl of great confidence, she claimed that her father was a judge who had been ruined by alcohol. Like

Ann Swinburne, 1914. She starred in Victor Herbert's operettas, including *The Madcap Duchess*, which had been written for her. She was ostracized when she ran off with the older, married, and very social Rudolph Schirmer in 1916. Elsie Cryder Woodward took up the young actress's cause, thereby opening to her the doors of society.

Mary Duncan Sanford (with her husband Stephen "Laddie" Sanford, heir to the Sanford carpet fortune) was a sensation in a number of Broadway plays in the 1920s, among them *The Shanghai Gesture*, in which she played the young prostitute.

Ina Claire, who was part of Elsie Woodward's salon, was married to John Gilbert and appeared in numerous Broadway productions, including *Bluebeard's Eighth Wife*, *Biography*, and *The Royal Family of Broadway*.

Prince Serge Obolensky, Elsie Woodward's escort and bridge partner at the St. Regis Roof, a nightclub in New York City. Obolensky was from the most prominent noble family in Russia, descended from Vikings, the princes of Kiev, and the first czar. His family assembled the collections at L'Hermitage and organized the ballet. Obolensky was born outside St. Petersburg, and three years after the revolution left Russia for the United States, where he married an Astor. He was a private in the U.S. Army during World War II and parachuted into Sardinia in his fifties. After his divorce, Obolensky went to work for his brother-in-law Vincent Astor, who owned the St. Regis Hotel.

thousands of theater fans, Elsie had watched her perform the comic operetta *The Madcap Duchess*, written for her by Victor Herbert. It was filled with charming clichés about French shepherdesses and disguises. At the opera's finale, Miss Swinburne hammed it up pretending to be a duchess at Versailles.

When the middle-aged music publisher Rudolph Schirmer left his wife for her, Miss Swinburne lost her toast-of-the-town status. This was when Elsie invited her to tea at the Plaza Hotel. Elsie wore her walking costume and gloves; she was just under thirty. During her first meeting with Elsie, Ann Swinburne began to imitate the older woman's grandeur. Elsie Woodward had a slender figure that looked athletic (although she was decidedly not), a noble carriage, long thin wrists and ankles, and fingers with scarlet nails. As tea progressed, Elsie laughed and laughed at Ann and lectured her about how she must do some charity work to enhance the Schirmer family name. For the rest of her life, Mrs. Schirmer sponsored music festivals and students. Elsie saw a reflection of herself in the young woman whose charms had won a distinguished husband. Ann Swinburne was ecstatic to have won Elsie Woodward's support.

Mary Duncan Sanford's husband, "Laddie," would be removed from the *Social Register* when they eloped. However, Elsie pronounced the stage and movie actress brilliant upon first meeting her at the Plaza Hotel. For a half century, Mary Sanford dutifully chaired events for Elsie Woodward's pet charities: the April in Paris Ball and a subsidized home for soldiers, sailors, and airmen. In later years, Elsie's friends included actresses Jinx Falkenburg, Rosalind Russell, Arlene Francis, and Joan Fontaine. Elsie did not seem to enjoy male actors as much, although Kevin McCarthy won her friendship. Perhaps it was based on affinity: she had made a good marriage mainly because her father had promoted her and her sister as theatrical oddities. Elsie's most loving feelings were for her sisters—and it was easy for her to fall under the spell of these beautiful young women.

4

WILLIAM WOODWARD, JR., ARRIVES

Well-born, well-dressed, and moderately learned.

—STATUTE OF OXFORD UNIVERSITY,
defining a gentleman, 1440

O n June 12, 1920, Elsie Woodward gave birth to the Woodward heir—after four daughters and sixteen years of marriage. The blessed event took place in her huge third-floor bedroom furnished with the palest yellow silk curtains and dark Queen Anne chairs and cabinets. Elsie was undoubtedly pleased to observe traces of her late father's lively countenance on her son, William Woodward, Jr. The Cryder physiognomy looked strong on a woman but better on a man.

Elsie was thirty-nine. Her daughters were now tall young ladies. Libby, considered the prettiest, was fourteen, and Sara was nine.

A few years before Billy was born, Woodward Sr. had left home for days upon hearing that his fourth child was yet another girl. He had refused even to look at little Ethel, bundled in pink satin and surrounded by chambermaids, footmen, pantry maids, the cook, and Putz. In honor of the arrival of his namesake, however, William Woodward dispatched several hundred telegrams to racing friends on both sides of the Atlantic.

At the age of forty-one Woodward considered his domestic duties over with the birth of his son. He could now escape from the hearth more and more. He also retired from active duty at Hanover Bank with a flourish of ceremonies. During one of his many trips to the English countryside he impulsively acquired a lovely filly he saw running in a field. He named her

Brown Betty and returned to New York to sleep at the Brook, one of his gentlemen's clubs.

Little Billy Woodward looked like a film star playing an English lord. He was plump only briefly. High-strung, he cried during the night. Like his mother, he ate little. He wept if forced by his mademoiselle or his four older sisters to sit sweating in his swimming costume at Newport Beach. He disliked tennis, tag, and football; his long bones were not buttressed by strong muscles. His shoulders were narrow.

When he was dressed, however, he looked like a drawing in *Vanity Fair* magazine. His nurse knotted a red-and-white Belair tie around his neck and slicked his hair back. Billy Woodward needed no waves or pompadours to offset the fine shape of his skull. He had the coloring, cheekbones, and jawline of a Frenchman, but he spoke—particularly in his early years—as though he had been born in London. On occasion Elsie Woodward invited the four-year-old child to sit in her drawing room, where actresses fed him candy.

Billy also loved to sit in his nanny's lap and turn pages of the family's worn calfskin-covered scrapbooks. The nursery was decorated with the official Central Hanover bank portrait of his fierce great-uncle James and a photograph of his dapper father in a bowler hat, sitting in his box at Belmont smoking a cigarette in an ebony holder. Billy would beg his nanny to tell him the story of how in 1919, his four sisters—accompanied by his father and President and Mrs. Wilson—frolicked on the White House lawns with a flock of lambs donated by his father. The tale carried a message to the boy: his father was very important.

It had been during World War I that Billy's father forced a reluctant President Wilson to accept a herd of prize Shropshire sheep from Belair's pastures. At first, President Wilson declined the gift, worried that a flock of grazing sheep would "injure the [White House lawn's] many flowers and shrubs." But Woodward persisted in a series of handwritten notes. The country needed wool; the sheep would be a morale booster. They would awaken the country to other belt-tightening measures. He joked that the lawns needed trimming anyway; the flock of sheep would save manpower for the war effort. After several months, Mrs. Wilson finally relented.

A year later, the President, Mrs. Wilson, and Woodward met to commemorate the success of the flock. President Wilson smiled wanly at the sight of his trampled crocus beds. Plucky and very English, Woodward's gift showed the world that the White House was no frivolous palace but a working aristocratic country home that could pitch in and produce that extra bit of wool for the war effort. Then the Red Cross auctioned off the wool at a charity event, raising $100,000 for rescue missions.

Nearly two years after the armistice, when Billy was six months old, the flock was returned to Belair. The framed letter of thanks from President Wilson hung in Billy's room. "Now that the sheep are returning to you, I want to send them with, as it were, a word of deep appreciation from Mrs. Wilson and myself of your kindness in supplying so fine and interesting a flock. We have enjoyed them and shall miss them very much, and while they were here they always reminded us of your generosity and kindness."

Woodward's handwritten response thanked the President for thanking him for the sheep. He concluded: "The memory of their stay on White House grounds will always be treasured at Belair."

The sheep were only the beginning. Billy believed his father owned the world. He had built the local grade school near Belair and owned the little ramshackle homes of some of Billy's favorite playmates, who were the children of tenant farmers. Billy traveled to Belair from his parents' homes in Manhattan and Newport on the Pennsylvania Railroad, which the little boy believed belonged to his father. The train whisked by Belair, unless Billy's nurse or one of his sisters whispered to the conductor, "The Woodward family would like to stop at their station at Bowie." At the tiny tree-shaded station, Billy's nurse and luggage would be loaded into several waiting Belair coaches pulled by pale Clydesdale horses.

Despite all the stories Billy heard about his father, Woodward was a remote figure to his son. Woodward often said that he preferred horses to trees, trees to people, and adults to any of his children. In later years, his red-bordered engraved Christmas cards featured portraits of famous Belair throughbred winners such as the American Triple Crown winner of 1930, Gallant Fox; Omaha, the winner in 1935; and Johnstown, who won two races of the Triple Crown in 1939.

As for his trees, Woodward employed four full-time tree surgeons and spent $10,000 a year on the upkeep of the hundreds of tulip poplars, more than 100 feet high, that lined the Belair entrance road. Each tree was fitted with its own lightning rod. While his father supervised the tree surgeons, Billy was permitted to watch from a respectful twenty-foot distance, flanked by his nurse and sisters. He looked like the perfect little boy in his loose dark pants, plain white shirt, loafers without socks, and small blazer with gold-plated buttons.

Billy would grow up in a series of austere American castles. He would never be a man's man—like his grandfather Duncan Cryder, he preferred to adorn a drawing room. His four older sisters fought his nurse for the right to dress him, hold his hand, and push his elaborate French pram along Fifth Avenue. One summer his sisters crowded around him, trying to teach Billy to swim in the shallow tides of Bailey's Beach Club at Newport. He inhaled seawater in terror. In later years, he remained so terrified by the experience that he refused to do more than wade in pools or oceans. Particularly around his sisters, Billy tried to suppress his feelings. If he felt a laugh coming, he'd purse his lips. He would snort, trying to pull the laugh back in.

Billy grew to dislike being with his father, who had little time to teach his son about his world. One day he accompanied his father to the stables after a race. Woodward Sr. began shaking hands with the stable boys and grooms, thanking them for their part in the training of the horse that had raced that day. The awed children stared as Billy surreptitiously got in line with them. Billy put out his hand to his father. Woodward stiffened and said pointedly, "These men worked, Sonny." Billy ran from the stable, mortified.

Whenever his father was home, the repeated injunction from Elsie, from his sisters, even from Putz and the nurses "to stay out from underfoot" caused little Billy intense unhappiness. As superior as Billy felt to most children and to the servants because of his father's wealth and station, he felt inferior to his inaccessible father. His father's enthusiasms for tennis and football made Billy shudder. Elsie raised an eyebrow after her husband's long monologues about the joys of playing fields. She joked, "Exercise destroys red corpuscles." Billy delivered the line for the rest of his life. Disappointed that his son was not like himself, Woodward backed away even further.

Billy tried to fit into his mother's life. It was not easy: the nearly 200 rooms in the four Woodward houses gave his mother ample hiding space. She announced in later years that she never cared for being a mother.*

Elsie Woodward stiffened at Billy's touch and would not permit him

---

*Of Elsie's children, the youngest daughter, Ethel, was most intimidated by her. Ethel would flee to live in Paris, where she finally established herself with a salon in her house on the fashionable Rue Weber. The highly placed government leaders who visited her would aid her sons' careers. Divorced from Pierre de Croisset, a Belgian Jew who was a friend of Proust and his circle, Ethel prided herself on an amateur interest in archaelogy. She was free to think for herself in Paris. But on a rare visit to her mother to ask for money, she obeyed Elsie like a child, although she was well into middle age. For example, she refused to attend a party of George Plimpton's because her mother insisted on an early bedtime.

to climb into her lap. Billy almost never got to kiss her good night or watch her do her hair, which the maid helped her put up into little buns and small wire clusters of curls. If Billy ever told his mother that he had a cold or was unhappy, she responded, "Well, then, be a dear and come back and tell me when you feel better."

When he was an adolescent, Billy particularly liked joking with the actresses at his mother's bridge salons. He played hooky from Buckley School rugby matches to eavesdrop on bridge games in the library. Filled with sun, the library contained gleaming antique English silver horse trophies and Woodward's leather-bound racing monographs. At first, Billy would casually stroll by the slightly opened library door. Elsie sat facing the side window with a view of trees in Central Park. Her house rules were strict. She insisted on high stakes: ten cents a point. Her sisters and she usually won. "Psychic," said actress Ina Claire, "the Cryder ladies used ESP." Another guest was the Russian prince Serge Obolensky, the former brother-in-law of Vincent Astor, now forced to work for a living doing publicity for Astor's hotels. Known for a flaming sword dance he performed for friends on the rooftop of the St. Regis Hotel, he was at that time one of Elsie's extra men. He was a bachelor and an entertaining addition to her dinner parties, although unlike most extra men, he was not homosexual. Elsie's bridge table was the perfect place for Serge to sharpen his wit, air his prejudices, and gossip.

Putz, who passed in and out of the library on his rounds, struck Billy as having illicit traces of the liquor cabinet on his breath. Irish maids wearing black uniforms with white organdy aprons entered the library bearing trays of teapots and honeycake.

Rewarded by a fleeting maternal glance, Billy would finally come into the library. He loved the scent of strong, brewed English tea. When the bridge game was going full-tilt he knew he must not speak. The hush of major bridge moments thrilled Billy. The society women wore jewels on their hands and enormous pearls at their throats. Among them was the cheery Mrs. Hermann "Dumpy" Oelrichs, who had married the penniless Prince Ferdinand of Liechtenstein.

Billy decided actresses were a privileged group and were—as his mother believed—much more stylish than his father's horse friends. They pronounced him the perfect child. Mary Sanford, who had starred on Broadway in *The Shanghai Gesture* as a fallen woman in a Chinese brothel, spoke frankly about the new wife of a wealthy man: "And I gather she learned everything she needs to know about that matter in a bawdy house in Paris." Otherwise, sex was a forbidden topic in the Woodward household. Nor was love a welcome part of the conversation. When Billy asked his mother, "Does Father love us?" Elsie replied, "That's a rather ordinary way of thinking."

Despite her own enjoyment of the company of actresses, Elsie Woodward was horrified a decade later when her son proudly presented such a girl as his prospective wife. She considered it a failure in his upbringing. What Elsie failed to see, however, was that unlike his mother, his father, and his grandfather Duncan Cryder, Billy was secure enough in his social status to feel that he could marry exactly whom he pleased. But Billy was a prince who was not being groomed by his father to be king, and he came to feel that there was nothing for him to strive for except exciting parties and romances.

Second to the bridge afternoons, Billy liked his mother's dinner parties. He preferred them, in fact, to children's play. They were held at a very long Georgian mahogany banquet table, a table long enough to seat fifty guests and narrow enough to permit conversation. It was decorated with some of William Woodward's silver trophies, silver chains, epergnes, Elsie's own yellow roses, and silver bowls of fruit on a long, mirrored centerpiece. After dinner, as chamber musicians entertained the guests, twelve-year-old Billy would sneak into the sumptuous ballroom, whose sixteen-foot ceiling was ornately carved. One night, before his mother could have him whisked away, he bowed to Ina Claire and whirled her from one end of the dance floor to the other.

Early summer was a rare time when both of Billy's parents were usually under the same roof. The Belair estate was also a wonderful playground for Billy and his friends whose parents farmed tobacco and corn. A caretaker's daughter lived upstairs in the stable in the mid-1920s; she and Billy picked buttercups together under the tulip poplars. Billy escaped his sisters to chase ducks around the fields. He and the caretaker's daughter chased a rooster. To impress her, Billy once trapped it against a fence. It pecked him hard on the hand, and Billy started to cry. The girl ran for her father, who took one look at Billy, grabbed the rooster, and wrung its neck. Billy never lost the uneasy sense of power that such episodes engendered.

Billy's favorite man was Uncle Andy Jackson, a wizened former slave who worked at Belair. Uncle Andy was in charge of the stables' sixty-one saddle horses as well as the Clydesdale parade horses. He also blacked William Woodward's boots, built the fires, and woke Billy's father at 4 a.m. to go fox hunting. Andy Jackson loved horses and small children.

Having been separated by slavery from his own family, he adopted "Mast'
Will." He taught Billy to play a good game of marbles. Every morning
Billy helped Uncle Andy hoist the red-and-white Belair flag up the pole
above a grassy hill. During the day, Billy conspired to escape the main
house. He deliberately got in the way until his exasperated mother ordered
him outside. He would seek out the old caretaker in his dilapidated cottage
by the brook and follow him on his rounds.

Billy promised not to tell his parents about the old man's crippling
arthritis because Uncle Andy feared being retired. Uncle Andy did not
force Billy to ride his gray pony bareback since Billy preferred sitting safely
behind it in a wicker buggy. Elsie assumed Billy would outgrow his childish
preference for playing with servants and farm children just as young English
aristocrats eventually stopped trailing their gamekeepers.

At Belair, Billy's father closeted himself in his study—decorated with
mounted deer heads—away from Billy, his daughters, his wife, and her
haughty sisters. He dictated pamphlets on thoroughbred breeding and racing and financed their printing. The most lively pamphlet was a memoir
with lots of quotes from the faithful Uncle Andy: "A Memoir of Andrew
Jackson Africanus, by William Woodward, in affectionate memory of long
and faithful service." Like his master, Uncle Andy possessed a clear memory for the ear shapes, faces, gaits, bloodlines, quirky moods, and weak-
nesses of hundreds of thoroughbred horses.

At the end of Elsie's dinners at which she served her famous Virginia
ham, British houseguests were startled by banjo strumming. Conversation
stopped as Andrew Jackson's tenor voice drifted in through the double
doors of the dining room. Billy would run down the wide polished staircase
in his stocking feet. The old man sang what Elsie and her husband referred
to as "darky ballads," such as "God Bless Old Abraham [Lincoln] who set
the Negroes free." Uncle Andy never "shooed" "Mast' Will" away until
Billy's father announced brandy in the library.

Billy looked forward to little Lady Sarah Churchill's annual trips to America. The first night of one of Sarah's visits, after prayers, Billy and his nurse
peeked under Sarah's bed for kidnappers. Billy was guarded by his nurse
and chauffeur like a crown jewel. That year, 1932, Charles and Anne Morrow Lindbergh's eleven-month old son had been kidnapped, held for ran-
som, and never returned. The two children were taken to the Ringling
Brothers and Barnum & Bailey Circus, accompanied by three protective
adults—her nanny, his nanny, and the Woodward chauffeur.

Elsie's hopes for Billy's splendid future included marriage to lovely little Sarah Churchill. The titled child was both an English royal and the heir to the Vanderbilt fortune.* Sarah loved to stare at Elsie Woodward and her sisters. She had never seen three identical ladies, although she could always identify Elsie Woodward by her manner.

In September 1932, Elsie arrived for the social season at the family's brick manor house in Brookville on Cedar Swamp Road, on Long Island's north shore. The chauffeur drove Billy, then twelve, out alone a few hours later in the station wagon. It was a few weeks before the boy's last year at the Buckley School. His schoolmates were the children of the leaders of industry and society, many of whom had avoided his parents' wedding. It was a very restricted little world, designed to provide Billy with a "good" circle of friends and business connections (if he had to work) out of which he would choose friends and a mate.

Billy was pleased to be only a half mile from Peacock Point, the home of his best friend in all the world, Grenville "Bean" Baker, the son of Elsie's friend, society hostess Edith Baker. The boy was called "Bean" because in a rare moment when his father had recognized his existence, George F. Baker, the chairman of First National Bank, of New York, had said, "That kid's got a good bean. He's smart."

Billy's mother had invited another of Billy's classmates from Buckley, Edward "Neddy" Patterson, for the weekend. Her secretary had hand-delivered an invitation to Neddy's mother, whose father gave the land for St. Patrick's Cathedral to the Catholic church. Neddy's mother thought the Woodwards were a bit grandiose. (She knew that they considered her "controversial" because she was a Catholic.)

Neddy was taken in the Packard past Oyster Bay surrounded by autumnal gold trees. "It really looks like the Gold Coast," said Neddy. The Gold Coast of Long Island was dotted with the opulent homes of the owners of banks, brokerage houses, and commodity markets in New York. Here they took tea and entertained in imitation of English country life.

The Woodward estate was sixty acres of hayfields, stables, gardens, meadows, and woodlands in which foxes ran wild. The property bordered that of Winthrop Aldrich, chairman of the board of Chase Bank and a

*The outspoken little girl was also a cousin of Winston Churchill's and the daughter of Consuelo Vanderbilt Churchill, the reluctant Duchess of Marlborough.

member of the Rockefeller family. Neddy arrived at the huge circular drive-way just before sundown. Miss De Tinguey, Bean Baker's Belgian governess with a flapper haircut, greeted him. Two gardeners clipped wisteria. They were among the ten servants who had been brought by private train from the Woodward estate in Newport. Behind them, the brick colonial house was still, except for brocade curtains almost imperceptibly stirring at the long windows of Billy's mother's bedroom. Billy's father rarely ever came here. He had no interest in either boats or Long Island house parties.

Neddy shook hands formally with his two classmates, feeling a little envious of their friendship. Bean was as close to Billy as a brother. Billy seemed to come to life in the company of the reckless Bean and his comic little griffon dog. Billy and Bean were an odd twosome: Billy, tall and so reserved he seemed unable to decide on anything, and Bean, six inches shorter, gleeful, swaggering, his head high, as though he were peering over a fence. The apple of his mother's eye, Bean would flirt so much with girls—waitresses, pre-debs, maids, his mother's dowager friends—that he often found himself surrounded by women. The two bank heirs had similar family problems. Their fathers were rarely at home and their mothers were far more interested in snagging dinner guests than in rearing sons. Bean was the wealthiest and most popular boy at Buckley. (His family endowed Columbia's football field and the Harvard Business School.) Bean was also a ringleader. The other boys admired his wild pranks. Everybody—and Billy most of all—loved the sound of little Bean's wild whooping laughter.

Bean had slept at Billy's house the night before Ned arrived. At five-thirty that morning, Bean had heard the fox hunters' horns blaring and awakened Billy. Billy tiptoed after him, wearing his nightshirt and short pants and holding his shoes. He liked leaving the house without having to account to his chauffeur, Putz, his governess, or a maid. The boys sprinted down the lawns behind the sleeping brick house, past the stable. They stopped to put on their shoes and then ran toward the hunters through pine and maple woods. Small and husky, Bean built up speed. It was still dark, and Billy complained that he was cold. "Pretend you are a horse—whinny, it will keep you warm," said Bean. Suddenly, the hunters were behind them. Horns rang out. In the nick of time, the boys scrambled up two trees. The hunters and their "whips" in pink coats rode by just under them.

Ned Patterson would never forget this last weekend of summer with his two best friends, both of whose lives ended in tragic gun accidents. It had seemed to Ned Patterson when they were all young together that the people he loved would live forever. "Woodward, make Neddy ride your pony," ordered the boisterous Bean, hopping from one foot to another. "We'll have a pony race."

Billy smiled nervously, stretching his lower lip until it trembled.

"I'm going to race cars next year. We can do anything we want on our own property. I don't care what Father says," said Bean.

Bean Baker had a morbid fascination with danger. He hid guns in his bedroom at home and sometimes had several guns hidden under his mattress and in his closets. Billy also owned guns. Bean and Billy would pretend to be white hunters in Bean's nursery—using loaded revolvers. Bean would disappear into the gun room in his family's thousand-acre Tallahassee plantation for hours. Billy had also taken to imitating Bean's habit of urging his chauffeur to exceed the speed limits.

"Let's go down to the barn now," Bean said to his two friends.

"What color is the pony?" asked Ned. His classmates had been right. The Woodwards and the Bakers were richer than anybody.

"Gold and white." Billy smiled uneasily. He felt like an imposter. It was too easy to impress his friends with his father's money, cars, racehorses, and travels. The Pell children and the little "count" Anthony Villa loved to play with his train set in the attic at the Newport house. The other Buckley students were amazed by his trip to England just to watch his father's horse win a race at Newmarket.

Bean led the other two boys outside to the barn. The dappled pony was standing in a large stall.

"Want to ride him?" asked Billy suddenly. Bean whooped with laughter.

"Well, no," said Ned uncertainly.

"Sure you do."

"Do it," said Bean.

Billy demonstrated how his guest should mount the bareback pony. Ned obediently jumped high and clung to the horse. A husky boy, he was known to be a much better athlete than Billy and years later would play varsity baseball for Yale. But the pony snorted and bucked. Ned was thrown onto the hard ground.

"Again," Billy said. "Ride him again."

Bean laughed. It was unheard of for Billy to take control like this. Ned smiled and hesitated. Billy's voice lowered. "Get it right." It was getting dark, and Ned had trouble seeing the expression on his friend's face.

"Well, it's harder than it looks," Ned said politely. He threw himself up and in the direction of the pony's back. With one shiver, the pony dislodged Ned and threw him to the ground again. The boy lay on his back, disoriented.

"What're you going to do?" asked Bean.

"Want to go inside?" Billy asked.

"Yes," said Ned.

"Well, you can't until you ride the pony."

Ned felt intimidated by Billy, who had, he believed, anything money could buy. Billy's father looked like an American Aga Khan with his flourishing mustaches. All the boys knew the Rolls-Royce with the silver horse on the hood. William Sr. alluded casually to the filly he had recently given to King George V.

"Get up," Billy said.

"In a second, okay?" Ned's body was aching. "I have to go in now, Billy."

"No, sir."

"I need a drink of water." Ned set out bravely toward the house. He heard Billy and Bean behind him in the tall grass.

Inside the house, Ned tried to look invisible when Mrs. Woodward passed on her way upstairs. Her dress was dark, plain, and old-fashioned. He lowered his head, unused to her attention. He saw clods of dirt on his white socks. What trick were the Woodwards going to pull next? Parents meant formal business, and they frightened Ned Patterson. "My dear, what a sight for dinner," Mrs. Woodward said. Her voice was clipped and almost as low as a man's. "Sonny, let's be sure Neddie plays less strenuously tomorrow. What will his mama say about our hospitality if we send her boy home looking such a fright?"

Ned sneaked a look at his schoolmates. Bean looked embarrassed. Billy had tilted his chin up like his mother's, imitating her proud smile. It would not have occurred to the boys that Ned might tell on them. It simply was not their code.

The following Monday morning in Manhattan, Elsie sat in her bedroom on silk and lace bed sheets drinking fresh coffee. Driven by the chauffeur, Billy traveled ten blocks south to join his classmates. He met Ned at 8 a.m. in front of Buckley. "Hello, old top," said Billy, shaking hands. Billy's shy eyes darted away. Ned was relieved to see that the dangerous bully had disappeared.

The boys were scrubbed, with fresh haircuts, and were dressed in waistcoat, jacket, peaked caps with the gold "B," Buckley school tie, and long pants. Until this year they had worn short pants; neither boy acknowledged their new symbol of maturity. Before they passed into a hidden side door, guarded night and day by a sharp-eyed black janitor, Ned greeted the Woodward chauffeur. Everyone was aware who came by chauffeur and big car, although it was also a sign of status among the oldest boys to walk to school alone.

If a Buckley student's father worked in a corporation, he was likely to own it. Billy's classmates included the son of the founder of Mack Trucks. There was also future mayor John Lindsay and his twin brother, and Orlando Weber, whose father "was" Allied Chemical. After the seventh grade, the students went on to Groton, St. Paul's, or St. Mark's, the top eastern secondary schools. They then found one another again at Harvard and Yale. Buckley was a strict school with an Episcopalian foundation and avowals of allegiance to democracy. The boys studied Latin and geography, recited the Lord's Prayer, and played soccer on the rooftop playground. They sang "America the Beautiful," not "The Star-Spangled Banner," because the eccentric headmaster and founder, B. Lord Buckley (a man who seemed to be falling out of his waistcoat and waving his pincenez), thought it too hard for the boys to reach the high notes of the national anthem. Buckley gave assembly speeches cautioning his students against "the decadences of the age." They must not simply admire the baseball hero Babe Ruth but play baseball themselves.

In 1935, at fourteen, Billy and Bean were separated. Bean was sent to St. Paul's School. Billy and several Buckley classmates were packed off to board at the Groton School in Groton, Massachusetts. Billy had been enrolled by his father at birth. Groton had a gilded reputation, and its graduates included Billy's father, Jock Whitney, and Averell Harriman. Billy was the only boy at school with his own checking account (at the family bank), and he was the first to own a car, a large Packard sedan. It was he who perfected the ritual of cigarette smoking in the woods and in the basement of his dorm. He held a short ebony cigarette holder between his two front teeth while he talked or between his thumb and ring finger. He was also the tallest boy, with a coltish beauty that he retained throughout his life.

Groton did not provide an entirely Spartan existence for its boys. Uniformed maids waited on them at table and made their beds. Although Billy had little taste for spills and bruises, the headmaster, the Reverend Endicott Peabody, made sure that he played football, as his father had.

Billy was frustrated to be following in his father's footsteps instead of discovering his own personality and tastes. Like his father, he became a dorm prefect and the business manager of the school newspaper.

When his parents visited the school, Billy found it difficult to share his father's enthusiasms. Woodward Sr. was pleased that Billy had joined the dramatic society, although he worked backstage as an electrician. Unlike both his father and his future wife, Billy lacked the force to stand in front of an assembly and recite, nor did he have the courage for self-parody. His father talked about the hit he himself had been as sexy Martha, the landlady. It was clear even to Billy that his father blamed Elsie for their son's lackluster athletic interests. Although she was hardly a devoted mother, it irked Elsie Woodward that her husband was pushing their son to be a chip off the old block.

Billy was relieved when his parents left. His mother did not want to be there, and his father was too much of a celebrity for his son's comfort. Woodward Sr. dazzled Groton students when he whipped out his gold toothpick carved with his initials to pick his teeth. When he was elected steward of the Jockey Club—the most important breeders' association, then limited to fifty members, all male, who controlled racing in New York and, to a lesser extent, the whole country—it was announced in the Groton student newspaper.

By now Billy's parents were making few public appearances together. This decade—the 1930s—was the worst in Elsie Woodward's life. Her husband was flourishing—but without her. Word still reached Elsie in New York that her husband was appearing at Newmarket in the company of young women. At fifty-five, Elsie looked dowdy in a photograph taken at Belmont Park racetrack. She wore a plaid raincoat too short for her brown skirt. Her fur stole was a raccoon whose head hung past Elsie's bosom.

Elsie's frequent escort during the thirties was a tall, flirtatious bachelor, a stockbroker named Robert Lancaster, whose family had owned a Springfield, Massachusetts, corset factory, the motto of which was "the tie that binds." Although Elsie was not one to show physical affection, her friends suspected an affair. Lancaster was lively. In fact, he may have been the object of Elsie Woodward's single marital infidelity. He was an extra man who lived with his mother on Park Avenue, enjoyed drawing room comedies, and was a fan of Mussolini's. Discussing adultery decades later, Elsie said, "In my day we had affairs with members of our own class; it made things ever so much easier."

Edward "Neddy" Patterson in the uniform of the Knickerbocker
Grays, the organization for young men in New York society, 1929.
Ned Patterson and Billy Woodward had met at the Buckley School
and remained close friends until Billy's death.

Grenville "Bean" Baker (heir to the First National City Bank) and his dog Griffon, with Priscilla (left) and Cynthia Howe, at the Greentree Fair on the Whitney estate, Manhasset, Long Island, 1933. "Bean" Baker was Billy Woodward's best friend.

Sally Woodward
Moore, one of Billy's
four older sisters, 1936.

Left to right: James "Sunny
Jim" Fitzsimmons, William
Woodward, Sr., and Billy,
1939. Sunny Jim Fitzsimmons
trained all of the Woodward
horses that raced in America.
He became the country's most
successful trainer (three
Kentucky Derbys and 225
winners, including Gallant Fox,
Johnstown, Bold Ruler, and
Sea Biscuit).

Left: William Woodward,
1945. *Below:* Elsie at Belmont
Park, Belmont, Long Island,
1935.

Few society members today will admit that Elsie Woodward ever looked or acted less than perfectly. An exception is Louis Auchincloss, who said in an interview, "Elsie Woodward was an ordinary woman who simply outlived her detractors."

Raised to be in society, Billy could not commit himself to the life of the church or to work as a missionary, although at Groton he did join the "missionary society." For a short time, he delivered food parcels to the poor, and even went to their churches. He knew "associating" with them any further went against his family's view of his place in society. Charity was done in small doses to enhance family names. But such token gestures were the province of wives.

Billy was, without even trying, the center of an elite clique at Groton. His classmates prized an invitation to his house in Manhattan. George Putnam tells how a footman unpacked his sweaty soccer pants and socks. He was embarrassed when they appeared washed and refolded in a drawer that evening. In New York, the boys also visited the magnificent houses of Billy's friends.

The Reverend Peabody gave Billy the assignment of writing an editorial for *The Grotonian* against cliques, elitism, and "the grinning fiend of Snobbishness." The wily reverend had picked the richest boy in the school for the task. Billy's editorial noted that cliques often begin because boys had come to Groton from the same school. Furthermore, a clique was usually based on "superficial markings, rather than genuine friendship." The editorial also railed against a guiding principle of his parents' lives— elitism. Billy knew well the words and phrases his mother, father, and sisters used to rank people: "not our sort," "controversial," "English," "fortune hunter," "social," "from nowhere," "the best family," "no family," "no background," "vulgar," "poor as a churchmouse," "in society," "used goods," "at home in the best homes," "breeds horses," "coloreds," "titled," "climber," "hebes," "tarty," "obvious," "no class," "pushy," "no money," and "not listed" [in the *Social Register*].*

In the mid-1930s, the most influential news event in Billy's life was the forbidden romance of King Edward VIII of England, who fell madly

---

*When a classmate, George Putnam, read F. Scott Fitzgerald's short story "The Rich Boy," he was reminded of Billy:

"Let me tell you about the very rich. They are different from you and me." The passage continues: "They possess and enjoy early, and it does something to them, makes them soft where we are hard, and cynical where we are trustful, in a way that, unless you were born rich, it is very difficult to understand. They think, deep in their hearts, that they are better than we are because we had to discover the compensations and refuges of life for ourselves. Even when they enter into our world or sink below us, they still think they are better than we are."

in love with a social inferior, the American divorcée Wallis Simpson. (The British press ignored the scandal for months.) The American newspapers had a field day when it was learned that the King wished to marry this inappropriate woman.

Bean Baker and Billy wanted desperately to love as extravagantly as the King. Born to extreme privilege, Billy and Bean took it lightly. Perhaps Billy dreamed of what fun it would be to give up the "Woodward stuff" for a beautiful woman who really loved him. But his parents were torn between their admiration of the English royalty and their belief that duty was more important than romantic love.

On December 10, 1936, the King of England declared his abdication. Bean and Billy got tipsy on sherry as Bean's father declared Edward a fool to give up his kingdom for sex. Mr. Baker instructed the boys on duty toward inherited burdens.

However, the teenage boys had been raised on movies. Joan Crawford may have only been a shopgirl, but she knew how to love her wealthy suitor. King Edward's romance was superior to the calculated mergers based on money and property. It was about true love. Billy was desperate to believe that the right woman could inflame him more than his proper mother inspired his father. As the years passed, Billy and Bean would declare society girls too "brown shoe"—meaning virtuous and dowdy. Bean swore if he were king he'd give up his throne for an evening with a waitress or dancer at Fefe's Monte Carlo.

When Bean Baker's remote father died, Bean began to behave erratically and to depend more than ever on Billy. He also inherited over $20 million. Bean lived on the upper floor of a brownstone next door to his mother on Madison Avenue. It took a police raid to inform Bean's mother of his gun collection, ordered through the mail, for which Bean held no license. He was once handcuffed at La Guardia Airport as he got out of a plane: he was carrying two unlicensed guns.

The showgirls at Fefe's Monte Carlo often looked like beautiful society belles. They tended to marry rich men; one even captured a titled Englishman. The black-lacquered stage was only a few feet from from the patrons in their dinner jackets. Bean liked to catch the 2 a.m. floor show. He also liked Woodward's admiration of his pranks. At three o'clock, the chorus girls finished dancing onstage and Bean and Billy bought dinner for several of them.

At Fefe's, Billy and Bean took up with "the king of the nightclubs," the handsome Ted Peckham. Peckham made Bean and Billy feel more grown-up. He could get them pretty girls from chorus lines and plays. Nobody told their parents about him.

Peckham also recruited young men for a paid escort service he ran by pasting notices on the bulletin boards at the Yale, Harvard, and Princeton clubs. Embarrassed by his own Western Reserve degree, Peckham believed that a Harvard man would always be a gentleman. He dined with Jean Cocteau, Louella Parsons, and Lady Mendl (Elsie de Wolfe) and insisted that nothing more prurient than the occasional marriage occurred between his escorts and the ladies who paid fifty dollars a night.

Billy Woodward's virginity became Ted Peckham's obsession. Bean, too, became dedicated to getting "Woodward deflowered." Peckham, who had a crush on Billy, conspired with Bean to introduce Billy to fast girls. Bean believed that the girls in their own set had little understanding of sex. He became obsessed with Spanish women and even with the language itself. On midterm break, Bean and Billy flew to Mexico City, where, Bean later claimed, he dated eight girls in a single four-day weekend. Despite secret tips to other Mexican girls, Billy remained chaste.

Billy and Bean did enjoy the friendship of a tall, young, pedigreed woman named Cassie Sands, whose forebears had founded the Long Island community of Sands Point, where her family still had its own private cemetery. Something of a tomboy, Cassie was six feet tall, as were Billy's sisters. Her father, Charles Sands, had been paralyzed from an illness and had married his nurse. Cassie lived on Park Avenue and in Oyster Bay. Billy always seemed to light up when she was around, but made little attempt to see her alone. He did everything in a group that happened around Bean. To their friends in the Long Island clique, Bean was deemed the most fun, but Billy was the best looking. Some girls thought Billy was homosexual, since he had so little sexual intensity. The boys played backgammon in the sand at the exclusive Piping Rock beach club on Long Island. A shabby wood shack served hot dogs and orange juice. No money changed hands. Billy signed "Woodward."

News of Germany's expansion came over the car radio between big brassy Jimmy Dorsey music. It made the future frightening. Billy watched military vehicles carting men and machines past Groton to a naval base up the road.

Unlike most freshmen, Billy did not think he needed Harvard. There was not a book in Widener Library he wanted to read. Billy missed the good-humored Reverend Peabody. The rector had taken it to be his duty to make Billy brush his teeth, write his compositions, and show up for football practice. At Harvard, Billy attended few classes, preferring to stay in bed in his good smoking jacket, drinking a gin martini as a late breakfast. He was considered a loner. An aspect of Harvard that pleased him was that once again he was a classmate of the irascible Bean.

Throughout his three and a half years at college, Billy turned off radio news about the war, saying he preferred listening to Benny Goodman. Bean wanted to run away to join the air force. William Woodward, Sr., formally told Billy to join the exclusive Naval Reserve, as had his friends' sons.

Billy reluctantly donned a tight NROTC uniform custom-made at Dunhill. He marched shoulder to shoulder with other reserve students in close-order drills until dinner. He was relieved to be following orders. Billy also sailed the old World War I battleship *Wyoming* to the Caribbean. The ship held gunnery exercises, towing a target behind. Another mandatory cruise was held on a private yacht commandeered by the navy, the *St. Augustine*, a ship that would be sunk during the war. The early morning risings, the uniform drills, and the quick maneuvers were sobering. Billy learned to navigate and chart a course. Staying up all night on watch and firing empty guns in drills, he felt as though he were in a war movie.

To pass the time at Harvard, Billy took his Packard and drove for hours, often exceeding the speed limit. His friends at the Porcellian, Harvard's exclusive social club, joked that the standard of living in the car was higher than anywhere else at Harvard. The dashboard, lined in burnished wood, suggested a chauffeur at the wheel. The leather seats were cracked but meticulously clean. No beer bottles rolled around. The car was fitted with a sterling-silver ice bucket. No longer forbidden, liquor was very stylish. Billy drank out of a slim pewter hip flask engraved "W.W."

Some afternoons he and Bean stopped off for stingers and planter's punch at the empty Ritz Bar under the Boucher murals of wood nymphs. As the wood tables filled for dinner, Billy and Bean left.

The two New York boys bought motorcycles and sped out of Cambridge, although Billy rarely made the Smith or Mount Holyoke College runs. Nor did he enjoy the local debutante parties and football weekends. Instead, he and Bean disappeared to New York to dance on the Astor roof with showgirls.

The other Harvard students admired Billy's style of dress: a scarf tucked into his collar, sometimes white trousers with his blue blazer. Billy arranged his classes so that he and Bean could fly or drive to Manhattan every Thursday. Bean proposed marriage almost as soon as he met Alicia Grajales, a voluptuous young Mexican showgirl at Fefe's Monte Carlo. She danced and sang in the late-night floor shows wearing a brief costume that included a cottontail and rabbit ears. When she smiled, she flashed a gold front tooth.

Alicia Grajales spoke almost no English, but her presence in the dormitory, Eliot House, convinced the other boys that Billy and Bean knew everyone in New York. Despite his engagement to Alicia, Bean was more desperate than ever, chasing Spanish-speaking girls and prostitutes. He woke up the owner of a West End Avenue brothel at midday to demand a party. And there was Billy behind him, almost too handsome, and sheepish. Bean went upstairs with a girl.

After his sophomore year, Billy moved out of the undergraduate dormitory. The dorms were too "public" for Billy, who, like his mother, needed more privacy. His politeness seemed—to some classmates—an act of generosity. He and Bean moved together to a sunny eighteenth-century Beacon Hill house. There was no hint that Billy and Bean were only student tenants. The big pieces of furniture were from the Woodwards' Newport home, which would be demolished in a few years. Bean stored his guns behind leather trunks in the closets. An Irish maid from Somerville stocked the refrigerator with liquor and threw away empty bottles. She served Bean's candlelit dinners. Billy had few female visitors. Despite his membership in the "right" social clubs like Porcellian and Hasty Pudding, he rarely socialized. He slept nine hours a night. Bean seemed to be waging a twenty-four-hour-a-day personal war to prove his manhood. He was also becoming a serious alcoholic.

Both boys were fighting panic.

Bean invited Billy down to Horseshoe, the Bakers' seventy-five room plantation house on 2,000 lush acres in Tallahassee, Florida. Billy's father, fearful of air travel, insisted they take the train. In their first-class compartment, a fat little boy stuffed chocolate caramels into his mouth and then cried to his governess because he had a stomachache. He was Edward M. Kennedy. Billy told him, "Stop eating those things and you'll feel fine."

Bean liked to shoot quail, duck, and possum at Horseshoe. He made guests such as Bing Crosby and the Duke and Duchess of Windsor laugh. Bean's bedroom was lined with gun cases containing antique French pistols,

.45-caliber shotguns, and rifles. In the town of Tallahassee, Billy followed Bean from pool hall to bar. Bean liked to go wild there. They often ended up at Whid's HighHat Bar, where brown-bagged bottles of homemade liquor were passed into their car window by teenage girls called "curb hops." Bean dated the girls, particularly Doris, who later married an electrician in Panama City.

When word reached the local gas station that Bean and his friend were in town and "catching tabs" down at Whid's HighHat, the street around the bar filled up fast.

The handymen, bartenders, juke-joint waitresses, and gas jockeys liked Bean—he never acted like a snob. In the cement yard behind the bar, Bean set a tin can as a target on a trash barrel. Billy enjoyed the danger of shooting freely in the middle of town and easily won the shooting matches.

"What's it like to be so damn rich?" one local boy asked Billy in a sweet nasal twang.

"You are as rich as I am," said Billy. He had heard his mother say this to a servant.

More than girls, Bean loved risking his life. At sundown, he made Billy put on a pair of high snake-proof swamp boots and two layers of leather clothes. "If I could shoot the way you do," Bean said, "I'd live in the swamps." Ted Peckham met the boys in Palm Beach for debutante parties. In his suite at the Lakeview Hotel, Billy kept his pallor and slept off hangovers. He maintained that the only reason to shave was to dance cheek to cheek. One night a tipsy C. Z. Cochrane (later C. Z. Guest) danced up to Ted Peckham. When he waved to Billy she asked him, "Help me marry Billy." Peckham obligingly set up dinners, but Billy was not interested. He wore an embarrassed smile and held his black cigarette filter high above his face. Girls like C.Z. did not mind his silences.

But the dance music stopped for Billy on Sunday, December 7, 1941, when Americans learned the Japanese had bombed Pearl Harbor.

As an editor of *The Harvard Crimson* wrote the next day, "We are aware that it is we who will be fighting this war. We know that after it is all over it will be some of us who will have our names engraved on the college's bronze memorial. We believe in our country and in the right and we believe that in the present war they are synonymous. In that belief we will fight and in that belief we will triumph."

5

NEW YORK

I may not be right,
But New York is quite
Wild enough for me . . .
Ours, the glitter of Broadway, Saturday night . . .
Ours, the mad brouhaha of the Plaza's Persian Room,
. . . Why don't we stay in Manhattan
And play it's all ours.

> —COLE PORTER,
> "Ours," from *Red, Hot and Blue*, 1936

Ann Crowell's dreams had been held in check for too long. But now, on a hot August morning in 1937, she stuffed the last box into her station wagon and was so elated she could barely catch her breath. Ann was twenty-two and she was leaving Kansas City forever. She was never going to clean up after her mother's boarders again.

The book of maps bounced on the front seat. She and Ethel had traced a line over roads and through cities Ann never heard of—all the way to the George Washington Bridge. Her fake alligator purse contained $400. Her mother had wrapped the bills with a rubber band.

Ann drove in her stocking feet, a habit she cultivated because she believed it looked sexy. At a filling station she washed her face and put on fresh makeup. She pictured herself talking to John Robert Powers, his wife, his receptionist. She was still thinking about a comment by the millinery buyer at Harzfelds. "You know Joan Crawford? Well, she made it in New York by sleeping with producers and agents. I guess it pays to sleep with a man if he helps your career." Ann had never had a sexual relationship, and her mother was proud that she was still a virgin, although when men looked up at her on the runway at Harzfelds her whole body tingled. Jack

87

Lescher, the millinery buyer, had kissed her a few times after he gave her the names of some modeling contacts at New York showrooms.

At midnight she pulled the car over and slept in the backseat behind a motel outside Cleveland. She locked the car doors and windows and hid under one of her mother's old bed sheets. There was a long journey ahead, and no one, least of all Ann Crowell, could imagine what was in store.

Six days later she was walking along Park Avenue in Manhattan in her four-inch spike heels and bright red dress, scanning *The New York Times*. On the front page was a picture of Anthony Eden, British foreign secretary, and Nazi leader Joseph Goebbels's declaration that the era of democracy was over. But international matters were not on Ann's mind; she was about to live out the fantasy of millions of American girls. Her fantasies had become Ann's only guideposts. She was endowed with an ability to recreate herself, most particularly her appearance. She had been forced to be a chameleon, working hard to adapt her personality to scores of different environments—including the middle-class Westport High and the upper-class thrift shop.

Ann Crowell was on the brink of the American dream of classlessness. Like her mother, she was not afraid to lie about her past, scramble for a job, put on appearances, and live in a constant state of crisis. Her goal would be "self-improvement"—it would be described by her detractors as nothing more than social climbing. But Ann was determined to work harder than anyone else. Her striking success in Manhattan would be based on an uncanny ability to imitate models and actors on the radio and on the screen, a lovely speaking voice, an extraordinary figure, an enormous will—and strong, blind ambition. Ann was eager to change what little self she had—at any cost—to suit New York style.

The lobby of the Powers Agency at 247 Park Avenue was filled with beautiful fidgeting girls from all over the country. Ann gave her name to one of the five secretaries and stared with envy at a real model walking by in a form-fitting suit. She carried her model's hatbox, filled for the day's assignments with makeup, a change of clothes, and accessories such as gloves and costume jewelry. Models checked the assignment chart hanging behind the counter. The secretaries on the telephones filled in the charts, writing the time and place of appointments and the required equipment and clothing.

John Robert Powers had started an industry of his own in the 1920s when, as a struggling actor, he overheard a businessman say he needed a group of attractive people to pose for a magazine advertisement. Powers saw that clothing looked better on tall thin women. He taught his models the grooming and style that made them known as "long-stemmed American beauty roses."

Ann wore a red secondhand shirtwaist from the Junior League Shop. At her hotel room the night before, she'd sewn a veil onto a white hat. The receptionist suggested that she take a seat. On the sofa, she leaned over with a big Kansas smile and greeted another girl. The girl and Ann arranged to meet at the Automat for dinner. After three hours, Ann was called to the long counter. The secretary told her to leave her pictures. Ann said, "There's some mistake. Mr. John, the hat designer, told Mr. Powers to see me in person."

"That's impossible."

Ann said, "Don't worry about me. I'm used to waiting."

By six-thirty, the secretary asked Ann to leave.

"I understand," Ann said. "I'll see you tomorrow."

That night, Ann decided to dress like the Powers models. The basic element was a suit as classic as a debutante's. But Powers girls wore their sober suits tight. For Powers, a girl's main ornament was her face and the outline of her figure. Her hat was for balance.

Ann sewed a new seam into a plain gray suit, nipping in the waistline. The next morning, after almost no sleep, she left an urgent message at Mr. John's office.

At the Powers agency, there was a new set of pretty girls. Ann was one of the few aspirants who was not wearing a bright dress. She sat for six hours. For two more long days she sat in the Powers office. At lunchtime, on the fourth day, she visited a clothing manufacturer recommended by Jack Lescher. Manufacturers used models to demonstrate their latest fashions to retail buyers. In the large room, she was surrounded by bolts of cloth and girls bent over sewing machines. She vowed she would never do that kind of donkeywork. The manufacturer asked her measurements.

She recited, "Thirty-six, twenty, thirty-four."

Although she asked him to leave the room while she undressed to try on one of his dresses, he refused. Unfortunately the dress was too tight in the bust. When Ann quietly told him she was going to be working for Powers, he let her try on a second dress. It was a better fit. "Maybe I'll call Powers and ask for you," he said. The next morning she went to Saks and filled out a salesgirl application. Jack Lescher's name opened doors. "I want to work Saturdays and nights," she said, telling herself it was just temporary.

She returned to the agency. The secretary shook her head, asking her to leave her pictures like everybody else.

Ann had probably rehearsed her response in front of the mirror. "I make a better impression in person," she said.

Four hours later, a man looked over his black-rimmed eyeglasses at her. "Come in, please." John Robert Powers told her to walk across the room. Ann walked with her pelvis first, as though her face, neck, fingers, arms, chest, and legs were separate and wonderful ornaments. At five feet seven, she was the right height. She kept her stomach tight, her shoulders relaxed. It was her blue-green eyes and the high, clean hairline that gave Ann Crowell her facial beauty. She had many different looks—important for a model. When she spoke of salary, she looked greedy. She projected something too strong that seemed sexual. When frightened, she resembled a little girl, although she had a strong chest and shoulders like Joan Craw-ford's. Her navy suit was tight. To John Powers, Ann Crowell with her big smiles undoubtedly seemed different from the parade of girls. She had something all-American about her. Most important, she seemed so enthu-siastic. She had also been clever enough to study the Powers dress and makeup style. Powers had to admire her initiative. He liked to say that 60 percent of modeling was personality and intelligence.

"Why did you persist?" he asked.

"I look better in person," she said.

He looked down at her glossies and told her she needed an operation to fix her nose. "Borrow the money," he said. "We'll recommend the doctor. He'll shorten it and take the bump off." He asked her why she had come to Manhattan.

"I want to be a model," she said. This was not true. It was movies that she wanted. But modeling was the first step.

He told her that her body was too generous for a fashion model; she would have to diet and exercise. However, she was full where she should be—in the chest—and small at her ankles, wrists, and waist. Her thighs were long. Her pride in her body added to her luster.

"You are applying for a salesman's job," he said, giving his usual lecture. "Whether it's toothpaste, mouthwash, or shampoo, you have to throw everything you have into it. A model needs to be an actress. Some days you will frown over your 'husband's' morning coffee or wave from your 'new' automobile." He lectured about practicing poses in front of a full-length mirror and was pleased by her hearty agreement; she was already doing just that. He listed Powers girls who had become famous in the movies, including Barbara Stanwyck, Kay Francis, Norma Shearer, Joan

Bennett, and Rosalind Russell. But she already knew those names. He also told her that Henry Fonda, Tyrone Power, and Fredric March had also worked for him.

John Robert Powers watched her talk. She probably smiled too often and spoke loudly. Her elation added to her odd quality. She was not an exotic or a chiseled beauty, but she would be good for toothpaste and soap ads and for bathing suits. She could pass for a debutante.

By coincidence Jack Lescher was in New York on a buying trip for Harzfelds. Ann went to see him in his hotel room to ask him for the money for her nose operation. He put his arms around her shoulders. Maybe I can do something for you." It was the most important $500 of her life. She smiled, wondering how she was going to escape his fondling and kisses. Three weeks later she worked a full Saturday at Saks selling millinery with a small bandage on her nose. Her head still ached from the operation, but she wanted to get the cash to repay Jack Lescher. He wanted to take her out to dinner. "I can't let you see me yet," she said. Her new nose made her look pert, like an actress, even though one nostril flared unevenly. The doctor said it was the best he could do. Her photograph was added to the large book that Powers sent to advertisers.

Ann competed at scores of auditions a week. She could never look tired or disheveled. She learned rigid rules of grooming. No matter how she felt, she had to smile. During her first months Ann complained, as did several of the other girls, that Powers kept fees for himself. When Ann spoke to Powers about it, her assignments dwindled for a time. Although Ann never got jobs at *Vogue* or *Harper's Bazaar,* she became a successful Powers model, posing in magazine ads for Lux and 'Camay soaps and Tangee lipstick. She was sometimes shown a sketch of the final advertisement. Her job was to assume the same facial expression and position as the sketch portrayed—and to pose for several hours under hot lights. The models acquired enormous working wardrobes. A request to appear in an evening dress usually meant "objectionables"—an ad for depilatories or deodorants. A call for her to wear an interesting neckline meant that Ann was going to model hats. Dark clothes and hats meant she would be modeling fur coats.

By December Ann had saved enough money to move into her own small penthouse apartment at 135 East Fiftieth Street. She refused to buy cheap furniture, preferring the empty white bedroom and living room walls and waxed floors. She papered her kitchen walls with menus from chic nightclubs and restaurants such as El Morocco, "21," and the Stork Club. She missed her mother, but decided not to go home for Christmas. Her life was all business. She took tap dancing and ballet lessons. She dated theater agents, who promised her introductions and bookings. They took her to "21" and to El Morocco to be seen with a Powers model. She dined with garment manufacturers, too—for her career. She flirted with them all over champagne and kissed them good night. Weekends, she called acquaintances to get news about theater auditions. On her twenty-fourth birthday, Ann felt lonely, even though her life had surpassed her fantasies. She impulsively threw a Christmas-tree-trimming party, inviting fashion models, casting agents, her acting teacher, a woman in her six-story building, and a man whose clothing line she modeled who knew a woman who worked for a Broadway casting agent. Ann's holiday blues disappeared when a model named Telde Getz arrived with a new friend named Malcolm Milligan, who played carols on the piano. Milligan had just arrived in New York. He was a slender young man, two inches shorter than Ann, twenty-three years old, with slicked-down black hair, dimples, and blue eyes. Sensitive, unassuming, Milligan was an honors graduate of Carnegie Mellon in acting. He was working as a confidential secretary and doing promotion for Philip Morris cigarettes. At the party friends persuaded Milligan to imitate the radio actor who would shout, "Call for Phil-i-i-p Morr-auris."

When Milligan learned that Ann was from Westport, Kansas, he told her that she would be perfect for a small but pivotal role in a new Broadway play he was reading called *Abe Lincoln in Illinois* by Robert Sherwood. The part was a poor Kansas farmwife whose husband is a boyhood friend of Abe Lincoln's. Ann asked him questions. The pioneer wife was named Aggie Gale, and she had one emotional scene, persuading Abe Lincoln to pray for her dying son.

Telde Getz glared at Ann, who was writing down Milligan's telephone number. She, too, was from Kansas City. "Malcolm," Telde said, "don't you have two other parties to go to?"

"Nope," he said, looking at Ann.

Later Milligan and Ann decided to cap off the evening with a drink around the corner at El Morocco. Ann was dancing with Milligan when she recognized the movie star Franchot Tone. He and his wife, Joan Crawford, had just split up. His Hollywood career had been floundering, according to an article that had just appeared in the tabloid newspaper the *Journal-American*.

An American aristocrat who looked like a matinee idol, Tone had been raised as a millionaire. But he had chafed under the overwhelming authority of his brilliant scientist father. A graduate of the Hill School in Pottstown, Pennsylvania, and Cornell (in three short years), Tone had taught romance languages for a year at Cornell. In the late 1920s he joined a summer stock company in Buffalo and then the New Playwrights Theater in Greenwich Village, where he was a success in *The Age of Innocence*, based on Edith Wharton's novel about nineteenth-century upper-class New Yorkers.

Tone was a serious artist and the "actors' actor" of his generation. He had been an original member of the experimental Group Theatre in New York in 1930, with Harold Clurman, Lee Strasberg, and Cheryl Crawford. When he left the theater for Hollywood, he planned only a short movie stint. Tone expressed contempt for the Crawford legend, but as soon as he spoke to Joan Crawford on a movie set, he fell in love with her. He won the most famous movie star of the era by catering to her obsession with bettering herself. He taught her table manners and wines. He sang opera to her.

Despite Tone's artistic ambitions, as the years passed, he was cast again and again as a Park Avenue type in light comedies. For seven years he had played second lead to such actors as Spencer Tracy and Gary Cooper. He yearned to play Aaron Burr or Thomas Paine. And his ego was deflated by fans who saw him as "Mr. Joan Crawford." Press photographers snapped photos of Crawford's black eye inflicted by Tone. When Ann first saw him, he was thirty-three years old and his MGM contract had just been canceled. He was desperate to prove himself again in New York as a serious stage actor.

Ann felt a kinship with Joan Crawford's climb to success. She had visited her house in Kansas City and had clipped articles from the Kansas City *Star* about how the abandoned girl had cleaned toilets at Rockingham Academy. Ann always felt that she had been abandoned by her father and left behind several times by her mother. She had cleaned bathrooms for the boarders. She understood what Crawford understood. Her new sexual attractiveness had given her a power over men who could help her realize her ambitions.

Franchot Tone was seeing a psychiatrist five days a week. He was angry at all women after losing Crawford. For breakfast he ordered one double martini after another. When asked why, he replied, "Because if I didn't I'd jump out a window."

Ann smiled hesitantly at Franchot Tone. "I'm sorry, I guess I wanted to meet you too much," she said.

His feelings shifted on his face. He was instantly attracted to her.

A moment passed. "Do you want to dance?" she asked quickly. Ann thought his date resembled Joan Crawford. Tone tossed back more champagne as he stood. He disliked dancing, but he told Ann that he was impressed by her nerve. But even drunk, he was a skillful dancer: Joan Crawford had insisted he take lessons.

Tone courted Ann Crowell for several months. They were both at their best in this phase before the passions of a sexual relationship seized them. Tone seemed paternal, although he was only nine years older than Ann. In the evenings at his suite at the Waldorf, he drank double martinis and read Shakespeare to her. Tone was also meeting with theater people. He asked Ann to read their submissions to him, saying that she had "intelligence of the heart." She told him she was honored by his presence in her life.

One afternoon Tone showed up at Ann's small apartment with a floral watercolor painting for her empty living room walls. He then escorted her to a screening room to watch *The Lives of a Bengal Lancer,* an adventure film in which he starred as a keen-witted British junior officer in India. Watching the film seemed to cheer him.

Tone seemed as pleased as Ann when they began a sexual affair. But after two months, he told Ann he thought of Joan Crawford while he made love to her. She read of his appearances at "21" with a series of other sexy "lowborn" girls. When he allowed it, Ann simply showed up at his hotel suite. She did not just love Franchot Tone; she undoubtedly wanted to be him. Although Tone hated to be seen once again as "Mr. Joan Crawford," he found it hard to talk of anyone else.

Tone decided Ann was sexually naive. She expected love. As their intimacy grew, she grew more demanding. Walking into rooms with Franchot made Ann glow: if she was at his side, she had to be beautiful.

Tone railed against what he called Ann's "shopgirl" worship of Hollywood, but he never ceased to be amazed by her shrewd mind. She was eager for his advice, and he advised her to dress in bright green and turquoise to bring out her eyes. It was he who suggested the braces that Ann wore at night to straighten her front teeth. He sent her to a professional Russian drama coach named Benno Schneider in Greenwich Village who taught the Stanislavsky "method." He was touched that when he used a word unfamiliar to her, she asked him to spell it and wrote it in her notebook. It made him smile that later she managed to use these words in conversation. But he did not tell her to tone down her heavy makeup. He perversely enjoyed looking at her when she painted her face. And he was probably smart enough to realize that Ann felt unattractive without it.

Ann asked him to coach her in *The Importance of Being Earnest.* She still had her high school copy of the play. He drilled her in breathing and phrasing. She made long lists of his acting tips, but he told her he did not think she would ever be a serious actress. He thought she was too removed from her parts. She memorized gestures but refused to search within herself for feelings. He urged her to read George Bernard Shaw's plays and to study elocution to diminish her drawl.

Ann was hurt when she read in the gossip columns that Joan Crawford was seeing Tone again, but divorcing him just the same. Ann did not understand that it was studio publicity designed to keep Tone from doing anything dangerous to himself, and thus to Joan Crawford's public reputation. Ann only reluctantly surrendered Tone to his one-night stands and his Group Theatre cronies. The women never seemed to last. He was in the habit of hitting women "because he cared too much," or so he explained it. Most of Tone's women ran from his physical violence. (He had a highly publicized fistfight over starlet Barbara Payton. The other man married Payton, divorced her, and later killed his third wife.)

6

THE TEN MOST
BEAUTIFUL GIRLS

Despite Ann's pleading, Franchot Tone procrastinated about arranging a screen test for her at MGM. He was ambivalent about life in Los Angeles, and he told Ann that she was wrong for Hollywood. He meant perhaps that her face was not photogenic enough for films. He feared she would lose whatever sense of herself she had there and suggested she find a man and start a family. "It didn't work for my mother," she said, smiling.

During the first week of November 1938, Tone had dinner at the Stork Club with an English girl who told him she wished she could be considered for a new Noël Coward musical revue called *Set to Music*. The show's star, Beatrice Lillie, would make her entrance singing Wagnerian opera and riding a real white horse. Coward had just arrived in Manhattan on the *Normandie* and was looking for the ten most beautiful girls in New York. Despite his misgivings about the frivolous nature of Coward's plays, at Sardi's a few nights later, Tone recommended Ann to Jack Wilson, Coward's manager and producer, as "the most beautiful girl in New York." He liked the idea of her playing a refined "hooker" in the Coward chorus. Coward's snobbish intellectual precision would be a good lesson for Ann. She was, after all, a talented mimic.

Auditions for *Set to Music* were hard to get: Coward planned to see only thirty girls and by invitation only. Ann was optimistic, although she had been turned down at a bewildering number of auditions. She had learned to shake off rejections, but pain hit her at odd moments. On November 29, two weeks before her twenty-fifth birthday, Ann Crowell waited with the remaining ten other girls to meet Noël Coward in a little office inside the Music Box Theatre on Forty-fifth Street. Ann looked like one of the youngest.

She recognized Toni Sorrel, a *Vogue* model who had danced in *Red, Hot and Blue* and clowned with Jimmy Durante. Toni was telling the girl next to her about having met Cary Grant when she was fifteen. "I told him I couldn't date him because I was a virgin." "You'd better be," he had told her. The beautiful girls in the room laughed. Ann also recognized red-haired Hilda Knight, a well-known beauty and the girlfriend of the man who ran the high society nightclub, Fefe's Monte Carlo. Hilda was also being kept by a financier named Jules Brulator. Ann had been taking singing lessons for a few months, but she doubted her ability to project into the balcony. Tone had dressed her for this event in a bright green blouse and hat. But compared to the other girls, she felt plain. Ann tried to make conversation with the top *Vogue* model—Helen Bennet, who arrived wearing a mink coat. She and Telde Getz were poring over instructions in a knitting magazine. They did not greet Ann; Telde was still irked by the way Ann had "taken over" Malcolm Milligan at her Christmas party. Today Telde wore a pillbox hat and a veil. Helen Bennet was said to have the best profile in Manhattan. She was a Brooklyn girl who never lost her accent. Helen's modeling minimum was eighty dollars a day. Her face was the model for Saks mannequins in store windows. She had high cheekbones and the flat, hollow cheeks favored by high-fashion photographers. Like Telde, she was a trained dancer, performing in every musical comedy at the Winter Garden Theatre for more than five years. Both girls' names appeared regularly in Walter Winchell's column.

Ann sang into an empty, dark theater. Afterward, an amused, self-congratulatory English voice thanked her. "That's charming, Miss Crowell," said Noël Coward, still invisible. "Luckily, singing is not the criterion for this revue." He sounded as though he were on her side. "Please pull up your skirt." This was routine. Her legs were an important part of these auditions. "You're rather refreshing to look at," he said after another pause. "You wear clothes well, too. Now walk around." Ann walked toward his voice. Even in the dark, the man commanded authority. "Please walk back," said Coward. "What work have you done?"

Ann cleared her throat and imitated him unconsciously. She described a busy career. "I model Lux and Camay soap ads, and I played Gwendolen in *The Importance of Being Earnest* at the Westport Theatre in Kansas." She omitted the fact that Westport was her high school.

Later she learned, of course, that her credits had been of no importance. Although her face was the least conventionally pretty of the chorus girls', Ann's vulnerability made her sexy. Coward made up his mind instantly at auditions. "Thank you. You'll be hearing from me shortly." He told her to leave her name and address with the stage manager. Unlike Coward, Ann did not consider the drawing-room lives of the rich to be material for comedy. The songs impressed upon her the fact that social climbing was infinitely worth it; she believed nobody was truly unhappy on the French Riviera.

In their third-floor dressing room, the "ten most beautiful girls" made themselves up. They were called the "Children of the Ritz chorus" and in one sketch played English prostitutes who strolled the Ritz Hotel lobby, awaiting male clients who had a yen for whores dressed as ladies. For another sketch they wore tunics and were literally a Greek chorus. Coward wrote them double-talk words that were fake Greek. At a dress rehearsal, the girls (including Ann) surprised Coward with dirty words to go in place of his "Greek" chant. Several phrases came through the masks loud and clear. While the forty other cast members screamed with laughter, Coward chose to be furious: "Girls, you are ladies."

Ann became obsessed with the English, reading books about London. Coward flaunted his friendship with Mrs. Anthony Eden by complaining that "going clubbing" with her was his least favorite form of entertainment. But as a loyal subject of the Crown, he did it for Britain. His comments gave Ann the idea for a new last name: Ann Eden. On the train to Boston for the first out-of-town preview, Ann consulted Coward about changing her name. The Boston programs had already been printed. But by the time the revue opened in Washington, D.C., in time for the 1939 New Year, she had taken the new name.

Ann tried to make friends with the English members of the cast. She chose to ignore the fact that they raised their eyebrows at her. She was particularly fascinated by Penelope Ward, whose mother had almost married the Duke of Windsor. But Penelope turned away Ann's overtures. There were those who whispered that the former English King was her actual father, as Ann wrote to her mother in Kansas City. The English cast members whispered that the models were kept by married men and gangsters. When Ann stepped out of a limousine one afternoon, sent by an admiring fashion photographer, they pretended to be scandalized. They also looked askance at the American models for their lack of dramatic training. Every afternoon the English sent word to the engineer to turn off the central heating because they liked the theater ice-cold. Except for Ann, the American girls shivered and went home. Ann mouthed the words to

Ann in New York, 1940. She worked successfully for three years as a radio actress, was voted "the most beautiful girl in radio," and acted in many radio soap operas, among them "Joyce Jordan, Girl Interne" and "Aunt Jenny's Real Life Stories."

Franchot Tone met Ann during his final separation from his wife, Joan Crawford (seen with him here in 1934), when he was in New York and was about to star in the Group Theatre production of *The Gentle People*.

The Group Theatre in 1936 at their summer retreat in Connecticut. Franchot Tone was considered by his colleagues and by critics to be the actors' actor of his generation. He was committed to the Group Theatre and helped to support them financially, as well as appearing in many of their productions.

Beatrice Lillie and (below, right) Penelope Ward in Noël Coward's *Set to Music*, New York, 1939.

Above: From the Noël Coward revue *Set to Music,* 1939. Ann, center, in the "Children of the Ritz" chorus. At left, Helen Bennet and Telde Getz.

Right: Malcolm Milligan, who had a small part in the Broadway production of *Abe Lincoln in Illinois,* fell in love with Ann while the play was on tour.

the comic ditties and jokes. Huddled in her winter coat, she memorized the entire revue. Later, Ann did imitations of Coward's breezy puns for Franchot Tone.

While the chorus girls awaited their cues, giggling and knitting, they excluded Ann. They did not want to see themselves in her. They said she was "not down to earth." When Ann repeated Coward's pranks and words of wisdom to the other girls, they resented her enthusiasm, making fun of the braces on her teeth and actually calling her "Miss Ambition."

One afternoon, Ann and the other girls were dancing a showy fox-trot to a song called "The Party's Over." Coward ran up the ramp to the stage and faced the empty house. Ann watched Coward as though he were an oracle. Coward snapped his fingers, motioning to the piano player: "I've got it, right. Ready to start. Everybody"—and Coward, every inch the dancer, paced out the steps. Once, twice, three times, he danced his routine. "The simple movements of the stage," he explained, and Ann nodded even though he was addressing one of the male English dancers, "only look spontaneous if they are studied over and over and over. You must know exactly how many steps to take to reach your partner, and you must take the same number of steps each time you do it." Ann rushed to her aisle seat to copy his words into her notebook.

She recounted stories of Coward in weekly letters to her mother. From Manhattan, her mother became a more benign presence. Ann invited Ethel Crowell to come watch them rehearse. Ethel stayed away, fearing that she might embarrass her daughter. She missed Angie desperately, but from a distance she was able to take pride in her success.

Ethel was now boarding in a dark wood house with a widow named Mabel Ostertag. Ann visited her mother at least once a year after moving to New York. Sleeping next to Ethel in the attic made Ann feel trapped all over again. The two women filled the Ostertag house with shouts and recrimination. Ethel pointedly refused to call her beautiful and increasingly unfamiliar daughter "Ann." "I named you Angeline, and darn it, that's your name," Ethel said.

Two weeks before the opening night of Coward's revue in New York, Elsie Woodward brought a group to a charity preview. At seven-fifteen, Mary Duncan Sanford, Herschel Williams, a playwright and extra man, and Alfred de Liagre, a theatrical producer, rode downtown in the Woodwards' silver Rolls-Royce. Other women who bought tickets to the benefit for the Berry School in Georgia were Mrs. Marshall Field, Mrs. Pierre Cartier,

Mrs. Cornelius Vanderbilt, and Mrs. Andrew Carnegie. They were the appropriate crowd to spread the good word about this musical. During intermission, an impromptu receiving line formed in the lobby to shake hands with Mrs. Woodward. She pronounced the show "great fun" and Coward at his best. Afterward, Mrs. Woodward and her party went backstage to congratulate Coward, who called each of them "darlingest." Then they went to El Morocco, where the maître d', Angelo, fought his way through the after-theater crowd to fuss over Mrs. Woodward.

Ann signed "Ann Eden" for an autograph hunter on opening night, January 18, 1939. Hundreds were turned away for standing room tickets. Downstairs, the men were in white tie. Tallulah Bankhead and her party, John Barrymore and his family, and Cole Porter in a leg cast had box seats. In the chorus line, Ann swayed and sang. Her hair was curled softly in some scenes and in others was gently pulled back. She looked like a sweet cornflower. At the end of the evening, Bea Lillie, lauded as "the miracle woman of mockery," received six standing ovations. Unfortunately, *Set to Music* received mixed reviews. Critics called it a jewel of a play with a dull finish. News of the war in Europe made it seem frivolous. Reviewers did say the girls were "stunning."

One night, after the cast had taken their curtain calls, Franchot Tone appeared backstage in white tie and tails. He and Ann were seeing less of each other. The English cast was very impressed by Ann Eden's "stage-door Johnny." Tone was an actor they respected. He had been standing in the stage-door entrance until he was recognized by Joan Crawford fans. After signing a few autographs, he ducked inside the cramped vestibule. When Ann appeared, he whisked her through the waiting crowd into a hired car.

At El Morocco, Ann hummed to the samba music as she entered ecstatic on Tone's arm. A month later, Ann could not attend Tone's opening in *The Gentle People*. It was February, and she was still playing in *Set to Music*. After the show, she joined Tone and his friends at Sardi's. Tone was praised for "radiant acting," but the reviews for the play were only lukewarm.

That night, Tone told her about his part in a new play by Ernest Hemingway called *The Fifth Column*. He believed that his role would reflect his own struggles to live according to his conscience. His character was a desperately unhappy man dedicated to a life of killing for an ideal.

The late 1930s were a good time for American theater. Lillian Hellman's play *The Little Foxes*, starring Tallulah Bankhead, was on Broadway, and

Katharine Hepburn was appearing in *The Philadelphia Story*. Ann auditioned for small speaking roles in several plays a week. The rejection that hurt the most was from the Broadway production of *Abe Lincoln in Illinois*. She listened enviously to production gossip from her friend Malcolm Milligan, who had won the small role of a soldier and was understudying one of Lincoln's sons. Then Milligan told Ann good news: the producers had decided to split the very successful show's cast in half and send two companies on the road. The role of Kansas farmwife Aggie Gale was available again—in the more prestigious road company headed by Raymond Massey.

The Gales were the salt-of-the-earth folk that Lincoln believed made America a good place. In contrast, the Noël Coward revue portrayed the superiority of the rich international set. Americans at that time even more than most seemed to hold both views. The conflicting sets of beliefs confused more people than Ann Eden and the Woodward family.

Abe Lincoln in Illinois presented Lincoln as a self-doubting man who was married to a shrewish wife and who drifted from job to job. It was a mix of realism and sentimental American history. The big scene for the character Ann wanted to play would take place in Westport Landing (the former name for part of Kansas City) on a moonlit prairie night. When Lincoln arrives, Aggie Gale appears in the back of the covered wagon, worried about her young son, who is burning up with fever. Lincoln is persuaded by her tears to pray for her little boy. The boy's fever drops, and Lincoln decides that he should be President because he can be of help to common folk.

Ann asked Franchot Tone to recommend her for the role to the play's director, Elmer Rice. When Ann met the forty-six-year-old Rice, he still looked like a precocious child despite his rimless glasses and thinning hair. Over lunch, Ann let him hold her hand as she told him about her father's homestead in western Kansas. Ann got the role with the touring company. The pay was thirty dollars a week, less than she'd get for one day of modeling or radio—but it was a chance to perform in a major piece of American theater. The other actors thought that Ann got her part by having a brief affair with Rice. The October tour started in Boston at the Opera House, where Ann turned to fellow actor Richard Allen and said, "I'd sleep with anybody if it would help my career." Although she was probably joking, he believed her.

Ann tended to her physical appearance more compulsively than usual. The other actors joked about the fact that Ann had to remove her makeup to go onstage. She always wore high spike heels and silk stockings with seams. Her tight clothes were made of sensuous fabrics. In addition to the professional trunk that each player was allotted, Ann's luggage on tour included six suitcases. She swung her hips when she walked, and the men were uneasy with her sexual power. They thought she was experimenting on them.

While they played at the Walnut Street Theatre in Philadelphia, Ann and Malcolm Milligan visited Betsy Ross's brick house. She felt like curling up in his pocket when he held her hand for the first time. She knew she was safe. Milligan was a big favorite in the troupe, even though, like Ann, he kept to himself. In her high heels and high hats, Ann towered three inches over him. Ann began a romance with shy, dimpled Milligan, who was again understudying Lincoln's son and playing a soldier. He was also an assistant stage manager and had the prestige of having been in the Broadway production. Milligan made the "calls," knocking on dressing-room doors and announcing "half hour," "fifteen minutes," "five minutes," and, finally, "places." He fell hopelessly in love with Ann. The other actors were amused by the way he ran for departing trains carrying her hand luggage. Throughout her life, Ann asked men to prove their love. She perhaps believed that if left to their own devices, they would neglect her. Ann usually selected two train seats far away from the rest of the actors, where she and Milligan sat, as their colleagues observed, "practically on top of each other."

7

SUCCESS

The troupe's 11,540-mile trip was scheduled for thirty-two weeks. Ann shared a happy moment with Milligan on the day after New Year's 1940, after having left Cincinnati. They were looking forward to settling down in Chicago for three months and performing at the Grand Opera. Ann noticed snowflakes rushing past the train. Changes in the weather affected her moods, as they had her father's. She peered out the windows, rapturously hugging Milligan at the sight. In Chicago the cast faced a cold winter. Ann and Milligan took separate rooms in a walk-up hotel and, like the other cast members, except for the stars, paid for their food and lodging from their thirty-dollar-a-week paycheck.

When a society suitor called Ann from New York, she was flattered. He announced he was stopping by to see her on his way to Los Angeles. She wrote him a letter explaining that she was in a moral quandary: "It is inopportune for you to visit me." When the young man appeared at the theater with flowers, Ann explained the situation to Milligan, who told her, "I would not do this to you." Afterward, Ann wrote Milligan daily notes asking his forgiveness. But he was furious for a full week.

Ann wrote her mother that she would be returning to Kansas City as a member of the troupe. They would arrive in town on April 5 to play the Music Hall on the fifth and sixth and then leave at six o'clock the next morning to travel all day to Wichita for a performance on the eighth. Ethel wrote Ann requesting a copy of the play. When Ann arrived in Kansas City, she did not sleep with her mother at Mrs. Ostertag's, even though it would have saved her two dollars a night. Instead, she checked into the Locarno Hotel. A Kansas City *Star* photograph showed her clasping one knee in a glamorous bathing-beauty pose. She looked elegant in her short pageboy, the pleated slacks that showed off her small waistline, a white shirt, and wedge sandals. She told the reporter that her mother lived permanently in the hotel.

Ann shared a dressing room at the theater with Augusta Dabney, who played Abe Lincoln's true love. Before they went on, the two stood at a long table, arranging their hair and ironing their costumes. Augusta liked Ann and enjoyed looking at her. She found Ann's face unconventionally beautiful. She also admired Ann's midwestern voice: she thought it was musical. Augusta sensed a certain mystery about Ann's past life and wondered if she was a society girl who had run away to be in theater.

After the performance in Kansas City, Ann dressed quickly and joined her mother and Mrs. Ostertag for a late-night cup of coffee. Ethel was impressed with the play and with her daughter's performance. She disapproved of Ann's eating restaurant food when she could have cooked her a home meal. Ann explained she had to get up very early in the morning to take the sunrise train to Wichita. But she knew her mother was proud of her, and that made her feel good.

That winter, Ann's maiden aunt, Lydia Smiley, was living with her parents in western Kansas. Every day she drove eighty-five miles over icy roads from Hugoton to teach children in Dodge City. Lydia was delighted to receive a note from her niece saying that she would arrive in a Broadway touring company for a performance in Wichita. Ann had also written to her mother's other sister, Edna Cobb, who worked in her husband's new pharmacy in Kinsley, Kansas. She offered to buy her relatives tickets at $3.36 each for the company's performance on Monday night, April 8. Grandma Laura Smiley felt things might work out for Angeline after all; she felt a little better about the fact that the poor child had never gone to college.

To see her niece perform, Lydia Smiley left school early and drove several hours with her mother to Kinsley, where they picked up Edna and her husband. Then they all drove another 100 miles to the center of the state. When Ann's aunts arrived in Wichita, it was too dark to take pictures. They bought a copy of the local newspaper that carried an interview with Raymond Massey.

The aunts did not know if Ann had seen her mother in Kansas City. They assumed a schism between mother and daughter. Ethel's stormy nature was a source of sorrow to them, and they had never forgiven her for dragging little Angie to Kansas City. They refused to discuss the Westport taxi business.

When the lights went down and Ann spoke her lines from the back of the covered wagon, the aunts marveled. "Why, dear me, she sounds just like herself," whispered Lydia. The scene was particularly moving for her family because they, too, had come to Kansas in a covered wagon. Ann wore no stage makeup, and in her plain sunbonnet and gingham apron she looked to her "tickled" Aunt Edna exactly as she had when she graduated from high school. After the performance, they all waited for Ann at a hotel near the theater to join them for a late supper that lasted past midnight. "I'm so proud of you, Angie," said Lydia, wiping her eyes.

Ann told them about her hopes to be a theater star. She was studying acting from a woman who taught Ann Harding. Her next stop would be a successful Hollywood screen test. She would work and work. Ann cried when she kissed her aunts good-bye. Only after she got home did Lydia realize Angie had gotten every member of the cast to sign the souvenir program, but had forgotten to sign it herself.

By the time the troupe reached Los Angeles in late April to play two weeks at the Biltmore, most of the actors were counting the days until the end of the tour. But Ann did not want the magic journey to end. She liked napping on trains. She did not mind sleeping in strange run-down hotels looking out on unfamiliar streets. As soon as they hit the out-skirts of a town, she pressed her nose against the window. These new stops reminded her that she was free to dream all kinds of new dreams. Always frugal, Ann had saved most of her weekly pay. She sewed her clothes and bought food in grocery stores rather than restaurants. In Hollywood she took Malcolm Milligan sightseeing. She went on studio tours and kept notes. She invited him to join her when she visited an agent in Leland Hayward's office who promised to set them both up with studio screen tests.

The next week, forty-three-year-old Ethel woke up in Kansas City with a bad sore throat. She picked up the phone, but she could not speak. The operator at St. Luke's Hospital asked over and over, "Is there anybody there who can tell me where you are so I can send an ambulance? Don't you have a neighbor who can tell me where you live?"

Malcolm Milligan took Lydia Smiley's telephone call in Ann's hotel room. Ann was napping with her black sleep mask over her eyes. The troupe had fourteen cities to play in the next five and a half weeks. Although as a minor actor without a run-of-the-play contract she could quit the tour without financial penalty, Ann knew it would tarnish her reputation as a stable performer.

Ann called Tone in New York, who advised her to consult a doctor at Barnes Hospital in St. Louis, who recommended Dr. Robert Graham to her. The doctor told Ann that she should bring her mother to St. Louis if she got worse. Then Ann made two more long-distance calls, while Malcolm Milligan watched in admiration. She called her two aunts in Hugoton and Kinsley. She asked if Edna and Lydia would go tend to Ethel in Kansas City until Ann was finished with the tour. Though Edna Cobb rarely communicated with Ethel, she knew her duty.

At the hospital in Kansas City, Edna and Lydia could see that whatever ailed sister Ethel, it had no effect on either her speech or her brain. Ethel was talking again. The Smiley sisters sat in folding chairs and reminisced about the time pastor Sam I. Smith had called Ethel the prettiest girl in the county. When Ann telephoned from San Francisco, Ethel said that she was just fine. "Don't leave that play," she told her daughter. Preoccupied with her mother's health, Ann grew more aloof than ever from the rest of the troupe.

After the tour ended, Ann hitched a ride from New York to Kansas City with three troupe members driving to Hollywood. One of them, David Clark, had paid $400 cash for a 1936 wooden Ford station wagon. Malcolm Milligan was going to be dropped off at his home in Pittsburgh, Pennsylvania.

When Ann showed up with her matching luggage, Clark grumbled as he loaded it. He also disapproved of how Malcolm catered to her by buying her soda pop at gas stations. It cost Ann exactly five dollars to travel halfway across the country—gasoline was twenty-five cents a gallon, and Clark charged his passengers a penny a mile. The men drove day and night in relays. They sang show tunes and Andrews Sisters songs: "Who stole my heart away? Who makes me dream . . . Dreams, I know, can never be true?"

Ann slept a lot in the backseat, and climbed out periodically to change her clothes. Clark resented Ann for not offering to drive. She kissed Milligan good-bye in Pittsburgh with a kind of finality. His unconditional love made her uneasy.

In Kansas, Ann joined Edna and Lydia, who were living in Mrs. Ostertag's attic. It would be Ann's next-to-last visit to Kansas City. She saw at once that her mother was very ill. Ethel seemed to have had all the anger knocked out of her. Ann read to her from the Bible by the hour. "You will get better soon," Ann told her.

Ann arranged to have herself and her mother driven in an ambulance to the specialist at Barnes Hospital. Her aunts were impressed by her efficiency. But Ethel's condition only worsened. The years of smoking, sleeplessness, anxiety, scrambling for a living, and severe winter colds had broken her resistance. Ethel passed her forty-fourth birthday under sedation, in an oxygen tent. Lydia came to St. Louis to lend Ann moral support. They took turns holding bags to Ethel's mouth to catch the phlegm each time she coughed. They read the Bible aloud and kept Ethel clean and her bedclothes fresh. Ann and Lydia were renting bedrooms in a private home, five minutes away. Ann snapped open her compact mirror several times an hour. It made her feel that she was doing something to improve herself and her mood.

Ethel continued to weaken. In June, Dr. Graham told Lydia to go home. He held out little hope for Ethel's recovery and told Ann and Lydia to expect that Ethel would choke to death on the liquid filling her lungs. Ann refused to accept this prognosis: "She must get better."

After Lydia left, Ann stayed in St. Louis for another month. She called Lydia with health bulletins. According to the doctors, Ethel had developed a rare lung disease that was common in cattle. Ann began to feel like a prisoner of grief in St. Louis. She saw her New York life ebbing away. Her entire existence was becoming the hospital room and her mother's agonized coughing. "I want you to get better," she whispered to Ethel as she watched her sleeping. "Pray for me," said Ethel, waking up.

By September, Ann had transferred her mother to a special lung unit of New York Hospital. By now Ann was trying to accept the fact that there was no cure for her mother's illness. She went to radio auditions and visited Ethel daily. Since Ann assumed all of her mother's hospital expenses, her savings were disappearing. The bills were several hundred dollars a week. Ann never asked her aunts or her grandmother to help pay them, but she quietly borrowed money from her friend Mary Borneau Taylor. Despite her mother's illness, Ann resolved to project good spirits. She had learned from her Powers training that this was important. At auditions and in her acting classes, she never mentioned her mother's health.

Most of Ann's New York male acquaintances had begun to recede from her life. Franchot Tone had returned to Hollywood. Ann enviously read fan magazine articles about his new fiancée, Jean Waleska, a wholesome Polish beauty. Ann began to miss Malcolm Milligan more and more. She wrote to the young actor, who had enlisted in Canada in the war. She was hurt when he did not write back. He had been too broken up by her rejection of his marriage proposal.*

Ann told her mother how she had introduced herself to the radio singer Lanny Ross at a Broadway musical audition in October 1940. Ethel looked impressed. The six-foot Yale graduate with gray eyes and light brown hair resembled Tyrone Power and was known for singing on Lucky Strike's "Your Hit Parade" and for his standing-room-only appearances at Town Hall and Carnegie Hall. Ann wrote Ross a polite note reminding him that they'd met and asking if he would visit her mother, who was very ill in New York Hospital. He agreed. Two nurses on Ethel's floor asked for his autograph. Afterward, Ross and Ann dated for a couple of months. She visited him during the week at his pied-à-terre, a duplex studio on East Fifty-seventh Street. He coached her in diction and singing techniques. He invited her for weekends to his 400-acre farm in Millbrook, New York. He was pleased Ann knew about crops and could ride a horse through the woods. Ann seemed comfortable in his four-room farmhouse. He went hunting for deer, and she accompanied him. When he lost interest in her, Ann was hurt, but she was also relieved. She had felt guilty leaving her mother alone all weekend. She tried to explain Ross away, saying it had been a fleeting New York affair.

In 1942, because of the hospital bills, Ann had given up her little penthouse at 135 East Fiftieth Street for a small studio apartment at 72 East Fifty-sixth. She lived out of cartons. Lowering her standard of living depressed her. Her acting lessons had also disappeared, and it seemed a long time since her life had been filled with magic. Right before Christmas Ann heard about a job that would allow her to visit her mother in the afternoons. She learned that "Fefe" Ferry was reopening his exclusive small nightclub, the Monte Carlo, on Fifty-fourth Street, near El Morocco and only two blocks from her new apartment. The Monte Carlo had catered to society men and Hollywood producers, until it had closed six months earlier. Fefe had also owned a club in Monaco and had been instrumental, along with Elsa Maxwell, in making the town of Monte Carlo into a watering spot for rich Europeans and Americans.

Determined to get an audition, Ann telephoned Ferry's girlfriend, Hilda Knight, who had danced with her in the Noël Coward revue. At the Monte Carlo, Ann could make fifty dollars a week dancing in the midnight and 3 a.m. floor shows; her days would be free to visit her mother, do Broadway auditions, and take her dance, acting, and voice lessons. The

*Milligan would commit suicide at age forty, a tragic parallel to the end of Ann's own life.

line at Fefe's club was also the best job for a girl interested in meeting Hollywood producers. The chorus girls were encouraged to mingle with the audience. A Broadway show audience would applaud and then disappear. The girls in the Copacabana line were fired if they talked to a producer.

For the audition, Ann wore a tight, bright green suit she had sewn, copied from *Vogue*. Three men stood on ladders painting the ceiling the color of the sky. The stage was a curved alcove close to the audience. There were only two steps down to the dance floor. Fefe Ferry looked immaculate in the middle of the construction clutter. He was under five feet five, and the gossip columns said he had the undersoles of his shoes polished. Fefe had closed the restaurant a few months earlier rather than admit patrons who were "just anyone." He asked Ann if he could see her legs. She lifted her dress to her thighs as though she were presenting a work of art. When Fefe asked if she spoke French, Ann ignored the question. "How soon does the job start?" she asked.

He answered, "No thank you, Miss Eden."

By the next morning Ann had thought of a plan. She had heard that mobster Frank Costello had financed the Monte Carlo club and had probably guaranteed Fefe's credit line in exchange for a share of the profits. During Prohibition, Costello had been the top bootlegger in the country and had lent hundreds of thousands of dollars on a handshake. As she had after her first interview with the Powers Agency, Ann returned to the Monte Carlo club the next day. Ann told Fefe Ferry that she was from Kansas City and that her family did business with Johnny Lazia. She asked Fefe to tell Frank Costello that she had served his liquor at her saloon and that she'd like to work with him again. Fefe did not necessarily believe her. However, like many Europeans, he loved "le jazz" and was romantic about Prohibition life. Ann Eden was hired for fifty dollars a week. She would be dancing at midnight and 3 a.m. She bought a large branch of dogwood to celebrate.

Ann had her eye on a new daytime career—live radio soap operas—sponsored by makers of soap. In 1940, radio was the major form of American entertainment. More people were listening to radio war news than were reading newspapers. During the day, 50 million housewives listened to radio as they vacuumed and dusted. They followed as many as six soap operas a day. The afternoon dramas about love, heartbreak, and money were more popular than "The Jack Benny Program."

Like Ann, the characters·lived out women's fantasies of the era. The stories were about playboys, social climbers, schemers, lovers, and poor orphans. Women in soap operas married above their station, but suffered. The soaps had a view of life as a crisis a minute. Like Ann, the leading character of "Backstage Wife" married a man who was a "catch" only to be plagued for years by other women chasing him. "Our Gal Sunday" described each episode as "the story that asks the question: can a girl from a little mining town in the West find happiness as the wife of a wealthy and titled Englishman?" The problems of "Just Plain Bill" were not unlike those of Jesse Claude Crowell. Bill worries about seeing his daughter for the first time in eighteen years. "She's been east with her aunt in fine finishing schools, and doesn't even know I'm her father. Is she going to be too good for me?"

Ann's first radio job was the popular quiz show "True or False." She was a member of a team of twelve women. Each contestant pressed a buzzer and got five dollars for a correct response. Ann knew a lot of answers, and her team collected $400, but she still dreamed of getting into the movies. She did not want to wait to be discovered at the Monte Carlo by a Hollywood producer like Walter Wanger or Joe Schenck. Though in New York, Ann answered calls for screen tests. Through Franchot Tone she tried but failed to get the part of a girl in a bathing suit in the Group Theatre's *Retreat to Pleasure* by Irwin Shaw. She decided that her talent was not large enough, so it was also a matter of pull.

Outside the Monte Carlo limousines were often double-parked along Fifty-fourth Street. Women in long gowns and men in white tie and tails waited in line. Many were turned away. Inside, the crowded bar was paneled in blue glass and decorated with blue violins and tangerine-colored fruit. The Latin and popular band music never stopped. The main room looked like the stage of a grand opera. Yellow, green, and scarlet draperies covered the walls.

Ann recognized Winston Guest, Brenda Frazier Kelly, John Hay "Jock" Whitney, and Michael Phipps in the Monte Carlo audiences. She sat down with Charlie Chaplin (and later glued his swizzle stick with an American flag on it into her scrapbook).

At midnight, lights dimmed in the white plaster chandeliers. A spotlight framed Ann and two other pretty girls on the small stage, who were dressed in white bathing suits, black net stockings, and high heels. They also wore pink and white rabbit ears and cottontails. While the band played music, the girls sang a patter song. Next to Ann danced Alicia Grajales, the Mexican girl who would marry Bean Baker. Alicia was living at the

St. Regis Hotel with a cousin. At that time her ex-boyfriend, a wealthy Spaniard, was being investigated by the FBI for spying. She was afraid that the U.S. government was looking for an excuse to order her to return to Mexico. Ann did not take these worries seriously until one night before a show two FBI agents interviewed her about Alicia's political sympathies.

Late one weekend night at the Monte Carlo, William Woodward bumped into his son, Billy, and Bean Baker. Woodward was still working on winning the English Derby. His stables now surpassed those of Jock Whitney, and his horse Johnstown had just won two legs of the Triple Crown. Woodward Sr. was probably relieved that his son had not caught him with a woman. To Billy's surprise his father drank him and Bean under the table. They stayed for the 3 a.m. chorus girl show. Bean kissed a cigarette girl. He asked the waiter to invite the "bunny girls" to their table. Ann and Alicia Grajales joined them. Woodward Sr. ordered Scotch whisky for the ladies. He then drank shot after shot. He enjoyed showgirls; young women brought out a bit of a paternal streak. He enjoyed lecturing them about racing. He explained the importance of filly inbreeding. Billy Woodward fell silent.

William Woodward invited Ann to see Johnstown out at the track. She accepted eagerly; these rich people lived lives out of her Noël Coward songs. Ann took the train to Aqueduct and joined a group of people for at least one early evening party. The group included some actresses, Woodward Sr., and Jock Whitney and his wife, Liz. The story circulated among the Whitneys and their servants that Ann was briefly the mistress of Billy's father. Liz told friends that Ann was the old man's girlfriend and that she had seen her often in his company at the track.

Like other showgirls, Ann accepted gifts of jewelry and "powder room money" (a twenty-dollar bill) from men. William Woodward, Sr., might have given her such gifts. Men had disappointed her mother; as a career girl Ann took care of herself. Ann did not trust the scores of men who called her, although her mood soared with their flattery. Rumors still circulate in the society crowd that Ann had been a call girl. But she was not.

One night a few weeks later, Bean reintroduced himself to Ann after the 3 a.m. show. He bought her a bottle of champagne. His fiancée, Alicia Grajales, was not dancing that evening. Bean told Ann that he was half-Castilian, but Ann knew he was the heir to the First National City Bank. She lied back, claiming her age was twenty-one, instead of twenty-seven, and spoke of Hollywood screen tests. They danced a samba. Bean made her laugh by singing Spanish-sounding phrases. They had similar desperations: Ann was willing to do almost anything to gain success, and Bean would risk all he had for fun.

The next night, Bean and Billy staggered into the standing-room-only Monte Carlo club around 2:45 a.m., just before the bunny chorus. To accommodate the two Harvard boys, Fefe asked two less prestigious customers to leave before dessert. Another night, the boys arrived in the middle of a game of musical chairs. The women in sweeping formal gowns and the men in white tie ran around the dance floor until the music stopped. The members of the bunny chorus jumped for chairs, too. Bean waved to Alicia. Billy stood alone in front of the turquoise mural of Monte Carlo beach. Years later, Ann told him he had looked almost literally like a wallflower.

A few moments later, Bean invited Ann and Alicia to go on to the Copa with him and Billy. Seated by Ann's side at the Copacabana, Billy behaved like a butler. When Ann finished her glass of champagne, he pulled the bottle out of the ice bucket. Ann caught him staring at her furtively. Something inside her jumped. He was a young man who had everything she lacked, yet he seemed so lost. She assumed Billy did not know that she had accepted his father's invitation to visit the track.

To Billy, Ann Eden probably resembled one of his mother's theater friends. She looked like a different species than his sisters. He could undoubtedly picture her in a movie playing Betty Grable's sister. He stared at the Copa girls in the floor show. On the dance floor Ann probably felt his body tension, but Billy Woodward was a better dancer than Franchot Tone. His tuxedo jacket had silk lapels. It had been tailored tight to his body. He had such straight posture that it seemed as if he were in the military. If she hadn't noticed his secret stares at the table, she would have assumed Billy was as cold as a mannequin. This man was subterranean, full of fears and secrets—like herself.

Back at the table under a white palm tree, she put a cigarette to her lips. Billy lit it. She began questioning him about his life. Billy told her about his airplane, his motorcycle, about Harvard College. He gasped at the bare-legged Copa girls walking by. Ann stubbed out her cigarette and vowed that when she became famous, men like him would bow at her feet. She checked her watch. "Really I prefer the Monte Carlo," he said, as though he knew her jealous thoughts.

Ann explained that it was 4 a.m. He walked her out to a taxicab.

One afternoon in March 1941, Ann, who was at the hospital visiting her mother, was told by the doctor to go home. It was eleven days past Ethel's forty-fifth birthday. Ethel did not say good-bye and indeed seemed not to recognize her daughter. Ann was turning the key in the lock in her apartment door at two-thirty when she heard the phone ring. Her mother had died peacefully ten minutes earlier. Ann chose the best funeral parlor in Manhattan, Frank E. Campbell's, on Eightieth and Madison. She signed "Ann Eden Crowell" on her mother's death certificate. She would not use the name Crowell again except on her marriage license. She gave her mother's occupation as "social service work." Ann arranged to ship her mother back to Pittsburg, asking Brenner's mortuary to have a hearse pick up the body at the train station in Fort Scott. Ann dressed in black for the long journey back to eastern Kansas. She would bring nothing of Ethel's back to Kansas except the old Bible in which Ethel had recorded Ann's and her brother's birth dates. Ann's immaculate appearance seemed at odds with her grief. A few wrinkles in her skirt, less makeup, or disheveled hair would have made her look like a daughter in mourning. But Ann could not tolerate bad grooming. For the rest of her life, she would perform the rituals learned in her days with Powers' regardless of how she felt.

Ann boarded the train at 5:55 on the afternoon of March 20 and bought a sleeper for the overnight trip. She brought with her several George Bernard Shaw plays, inscribed to her by Franchot Tone. She awoke in the caverns of Union Station the next morning at 6:30 and looked out at Kansas City, a place for which she felt no warmth or nostalgia. An hour later, at the Fort Scott station, she kissed her aunts, Lydia Smiley and Edna Cobb. A polished station-wagon hearse was parked nearby. George Brenner, the mortician, introduced himself to Ann as he and the conductor carried the coffin to the hearse. He had been a student in Ethel's social studies class at Pittsburg Senior High School.

Her aunts fussed over Ann's hat as they settled her into their gray Dodge. Ann felt as though she were suffocating and instinctively rolled down the window. She loved her aunts, but she did not want to be in this family. They admired rich people and movies, but they seemed hopelessly stuck in dreary defeat and poverty. That they loved her only made her feel worse. Ann tried not to look at the drab landscape; in only forty-six hours she would be back in New York.

She checked into the Bessie Hotel in Pittsburg. She hugged her aunt Fannie Flower, Grandma Laura, and her uncle Hugh (her mother's only brother and the only Smiley sibling who did not go to college). Aunt Edna was proud they could afford to stay at the hotel, an eight-story brick building across the main street, Broadway, from Brenner's mortuary.

Ethel was barely mentioned. Her sisters assumed that it had been her life outside respectable society that had killed her. Edna had no desire to know what had caused her sister's death. "I don't know and I won't ask," she said decades later in her gruff country twang. Ethel's New York death certificate states that she died from a "non-communicable disease." George Brenner told each family member that Ethel was a very good social studies teacher—the best. Ann told Brenner that she would not have had the gumption to go to New York to seek her own fortune if it hadn't been for her mother's example.

During this visit, Ann went to the Crowell drugstore to visit with her second cousin Paul, from the prosperous side of her father's family. At sixty-seven, Paul Crowell was old enough to be Ann's father, but he was a ladies' man. Edna Cobb shook her head when she saw him talking so much to Angie. Edna had seen him at two Kansas State University football games with women who were not his wife.

Paul remembered Angeline as a pale solitary child who dreamed of movies and movie stars. She reminded Paul that he used to give her free ice-cream cones. He had done it, he told her, because her father, Jesse Claude, was always asking after her. Paul jokingly asked her if she still had big eyes for Hollywood. She said her modeling career was only temporary. The movies were still her goal. She told him that she would not marry unless she fell madly in love and was absolutely sure that the marriage would last. Neither of them spoke of her mother's two divorces.

At two o'clock on Saturday, the twenty-second of March 1941, Ann delivered her mother's eulogy after prayers by the Reverend C. J. Haskins. To an almost empty church, Ann repeated that it had been because of Ethel's example of courage that she had had the strength to go to New York and into show business. Ann's audience consisted of a few pallbearers, Paul Crowell, the Smiley sisters, their brother, and their mother. Ethel's sisters marveled at how beautiful Ethel looked in the coffin, with soft white curls framing her face. In Manhattan, the mortician had done his job well. Ethel was buried in Mount Olive Cemetery that afternoon, in the Crowell family plot next to her infant son. Before she left town, Ann asked Paul Crowell to keep an eye on her mother's grave.

"When are you coming back?" he asked.

"Soon." But Ann never returned, not even to bury Grandmother Laura in 1962.

Jesse Claude wrote to his cousin Paul for news about the funeral. He told Paul that he had sent Angie money—but that he believed her mother had intercepted the letters. Paul Crowell became confused by all the Hollywood stories. A few months later he told Jesse Claude that Angie had become the actress Eve Arden. Jesse Claude was proud that his Angeline was a big radio and movie star, and he went to see *Mildred Pierce* in Detroit. It was easy for him to believe that Eve Arden was Angeline, because she resembled his first wife, tall and blond with strong facial features.*

Paul Crowell bragged to his neighbors about his second cousin Eve Arden. For the next fourteen years the Pittsburg *Headlight* carried news of the actress. Paul told Jesse Claude how she took "Eve" from a romantic novel and "Arden" from a bottle of cold cream. In movies she played the heroine's best friend. People in Pittsburg liked the idea; Angeline Crowell had been so poor. It was proof that America was a wonderful place.

On Wednesday, June 18, 1948, an article appeared in the Pittsburg *Headlight* written by the newspaper's publisher. It illustrated the broken lines of communication in Ann's life. "It must be surprising to some local residents to know that Pittsburg has its own movie star born and reared in this section. Evangeline Crowell is her name.

"Never heard of her? That's not surprising, for like most other movie stars she has a flicker name in addition to her real name.

"The screen name of the former Pittsburger is Eve Arden. Remember her now? Her last appearance in Pittsburg was as the flighty gold-digging co-star of "The Voice of the Turtle" film version. . . .

"Miss Crowell attended rural and Pittsburg grade schools during the early days of her life, but moved to Kansas City with her mother when she was twelve. There she was graduated from Northeast High School, and was an extra model at one of the exclusive Kansas City stores. It was from this modeling that Miss Crowell or Miss Arden got her first push toward the big time. . . .

"In New York, she made several short films using the name of "Ann Eden."

"In March 1941, the mother died in New York, and Miss Crowell had Paul Crowell make funeral arrangements in Pittsburg. . . .

"At that time, she informed her Pittsburg cousin that she was en route to Hollywood with a film offer, and she has been there ever since.

---

*Eve Arden (born Eunice Quedens on April 30, 1912, in Mill Valley, California) had appeared in the 1934 *Ziegfeld Follies*, where she was discovered and cast in her first Hollywood picture, *Oh, Doctor*, under her new name. She married Edward Bergen in Hollywood in 1939 and appeared in countless movies, including the Marx Brothers' *At the Circus*. An excellent comedienne, her radio hit, first broadcast in 1948, was "Our Miss Brooks," in which she played a caustic, very smart schoolteacher. She would also play the popular role on television.

She changed her film name to Eve Arden shortly after reaching the movie capital. . . .

" 'Eve has a summer home in Phoenix, Ariz., and is doing right well by herself,' Mr. Crowell said."

It would not be until after the publicity surrounding Billy's death that Ann's father discovered his error about her identity.

Ann returned to New York and began new acting lessons and auditions. In June 1941, she landed a daily role as a nurse in an afternoon serial called "Joyce Jordan, Girl Interne." She moved to a small penthouse at 141 East Fifty-sixth Street. Like her mother, she believed that moving was always the answer to life's rough spots. A week before she started "Joyce Jordan," she clipped a brief notice about her job from *The New York Times:* "Ann Eden is now turning her talents to WABC's 'Joyce Jordan, Girl Interne' and will be heard Monday through Friday at 2:30."

To celebrate the return of her luck, she decorated her apartment from top to bottom, coordinating the wallpaper with the down-cushioned couches. She built mirrored bookshelves and had the bedroom painted a flattering pale coral. She selected a chintz with big coral birds and green flowers for the couch. The apartment barely looked lived in. Everything looked as well ordered and clean as if she had a full-time servant. Ann made her bed after she slipped out of it.

Every morning, Ann set her hair, wrapped it in a silk turban, and a few hours later walked, oblivious of the heat, to the CBS building at Fifty-second Street and Madison Avenue. Within minutes, she was sitting on a tall leather stool in the control room humming a scale and surrounded by five other actors, each with a typed script in hand. Then they trooped into a small soundproof room and stood in a circle around a microphone hanging from the ceiling. The lights flashed. They were on the air.

It was two-thirty Eastern Standard Time. The show would be broadcast live around the country for the next fifteen minutes, and rebroadcast on tape at six o'clock. Ann had nothing to memorize. For a week of fifteen-minute days, she earned thirty dollars. A chorus girl who performed five nights at the Copa received fifty dollars. Radio soaps were perfect jobs for a girl who dined and danced at the Stork Club.

The announcer leaned into the microphone; the sound effects man hit a bell: "Calling Dr. Jordan—bong-bong—" Then there was a thrilling glissando on a small harp. "General Foods presents Joyce Jordan, Girl Interne, a woman alone in a man's world."

Dr. Joyce Jordan had to fight for challenging cases. Men were always trying to grab her, and she rued the fact that she was assigned to be a scrub nurse instead of taking part in brain surgery. Ann played a surgical nurse who befriended Dr. Jordan. She practiced elocution in front of her mirror by the hour. Although she hated the sound of Kansas in her voice, she did not have a twang. In fact, her words had a drawling ease. She was also able to produce a good-humored laugh, leaning back from the microphone. She sounded, one fan wrote, like the girl next door. The network publicity department announced that Ann was "the most beautiful girl in radio." Her pinup photos in the control room received wolf whistles.

In the last weeks of December 1941, Ann landed a part in "Lincoln Highway," starring Ethel Barrymore on NBC, one of the best dramatic programs on radio. She was cast as a forlorn hitchhiker from Nebraska. "Lincoln Highway" was a weekly series of "true-life" stories that had presumably taken place along U.S. Route 30.

An NBC bio was released six months later: "Tall, blond Ann thinks everything is fun. First-rate radio acting is 'exciting.' Designing her own apartment gives her 'a thrill.' Riding a horse in Central Park is 'swell,' and dancing at the Stork Club is 'the tops.' She is fascinated by medicine and finds watching an operation one of her most exciting thrills." The last sentence was the public relations department's own creation.

Although he was back in Los Angeles, Franchot Tone was indirectly responsible for Ann's continuing good fortune. He had introduced her to some of the regular actors on the show. Ann was proud to be a member of the cast. "Lincoln Highway" was as close to serious as daytime radio got in the 1940s. It started broadcasting February 10, 1942, and ran two seasons, attracting an audience of more than 8 million:

> "Hi there, neighbor,
> Going my way
> East or West on the Lincoln Highway?
>
> Hi there, Yankee,
> Give out with a great big 'Thankee';
> This is God's country."

For her first segment, Ann played a young girl much like herself, a hitchhiker running toward the bright lights of a big city. Along the way, kind people saved her from catastrophes at the hands of men. More radio parts followed her work in "Lincoln Highway." She was soon considered a successful radio actress who added prestige to a program. Over the next two years, she played on "Bright Horizon" on CBS and "Aunt Jenny's Real Life Stories" and "Portia Faces Life" on NBC.

In March of 1942, Billy Woodward, then in his junior year at Harvard, bumped into his father at their house on East Eighty-sixth Street. The two had not seen each other in weeks. When his father asked if he had been to any nightclubs, Billy nodded. "Do you have a regular girl?" Billy's father, while preoccupied as usual with his horses and his travels, was also worried about this aspect of his son's development.

"No, sir."

Woodward Sr. suggested that Billy ask Ann Eden, the girl they had met at Fefe's Monte Carlo, to dinner. Neither mentioned that he had seen her after that first meeting.

"Yes, sir."

Woodward Sr. may have been passing along a mistress to his son in the Edwardian fashion. Several of the senior Woodward's friends believed that since Ann had been the father's mistress, he knew she would be right for his son as well. This is a story that is hard to prove or disprove.

A few nights after his father's suggestion, Billy took Ann to the "21" Club at 21 West Fifty-second Street. Their twenty-dollar dinner was considered one of the best in town. Both young people were known to the waiters. Billy liked the way Ann ducked her head shyly, reminding him of girls he grew up with. Ann did not say that she had visited his father's house at Saratoga.

Billy ordered a bottle of champagne. He was too nervous to eat. Ann was always on a diet. The dinner menu included venison and flaming crepes suzette. The restaurant was filled with members of café society, such as Captain Isaac Emerson (the founder of Bromo Seltzer), the Jack Warners, John O'Hara, Moss Hart, and the young Gloria Vanderbilt. Throughout the next thirteen years of his life, Billy would nod at hundreds of such people at restaurants and parties. His and their lives were social—involved with seeing and being seen by "the best people." Relationships with deep feelings were not the point.

On their first formal date, Ann told Billy about her mother's death. Watching him fidget must have made her impatient. His life seemed so charmed. She felt much more than five years older. When he asked her to dance, she refused. Billy nodded his head sharply, making a small European bow, but he looked discouraged. His misery made her confident. She decided to make the best of it and asked him to dance.

"Absolutely," he said. The word sounded like a promise. Her spirits rose. Maybe he would show her the secrets of the rich Manhattan life. Back at the table, she was surprised to find herself confiding in Billy. She told him she actually missed the hospital room. She told him that as a girl she had fought with her mother. This seemed to impress him. He told her he dared not fight with his parents. She told him she was on her own. He looked at her only when he lit her cigarettes. She deliberately smoked a lot of them.

When Ann brought up the Woodward horse Apache, Billy was surprised that she pronounced it correctly. (His father did not say the final "e.") The horse had captured the country's imagination by his habit of starting a race in the lead and often losing it.

"Come to Saratoga and see him," said Billy. His father had ordered Billy to Saratoga for the big weekend of August 15, when the famous brown-and-white three-year-old would be running the Wilson stakes. Ann laughed with delight. Her enthusiasm made Billy wonder why he had never thought Saratoga the most exciting place he knew.

Ann was touched that he wanted so much to be with her and surprised at how little he tried to make it happen. Ann had worked so hard to make things happen in her life. After a few more dinners, she invited him to her apartment and changed into a blue peignoir. It was clear that he had never been with a woman. Ann had memorized scores of movie seductions. She imitated Cary Grant. "Nothing in life is more important than love and being in love," she said, and kissed him. No woman had ever been so aggressive with Billy Woodward. Many in Billy's crowd believed by now that he had a male lover.

Billy was instantly smitten. He had found part of himself in Ann; he thought there could not be another woman who would have had the gumption to seduce him. He would remain sexually keyed into her for the rest of his life, no matter how badly he wished to escape. There was a Spanish print in Ann's bedroom of a monkey and a donkey. They began calling each other pet names, "Monk" and "Dunk."

Ann asked him for a photograph of himself. She cooked his meals, and he brushed her hair. She cut her elocution classes and asked questions about his travels to racetracks in England, quail hunts in Scotland, combat in the navy, and the Porcellian Club at Harvard. He took her to Bergdorf's and asked her to choose good pearls. He kissed her hand. She loved his

English-sounding voice and exquisite manners. She was probably flattered to be invited to the track by so patrician a son and father. Ann found a large hat at the John-Frederics wholesale showroom for the racing weekend. It was black velvet, with a big green bow. Even though the nation was at war in 1942, the country was swept up in a passion for horse racing. It was one of the great national escapes.

On Thursday, August 13, 1942, Elsie Woodward boarded the train for Saratoga, reluctantly leaving her two sisters at White Sulphur Springs. *The Saratogan*'s society page would herald her rare appearance, noting that as a Cryder triplet her debut had been one of society's most brilliant affairs. Billy was unaware that his mother was coming to Saratoga. He was in love and could think only of Ann. He hoped he would appear dashing to her in the boisterous streets of this old Victorian resort. He told her of Diamond Jim Brady and that his father and mother had met at Saratoga. He was looking forward to showing Ann off at Saratoga, a masculine environment. His father's "bachelor" cocktail parties in the rented yellow house were sometimes quite wild.

The day of the race, Saturday, August 15, dawned hot and clear. Billy and Ann sped along the New York highways in his black souped-up Packard. He wore a red-and-white bow tie in the Belair colors. She wore a green filmy dress and her new large-brimmed John-Frederics hat. Billy was one of the few who at a time when gasoline and tires were rationed were still able to drive a car to Saratoga.

In Saratoga, he parked near the Grand Union Hotel and took Ann to the Broadway Spa for eggs and black coffee. Eating before lunch helped Billy believe in his independence. Unfortunately, the meal made them late for his punctilious parents, who saw Billy's tardiness as a vice.

Ann looked longingly past apple trees around the white Victorian clubhouse and out onto the green curves of the track. The setting conveyed such security that she felt as if she were part of it; she would never be frightened again. Looking at Billy in the sunlight, Ann thought it was a miracle of a day. He guided her inside the clubhouse, which was filled with the richest people in America, the owners of railroads and banks.

Racing enthusiasts in attendance included W. E. Boeing, of the aircraft family, Walter Chrysler, Jr., from Detroit, and two women breeders, Isabel Dodge Sloan and Mrs. Payne Whitney. It was Ann's first glimpse of Mrs. Harrison Williams, wearing her magnificent pearls at her wrist and throat. Harrison Williams, a former utilities magnate, had been one of the richest men in America until the stock market crash. The couple still lived lavishly on the gifts he had given his wife.

Elsie Woodward extended her hand to Ann with eyebrows raised. She presented Ann with a racing program. William Woodward, Sr., sputtered his greetings, rolled his mustaches with his thumb and forefinger, and reached for a gold toothpick from a leather case. Ann had decided he resembled a country squire and complimented him on his Belair stables. He looked uncomfortable and did not respond. He perhaps wondered how much his wife could possibly guess about the situation. He doubted his son was aware of his own interaction with Ann. Why bring the girl otherwise?

Ann shook hands with Billy's sister Edie and smiled a lot at Billy's father. Ann had known William would be there, but she had not anticipated that he would be this nervous about her presence.

Elsie put on her sunglasses so that she could scrutinize "the cut of the younger woman's jib." ("One look and I knew the whole story," she would tell bridge friends and extra men such as Robert Leylan years later.) Her peers and their descendants still speak of her first impression of Ann. It is legend. Mrs. Woodward could foresee the future. In respect to Ann, she had ESP.

The Woodward myth—evolved out of gossip and Truman Capote's fiction—endows Elsie Woodward with superhuman powers. The tale of love, murder, and social climbing has become proof to many American WASPs that they are part of an aristocracy. The Woodwards are a kind of standard, demonstrating that in the past, anyway, aristocrats were truly superior. According to myth, Elsie never swerved in her view that the bold and attractive Kansas girl ruined Billy's life with her powers of sex. Mrs. Woodward fueled the story by declaring that her son's tragic shooting was rooted in the fact that Ann was not his social equal. Elsie deemed anybody not of her class as improperly dressed and was appalled by Ann's smart clothes. She spoke her mind at length in later years about Ann's fashionable hat, calling it a "vulgar up-to-the-minute shopgirl's bonnet."*

At the Saratoga clubhouse, the Woodwards accepted the expressions of support from well-wishers. Ann refrained from smoking and indeed

---

*Elsie's reaction was similar to that of a property-loving nineteenth-century English family described in a volume of *The Forsyte Sage*, by John Galsworthy. A penniless man was introduced as a young woman's fiancé at an "at home" party. The family decided that the problem was his unpresentable hat: "Soft, gray, shapeless, it made them feel in contact with some strange unsafe thing. Nearsighted Aunt Hester tried to shoo it off the hall chair taking it for a strange disreputable cat. The hat was a harbinger of evil to come, a significant trifle, in which was embedded the meaning of the whole matter."

would soon give up the habit altogether. She did, however, insert a red rose in Billy's lapel. When Elsie frowned, Ann feared it had been ill-mannered to have disturbed the table flowers.

Because of the war, there were few young men present that morning at Saratoga. Captain Stephen "Laddie" Sanford was home on leave. Ann was thrilled to meet him and his wife, Mary Duncan Sanford. During lunch, an assistant from a movie then being filmed—*Saratoga Trunk*, based on the Edna Ferber novel—approached their table and asked Ann if she would help them out. They needed a pretty girl to stroll out the clubhouse door in front of the camera. Billy squeezed Ann's elbow with pride. When she returned to the table, Ann got the impression from Elsie that she had once again transgressed.

After lunch, Ann and the Woodwards sat down in the front row of green folding chairs. The family box was a few feet from the finish line. Members of the racing establishment waved and continued to wish the Woodwards good luck. William Woodward had pulled Apache from several recent races because the horse had lost the Kentucky Derby and then the Preakness—where he led the pack for a mile but finished ninth out of ten. But the two-month rest had paid off; Apache had just won the Empire City Handicap, taking home $20,100 and another handsome trophy for his owner. Woodward Sr. lectured Ann about the race. It was, he explained, a short track, only one mile, and that would count in Apache's favor. He was confident Apache would hold his lead this time.

Looking around her, Ann noticed that few women in the boxes had her flair for fashion, not to mention her figure. In fact, Ann observed, most of them dressed in what she considered a matronly manner. She recognized designer originals by Worth, but the dresses were not from contemporary collections. Elsie tapped her son on the shoulder to direct his gaze to a girl he knew from Brookville.

Ann decided that Billy was the main catch of their crowd. He stood and bowed slightly as girls greeted him. The girls looked enviously at Ann's hat and face. Ann had the confusing impression that Billy and the girls had been to the same parties for the last decade. Later, Sister Bird, a Boston society woman, summed up their impression of Ann and Billy: "Woodward was not interested in us. He wanted glamour. He was like the Prince of Wales. He could break any rule."

Elsie tapped Ann's shoulder just before the race began. "Your hat, my dear." Ann smiled. "Take it off, it is not made of glass," said Elsie in her firm way. Ann kept forcing her smile. She pulled the hat off in a girlish gesture, and her chignon loosened in a tumble of blond curls.

Eve Arden, circa 1940. Ann Eden's father, Jesse Claude Crowell, and the residents of Pittsburg, Kansas, mistakenly believed his daughter had gone to Hollywood, changed her name to Eve Arden, and made a big success in the movies.

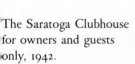

The Saratoga Clubhouse for owners and guests only, 1942.

Left to right: Edith, Elsie, and
William Woodward, Sr., at the
track the day the Woodward horse
Fighting Fox, the year's outstanding
Derby candidate, won the Wood
Memorial in Jamaica, New York,
1938. Woodward's stud farm in
Bowie, Maryland, was considered to
be one of the two best in America.

The Woodward horse Apache, 1942.

At the starting gate, Apache, as usual, took the lead. He surprised even his fans by running so fast that he finished six lengths ahead of the rest of the horses. He came within four fifths of a second of a track record. Apache added $5,250 to his earnings of $44,600 for the year. "Best damn horse I ever saw," said a man sitting near them. Ann noticed that the word "best" was used again and again to describe the Woodwards and their possessions.

Afterward, Billy took Ann to dinner at a little Dutch restaurant two blocks from the track. Ann and Billy strolled over to watch the annual Fasig-Tipton horse auction. The silent ushers registered sums in the thousands. The year before, a young horse named New Broom had brought $70,000. A. B. "Bull" Hancock, Billy's father's partner at Claiborne Farm in Kentucky, was selling ten colts tonight. Alfred Gwynne Vanderbilt, then in the navy, sold twenty. Though the atmosphere was charged with excitement, no one spoke except the auctioneer into his microphone.

Ann watched two servants brush a shining colt. A third stable boy swept around him. It struck Ann that the thoroughbreds were a little like Billy Woodward, nervous and leggy. A lot of girls who had passed her today would like to bid on him. "You belong to me, Annie," Billy whispered in her ear as they danced at El Morocco a few nights later. Ann had never been in love like this.

In the weeks that followed, Elsie took the step of hiring a private detective to follow Ann. Elsie's social stability was based on the credo that sex and love were secondary to family background. To Elsie Woodward, inappropriate sexual liaisons were not merely disgusting; that Billy had even thought to invite such a girl to the family box meant that his upbringing had failed. Elsie had failed. Now she must take steps to insure that the money and social standing for which the Cryders and Woodwards had struggled would not be diluted.

The report on Ann's romance with Franchot Tone confirmed Elsie's suspicions. She read of Ann's skimpy bunny costume at Fefe's with horror. Ann's brief affair with singer Lanny Ross was also uncovered.

"I am worried," she told Mary Sanford. "Ann is too gay. She has gone with too many men." Mary offered Elsie her sympathies. Prudently, Mary did not mention that she herself had been in the same predicament before she married polo-playing Laddie Sanford. Nor did she remind her friend that Elsie had championed her at the time. The detective also reported that Ann was wearing an antique gold bracelet. It was said to be a gift from Billy. In fact, Elsie discovered that the bracelet had been presented by Billy's uncle James to Billy's grandmother at the turn of the century. Elsie had never been so angry at her son. If he gave family heirlooms to tarts, then he might give away the family name. Elsie dispatched the detective to Kansas to find out more about Miss Eden.

Elsie decided a maternal warning was in order. She invited Billy into the library for afternoon tea and asked him to invite his old friend Cassie Sands to dinner. Billy most likely did not say that such girls held no appeal for him. There was no way to tell his mother how excited he was to finally feel the power of love and sex. He did tell his mother that Ann Eden thought Elsie Woodward was splendid and very like the heroine of an Edith Wharton book.

Elsie told him she hoped he was seeing lots of girls. "Father likes her," Billy said. He did not say that Ann reminded him of his mother's lively collection of actresses. Elsie did not speak of Ann's vulgarity. She undoubtedly realized that Billy was too infatuated to forgive such a statement. Elsie told her son that Franchot Tone had had an affair with Miss Eden while he was married to Joan Crawford. Elsie's revelation had exactly the opposite effect from what Elsie had intended. Billy was impressed. It made Ann seem even more of a catch. He wondered why such a wonderful girl would give him the time of day.

"These girls from nowhere can be dangerous to families," Elsie said. She explained that inappropriate liaisons could destroy generations of tradition. Billy might resemble his grandfather Duncan Cryder, but he did not understand at what price his place in the world had been won. Elsie reminded her son that the Woodwards had a long tradition to protect. Billy was the one who would carry the family name. He told Ann afterward that he had resisted an impulse to tell his mother that by his reckoning the Woodward tradition was not as lengthy as she implied. Billy said that he was disappointed in his mother. He had been proud of her support of the Duke of Windsor's marriage to a divorced American. He and Bean were still impressed that Elsie had been so modern in her thinking. "Wallis Simpson was a lady," said Elsie, closing the meeting.

That night Elsie Woodward enlisted her husband. The subject was explosive. Elsie suspected her husband had similar girlfriends. But William Woodward, Sr., did promise to have a heart-to-heart talk with Billy. Elsie blamed her husband for the Ann Eden affair—but for the wrong reasons. She believed it had occurred because William Woodward, Sr., had not been around to provide an example to Billy.

Billy and his father faced each other inside the closed library. William sat in his tie and short double-breasted suit jacket behind his burnished Queen Anne desk. William explained the double standard. Girls like Ann were not meant to be taken seriously. Billy must never expose showgirls to his mother and sisters again. Billy asked his father not to insult Ann. He did not say that each time he made love to Ann, it was a defiant pleasure. He later told Ann he had said, "I would rather spend one evening with Annie than a life with any of the local crop of debutantes."

The strain of the frank conversation probably exhausted both Woodwards. William Sr.'s plan had misfired. He blamed Elsie. The boy should have been more athletic. He was no chip off the old block. He was no Woodward.

The only person who understood Billy was Bean Baker, who was drinking more heavily than ever. On leave from the Eighth Air Force Division, Bean had given Alicia Grajales an emerald engagement ring— similar to the one owned by the Duchess of Windsor. Bean made Billy laugh about the look on Edith Baker's face when he brought his Mexican bride-to-be to dine at his family's Chinese Chippendale table in Peacock Point. Bean believed that he had solved the problem of gold diggers that obsessed their parents: "If I marry a rich girl because my mother thinks it's a proper match for our family fortunes, then I'm a gold digger." Billy agreed: "You're both marrying for money, not love." Bean said, "Quite right. And if I fall for a beautiful girl who truly loves me, then she's not a gold digger. And neither am I. We're in love."

Elsie ordered Billy to sail to Newport. His father offered him a new car. But Billy still disappeared for days to live with Ann.

Neither of his parents could remember Billy disobeying them as he did now. His past rebellions had been hidden. Billy Woodward's position in the household changed from his mother's favorite to her problem child. Elsie Woodward produced documents from the detective. Ann had no money. But Billy believed he had no choice; he was not attracted to any other women. His love for Ann was all-consuming. He had awakened from his slumbers with a jolt. If Billy was subconsciously angry at his mother, Elsie's extreme reaction fueled the situation. To Elsie, he seemed demented, smiling at the mention of Ann's name. Billy shrugged off his mother's threats of disinheritance. He did not believe he could ever be poor. He was willing to sacrifice everything Elsie believed in.

8

WAR BRIDE

In January 1943, Ensign William Woodward, Jr., was home on leave for a week from the Todd Shipyard on Puget Sound near booming Seattle, Washington. He had been training for the war in the South Pacific. Despite his mother's disapproval, he slept at Ann Eden's small penthouse apartment. Their relationship, the major rebellion of Billy's life, broke so many taboos that he was elated. With Ann, a grateful Billy had begun to discover his lifetime habit of making love during the afternoon cocktail hour, when liquor had lowered his usual inhibitions. He and she then napped and went off to El Morocco.

Billy loved the way she whispered in his ear just before they made love. Ann mixed witty Noël Coward lines with earthy words she had learned from the Kansas cabdrivers. It was an original verbal style for a woman. She took pleasure saying things most women dared not mention. There was a continuing story she made up for Billy, about adventures they could have had on a remote desert island. "You are the only girl I feel comfortable with," said Billy, "the only girl I have ever loved."

Both Ann and Billy undoubtedly felt as if they were living out roles defined in popular songs and movies. They were young lovers; he was a rich heir and she was an actress. They had fallen madly in love despite terrible obstacles. Finally, after he had enlisted in the navy in December 1942, they were lovers haunted by the specter of Billy's dying in a faraway Pacific battle.

His love was a narcotic to Ann. She wanted to make a place for herself with this grateful boy more than anything else she could think of. She believed she loved him for himself. She probably did not realize how desperate she was to belong to a world more sustaining than the one she was carrying inside her. When Ann did anything she did it completely. Her success as a model, a showgirl, and an actress was based as much on her determination as on her beauty or talent. But Ann Eden did not realize how high the walls were that surrounded the Woodward family.

When she came home one afternoon at four, after her "Joyce Jordan" broadcast, Ann expected to find Billy lying as usual in his black silk bathrobe. He had joked all week that he disliked going out in daylight. But Billy was dressed in his navy uniform. He had received emergency orders to return to gunnery school in Tacoma. The war had become another test for him, a chance to prove his masculinity. Ann could not bear saying good-bye. "Annie, please, it's a war," he said. "I don't care," she sobbed. Then she told him about her nightmares in which he was caught in submarine battles underwater. Billy was flattered. They undressed and made love.

Until Ann had entered his life, no woman had been emotional about Billy Woodward. To live his own life, Billy wanted a warrior woman whose anger and passions were equivalent to his own buried feelings. She was like his mother in fierce willpower. What he could not put into the equation was what would happen when he and Ann turned on each other. Billy also failed to take Ann's shifting temperament into account. His mother's great strength was her dispassionate stability.

In her small penthouse, Ann refilled Billy's martini. She asked him not to leave her behind. Solemnly, he asked her to live with him in Tacoma. "Marry me now," she whispered, "or go away forever." Billy knew Ann had been envious a few weeks earlier when Bean Baker eloped with Alicia Grajales. Before leaving for the air force, Bean had urged Billy to marry Ann: "It's worth the price of the license alone to watch your folks go round the bend."

Billy promised Ann he would think about marriage. "But no more arguments," he said. For Ann, fighting and making up with Billy was like coming home. She did not trust anybody to love her—and demanded constant proof of affection.

Billy flew back to Tacoma alone. He was living off the base at the best hotel, the Tacoma. He found the officers' quarters too Spartan. At night he ate a one-dollar dinner in the Officers Club with a Harvard Naval Reserve acquaintance, the cheerful Jack James. Many of the young officers were rushing into wartime marriages.

In Manhattan, Ann wept at odd moments and told herself only a fool would assume such a boy would marry her. She gave up. She called

him to say that she would live with him even if he did not think she was
good enough to marry. She apologized for having suggested marriage. She
said she would give up her four jobs on the radio. Billy was disarmed. After
a long pause, he asked Ann if there was somebody in her family whose
permission he should ask to marry her. "No," Ann said, "I'm an orphan.
Just ask me."

Although terrified that one day she would be found out, she had lied
to Billy, telling him that her father was dead. It was a lie her mother had
often told. And it was easier than explaining her father's disappearance from
her life and his job as a streetcar conductor.

A formal letter to Ann followed. Since Billy was stationed out in
Tacoma, the wedding would take place there immediately. It was a logical
step. Billy fantasized somebody at home missing him while he dodged
Japanese fighter planes. Ann filled the bill to perfection. Billy sent a formal
telegram to the Porcellian Club steward at Harvard: "Please advise that I
have become engaged to Miss Ann Eden Crowell of Kansas City." His
father had announced his engagement the same way. Usually, the young
woman named was known to everybody at the Porcellian.

Billy wrote his parents a letter every few days. "I have asked Miss
Eden for her hand in marriage, and she has honored me by accepting." He
added that since both her parents were dead, he had asked only her for
permission. William and Elsie telephoned Tacoma at once. "It's a matter
of money," said Elsie clearly in the background. "That's what she's really
after." In Elsie's mind, money and the Woodward name were the absolutes.
Her son's charms were of no importance in a marriage negotiation. Elsie
Woodward suffered a rare loss of temper and told her husband to disinherit
Billy. Since Billy had just turned twenty-one and was now the beneficiary
of a trust fund that paid him over $4,000 a month, he was not shaken by
his mother's threat.

"There's no emergency?" Billy's father asked him.

"We want to get married now," said Billy.

"I'm asking if Miss Eden is in the family way," William said. Billy
replied that Ann was not. "Then buy her an apartment and give her an
allowance," said his father. "That's how a normal man would behave."

"No, sir." Billy had never before stood up to his parents. He wrote
Bean the whole story.

William worried that his son might be emotionally defective in some
way and would, if penniless, embarrass them further. But before he boarded
the cross-country train to attend the wedding, he met with the family
lawyer, Walter Dunnington, to make certain that the Woodward money

Alicia and Grenville "Bean" Baker, seen here at El Morocco in the mid-1940s, first met when Alicia Grajales was a dancer at Fefe's Monte Carlo nightclub with Ann. (During the war, Alicia was investigated by the FBI as a possible Fascist spy; she was not.)

would stay in the family. The young woman would not inherit Billy's share were he to die at war.

At the same time, Ann Eden announced her news to her acquaintances. Billy Woodward offered love and success—her theater and radio life seemed empty. She quit "Joyce Jordan" and "Aunt Jenny" and her other soap operas. She gave her landlord notice and began packing her trunks. She taped cheerful notes to the furniture and kitchen supplies, which she gave away to friends. The exit took her four days. Ethel Crowell had trained her well.

Elsie invited Ann to tea late one afternoon. Putz led her into the reception area. Elsie greeted her, flanked by two of her tall daughters, who looked Ann in the eye. At five foot ten, they wore flat shoes; Ann wore very high heels. The sisters also wore small hats, loose suits, and no lipstick. Ann's hat was small, and she wore a tight blue suit that left little to the imagination. Ann felt embarrassed when she shifted her legs. The Woodward women seemed to disapprove of her figure.

Elsie explained that they would not be able to leave their families to travel to the wedding. Her daughters murmured, "Our thoughts will be with you." Ann thanked them and began to imitate the American stage accent of her future mother-in-law. For years to come, Ann would study the imperious hand flutters of her mother-in-law as well as her contained smile. Like most Americans, Ann believed that upper-class style was superior to her own.

She told Elsie, "I am looking forward to meeting your pastor, Reverend Kinsolving." She gulped down her cup of tea. Then she watched Elsie take only one small sip.

Elsie mentioned the family position and how important it would be to entertain the right people. Ann knew at once that she must relinquish actors and showgirls. She would stop writing to Franchot Tone, although he would have been welcomed by Elsie were it not for his romance with Ann. Elsie handed Ann a few small packages to take to Billy in Tacoma, including a Tiffany's album for their wedding pictures. "You're both quite young," said Elsie sadly. She did not confront Ann with the detective's information, which included Ann's birth certificate. Ann flushed as Elsie asked, "How old are you, my dear?"

"Over twenty-two," was Ann's discreet reply.

Elsie closed the meeting by telling Ann to draft a marriage announcement. Ann startled the older woman and her two daughters by kissing them good-bye and promising to make them proud of her.

Ann wrote to Billy that the tea had gone wonderfully. She asked to join him immediately and not wait to travel west with his father. Billy agreed. He did not know when he and his fellow naval officers might suddenly ship out. She packed four new Saratoga trunks and took the cross-country sleeper train to Chicago, changing to a Great Northern train for Seattle.

With its new airplane plants and a navy yard, Seattle was one of the country's major boomtowns. Spotting Billy in the crowd at the train station, Ann put her hand on her hat and jumped up and down like a cheerleader. He took her to the Officers Club, where she met Jack James, who made a point of telling her that he had lived in Kansas, had gone to Harvard on scholarship, and was honored to have been asked to be their best man.

Billy brought Ann to the bridal suite at the Tacoma Hotel, where they locked themselves away on a prenuptial honeymoon. They also made arrangements to move into their first home, lent to them by friends of the Boeing family's.

William Woodward, Sr., arrived a short while later, hinting that he would have preferred to be with his horses. He gave Ann a booklet tracing the Woodward genealogy back to England. He tried to convey his own acceptance of the match. It was his wife and "the girls," he said, who were uneasy. Ann took his hand and swore to him that she would change their minds.

The night before the wedding, on March 10, 1943, Ann listened to the senior Woodward's monologue at dinner. He spoke of his wife's ancestors and his own, who had settled Annapolis, Maryland. Ann was too blissful to feel the sting of reproof. Billy sat through the speech with his eyebrows raised. His expression was similar to his mother's. Of course the Woodwards were superior. But Billy could see no point in speaking of it now. Since coming out to Seattle, Billy had felt less threatened by his father. He was even able to joke to Ann that his father seemed to speak of his own breeding in the same way that he discussed the lineage of his favorite horses.

Ann bought her wedding dress in the bridal shop of Seattle's major department store, Bon Marché. She doubled the lace train over and pinned it in her hair so that it formed a raised crown. It trailed three feet behind her when Jack James escorted her up the aisle of the Lutheran church. Her exuberance filled the small chapel. But on the marriage license Ann was less confident. She had problems writing her age. She began to write "23," crossed it out, and wrote "over 21." (In fact, she was twenty-seven and a half.) The small reception after the ceremony took place at the Tacoma Hotel. Wartime protocol dictated that William Woodward, Sr., wear a business suit. He hugged his son, but Billy was embarrassed. He wore his navy dress uniform with a single gold stripe on the sleeve.

Elsie Woodward did not announce her only son's marriage in *The New York Times*. A nine-line announcement was buried in the catchall column of the Newport *Mercury and Weekly News* on Friday, March 12, 1943. Ann had invented a World War I record for her father, Jesse Claude, moved him to Kansas City, and omitted the fact that he had been divorced from her mother. Ann Eden Crowell was announced to be the daughter of the late Colonel and Mrs. J. C. Crowell of Kansas City.

One week after her wedding Ann E. Crowell Woodward wrote a letter from their hotel suite in Tacoma to one of her favorite relatives, Grandmother Laura Smiley in Hugoton: "Dear Grandmother, Just to tell you I was married on March 14 to the most wonderful boy anywhere, William Woodward Jr. He is an ensign in the Navy and stationed out here in Tacoma Washington. I closed my apartment . . ."

Ann made a serious tactical error with Billy soon after their marriage. She told her new husband that she had seen the horse Johnstown run. When Billy questioned her, he elicited the fact that his father had asked her out and that she had attended parties with him at Aqueduct. Ann swore on a Bible that her encounters with William were innocent, but Billy felt humiliated.

Two weeks later she wrote her grandmother again, revealing the first signs of marital discord. Her handwriting slanted in several directions. "Just because two people have had a marriage ceremony, it doesn't constitute a real marriage. I am trying hard to adjust myself to William and to build our future on a solid foundation. I really am the luckiest girl in the world to have gotten such a truly wonderful husband—now I feel it is up to me to make it work." She insisted to her grandmother that under no circumstances (she underlined these last three words heavily) was any member of the Smiley family to tell her father about the wedding. She did not explain that the last thing she wanted was his reappearance in her life.

She gave her grandmother strict orders to let the entire family know that they must not visit or write to Ann until she gave the word: "That will have to wait." She wanted time to win over her in-laws with no interference from her Kansas relatives. She made it painfully clear that it was going to be a difficult job having Billy's family accept her, but characteristically wrote, "I am determined to succeed no matter how long it takes, or what it involves."

The newlyweds moved into a five-bedroom Tudor-style house overlooking misty Puget Sound. Ann awoke each morning amazed by the gray light reflected off the water. The house was furnished with nineteenth-century copies of Queen Anne chairs and tables. She had never lived in such luxury. When Billy left each day to go to the navy yard, she walked from room to room opening windows and closing them. She bought pale blue dressing gowns that coordinated with the damask-covered divans and chairs.

Ann was told by her mother-in-law that Billy expected a servant to cook and clean daily. She followed Elsie's instructions and began her life-long habit of writing household notes in a lavish leather-bound notebook, referring to herself as AEW. She planned menus and began an album of clippings about the Woodward horses. She also devoted hours to finding places in the house for wedding gifts that came by mail. She kept stacks of congratulatory cards marked with the date of her thank-you notes. For example, on one she wrote: "a spode cup and saucer circa 1810, the gift of Mrs. Richard Whitney, Boston, thanked 4-10-43." Another card read, "best wishes, Ethel and Philippe," and Ann wrote "4-11-43" and that it had accompanied a silver tray from Cartier sent by Billy's sister and her husband, Pierre de Croisset. Ann saved these little cards her entire life. They were proof of her contact through Billy with the mysterious world of the upper class. This should have been a rare period of security for Ann. Her worries about money were over, and she had the handsomest man in the world as her husband. But she knew that at any moment Billy would leave her to go to the war.

Ann was still improving herself day and night. She read books about English and American antiques, learning the difference between Queen Anne and Georgian furniture. She took Spanish lessons in the early afternoon from a local teacher. Ann used a sunlamp to keep tan despite the foggy winds off Puget Sound. She studied etiquette books and copied recipes. She mailed Elsie Woodward pictures she'd taken of Billy and inquired about Elsie's health.

Each evening after cocktails, Ann teased and encouraged Billy. She knew that sex was her hold on him. Many nights she and Billy would attend dinner parties in the modest homes of other officers. Neither Billy nor Ann ever relaxed at these parties. Billy seemed too good for the crowd, as he cocked his head and listened. Ann seemed frightened of her new role, but she savored the spell she cast on Billy's male friends in her dramatic décolletage. She blazed with excitement, a rare volatile blonde. The other officers' wives faded in her presence.

Billy began to stare unhappily at her in public. Sometimes she stopped in midsentence. "Darling?" At first he would turn away. But at one of their dinner parties, he mumbled a reproach that sounded like his mother: "Stop eating as though there is not enough food to go around, darling. It reflects on our hospitality."

He also began to complain that she pronounced words incorrectly and told her she flirted like a tramp. Although Ann argued with his criticisms, she always sought to improve herself.

When she tried out her Spanish in front of another couple, Billy laughed and said, "Hey, stop that Kansas Spanish." Ann smiled brightly, determined to improve her accent.

The sad truth was that Billy felt lonely with Ann. He felt less free to strike his ironic attitudes toward the "lower classes." Most important, in her eagerness for self-improvement, his flamboyant new wife betrayed exasperating insecurities. He had hoped that Ann would stand up to his parents for him—not knuckle under and imitate them. Instead of encouraging her, he poked fun at her aspirations.

Ann and Billy had a public fight after a dinner party at the home of Ensign John Karkoff and his wife, Geraldine. It started when Ann's laughter rang loudly at another reserve officer's joke. Billy ordered her to an adjoining room. He was slightly drunk and jealous of his bride's enjoyment of the wit of another man. He announced, "I think you have a drinking problem." Ann did not answer. Jack James, hearing their words from the next room, wondered why Billy was being so cruel. When Billy cited rules for proper behavior, Ann broke down. She did not reappear, but Billy bid a wry, smiling good-bye to his embarrassed acquaintances. The other young couples whispered later that Ann had not seemed drunk to them.

During the first months of the marriage, notes written in large calligraphic hand on somber gray stationery arrived from Elsie Woodward addressed to Ann. Elsie's letterhead was not engraved with the Woodward name, only "9 East Eighty-sixth Street." The sentences were alternately printed and written and showed no concern for punctuation. Ann saved these, too, for the rest of her life, in a folder marked "AEW, Personal." On May 12, Elsie wrote Ann, thanking her daughter-in-law for writing. After commenting on the weather and the war news, Elsie wrote, "You sound like a first class manager of your household—At your age I was such a dumbbell that I wonder how W. lived through it. Poor Ethel is going through the vagaries of the colored servants. Cook didn't appear as she had swollen legs and asthma & pains of a variable nature. Then the maid didn't turn up—had a tooth [underlined] extracted and 'wasn't resting well'—''

Elsie concluded that family news such as the scarlet fever contracted by Edith's boys probably wasn't much fun for Ann but "you may as well get used to it early—my dear—I am glad my Bill looks well—I haven't seen him for so long—I probably will not recognize him—

"Love to you both

"Ma"

The polite notes contained no whisper of the family's displeasure at the marriage. Although Elsie was only doing her duty, Ann assumed that her mother-in-law was bringing her into the fold.

In May, Billy left Ann for a week to go to gunnery school. Ann seized the opportunity to enroll in an accounting class. On May 23, Elsie wrote, sympathizing that Ann was all alone. She suggested that Ann get a friend to come out and live with her. Elsie was still proposing a visit to Billy and Ann in July. She turned down Ann's invitation to stay with them, saying she preferred a hotel. "I never stay with any of the girls and prefer to be independent." She thanked Ann for the snapshots of Billy that she now was carrying in her purse to show friends. She signed off, "Much love to you both, Ma."

Jack James enjoyed visiting Billy and Ann on Sunday mornings for coffee. Once, the Woodwards introduced Jack to an elderly Tiffany's employee who had traveled from New York with several hundred thousand dollars' worth of loose emeralds. Billy and Ann selected a single stone worth $25,000. To Ann, the money and jewelry were not merely luxuries. They represented a kind of medication that she always hoped would cure her of her childhood deprivation.

By May 30, another note from Elsie implied she was having second thoughts about the long train trip west. Could Billy get a leave instead and come to visit her before he was shipped out? Her daughters in New York were also eager to see Billy, she explained. She signed it, "Much Love Ma." But then the war intervened. Billy was ordered to San Francisco in mid-June for training. He would ship out on the new small aircraft carrier *Liscome Bay*. The senior Woodwards hurried to Tacoma for what they feared might be their last visit with their son. Before he left, Billy presented Ann with a set of diamonds and a large pearl necklace and earrings from

Harry Winston worth almost $50,000. He also gave her a $10,000 U.S. savings bond that would be due twenty years later.

It was just as well that Ann and Billy were forced to entertain his parents. Billy had lashed out at Ann for misplacing some magazines he had wanted to take to San Francisco. He clenched his hand until the knuckles showed white. He was terrified of what lay ahead for him. To Ann, the weekend with Billy's parents had the quality of a picture postcard. These people had a supernatural authority. Ann tried to relax, imitating the senior Woodwards, who were seeking to diffuse their tensions over Billy's departure by discussing how they could find Ann a house in Port Blakely on exclusive Bainbridge Island, Washington. She snapped photographs with her Rolleiflex.

On her trip home, Elsie wrote a letter on Drake Hotel stationery, complaining that the old Northern Pacific was better than the new train. She again commiserated with Ann for her solitude. Ann had moved to Bainbridge Island on her own. Her new house faced a golf course and a beach. The isolated island was the first of many on which Ann would establish a household.

In her next letter, Elsie promised "to find Ann a radio with an alternate battery outlet." Ann's household was suffering electrical blackouts. Elsie also wrote that she had even talked to the Zenith and Philco people, who said there were no radios to be had except one cabinet-sized secondhand model. Instead Elsie had sent Ann her own small radio. "However, if that isn't all right, I will put a friend at a shop called Liberty on 67th Street to work on the project of finding a radio for you."

After a few weeks alone, Ann discovered she was pregnant. At almost the same time that he learned Ann's good news, on September 10, Billy shipped out on the *Liscome Bay* for Hawaii and the South Pacific. He asked Ann to stay with his family in New York. There was an apartment on the fourth floor. Ann told Billy she preferred to wait for him on the West Coast. She loved walking on the beach. Then Elsie called. In a few months, it would be hard for Ann to travel at all. She told Ann she must come home now.

Ann was lonely in the big silent New York house. She disturbed her mother-in-law by ringing too often for Putz's services. She needed company, and he seemed the only available human being. Elsie coached her on table settings, floral arrangements, correct notepapers. But after a short time, Elsie began to keep her distance. It probably irked her that this ordinary girl was giving birth to a Woodward. Ann yearned to go out to restaurants, but dared not. She put herself to work photographing the small details and splendid large areas of the house: the Queen Anne chairs by the soaring staircase, the Roman busts carved into the library walls. Ann presented her mother-in-law with a book of the photographs. Elsie accepted the gift without enthusiasm.

In late October, Billy sailed for Pearl Harbor. He was excited by the prospect of battle, but disliked the sound of the bells that called him to duty. He grew accustomed to the arduous four-hour sleeping/eight-hour working shifts. The *Liscome Bay* was one of several escort carriers surrounding the warship *New Mexico*. It was a "baby flattop" with a large 512-foot landing field. The *Liscome Bay* was carrying twenty-one airplanes, 932 men, and thousands of pounds of bombs, TNT, and torpedoes—many of which were thin-walled and delicate—in the hatch. The new untried ship had been built by Kaiser and could travel only fifteen knots.

Despite his dislike of hard work, Billy ran up straight metal ladders and stooped to get through the round-cornered four-and-a-half-foot metal hatches. He read radar, radio, and navigational compasses set in low boxy consoles.

A month later, on Thanksgiving, the *Liscome Bay* was off the Gilbert Islands in the South Pacific, taking part in the complex invasion of the once idyllic islands now held by the Japanese. For five days, the *Liscome Bay* had been sending airplanes to bomb Makin, a nearby coral island. One plane had crashed at sea the day before.

At 4:40 in the morning, USNR Ensign William Woodward was officer of the deck, in charge of the ship, while the captain slept. The safety of the ship and her crew had been in his hands since midnight. He was in the navigation room, high on the bridge of the ship, above the large landing deck. It was his job to give directions to keep the ship parallel to the other aircraft carriers in the task force. The ship was surrounded by the silent dark ocean, filled with both American and enemy ships and submarines.

Billy felt exhausted but pleased. He had been in command of the *Liscome Bay* for four and a half hours. His directives were transmitted by messengers or bullhorns. Billy gave the orders for reveille and then the general quarters command. When it was heard throughout the ship at 4:50, the men awoke and took their positions at the guns or began to ready the airplanes for takeoff. The Pacific was calm and the winds light. The clouds had passed in front of the crescent moon on the horizon. As Billy wrote later, "I had just sent a messenger below to wake Captain Wiltsie at 0500 in accordance with his night orders."

Then Billy ordered that the ship be turned sixty degrees for morning flight operations. He wished Ann and his family could see him ordering the ship around. Shortly after five o'clock, he saw that one of the destroyers had gone to investigate a dim white flashing light. An unidentified aircraft some thirty miles away had been spotted by a carrier ship in their fleet. At 5:07, the remaining boats began regrouping to close the gap left by the investigating destroyer. Woodward gave orders to turn the *Liscome Bay* another sixty degrees.

By 5:11, Billy looked back at the closed door, wondering where Captain Wiltsie was. Then suddenly, without warning, an explosion lifted Billy up three feet and threw him to the floor. Stunned, he waited for someone to tell him what to do next. He still had responsibilities. He knew he should be attempting to steer the ship into a safe position so that she would not be hit again. He should be sending messages to emergency crews to order them to discover the extent of the damage to the ship and to begin to repair it.

What Billy did not know was that a torpedo from a Japanese submarine had torn into the hold, where the ship's thousands of pounds of volatile bombs and torpedoes were stored. Lieutenant Commander Oliver Ames was now the ranking surviving commanding officer. (Ames was a Boston cousin of Billy's. His mother was Elsie's triplet sister Edith.) In the flight control room Ames saw the thousand-foot column of pure yellow flame and concluded that an underwater torpedo had scored a random hit on the *Liscome Bay*.

Billy heard the cries of the dying men below him on the flight deck. As he tried to stand up, he cut his palms on the glass and bits of metal on the floor. Engulfed by heat and smoke, he went into shock. The *Liscome Bay* was sinking rapidly. The bullhorn was broken, and the telephone lines were down. Even if he had wanted to, Billy could not have issued an order to abandon ship.* He feared that crew members might not jump unless they received orders.

Billy was not only in shock; he was also unprepared emotionally to act. He did not help his wounded and trapped shipmates, as many others did. Flames leapt around him, and the boat tilted. The first explosion had blown an elevator loose from its moorings, causing a large fire that enveloped the bridge. There was no water pressure to put out fires. The flight deck below him began to tear.

Then another explosion followed from deep inside the *Liscome Bay*.

---

*This important command had to come from the officer of the deck or the captain.

The ship's hull was not sufficiently armored to protect 135,000 pounds of explosives in the hold. It blew up, tossing men, planes, deck frames, and molten fragments. The *Liscome Bay* appeared to fold in half like a cracker box. An instant later, a wave of debris hit the deck of carrier U.S.S. *Hughes*, 1,500 feet away. Fragments of metal and human flesh also showered the decks of the *New Mexico*—1,500 yards away.

Around Billy, the bridge erupted with fire and steam.* Everything was melting. His heart sank as he wondered if a better officer of the deck would have maneuvered the ship away from the second hit. (He would torture himself for three more days over this until he learned that the second explosion had not been a hit at all.)

The sea was aflame in front of the heaving *Liscome Bay*, as Lieutenant Commander Ames pushed his way to the bridge. Billy was gagging on the heat, smoke, and stench of burning flesh. Still in shock, he mistook his cousin from Boston for Captain Wiltsie. In his report, he wrote that Captain Wiltsie appeared and "helped him untie the knots on a rope, and to escape."

Ames told Billy to follow him. Billy crawled through a foot of oil and water toward a steep metal ladder that had been partially destroyed and was blocked by wounded men and debris. Some men nearby jumped into the sea sixty feet below. Most died in the fall. Others started throwing boxes of ammunition overboard to keep them away from the fires. Still others restrained the men, because the boxes were exploding in the water, where survivors were swimming.

Commander Ames told Billy he had seen the torpedo hit. They were perhaps the only survivors who had any inkling of what had happened. They watched sailors throw knotted lines over the railing, then climb thirty feet down these emergency ropes to the shattered flight deck. The sailors then jumped the final thirty feet into the flaming sea. Ames recognized that Billy was in shock but urged him to jump. He shouted at him to keep on his shoes, uniform, shirt, and trousers. "They will be useful on the beach," he said.

His face covered with oil, and nearly suffocating from smoke, Billy jumped into the burning sea. Miraculously, he missed the floating deck beams and cork. Tracer bullets from the ship's exploding ammunition stores filled the air. Fires on the ship lit the ocean. For forty-five minutes, he tried

---

*As Billy wrote later, "I was thrown to the deck by the explosion. Within less than thirty seconds the whole of the ship was aflame, and those on the bridge had to stay below the coaming [ceiling] because of the excessive heat."

to swim away from the ship. His sodden uniform made swimming even more difficult. He pulled off his gloves with his teeth, kicked off his overshoes, and ducked underwater to cool his face.

The sun rose with a slash of pink, but it was dwarfed by the flames of the *Liscome Bay*. Behind Billy the hissing hull was fast disappearing. Some men still stood on the long flight deck. They went down with the ship, afraid to jump.

One explosion lifted the survivors completely out of the water. The shock sprained Billy's back. He wrote later, "At a safe distance, I observed that the whole after [back] end of the ship was gone, and the rest of the ship was solid flame except for a small portion of the forward [front] edge of the flight deck. I joined up with several men on a life net. At about 0530, she raised her bow, rolled over to starboard, and slipped beneath the waves."

At 5:25, the nearby U.S.S. *Hughes* was finally ordered to pick up survivors from the crippled ship. The *Hughes* had first been ordered to search only for submarines. At 5:33, a blip on the radar screen of the *Hughes* signaled that the *Liscome Bay* had disappeared. In twenty-three minutes, the 512-foot-long ship had sunk. Two thirds of Billy's fellow sailors were killed. Fifty-five officers and 217 enlisted men were rescued by the *Hughes* at approximately 6:15. The sinking of the *Liscome Bay* came to be considered one of the greatest tragedies in the Pacific campaign.

Billy and his wounded mates were laid out on the floors of the mess hall of the *Hughes*. Billy was treated with boric acid ointment and his head was wrapped in towels by emergency "burn teams." He asked about Captain Wiltsie, refusing to believe he had died. He was given shoes, a shirt, dungarees, and a berth in the officers' area. He kept waking up, his burns throbbing, believing he was still on duty and that another torpedo had hit. At 10:10, Billy and the other survivors who could walk were transferred to a hospital ship.

A few days later, Billy Woodward, wearing dungarees, stood with his fellow survivors as the flag-draped coffins of their dead shipmates were slid one after another into the dark sea. A bugle played taps. The sinking assumed nightmare proportions in Billy's mind, as he continued to blame himself for the deaths. It did not help when, in the next month, he was decorated as a hero, receiving several ribbons and the Purple Heart. The real cause of the sinking remained a naval secret for years: the *Liscome Bay* was badly designed; the ammunition in her unprotected hold took the torpedo hit, exploded, and destroyed her.

Like most men of his generation, Billy's major adult experience was

the war. It was a commonly held belief that the military made boys into
men. For the next several years, Billy mumbled to attractive dinner partners
about the famous loss at sea. They believed the incident had made a man
of him. But in fact it made him doubt his powers. He believed, for example,
that Bean Baker would have saved his wounded mates and then gone down
with the ship like a true hero. His brush with death only increased Billy's
self-doubt and impelled him to take life-threatening risks. Billy would try
to replicate the rush of adrenaline that came in part from surviving death.

In keeping with a new navy policy, news of the ship's sinking was
not immediately released. Nor were families notified about casualties; the
navy had decided to put together a complete survivors' list before contact-
ing relatives. But two days after the incident, an ominous hint appeared.
Many newspapers stated that Admiral Henry Mullinix had been visiting
the ship and was missing in action. William Woodward, Sr., called the
White House for information. Ann told herself that the Woodwards were
too fortunate to have their son die at war. In that week, she and the
grandchild she carried seemed to gain a new status, as perhaps the family's
last links to Billy Woodward.

By December 2, horrified reporters were filing front-page stories of
the catastrophe of the *Liscome Bay*. The fallen ship made the Gilbert Islands
invasion one of the bloodiest in the Pacific. When Ann read these newspaper accounts, she began to panic. But then William Woodward received
word from the War Department that Billy was neither dead nor missing in
action. The family relaxed and seemed to embrace Ann as a fellow suf-
ferer—as a Woodward, in short. Elsie and her husband soon heard from
their only son. Billy had taken the "best" suite at the St. Francis Hotel in
San Francisco.

Desperate to put his nightmare behind him, Billy began to celebrate.
While Ann prepared to cross the country to join him, he ordered cases of
liquor and invited several secretaries to his suite. He called Jack James in
Tacoma. "They are all willing," he said shakily. "This hotel is full of pretty
girls, and I'm having the time of my life." Billy held a weeklong party. On
one memorable night, he had two women in bed with him. "There are so
many beautiful girls, and they love a uniform," he said over the telephone
to James.

9

AFTER THE HONEYMOON

Billy was assigned to Norfolk, Virginia, as an office aide to Admiral Patrick Niesson L. Bellinger, a job arranged through his family's political connections. He had been relieved of active duty. His pregnant war bride looked to him like a pretty stranger. Within two weeks, he and Ann had moved into an old white Colonial house with a Woodward family friend, Jo Hartford Douglas, and her husband. Jo was the daughter of the founder of the A & P supermarket chain and the sister of Huntington Hartford. Her husband, Barclay Douglas, also worked as an aide to the admiral.

When she was young, Jo had spent many hours with William Woodward, Sr., learning about horse breeding and racing. Unlike Billy, she had found Woodward a generous and agreeable teacher.

In Norfolk, the two naval aides left the house at seven-thirty every morning to drive to the base, returning together at six-thirty in the evening. His navy duty was Billy's only stint as a workingman, and without the excitement of battle he found the routine deadly. Since it was wartime and there was a labor shortage, Jo Hartford had no household help. She had never cleaned her own house before. Jo pulled dinner together with carrots, potatoes, squash, and tomatoes from her victory garden.

Ann and Billy did not pitch in. They were younger than Jo and Barclay, and Billy had probably decided to let Jo mother them. Jo resented Ann for ignoring the chores, but no one resented Billy, who in their circle could do no wrong. Ann's past intrigued Jo. But whenever she tried to ask Ann where she came from, Ann would reply, "Oh, you wouldn't be interested."

Still, Jo found Ann sympathetic in some ways. As she said decades later, "She wasn't what you'd think—ostentatious or cheap. She was a little girl who had not had very many opportunities in life. I don't think she planned to marry a rich man. Oh, she was experienced all right, but she was not vulgar. She was not the kind of calculating woman we've all seen around New York. She was obviously crazy about Billy Woodward, and dying to break into his world."

Jo noticed, though, that the Woodwards bickered about everything—from when to telephone Billy's parents to when to go to sleep. Jo excused Billy's outbursts as war nerves and blamed Ann. Jo did not realize that the rages were often intentionally brought on by Billy himself. He might simply admire another woman and flash a look at Ann, who would become furious. In fact, Ann did begin to lose her balance: her self-image depended almost entirely on Billy's assessment of her. The battles would rage until Billy and Ann retreated to their bedroom. Suddenly, there would be silence throughout the house. Jo and her husband knew then that the shouting would stop for a while. These reconciliations became a ritual, the most satisfying part of Billy and Ann's life.

When Ann gave birth to their first son, William Woodward III, on July 27, 1944, she was living at Billy's parents' house in Manhattan. Billy was stationed in Philadelphia, still connected to the admiralty office. That September Billy gave Ann a necklace of square-cut sapphires and bought her a second treasury bond that would be worth $10,000 seven years later. That November, he gave her a gift of securities worth more than $200,000.

When Billy returned in 1945, he did not want to go to work at the bank. He was relieved to be taken care of by Putz and the maids in his parents' well-ordered home. Although his mother was proud that he did not need to work (a point of view she was determined to give him, in honor of her father's beliefs), Elsie was desperate to interest him in something other than parties and chasing women. She urged him to go to meetings at New York Hospital, to which the Woodwards gave about $10,000 a year.

Billy preferred to stay in bed with his breakfast tray until eleven, recovering from a hangover. Not wanting to start that day's fight, he would tell Ann it was too early for him to talk coherently. He'd dress in a navy suit—without shaving. He would drive his Commander model Studebaker downtown. Designed by Raymond Loewy, who was also responsible for the Lucky Strike cigarette package, the handsome car was souped up with a Cadillac engine and called a Studillac.* Billy parked it and walked to the Ritz Hotel at Fiftieth Street and Madison Avenue. The Ritz had particular appeal to Manhattan's elite WASP establishment, reminding them of the Ritz in Paris. It was owned by the prosperous old Manhattan family, the Goelets.**

By 11:30 a.m., Nick Biddle and several others of Billy's Buckley classmates had gathered at the small round tables near the bar for prelunch cocktails. Billy Woodward was not the only man in his set who had returned from the war wanting to act as if he were still twenty-one—even hardworking Neddy Patterson frequented the Ritz Bar before he took a job on Wall Street. The young men bragged that it was the only bar in the whole city in which an unescorted woman could have a drink undisturbed by rude men.

When Billy spotted Bean Baker working his way through the crowd, his face brightened. Like Billy, Bean did not have a clue about how to follow in the footsteps of his hardworking forebears. Although neither of them would become embarrassingly drunk, they often drank at the Ritz into the evening. They broke only for lunch downstairs in the exclusive hotel restaurant with its wall of live ivy vines.

The long afternoons with Bean Baker made Billy feel less lost. They talked of their women, their disinterest in banking, Bean's pilot days, and the *Liscome Bay* sinking. As an aviation cadet Bean had been stationed near Cape Girardeau, Missouri, where he and Alicia sometimes lost as much as $5,000 a night playing cards. He told stories of FBI agents questioning him about Alicia's being a foreign agent. Bean seemed a genuine war hero; he had flown thirty-five bombing missions over Germany and had attained the rank of captain in the air force. But, like Billy, Bean made little sense of his close calls with death. Billy spoke of having failed to do his duty to his shipmates as the officer of the deck on the *Liscome Bay*. Bean dismissed Billy's remorse and pronounced it heroic to have jumped off the ship into the floating fires.

Although Ann tried to join Billy's lunches at the Ritz, she was always told, "Sorry, men only." Bean sometimes brought Shadow, a Labrador he

---

*Loewy's work for Studebaker helped pave the way for modern automotive design. Other designs by Loewy, who virtually founded the profession of industrial designer, include costumes for Florenz Ziegfeld's entertainers; the Greyhound Supercruiser; Air Force One for President Kennedy; the Carling Black Label beer can label; Oreo, Ritz cracker, and Nabisco Shredded Wheat packages; the Exxon sign; and logos for Exxon, TWA, Shell, International Harvester, *Newsweek*, Canada Dry, and many others.

**Mary Goelet was the woman courted by young William Woodward, Sr., in London.

had trained to wait for him on street corners. Billy and Bean would emerge unsteadily into the dim evening light on East Fiftieth Street and call the dog, who would run to them.

Billy and Bean dressed very much alike. Their suits and shirts were custom-made at Dunhill. They bought their hunting ammunition at Abercrombie & Fitch. They paid dues to the exclusive men's clubs of their fathers and grandfathers, the Metropolitan, the Knickerbocker, the Brook, and the Creek. They kept airplanes and were also members of the Aviation Country Club in Hicksville. Each man also kept about a thousand dollars in credit at a jewelry store on Fifth Avenue owned by Fulco di Verdura, a fashionable homosexual Sicilian duke. It was fun to breeze in with a girl and buy one of his gold pieces without ever having to open a checkbook. Neither young man was easy with his prewar commitment to his wife. Ann and Alicia were sexual exotics to Bean and Billy—not soul mates. Nonetheless, Billy had already given Ann property and securities worth more than $400,000. Billy told Bean that Ann was so interested in money that she had refused to take his father's accountant's advice about investing. Instead, she enrolled in a business course at Bernard M. Baruch College. Billy and Bean enjoyed complaining to each other about their similar marital battles. Bean described his marriage to Billy: "She is like a drug. I can't live with her and I can't live without her." After Alicia left to visit her family in Mexico City, Billy accompanied Bean to Nassau to snorkel and paddle around. Away from their wives, Bean and Billy went out on dates.

Meanwhile, William Woodward, Sr., attempted to guide Billy toward a business life. He gave him the remainder of a trust fund of $3 million in blue-chip stocks, thus increasing Billy's monthly income to $10,000. A more prudent father might have waited for Billy to achieve something on his own before rewarding him.

Billy now sat on the boards of two companies—Turner Halsey textiles and United Shoe Machinery, the firm that held the international monopoly on leasing and marketing equipment for manufacturing shoes. United Shoe dated back to the Civil War, when it leased machinery to manufacturers making shoes for soldiers. By 1946, it was known as a "widows and orphans" stock because it was considered so safe. As a director, Billy was responsible for voting on dividends, expansion, and antitrust litigation, but he turned up only once to tour the New York offices.

At a Turner Halsey board meeting, Billy once pitched a sales idea. Turner Halsey supplied a heavy cotton duck that was used in work gloves, awnings, and industrial belting. Billy urged the directors to manufacture canvas tops for convertible cars in colors and plaid patterns. Since the large

textile producers did not want to make custom items for wealthy sportsmen, Billy's interest in the company flagged.

In these years, Ann decided that it was her responsibility to provide
amusement for her husband. She found a restaurant in Greenwich Village
with transvestite waiters and planned trips to Cap Ferrat to lift his mood.
Like her short stint on Puget Sound, these trips to the Riviera were the
beginning of her lifelong affair with the sea. She photographed Billy in
front of old white walls covered with scarlet bougainvillea. Billy disapproved of Ann's sunbathing and said he was not interested in losing his
patrician pallor. Ann hummed her Noël Coward songs about decadent
antics at "mahvelous parties" in Billy's ear. Her overwhelming hunger for
things he took for granted began to tire him, much the way his father's
football and racing obsessions had. Billy complained to friends like Alfred
Gelardin about Ann's interest in titled Europeans. Yet before Billy would
agree to attend a party, he, too, insisted on knowing which important titles
would be there.

In Manhattan, Billy showed little enthusiasm for Ann's eagerness to
have their own home. The young Woodwards were still living upstairs in
the apartment at his parents' house. Ann's feelings were similar to those of
Elsie forty-five years earlier, when as a newlywed she had had to play
second fiddle at her mother-in-law's parties.

Elsie criticized Ann's trips to Paris, implying that Ann was not a good
mother. Elsie took it for granted that Billy would show no interest in
fatherhood. She introduced Ann to Mainbocher, whose suits were inspired
by the paintings of John Singer Sargent. To Ann, his clothes looked
dowdy.

Ann hired Count Lanfranco Rasponi, a public relations man, as her
tutor.* Rasponi, a handsome escort of Elizabeth Arden's, lacked the money
to live like the rich restless people he adored. His clients, such as Mrs.
Randolph Hearst, usually asked him to arrange flowers, find exciting lo-
cations for parties, and make up the guest lists for their parties—and, of
course, to help them break into society columns like Cholly Knickerbocker's. (Ann was dubbed a "Cinderella girl" by the society press during that
period, as was "Bobo," Mrs. Winthrop Rockefeller, a girl from the Midwest.) Ann took notes on Rasponi's rules. He told her she should have

---

*By 1960, Rasponi was to write *The International Nomads (Today's Jet-Set Society, Who It
Is, and How, Why, and Where It Functions)*, in which he itemized the most social meeting places
in Sardinia, St. Moritz, Gstaad, Klosters, Paris, Madrid, Marbella, Venice, and Rome. He would
group his socialites by first names and specify which name should be dropped in which countries
at particular seasons for the best impact.

cards engraved like Elsie Woodward and must make arrangements for after-dinner musicians. In later years, even her critics said that Ann entertained flawlessly.

In addition to learning whom to cultivate, Ann learned whom to cut: people who had been involved in a scandal or who had lost their money or their titled mates. She learned to condescend to those less important than the Woodwards.

It was 1945, and Billy had not been back from the war very long when Ann bought her first Charles James evening dress (later donated to the Metropolitan Museum of Art). She had fasted and exercised to regain her figure after her son William's birth. She discovered that the great designers were eager to please her. She was a walking advertisement at Long Island dinner parties and charity balls. James's sculpted evening creations, which were sold at the Elizabeth Arden salon on Fifth Avenue, resembled the extravagant ball gowns of the late nineteenth century. Charles James had dressed such women as Dolores Del Rio, Claire Luce, Doris Duke, Gypsy Rose Lee, and Marlene Dietrich. But for the most part his clients were titled Europeans. Ann was one of the first young American society women to support him. She soon made the best-dressed lists in his creations. Within four years, others such as Babe Paley and Eleanor Whitney would follow Ann's lead.

Predictably, Elsie disliked the huge rustling James creations. On one particular evening, Ann sat at Billy's father's feet, arranging her stiff black satin skirt in a puffy circle around her. William lectured her on Belair horse lineage. Even Libby, the "beautiful sister," wore drab evening dresses. Ann's dramatic presentation was a constant reminder of why Billy had broken with the family.

Charles James and Ann saw eye to eye. He enjoyed dressing her more than almost any other client. Under the crystal chandelier in his chaotic, cluttered sewing rooms at 699 Madison Avenue, James knelt to drape fabric on Ann and to insert wires. Five assistants spoke terse instructions to each other. James once ripped a dress apart while Ann was wearing it; a seam was misstitched. He ranted about plumb lines and pure architectural principles. Another time he discarded a completed skirt after discovering a new beige satin upholstery fabric that glowed gold in the folds. Gold picked up the highlights of Ann's hair. In 1947, James invited Ann and Mrs. Randolph Hearst to model his gowns for an article in *Vogue*. Ann looked regal in the "parachute" dinner dress—and maybe a little too professional holding the beige satin skirt. Her face was in profile, her hair austerely held in a bun. The black velvet V-necked bodice was open in back. But Elsie Wood-

ward felt it was unseemly for her daughter-in-law to advertise fashion designers. Ann promised to be more conservative.

To that end, she made friends with Peter Pels, a dictatorial salesman
at the Maximilian fur salon, which catered to Helena Rubinstein and the
Duchess of Windsor and would later provide furs to Jacqueline Kennedy
and Claude Pompidou. Pels permitted Ann to visit him on matters other
than fur purchases. There was, he taught her, only one right way to wear
clothing. "Sable is dark, but not too dark," he advised her. She had the
feeling he was telling her she was all wrong, but she kept asking questions.
Ann showed Pels her pocket-sized leather notebooks filled with swatches
of fabric and her own stick-figure drawings of jackets, gowns, and blouses
that she had seen at Dior, Chanel, Givenchy, and Jacques Fath. Pels was
impressed. He found that she had good taste, but she seemed to need
constant reinforcement of her judgment. "Which is good for me?" she'd
ask him eagerly. He shuddered the day Ann appeared wearing red shoes
and a blue dress. His ladies wore "finished combinations"—coordinated
gloves, scarves, shoes, and stockings. He dictated pastel blues, textured
grays, and soft greens for her pale blond skin tones. Hemlines had to be
appropriate to her social position. He politely broke her of the habit of
bright colors—especially her favorites, turquoise and kelly green, which
changed the color of her eyes. Pels ruled her selection of furs. She bought
a pale dyed "caramel" Persian lamb coat, a gunmetal gray mink coat called
a Lutitian mink, and a sleeveless leopard jacket. Ann was fascinated by the
Duchess of Windsor and asked for a black broadtail straight skirt and
blouse that had originally been made for her by Maximilian. ("All chic
things are straight," said Pels.)

Ann's diaries from this period are filled with Pels's mandates about
hats, clothes, gloves, makeup, and jewelry. She seems to have been an
actress dressing for a role or an anthropologist trying to join in an alien
culture. In the middle of a page describing an ensemble of a dark brown
dress, cape, hat (pictured in an ink drawing), and belt, all by Givenchy,
Ann printed: "SEVERE: THIS IS ELEGANCE."

> FUR COAT PERSIAN
> BROWN WOOL
> Do not wear fur with same color dress.
> Make up base Helena Rubinstein
> Lipstick Dior #99
> Can always use Dior #5 over if think too orange to finish
> makeup Helena Rubinstein Blush Peach

On one page she wrote in big letters:

<u>AEW</u>
"DRESS ALWAYS
 SOFT
 SEDUCTIVE
 (possibly) CONSPICUOUS"
[The word "possibly" is added in a darker pen.]

10

PRINCESS MARINA TORLONIA

*"Who stole my heart away? Who makes me
dream . . . Dreams, I know, can never be true?"*

—JEROME KERN,
  "Who," from *Sunny*, 1925

*"There was nothing more important to Billy than
chasing women. Sometimes he had been in love with
Ann and loyal to the boys—but it was not his way of
life. He felt that extracurricular activity was his pre-
rogative as a man. There were three words to describe
Billy Woodward: selfish and egotistical and well-
mannered. I don't ever recall Ann being at peace with
herself. Everything was always a crisis. She was inse-
cure but he gave her that feeling."*

—JACK JAMES, best man at Billy's wedding
    and fellow Naval Reserve friend from Harvard
    and the war

*"When you're in trouble, hire a Jew, a lawyer like
Sol."*

—ROBERT LEYLAN

In the late forties, Billy Woodward was a star of New York society
nightlife. Every night he wore black tie; Cholly Knickerbocker wrote
about Billy and his beautiful wife, who appeared at theatrical openings
and charity balls. During this time, Ann seemed to lose more and more
ground in the relationship. Amusing Billy became her main obsession—

particularly as her sexual hold on him weakened. And since she took on the responsibility, Billy, instead of coping with his own emptiness, blamed her for his ennui. He became convinced that if he had married a woman of his own background, their social life would not have been filled with what he called squalid negotiations. Ann began to suspect that there might be another woman.

The autumn of 1946 marked the end of any serenity in the Woodward marriage. Billy met Princess Marina Torlonia, a sinewy beauty several years older than he. At Billy's sister's party, Marina overwhelmed Billy with her chitcat, which usually included such anecdotes as an account of a hospital visit to her close friend Oona O'Neill Chaplin. Oona, who had just given birth, confided in Marina, "You know, I love him dearly—but Charlie's got some of the damnedest ideas. He made me eat the placenta. He says dogs do it and it's terribly healthy."

Marina's mother was a Connecticut WASP—she had the added spice of an Italian title on her father's side. An artist who painted Marina's portrait described her as a great beauty, long-limbed like a Russian wolfhound. She was tall, with regal posture, a Roman nose, and a long neck marked by tense tendons. She commanded a room and with her emphatic manner seemed more Italian than American.

At that time, Marina was married to the internationally known tennis star Frank Shields. She had a history of aggressive, turbulent relationships with handsome men. She had fallen in love with Shields as soon as she saw him on the tennis court. "I must have him," she said. "He will be the father of my children." Shields was six feet six inches tall and very thin, with a full sensual mouth and high cheekbones, large melting Irish eyes, and black eyebrows.*

In late 1939, Marina followed Frank Shields from tennis match to tennis match.** She moved to Hollywood while Frank took screen tests and proceded with his divorce. They were together constantly.

Marina Torlonia had more glamour and sparkle than most American debutantes. Most important to Billy, however, was the fact that Marina

---

*In his white V-neck tennis sweaters, he looked like a fraternal twin of his granddaughter, the 1980s movie star Brooke Shields.

**A poor Irish kid who came up the hard way, Shields had superb athletic talent, but his physical grace hid a great deal of self-destructiveness. His friends reported his alcoholic confusions as great escapades. While in France for the Davis Cup matches in 1938, for instance, he disappeared after a defeat in a preliminary match. Carrying champagne bottles, he had gone to a farewell party for friends who were sailing to America on the *President Harding*, passed out, and awoken at sea.

was a woman of his class—and an acquaintance since childhood. Her background gave her the authority that Ann lacked. She broke rules of etiquette
without compromising her extraordinary status. Walter Pidgeon, the Hollywood actor, and his wife, Ruth, were surprised to be served Ritz crackers
out of a box at Marina's cocktail hour. But then they wondered if they
should continue to serve fancy hors d'oeuvres. In Los Angeles, Princess
Marina seemed undaunted by financial hardships. Nonplussed guests found
it amusing to help her wash dishes.

Marina told shocking stories about her difficult brother and sister—
both homosexual (although Prince Alessandro had married Infanta Beatriz,
daughter of ex-King Alfonso and Queen Victoria of Spain) and turbulent
in temperament. Marina reported that Alessandro charged her rent when
she went to stay at the fifty-room marble Torlonia palace in Rome. Her
sister, Princess Cristiana, once killed a child in a hit-and-run accident in a
small Italian village. Marina liked to tell how she herself was greeted on
the Lido by an American woman, Princess San Faustino, who had married
an Italian nobleman. "Tell me," the woman had asked, "which Torlonia
are you? The murderess or the wife of the tennis player?"

Living in Beverly Hills, Marina found excuses to fly to see Billy in
Manhattan. She openly chased him, arranging afternoon liaisons at the
Lowell Hotel. The two began an intimate correspondence. Marina treasured their long-distance courtship as an escape from the difficult times
with her husband. Her California friends were amazed at the girlish excitement with which she received her nightly telephone calls from Billy. Bean
and Billy met less frequently at the Ritz Bar during the next two years.
Bean had also fallen madly in love with a woman of his own class. Both
young men changed their wills that year to give their wives smaller shares
of their estates.

Ann decided a second honeymoon would persuade Billy to forget his mistress. Lady Sarah Churchill and her husband, Ed Russell, were renting a
beach cottage at Lyford Cay, near Jo Hartford Douglas and her husband.
Ann persuaded Billy to go, despite the fact that she was pregnant again.
She packed up her son and the three of them sailed to Nassau, even though
traveling with two-year-old "Woody" made her feel less able to focus on
pleasing Billy.

It was a sunny spring with flowers blooming on the beach, where a
row of bungalows faced the sparkling sea. No matter how badly things
were going with Billy, Ann sat alone in the early morning with her shoul-

ders raised toward the sun, sifting sand through her fingers. The sea air made her hungry, but she was determined to keep her figure throughout the pregnancy.

Several of Billy's Harvard friends were in Nassau, many still bachelors, playing tennis and golf. But Billy was still trying to define separate interests from his very sporting father. He played two holes of golf with Ann, then walked off the green. He acted as though he had invented a Woodward style of golf. Ann followed, proud to be playing with him. But Billy seemed more and more part of the crowd with whom he had grown up—rather than Ann's husband. Moreover, despite the fact that Ann was intent on making a good impression, Sarah, who was also pregnant, found her ill at ease around Billy's friends. It upset Sarah that Ann considered the beach a place to present herself sexually, in makeup and a glamorous bathing suit. Ann would never simply sit down and companionably read a book or chat on the sand. Waiting for Billy, she would be a restless blur—putting on mascara, powder, and lipstick and looking in the mirror to brush her hair. Sarah found it difficult to talk with Ann about anything other than Billy. Billy's friends thought that he felt more comfortable with the far more relaxed Sarah.

On the beach at sundown Billy asked Sarah to be the godmother of his next child. Ann learned of his request and was furious that she had not been consulted. Sarah and her husband asked him to a beach picnic with John Sims "Shipwreck" Kelly and Brenda Frazier. Billy agreed, again without consulting Ann. Ann sulked. Billy went without her.

One night the two couples and the Kellys were invited to a small dinner party at Jo Hartford Douglas's house. Billy enjoyed dancing to the live music. Ann was a popular dance partner, but she could not stop staring at her husband. Before midnight, Sarah asked her husband to take her home because she was feeling unwell. He did, then returned to the party. Ann saw them leave and asked Billy to take her home. Inside their beach bungalow, Ann hugged him and said she was ready for bed. Sex was at her instigation. But Billy wanted to go back to the party. He still felt like dancing. "Darling, stay with me," said Ann.

Billy felt guilty, but dancing with debutantes like Brenda Frazier, whom he had known since childhood, was his favorite physical recreation. Ann watched him raise his palm. "Go ahead, hit me," she said. Their sexual connection was frequently made after Billy hit her and felt contrite. But this time, he simply heaved an angry sigh, yelled, "Get out of my way," and pushed her to one side of the door.

One bungalow away, Sarah was in bed when she heard someone open her front door. Ann entered her bedroom weeping and swept a hairbrush from Sarah's bureau. Ann took off one of her pumps and threw it, shattering a wall mirror, then stood looking at her broken image. Although terrified by Ann's violence, Sarah gave her a tentative smile: "My God, what's happened?"

But Ann rushed out. Then the front door slammed, and she was back. Her anger was dissipating. "I don't understand you people. Why did you let Ed go back to the party?"

Sarah saw that it was a fit of jealousy. Ann was not drunk. "Oh, God, I'm sorry," Ann said, and turned to flee again. "Billy will be furious."

Sarah got out of bed to sweep up the glass with a short broom. She was still at it a few minutes later when her husband returned. "What the hell's been going on here?" he asked. Sarah did not say a word.

On January 14, 1948, little James Thomas Woodward was a year old and Ann had fulfilled her duty by delivering, in the British phrase, an heir and a spare. Upon hearing of Jimmy's birth, his godmother, Lady Sarah Churchill, had sent him a leather-bound novel, as she would on every birthday until he took his own life at the age of twenty-seven. Named for his grandfather's brother and mentor, the gruff man of business, Jimmy was a beautiful, towheaded baby, who looked startlingly like Ann's brother, little Jesse Jr. ("I'm a mongrel," Jimmy would tell people, smiling, as he grew older, "a mix of blue and red blood.") He was a sensitive boy, determined to do something for humanity and not marry "a bitchy girl after my money." The child inherited Ann's father's love of nature and his magnetism. His well-mannered older brother, Woody, seemed more like a Woodward.

Although his parents were too busy traveling and fighting with each other to give him much attention, Jimmy elicited protective feelings in others. Livio "Lee" Principe, the Woodward chauffeur, hugged him often, bought him licorice, and took him for rides. The two little boys had a strict Scottish governess who made schedules for them on blackboards and gave them stars for promptness and penalties for speaking too loudly. As a preschooler, Jimmy was operated on for flat feet and spent months in a wheelchair, his feet and legs in casts. Jack James and his wife wondered why the Woodwards made him endure so much pain for such a small problem. The birth of their second son did not bring Billy and Ann closer. Billy continued to leave his young family for long weekends with Marina Torlonia in Los Angeles.

Elsie now believed that Billy was the black sheep of the family. He seemed chronically bored and disappointed. Any respect he had ever achieved had come to him from the impact his father had had on the world—not for anything he had accomplished. He had decided he was not good enough to compete. One afternoon, Elsie ordered Ann to come downstairs to tea. Ann, Billy, and their sons were still living in Elsie's house. "The boys are running Mr. Putz ragged," Elsie announced, as she poured the tea into china cups decorated with portraits of Belair horses. She was tired of having Ann and her grandsons underfoot. "It is time Billy was the head of his own home," Elsie said. It would have been less of a problem, she implied, if Ann and the boys had a separate entrance.

Ann soon found a five-story town house on East Seventy-third Street. It had an intimate feel and splendid, tall windows. Billy had mixed feelings about leading a household of his own, but he agreed to buy it, just before making one of his frequent escapes to be with Marina. The granite mansion fulfilled Ann's fantasies, although she would later recall the time spent as a newlywed on East Eighty-sixth Street as the happiest in her life. Ann filled the new house with eighteenth-century French furniture and soft, pastel silk brocades, a decision that irked Elsie, who preferred the English style.

The dining room's eight tall French doors, draped in heavy pale silk, overlooked a shaded, barren garden. The sparse hedges became dirty in the New York grime. Ann complained about the garden instead of about her marriage, finally cementing most of it over. The third floor included a pale blue master bedroom suite with two dressing rooms and two bathrooms. Ann's three-way mirror hung in her bright blue tiled bathroom. Billy often slept in the next room, the paneled library. The small fourth floor was the children's floor, with bedrooms for Woody, Jimmy, and their governess. An exercise bar was mounted in the doorway of Jimmy's bedroom. The cramped fifth floor was the servants' quarters.

Although Billy's trust fund did not permit a full staff, the family had a cook, a maid who took care of Ann's wardrobe and also waited on table and cleaned, and a series of English butlers.

Ann designed a wrought-iron gated elevator. As was the fashion, she installed a smoked-glass mirror on the entire staircase wall. The fireplaces were pink mottled marble, a color Ann told Billy was sexual: it reminded her of the intimate parts of the body. Across from the elevator on the second floor there was a closet bar and next to that, behind a door, a six-foot-high metal safe.

In the library, Ann installed two six-foot fish tanks. Billy would spend hours staring at the fish—often while drinking brandy with guests. After about a year on Seventy-third Street, Billy whispered to Jack James in the drawing room, lit only by the fish tanks, while their wives sat sipping coffee, "Look, that gray fish is crazy. It's both a boy and a girl. It doesn't need a mate. It just screws itself."

Ann could no longer sleep well. She began to eat sweets and gained ten pounds. By April 1948, she was taking codeine for her insomnia and head-aches, marking the beginning of her dependency on drugs. She said she used them to strengthen herself in her fight to keep Billy. Despite Ann and Billy's troubles, parties at the Woodwards were splendid affairs. Billy, who was socially ill at ease, depended on Ann, challenging her to rival his mother's skills as New York society's outstanding hostess. Ann rehearsed her dinner parties during the afternoon, treating them like dramatic events. She called Lanfranco Rasponi and wrote pages of notes, including lists of courses and diagrams of china and silverware settings.

In the next several years, the young Woodwards gave large dinner parties for the Duke and Duchess of Windsor. The fireplaces blazed. Ann drenched candles in Chanel No. 5, a practice she had learned in the south of France. Guests at small tables enjoyed the music of a pianist and a strolling violinist named Henry Rosner, who played romantic Hungarian songs on his violin. He liked Ann: when he sent her a bill, she always added at least $50 to his fee.

At one of the parties for the Windsors, a butler discreetly summoned Ann to the kitchen, where he showed her several burnt baked Alaskas. "Can't you manage anything right?" asked Billy, just behind her. Dis-traught, Ann apologized profusely to the guests. The inebriated Duke of Windsor did not care for baked Alaska. Billy winked and shrugged off his questioning stare. Ann's mood improved after dinner, when her guests applauded as Ethel Merman and Russell Nype entertained with songs from their hit show *Call Me Madam*.

When, at another party, Billy commented that the servants had failed to serve the cake on the new Spode china, Ann threw cake plates at the cook.

Ann's problem as a hostess was her lack of calm. She stared at guests as if willing them to enjoy her party. She would repeat bits of casual praise for her floral decorations or scented candles to Billy. Although Billy sus-pected that the guests' remarks were mere politeness, her efforts to please sometimes touched him.

Billy did not feel the same pressure to be polite. Once, after dinner one evening, the young Duke of Marlborough went upstairs to use the telephone, and Billy said, "I bet he's up there sponging on us, England being in such a bad way after the war. I have a feeling he is calling overseas." Billy telephoned the overseas operator. "In the last five minutes, have you booked any calls to my number?" Billy told the Duke, "Please pay me the charges."

Billy usually kept his entertaining with Ann and his ongoing affair with Marina in separate spheres. But at one cocktail party his two worlds collided. It had been going well for about two hours. The liquor was flowing. David Selznick and his wife, Irene Mayer Selznick, were the center of attention. Then, just before the guests began to leave, Putz, on loan for the evening from Elsie, ushered in a dramatic late guest—Princess Marina Torlonia Shields, just back from Rome. Conversation stopped as Marina, in a regal black dress, entered on the arm of Bean Baker. "We're on our way to dinner," Marina said.

Ann clutched Billy's elbow: "I want that Italian whore out of my house." "You've been flirting so hard all afternoon I'm surprised you even noticed her," said Billy. He looked excited to see the two women in the same room. Marina retreated up the stairs to the drawing room. Then she pulled Bean up by the hand, and they ran down the stairs and out into the night.

After the party, Ann and Billy faced each other in front of a pink marble fireplace. Butler Sidney Mutum was retrieving cocktail glasses. "How dare you invite her?" asked Ann.

"I didn't."

"You liar."

As Mutum carried his tray of daiquiri glasses toward the kitchen, he heard Billy hit Ann and turned to see Ann hugging Billy.

Ann told her friend socialite Natalie Sherman that she was unhappy. "But why?" "Why?" said Ann. "Well, if C. Z. Guest is greeted at a party by somebody she doesn't want to talk to, she turns her back. Nobody says she's been impolite. Nobody even whispers that she's not a wonderful person." Natalie Sherman was aghast. "Ann, that's not nice."

Ann had broken a taboo by discussing the social pecking order. Superior caste gave C. Z. Guest and the Woodwards unlimited authority. As a young woman, C. Z. Guest had danced in the *Ziegfeld Follies* and had gone to Hollywood under contract to Fox, made no movies, but had romances with Victor Mature and Errol Flynn. Flynn's drinking buddy

Diego Rivera painted her in the nude; the picture hung behind a Mexican bar. However, unlike Ann, C.Z. was accepted by the Long Island social set. Winston Guest had been confidently told about the nude painting, and friends say he gallantly purchased it. C.Z. simply had what was viewed as "class": lovely manners and a "good" family name.

By the winter of 1948, Billy was spending long afternoons with Marina. One day, at lunch on Wall Street, he told Jack James that Frank Shields's wife was inviting him to hotel assignations. James had a pang of worry about Ann, who struck him as more and more frazzled. Jack also noticed that unlike other restaurant patrons, Billy had not shaved. When asked why, Billy explained, "I don't shave unless I have an afternoon romantic appointment. Otherwise I shave at night for parties, when it counts."

By the time she fell in love with Billy, Marina Torlonia Shields was a disappointed wife. Frank chafed and drank and disappeared to parties "for business reasons." He was also using his fists in public fights and on her. His many loves included Merle Oberon, Joan Bennett, Norma Shearer, and Marilyn Monroe. To Billy's delight, Marina proposed marriage to him. She knew, as Ann had learned years earlier, that to keep Billy's attention a woman had to take the lead. Although he stalled about marriage, Billy continued to send her love letters.

In the spring of 1948, Marina's best friend, Audrey Chapin, flew to Los Angeles. The two women loved to tell about their adventures, laughing. Marina later told Billy how that particular visit had been the final blow to her marriage. Frank Shields had given up on screen tests and was trying to sell insurance to Louis B. Mayer, still head of MGM. When during dinner Audrey inadvertently insulted Mr. Mayer, both women had a fit of giggles and Frank threw them out. Marina was glad to be set free.

Marina and Audrey and the Shields children flew to the Torlonia palace in Rome, which was owned by her brother. Marina telephoned Billy immediately and invited him to join them.

After accepting Marina's invitation, Billy suggested to Ann that he accompany her to Paris to the collections. He knew he would be able to escape to see Marina. Soon after Billy and Ann arrived in Paris, they received word that Billy's father was too ill to attend the St. Leger race in Doncaster, England, where his prize stallion, Black Tarquin, was racing. Billy turned down his father's request to represent the family at the race, dispatching Ann instead. She was thrilled. Black Tarquin won a decisive

Mrs. William Woodward, Jr., in a gown by the designer Charles James, photographed by John Rawlings for the December 1, 1945, issue of *Vogue*. Ann and Billy had been married for two years and were still living with his parents, Elsie and William Woodward.

Princess Marina Torlonia with her husband, tennis champion Frank Shields, Los Angeles, 1944. (Note his resemblance to his granddaughter, actress Brooke Shields.) Marina had been the object of the first international custody battle, between her mother, a member of the Moore family of Connecticut, and Prince Torlonia of Rome.

Woody and Ann (holding Jimmy, who was then nine months old), Long Island, 1945.

victory at St. Leger, for which the Woodwards collected 15,260 pounds. Ann accepted the trophy as the crowd roared approval, and she was presented to young Queen Elizabeth.

Meanwhile, in Rome, Billy, Audrey, and Marina laughed about Ann putting on airs in England. Billy stayed at the sixteenth-century Torlonia palace, near the Spanish Steps. The palace was as big as a Manhattan block. Three elegant shops filled the first floor. Twenty-five-foot-high gates opened into the marble courtyard that held an ancient stone fountain. When Marina's mother married Prince Torlonia, her family had paid hundreds of thousands of dollars to refurbish the palace. Billy's bedroom overlooked the lively Via dei Condotti, a fashionable street. The second floor included formal ballrooms and a chapel with stained-glass windows. The ballrooms and dining room had intricate parquet floors and twenty-foot ceilings embellished with clouds and cherubs.

Marina, Billy, and Audrey tormented Prince Alessandro, their reluctant host, who had recently fallen in love with his young chauffeur. One sunny afternoon, they had the chauffeur drive them to a nude beach on the island of Capri. At sundown, they found that the hotels were filled. The chauffeur slept in the car, while Billy, Audrey, and Marina shared one small bed in a beachfront hotel room, with Billy in the middle. The laughter and frivolity reminded Billy of his lost week in San Francisco after the *Liscome Bay* sinking. The next day, Prince Alessandro appeared in Capri and demanded that the young boy return to the palace. Marina and Billy contrived to travel back to the United States on the same ship after Billy cabled Ann to return to America directly from England.

In the fall of 1948, Marina moved to New York to be near Billy. Her sons, Frank and Willy, were enrolled at the Buckley School. They moved into the Volney, a residential hotel at Seventy-third Street and Madison Avenue, until her furniture arrived. Soon they would rent an apartment at 70 East Seventy-seventh Street, adjacent to the Carlyle Hotel. Marina brought her Steinway piano, her Roman family portraits, and antique cabinets filled with carved ivory animals. She reupholstered her cream-colored sofas and chairs.

One night, after Billy had hinted that he had not been in Rome alone, Ann insisted on all the details. She was particularly hurt by the Capri episode and asked Billy if he still wanted two women in bed with him. He said yes. As usual, Ann converted the heat of the fight into a steamy seduction. That fall Billy was on the verge of agreeing to marry Marina. His encouragement gave her the impetus to institute divorce proceedings against Shields. Meanwhile, Ann had hired a detective, who had photographed the lovers walking hand in hand in Central Park. Ann kept the photograph in her handbag.*

Billy came home late one night and slipped into the library across from the master bedroom. Brandishing the photograph, Ann strode through the door. He tried to grab the snapshot out of her hand. When she held it behind her back, he punched her arm. They exchanged blows until Billy said, "Let's get it over with. I want a divorce." Something had changed between them. "No, please, no divorce," Ann said. The photograph fell to the floor.

At about 2:30 a.m. Maurice Page, the butler on the fifth floor, heard screams. "You no-good bastard," Ann was yelling. "Go to your wop princess." Billy grabbed her nightgown and pushed her away from him. The sounds of the fight tumbled out into the night through an open window. A neighbor called the police.

Ann hid upstairs, while Billy sat with the police in the dining room, sheepish and smiling his apologies. As soon as they left, Billy raced out into the night. Ann screamed after him, "I'll never let you go."

---

*In late October 1955, Ann reluctantly answered questions about Marina Torlonia. Her interrogator was the Long Island chief assistant district attorney, Edward Robinson.

ANN WOODWARD: Her whole name was Marina Torlonia Shields.

EDWARD ROBINSON: Do you know where she lived at that time?

ANN WOODWARD: She lived near the Carlyle Hotel.

EDWARD ROBINSON: The name that you have given me includes her married name, or do you remember?

ANN WOODWARD: Shields is her married name. Torlonia was the name—her maiden name.

EDWARD ROBINSON: Do you know where they live now?

ANN WOODWARD: She has since divorced and I don't know where she lives now.

EDWARD ROBINSON: Do you know whether she still goes under the name Shields?

ANN WOODWARD: No. She married again.

EDWARD ROBINSON: Does the name Slater mean anything to you?

ANN WOODWARD: Yes, sir.

EDWARD ROBINSON: Is that her present married name?

ANN WOODWARD: Yes, that's it. I knew it was something that began with s.

EDWARD ROBINSON: Was there any trouble brewing between you and Mr. Woodward because of these things? I want you to be very frank with me, if you can, Mrs. Woodward.

ANN WOODWARD: Well, there was, because he saw this woman for rather a long—I mean a long period of time. And I think she may have very much wanted to marry my husband. My husband was very attractive. I can understand that.

The Brook Club butler in gray uniform with red piping looked the other way when Mr. Woodward made his 3 a.m. entrance. At the Brook, Billy wore slippers with the club crest, took martinis from butlers' trays, and imagined he was a boy again, living in the protected splendor of his parents' domain. (The same architect designed both buildings.) The club was open twenty-four hours a day: members could eat a solitary meal, cash a check, or move in. Billy called Marina at 4 a.m. and told her they would be married. He telephoned Maurice Page and asked him to pack his bags.

The next morning, Ann barricaded herself in her bedroom to hide her swollen face. She rang the butler for an ice pack. When Jimmy knocked to say good-bye before he left for school, she refused to let him come in. At noon, Ann instructed a locksmith to change the locks on both front doors. She took no phone calls. In the late afternoon, her physician, Dr. John Prutting, was admitted to her bedroom. Dr. Prutting attended her for years, listening to her woes and acting as her informal psychiatrist. He also supplied Ann with tranquilizers, sleeping pills, antidepressants, and amphetamines. "I fell down the stairs," she told him. He diagnosed a mild concussion.

Ann called the society divorce lawyer Sol Rosenblatt. He told her not to allow Billy or his parents to see their grandchildren. The next afternoon, Billy's father pulled up in his Rolls-Royce. Ann hysterically instructed the butler not to admit him and had the maid lock the children in their bedrooms. "I would like to see my grandchildren," said William Woodward, Sr., at the front door. Page knew that the famous sportsman had financed the house. He had little respect for Ann, who seemed hysterical most of the time, nor did he think much of her husband, an odd duck who always appeared smiling after their fights. So he risked his job to take old Mr. Woodward up on the elevator to see his grandsons. Woodward left after assuring himself that the boys were fine.

By the end of September 1948, Billy and Ann had officially separated. Ann had hired Rosenblatt as her matrimonial lawyer because he was known as a fixer in Billy's crowd. Rosenblatt was brilliant, Oklahoma-born and Harvard-educated, and the only Jewish member of the circle. He adored society people. His wife was the elegant international beauty Estrella Boissevain. Rosenblatt had a mystique: he had been shot in the leg by a hit man during a court case contesting the J. P. Morgan will. He had connections and was said to be an important man to know when things got hot. Louis B. Mayer had hinted that Rosenblatt had once been a big help in a crisis involving unions. He was invited to Clare Boothe Luce's dinner parties and was a close friend of both Governor Averell Harriman and political boss Carmine DeSapio.

Adept at extracting satisfying sums of money for the discarded wives of wealthy socialites, Rosenblatt did everything he could for his clients, who included his wife's best friend, Marlene Dietrich, as well as Eleanor Whitney and Elsa Maxwell. He provided a handkerchief for Ann's tears during intimate lunches at the Côte Basque and offered help with taxes and travel plans. When the dust settled, Rosenblatt set expensive terms. Ann asked for another chance or $2 million. Since Billy had only his income from the trust from his grandfather's estate, it would be up to his parents whether to bail him out by paying Ann the $2 million.

During the first two months of the separation, Ann lost weight until she looked, as she called it, "sexy skinny." She scrambled to go to parties to show Billy that she was desirable. She seemed to regain some of her old drive and sparkle.

In October she appeared alone at the Bal des Symphonies at the Plaza Hotel, where other guests included Mrs. Lytle Hull, the Alexander Cushings, Adele Astaire Douglas, William de Rham, and Prince Serge Obolensky. Ann looked ten years younger than she had six months earlier. She was now taking Dexedrine for dieting and as an antidepressant. Her blond hair was pulled back tight, her face taut. After dinner, she created her own party in a revealing green sheath dress with horizontal pleats. She dipped with dancing master de Rham. She also danced up to Obolensky, who was doing the tango with Adele Astaire Douglas.* A surprised Adele allowed Ann to cut in. It was not hard at such times for women to dislike her, nor for men to imagine her in bed. The gossip that night was that Ann had simply been too much for poor Billy to handle.

Soon after Billy moved into the Brook, he changed his will again. He had originally left one third of his estate to his wife, as well as a bequest of $2 million. But he reduced Ann's inheritance to income on one third of the estate and the minimum widow's stipend of $2,500, required at the time under New York State law. For every dollar Billy decided not to give to Ann, the state and federal government would take seventy-five cents. By the time of his death in 1955, at which time his December 14, 1948, will was still in effect, his estate was worth well over $10 million—and his executors were required to pay over $2 million more to the government because he had not left a larger sum to Ann.

---

*She was an early partner of her brother, Fred Astaire.

In December 1948, a few days after Ann's birthday, Billy formally asked Ann for a divorce. Marina's friends crossed their fingers for her. Billy's parents grumbled but agreed to pay the $2 million for his freedom. The separation agreement was signed.* Billy's idyll with Marina was more a romance than a sexual obsession. Ann's detective, Walter Kerr, watched them dance cheek-to-cheek at El Morocco and laugh as they walked up Madison Avenue. But he saw them enter the Lowell Hotel only on rare occasions.

As Ann became more terrified of life without Billy, she began pinching pennies. She had her butler drive her to Loehmann's discount store in Brooklyn, where she bought suits and gowns into which her seamstress sewed her old Balenciaga and Dior labels. Ann discovered that Billy, too, had hired a private detective, who was now tapping her telephone. If he could prove that Ann had committed adultery, under New York law at the time, he would not have to pay her the $2 million specified in the separation agreement. When Jack James's wife visited, she and Ann sat sipping tea on the green silk divan with the radio between them playing at full volume because Ann knew Billy had had the entire house bugged.

That December, Billy felt uneasy sharing Marina's elaborate Christmas with her boys. Instead, he went to Bermuda to visit Prince and Princess Kyril Scherbatow (whose ancestors were princes of Kiev and Chernigov more than a thousand years ago). At that time, Bermuda was a paradise. The terrace of the Scherbatow estate, High Times, was only six feet from the sea. The Early American furnishings had been brought from Newport on Vincent Astor's yacht, the *Nourmahal.* Feeling relaxed and rakish away from his family, Billy sat by the hour on the coral beach. He unbuttoned his white shirt, tying the tails over his flat bare stomach. He flirted with the beautiful Constance Woodworth, a few years his senior, who was a *Journal-American* gossip columnist, former model, and girlfriend of Serge Obolensky. They took long afternoon walks in the woods.

Meanwhile, Ann flew off to Paris and on to the French Riviera to accept a long-standing invitation to have a fling with Prince Aly Khan, whose father, the Aga Khan, was the spiritual leader of 15 million Moslems.** Aly Khan was the foremost playboy in the world, a charmer of

*The existence of this signed agreement is at odds with the story told by many New York socialites concerning the Woodward shooting, who insist that the senior Woodwards made a $1 million counter offer, which Ann turned down. They claim that this was the actual reason why Billy stuck with Ann, thus making Ann's greed into myth.

**Aly would never become the Aga Khan. His tempestuous courtship, marriage, and ultimate divorce from Rita Hayworth, as well as his gambling debts and flamboyant living, caused his disapproving father to pass him over in favor of his son, Karim, a handsome Harvard student with a strong sense of privacy and public decorum. Aly never recovered from the shock.

women, an expert polo player, gentleman jockey, and horse breeder. He gave Ann a sari made from eighteen-karat gold thread. At the time, Aly was about to marry Rita Hayworth, who was then living with him.

In one important way, the dissolute Aly Khan was like Ann: he was, for all his fabulous wealth, an outsider. He, too, had used sexual seduction to fight his way into high society. His mother had been an Italian dancer with the Casino ballet in Monte Carlo. A woman had once refused to be seated next to his father at dinner. "But it is the Aga Khan," said her hostess. "I don't care what it is," she replied, "it's black." In 1898, the old Aga Khan had had to live with advertisements in English buses that declared a brand of chocolate to be "rich and dark like the Aga Khan." Aly had encountered similar hostility as a boy, in particular because the Aga Khan was determined to become an English gentleman. To the British upper crust, Aly was still known as a "wog, a greasy green wop." In middle age, he delighted in telling people, "They called me a bloody nigger, and I paid them back by winning all their women."

Part of Aly Khan's legend was his ability to have sex for hours. His secret was that he stopped to douse his wrists and penis with ice-cold water. Like most great seducers, his appeal was his enthusiasm.

Ann was photographed during that week beaming and suntanned on Aly's yacht at Cannes. (Rita Hayworth could be seen in the foreground.) Ann's halter showed off her taut midriff. Her hair was long and flowing like a girl's, the style that most became her.

Although the Aly Khan affair gave Billy the ammunition with which to divorce Ann without paying the $2 million, it had the opposite effect: it quickened Billy's interest in her. Billy soon found an excuse to visit his Seventy-third Street home, and Ann propeled him into bed. While he continued to squire Marina about town, he began to see Ann secretly as well. Ann persuaded him to tell her all about his relationship with Marina. Putting aside hurt feelings, she bound Billy to her more intimately than ever by extracting these confidences.

11

BILLY COMES BACK

As 1948 drew to a close, Bean Baker was twenty-seven years old and desperate. It surprised no one that his marriage was on the rocks. Bean had used Alicia's trips to nurse her marital wounds in her native Mexico as license to get drunk and go out with more girls. Like the Aly Khan, he was a Pied Piper to women. Like Billy, Bean had recently proposed to a society girl. Both were returning to the rules of their class. When Alicia heard that Bean's mother had received the girl to whom he had proposed for luncheon at their home, she agreed to a divorce.

One night in January, Bean had been drinking and carousing in Tallahassee with his buddy, saloon owner Floyd "Shorty" Whiddon. Bean's other companions included Shorty's wife, Helen, their dog, and a girl named Thelma "Puddin' " Griffiths, the divorced wife of a letter carrier. She was twenty-one and had waited on them earlier that evening at a juke joint. Bean invited her to put down her apron and join them. After dinner, Bean drove the Whiddon car seventeen miles to the 13,000-acre Horseshoe plantation owned by his family. They turned off the Thomasville highway onto a private dirt road, past tall trees hung with Spanish moss. It was after three in the morning, and the household was asleep.

After a visit—of disputed length—Bean asked Puddin' to ride with him back to the highway. As the Whiddons drove off, Bean backed his army jeep out of the garage. Then he raced to catch up with Shorty on the dark road. He gave the girl his jacket; she was cold. She held tight to the side of the open jeep to keep from bouncing out. Bean asked her to hand him his customized .38-caliber gun from the pocket of the jacket she was wearing. He fired a shot at the sky, signaling Shorty. Suddenly, Bean lost control of the jeep, which jumped an embankment.

When the girl regained consciousness, she saw Bean lying facedown in the middle of the road. She ran to the highway to tell the Whiddons. Meanwhile, Bean also regained consciousness and turned off the jeep motor. He shot the gun, in an apparent attempt to summon help. As the police reconstructed it, however, because he was drunk and in shock, he shot himself in the head.

Moments later, his mother, Edith Baker, found him, mortally wounded, brought him up to the house, called the police, and began to cover up Bean's problems. She asked reporters not to mention his drinking, his fanatic interest in guns, or his drinking companions on his last night. Mrs. Baker told the press that Bean and Alicia had been happily married, that Alicia had come from a wealthy family and had always been graciously accepted by the Bakers.

Cholly Knickerbocker, the society columnist protested the Baker family cover-up: "The mysterious death of Grenville (Bean) Baker remains the No. 1 topic of conversation everywhere you go in New York. Naturally all my sympathy goes to his mother, the socially omnipotent Mrs. George Baker. However I must disagree with statements issued by the family that Alicia and the young banking heir were not estranged. The fact is that the matter of a divorce had been all but settled and Alicia was prepared to go West to obtain it. . . . On Bean's recent visits to New York, he told friends of his adamant desire to terminate the marriage. Alicia was the one who tried to talk him out of the divorce."

Mrs. Baker's friends, peers, children, and grandchildren swear to a kind of Bean Baker myth. They say that Bean was murdered by a "colored" foreman for "fooling around with the man's wife." They believe Mrs. Baker lied to keep scandal from her family name and that she had the money and power to divert the course of the criminal justice system.

The day after Bean's death, his older sister, Florynce, telephoned the Woodward house on East Seventy-third Street. She told Ann, "I'm calling to tell you and Billy that Bean died in a freak accident at Horseshoe." Shocked, Ann replied that she and Billy were separated. Florynce had heard talk about the Woodwards' fights. Like Alicia and Bean, they seemed to be able to live neither together nor apart. "I'm sorry, Ann," Florynce said. "Please call and tell Billy that Mother wants him to be an honorary pallbearer."

Left to right: Christian Dior, Estrella Boissevain, Marlene Dietrich, and Sol Rosenblatt at a ball at the Plaza, New York, 1947.

L'Horizon Château at Cannes, 1948. Ann Woodward (standing, center) was invited as the guest of Prince Aly Khan (seated, left), who was to be married to Rita Hayworth (seated, right) in May 1949.

Billy Woodward with Constance
Woodworth at the estate "High
Times" of Prince and Princess
Scherbatow, Bermuda, 1948.
During this time, Ann and Billy
were separated. Constance
Woodworth was a gossip colum-
nist for the *Journal-American*
and was said to be romantically
involved with Serge Obolensky.

Serge Obolensky's junket to Bermuda for the gala opening of Conrad Hilton's
Bermudiana Hotel, 1949. In the crowd, Conrad Hilton, T. Reed and Diana
Vreeland (top of stairs), Ann Woodward (leaning against stairs), Serge
Obolensky (kneeling).

Conrad Hilton dancing the Mexican hat dance (his favorite) with Ann Woodward at the Bermudiana Hotel ball. Ann and Billy, no longer separated, were on their second honeymoon.

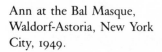

Ann at the Bal Masque, Waldorf-Astoria, New York City, 1949.

Billy Woodward's closest friend from childhood, Grenville "Bean" Baker, accidentally shot himself in the head while drunk at his family's plantation, Horseshoe, in Florida. Baker's body arrived at Pennsylvania Station, New York, on January 19, 1949.

Ann took a taxi to the Brook Club, where for several hours she waited for her husband's return. At the sight of his wife, Billy looked furious. But when she told him why she was there, he sagged. Billy did not resist her embrace.

In fact, Bean's death distanced Billy from Marina, perhaps in part because she had not known Bean well. The affair with Marina now seemed suddenly dangerous to Billy: he believed that if Bean had stayed home with Alicia he would still be alive. Billy postponed the divorce and told friends that Ann had asked for too much money.

Their friends believe, however, that Billy stayed married because he was a Woodward, a gentleman, whose wife never gave him permission to divorce.

On January 21, 1949, Ann accompanied Billy to Bean Baker's funeral. The day before, Billy and Ann had spent hours rummaging through piles of photographs of Bean. Elsie Woodward attended the service with her daughter Libby. The body had been shipped by train from Washington, where the FBI had performed an autopsy. It was brought to the All Souls Unitarian Church on Lexington Avenue and Eightieth Street, which Bean's grandfather had given the money to build.

Six hundred friends and members of the Baker family filled the church. Ann guided Billy to Alicia, who wore long black veils. Billy walked out beside the gray coffin, adorned only with a cross of white carnations, along with Eustice Paine, Jr., Grenville McVickers, and Anthony Villa. Ann rushed after him, even before the rest of the crowd left the church.

The finality of Bean's death terrified Billy. The two boyhood friends had always assumed they were too rich to get hurt. After all, they had emerged unscathed by the war. The name Horseshoe now seemed suddenly ironic.

Billy was deeply joined to Ann. Their intimacy included his free expression of revulsion. The fights they had had now seemed to them like amusing anecdotes. Billy even told Ann that he was flattered to have been followed by her private detective. Ann laughed about Kerr's blurred snapshot of Billy and Marina. They felt that their tempestuous romance had strained civilized bonds, but never died. Ann swore on her mother's old Kansas Bible that Billy was the great love of her life. He knew she was telling the truth. Ann took on a protective role. "I can't talk now," she would tell acquaintances who telephoned. "Billy needs me." She arranged to spirit her husband away to Hawaii with the children.

But soon afterward, Billy asked Ann to allow him to have affairs. In return, he would not divorce her. Ann tacitly consented. But though she tried to prevent him from straying, it became accepted practice that Billy spend a weekend alone at Belair or a night at the Brook Club.

In the late winter of 1949, Serge Obolensky invited the handsome young Woodwards to the opening of the Bermudiana Hotel. Curious about Billy's enthusiasm over his Christmas trip to Bermuda, Ann decided that she and Billy should accept and turn the trip into a winter honeymoon. Ann looked like a beautiful upper-class Englishwoman in her plaid skirt and sensible pumps. A feather curled above her small hat. She carried a small straw-colored suitcase for touching up her makeup en route.

The gala international party signaled that New York society had discovered Bermuda. Prince Obolensky had divorced Mary Astor and was now employed as a hotel publicist by her brother Vincent and by Conrad Hilton. His glamorous guests included Horst, the fashion photographer; Diana and T. Reed Vreeland; New England socialite Sally Iselin; extra man and *Family Circle* society writer Harry Evans; and Conrad Hilton's son Nicky, who would later marry Elizabeth Taylor. Ann made a conquest in Bermuda. At the ball, Conrad Hilton bent to her with a shy smile. Ann looked radiant in a strapless pale gown with a black lace Spanish mantilla tied over one shoulder. Billy glared, trying not to look impressed. Then Ann asked Hilton to dance the Mexican hat dance. Arms entwined, they skipped to the fast music. Stopping to greet Mrs. Anthony Eden, Ann felt a secret triumph. After taking the elegant name Eden for the stage, she was now within the golden circle.

One summer night in 1949, the butler drove Ann and Billy, in formal dress, to the exclusive Meadowbrook Club on Long Island. The club was a plain Colonial house set in large fields where, it was said, the best polo in America was played. Returning from the powder room, Ann saw Marina Torlonia on the porch, wearing her trademark black evening dress with a single large pearl on her prominent collarbone. Ann had sipped champagne. Liquor did not mix well with the pills she was taking: Dexedrine to curb her appetite, Thorazine to calm her nerves, and Seconal to put her to sleep.

Before Billy knew what Ann was doing, she strode outside to Marina. "Stay away from Billy," Ann said. "It's Billy you should speak to, is it not?" asked Marina.

A moment later, a waiter murmured to Billy, "Two ladies on the porch, sir, are fighting." Several waiters went outside. Ann and Marina were crying and hitting each other. After several minutes, the fight was stopped.

It was Ann's tantrum that ended Marina's relationship to Billy, although New York society would loyally maintain that Ann's scheming greed had caused the tragedy of Marina's life. To the ex-debutantes and their husbands, Marina was not "the other woman" but Billy's social peer. That gave her a moral position superior to Ann's claim on him.

A year later Marina ran into Ann at an annual fund-raising ball. This time Marina escorted her new husband, Ed Slater, over to meet Billy. Ann had been dancing with Serge Obolensky, but excused herself and went to her husband's side. It was clear that Marina was trying to show Billy that she was attractive to another presentable man.

Elsie decreed that Ann and Billy should go to Newport the following summer. Little Jimmy was one and a half years old and played in front of Bailey's Beach Club by the sea. It was there that society gathered for sunbathing, swimming, and tea sandwiches. Woody was only five, but he already had the flawless Woodward carriage. Although Billy had taken Ann back, Elsie had not. When Doris Duke organized a benefit to restore the navy buildings on Newport Beach, Elsie asked that Ann be "excused." The reason given: Ann needed to spend more time at home caring for her family.

One person in Newport society sympathized with Ann. Elaine Lorillard, who had also married into a wealthy family, saw that Ann was mortally frightened of Billy, who often accused her of doing or saying the wrong thing.

Billy impressed Elaine as a playboy, always looking for a good time, someone who had great energy, but who never channeled it. She saw him as clinically hyperactive. There almost seemed something wrong with his metabolism. He talked too fast, invariably about himself. Every night he had to go to the theater or to a nightclub.

Ann also worried about looking too old. Billy was thirty years old. One day Ann—who was thirty-six—and Elaine were having luncheon outdoors at the Clambake Club. Elaine was surprised to see in the sunlight that Ann had a good deal of gray in her hair. Perhaps Ann had been too distracted by her problems with Billy to have it dyed.

After the Newport summer, Elsie decided she was tired of her little grandchildren visiting at her Georgian manor house on Cedar Swamp Road in

Long Island. It was time for her son's family to find their own second home on the North Shore. Ann and Billy agreed with Elsie that the boys would be safer living in the country. And they liked the fact that that Long Island's North Shore was only forty-five minutes from Manhattan.

So in the summer of 1951 Ann began looking at houses that had been owned by J. P. Morgan, Ring Lardner, Basil Rathbone, and Leslie Howard. She chose a large yellow stucco Italian "Playhouse" to rent, one of twenty or so on the North Shore built not as residences but to protect clay tennis courts some 160 feet long, 80 feet wide, and 60 feet high.

Built by the heirs of the Woolworth family on their estate Sunken Orchard, the Woodward Playhouse had a magnificent exterior. It looked like a Roman country villa set among formal lawns, sculptured rose gardens, trellises, statuary, and a majestic swimming pool. A half mile from tranquil Long Island Sound, it was surrounded by pine forests. Tennis balls from the adjoining Pine Hollow Country Club bounced down the lawns.

While the grounds were splendid, the interior of the Playhouse was a warren of small dark rooms and two large unlivable spaces. Neighbors called it "the maze." The Woodward family lived in the front of the house, in quarters more cramped than a middle-class ranch house. In the back of the house was a nest of even smaller servants' quarters, where only the chauffeur slept. Also in the back, a musty music room was used to store a collection of the Woolworths' priceless Oriental rugs. It was paneled in dark oak taken from the fifteenth-century Scottish castle of the Duke of Essex, and the vaulted ceiling was more than fifty feet high. Ann had visions of turning it into a ballroom and throwing grand parties, but this room was not included in the $200-a-month rent.

Ann closed the balcony that overlooked the tennis courts and turned it into a living room. She transformed the ground-floor changing rooms into separate bedrooms for Billy and herself. Their rooms were joined by an eighteen-foot-long hallway. Billy's small bedroom had French wallpaper and an English rolltop desk. Ann installed an imposing metal jewelry safe in her closet. Her bedroom was furnished with French provincial pieces. But no matter what she did, the house retained a cramped, eccentric feeling.

The Woodwards were not the only tenants. The Woolworths rented the huge glass-enclosed tennis court to Cinerama Corporation for recording sound tracks to such films as *Around the World in 80 Days*. Sometimes as many as a hundred musicians traipsed over the grounds.

A year later, Billy and Ann bought the Playhouse and two acres of land from the Woolworths for $125,000. The title to the house was in Ann's name (in return for which she gave Billy an IOU in that amount).

Ann and Billy bought the "Playhouse" built by the Woolworth family in Oyster Bay Cove, Long Island. The Playhouse was originally designed to enclose a huge indoor tennis court (above, at left). The spectator and changing rooms were used by Ann and Billy and their children as living quarters (below). The back of the house was an enormous music chapel.

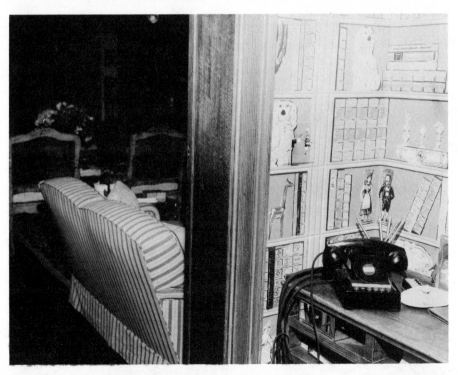

Above: the treillage in the Palladian gardens that surrounded the Playhouse.
Below: the Woodwards' pool. The main house of the estate, built by the daughter of F. W. Woolworth in 1927 for an estimated nine million dollars, was separated from the Playhouse by twenty-five acres.

In 1951, she paid another $60,000 for an additional twenty-three acres of pine forests. It was Ann's decision to keep Cinerama as a commercial tenant for tax purposes.

Ann took enormous pride in owning the estate. It made the constrictions of her new life worthwhile and helped her bury her memories of how she had lived in Kansas. She proudly told summer guests that the cobblestones in their circular driveway had been trod by Mary, Queen of Scots, on her way to her execution at Fotheringhay Castle.

That fall Ann and Billy left the boys at the Playhouse with their governess to attend Green Vale School while they traveled desperately—and sometimes separately—to parties around the world. The little boys took horseback riding, sailing, swimming, and tennis lessons at the nearby Piping Rock Club. Chauffeur Lee Principe drove Woody and Jimmy to school and in and out of Manhattan for weekends while Ann concentrated on pleasing her husband.

Principe adored the boys. Before the Woodwards hired him as chauffeur and handyman he had been a "grasshopper," mowing lawns. He had lived in the servants' quarters on the estates of Nelson Doubleday and Jay Gould. As a child he had helped his father milk cows on Theodore Roosevelt's Sagamore Hill.

Ann became known for giving the best children's parties on Long Island. For Woody's birthday in 1952, she asked Poppy Thomas, whose husband, Joseph, worked at Lehman Brothers, to bring a rare baby African antelope, called a duiker, which she had just received from Gussie Busch, the head of Anheuser-Busch. Mrs. Thomas wove a wreath of garden flowers for the animal's neck and drove it over in her station wagon. Ann, a butler, a cook, and a footman were chasing puppies, kittens, and little children all over the lawn. The little antelope joined the group, entering the garden near the trellised rose bushes. It was the hit of the party.

Ann often invited Poppy Thomas to play golf at Piping Rock. Ann thought they had much in common because they were both outsiders to Long Island society. But Mrs. Thomas did not wish to be friends. In her opinion, Ann played the Woodward role with too much force; not only that, she revealed too much bosom.

One stiflingly hot night, Ann and Billy's guests were dining on beef Wellington and champagne at four small white wrought-iron tables on the Playhouse lawn, overlooking the rose garden. The centerpieces were enormous cabbage roses. Battery-operated lanterns cast a romantic glow. A violinist strolled, playing central European songs. Joan Patterson, E. F. Hutton's favorite stepdaughter, told Mary and Laddie Sanford about her

Hudson River School paintings. Her husband, Ned, chatted with Fern Tailer Gimbel, a Baker heiress and beautiful leader of the younger social set. Harry Guggenheim and his wife, Alicia Patterson, spoke about the problems of building the circulation of her family's newspaper, *Newsday*.

Throughout dinner, guests felt grateful for the cool winds off Long Island Sound. Ned Patterson found Ann dazzling, with her unwavering turquoise eyes, as she began to question him closely about his work on Wall Street. She even wrote down a stock Ned liked. Ann imitated Elsie Woodward's manner of listening to an admired guest, her eyes fastening on his face. Like Elsie, Ann sometimes looked down to one side, as if provoked to thought. She asked intelligent questions and tried to guide the conversation toward the expertise of her companion.

At Billy's table, the conversation moved from quail hunting in Scotland to Beatrice Lillie and Joan Fontaine to fighting with gun makers in London over a short barrel. Billy's rapid-fire pattern of speech made one acquaintance remark that he was "overbred, like one of old Woodward's thoroughbreds."

Suddenly, young David Gimbel left the table. Ann quickly followed him to the Playhouse. After a moment Billy asked, "Where's my wife? Where's Ann?" He peered into the darkened grounds of his estate, alarmed that his handsome friend had also disappeared. Watching him, Ned Patterson got the impression that, without Ann, Billy lacked a host's authority. When Ann returned, she explained that David had taken ill. Since the chauffeur was busy, Ann had driven him home herself. "He didn't want to bother you," she told Fern.

"That's my wife," Billy said.

12

THE BEST TIMES

By 1952, Ann was filling her third leather-bound clippings album. Turning the pages kept her dream alive. The articles concerned such events as the horse set's prestigious Belmont Ball. Each time she saw herself written about as the "lovely society hostess Mrs. William Woodward, Jr.," it confirmed to her that she was an important person.

Before a party, she usually took a Dexedrine. As she entered, the photographers flocked to her. She arched her back, swinging around columns, and offered armfuls of flowers to the camera. There were no unflattering photos of Ann Woodward. Although Billy continued to belittle Ann's "social climbing," her publicity impressed him; after all, he was Mr. William Woodward, Jr., and his wife's beauty enhanced him.

His afternoon "dates" learned to accept these "silly social obligations." After a flirtatious cocktail hour at the Taft or Lowell hotels, he excused himself and returned home to dress for yet another public appearance with Ann.

At one dinner party, in the winter of 1952, Billy observed Ann and announced, "She looks ten years older than I." Ann soon began spending her mornings in consultations with plastic surgeons and dermatologists. She continued to put up a brave front, however, carrying herself like a beautiful young woman. Later in 1952 Ann was vindicated. She was named one of six great American beauties by *Vogue*. The other five women were all younger than Ann and born to great wealth.

Billy continued to appear with Ann in public, but he was merely following in the Edwardian tradition of his father, who functioned this way for decades with Elsie. Ann took his public appearances with her as encouraging signs of affection. But that winter she confided to Dr. Prutting that Billy might "fire her" at any moment. She begged in his quiet Park Avenue office until he increased her regimen of pills. "I need to be the strongest woman on earth to fight for Billy," Ann said.

In October 1952, Ann convinced Billy that he should take her to India. They were the guests of the Maharaja of Jaipur. During her separation from Billy in 1948, Ann had met the "Jai" in Paris through Aly Khan. Jai was India's outstanding polo player. Once, after his team had won a match near Paris, he placed Ann's hand in the crook of his arm and took her around the field. He spoke flawless Oxonian English, laughing with her over the fact that his daughter's wedding was listed in the *Guinness Book of Records* as the most expensive of all time.

Like Billy, Jai lived a life of leisure: tiger hunting, palaces, and jewels. Jai's ceremonial position was more frustrating since he had been the absolute sovereign of Jaipur until a few years after World War II. The polygamous Jaipur had also been known as a womanizer. Recently, people had spoken of his devotion to his new wife, the beautiful Ayesha. Ann and Ayesha never became friends.*

Ann and Billy lingered in Jaipur for six weeks, tiger hunting, sightseeing, and sipping sugared yogurt drinks in imperial splendor. They lived at the vast Rambagh Palace. Four hundred servants in bright pink turbans waited on Jai and his guests. The palace had been designed by Jai himself. The drawing rooms, bedrooms, verandas, cupolas, and scalloped arches were arranged around Lalique fountains and a courtyard. Ann and Billy stayed in the Mountbatten suite. An ancient jeweled bird with an emerald beak was poised on the mantel. Ann's dressing room alone was as large as her Oyster Bay bedroom.

Jai made Ann laugh when he greeted her in the morning by saying, "How's my wonder girl?" At breakfast in the garden, he amazed his guests by enticing peacocks to eat from his hand.

While Billy was content to sleep through breakfast, Ann was chauffeured each morning before sunrise past the old walls of fortresses and rare blue jacaranda trees surrounding the city. She photographed the lake that reflected the palace. Jaipur showed her his stunning collection of gems but did not permit her to photograph it.

In the afternoons, as she wandered the streets of Jaipur on her own,

---

*In 1975, Ann clipped a piece from *The New York Times* about how Ayesha, one of the most glamorous and wealthy Indian aristocrats and a member of Parliament since 1962, had been jailed as an outspoken critic of Prime Minister Indira Gandhi.

The Fan Ball at the Plaza Hotel, winter 1950. Ann Woodward (far left) with (back row) Mrs. Herbert Weston, Mrs. Igor Cassini, and (front) Mrs. Byron Foy, Mrs. Charles Amory. Other guests included Lady Sarah Churchill, Cecil Beaton, Fern Tailer Gimbel, and George Gene Nathan.

Ann Woodward, Claude Cartier, and Elsa Schiaparelli, 1951.

The Maharaja of Jaipur (photographed by Ann Woodward) was a ceremonial ruler who invited international society to his Rambagh Palace in Jaipur, India.

Jai, his wife Ayesha, and their son, with Ann, 1952.

Billy Woodward on safari, photographed by Ann, India, 1954.

Ann received salacious stares. She seemed to luxuriate in the hot sun, unlike most Westerners. She took hundreds of photographs of tigers and snakes, as well as of people in red, yellow, and pink turbans and robes. She bargained for gold silk and took pictures of the silver-and-gold ceremonial jewelry worn by the elephants on their feet and their foreheads. Wearing a tinkling anklet like the Indian women, she sat in a jeep and photographed Jai, high on his horse, playing polo against the sunset.

During the first week of the trip Billy disappeared to Jai's tiger-hunting camp some forty miles away from the palace in the foothills of the Himalayas. Even though it was customary for the men to hunt alone, Ann still felt abandoned. The following morning she had herself driven to the camp. Hoping to become Billy's hunting companion, Ann took shooting lessons and shot a double-barreled shotgun at targets stuck on banyan trees. The gun bearers joked fearfully at her wild aim. But, as always, any self-improvement project gave Ann hope.

The Woodwards were accompanied on that first trip to India by Los Angeles oil magnate Russell Havenstrite and his wife. The Havenstrites poked fun at Ann's "inability to pick up a water glass without help if it was more than a foot away from her." The night before the Havenstrites flew back to America, they witnessed a fight between the Woodwards. The two couples were staying in Delhi, at Jai's town house. Ann decided not to go out to a restaurant for dinner because she was experiencing severe menstrual cramps. Billy kissed her good-bye, promising to bring her some chicken and rice. When he returned, she came out of their bedroom, yawning, saying she was feeling better. "I'm starved," she said. "Where's my chicken?" Billy spread his empty hands. "Tough luck. I forgot, Annie." Ann burst into tears. "How could you? You never think of me."

Before leaving India, Ann and Billy celebrated the Hindu New Year, the Diwali festival, which fell in late October. As an American wife, Ann refused to stay back at the palace with Princess Ayesha and her ladies-in-waiting. She and Billy followed the Maharaja, who paid ceremonial visits, surrounded by his nobles. Later, the party returned to the palace to drink champagne and play roulette until dawn.

The Indian sojourn ended when Billy suddenly developed a fever. The palace doctor diagnosed a case of hepatitis. Ann had him rushed to the airport on a stretcher and flown by chartered plane directly to New York. His life was in danger for a week.

As he recovered his health, Billy escaped Ann's nursing to become involved with a six-foot-tall, platinum-blond French countess. Fernanda Montel swept into town in February 1953 to sing at the St. Regis Maisonette—and Billy was one of her conquests. Her nightclub act involved suggestive hip swings and romantic monologues about what men needed. Her low voice was the least interesting part of her camp presentation. *The New Yorker* called her work a curious combination of narcissism and humorous self-deprecation, saying appreciatively, "Miss Montel's striking physique and her deep husky voice . . . [seem] forever in danger of becoming too impassioned. Miss Montel is, after all, a true Frenchwoman, from her sharp fingertips to her spike heels." The review concluded, "Undulating about the small floor, she often gives the impression that her singing is an afterthought, and in fact she has very little in the way of voice." Fernanda Montel appeared in one of her ten floor-length mink coats over a sequined gown. She wore clothes with the same panache as Ann, kept herself tan and thin at the waistline, and, like Ann, she loved to laugh.

Dancing with her, Billy looked boyish and slight. She told him that his gifts to her must come only from Cartier and that her formal title was the Countess de Castro Monte. That she was a known lesbian added to Billy's appreciation of her. While Fernanda was in town, Billy stayed at the Brook Club. If it came to divorce this time, Ann would get no further dirt on him. Ann resented the Brook as she might another woman. After three days, she began to telephone him, but Billy ignored her. Using a men's club was a Woodward family tradition. After all, his father did not always sleep at home after a long victorious racing trip. Meanwhile, Ann was having Billy trailed as far away as the Ritz Hotel in Montreal. By now Billy was keeping a dinner jacket, two dark suits, shoes, evening slippers, a duplicate bathrobe, underwear, and shirts and ties at the Brook.

On the fourth day of Billy's absence, Ann took a taxicab to East Fifty-fourth Street to the Brook. With the cab waiting in front, Ann ignored the "strangers' room" (where she was told to wait) and climbed the spiral staircase to the third floor. There she found herself in front of a small group of men silently eating dinner at a thirty-foot baronial table under a famous Gilbert Stuart portrait of George Washington. Billy jolted to his feet, looking at Ann with a combination of fear (she had violated the club's prohibition against women on the premises) and admiration.

"Darling, the car is waiting," said Ann. Billy propelled her out by the elbow. Then they ran down the staircase giggling. The coatroom butler did not speak. The rules, as always, bent for Billy Woodward. Back home, however, Billy locked himself in the library across from their bedroom. After changing into an apricot silk bathrobe, Ann began to bang on the door until he relented. As so often with them, rage had become foreplay. Later that night in bed Ann described her illicit entry. She had encountered a frightened butler in a gray cutaway on the staircase. Billy toasted her as the only woman in club history who had dared such a feat.

Ann had met Salvador Dalí at the Park Avenue apartment of her lawyer, Sol Rosenblatt. Dalí told Ann she made his mustache vibrate. "If I were a beautiful woman, I would be you," he whispered, kissing her hand. She commissioned him to paint her portrait. Ann had just finished sitting for a portrait by John Klett that showed her wearing a low-cut white evening gown and three strands of pearls. The artist took years off her face, highlighting her cheekbones and enlarging her crimson mouth. This portrait resembled the photographs of Joan Crawford sold in Woolworth picture frames. It also showed Ann's uneven nostrils, making her look like a sexual animal in refined evening garb. The finishing touch was a nosegay of violets held between the tips of her long polished fingernails. But the painting was not a work of art, and C. Z. Guest was having her daughter painted by Dalí.

Dalí and Ann Woodward had temperamental similarities. They were both unabashed show-offs who loved to see their names in the newspapers. They felt most alive when hobnobbing with the rich and famous. Each had a manic-depressive streak, a stubborn will, and an intensity that would later exhibit itself as paranoia. They both depended heavily on sleeping pills, Dexedrine, and tranquilizers. Ann arrived at Dalí's room at the St. Regis for her first sitting wearing an evening gown under her ermine coat. Dalí helped her choose her emerald engagement ring and her diamond sapphire necklace. She confided that she wanted to give the portrait to her son Woody—it would be a valuable work of art.

Dalí asked, "What are your favorite colors?"

She listed the colors that Peter Pels had selected for her years before. "Pastels—blue, beige, green, and gray."

"And your favorite place?" Ann described a beach by the sea.

"I, Dalí, will paint a masterpiece," he said, serving her a glass of orange juice.

Alas, Dalí was no longer painting masterpieces. He preferred to make money by painting quick portraits of socialites and by supplying drawings to advertise Wrigley's chewing gum. After the third sitting, Dalí told Ann he was leaving for Spain. In one year—by the spring of 1953—her picture would be complete.

Few society people minded if Dalí painted them with lizards instead of hair. He had painted Mrs. Harrison Williams, once called the best-dressed woman in the world, barefoot and in a ragged Grecian tunic. Helena Rubinstein appeared as if projecting from a rocky cliff.

Thirteen months later, in April 1953, Dalí telephoned Ann. "I have finished a masterpiece," he said, referring to his portrait of her. A day later in his St. Regis suite, Dalí lead her proudly to the painting. "I unmask you," he said.

"It's ugly," she said. After two seconds, she turned her back on the portrait of the homely woman standing at the mouth of a black cave by a gray sea. Dalí had enlarged her face, making it look like a mask, shortened her neck, and lengthened her already long upper lip. She resembled an amused and predatory pig. Her mouth was bright crimson. He satirized her riches by showing her wearing an evening gown and the emerald engagement ring against a grim rocky beach, suggesting she had not always been at home in the drawing rooms of the wealthy. The gown bared the outlines of her lush breasts. Her long thigh pressed against the flowing skirt. She did not seem to notice a tiny male figure in the far distance, probably Dalí.

Further, he portrayed Ann surrounded by nightmarish sexual images. Ann's shadow and the cave are linked, as Dalí hinted that the horrifying mouth of the cave may be her true form. A lonely conch shell, suggestive of female genitals, is tossed on the sand at Ann Woodward's feet.

Although he had waited a year to show it, Dalí had painted the portrait in less than twelve hours. The picture uses the same images as Dalí's early nightmarish masterpiece about his terror of women called *Spectre of Sex Appeal*. In that painting, he showed a headless female figure propped on a gray beach with rocks behind it. This work, too, contained a tiny realistic figure in the background. Dalí wrote of the painting, "The child Dalí is terrified by the giant specter of the eternal feminine." He added, "The eternal . . . feminine is perhaps a phobia."

Several months passed, and Dalí did not hear from Ann. His wife, Gala, telephoned the Woodward house several times to demand the unpaid fee. "I owe him nothing," Ann said. "I hate the picture, and I don't want it near me."

That August, Dalí sued Ann and Billy for $7,000. The Cleveland *Plain Dealer* ran an editorial noting that "a New York socialite, Mrs. Ann Eden Crowell Woodward . . . learned that art is a dangerous thing to Dali with." The editorial chastised Ann, observing that great artists need not boast a photographic touch. Ann filled a scrapbook with Dalí-Woodward articles. At a press conference, Billy took the offensive, saying of his wife: "She walked away as though from a monster. It is a heck of an unpleasant picture, depicting Ann against a rock with shells around, sort of slapped together in unpleasant gray grim colors."

A wealthy Peruvian diplomat named Ernesto Ayulo called Cholly Knickerbocker and volunteered to buy the painting. Knickerbocker published a photograph of Ann. Ann prized the clipping that stated: "The South American diplomat says he considers the junior Mrs. Woodward one of the outstanding beauties of our times."

Dalí's suit against the Woodwards went to the New York State Supreme Court. Before the hearing, Dalí asked the Woodwards to admit they had hired him and had agreed to pay him a reasonable fee of $7,000. The Woodward lawyers admitted only that Ann Woodward had hired Dalí to paint to her personal satisfaction. They argued that Dalí had no written proof that Ann had agreed to pay him. They asked him how many hours he had worked on the painting and where he worked on it. Dalí responded that a work of art was not measured in value by the number of hours or brushstrokes he had put into it.

When the Woodwards paid the $7,000 fee to avoid a protracted trial, the New York *Post* headline declared, "Horrified Lady Can't Brush Dalí." The famous painting was offered for sale at Carstair's Gallery, but no one bought it. It was stored in a fifth-floor closet on East Seventy-third Street and was ultimately inherited by Woody.

When Billy strayed, Ann often sought his attention by going off on her own. Packing suitcases always gave Ann a lift. It was similar to the way she and Ethel Crowell had felt leaving little Kansas towns. In England, Ann began a romance with Lord William Astor, then forty-four, whose family owned vast real estate holdings in London, Manhattan, and the Bronx. Through Astor she found herself in the center of a coterie of Britishers who paid young girls to play sexual games with them.

Lord Astor was not exactly dashing: his ears stuck out. But socially, he was a more impressive catch than Billy. In keeping with the dictates of his class, he never entered commerce, but did have charity interests, a string of thoroughbred horses, and he played polo well; he had picked it up at Eton. Astor's title and money blinded Ann to his emotional problems.

Like Billy Woodward, Astor was a profoundly unhappy man who, by the time Ann knew him, expected his life to turn out badly. She had first met him in 1951 during one of his frequent trips to Manhattan to consult American orthopedists about a condition prompted by a fall from a horse.

At Ann's invitation, they saw each other several months afterward, in late 1952, for cocktails at the elegant Palm Court of New York's Plaza Hotel. Ann was in despair, having been reprimanded by her mother-in-law for tarnishing the Woodward name in the public dispute with Dalí. Discouraged by Billy's lack of interest and Elsie's criticism, she had given up classes in interior design, her latest effort at self-improvement. Her spirits were renewed by Astor's flattering attention. She resolved to enroll in courses on gardening and English history at Hunter College.

Ann preferred to focus on a man's needs, rather than to dwell on her own bleak feelings. To her Bill Astor was simply better than she was. When he looked into her eyes after several drinks, he seemed to invite her to be herself. She found herself complaining that Billy forbade her to wear her low-cut chiffon blouse under her jacket. Astor told her that he had decided to divorce his wife for her adultery. He invited Ann when she was next in England to stop at his home, Cliveden-on-Thames. Cliveden was surrounded by the finest flowering gardens in England. Far grander than the Woodwards' Belair stud farm in Maryland, the estate had a ten-mile approach lined with poplar trees.

Astor probably did not tell Ann that he was depressed, nor that he not inherited his father's property, as he had always assumed he would. His father, Waldorf, had died only recently, leaving Bill his title. Waldorf's impressive estate was bequeathed to the National Trust, and the family's newspaper, the *National Observer*, to Bill's younger brother, David. Bill Astor lived out the rest of his life in this public humiliation. Although he was allowed to live at Cliveden as a tenant, tourists were permitted on the grounds during the holiday season.

His mother was another source of misery. The outspoken American-born Nancy Astor, the first woman to take a seat in Parliament, was cold and cruel at home and ignored Bill in favor of his brother. Astor was even more repressed than the average upper-class Englishman. This lack of warmth at home seemed to have created in Astor a lifelong inability to become truly intimate in his relationships. In this trait he resembled Billy Woodward.*

---

*Astor's family was far richer than the Woodwards. In the eighteenth century, Johann Jakob (John Jacob) Astor, the son of a German butcher, had come to America to work as a baker's assistant. He saved his earnings and began buying bits and pieces of land and then farms on Manhattan Island. Soon, waves of immigrants moved into tenements on Astor landholdings.

Lord Astor's father, Waldorf, who lived in splendor in England (carrying the Anglophilism of his American forebears to an extreme), was the richest absentee landlord in the world; rents from his Manhattan holdings alone totaled close to $10 million a year. Whenever the Astors sold land, they bought new farms. By the turn of the century they had started to buy farms in the Bronx. In Manhattan, the Astors had built and owned the Sherry Netherland, the Waldorf-Astoria, the Knickerbocker, the St. Regis, and the Astor hotels.

Bill Astor was delighted a few weeks after their Palm Court cocktails when Ann rang him from London and told him she had come to England just to see him. He invited her to Cliveden. Astor was under the sway of Stephen Ward, an osteopath. Ward's capable fingers massaged Astor's physical pains. In exchange for introductions to women and the pleasure of Ward's company, Astor lent Ward thousands of pounds and paid the rent on at least one call girl's London flat.*

At first Astor did not invite Ann to sample his idea of pleasure. While there was something about her that invited his candor, she was a girl from Kansas, and when she spoke of her husband and little boys she could not hide her homesickness. Ann finally agreed to attend a party, but only as an observer. She saw it as a kind of theater. Lord Astor did not refer to his parties as orgies. But typically, a girl would begin with a striptease or a belly dance. Other girls would follow suit, and they would soon disappear with male guests in pairs and in triplets to the bedrooms. Other parties were devoted to sadism. Naked girls were tied up and gagged all around the room while the other guests dined, drank, and smoked cigars.

Ann learned the code of Astor's world—and wore the correct hat to high tea and to Ascot. She greeted racing friends of Billy's father's from the Astor box, near the royal enclosure. It was reckless to flaunt the romance, but she was eager to show Billy that she could scale the social heights of English life. Ironically, in England she received more respect as Mrs. William Woodward, Jr., than she ever had in New York. Billy's father's drive to win the Derby was known in virtually every upper-class English home.

Ann took lessons in riding to hounds from one of the grooms. It was here, riding in full regalia, that she developed a passion for shoots that lasted the rest of her life. Ann loved weekend hunting parties at Cliveden. In his memoir, Stephen Ward described the traditional luxury of Astor's

---

*Ann met Ward on her first trip to Cliveden in 1953. Nearly a decade later, Ward's "best friend," Bill Astor, would allow him to take the fall for their roles in the Profumo affair, the biggest sex scandal in English government history.

The Profumo scandal has been recently linked to Astor's efforts on the part of one branch of British intelligence, MI-5 (efforts that backfired in this case), to blackmail foreign dignitaries. Government files show that Cliveden, one hour from London, was used as a "honeypot," a place where foreign representatives were introduced to girls, compromised, and thus blackmailed or eventually "turned" by the British government.

The scandal surfaced as Dr. Stephen Ward was accused of procuring girls for Astor, for British secretary of state for war John Profumo, and for a Russian agent. When the same girl was found to be sleeping with Profumo and the Russian agent, the scandal became a matter of government security. It forced the resignation of Profumo and brought down a Conservative British government in what was considered the most public shaming a government had endured in this century. Lord Astor, looking arrogant in public, pretended innocence.

entertaining: "The Visitor's Book reads like Who's Who. After changing for dinner, the guests usually meet in the Long Drawing Room. Champagne and cocktails are always served here . . . and the guests always include at least one Duchess. Dinner is announced by the butler, and the guests drift into the huge and ornate dining room, from Madame De-Pompadour's hunting lodge."

Ann could see at once that she would have to win over Stephen Ward, a permanent part of Astor's domestic ménage. When Astor invited her up for a weekend to hunt, he asked if she wanted a free session with Stephen to cure any aches and pains.

At first Ward reminisced with Ann about his school days in Missouri. He gave her treatments to soothe the tension in the small of her back. The two of them had in common an intense, almost erotic desire to infiltrate the upper classes.

Ward encouraged Ann to confide in him. He was fascinated by her marriage and told her how brave she was to keep trying to win the Woodwards' approval.

That Ward and Astor had decadent sexual practices made perfect sense to Ann, given what she knew of upper-class British life. But after a few weeks, she grew tired of the constant presence of Stephen Ward and his young girls. It was increasingly clear to her that these girls were available to anybody, including Lord Astor.

Despite the bevy of girls, Astor began to fall in love with Ann, partly because of her unbounded enthusiasm for him. Ann saw Astor as her great opportunity. He was a shield against Billy's threats to "fire" her. Astor was grateful for her flirtatious affection—and responded by proposing marriage after Ann had been in England only a few weeks. It was a stunning conquest.

But once she had won him, Astor began to please Ann less and less. Billy Woodward was still her greatest obsession, and she telephoned Kerr, her private detective, for news of his comings and goings. When she called Billy, he told her his father was dying. He needed her—but this he would not admit.

The more she gained in Astor's affections, the more Ward competed with her. Ward had infinite patience in battle. He used "men only" language to silence Ann. He pitted her against his women friends, who were either former prostitutes to whom he had taught manners or intellectual lesbian bohemians like the painter Gwen Le Gallienne, who had been in British Intelligence service during the war and had been the mistress of the socialist writer John Reed.

Ann Woodward painted by Salvador Dalí, 1953. Note the masklike face.

Nancy, Lady Astor (above left), one of the beautiful Langhorne sisters of Virginia, who married Waldorf Astor (they met abroad, fox-hunting). Nancy's father-in-law gave them Cliveden-on-Thames (below), the great Palladian house that had been bought from the Duke of Westminster, as a present. Lady Astor became the first female member of Parliament. Her son William (above right), who fell in love with Ann, was implicated in the Profumo scandal that brought down the British government in 1963.

When Ann asked Astor if they could be alone at Cliveden one week-end, he refused. Perhaps she realized she had more control over her life with Billy Woodward than she ever would with Bill Astor.

After four weeks in England, Ann returned to New York. She dropped hints of Astor's interest; Billy feigned disgust, but he was nonetheless impressed. Elsie was outraged. Wives were not equal in sexual warfare. She wondered why Ann had returned if Bill Astor had proposed and recommended that Billy finally get a divorce. The truth was that Ann was still able to reach Billy in a way no one else ever had. His freedom to express his dark side made her essential to him. Ann accepted him unconditionally. He believed he could do anything to her and she would remain his.

That June, Ann and Billy flew to Paris at the height of the social season known as *la grande semaine.* They stayed with Billy's sister Ethel de Crois-set, who had established herself in a town house on Rue Weber near the Arc de Triomphe. The most emotional of the Woodwards, Ethel was more comfortable away from her mother.

Ann and Ethel de Croisset had a modest rapport, partly because they both enjoyed international society, but also because they shared Elsie's disfavor. Ethel filled her Parisian drawing room with society people, artists, and politicians. As a girl, she had been rebellious, too. Her former husband, Philippe, was a Belgian Jew whose father was said to be one of several decadent men who were models for Proust's character the Baron de Charlus in *Remembrance of Things Past.* (Some of Elsie's friends blamed the failure of Ethel's marriage on the fact that de Croisset was a Jew.)

Upon arriving in Paris, Ann began telephoning the Baroness Terry von Pantz, the Avon heiress, and others, to make sure she and Billy would be invited to parties being given by Aly Khan, the Marquis de Cuevas, and André Dubonnet. At Aly Khan's party, Billy flirted with a French-woman. Piqued, Ann disappeared the next afternoon with the elegant An-dré Dubonnet,* the blond heir to the great French aperitif fortune, who

---

*Dubonnet was cited by Lanfranco Rasponi as the most important name to drop when discussing a recent visit to Paris. The clubs and restaurants all vied for his patronage. In Paris, pretty American girls at chic all-night clubs like L'Elephant Blanc, with its turning stage, would, when presented with a check for twenty dollars for a drink, whisper to the waiter, *"Non, non, non, je veux le prix de Monsieur Dubonnet."* (Having dined with him, they knew his privileges.) Thus, the check would be corrected to $3.50.

had a weakness for American women. His fortune was fast being dissipated to underwrite his womanizing, bridge playing, and glorious *train de vie*. He lived in a large modern apartment overlooking the Bois de Boulogne and kept a second house at Antibes in the south of France. He had just left his American wife for his mistress, Alyse Hunt. He owned two houses in Paris—one for each woman.

It was Dubonnet's smile that made him attractive. He spirited Ann to lunch at the Hôtel Bristol. Ann and he repaired upstairs for a romp. She tried to remember details like the nearby French President's mansion and the old lace on the bedcover at the Bristol to impress Billy. In fact, for Ann the most pleasurable part of the Dubonnet escapade was her confession to Billy. Her detailed descriptions of adultery with a significant member of international society enraged her husband, made him jealous, admiring. Their shouting match ended in sex.

On the same visit, Ann made certain that Elsa Maxwell invited them to a big ball in Biarritz to help revive the resort as a playground for the international set. Elsa Maxwell had been hired by several hotel owners to promote Biarritz. The Marquis Georges de Cuevas had been asked to give the ball at Schuberta, his house near the magnificent municipal gardens. Ann's enthusiasm and sheer exuberance lured a reluctant Billy onto the airplane. She swore to him that she would make the masquerade party better than a honeymoon.

The Woodwards checked into complimentary rooms at the gilt and marble Miramar Hôtel, whose long windows opened onto the Mediterranean. Each morning, while Billy slept, Ann made her way to the beach to tan herself. Lying in the sun calmed her. It would improve her appearance for the party, and, as she said, "It warms my blood." The de Cuevas masquerade party required historical costume. Elsa Maxwell set the tone by announcing she would appear in the armor of Don Quixote's sidekick, Sancho Panza.

Despite the heat, Ann turned the hotel suite into a costume room, pinning and sewing. Billy would dress as a French musketeer in plumed hat and velvet knickers. Ann told everyone she was going as her secret persona: Anne d'Autriche, beleaguered Queen of France.* Her costume was a long velvet gown with puffed sleeves. She twisted long ropes of fake pearls down to her waist. Her hair was pulled away from her face with a

---

*Anne, born in 1601, the daughter of King Philip III of Spain, had loved her husband, King Louis XIII, too much. Anne was considered an alien in France. Persecuted by Cardinal Richelieu, who was in league with her mother-in-law, Queen Anne held her power in spite of her husband's lack of support.

long fall of curls attached at the nape of her neck. A rhinestone tiara completed the regal portrait. Ann Woodward's choice of her model was both grandiose and telling. It seemed to show off her fight for her place as Billy's wife. Queen Anne was a woman who battled enemies to stay at her husband's side as his consort.

The first awkward incident at the de Cuevas ball occurred when a drunken Irish poet in Spanish military uniform shouted to Peter, the former King of Yugoslavia, "We have only one King here—me. I'm the King of Ireland." Music drowned his cries as he was evicted.

After midnight, Billy began shimmying to a samba with a beautiful Chilean, Carmen Sainte, the lithe young wife of Daniel Sainte, a French financier. Ann stared at him in the moonlight from a nearby table, unable to pay attention to her companion, Jacques Cartier—heir of the jewelers. Suddenly, Carmen Sainte tossed her black mantilla over Billy's and her own head. The two were dancing in a private tent. Ann was horrified. Some later said that she had also had too much champagne. But her reaction was more complex. It stemmed from her jealousy and her desire to show Billy how much violence and public embarrassment she would risk to keep him.

She tried to pull the woman's mantilla off Billy's head, ripping the delicate lace. "Ann, stop it," said Billy, trying to grab her.

"He's my husband," shouted Ann, as the women fought with each other in the half-light of the dance floor.

Around them, couples stood speechless as Ann's pearls snapped and rolled on the ground. Two employees in evening jackets separated Ann and Carmen Sainte. Ann ran into the crowd in her stocking feet and into the hotel. She entered their room, bolting the lock. Billy banged on the door, shouting, "Dammit, let me inside."

"Go away," said Ann. "Why didn't she throw her skirt over your head?"

After another minute, Billy gave up and left. Back at the party, Billy danced with his old friend Jo Bryce, who recounted Ann's temper displays back during the war when he and Ann shared Jo's house in Norfolk, Virginia. Billy danced until dawn. At about 7 a.m., he knocked on the door of their bedroom. Ann let him in. "Are you sorry?" she asked. "You should be sorry." When she lunged at him, he threw two quick punches. She ducked and hit her head on a wall. "You gave me a concussion," she said.

After ten minutes of fighting, Billy was locked outside in the corridor in his pajamas. Ann threw a shirt and shoes and sport pants out after him. She spent that day pressing ice wrapped in towels to her bruised face. Her shoulder ached, but her dress would cover the bruises. Before dinner, Billy knocked again. His dinner jacket was inside. Ann shrieked, "Go dance with your South American bitch!"

"I am getting the manager," said Billy. "He will open the door." Instead, Billy went to see several friends to have a drink and try to borrow a dinner jacket. He could have rented a tuxedo, but he liked displaying himself in the role of the wronged but cherished man. He relished discussing the calamitous public event and finally borrowed a dark blue jacket and tie.

At the beginning of dinner, everybody stared at Billy, who sat alone. Some said Ann had ripped the entire front of Carmen Sainte's ball gown. Ann and Billy greeted each other with stiff public kisses. After dessert, the Woodwards held hands and strolled with their long strides to the dance floor. They moved through circles of hush.

At an after-theater party at the "21" Club, February 1950. Back row, left to right: Mrs. Rudolph Shirmer, Mrs. B. Bertlschman, Mrs. William Woodward, Jr., Mrs. David McConnell. Middle row: Mrs. John Hammond, Mrs. Nathan Milstein, Mrs. Baldwin Dillon, Mrs. Thomas Phipps, Mrs. Donald Straalem. Front row: Mrs. John R. Topping, Mrs. Clyde Newhouse, Mrs. Mortimer Rogers.

Biarritz, a masked ball given by the Marquis de Cuevas. Ann went as the French queen, Anne of Austria.

Above left: Elsie Woodward with Lanfranco Rasponi at a dinner given by Earl Blackwell in 1961. Other guests included Serge Obolensky, Joan Fontaine, Anita Loos, Adele Douglas, and Tilly Losch. *Above right:* Elsie Woodward and (standing) Elsa Maxwell, 1961. Elsa Maxwell organized parties for international society occasions. At times Elsie Woodward assisted her financially.

Billy with Sunny Jim Fitzsimmons, 1955.

Nashua
BELMONT FUTURITY WINNER·1954

Seasons Greetings
from
Belair

Left: Nashua, featured on Ann and Billy's Christmas card, 1954. *Below:* Nashua, Billy, and Ann in the winner's circle, Arlington Park Racetrack, Chicago, after Nashua won the Arlington Classic, July 1955. Notice Ann's ease before the camera; much to Elsie's annoyance, in photographs and in newsreels and on the relatively new form of entertainment, television, Ann overshadowed Billy.

13

MATCH RACE

During the summer of 1953, Billy's seventy-seven-year-old father was ensconced in the second-floor ballroom dying of heart disease. He had resigned from the board of the Hanover Bank, and as chairman of the Jockey Club after twenty years, and turned both positions over to Billy.* Elsie refused to surrender her husband to New York Hospital. Instead, she set up a fully equipped hospital room in the ballroom.

He had not realized his life's dream of winning the English Derby. When William had shipped his horse, Prince Simon, to England a few years earlier, the yearling was not taken seriously because of his stiff knees. But one morning he galloped past a champion on Newmarket Heath, in the most impressive performance by a two-year-old that his trainer had ever seen. Captain Cecil Boyd-Rochfort wrote to Woodward: "I think he is perhaps one of the best you have ever had, and you may have the animal you have always longed for." Prince Simon created enormous excitement in England. "Every newspaper has been after me," Boyd-Rochfort went on, "photographers looking around every corner to take his photograph. You would have thought he was Greta Garbo."

Woodward had been too sick to cross the Atlantic to see Prince Simon run in the Derby, but he consoled himself that he would have better luck from a distance. He cabled his anxieties about the animal's knees,

---

*Woodward Sr. had just given $80,000 to the Cathedral Church of St. John the Divine, near Columbia University, for a forty-foot-wide rose window containing over 10,000 pieces of glass (bigger than that of Notre Dame Cathedral) as a memorial to his uncle James and his parents. His uncle James T. Woodward had bequeathed money to build the church.

appetite, aches, and moods. Woodward believed that if a horse he had bred could finally win the Derby, he would die a happy man.

Ten days before the Derby, Woodward continued to worry. "We ought to have a watchman with Prince Simon," he wrote to Boyd-Rochfort, "throughout the Epsom trip, and also protect him going to the paddock, so please do not let that slip out of your mind. Also don't let the box be arranged so that some marauder can throw a poisoned apple in through the back window. Enough said."

On May 27, 1950, the day of Prince Simon's Derby, Woodward listened to the race on the radio in White Sulphur Springs with his wife and daughters. Billy was in England representing his father. Ann had not been invited. With her sons she, too, listened to the broadcast of the race.

Victory seemed certain. Throughout the second half of the race, Prince Simon—the outstanding favorite—looked like the sure winner. With only a furlong to go, Prince Simon shied at the sight of the huge racing crowd and lost to a French horse by a head.

Ann telephoned the Woodwards immediately to offer her condolences. William answered the phone, sounding utterly defeated. He told Ann that the ambition for which he had been striving for thirty years was now beyond his grasp. For years afterward, Prince Simon was known in England as the "best horse never to have won the Derby."

When on September 26, 1953, Billy learned of his father's death, he was unable to shed a tear. Ann cried for both of them.

Flags flew at half-mast at racetracks, at the Hanover Bank, the Knickerbocker and the Brook clubs in New York, and at White's in London. William Woodward's obituary in *The New York Times* enhanced history. Instead of reflecting on his father and uncle's nineteenth and twentieth-century fortunes, the family looked further back. The only antecedent referred to in the obituary was his grandfather's rich relative who had at one time owned the land that Annapolis now occupied.

Despite his contempt for his son, Billy's father did what he probably felt was his duty and left Billy the magnificent horses, the 3,000-acre stud farm in Maryland, and $1 million.* The majority of the $30 million Wood-

---

*In formal language, Woodward expressed an uncharacteristically warm wish to share the joys of his empire with Billy: "As to the estate known as Belair, Prince Georges County, Maryland, received by me from my uncle James T. Woodward, it is my wish that it may mean as much to him [Billy] as it has to my uncle and myself and that he may spend many happy days there maintaining the place in a modest and simple way as has been our habit."

ward fortune was still in trust for his mother; Billy would inherit three sevenths of half of the estate—nearly six and a half million—only upon Elsie's death.

William left Elsie the East Eighty-sixth Street house (with the proviso note that she not feel obligated to "maintain my said residence as her home"), $100,000 outright, and a lifetime income from his estate. He had already established trusts of more than $10 million for his wife and children. He also gave $100,000 to the Society of New York Hospital to start a Woodward fund and $50,000 to the trustees of the Groton School to provide bonuses to outstanding teachers.

Billy Woodward had never been groomed to take over the Hanover Bank. The new head of the family was immature for his thirty-three years and had never learned work habits. He had not dared to compete with his father, an endeavor he viewed as hopeless. His philosophy consisted primarily of a code of manners, which taught him that at parties and other casual encounters with his peers, he must put their interests ahead of his own.

Like many dowagers, Elsie was reluctant to relinquish her empire to Billy. He was a victim of what the English call the Prince of Wales syndrome. As he grew up, there was no role for him in his father's empire. Now, suddenly, Billy was overwhelmed by adult responsibility. At Ann's urging, he brought his sons back to Seventy-third Street from Oyster Bay and enrolled them in the Buckley School.

Elsie urged him to divorce Ann, failing to see how badly Billy needed Ann during this emotional transition. No matter how low an opinion Billy had of himself, Ann was always there to adore him. He could always abuse her, with her approval. At first Ann had been his proof to the world that he had guts. But by this point, his contempt for her often equaled Elsie's. His contempt, however, often turned into raw sexual satisfaction.

After her husband's death, Elsie was still working on the Woodward image. William had asked her to donate his collection of English paintings of horses to the Baltimore Museum of Art. She hired Billy Baldwin, the society decorator, to design a special museum wing. They rode to Baltimore together in a railroad dining car; Baldwin was scandalized by Elsie's miserly tips. She told him that she and the late Mr. Woodward had been barely compatible.

Elsie had come to be known as a dutiful wife who stayed in the background of her husband's racing and banking achievements. Acquaintances assumed her background was Bostonian; she had a reticent quality. (She did not play up her connection to the Adams family of Boston; perhaps she felt diminished by them. When she spoke of her illustrious antecedents, it was the Pilgrim John Ogden who had once, she said, owned most of what was now Southampton, Long Island.)

At first Billy did not seem to be a part of the world he inherited from his father. He shunned Belair and claimed that owning racing stables and breeding racehorses was sheer snobbery, a way of flaunting the prestige that a handful of wealthy Americans claimed as their right.

But as part of Ann's perpetual fight against Billy's boredom, she urged him to give his horses a chance. His oldest sister, Edie, who had been supervising the farmers and grooms, was bitterly disappointed when he announced he would take over directing the stables. After all, Edie had stood by her father's side for decades, memorizing his guidelines of horse breeding. But she was a woman and, to her father, an inappropriate heir. Neither she, her sisters, nor their mother could bring themselves to believe that either Billy or Ann was capable of continuing the proud tradition of the preeminent Belair stud. But Billy gave in to his wife's urging, and soon after his father's funeral in 1953, on a fine day of dazzling red-and-orange autumn colors, chartered a plane and flew to Belair.

Billy barely knew his father's legendary American trainer, seventy-nine-year-old James Fitzsimmons, although the former jockey had made all the major decisions about training winning Woodward horses for thirty years. Although plagued by severe arthritis, "Mr. Fitz" was to be the key to Billy's new empire. He talked to the horses and seemed able to read their minds. He never blamed a horse for losing and would tell the animals so.*

The breeding of Nashua had been the culmination of a lifetime of study and careful purchasing. To bring his American thoroughbreds up to the standards of English horses, Billy's father had chosen his prize mare, Segula, the daughter of Woodward's champion stallion and 1939 Kentucky Derby winner, Johnstown. He mated Segula with the Aga Khan's strong temperamental "rogue" Irish stallion Nasrullah, who arrived in this country from Ireland in 1950. The horse had been retired to stud because he

---

*Fitzsimmons was a quiet sports hero who shunned the spotlight. He claimed that his physical deformity—a severely hunched back—gave him no pain and, in fact, gave him luck. After races, Mr. Fitz never went to the winner's circle, but returned to the barn to discuss the race with his great-grandsons, grandsons, sons, stable boys, and the horses.

Sportswriters loved Fitzsimmons, as is clear from Jimmy Breslin's excellent memoir, *Sunny Jim*. He earned close to half a million dollars a year, but had lived for decades with his wife in a working-class neighborhood in Ozone Park, Queens, in New York City.

was too difficult to handle as a racehorse. Though capable of legendary speed, he was ill-tempered in his stall, unresponsive on the track, and a risk as a sire. Nasrullah did not respond to the whip; he did whatever he pleased.

Woodward Sr. was one of a small group who imported Nasrullah to stand at Claiborne Farm in Kentucky to improve the stock of their American mares. It was an inspired decision. As a stud, he was record-breaking. He sired Never Say Die (not a Woodward horse), who won the English Derby and the St. Leger in 1954—and two of the great American racehorses of all time: Nashua and Bold Ruler.

At Belair, Billy joined Mr. Fitz in the Ford truck, and they sped off to inspect the new yearlings—an annual ritual from which his father had usually excluded Billy.

The colt Nashua trotted to the fence as Mr. Fitz and Billy approached. Jimmy Breslin wrote in *Sunny Jim*: "[Nashua] then wheeled and pounded back toward the center of the field, his feet sending clods of dirt into the air. He would not be two years old until the end of the year, but he had a chest on him, and his legs looked like they could kick their way through a brick wall. You look at a horse such as this and it does something to you, even if you are not used to breeding horses."

Fitz explained, "Nashua gotta be the best yearling colt your father bred. He's headed for England in a week's time for training for the Derby."

In his final trip to Belair several months earlier, William Woodward had also been driven to this pasture. William had been eager to do something special with Nashua, named for the river that flowed past the Groton School. He told old Jim Fitzsimmons that Nashua would be the colt sent that year to England to race. "I like the breeding," he said. "He looks fine," said Mr. Fitz.

That October afternoon, in the chill of the setting autumn sun, Billy chose for the second time in his life openly to defy his family. He did not share his father's dream of winning the English Derby with a Belair colt. Unlike his father, Billy wanted Nashua to race in America, despite the colt's big chest, which promised great stamina for the longer English courses.

During the next weeks, Mr. Fitz sent Nashua to a Long Island horse farm to be broken. Mr. Fitz believed he suddenly had the best horse of his life. He called him "Mickey" because his father was Irish, and told him that he would become a champion. At first when Nashua raced, Billy came to watch only occasionally. His father had been the grand old man of American racing, and it did not seem possible to step into his shoes. Reporters still called Billy "young Woodward" and "Junior" and whispered that he was hostile and distant and had not earned his stripes.

But then the great horse Nashua began to win races. Billy started waking up in the mornings, showering, and dressing in a clean white shirt and blazer to read bloodstock magazines. He took an owner's pride in the strong bay colt and finally began to believe it was his, even though it had been bred by his father. The stallion promised to break all Woodward records.

The society and sporting press suddenly discovered the young Woodwards. Ann was chic; Billy was handsome and debonair and carried no money in his pockets. But they also seized upon Nashua's flaws: he liked to run lazily until the end of a race and rarely won by more than a few inches. His jockey, Eddie Arcaro, usually hit him hard until well past the finish line. Nashua was rumored to be a mean horse, biting people and suddenly rearing back on his hind legs. However, Mr. Fitz said the colt was "just playful." He said Nashua was by no means as difficult as his sire, who on some days even refused to run.

In the next two years, the horse would become the second largest money-maker in history, winning every race but the Kentucky Derby.

The spectacular success of Nashua was like a tonic for Ann and Billy's marriage. The horse made them feel lucky for the first time in years. Elsie said grimly to her son, "If it weren't for the horse, Ann would have left you by now."

Even though Elsie still controlled the major part of the family's $45 million, it chafed her that the prized public role for which she had sacrificed so much of herself had been usurped by Ann, who was now becoming the famous Mrs. William Woodward. Ann began to stand for the good life in the media. The sports press adored her. She became adept at talking with great authority about horses.

After Nashua's races she never forgot to shake the jockey's hand, and she had a knack for thanking the most obscure members of the horse's entourage, down to the exercise boy and the groom. The world around a champion racehorse reminded her of a Broadway opening, and she relished it. Her experience as a radio actress and Broadway chorus girl was useful when she was in the winner's circle. With her smiles and graceful gestures, she pleased the camera. Billy was usually holding the reins of the champion horse, but he seemed to be secondary in the news photographs. He was torn between his well-bred labors to appear inconspicuous and his own desire for the limelight. Ann became his competitor.

*   *   *

At the track, Billy finally found a successor to Bean Baker in a tall, fine-featured playboy named Charles Wacker, Jr.* Wacker loved the sport of racing and had his own string of horses. His champagne and hundred-dollar-bill pranks reminded Billy of Bean. Society columnists described Wacker's nightclub life with celebrities like Kim Novak. It flattered Charlie Wacker to give Billy training advice, and he soon became a fan of Nashua's. He was so impressed with the horse that he began carrying a picture of him in his wallet.

Wacker and Billy were young to be racehorse owners. Wacker convinced Billy that the Jockey Club preserved racing as "the sport of kings," and that the sport should "go democratic." He wanted the Jockey Club to make a lot of money by organizing off-track betting for rich and poor people. In Wacker's company, Billy began to smile more. He and Wacker watched Nashua win purse after purse.

In early March 1954, Billy went south to prepare for the Florida Derby. Although for past races Ann and their sons had stayed in a little cottage at the Golden Beach Bungalow Hotel, that spring Billy was alone. When his friends saw him with local women, they assumed he and his wife were separated, but they were not. Still, Wacker maintains Billy had no serious love affairs.

Billy spent long days at the racetrack and in the evenings went out with Laura Monroe, a striptease entertainer. At a Miami nightclub, Billy taunted a stand-up comic by putting a teddy-bear puppet on the stage. As Wacker cheered, Billy gleefully squeezed a tube hidden in his lap, making the puppet jump. When Ann arrived two days before the Florida Derby, she set out to win over Charlie Wacker: she was jealous of his influence on Billy but was determined to make him her ally. Her roughness impressed him. "What do I have to do to get the Woodward women to accept me?" she asked.

On March 26, 1954, six months after his father's death, Billy became a national sports hero. It was raining hard and the track was slippery and dangerous. Many owners would have withdrawn a horse as valuable as Nashua. Mr. Fitz's arthritis had kept him from traveling to Florida, but he and Billy conferred by telephone a few hours before the race. "Walk the track," he told Billy. "See if you think Mickey will slip or fall."

Billy was photographed with neither hat nor umbrella, splashing in

---

*He came from a Chicago family whose nineteenth-century fortune had begun with breweries. Most recently, his philanthropic father, Charles Wacker, Sr., had been awarded prizes as the force behind the planning of the parks and railroad stations of modern Chicago. Wacker Sr. had helped build Wacker Drive, a major double-decker boulevard.

the mud all the way around the Gulfstream track in the pouring rain. Reporters wrote how he wore his usual custom-made loafers, a single-breasted dark gray suit, white cotton shirt, and his customary striped "lucky" tie.

Eddie Arcaro followed Billy. By the end of their walk, Arcaro was convinced the precious horse would not be entered in the race. Billy was still undecided. Arcaro knew better than anyone how much was at risk. In the rain and mud Nashua would be harder than ever to control and thus in great danger.

Ann arrived for the race; she took off her hat and, still wearing her gloves, tossed back her hair in the rain, while photographers took hundreds of pictures. After Billy telephoned Mr. Fitz, he told reporters, "Nashua belongs to the people and they're anxious to see him run." Billy deferred to the racing public, saying, "Hell, I can't scratch Nashua and disappoint all those people who will be out here on a day like this to see him run."

The Florida Derby was harrowing. The temperamental horse gave Billy new cause for worry. Although Nashua was in the lead, at the last possible moment he suddenly made the kind of move that loses races. Right before the finish line, he "propped"—threw his front legs forward stiffly and tried to stop dead in his tracks. Arcaro beat him frantically to keep him moving.

To the surprise of all who witnessed the race, Nashua won the first prize of $148,750. Mr. Fitz declared him the best horse he had ever trained.

That night Mary Sanford gave a party for the winning couple. The centerpiece was the large winner's wreath of white carnations. Billy and Ann spent that night at the beach house of C.Z. and Winston Guest. In the middle of the night, the Woodwards woke the household with one of their loud fights. Ann was jealous of Laura Monroe. She wept, clasping his hands. He flung her away. She begged him to tell her how she could be a better wife. "Keep a lower profile at the track," he said finally.

Unable to sleep, Ann took a late-night walk on the beach. Usually, the house was clearly visible from a great distance. But rain clouds covered the moon that night. She panicked and ran in several directions. When she eventually returned, sandy, tears running down her face and her feet scratched from running on seashells, she pounded on a side door, waking everyone in the house. But her hysteria only engendered sympathy for Billy.

One evening a few days later, guests at the Golden Beach Bungalow Hotel in Miami heard a woman crying for help. The fight had started when Billy accused Ann of paying too much attention to Laddie Sanford at dinner. "You are a cheap flirt," Billy shouted. Ann shrieked, "I like talking to Laddie. He treats me right. I'm tired of you and your mother's lessons on what I can and can't do."

Billy punched her. "I hate the sound of your voice."

She fell back and hit her skull against a wall. "I'm not afraid of you," she announced. Ann lunged for him, tripped, and hit her face on a sharp edge of a table. She fumbled for an ashtray and threw it. It missed him, crashing into the floor lamp. "Be quiet, for God's sake," said Billy. Ann screamed for help.

Billy knelt, grabbing her by the throat. Woody, age nine, and Jimmy, age seven, in their adjacent bedroom overheard the fight. Suddenly, police were pounding the door. Billy opened it, looking disheveled.

"No problem," said Billy in his formal social way. He did not turn on the table lamp. Ann made no effort to detain the police. These fights were private events. Ann never discussed them with even her closest friends until long after Billy's death.

"Good night then," said the police. "Good night," Ann said, trying to clear her throat. Then she dragged herself into an armchair. The two were breathing hard. He locked eyes with her. "Annie, God only knows," he said sadly. "I feel so bad, I could kill myself." "You're all I have," she said in a similar tone of voice. It was time to make up in bed.

The next day the Woodwards awoke up late in the afternoon. Ann's tanned face was swollen. She dressed very slowly for a charity polo match in West Palm Beach. There was no question of missing the event. She and Billy were to be the guests of the Duke and Duchess of Windsor, the most important figures in Elsie Woodward's social circle. They understood that their newfound social cache was based on Nashua, but they did not mind.

Ann applied her darkest red lipstick over a bruise in the center of her lower lip. It was still clearly visible.

It was raining slightly when Ann and Billy greeted the Duke and Duchess of Windsor, Charlie Wacker, and Mary and Laddie Sanford. Both Ann and Billy were squinting, as though they had not slept the night before. Sitting in a folding chair, Ann hugged herself in the folds of her white cashmere overcoat, her collar turned up to hide the raw patches on her neck. She observed that the melancholy Duke looked more and more like a fragile old lady, while square-jawed Wallis looked more like a man. The Duchess liked strong American women and recognized in Ann and Mary Sanford fellow social climbers' pluck. In turn, Ann was especially fond of the Duchess.

Ann seemed dazed, for once not playing to press cameras. She was careful not to twist her sore body even when the Duchess, holding an umbrella over her head, leaned across Mary Sanford to whisper to her.

Billy paced behind Ann's chair in the light rain, still overwrought from the evening before. He kept smoothing back his damp forelock, brightening at Wacker's wry jokes.

That August, the Woodwards traveled in opposite directions. Ann attended the Paris collections. Billy visited Charles Wacker in Chicago, where Nashua won another race, the Arlington Classic.

During the winter of 1955, Ann was sleeping fitfully between crying jags. She often woke before dawn in a state of anxiety and swallowed more Seconal. She relied increasingly on Dr. Prutting. She refused to see the Woodward family doctor, Ben Kean, who she suspected might report her problems to her mother-in-law. Dr. Prutting administered a variety of tranquilizers, including Tuinal. She took them in her locked bathroom with a few cans of beer each night to fully knock herself out. In time, the drugs made Ann more agitated. Billy and his family would "fire" her if they learned she was taking them.

That January, Dr. Prutting was called out of his office on an emergency. He instructed his wife, Dr. Jane Oldden, who was also a physician, to give Ann a basal metabolism test for emotionality and hyperactivity caused by a hyperactive thyroid. Dr. Oldden felt protective toward Ann, who was very agitated. After several attempts to administer the test, Dr. Oldden said, "I'm sorry, but we cannot do the tests now while you are so nervous."

"Can't you call somebody else to do it?" Ann asked. Dr. Oldden realized that Ann felt rejected by her.

Yet even after this difficulty, Ann refused to go to Pratt Center for a thorough metabolic examination. The Woodwards must never suspect there might be anything wrong with her. In fact, when she finally agreed to check into the clinic, she used a false name. But the tests proved inconclusive, and Ann continued with her drug regimen.

There was less and less sensuality about Billy in his middle thirties. Although still very handsome, his face looked stretched and he had developed a squint. He had become more fastidious, bathing and changing his clothes several times a day. Billy was in the habit of long pauses before he answered reporters' questions. It was very hard for him to look at a television camera.

At about this time, Elsie Woodward began a new campaign. When Jeanne Vanderbilt separated from Alfred Gwynne Vanderbilt, Elsie championed her. "Unlike Ann, Jeanne is a wonderful mother," said Elsie to Billy, "and has been, despite her difficult husband, a perfect wife."

Elsie invited Jeanne to dinner, thinking she would make an ideal second wife for her son, but the younger woman, still distraught about the dissolution of her own marriage, did not attend.

When Ann learned of the invitation, she confronted Billy. He accused her of seeing enemies everywhere—particularly in his family.

On April 23, 1955, a huge crowd cheered as Nashua trotted out of his stall to run the Wood Memorial in Jamaica, Queens, New York. Ann was once again at Billy's wide, and the crowd cheered them, too. It was Nashua's first important race as a three-year-old. The overflowing crowd of 41,721 fans trampled the flower beds around the tote board. They had flocked to see Nashua race five horses in what insiders called a preview of the upcoming Kentucky Derby.

Billy had received permission to watch the race from the clubhouse roof and took Charlie Wacker with him. Throughout the race, Eddie Arcaro whipped the stubborn horse. Mr. Fitz had picked Summer Tan, the popular favorite, as Nashua's most serious rival. Fans were touched because the horse had almost died from a blood clot.

Billy watched Nashua come from behind with five great strides to beat Summer Tan in the last furlong of the race. The fans cheered Nashua in a heartwarming roar, and the applause made Billy feel as if he owned the world. Nashua had just won $75,100 and moved into fifteenth place on the list of all-time money winners.

A week later, on the morning of Saturday, April 30, rain drenched the barns and the deserted track and grandstands at Belmont Park. Reporters and photographers huddled in cars waiting to catch a final glimpse of Nashua before he was taken to Louisville for the Kentucky Derby. *The New York Times* devoted sixty lines to the departure of the local hero.

Billy had never tasted such success. Television had made him far more famous than his father had been after four decades in racing. All of middle-class America was now cheering Nashua on, as though they were watching from prized box seats rather than on their own home television sets. Billy was receiving hundreds of fan letters addressed to the Aqueduct Racetrack from women, who enclosed photographs. Walking along Madison Avenue he was slapped on the back by complete strangers and stopped to sign autographs. Ann was getting letters about her clothing and her sex appeal. And Nashua got more mail than both Woodwards combined.

Photographers tumbled out into the rain as a horse van drove up. Mr. Fitz called out, "No, boys, not yet." The arriving van contained only Mr. Alside, Nashua's horse companion for the trip. When Nashua arrived, the reporters cheered him. Billy and Mr. Fitz smiled as the grooms loaded the horse onto a train.

Billy then flew to Louisville to meet Nashua's train and oversee the unloading. He discussed with reporters his plans for Nashua to try out the Churchill Downs track. The Kentucky Derby strategy for Nashua was now taking shape. Mr. Fitz decided that once again Nashua would concentrate on beating Summer Tan. Despite raves from Western racing enthusiasts, he ignored the threat of Swaps, a red colt from California.

On May 7, during the fabled Kentucky Derby, Nashua dawdled as usual, then cut loose and desperately chased Swaps in the stretch. Ann jumped up and down, and Billy clung to her with both arms. But the big black horse failed to catch up. The chestnut horse upset all predictions in front of a cheering crowd of 100,000 and became the second horse from California to win the prized Derby. Swaps beat Nashua by a length and a half.

Billy and Ann stood a few inches apart, not touching, each in private agony. Billy felt that he had been very bad and was now being punished. Would his father have known to ask Mr. Fitz to focus on beating Swaps? Ann took his elbow. He did not seem to notice.

From Belmont Park, too frail to travel south, Mr. Fitz graciously took all the blame for the mistake, although he never took credit when his strategy and training helped a horse win. He had dismissed the newcomer, Swaps. He said he had told Eddie Arcaro to run the race against Summer Tan.

Moments after he lost the Derby, Billy stood bareheaded in the paddocks near the barn. He remembered his manners, of course, and congratulated Rex Ellsworth, the owner of Swaps. The horse was being hosed down to cool him off. This was a practice abhorred by East Coast trainers, who considered it rough treatment. After watching for a minute, Billy acted on an angry impulse. He said, "I'm thinking of coming to California. If I did, would you be interested in a match race?"

Within earshot of reporters, Ellsworth responded, "I would be happy to have one."

Billy was proposing an unusual historic racing event, a two-horse race—in effect, a rematch. It was not something his father would have done; a match race required more strategy. Time and place were crucial.

No one was more surprised than Ann at Billy's impetuous suggestion of a match race. Her husband finally cared about something. She told him proudly that she had been right to encourage him to take an interest in his inherited horses.

Sportswriters went wild over the idea of the match race. The Eastern press seemed as hurt as Billy by Nashua's defeat. But the very idea of the match race was the last straw for Elsie. It was bad enough that her daughter-in-law had usurped her public position as the mistress of Belair. Now her inexperienced son, Billy, was risking the reputation of his father's racing colors.

14

INDIA

That spring Billy and Ann were invited to India for another tiger shoot. Hours before the plane left, however, Billy declared he could not leave the match race negotiations. He also wanted to be in town on May 13, when the Jockey Club would induct him into the select group of directors of the New York Racing Association. Billy hoped to lobby the stuffy members to organize off-track betting, as Charlie Wacker had suggested. He urged Ann to go to India without him. Ann suspected a new girlfriend, unable to forget his romantic idyll in Rome while she was off in England collecting the St. Leger trophy. Billy denied everything.

The next morning, Ann greeted their traveling companions, the Russell Havenstrites, with uncharacteristically candid remarks about her husband and other women. It was obvious that things were going badly between them. "Stay home," said Mrs. Havenstrite.

But Ann decided to fly to Karachi, Pakistan, without Billy, hoping he would miss her. She left instructions with her private detective, Walter Kerr, to trail Billy. "I love my husband," she said.

Kerr soon confirmed Ann's suspicions. A week earlier, Billy had drifted into a New York cocktail party given by Buckley friend Gordon Lyle and had become infatuated with a society beauty named Sally Parsons Oriel, who was recently divorced. Sally had been glad to see him again after such a long lapse of time. Billy kept making excuses to stand near her. Sally had been a top debutante of Billy's generation, with a heart-shaped face as beautiful as young Hedy Lamarr's. Like other women Billy admired, Sally was known for her electrifying entrances to parties.

As one friend described her, "Sally came on as the baddest thing east of the Rockies. She pulled it off, she had style. She was naughty, beautiful, crazy, and a fantastic dancer."

Sally came from an old New York family. Robert Livingston, one of her forebears, had administered the oath of office to George Washington. Her mother, like Elsie Woodward, claimed descendance from King Robert the Bruce of Scotland. Billy had first met Sally in Newport in the summer of 1939 at her coming-out luncheon, an outdoor affair for eighty people given by her godfather. Billy had invited her to the Harvard Hasty Pudding show of 1940, but she had a "heavy beau" and was swamped with scores of invitations. Nineteen forty was the last great prewar debut party year. Sally and Billy danced under striped tents in Far Hills, Locust Valley, and Newport.

Two days after they met again, in May 1955, Billy called Sally late one night to talk. "I'm sitting next to Elsa Maxwell, and I'm bored." He also told her that his wife had a maharajah on a string and was off to India. That week Sally and Billy stopped by his house on Seventy-third Street, where she met his sons. If Ann had ever brought a man to meet the children, it would have been triumphantly cited as an example of her lower-class behavior.

After dinner, Sally told Billy he could kiss her. A gentleman, Billy refused, saying that he knew Sally was in love with someone else, and that he could be in love with her, but he would wait his time.

Shortly after that, Billy called Sally. "You wouldn't be interested in getting up early tomorrow, would you, just to see Nashua work out?"

She met Billy at 6 a.m. to drive in the Studillac to Belmont Park. He asked a groom to bring Nashua out into the paddock. Sally saw that Billy was terribly proud of him.

Sally's father would have liked her to marry Billy. He had opened the Seventy-second and Madison branch of the Central Hanover Bank and knew William Woodward, Sr. Sally framed a photograph she had taken that morning of Billy and Jim Fitzsimmons with Nashua at Aqueduct. Later that week, Billy asked Sally to meet him at a restaurant near Bloomingdale's, where he presented her with a little silver pin from Buccellati's, and she was very touched.

When, several days later, Sally suggested they go to a game at Princeton, Billy exclaimed, "Oh, I haven't been to a game in some time." Sally assumed that this was because of the social whirl into which Ann had plunged him; in fact, sports were not an interest of Billy's. But he enjoyed himself that day at Princeton. During the game, however, Billy became disturbed by the spectators who booed when a player made a mistake. He asked Sally, "Could we do as well if we were down on the field?" Perhaps he was thinking of Nashua's racetrack fans and what would happen if Nashua lost the upcoming match race.

After the game, Sally and Billy went to the Ivy Club. They were with people of their own set. Sally ran into the man she was crazy about and was proud to have the famous young sportsman at her side.

Meanwhile, in Jaipur, Ann did not have the heart to take photographs. Nor did she tan herself. Although she bought an apricot sari with gold threads, she did not feel like shopping. Instead, she spent an entire hour before she went to bed telephoning Billy and her detective. She was close to mental collapse, not sleeping, and asking repeatedly for iced tea, beer, and sweet papaya juice from the scores of servants.

Since it was polo season, Jai escaped to Delhi and Bombay to play at the matches. He gave instructions for Ann and the Havenstrites to hunt at the jungle camp at Swammandpor, ten miles to the south, for twelve days. The large Bengal tigers were terrorizing the nearby villages. They were hungry and eating people as well as other animals. The hunters were welcomed as a means of chasing them out of the area.

The white hunters slept in lavish white tents decorated with wall hangings. At night, Ann paced the silk carpets, worrying about her husband. There was plenty of space in the main room of her tent for a large bed, several chests of drawers, a desk, and a cupboard for clothing. Alcoves of the tent contained the toilet and the bathtub. Four servants took care of the needs of the five Americans. They emptied the toilet, brought water for the bathtub, and washed Ann's clothing by hand.

Bolstered by tranquilizers, Ann went shooting. The first afternoon, the group shot birds from a station wagon. But the guns rattled Ann. Russell Havenstrite was terrified by her desperation to shoot and her lack of expertise. The Havenstrites alerted the Maharajah about Ann's habits with guns. A number of the Indian men were scared to go hunting with her. In response, the Maharajah told his head guide that Ann was inexperienced and dangerous and that she should have someone with her at all times.

Ann agreed to let the head guide stand by her in the jungle. He would keep her hidden and on the side until it was time to shoot. The man fell in love with her. Ann and the guide shot at tigers from a platform on a high branch in a banyan tree. The tigers were lured by a goat kept tied to the trunk of the tree. Ann would wait for hours, overheated and anxious, until a tiger approached the goat.

Although the hunting party grew increasingly terrified of Ann, the group flew six hours in Havenstrite's airplane to shoot tigers in Cooch Behar. During the plane ride, Ann brooded, "I should be by Billy's side. I'm scared he is going to divorce me." The Havenstrites urged her to return to him.

Upon landing, the group drove a couple of hundred miles to a camp in the foothills of the Himalayas. It was a hot and humid May. The Americans watched the bright colors of the cloth and jewels worn by elephants in the Puniya festival, but Ann was not enjoying herself. The morning after their arrival, she received a brief letter from her private detective describing Billy's date near Bloomingdale's with Sally Parsons Oriel.

Distraught, Ann returned to camp to dress for the hunt. Despite the humidity and a temperature of nearly 120 degrees in the shade, she donned a cold-weather Abercrombie & Fitch loden wool hunting suit lined with white chinchilla. She was in such private anguish that her physical discomfort was immaterial to her. The jungle was dense with hanging vines and ten-foot-high grasses. Ann was too absorbed in her problems to enjoy the scent of the mustard flowers and the view of the white half circle of the Himalayas.

She was furnished with two elephants for the hunt. According to custom, the first carried several mattresses on which the hunter rode lying down or sitting sideways. The gun bearer sat on a seat behind Ann. Her second elephant was ridden by another guide, who shielded her from the sun with an enormous parasol.

One morning, the beaters drove a flock of pheasants toward the hunters. Ann swung around fast and fired too low, showering four elephants by mistake with buckshot in the sides and in the faces. The Indian keepers were horrified at the sight of the bleeding, thrashing, and trumpeting elephants. She had almost caused a fatal stampede. The Havenstrites tried to console Ann. They told her that rough hunting required more experience. Defeated, she agreed to go home. But after a sleepless night, she insisted she must shoot a tiger for Billy. Ann's shooting skills seemed to deteriorate. The next day the guides put the rich Americans up in the trees and drove leopards toward them. An animal was driven ten feet from Ann, but she missed it. Then it lunged under her; she missed it again.

But after several more days of practice shooting at targets on banyan trees, Ann finally succeeded. At 6 a.m., her admiring guide woke her from a sound sleep and took her 200 yards away from camp. He tied a goat to

Sally Livingston Parsons (later Sally Parsons Oriel), left, photographed for *Vogue* with Eleanor Frothingham at the National Horse Show, Madison Square Garden, 1946. Sally was a popular and beautiful debutante, and she and Billy became close friends in the last years of his life.

Ann, India, 1955.

a stake for bait. After only ten minutes, Ann shot and killed a leopard. The Havenstrites photographed Ann beside her kill, holding a rifle and wearing a hunting suit.*

Havenstrite marveled that Ann's temperament was so ill suited to hunting. He later wrote, "Sometimes the guide would have to grab the gun away from her, she would get so nervous and out of control shooting it. I would not go near her when she was shooting. She was very erratic with a gun, she had almost no idea of what she was doing. She was very nervous and high-strung whenever there was any shooting going on at all. I don't think she is a very stable person around firearms."

Ann was home by May 29, emotionally held together with tranquilizers. As they posed for photographers before Nashua ran the Preakness, she clutched Billy's arm. Billy longed to share these exciting events with Sally, but public appearances with Ann were his duty. Sally studied the pictures of Ann and wondered why any woman would be foolish enough to leave Billy alone so much. From remarks Billy had made, Sally was convinced that Ann had been in India to sleep with the Maharajah of Jaipur.

In the Preakness, Nashua seemed to exert himself only during the last third of the race. Ann and Billy jumped up and down when he won by a fifth of a second. "You're lucky," Ann shouted to Billy. He held her tight. Nashua had set a new track record. He ran the one and one-sixteenth miles in one minute fifty-four and three-quarters seconds and earned $67,550 for Billy. (Billy earned a total of $113,350 that day in the world of racing because his horse High Voltage also won a race at Belmont.)

In the winner's circle, the temperamental horse refused to let anyone drape the floral wreath on him. He kicked and wheeled until Billy angrily cut off that part of the ceremony. He almost canceled the next step of the victory celebration. But Ann urged him to continue the Preakness tradition. So an hour later, they had a station wagon filled with iced champagne driven to Nashua's stall for a small party. The next day, also according to custom, the old weather vane on top of the clubhouse was repainted with Nashua's winning number in the red-and-white colors of Belair.

At the victory party at Nashua's stall, Eddie Arcaro spoke to reporters, again challenging the owners of Swaps to a match race: "Nashua could have run all day. I wish we could get another crack at Swaps."

*This portrait (donated by Havenstrite) would be flashed around the country in the week after the shooting of Billy Woodward.

*   *   *

That June, Ann and Billy flew to Paris together for dinner at the chateau 4 Rue du Champ d'Entrainment, home of the Duke and Duchess of Windsor. Billy and Ann stayed at the Ritz. For their evening, Ann wore a gray floor-length taffeta dress, deciding against her blue gown just in case the Duchess wore one of her preferred "Wallis" blue dresses.

When they could not find the gates of the Windsor château behind tall hedges, Billy blamed Ann for getting them lost. Finally, the driver spotted the gilded gates. The royal pavilion was surrounded by oak, weeping willows, and blooming roses. Gloved footmen wore red-and-gold cutaway jackets. Ann's spirits began to soar as they entered this celebrated world. The invitation was for 8:45, and she had timed their arrival to be a few minutes early, as usual following Elsie's social injunction to be "prepunctual."

The house was a large reproduction of an eighteenth-century French château. Ann memorized details, some of which she would sketch in her notebook. High above the huge vestibule was a ceiling painted with clouds and flying geese. A faded royal silk banner hung from the second floor. A tiny perfume burner scented each room.

The Duke appeared in his ink-blue evening jacket. The bone-thin Duchess wore a short black evening gown of the sort she had made fashionable. Ann thought she recognized the Duchess's legendary ruby and diamond necklace with matching bracelet.

The American Duchess smiled when Ann complimented her on the floral room scents. In the vestibule, the Duchess and Ann agreed on the advantages of buying the new French couturier ready-to-wear. The Duchess's success made Ann feel better about herself. A plain woman who had created her own legendary chic, the Duchess, too, had snagged an important man with her charm. Like Ann, she was said to have come from "the wrong side of the tracks" and to have been raised without a father. The Duchess seemed too easily threatened by the lower classes to have been an aristocrat. But at least, as Ann told acquaintances later, "she was honest." Everybody complained about Negro servants, including Elsie, but few had the Duchess's frank hostility.

The Woodwards followed their hosts into the silver-blue salon, where the other guests had gathered. Ann sat on one of the gold Louis XVI chairs next to André Dubonnet, the Parisian with whom she had had an afternoon dalliance. Dubonnet was served his favorite cocktail without being asked his preference.

The Duchess of Windsor asked Ann a few questions about her friend Elsie Woodward and about the famous Nashua. Ann refreshed her lipstick when the Duchess snapped open her Verdura compact. She seemed unconsciously to mirror the Duchess, laughing and smoothing her skirt whenever the Duchess did.

Ann was hypnotized by the Duchess's eyes. She vowed to lose weight as she grew older, although she savored Billy's pride in her large breasts. She looked closely at the Duchess's flat figure; it was obvious that she was wearing a one-piece full-body elastic corset. Ann's midriff had thickened to the point where she, too, was probably encased in an uncomfortably tight sheath of elastic. Neither Ann nor the Duchess had a hair out of place. At such events, they looked like retouched portraits of themselves.

Both Ann and the Duchess had been controversial choices as wives. They were denounced for stealing their husbands from families of their "betters." Ann, who had devoted much thought to the Duchess, believed that the great difference in the two women's lives was their husbands' attitudes toward them. The Duke accorded his wife every honor, calling her "my romance." He added her American intonations and pronunciations to his conversation, answering the telephone, "the Doook speaking."

Billy, on the other hand, had slowly taken on his mother's attitude toward Ann. Except in bed, most of the qualities he had liked about her at the beginning now appeared distastefully common.

In fact, there was very little left on Ann's surface that resembled Angeline Crowell. There was her exuberant smile, her sexual appeal, and her will. Her Kansas drawl, however, had long ago been masked by mid-Atlantic vowels. She had finally perfected Elsie Woodward's throaty chuckle and would never dream of throwing her head back now to roar with laughter. She knew the rules about how to coordinate cloth napkins with sets of dishes.

At the Windsors that night, as usual, Billy disliked the way Ann scrutinized his face to see if he was having a good time. If he smiled, she exuded pride.

Billy and Ann were seated at different tables in the dining room, with its blue-and-gold silk drapes and red Oriental carpet. Ann furnished her next dining room with similar antique Chinese wall panels. She was seated next to Dubonnet, not because the Duchess knew of their brief affair, but because of his known preference for American blondes. When Dubonnet whispered to Ann that the great pleasures of sex were never in the marital bed, she put her hand on his wrist, smiling. The Duchess's knowing eyes seemed to gleam in her direction. Ann noticed with satisfaction that Billy was stuck with an elderly Swiss woman.

There was no real need for Ann to use French; the other guests and the Windsors all spoke English. But Ann had been studying conversational French at Berlitz. She thought nothing of making small errors in tenses and had picked up the British upper-class way of speaking without French intonations from Bill Astor and his friends.

Billy was not pleased by this conceit. Ann was only a poor girl from Kansas. To Billy, French was his mother's province. Elsie had, after all, been told by an old French duchess that her accent was positively eighteenth-century.

The meal was reaching its end; the Duchess had revealed her probably homemade savory, a rich frozen Camembert ice cream baked in hot bread crumbs. André Dubonnet looked longingly at it. Ann murmured something.

"Stop that Kansas French," Billy said from the next table. Ann looked as though she'd been hit.

But from the other side of the table, the Duchess spoke grandly, "But Ann, you must do as the Duke does. After all these years in France, he just doesn't bother to speak French at all."

Ann turned back to Dubonnet, trying to smile.

For the rest of the evening, the Duchess laughed approvingly in Billy's direction whenever Ann spoke. She seemed to bless the young couple in a way that few among Billy's relatives and friends cared to. Billy marveled that his wife had gained the protection of the most illustrious woman in their circle. It was a curious kind of evening, dedicated to display and stilted ceremony—and Ann had triumphed.

After dinner the Duchess led her guests in a conga line while the Duke played the piano. When she passed, Ann smiled at the frail former King. There was something about his melancholy Saxon face that touched her.

Finally, she strode over to him and made her invitation. The Duchess joined Ann, urging, "For God's sake, David, dance with her."

Ann stood ramrod straight, towering over her partner. Billy's eyes were glued to them as they executed an extravagant, arm's-length waltz. As they danced, the Duke invited Ann to see his country garden of sweet peas and white petunia beds by a mill stream in nearby Chevreuse.

After some of the elderly guests departed, the Duchess packed the Duke off to bed and took her remaining guests in several of the Windsors' cars to a nightclub called Scheherazade. Dubonnet continued to pay court to Ann.

When she relayed his flattering words to Billy later that night, he refused to speak to her at first. Then he announced that he wished to return to America immediately without her: "I want a divorce and get this thing finished."

That evening the Woodwards fought once again. But Billy did not leave Ann. They flew home bruised, but together.

15

HOME IS WHERE
THE HEART IS

During the next six months, Billy continued to see Sally Parsons Oriel. He brought her a small Victrola, carrying it up three flights of stairs to Sally's apartment on Seventy-second Street. Sally was impressed with his labor. "How nice," she said to him, "that someone with all your advantages would carry it up all those stairs."

Still, on July 2, Ann and Billy appeared together as Nashua entered the starting gate at Aqueduct, his forelock braided with red ribbon. It was a three-horse race; only two other owners dared challenge Nashua. This time Nashua really raced: he finished first, five lengths ahead of one horse and an amazing forty-five lengths ahead of the other. On top of the world again, Billy and Ann beamed as they collected $37,200 and another cup.

At the Arlington Classic in Chicago on July 16, Nashua took an early lead, but then fell substantially behind. At the last possible moment, he spurted across the finish line to win. Arcaro commented to reporters, "Nashua was not at his best, to say the least." Later, Elsie Woodward asked her son to curb the jockey's public statements about Nashua.

Meanwhile, behind the scenes, newspapers exaggerated the match race feud. They portrayed Rex Ellsworth as a rich former cowboy who owned the big red Swaps, unbeaten in five races that year, the finest thoroughbred to come out of the West, and Billy as the handsome playboy owner of Nashua. The two horses were written about as if they possessed emotions of love, conflict, depression, and pleasure.

Hollywood Park in California offered a gold cup and a winner's purse of $100,000 for any reasonable date in July. Newspaper headlines began billing the proposed match race as "the race of the century." The race would promote horse racing; millions would watch it on television.

The confusion mounted when the match race was announced for August 6 by Ben Lindheimer, owner of the Arlington track in Chicago.

As it turned out, Rex Ellsworth called off the race. Ellsworth telephoned Billy on June 10 to say that despite rumors to the contrary he had not agreed to ship his horse to Chicago. His horse would not be ready by August 6. Then Ellsworth called a reporter and claimed that during their most recent telephone conversation, Billy had finally agreed to a rematch in Hollywood Park, with a winner-take-all purse of $100,000. He said they promised each other not to say anything to the public until their horses had run their next races.

In a formal public statement published in hundreds of newspapers, Billy replied that he had never agreed to ship his horse to Hollywood Park.

Billy announced, "Although I am very much in favor of a meeting between the two horses, which the public demands, it is my belief that it would be unfair to Nashua and the public if we shipped him 3,000 miles at this time. I would prefer not to commit to a meeting between the two horses until August 1. If at that time, both horses are fit to run, the race should take place in a few weeks after both owners accept. I regret that statements I made in my conversation over the telephone on Friday with Rex Ellsworth were misinterpreted. I had no intention of indicating we would ship Nashua to California."

Despite Billy's decision, one night soon thereafter he and Ann bumped into movie star Don Ameche at the Stork Club, and Ameche convinced Billy to recommence negotiations.

Nashua continued to amaze his owner. During a dawn workout, Billy and Charlie Wacker clocked him. The horse broke the record for five furlongs with a time of fifty-six seconds. But Arcaro dismounted, complaining, "I couldn't get him to do anything." Nashua had run with such little effort that Arcaro had not even realized that he had just broken a record. "I'm going to bet big on this horse for the match race," Wacker told Billy.

Mr. Fitz described Nashua while the horse was cooling down after a run: "He's sound as a bell. He doesn't have a blemish on him. He has a wonderful conformation, a wonderful disposition, and a wonderful constitution. He's tall, he's got good wide legs, and a good wide jowl. He's got a good strong forehead and the thighs are the same way. He's long enough to go a distance and has muscles enough for speed. He's a perfect horse, even though he's not too pretty in the head; those lop ears are not so nice.

He's very intelligent; he's a long way from being the dumbest animal in the world. And he's as good a bred horse as you can have."

On July 18, hundreds of flashbulbs exploded at Billy and Ann as they waited at the Saratoga train station for Nashua to arrive. Billy's whim had turned into a national event. The match race would be run in Chicago five weeks later, but Mr. Fitz wanted Nashua to train on the deep, slow soil at Saratoga.

As was becoming his pattern, Billy had awakened during the previous night frightened that the race was a horrible mistake. Elsie Woodward's criticisms of Nashua and the match race infuriated and worried him; he still expected disappointment. Fame, however, was changing him. He was becoming less shy in public. This new attitude seemed to make him more attractive than ever to women.

At the train station, boisterous sportswriters were swarming around Mr. Fitz. Doubled over in pain from his arthritis, Mr. Fitz talked quietly about how he was going to spend the next five weeks trying to pour his sixty years of experience into getting his champion ready for "the race of the century." After more than a month in Saratoga, he hoped Nashua would hit the hard Chicago track with the sudden freedom of a baseball player who had been training with a heavy bat but who steps up to the plate with a far lighter one.

A half hour later, Nashua ambled off the freight car. Cameras snapped as Billy wiped his face with a handkerchief. Nashua was going into the match race with winnings totaling $782,545. If he were to win the match race, he would get a winner-take-all purse of $100,000 and jump into second place among purse winners. There was little for Billy and Ann to do for the next weeks except hover and worry.

While Mr. Fitz trained Nashua, Billy and Ann drove down to Southampton to the forty-four-room Wanamaker beach cottage for one of the most extravagant parties of the decade. "A Night in Baghdad" was given by Fernanda Wanamaker Leas, a long-haired blond department store heiress whose costume was a transparent harem outfit with a gold crown adorned by four long ostrich feathers. Camels wearing garlands of flowers roamed the grounds.

Guests included Gary Cooper, who was awarded first prize in the men's division for his Turkish costume—and for being Gary Cooper. Serge Obolensky wore harem pants.

Billy Woodward had planned a strange costume. He explained to fellow houseguest Francis Kellogg that he was dressing as a blackamoor to look invisible: "If I paint myself black, the *Life* magazine photographer won't be able to take a picture of me." Although he loved escorting women who made dramatic entrances, Billy himself pretended to disdain exhibitionism. But emboldened by his recent fame, he was planning to make a splash of his own.

Ann had helped Billy assemble his costume, but they quarreled over whether he should wear her long pearl necklaces. She said no. He refused to let Ann apply the very dark Pan-Cake makeup. Instead, society photographer Jerome Zerbe smeared it on Billy's back. Except for a turban, necklace, and large earring, Billy was naked and black from the waist up. A wide white cummerbund cut into the flesh of his stomach. He wore a long, wide sari skirt, and his gilded turban had a plume.

One result was that Billy left inky palm prints on the bare shoulders of his dancing partners. He was the talk of the party. Guests said he—and not Gary Cooper—should have won the prize for the most outrageous costume. In his column, Cholly Knickerbocker reported Billy's outfit as most interesting.

Ann had dieted and lost more than six pounds. Her hair swung free of pins, almost electric. Early in the evening, she discarded a gold-and-silver blouse to display her flawless skin in a brief gold satin halter top. Her midriff looked firm and her stomach flat over rough white cotton harem pants. Her sapphire-and-diamond necklace gleamed on her bare collarbone.

Serge Obolensky was one of Ann's first dancing partners. Ann also danced with Harry Evans, the short, smiling extra man, who managed not to trip over his silly striped bathrobe. Evans, a columnist at *Family Circle*, kept the respect of his employers with his society connections. Although they rarely spoke, Billy greeted Evans at parties as if they were good friends.

During the August horse season, Billy visited his childhood friend Jo Hartford Douglas Bryce at her Vermont farm, fifteen miles from Saratoga.

She and her English husband, Ivor Bryce, collected beautiful houses. Nowhere was this more apparent that at Black Hole Hollow farm, in a region once known for dairy farms. Shaded by ancient trees, the one-story farmhouse had thick stone walls and more than twenty-five rooms. To the old-fashioned, low-ceilinged farmhouse, the Bryces had added spacious guest bedrooms, a music room, a dining room, and a bar and sun lounge.

As Nashua went through his paces in Saratoga, Billy drank a martini for breakfast, then sat in the pink guest bedroom, chain-smoking and reading racing charts to learn more about Swaps's lineage and performance. He did not swim in the pond surrounded by blueberry bushes or play tennis. At Ann's prodding, he drove to Saratoga every other day. Ten years had passed since Billy and Ann had stayed with Jo Bryce in Norfolk, but Ann's efforts to talk to the older woman were still met with an amused silence. Jo blamed Ann for the Woodwards' ongoing quarrels.

While Billy and Ann visited, a third houseguest was the British writer Ian Fleming, then forty-six, who was in America for the simultaneous publication of three James Bond thrillers. One friend described Fleming's face as he grew older as a "sculptured mask of melancholy." The disinherited grandson of a millionaire, Fleming was surprisingly similar to Billy. His family money had also been made in the American Civil War. Both men had been raised in homes from which their hard-driving fathers had been absent. Fleming's father had died a hero in World War I.

He and Billy had precise table manners and sported short Dunhill cigarette holders. They shared interests in fast cars, women, and expensive clothes. Although both were married, they had bachelor airs. Neither believed that a sexual partner had any necessary claim on his affections. Fleming often described his wife as the former wife of Lord Rothermere. Much of Fleming's life, like Billy's, had been devoted to pretending he did not particularly care to succeed at anything. He had posed as a kind of British public school dilettante. Fleming was emerging from a long dormant stage and writing books for the first time in his life as an antidote to a difficult new marriage.

Billy had a strong sense of hero worship in him, and he was ready to take on an intense two-week friendship with Ian Fleming. The writer had a smug and watchful attitude around Americans. They came on too strong. But Billy was a welcome relief. Fleming joked affectionately about Billy's habit of cocktails before lunch, pronouncing him one of the best Americans he had ever met.

When it came to glamour, Billy was in a class with James Bond himself. Fleming was impressed with Billy's old money, his ex-showgirl wife who had him on a long leash, and his racehorses. In *Diamonds Are Forever*, which Fleming wrote that summer, James Bond has a partner named Felix Leiter, who has several things in common with Billy. Bond and Leiter crush

A charity polo match, West Palm Beach, Florida, 1955. Seated, left to right: Ann Woodward, Mary Sanford, Mrs. Mario Pansa, Charles Wacker, Jr., the Duke and Duchess of Windsor. Billy Woodward is standing behind his wife, who has a bruised lower lip. Elsie Woodward said of the Duchess of Windsor, "My poor sorry Duchess, she married that boring little man and now she has to live with him."

"A Night in Baghdad" costume party, Southampton, 1955. Left to right: Serge Obolensky, hostess Fernanda Wanamaker Leas, and Gary Cooper, who won the prize for best costume (a bright red fez and Turkish garb).

Ann and Billy at the same costume party. Other guests included Angier Biddle
Duke, dressed as an Indian prince, and the Duke of Marlboro as the Duke of
Marlboro.

an illegal international diamond export scheme and save a horse race fixed by American gangsters. The novel was dedicated to three people, including Billy: ". . . to the memory of w.w., jr. at saratoga, 1954 and 1955."

The "Billy" character is Bond's true American friend, a former Secret Service agent. In the novel Fleming describes a speeding car trip as part of the good life: " 'I didn't know the Studillacs had it in them,' said Bond. There was a straight patch of empty road in front of them. Leiter gave a brief glance in his rear-view mirror and suddenly rammed the gear lever into second and thrust his foot to the floor boards. Bond's head jerked back on his shoulders and he felt his spine being pressed into the bucket seat. Incredulously he watched the hooded speedometer. Eighty . . . Ninety, ninety-five, six, seven—and then there was a bridge and a converging road and Leiter's foot was on the brake and the deep roar of the engine gave way to a steady thrumming as they settled down into the fifties again and swept easily through graded curves."

Like Billy, Leiter describes how his swift souped-up Studillac will outwit the police: "We'll take the Taconic State Parkway. . . . There's a fifty-mile speed limit in most of New York State, and the cops are fierce. I can generally get away from them if I'm in a hurry. They don't book you if they can't catch you. Too ashamed to show up in court and admit something is faster then they are."

Later, Leiter points out the great trainer Sunny Jim Fitzsimmons and the Woodward horses, most of which, Leiter explains, will be winners at Saratoga.

In chapter ten, titled "Studillac to Saratoga," Fleming wrote that the two horses predicted to win at Saratoga were thoroughbreds owned by C. V. "Sonny" Whitney and by William Woodward, Jr. The plot turns on the fact that the gangsters have substituted another horse for one that is scheduled to run against Woodward's horse. Leiter convinces the jockey of the substituted horse to throw the race, and the Woodward horse is declared the winner. He also introduces James Bond to American vermouth for martinis, a preference of Billy's.

At the end of the book, Leiter drives the Studillac to Las Vegas, just in the nick of time to save Bond from gangland criminals. The duo then drive to Los Angeles: "Then they were rolling easily along Sunset Boulevard between the palm trees and the emerald lawns, the dust-streaked Studillac looking incongruous among the glistening Corvettes and Jaguars."

It was clear to Ann that Ian Fleming disliked her. But because Billy was enamored of him, Ann laughed at his jokes and sought to humor him by asking for advice on hunting in Europe. Fleming suggested she visit

Schloss Mittersill, a shooting and social club in the Bavarian Alps, adding that he was one of the few nontitled members. Ann booked a late summer week.

Hunting was becoming an obsession to Ann. She was dismayed that she had been excluded when Billy and his boyhood friends Eustice Paine, Jr., and Anthony Villa hunted birds along the Hudson River. Unlike Elsie, who viewed these shoots as masculine pursuits, Ann was determined to accompany her husband on shooting trips. To Elsie, Ann's eagerness to shoulder a gun alongside Billy was just another example of her commonness. But Ann loved the look of admiration on Billy's face when she told him of shooting a fox with Bill Astor.

A year earlier, in the summer of 1954, Billy had presented Ann with a custom-made shotgun from E. J. Churchill in London, the official gun makers to the Prince of Wales. That August, on her way to Paris, Ann had stopped at the gun works on Orange Street in Leicester Square, London, to be measured. The barrel was twenty-five inches long and customized to her arm length and comfort. The purchase price was $250 and included gold leaf inlay on the barrel.

After Ann's departure, Billy asked Fleming for advice about his marriage. Should he divorce her? It seemed that he and Ann were always either at each other's throats or in bed. "Yes, divorce, my good man," said Fleming.

The first morning without Ann the cook and butler brought Billy what he needed for breakfast, which was coffee followed by a martini and a hot buttered scone. At lunchtime, Billy appeared on the front porch. Jo Bryce was back from her morning at Saratoga.

They sat down to a light lunch on a huge glass table surrounded by blue irises and honeysuckle. The Bryces and Billy sipped spiked ice tea with wild mint leaves and laughed as Ian Fleming described his arrest by a local police chief. Fleming had driven Billy's Studillac through town at 100 miles an hour. The chief had questioned Fleming at his kitchen table for hours, unable to understand his accent.

After lunch, Billy sped ahead of Jo, at nearly 100 miles an hour, over an ancient covered Vermont bridge to see how loud it would rattle. At the Saratoga paddock, Billy paced around old Mr. Fitz, who sat in a folding chair. Mr. Fitz said, "I want to get the horse screwed tight. I want that horse to run like a bat out of hell from the starting gate. I believe a match race is won in the first three quarters of a mile—when a horse sets a pace and forces the other horse to keep up with him.''

After the fourth race, a loudspeaker announced "Nashua" and the crowd stilled: this was Nashua's final public workout around the track before being shipped to Chicago. At first Eddie Arcaro, wearing only a white T-shirt and blue jeans, urged the horse into a slow gallop. But suddenly, on the backstretch, the jockey's arms began to pump. Nashua's legs became a blur. The horse was running his heart out, and the crowd knew it. Billy cheered with them, at the top of his lungs.

16

BOAR HUNT

Billy decided to join Ann at Mittersill just before the match race. The famous young sportsman was beginning to believe in himself. After all, the race was being hailed in the United States as the sporting event of the century. Ann insisted it was proof he was a sportsman with great instincts. "It's in your blood," she told him. He was a winner, just like Nashua. It was a heady thought.

As soon as Billy arrived at the Tyrolean village near Salzburg, his driver cautioned him to use a guide like the other tourists. Only local hunters stalked wild boar and chamois on their own in the steep Alpine forests.

The moss-covered Schloss Mittersill was an imposing sight. The restored twelfth-century castle had 100 rooms and a subterranean labyrinth of dungeons. Baron Hubert and Baroness Terry von Pantz had spent at least a million dollars to convert the castle into a hunting club. Prince Alex Hohenlohe and his trained local guides ran the hunting parties. Hohenlohe was short on funds because his vast East German empire had been taken over by the Communists. His wife, Princess "Honeychile," was a former chorus girl from the American South who had been in Bob Hope's troupe. Ann was thrilled to greet the thirty titled Europeans, who had each paid a thousand dollars initiation fee for the right to fish, hunt, and socialize here.

On their first night, the Woodwards took cocktails with the Duchess of Westminster and Sir Francis and Lady Peek, who had renovated areas of the castle as apartments. Other guests included Billy's friend Count Peter Salm (whose mother was Millicent Rogers), Prince Charles D'Arensberg,

Prince Johann Turn und Taxis, and Princess Marie Christine de Bourbon Parma. Ann noticed how pleased Billy was with his pretty dinner partner, Lady Marilyn Peek.

The next day Ann and Billy rose before daybreak to hunt boar in a group of guides, dogs, beaters, gun bearers, and servants. All the guests wore loden green hunting outfits. In her Tyrolean felt hat, Ann was one of the most stylish women at Mittersill.

Prince Alex Hohenlohe went over the Mittersill rules. The hunters, accompanied by their jaegers, beaters, and other servants, would hike to a small hut a few miles away. But Billy had a more sporting idea. He wanted to hunt the wild boar and stag alone in the steep woods and tree-covered ravines—without any guides at all. Ann summoned Hohenlohe to ask for a private hunt.

Hohenlohe was appalled.

"But, no, my good woman, never," he said. "No guest is permitted such foolishness. I personally forbid it."

In fact, Prince Hohenlohe himself hunted without a local guide. But he had been hunting here since boyhood and knew every valley and sharp precipice.

Hohenlohe laid down the law. "I will not be responsible for your injuries or death. My good woman, you and your husband might easily slip and fall three miles down a ravine. It is madness to think you can just wander around on your own in an unfamiliar country looking for things to shoot at."

"Oh, but my husband is a great hunter," said Ann. "He isn't afraid because—"

"I forbid it. By mistake, you may shoot an animal in mating season and that is illegal to kill, or an animal that is too old or rare."

Hohenlohe walked away saying, *"Quelle bêtise.* And dangerous too!"

That morning, with the guides, Billy shot two animals. Ann shot nothing. Billy mocked her for her poor handling of the shotgun.

The second night at Mittersill, Ann's high forehead and bare back glowed in the candlelight from an iron chandelier, purportedly installed by Himmler during the Nazi occupation of the castle. Her green skirt trailed along the stone floor. It was all more glamorous than she had ever dreamed possible. She was still the beautiful young Mrs. William Woodward, Jr., in an ancient royal castle.

At dinner Ann sat next to Prince Alex Hohenlohe. At a different table, Billy kissed the hand of Princess Honeychile Hohenlohe. Ann was shocked to see that on Billy's other side was again seated the beautiful Lady

Marilyn Peek. Ann suspected that Lady Peek had asked to sit with Billy for a second time. That sort of subterfuge was par for the course in international society. (In fact, Baroness Terry von Pantz had put Billy Woodward and Marilyn Peek together because she was young and pretty and he was young and handsome.)

Ann had difficulty paying attention to Prince Hohenlohe's conversation about Alpine storms. By the time the soup course was cleared, Billy faced Lady Peek. He whispered in her ear. Marilyn Peek laughed.

Picking up her long green satin gloves, Ann strode around the table to stand behind Billy. "What's going on?" she demanded.

The familiar look of admiration and fear filled Billy's eyes.

Ann shouted across him to the startled Englishwoman, "Well, Lady Peek . . . Lady . . . Lady Prick, he's my husband and thank you I will sit with my husband."

Marilyn Peek flinched and stood. Ann slid down into the empty chair next to her husband. Her eyes were shining with unshed tears. Nobody moved until Honeychile beckoned to Marilyn Peek to take Ann's empty seat next to Prince Alex. The guests watched Ann to see what she would do next. But Ann had made her point. Tactically, she had learned that the best time to confront Billy was in public, where his manners inhibited his reactions. Ann went further each time.

Afterward, the guests and the Hohenlohes went to the living room. The walls were hung with a hundred mounted stag heads. Ann sat alone on a medieval leather throne chair. The atmosphere relaxed, people played backgammon, stood by the bar, or danced to the waltzes played by the orchestra.

"Why did you behave so badly?" Princess Honeychile asked Ann.

Still seething, Ann said, "Who arranged the seating? That woman is trying to steal my husband. Why does she sit next to my husband at every meal?"

"Now wait a minute, the seating was coincidental," said Princess Honeychile. She looked into Ann's wild turquoise eyes. "But you're insane," she told her. "You need help."

Princess Honeychile had heard that Billy was trying to divorce Ann; it sounded like a good idea. It did not dawn on the Princess that Billy's divorce threats might be part of what was driving his wife into jealous rages.

Honeychile called to her husband. "Talk to this woman," she told him. "She's insane."

After consulting his wife, Alex Hohenlohe knocked on Billy's bed-

room door: "Bill, your wife's insane. You must get some help for her."
After a pause, Alex said, "You must get off this holiday and take the woman
to a hospital to get some help."

That night a maid summoned Prince Hohenlohe to hear screams
coming from the Woodwards' large bedroom. Inside, Ann was begging
Billy to tell her he was not infatuated with Marilyn Peek. Billy refused
and pushed her against a table. She cursed and threw a vase at him. Outside, Alex Hohenlohe heard glass shatter. "Damn you, Woodward,"
screamed Ann.

The next day, after conferring with Princess Honeychile and Baron
von Pantz, Alex Hohenlohe spoke firmly to Billy. "Unfortunately, I very
much want you to go." He offered Billy a dignified exit. "Wait a day if
you wish."

When Billy returned to their room, Ann was lying in bed, numb
from barbiturates. She apologized abjectly when Billy accused her of ruining their vacation. Billy walked over to her. He saw that her face was
bruised. "Jesus, Annie, let's forget it." Without removing her sleep mask,
she opened her arms, as he collapsed down on the bed. "That pompous
bastard Hohenlohe," said Billy, hugging Ann back. The next morning the
Woodwards were on their way home.

Driving rains pelted the hard Chicago track for two days before the match
race. Mr. Fitz thanked providence: wet weather would soften the track and
favor Nashua. Ann arrived in Chicago with her array of Louis Vuitton
garment bags, suitcases, and trunks. Billy's friends whispered that she was
an ostentatious clotheshorse.

In reality, the suitcases were evidence of Ann's latest problem. Elsie
had issued an order. Billy must do something about Ann at the races—or
else. Billy obediently told Ann that in the future he would go into the
winner's circle without her unless he selected her clothes. Neither mentioned the recent *Sports Illustrated* spread on Ann's outfits at the races,
which referred to her as the "best-dressed woman in sports."

In New York, before she packed for the match race, Ann had asked
Billy to choose her ensemble. "Too busy," said Billy. As she jammed ten
new dresses and suits into travel bags, Ann was certain that Billy would
have an adequate selection in Chicago.

Three nights before the match race, Ann hung her clothes around a
guest room in Charles Wacker's Lake Forest estate.

"What should I wear to the race?" she asked Billy.

"Tomorrow, I'll choose a dress," said Billy. He was keeping her as off-balance as he felt himself. The race was out of his control, but he believed his life would be destroyed if he lost it.

Ann had become more worried than ever about her appearance. Every morning, she begged Billy to choose her dress for the day. When he did, she thanked him repeatedly. In her mind Billy's selections looked better, even if they only matched up her familiar blouses, suits, and gloves. Ann felt beautiful walking into a party or a press conference with his approval as the final touch to her ensemble.*

In the hectic days before the match race, the track in Chicago was packed with television, newspaper, and magazine reporters. Billy was still awkward facing reporters and crowds. At these moments even Elsie could not tone down Ann's high spirits. She knew just what to do. Ann dazzled reporters by reciting Mr. Fitz's views of Nashua's regimen and progress. Soon she was trading racing information with reporters. Though Swaps was the four-to-one favorite, Ann told the press that she believed there was not an animal alive who could beat Nashua.

One afternoon just before the match race, Nashua gave everyone a scare. His groom had saddled him and was walking him around the turf in front of the racecourse grandstands to get him more accustomed to the crowds. Suddenly, something spooked Nashua and he reared back on his hind legs, his head high, tossing his mane like a wild mustang in a cowboy movie. He lost his balance, looking as though he were going to topple back and crack his spine. People in the grandstands groaned. Twenty feet from the horse, Billy grabbed Ann's hands and held hard.

Miraculously, the groom held the reins tight, and Nashua finally landed on all four feet. Billy was shaken by the near disaster. But Ann assured the reporters, "This is all part of the training to calm him down."

At three o'clock on the morning of the race, Billy awoke with a start. Despite her face mask and earplugs, Ann woke up, too. Billy told Ann that the horse should be winning races in England.

---

*Lydia Smiley had traveled to New York to visit her niece Ann just before the match race. She was appalled by Ann's misery and remembered her saying, "I'm always wrong. It doesn't matter what I do, they don't think I have style." Lydia recalled, "Ann wouldn't wear a dress if Bill didn't like it; he used to pick out each and every one for her. If she bought a dress, and he didn't like it, Ann returned it that same afternoon."

In New York, one night before a party, Ann was crying and unable to dress herself at all. Her aunt suggested she was working too hard to please her husband. "You are a pretty girl, nobody can take that away from you no matter what dress you wear," said Aunt Lydia, kissing her. "A wife is obedient, but you're acting to extremes."

"He'll win here," said Ann.

Billy put on his long silk pajama top, listening to the soft rain. Ann slipped on a filmy blue robe and applied lipstick. Billy was worried that the press would criticize him because the tickets to the race cost too much. Mr. Fitz had not been happy about the rise in prices. The fans were going to cheer Nashua from grandstand seats that cost $2.00 instead of $1.20; admission to the clubhouse area was now $4.00, up from $1.75.

"But people want to pay the money," said Ann.

They listened to the rain pelting the windows. Billy put a cigarette in his holder. "That rain will ruin me. He'll slip and fall."

"Mr. Fitz never saw such a good horse," said Ann.

"He can't run in the mud." Billy sounded as scared as if he were going to run the race himself.

"He ran in the mud in Florida."

Billy refused to take comfort. He was out on a limb. He hated thinking of how his mother would take a loss. She had refused to come to Chicago.

Moreover, Mr. Fitz, who also disapproved of the race, was finally treating Billy as though he deserved to own the Belair colors. Losing would be a disaster.

Billy was still nervous when he called the paddock shortly after 8 a.m. The track was muddy and slow, but at least the rain had stopped. Both horses were taking a romp. Nashua seemed fine.

The two horses took a turn around the track with their exercise riders. Billy was unaware that Swaps's owner was disturbed over his horse's back foot. A tape bandage was prepared to hold a protective leather pad on top of his shoe.

The track gates opened at ten o'clock. While Swaps had been undefeated in eight races that year, Nashua had been beaten only once in nine starts—and that was by Swaps himself in the Kentucky Derby.

After their breakfast trays were cleared, Ann asked Billy if he had decided which dress she should wear. Billy ignored her. Ann pulled a pink cotton-and-silk dress over her head, imploring him to like it. When he called it "too youthful," she became unhinged. They rushed to the window when they heard Charlie Wacker's little airplane landing out on the lawn.

"Better hurry," said Billy. The diversion was working; his amiability had returned.

Downstairs, the Wacker family was startled as cries came from the Woodward bedroom.

Upstairs, Ann did not know what to do. She finally lunged at Billy, her hand raised. He threw her onto the chaise on a mound of satin travel bags filled with brassieres, slips, and stockings, and left her sobbing, begging him to choose a dress. They were already ten minutes late for boarding the plane.

Downstairs, Billy said, "Ann's having a dreadful time dressing. She can't seem to decide what to wear."

"Don't worry about us," said Charles Wacker with sympathy. Everyone had heard enough to assume that Ann was at it again. Poor Billy was a saint; he put up with such hell. After all, it was Billy Woodward's day and Ann's vanity was ruining it for him.

"I hope Annie makes it today," said Billy. He probably had no intention of attending the race without Ann. He needed her help when he panicked in front of a television camera. He prolonged his private game as long as possible, however.

The hour of departure came and went. Billy did not mind. The race did not start until five that afternoon, and he preferred to arrive as late as possible. Pacing the paddocks and listening to the crowds was unnerving.

"Where is Ann?" Billy asked as if he had suddenly lost patience. He ducked upstairs, cursing Arcaro's loss in the fourth race on a horse named Mighty Moment to Willie Shoemaker, who would ride Swaps. It was bad luck. Ann was slumped on the bed waiting for him. She wore a black brassiere and girdle. "It doesn't matter a bit about the jockey," Ann said. "The horse will win for you."

Billy brightened. "Oh, wear that," and he waved at the dress on the bed.

Billy smoked a cigarette in the hall while she dressed. Ten minutes later, they appeared in the doorway to the huge living room. Billy enjoyed sharing the spotlight of her dubious entrance. The low-cut black cocktail dress was utterly inappropriate. Billy watched several women shake their heads. They wore buttoned-up pastel shirtwaist frocks or sweet summer suits.

In another minute, Billy and Ann and the other guests were on their way across wide lawns to the plane. Billy's nerves were taut. Nobody spoke to Ann during the ten-minute flight. When they landed, Billy learned from the swarm of reporters that Nashua was still the underdog in the betting. If he won, he would pay $4.40 on the dollar. Ann and Billy joined festive crowds walking to the gates. Fans wished Ann luck. "Thank you so much," she said, waving.

Such was her physical charisma that the press did not criticize her clinging black dress. She greeted a reporter. He asked her what she thought about Willie Shoemaker's having beaten jockey Eddie Arcaro in the earlier race. "My husband is very optimistic," said Ann.

The match race was the seventh race of the afternoon. At 4:45, after the sixth race, the noise of the crowd deepened as the rival three-year-olds were led from their stalls to the track. Nashua's lead pony, Francis, was with him. The pampered blueblood was covered with a light cashmere blanket.

The two jockeys weighed in. Willie Shoemaker was only twenty-four years old, a little man with cold dark eyes and black hair. Eddie Arcaro was thirty-nine, four feet ten inches, and known as the "master of the whip." A driving competitor, he was a veteran of twenty-four years' experience and had been the first American to win 3,000 races, five of them Kentucky Derbys. Today his saddle was twice as heavy as usual. He had filled it with the lead he needed to meet the jockey's minimum weight standard for the track.

At 5:18 the horses moved off the grass to the starting gate. Nashua was in stall number two, Swaps in stall number four. Arcaro looked down the track at little paths made in the drying mud. He found one leading from stall number three. Arcaro decided to get himself on that path and hold it. The stands suddenly fell silent.

The gates flew open. Before the crowd could make a sound, Arcaro had shrieked at Nashua and whacked him. Fans said later that Nashua sprang out of the gate at the sound of the bell as though he had been stuck with a tack. Shoemaker was surprised; he had expected Nashua to start slowly as usual. But Mr. Fitz had devised a new strategy for Billy's temperamental colt.

At the quarter pole, Arcaro hit the horse six times. He looked back at Swaps with satisfaction. (At the Kentucky Derby the Californian had been a length and a half ahead of him at this point.) Today Swaps made several attempts to catch up, but Nashua just seemed to lower his belly and gallop faster.

Although Nashua was four lengths ahead on the home stretch, Arcaro went wild. (Some said he was a man who believed that horse racing would be better if you could eliminate the horse.) He began to switch the whip from one hand to the other, beating Nashua, kicking him, and riding as if the two horses were neck and neck. Near the finish line, Ann and Billy were locked in an embrace, jumping up and down. Nashua went under the wire six lengths ahead of Swaps, with Arcaro still whipping him.

The two Woodwards faced the cameras, hugging each other like a storybook couple. "You played it right," said Ann euphorically. Billy bit his upper lip hard. "I won, I won."

For William Woodward, Jr., the few seconds after Nashua won were probably the best of his entire thirty-five-year life. The win confirmed his skills as an adult and a sportsman. Members of the East Coast racing establishment surrounded Billy and Ann. Nashua had vindicated them. Most people now believed Nashua to be the better horse; he would soon be selected "horse of the year."

Even Elsie had to admit that Billy had played it right.

A television commentator announced Nashua's ninth victory in ten starts that year. The $100,000 purse boosted his season's total winnings to $689,700, making him the second largest money-maker in thoroughbred history.*

Billy led Nashua and the mounted Arcaro into the winner's circle. Ann beamed, ecstatic to be sharing this event as Billy's wife. Nashua shied away from the man who tried to drape the flower wreath around his neck. He was wired up. But when a television camera emerged, Ann extended her arm high toward the horse to shake Arcaro's hand. Nashua snorted and kicked out with his left hind foot. The reporters swarmed forward as Ann jumped away, planting one hand on her wide-brimmed black hat. Ann patted the horse and reached up again to shake the jockey's hand. The journalists began to interview her as though she were the sole owner of the horse.

Unhappy and ignored, Billy held the horse's reins. He seemed to be counting the seconds until the embarrassing ordeal was finished. Illinois governor Lyle Stratton awarded the trophy. Arcaro dismounted.

As Billy led the horse from the winner's circle, Laddie Sanford whispered to him, "She's going to be in every newspaper in America hanging out of that dress." Billy nodded.

But more controversial than Ann's décolletage was the owner's assertion that Swaps may have entered the race with a sore foot. At the paddock, Rex Ellsworth was telling reporters the race had not been a fair test. Billy and Charlie Wacker said he was lying. Nashua had proved fair and square to be the better horse.

Mary and Laddie Sanford, C.Z. and Winston Guest, and the Iselins toasted one another and Billy and Ann and Nashua well into the morning at a party in the Ambassador Hotel. Nashua's victory reinforced their deep

---

*Bing Crosby's son Gary wrote in the *Herald-Tribune*, "Nashua beat Swaps in everything this afternoon in the Match Race for $100,000, winner take all."

belief in their class superiority. The television fame of the Woodwards and the horse also impressed them, despite their desire to keep the general public distant from their elite sport.

Elsie was conspicuous by her absence. Still mourning, said friends, referring to the death that year of her sister Edith Ames Cutler. As Billy expected, his mother spoke sharply about Ann. Elsie tended to pronounce her words even more authoritatively on the telephone: "That black dress was ghastly. I don't want her in the winner's circle anymore." Elsie Woodward could see that the prize-winning horse upstaged her son, and Ann was a close second.

At the Ambassador party, Billy reported this latest order from Elsie to Ann. His friends noticed a new silence from Ann. Her eyes followed Billy as though she were waiting for the next round of a losing fight.

Even at the height of Ann and Billy's fame with Nashua, Ann was nagged by a presentiment of loss. "Unhand my man," she told Joan Fontaine, who was dancing with Billy at a party on Manhattan's West Side. After a snowstorm, the winter before the match race, Ann had walked out of El Morocco and clutched her ear. Her diamond earring was gone. She knelt searching in a snowdrift.

The missing earring confirmed her worst fears about how easily her life might evaporate. The next day she and a maid dug in snowbanks outside El Morocco, but Ann never found the earring. She insisted that nothing lit up her face like that diamond-and-pearl cluster. It was as if she had lost some part of herself.

While Ann and Billy were away a month later, the East Seventy-third Street town house was burglarized. Ann instructed John Ludewig, her husband's secretary, to change the locks. Forty thousand dollars in jewelry was missing, along with their bedroom safe. Even though the jewelry had been insured, Ann experienced emotions similar to mourning. She felt the robbery had been her fault. Ann spoke of the loss of a platinum-and-diamond "preengagement" ring as though it had been a living thing. It was an early gift from Billy and was valued at less than $1,000. Ann interviewed former servants, fearing that one of them had stolen the jewelry. It was easier than speaking of her real and growing fears of losing Billy.

17

WINNER TAKE ALL

September 2, 1955, Aqueduct.

It was a glorious day for New York racing, and the glory was all Billy Woodward's. Four hundred fans waited as the victory train slowed. The great horse was coming home from Chicago. The crowd had recognized Billy from television and movie newsreels. He lit a cigarette with his gold Dunhill lighter. For a rare moment, his anticipation was so intense he forgot to be self-conscious about the Americans staring at his upper-crust English style. The train door opened to cheers from the crowd as the most famous horse that ever raced pranced down the gangplank.

Twenty minutes after Nashua arrived, Billy and a cavalcade of reporters trailed the horse van to Aqueduct Racetrack. At all four automobile entrances to the track, signs proclaimed: AQUEDUCT, HOME OF NASHUA.

The stablemen stood at attention by the barns. The nostrils of the high-strung horse flared as more flashbulbs popped.

Sometimes Billy's new pride made him high and happy. One morning that week, he swore eternal love to Ann by telephone to Paris; he liked her better when she was away. He told her that he had ordered a $100,000 diamond necklace from Cartier for Christmas.

At other moments, Billy hated everything about Ann. He gagged on the scent of her White Shoulders perfume. But, perversely, it was then that he desired her most. He enjoyed taking her violently. Recently, to Ann's dismay, Billy had added a new twist, a carousel of male pornographic films borrowed from a friend, to watch before they made love.

*　　*　　*

September 3, 1955.

Fresh from the airplane from Paris, Ann was looking forward to the weekend with Billy in Oyster Bay. But Billy was irked by the rain and the Labor Day weekend traffic jams. When they arrived at the Playhouse, the boys were out riding ponies with Barney Balding, the local riding teacher.

Billy looked around and announced, "The house is a mess." Although Ann was ashamed of the Playhouse's unfinished, dusty appearance, there never seemed to be time to arrange for a decorator.

Billy continued to criticize Ann, repeating with some relish Elsie's latest criticisms about her as a mother. His mother, who was still singing the praises of Jeanne Murray Vanderbilt, had mentioned Ann's "vagrant" quality to Billy. "She would not be around at all," Elsie told Billy, "if not for that horse."

Not satisfied, Billy fired another round. He mimicked Ann's complaints to Jack James's wife about Billy's request that Ann have sex with him and another woman. Ann realized with dismay that Billy was tapping the telephone on Seventy-third Street. She countered with details, gleaned from her private detective, of how Billy had taken a date to Aqueduct. It was a familiar fight.

Ann shouted, "Why not get a man in bed with us? That's what you really want."

Billy slapped her hard. She swung back at him but missed. He shoved her against a wall. Pushing Billy away, Ann scratched his cheek. Horrified to see his blood, she covered her face with her hands, begging forgiveness. She rushed for the bottle of iodine. The relationship was still alive because she and Billy could still find new ways to hurt each other. Billy slapped the iodine out of Ann's hand, then knocked her to the floor. She lay still, the wind gone out of her. A contrite look passed over his face.

After several minutes, they were undressing in front of Ann's bed. Ann closed the satin curtains. She and Billy still referred to afternoon sex as "taking a nap."

Two hours later, Ann sat in front of her littered dressing table blotting her eyeshadow with powder. "AEW: conservative, sexy, and glamorous," she had written in her notebook. She often wore a bra to sleep at night, believing that it would help to preserve her figure.

She applied makeup base to her chest and neck. Night had fallen, and the cavernous house seemed deserted. It had never been much of a home. She had not been in the smaller rooms on the second floor for months. The music room in the back was an embarrassment now that the Metropolitan Museum of Art had borrowed the piles of the Woolworths' Oriental rugs for exhibition. It smelled of rot. The floor was covered with mouse droppings. The walls were soggy from leaking rainwater. Only Jimmy, from time to time, sneaked in to test the keys of the pipe organ.

Ann dreamed of turning the indoor tennis court into a vast room for elegant parties. She wanted an indoor tropical garden, birds, and a fountain. But consultation with Billy Baldwin had not met with Billy's approval: he thought Baldwin's ideas too costly. He would not invest in the Oyster Bay house, which had been purchased in Ann's name.

Alone in his green-and-black-tiled bathroom, Billy finished shaving and applied a small Band-Aid on his face over Ann's long scratch.

An hour later, Ann sat in the pale blue Thunderbird, eager to see Gertrude Whitney's sculpting studio. It had been built to the specifications of an ancient and vast Roman palace. The party was given by several Whitneys. Billy derided Ann's excitement about the party, but she would win him over. They were keyed together.

Greentree, the Whitney family compound, was one of the largest estates on Long Island. Guards checked their name at the imposing gate. The formal fall bash for 150 started with a cocktail party by the indoor pool under enormous potted trees. In Paris, Ann had put several pounds back on, so she wore a blue-and-silver lace stole over her backless dress. She and Billy greeted Grace Kelly.

When he was asked about the Band-Aid on his face, the glamorous young owner of Nashua joked, "I walked into a door." Several people congratulated Ann on being named the best-dressed woman in sports. Declining offers of champagne, Ann mounted a spiral staircase. On the landing outside Gertrude's black-and-white bedroom hung a portrait of her in an exotic black-and-white tunic and orange harem pants.

Ann envied the indulgence and the money that allowed Gertrude Whitney to build this fantasy palace with its soaring glass roof. She believed that if Billy's parents had approved of her, she could have spent hundreds of thousands to decorate the Playhouse. Downstairs, she found Billy in the carved topiary, talking to Grace Kelly as dinner was announced. "Sorry to break this up," said Ann, pulling his arm.

Ann's mood picked up when she discovered her printed place card next to Charles Shipman Payson, the brother-in-law of Jock Whitney. This was clearly one of the best tables at the party. A 100-piece orchestra played as Ann paid her more important dinner partner the compliment of ignoring the other. Payson was married to Joan Whitney Payson, who ran the Greentree Stables and would later own the New York Mets. Ann did not "turn with the roast"—that is, shift her attention to Mr. Robert Henry, an attorney on her left, as a new course was served.

Nevertheless, at the end of the meal Henry asked Ann to dance. Ann seemed not to hear him and literally turned her shoulder. Payson asked another woman to dance, and in the candlelit gardens, Ann caught sight of Billy dancing with a stranger. "Dance with me," she said suddenly to Henry. There was a sexual desperation in her command.

Sometimes at these parties, Billy fell in love with Ann all over again. He liked watching her from a distance, as she dazzled other men. But that night, driving home from the party, Billy tormented her by going on and on about Grace Kelly.

September 4, 1955.

At midnight, Ann swallowed several Seconal and Thorazine with a glass of beer. But she tossed for hours, believing that she heard "forest creatures."

She rushed down the eighteen-foot corridor to Billy's bedroom door. "Let me in," she said. "I can't sleep." Nothing happened. "Billy, please, Billy," she said. Then she ran toward the heavy front door. It was 5 a.m., and she flicked on the lights, illuminating the courtyard down to the brick entrance pillars.

The lights awakened the Cinerama night watchman, Steve Smith. He did not get out of bed. It would not be the first time he had heard Ann in the garden during the night.

Ann groped her way past the topiary, the rows of trees meeting overhead, and the neoclassical marble temple. Usually, she went no further than the domed gazebo with its misting fountain. That morning, though, she walked into the forest.

Ann was groggy in the late morning as her maid served her coffee in bed. But Billy was amiable at lunch with the boys and complimented her on the flowers she had placed on the table.

As summer turned to autumn, Ann fired the children's governess, Ingeborg Sorenson, and had the maid, Ann Gorney, look after the boys. (Sorenson had come to the conclusion that Ann was "sick, mentally ill" because of the way she lost her temper around Billy.) And even though

Gorney had only arrived at the beginning of the summer, she was already looking for new employers.

September 24, 1955.

Although Nashua was favored five-to-three to win at Belmont Park, the horse shocked Billy and millions of spectators by losing the Synsonby Race. Fans booed the Woodward horse. The loss rocked Billy's fragile confidence. Ann, too, was devastated.

October 16, Belmont Racetrack.

Despite his earlier loss, Nashua was still the four-to-one favorite to win the Jockey Club Gold Cup and $52,850. Nashua sloshed around the muddy Belmont track, then shot ahead to win by five lengths. A sportswriter described the horse "splashing home with the assurance of a duck." Ann and Billy ran hand in hand to the winner's circle.

The newspapers heralded the fact that Nashua had won more money that year than any horse in America ever had before. He earned $752,550, putting him second in total lifetime purse earnings only to the former American champion Citation.

Billy and Ann had been invited to a dinner party to celebrate Ned Patterson's thirty-fifth birthday at his house on Valentine Lane. It was still rainy and cold in exclusive Locust Valley. The Pattersons were not really part of the international set. In contrast to Billy, Ned went to work every day on Wall Street. Ned looked like a banker in a Cary Grant movie. He dressed in loose Brooks Brothers suits, and despite his Buckley School education, his "r"s were barely dropped; he sounded American. His wife, Joan, was an attractive woman whose picture at charity balls that she organized occasionally appeared in *Vogue*.

That evening the radio and television were full of interviews with Billy. The Pattersons did not expect the golden couple to make it to the party. But the forty members of "the old crowd" were thrilled to see Billy and Ann arrive in the front hallway.

Ned was sympathetic to Ann's concerns about Billy. But even Ned, who always saw the best in everybody, knew that Ann sometimes lost control. He wondered why Billy did not reassure her more. Ned Patterson also thought that Ann put women off. It was as though she were broadcasting a message that if they left her alone, she'd leave them alone, or she would meet them halfway if they met her halfway. There was also some forbidden territory surrounded by no-trespassing signs and wire fences a hundred feet high—behind which she wanted Billy to be. He thought her message to other women was, "Stay away from him, he belongs to me. And if you do all these things, I'll be your friend."

That night Patterson told her, "I see good in you and I see you have a hard time in this crowd. It's just hard for these people to take to somebody new." He added, "It's not easy making sure Billy doesn't make mistakes." Ann lowered her turquoise eyes. She said, "Oh, but go on, give me specific examples."

Patterson said, "Well, Billy doesn't get too drunk or get into anything too deeply." (Here, Patterson was alluding indirectly to flirtations.)

Not referring to any specific incident, Ann said, "It's funny that you should say that, something like that happened the other night."

Then suddenly at the other end of the table, Billy began laughing with a good-looking girl next to him. Ann said gamely to Patterson, "Well, he's having a good time."

Then she called down the table, "What's going on, Woodward?"

Billy kept laughing.

"Don't worry, Ann," Ned said. "He heard you, and that girl he's talking to is happily married."

"I hope you're right," said Ann.

After dinner, they gathered in the living room to watch a sixteen-millimeter print of Alfred Hitchcock's *The Thirty-nine Steps.* Guests seemed to prefer talking to Billy and Ann about Nashua.

Looking back on that night, Patterson would say he felt a new recklessness in Billy. "Sometimes I thought he had dangerous, angry stuff buried inside him. He was testing new limits."

October 19, 1955, Wall Street.

Billy telephoned Stewart Clement, an old Groton acquaintance, for advice about buying a new airplane. His twin-engine Beechcraft model 18 could not land on his back lawn. Clement recommended a Helio, an airplane just invented by a professor of aeronautics at MIT. There were only a few of the small four-seater, 3,000-pound planes in existence. It would cost $10,000.

As they strolled down Wall Street to lunch, racing fans in their three-piece suits congratulated Billy; everyone loved Nashua.

"It's called the tennis-court airplane because it can take off and land from very small spots," explained Clement.

"Perfect," said Billy.

Over lunch, Billy learned that only one Helio was manufactured a week. "Where are they made?" he asked.

"Pittsburg, Kansas," said Clement.

Laughing, Billy said, "My wife was manufactured there, too."

This coincidence struck Billy as proof that the airplane was his destiny. Billy could not wait to tell Ann the amazing story. She listened expressionless while he explained that the Helio was built on West Fourth Street in Pittsburg.

"Two miles from our farm," she said. Ann had not been back to Pittsburg since she was eleven. Her grandmother's unpainted house on Second Street would only depress her.

"Maybe I'll go out there to pick one up," Billy said in a teasing way, "and learn the truth about you."

"I'll go with you," Ann said without enthusiasm.

Billy became impatient to own the airplane. The Helio was going to improve his life. His father, who had hated planes, could no longer veto such a dangerous toy. With the little airplane, Billy could fly from Oyster Bay to Belair. He would not even have to book hangar space in private airports. He asked the groundskeeper to begin building a small airstrip behind the Playhouse immediately.

He might fly down to South America with Ann, in a few hops, landing on the cattle ranch of friends in Brazil. But Billy was a little manic. The winning horse was a piece of luck, not a testimonial to his intelligence.

Clement arranged for Billy to try out a Helio. He asked Dr. Lynn Bollinger, the chairman of the company and a professor at the Harvard Business School, to fly a plane down to Flushing Airfield.

October 20, La Guardia Airport.

It was a clear day with gentle northwest winds, good for flying. Billy and Stewart Clement took the Studillac to La Guardia Airport. Shocked at how fast Billy drove, Clement gasped, "Gee, this is pretty souped up." Clement was saddened by Billy's comments about pursuing women.

When they went up in the closed-cabin airplane, Dr. Bollinger sat in the pilot seat. Billy sat next to him, with Clement in back. They flew around, admiring the Manhattan skyline. Clement asked Billy, "Do you understand how slowly this plane can fly and still be under control?"

Billy did not reply. Instead, he reached to the overhead controls, cranked the flaps down and forward, and threw the throttle back. They began climbing slowly, at an impossibly steep angle. The airspeed needle was quivering. Billy looked elated. Clement was terrified. He knew that flying so slowly and steeply, the plane could easily stall and flip over. Clement was even more shocked when Dr. Bollinger ordered Billy to turn to the left. This finally scared Billy. Billy hesitated. "Go ahead," challenged the Helio's inventor.

Billy gingerly turned to the left. He was scared. Dr. Bollinger took over and demonstrated in how little space they could land. They slid about ten feet and stopped. Euphoric, Billy made plans to fly to Pittsburg, Kansas, to pick up a plane of his own and pilot it home.

That night Teddy Bemberg gave a dinner party in his Park Avenue duplex in honor of Vincent Astor and his wife, Brooke.

Billy Woodward stepped off an airplane at Atkinson Municipal Airport in Kansas. Vernon Marsh, the midstate Helio plant manager, drove Billy two miles southwest, past run-down farmhouses and muddy fields. Billy told Marsh that his wife, Ann Eden Crowell, hailed from Pittsburg.

The man assured him that the town had not changed since the Depression years. Marsh recalled that Ethel Crowell had been a good-looking girl and a respected social studies teacher. It was the sort of town one of Billy's servants might have come from. Billy stared at open porches with old gliders and rocking chairs. Backyards were littered with cars and broken furniture. There were few sidewalks. Telephone wires stood out on the treeless Pittsburg streets. Billy learned that the old Crowell ranch was still standing, a mile south on Quincy Road near some quarries and abandoned coal mines, but he did not ask to see it.

After dropping off his Vuitton duffel at the Bessie Hotel, he and Vernon Marsh drove a mile west of town to the cement-block factory with its grass landing strip. Marsh took Billy on a thirty-minute tour of the plant, where 125 craftsmen had been working for the past week on Billy's new airplane, only the fifteenth ever made. They would not take a test flight until the rain stopped. Billy hung around the plant that afternoon and watched them build another Helio. The Helios had lightweight steel bodies covered with aluminum. Silver-painted fabric was stretched on the wing frames. Billy saw a wrecked Helio that had been shipped back from Michigan. It had pontoons under the body for water landing. Billy swore his plane would never get a scratch.

Billy bought a local newspaper with a page-one picture of a dentist being honored for pulling teeth for fifty years. He went to the front desk and asked for directions to Ann's cousin Paul Crowell's drugstore.

In the small drugstore, he sat at the soda fountain and drank a Coca-Cola. The soda jerk said he did not want to repeat "women's talk" about Ethel Crowell, but Billy pressed and learned of Ethel's two failed marriages. She had once chased Mr. Jordan down the street, the youngster said, hitting him over the head with a pot. Ethel had also told a lady he knew that Mr. Jordan had given her the clap. Mrs. Crowell had disappeared from these parts, still owing folks money.

With encouragement, the soda jerk told Billy that Jesse Claude Crowell was a retired streetcar conductor and probably alive. This was far worse than Billy had feared. What would his mother say? Billy decided to ask his lawyer if this could be grounds for divorce.

Back at the hotel, Billy telephoned Ann. "They smile too much here when they talk to you," said Billy. He used to tell Ann that he liked her big Kansas smiles. "I got some dirt on you for my lawyers," he added a moment later.

"Oh, Billy, nobody remembers me in Pittsburg," Ann answered.

"I just learned that my father-in-law is alive and a streetcar conductor in Detroit. He's never been a colonel," Billy said. "You lied to me."

"My mother told me she was a widow," Ann replied.

"I'll believe he's dead when I see his grave in the cemetery."

The Helio test pilot, William Carpenter, picked Billy up at the hotel. Despite the light rain, Billy was bareheaded. He wore a Dunhill khaki safari jacket. Carpenter loved airplanes and told Billy he did not mind working weekends to train new Helio owners. Billy thanked him, then said, "I would like to see the condition of my wife's family plot." Carpenter obligingly headed toward Mount Olive Cemetery. Billy had not slept much. He felt a head cold coming on.

Inside the thirty-three-acre cemetery, the graves lay in tightly banked ascending rows. But there was no custodian, and they could not find the Crowell graves. Billy finally gave up the search. In his polite way, he said, "All I can do is go back and tell my wife that the entire cemetery looks nice, so I know the grave is well cared for."

"What business are you in?" asked Bill Carpenter.

"Banking," replied Billy Woodward.

*   *   *

October 24, the Carpenter house.

Billy heard hymns from the new white Mormon church. Carpenter asked him to dinner, as he did most Helio buyers. It seemed like the right thing to do for anybody stuck in Pittsburg for several days.

When they arrived at the one-story Carpenter house, Mary Carpenter was pleasantly surprised by the unexpected guest. Toys littered the front room. Nobody offered Billy a cocktail. Carpenter rarely drank if he was flying the next day. Mary Carpenter soon realized she had never had such a famous guest. "Horses. My, my. Racehorses?"

"I own Nashua," said Billy. Bill Carpenter and his wife were astounded when Billy told them, matter-of-factly, that Nashua was given bottled water and boiled vegetables.

Billy Woodward seemed much more interesting than the men from Venezuela and Argentina, of whom Mary Carpenter had asked questions until three in the morning.

The dinner was served on the rectangular kitchen table between the sink and a window that overlooked a clothesline. There were no trees on the property. Bill Jr., age two, and Karen, age four, bowed their heads and said grace. "Karen is in kindergarten at St. Mary's," said Mary proudly.

Billy told the Carpenters he hoped to fly his new plane to racetracks, land in the infield, watch the race, and then fly right out. For dessert, Mary served chocolate chip ice cream. "My favorite," Billy said.

Mary wondered if it was the first time Woodward had eaten in a kitchen. Billy showed his manners by helping her dry the dishes—an unfamiliar task. There were no complaints about Ann to these happily married Kansas folk. He invited little Karen to sit on his knee and talked to her. The Carpenters were surprised that such a famous rich man would not seek to dominate the conversation. Billy told Mrs. Carpenter that he and his wife, Ann, would take the Helio to Brazil. She also liked guns and had been on safaris. "Gee, a woman hunter, that's odd," said Mary, but then she apologized, saying, "Everybody does not have to be like me."

After the children were put to bed, Billy, the Carpenters, and Mary's brother played canasta on the kitchen table until eleven.

October 25, Pittsburg.

Employees cheered as the gaily painted plane finally rolled out of the factory. The rain had stopped, and after three days Billy was eager to leave the heartland. He threw his duffel into the plane behind William Carpenter and took off. Billy laughed as he watched the pilot manipulate the controls. They pointed the nose down and let the plane speed to 220 miles an hour. Below, the square brown patches of farms covered the flat landscape. After landing, the plant manager and engineer ironed out the last bugs.

That afternoon, Carpenter and Billy said good-bye on the landing strip. Billy's cold made him sneeze. Smiling, Carpenter said to Billy, "Gosh, I don't believe I've ever worked with anybody as rich as you."

As Woodward was stepping into the cockpit, he said, "I think you're twice as rich as I will ever be."

Billy Woodward flew east out of Pittsburg in his new airplane, having sown the seed of one of the many myths surrounding his bizarre murder.*

When a friend asked why he had gone to Kansas, Billy had replied, "To get dirt on Annie."

October 26, Belair.

The next morning, Billy Woodward swooped the Helio down into a flat pasture, where a waiting group of tenant farmers and servants applauded. Billy made an impromptu speech: "I have bought this revolutionary new airplane to make it easy to come down here every weekend." He explained that the plane had coasted less than fifty feet as he landed. He giddily predicted it would one day make airplanes as commonplace as cars.

Hoarse from a cold, Billy led his employees on a triumphal tour of the stable and pastures, announcing that Nashua would be arriving in three days. He vowed to make Belair a profitable venture for the first time in history. "Since my father passed away, I've been trying to figure out ways to get our farm out of the red. I am building a more lucrative herd of Shorthorn beef cattle—prize bulls and a herd of brood cows. We're going

---

*Truman Capote would use Billy's coincidental visit to Ann's birthplace to supply a fictional "Ann" with a murder motive.

Capote authoritatively told friends that Billy went to Pittsburg because his detective had found Ann's real husband; he did not know of Billy's purchase of the little Helio. Capote claimed that in Kansas, Billy learned that Ann was a "two-bit bigamist" who had never bothered to divorce her high school sweetheart, now an Oakland cop. Capote did not realize that Ann had left Pittsburg before she went to high school. Since Ann was a bigamist, said Capote, her marriage to Billy was illegitimate and to divorce her Billy did not have to pay a penny in alimony.

Capote soon began making notes for his novel *Answered Prayers*. Part of the book was to be a thinly disguised account of the Woodward shooting, portraying Ann as a calculating killer. The fact that Capote fabricated the story out of their gossip was never understood by most society friends of Elsie and Billy. No record has been found of an earlier marriage.

to increase the facilities for grazing and resting young thoroughbreds, and we'll grow soybeans, too."

That afternoon, the servants watched the Helio take off for Claiborne Farm in Kentucky. There Billy would inspect his twenty-five broodmares. He canceled a trip to Ireland with members of a horse-buying syndicate he had joined, preferring to fly his new plane. The syndicate planned to buy Tuylar, the Irish stallion assumed to be the second greatest horse in the world.

October 27, Zahn Airport, Long Island.

From Kentucky, Billy flew five hours to Amityville, Long Island, where he reluctantly left the airplane at the Zahn hangars. He called Ann to say he would be back in Oyster Bay Cove in two days to inspect the new Playhouse landing strip. "Please come home now," she said. "I miss you."

But he still felt troubled by the thought that his wife was the daughter of a streetcar conductor. He had a driver take him from the airport to the Brook Club, where he spent Wednesday sleeping off his trip.

October 28, Brookville, Long Island.

Harriet Aldrich Bering was awakened from a sound sleep by a noise in the night. Harriet Bering, a Rockefeller, was Elsie's next-door neighbor. All that week in October, she had been alarmed by police reports of a prowler among the large wooded estates.

Someone was fumbling at the front door. She grabbed her shotgun as the door opened and closed. Stealthy footsteps approached. She pointed the gun down the stairs as the entry lights clicked on. She found herself aiming her gun at her apologetic father. It was weeks before she could tell friends what she had done.

October 29, 111 East Seventy-third Street.

Ann had called Billy every half hour at the Brook Club. At midday, Billy took her call, announcing he was canceling the Oyster Bay Cove weekend in favor of what was being called "the world's richest race." He would go alone to Garden State Park in Camden, New Jersey.

Ann persisted, telling Billy it would be bad form to back out on Bean's mother's Saturday night party for the Duke of Windsor. Billy finally agreed to go, but he did want to check out the Helio, hangared only twenty minutes from the Playhouse.

Ann gave him a hero's welcome at their East Seventy-third Street home that Friday afternoon: he had flown halfway across the continent on his own. When he said he wanted to skip another cocktail party and "take a nap," she happily telephoned their regrets to the party's host and got into bed with him.

A few hours later, Ann packed her gray maribou-edged ball gown and her collection of pills. She took one more pill than usual for her menstrual cramps. Meanwhile, the boys were packed up by Lee Principe, the chauffeur. They waited in the station wagon on Fifty-seventh Street, while Principe took the elevator up to the Maximilian fur salon to pick up Ann's sable coat. The coat had been custom-made for Ann the previous winter for a racing appearance. In June, Principe had brought it back, and now the double silk lining was properly in place.

Ann and Billy sped through the rain to Oyster Bay Cove. Neither knew anything about the prowler who was stealing food in the Cove. Ann teased Billy that he flew the rain clouds in from Kansas. She explained that actresses like Ann Harding routinely glamorized their backgrounds. She had pretended her father was a colonel only to please his family. Billy was temporarily silenced. They stopped for dinner and a truce at Rothmann's, a bar on Route 26.

October 28.

In Oyster Bay Cove, while Billy and Ann slept in their separate ground-floor bedrooms, four detectives from nearby Brookville were searching the estate on the trail of the prowler, who had reportedly been stealing food and cars in the area for months.

When, at 4 a.m., Nassau County detective Ray Soper slowed on Berry Hill Road, leading to the Playhouse, he saw local police running. Like them, he had received word on the radio that the prowler was in a nearby barn.

He did not join the chase. Since he answered to the same description as the prowler, six feet two and blond, the out-of-uniform Soper was afraid he might be shot by mistake.

At the Playhouse, the Cinerama night watchman, Steve Smith, showed Detective Soper where the prowler had broken into the garage. Woodward's briefcase was on the floor. By the pool cabana, Detective Soper saw empty cases of shotgun shells. "The prowler has a shotgun," said Soper.

Soper drove to the barn, which was by now surrounded by local police. Other policemen searched the shrubbery and bushes. Unbeknownst to them, the prowler, Paul Wirths, was hiding under a large bush near the barn. A Brookville policeman almost stepped on his hand.

At seven that morning there was little sun. It was cold for October. Soper stopped by the Woodward estate again on his way home to talk to Billy.

Steve Smith was still the only person awake.

"Tell Woodward to call me," said Soper. "He's the one who sustained the loss."

October 29, the Playhouse.

When Billy awoke, Lee Principe told him a prowler had spent the night on the property. He showed Billy that the man had broken into the garage and how he had stolen canned soup from the pool cabana. Billy telephoned Oyster Bay Cove police chief Russell Haff, who said that the Nassau County Police suspected a young out-of-work German who had been arrested in the past for burglaries in the area.

The next morning, Woody, who was then eleven, telephoned his regrets for a Halloween party to his friend Robert Straus, age ten, who lived across from the Woodwards on Seventy-third Street. The maid, Ann Gorney, had already told the Strauses' butler that Woody would not attend the party. Then Woody went off with his dad to Amityville for a short spin in his new airplane.

EDWARD ROBINSON: I think you told me before that you slept much later than Mr. Woodward.

ANN WOODWARD: Yes, but I don't know exactly when I got up, no. I just remember my husband coming in my room and smiling and being glad that I was awake. (Witness sobs.) . . .

EDWARD ROBINSON: Did you get up then and dress?

ANN WOODWARD: I think Woody our oldest boy was with him, and I think the three of us talked.

EDWARD ROBINSON: Up to that time had there been any talk of prowlers at all?

ANN WOODWARD: As soon as Woody went out of the room then [my husband] told me that somebody had broken into his car the night before . . . into the glove compartment and the gardener had—or he had heard from somebody about the prowler being all around the place during the week before. . . . I was terrified and he was terrified, too, because we had come home the night before. He had gone out to the garage and put the car in the garage and the man, whoever it was, might have been right there.

EDWARD ROBINSON: Yes?

ANN WOODWARD: And then I don't know whether my husband talked— he must have talked to the police and I thought there were police guarding the whole property all the time. . . . And I said, "There are so many different entrances to this property."*

EDWARD ROBINSON: What did you notice when you went outside, then, with Mr. Woodward?

ANN WOODWARD: Well, we searched all around the property. We went down to the swimming pool and we found that the bathhouse had been broken into—not the men's dressing room or the ladies' dressing room but another room that has an ice box and like a little bar and a sitting room, sort of, inside.

And we found that the window had been broken into.

I said, "Couldn't we pay to get somebody who would guard the house for about 24 hours until the person was located?" Because we had seen where this man had made himself a bed, and he had taken one of those swimming pool chairs, you know, those long chairs that you stick your legs out on, and he had pulled it inside and he had eaten everything in the ice box except one can of grapefruit juice.

EDWARD ROBINSON: This ice box was in the building there at the swimming pool?

ANN WOODWARD: Yes. I mean, we were terrified to the point that my husband and I sat there and spoke French. I mean, I was afraid to speak English. I thought the prowler was right there, behind me or

---

*After the murder, Oyster Bay police chief Russ Haff reported to members of the press that Billy had called him at 1 p.m. that Saturday, about twelve hours before his death. "Mr. Woodward was concerned," said Haff, "that the man lurking around his property might be a crackpot from the track who'd lost a bet and was nursing a vengeance against the Woodwards because of Nashua's success."

over my shoulder, practically. I was so frightened. And I kept speaking French to my husband because I thought the prowler might be listening—that close.

But we stayed there and found a box out in front of the bathhouse with some cans that the prowler had used that had come out of the ice box.

And I was frightened as anything then. I said to my husband, I said, "Let's go back to town. Let's don't stay out here. Let us get the children and go back to town."

EDWARD ROBINSON: What other parts of the place did you look over?

ANN WOODWARD: Well, we went everywhere and we saw that both of the garage windows had been broken into. In the same way.

And we saw that the prowler had pulled a whole box of shells over to the window on the shelf, and he had taken a rock which my husband and I saw outside of the window, and my husband said to me that he thought that the prowler must have used that rock to try to break the top in of the shells, because the wooden part was broken into.

So that we were even more alarmed, because we realized that the prowler must have a gun.

EDWARD ROBINSON: Did Mr. Woodward have a briefcase out there?

ANN WOODWARD: It was in the car.

EDWARD ROBINSON: What part of the car?

ANN WOODWARD: I don't remember that. I know that the glove compartment in the car had been completely broken into.

EDWARD ROBINSON: What car was that, the Studillac?

ANN WOODWARD: The Studebaker, the car that we had gone from New York in the very night before had been broken into just as soon as we had parked it in the garage. So again the prowler was just right there, right at the place. So my husband said—I mean, that the prowler had a gun if he tried to steal shells; and that we had better arm ourselves and be prepared for the prowler.

EDWARD ROBINSON: Did he talk about putting a guard on or anything?

ANN WOODWARD: I really suggested getting a guard or at least getting a line of men and going through the woods and combing the woods.

You see, we've got nearly—oh, over twenty acres of just virgin woods with fallen trees and branches and anything that he could hide behind.

EDWARD ROBINSON: . . . Ann [the cook] tells us that she served breakfast and lunch to both you and Mr. Woodward and the boys. There was some conversation between you and your husband about some flowers.

ANN WOODWARD: The only conversation that I can think of is if he said something about a bill for flowers we had just put in at the swimming pool. Because he always checked everything with me before we paid for things.

EDWARD ROBINSON: Well, had you picked some flowers that morning?

ANN WOODWARD: Had I picked flowers?

EDWARD ROBINSON: Yes. Ann tells us that he made a remark about how nice the flowers were, and that you said something about you knew he liked those flowers. The flowers that were on the table, the cut flowers.

ANN WOODWARD: Yes. Well, he always liked the flowers that I planted.

EDWARD ROBINSON: The cook tells us that he made some remark about the flowers and you in turn remarked that you knew he liked those.

ANN WOODWARD: Well, I always tried to have everything in the house the way he liked it . . .

EDWARD ROBINSON: Do you recall what you had for lunch?

ANN WOODWARD: I remember sitting at the table but I don't remember what we were eating.

October 29, Oyster Bay Cove.
    Charles Wacker and Billy spoke by telephone for an hour about a wildcat oil investment and horses. Billy mentioned the prowler. "Oh, Ann's all upset, she thinks there is a prowler, you know."

ANN WOODWARD: He [Billy] took his gun with him [that night] when we went out to dinner. We were, oh, very frightened, and he said, "He must be very desperate and very dangerous." He said, "We couldn't even think of going out to dinner if we didn't have a gun with us."

EDWARD ROBINSON: Was it a pistol?

ANN WOODWARD: Yes.

EDWARD ROBINSON: Not a long gun?

ANN WOODWARD: No. And he took it with him in the glove compartment when we went to dinner. We didn't know whether to go back to town or whether to stay in the country or what to do—

EDWARD ROBINSON: Well, what precautions did you take in connection with the care of the children in view of this prowler situation?

ANN WOODWARD: Well, we instructed the cook very definitely and clearly before we went out to dinner that she should wait for the children and be sure to lock the front door when the children came in—a lot of time we didn't lock the front door.

EDWARD ROBINSON: This is a very personal question, but I have to ask it, Mrs. Woodward: did you have sexual intercourse with him that night?

ANN WOODWARD: Yes.

EDWARD ROBINSON: You said yes?

ANN WOODWARD: Yes. Before the party.

18

THE DINNER PARTY

There was no prowler. Ann made him up. She tried to protect herself because she murdered Billy Woodward in cold blood. Everybody at that party reported the fight they had to me. It was awful.

—Liz Fondaras, society person, 1986

Everybody was scared about the prowler starting a few days before the shooting. We lived in Mill Neck, twenty minutes away, and went to the same club, Piping Rock. I was particularly nervous about him. I started locking the front door.

—Mrs. I. Townsend Burden, 1989

The crowd was like that, I mean the affairs and the scenes and so forth were legendary. Just about all of the women below a certain age in that crowd were available. The men, too. Laddie Sanford adored Mary, but he managed to bed down every sweet young thing that arrived on the scene. It was a simple matter of making a deal, then going to visit for a luncheon salad and then having sex and splitting without making a big disruption in your day.

—Michael Butler, February 1987

Most society people never heard about the police catching the prowler. They just heard Capote and others say he never existed.

—JOHN RICHARDSON,
author and friend of
Elsie Woodward, 1981

Oh, I discussed the prowler with nearly everybody that I talked to, at the party anyway, and Bill talked about the prowler, and I said that's all we had been thinking about the whole day. I think Bill said that he brought a gun and he had put the gun in—and he was going to protect us on the way over and back.
. . . John Schiff lived right across the road from us and we said that he was as much in danger as we were about the prowler, and we said that as the prowler was stealing food we might put some sleeping things or something in the food, and maybe if we did that, that the prowler would eat the food and then we could get the prowler or catch the prowler. But my husband said that he was not taking any chances, that he was armed.

—ANN WOODWARD,
police report interrogation,
November 1955

EDWARD ROBINSON: Did you have anything to drink at all at the party?

ANN WOODWARD: Well, I did what I always do, as I remember. I sip a drink. I always take something that is offered, as being polite, and then I hold it in my hand and sip at it.

EDWARD ROBINSON: Tell me, did they serve cocktails or long drinks, or both?

ANN WOODWARD: Well, I believe they just asked you what you wanted.

EDWARD ROBINSON: Well, I will ask you point blank: were you intoxicated at all that night? You, I am talking about.

ANN WOODWARD: I don't think so. No.

EDWARD ROBINSON: How about your husband? Did he have much to drink, do you know?

ANN WOODWARD: Well, I don't know what my husband had to drink because, I mean, if you are at a party each one is talking to different people, you know.

> —police report interrogation,
> November 1955

Ann was not tough or strong enough to have murdered Billy.

> —NED PATTERSON, 1982

He was my best friend. I talked to those people at that party. You talked to them, too. She had him going about that prowler. There wasn't any prowler. She was plotting the murder. I'm convinced it just gave her an excuse to go get that shotgun and have it by her bed. He didn't care about the prowler. She invented the prowler and talked it up. It was all part of her premeditated plan to murder Billy. I knew her well. She was a strong lady and she could carry off something like that once she decided on it.

> —CHARLES WACKER, 1987

Except for the fact that everybody knew where and what she started off from, the Nick Dunne book *The Two Mrs. Grenvilles* was fiction. Everybody knew that prowler was in the neighborhood. I had no conversation afterward with Elsie or anybody else about standing by her. The police just called and asked if we had anything special to say. We didn't. We had just been to the Bakers' and we said that we and everybody were talking about the prowler.

> —MRS. CHARLES SCHWARTZ,
> Baker party guest,
> interview, 1987

She never meant to kill Billy. I had told Laddie to shut up the house and go right back to New York. I was scared silly of that prowler.

> —MARY SANFORD,
> Baker party guest,
> interview, 1981

Audrey Chapin [Marina Torlonia's best friend] always thought it was Marina on the telephone at the Baker party that night after we heard about the murder and the telephone call.

—MILO GRAY,
North Shore socialite, 1983

The shooting was a misfortune, and people like to imagine all sorts of things that aren't true about misfortunes.

—MRS. JOHN WINSLOW,
Newport socialite and
Baker party guest, interview, 1986

Sometimes a cigar is just a cigar.

—SIGMUND FREUD

Billy had begun a search for the prowler. If locks and lights didn't scare the prowler from his estate, he knew it was within the law for him or Ann to shoot a person trespassing on his property in self-defense. Billy's manic mood was contagious. The presence of a lurking prowler seemed to bring him and Ann together as a team. They could see the headlines: "Millionaire Sportsman Shoots Prowler in His Own Home."

They spent an hour inspecting the closets, unused rooms, and empty corridors of the Playhouse. Ann was sure the prowler was watching them from somewhere like a dark closet.

Ann and Billy hunted for the prowler around the edge of the woods, whispering to each other in French. Billy carried a gun because it was known that the prowler was armed. For once Billy did not make fun of her accent. Because of the prowler, Billy had not mentioned Kansas or her father for several hours.

At cocktail hour, Ann seduced Billy. She knew the idea of the prowler had turned him on. As long as she could take Billy to bed, it meant he still loved her.

As they left the Playhouse for the Baker party, her spike heels slipped on the wet leaves. She listened for other footsteps. It was raining lightly. She was carrying her opal-and-diamond necklace and emerald ring in a pouch. She jumped as if someone had shouted "Boo!" "What's that?" she said.

In front of her, Billy pointed his revolver. It made him furious that someone could break into his private domain. He shined a flashlight into the Studillac. A moment later, he drove slowly down their lane, the unhols-tered gun on his knee. The jewelry pouch was on Ann's lap. Billy flipped a switch and illuminated the empty cobblestone courtyard behind him. The prowler would have to break into their home under bright lights.

Billy put the revolver in the glove compartment. He was speeding past the sandy coves at seventy-five miles an hour, on his special route through sleepy East Norwich, down a steep hill on Skunk's Misery Landing Road.

Turning in her seat, Ann examined her husband as if for the first time. Tonight, in his evening jacket, he resembled his photographs in *The New York Times*. Ann watched him bite his black cigarette holder. "Billy Woodward," she said, "you're my best jewel." Ann's hyperbole usually unnerved him; nobody in his family spoke with such unbridled emotion. Despite the wet road, he declared, as he often did, "This is the best time yet between us and Bean's place."

It was de rigueur to wear important pieces at a party for the Duke and Duchess. Ann slipped her emerald engagement ring on her finger in the dark. The Duchess had always made it clear that her husband's love would be demonstrated by the jewels he gave her.

Billy asked Ann not to wear the ring, which was a copy of the engagement ring the Duke had given the Duchess. It was slightly embar-rassing to him.

"Suppose she doesn't wear hers," said Ann.

"It's still bad form," said Billy.

"It's a compliment and you know it," said Ann.

The Duchess set the style. Ann's favorite suit was a copy of a fitted Russian broadtail suit that had been designed for the Duchess by Balenci-aga. The Duchess also collected little petit-point pillows with phrases em-broidered on them. Ann had recently given Billy a copy of a favorite of the Duchess's which read, "Never explain, never complain."

Billy slowed, looking through the fog at the familiar sight of Peacock Point, the ivy-covered Georgian manor house owned by Bean's mother. He checked his gold Omega watch; it was just eight o'clock. Inside, the Duch-ess was upstairs with the Duke. The royal couple had brought three pug dogs, many large trunks and suitcases, and a personal maid who cleaned up after the dogs. Other houseguests of Mrs. George Baker's included Mrs. Byrnes MacDonald of San Francisco, Mr. and Mrs. Charles Schwartz, and C. Z. Guest.

The Duke of Windsor was refusing to go through another dull sub-urban dinner party. He wanted to lie down in bed next to the little rag doll his late mother, Queen Mary, had stitched for him.

Edith Baker and the Duke of Windsor at the Green-briar Golf Course.

Harry Evans and Adele Astaire Douglas.

Michael Butler (1954) was the Duchess of Windsor's favorite extra man, and was her escort at the Baker party.

The Duchess informed her hostess of what she archly called the Duke's latest "abdication." It was decided that the Duchess would be escorted by her new favorite young man, twenty-four-year-old Michael Butler, who had been introduced to her in Paris by C. Z. Guest. He was the handsome paper heir and polo player* from Chicago—and less than half the Duchess's age.

For the Duchess, the ebullient Butler was probably a welcome relief from the Duke. But Butler had his own agenda. Tonight he was here for a rendezvous with Mrs. Baker's granddaughter, Bean's niece, Fern Tailer Gimbel.

In the courtyard, Ann stepped out of the Studillac holding her heavy taffeta skirt high over one elbow. Billy stayed in the car, turning the dashboard clock back an hour for the start of daylight saving time at midnight.

"Please hurry," said Ann.

Ann waited for Billy under the doorway of the vast brick house. It had been built in 1914 by Bean's father, the late George F. Baker, owner of First National City Bank. Beyond the house were several formidable "cottages" and bathhouses.**

Bean's fifteen-room beach cottage sat on a cliff overlooking the sea, a five-minute walk from the main house. Bean had had his own cook, but he enjoyed calling the main house on the master switchboard to command a parade of his mother's servants with brandy bottles, flambéed desserts, fresh fruit, and cut flowers.

Billy handed the Studillac keys to the borrowed butler, Sidney Mutum, who wore a white double-breasted jacket. Sidney was shocked to see Billy check a pistol in the glove compartment. "The local prowler has frightened my entire family," said Billy. "I need this for protection."

"Yes, sir."

"Bit early for the party, I'm afraid, sir," said Sidney.

It was 8:05. The party was not scheduled to begin until 8:30. It did not embarrass Billy to be too early, but he was annoyed with Ann for the error. "Duke's under the weather, sir," said Sidney. "He's a no-show tonight."

---

*Most of the men in "the Duchess of Windsor set" were identified as polo players. It was synonymous with "playboy," a man who had inherited enough money to own a string of polo ponies and not have to work.

**Mrs. George Baker lived in great luxury. Her entire bedroom was swathed in white satin, and the walls were adorned with three-dimensional tropical flowers. Entertaining and bridge were her principal interests. Her daughters believed they were denied her recipes because she preferred her dinner parties to them. Her favorite books were the Albert Payson Terhune children's tales about heroic collies.

"What do you and the Windsors talk about?" Mrs. Baker was once asked.

"Well, where they've just been and who they've just seen," she said.

Billy sighed aloud. It was not easy for him to enter the Baker house. There were many memories of Bean and previous autumns. As children, they had ridden tricycles in the huge toy room on the first floor.

Ann swept a few steps up to the great hall. Her audience was two butlers, the maids, and the musician Stan Freeman, a familiar figure at these parties, who waved at Ann from the top of the wide angular stairway. He had not yet begun to play the piano, but had been staring out a window at foggy Long Island Sound. Ann made a lovely sight, framed by the chrysanthemums in huge vases on either side of her. Later, Freeman would recall that single image of her, saying that chrysanthemums were known in Europe as "the flowers of death."

Ann's gray gown suited the décor. Billy had chosen it to blend with the sixty-foot-long blue, gray, and beige Chinese carpet in the great hall.

Instead of attempting the stairs under Freeman's scrutiny, Ann ducked into the ladies' room. She could spend a good ten minutes here until more guests arrived. Standing on a pink silk Aubusson carpet in the mirrored room, she smoothed her skirts. A month shy of her fortieth birthday, Ann worried about getting fat. She was still doing the morning exercises she had learned as a Powers model, but she had lost the suppleness in her torso. Nor had the firming exercises with the Swedish masseuse helped to tighten the sagging skin under her chin. She wore a heavy makeup base, and in such bright light it appeared caked in the lines around her eyes. Her eyelids looked puffy.

Ann snapped open her new heart-shaped quartz compact. It had been designed by the Duke Fulco di Verdura and was similar to the Duchess's. Di Verdura had been discovered by Coco Chanel in Paris in the 1920s. Ann dabbed White Shoulders between her breasts from a silver flask. Then she powdered her chest to hide the shine. The third guest of the evening, Mary Sanford, swept into the powder room.

"Hiya, darlin'," Mary greeted Ann. Mary was Elsie's special friend. "Billy here? Laddie's got a terrible col' so he's at home by his lonesome."

Mary wore a too-low-cut black ruffled dress and scarlet lipstick. Ann knew that if she wore such a dress, she would never hear the end of it from Billy. Ann consoled herself with the knowledge that Mary's status with Elsie was possible only because she had not married Elsie's son. Mary accidently dropped her gold-mesh evening purse, and her compact smashed. Pink powder floated onto the carpet. Ann shrieked, caught herself, and turned it into a giggle. "It's the prowler," Ann apologized. "Whenever I walked outside today I could feel him looking at us."

"My dear, I know. I hear he has a gun," said Mary. "I tried to get poor Laddie to lock up the house and rush home to New York, but Laddie has the sniffles."

"The man took ammunition and food from our pool house," Ann told her.

"You must be terrified."

"But we have a plan to catch him," said Ann. "Billy has been carrying a gun."

Stooping to pick up slivers of her compact mirror, Mary laughed. "Don't worry, dear Ann," she said, "it looks like I'm the one who's going to have seven years of bad luck."

"Don't tell Laddie I'm here," Mary said to Ann, smiling. "I fibbed to him. He thinks I'm visiting my sister." Mary and a beau were planning to fly away at midnight to Washington for the rest of the weekend. Ann smiled at Mary. Everyone applauded the way the amusing Sanfords enjoyed tricking each other.

Upstairs, Billy shook hands with Stan Freeman. The white-gloved footman, Joseph Chaprionière, brought Billy his usual gin martini on a silver Georgian tray. Freeman did not want to sit down at the grand piano just yet. It was exciting to be alone with the famous Bill Woodward. Freeman offered his congratulations on Nashua's showing at the Belmont Futurity. "The horse has a temper," he said.

A footman trailed by with onion dip and potato chips.

Billy brightened when Freeman mentioned new romantic problems in the English royal family. It was delicious conversation with the Windsors upstairs. The newspapers said that Princess Margaret had escaped for a second weekend in the country with unsuitable divorced commoner Captain Peter Townsend. Queen Elizabeth was said to be resigned, but the Archbishop was upset. If she married him, Margaret must give up her succession right to the throne. The year before, Billy had dined with Princess Margaret and the Duchess of Westminster in Newmarket. "Funnily enough, I hope she marries him," said Billy.

Billy greeted Harry Evans. As usual, Evans was planning to dance with all the wives. Stan Freeman brightened. A jolly guest like Harry Evans made his job that much easier.

"Is Princess Papula going to dance for us tonight?" asked Billy, smiling. He loved outrageous behavior in others. Evans obliged with his imitation of a Hawaiian girl. Bending his knees, he did a hula swing with his hips, and sang in a falsetto voice:

"Princess Papula
Does her rather wild hula,
Under the stars alone,
A long night of Hawaiian love."

Billy mentioned the neighborhood prowler. "I'm prepared for a fight if he shows up again."

Evans laughed, "Of course he'll be no match for you."

"I hope you're well armed," Freeman said.

"Rather," said Billy. "I have a pistol. I'll take care of him."

Charles Cushing, Mrs. Baker's paramour, lived at the house, sleeping in a modest gray-and-brown bedroom near Edith Baker's enormous suite. Mrs. Baker's children knew Edith Cushing had to go to an office, but nobody had asked him what he did.

Cushing looked upset. He told Billy the Duke was not coming downstairs. "Feeling under the weather."

Billy raised his eyebrows. "Most likely bored, I should suspect."

"Ate something that disagreed with him," said Cushing.

"Only very impolite food dares to disagree with the Duke," joked Evans.

The Duchess of Windsor and her maid were finishing her toilette in a pale green bedroom overlooking the garden. The Duchess had decided to wear an amethyst-and-turquoise bracelet. Unlike Ann and Billy, she would not arrive until her entrance could be admired by all fifty-seven guests. Finally, Edith Baker descended the stairs. She dared not be late for the Duchess.*

---

*To the Duchess, the Baker manor house and Florida plantation were fitting places. Edith Baker obediently submitted her guest list to the Duchess, who crossed out names.

The final guest list was made up of Mr. and Mrs. Michael Phipps, Mr. and Mrs. John Clark, Mr. and Mrs. John Rutherfurd, Mr. and Mrs. Winston Guest, Mr. and Mrs. George Leib, Mr. and Mrs. A. Charles Schwartz, Mr. and Mrs. Joseph Thomas, Mr. and Mrs. Winston Frost, Mr. and Mrs. William Woodward, Mr. and Mrs. Edwin Fish, Mr. and Mrs. Charles Blackwell, Mr. and Mrs. Byrnes MacDonald, Mr. and Mrs. John Schiff, Mr. and Mrs. David Gimbel, Mr. and Mrs. Thomas Phipps, Mr. and Mrs. Richard Myers, the Duchess of Windsor, Mrs. Lyon Slater, Mrs. Brooke Howe, Mrs. Lorelle Hearst, Mrs. John S. Kelly, Mrs. Whitney Choate, Mrs. Stephen Sanford, Mrs. Thomas Hitchcock, Mr. Denniston Slater, Mr. Charles G. Cushing, Mr. Milton Holden, Mr. Harry King, Mr. Michael Butler, Mr. Harry Brooke, Mr. Whitney de Rham, Mr. Roy Atwood, Mr. Harry Evans, Lord Cowdray, Mr. Spotiswood White, Mr. Samuel Vallance, Mr. Robert Chatfield-Taylor, Mr. J. McCore.

After-dinner guests included Mr. and Mrs. John Winslow, Mr. and Mrs. Henry Reed, Mr. and Mrs. Ross Baker, Countess Willaminez, Mr. Fulton Cutting, and Nancy Graham.

And then a hush came over the room. The Duchess was descending the stairs wearing a tight floor-length navy dress that showed off her hip-bones and jewelry. The Duchess insisted on a royal reception. She entered the room ready to be kissed by her friends but did not return the kisses.

A breathless silence continued as a tribute. Then a line of people began moving past the Duchess. Ann walked to the front ranks and watched proudly as Billy made the Duchess smile.

"Dear Ann," murmured the Duchess a moment later, her eyes dropping to the huge emerald ring. Her face remained neutral.

"Please come see us soon," said Ann.

Ann strolled into the wood-paneled grand salon, pausing at the sixteenth-century auctioneer's desk. Billy had shown her secret drawers where Bean used to hide dollar bills and broken seashells.

At the fireplace she chatted with producer and composer Richard Myers and his new French wife, Comtesse Suzanne de Gozalow. Ann mentioned that Ethel Merman, the star of *Call Me Madam*, had sung at her house. She told Myers about the prowler.

Mary Phipps, standing near them, asked, "Is he dangerous?"

"If he bothers us, we'll be armed," Ann said, warming her back in front of the roaring fire.

Freeman began to play Cole Porter ballads. Michael Butler joined Fern Tailer Gimbel. Harry Evans passed around an article in the next day's Sunday *Daily Mirror Magazine* that dubbed Ann, C. Z. Guest, Fern, and Babe Paley "society's box-office beauties." Ann led the list of the rich ladies who were invited to charity balls to promote tickets. She was shown in her gilded halter top standing behind a camel at the Wanamaker costume party in Southampton. The article called Ann the "daughter-in-law of one of New York's most distinguished hostesses and a noted hostess in her own right."

By nine-fifteen, the kitchen was ready and butlers were helping guests find their place cards at the tables. The seating took twenty minutes. Billy and Ann were seated at separate young people's tables in the grand hall. Four tables had been set with floral linen cloths and pale flowered china, silver candelabra, and vases of the last mums of the season.

Ann waved to catch Billy's attention, and checked out any threats at his table.

Billy was seated near the little wallpapered telephone "booth." The small room with a bench was used for telephoning by houseguests. Ann watched Billy taste the first course, lobster pullman. He was listening intently to Lorelle Hearst, seated on one side of him.

Lorelle was too self-absorbed to be a real threat. The former Mrs. William Randolph Hearst was a tough-talking, statuesque blonde known on the North Shore as "an ex-chorus girl from the sticks."

Ann wished Billy would talk to Mary Phipps, seated at his other side, or Martha Frost, daughter of an aviation financier, across from him.

Also at Billy's table were his neighbors Mrs. John "Titi" Schiff and David Gimbel, the Saks Fifth Avenue and Gimbels department store heir. David was the twin of Bernard Gimbel and the husband of Fern Tailer Gimbel. Billy smiled broadly at Bean's favorite sister, Titi, who looked remarkably like her late brother.

Harry Evans and C. Z. Guest rounded out Billy's table.* C.Z. promised Billy that she and her husband would visit him at Belair for the International Races on November 11.

Ann did not touch the second course, beef fillet. Staring at Billy, she was having trouble listening to Denny Slater, seated to her right.

Michael Butler sat on Ann's other side and devoted himself to Fern Tailer Gimbel. The host, Charles Cushing, the only older person at the table, asked Ann about Elsie Woodward, who had just started to come out of mourning for her husband, but was not present at the dinner party because she was still upset by the death of her triplet sister from Boston, Edith Ames Cutler.

Fifty feet away, in the dining room, surrounded by thirty-five candles, sat Edith Baker. Exquisite Chinese rice wallpaper was set in arched panels, similar to those in the Duchess's château in the Bois de Boulogne. On the mantel stood carved ivory Chinese horses.

It was important never to seat the same person next to the Duchess of Windsor at succeeding dinners. She was addressed as "Your Grace," but curtsies were not required. Tonight, the Duchess was served first. Usually, Mrs. Baker deferred to the Duke, and the Duke would defer back to the Duchess and so on until the footman was dizzy.

Seated in the grand hall, Billy turned from Lorelle Hearst to Mary Phipps, telling her he planned to catch the prowler.

Ann sipped sparkling water and turned to Denny Slater. The news-

*The police report describes an interview with guest Martha Frost at her home on Stone Hill Road in Old Westbury on Wednesday, November 2, 1955: "Present at this address, interviewed Mrs. Winston Frost and she stated that she and her husband did attend the Baker party together and that during dinner she sat at the same table as Mr. Woodward but not next to him. She said that Mrs. Thomas Phipps did sit next to Mr. Woodward and that Mrs. Phipps had told her a great deal about Woodward's worries due to the prowler and that he and his wife were afraid of him and that he felt that the prowler might revisit his estate. He also told her he had brought a gun in his car for protection."

papers had been full of stories about him and Fernanda Montel. Tonight, instead of bringing her, Slater had escorted his mother. Ann wondered if Slater knew about Billy and Miss Montel.

"Have you heard about our prowler?" asked Ann. She tended to repeat her opening lines at parties.

"Well, a bit," said Denny.

Ann described the feeling of being watched by the man. "Billy wants to shoot him," she said.

Ann said to Michael Butler, "Let's dance between courses," although she knew it was not really a dancing party. But Michael Butler's energy was focused on Fern Tailer Gimbel.*

Cleveland Amory attacked the loose sexuality of the crowd. "[In this set] relations between the sexes are so complicated that the only way one can tell if members of the set are 'going together' is if they're married. Then, almost surely, they are not."

Snubbed by Butler, Ann turned to Thomas Phipps, but they spoke little. She was also distressed by the presence of Mrs. Byrnes MacDonald, a friend of Princess Marina Torlonia's.

Then Ann asked Billy to dance. Afterward, she clutched his arm as Charles Cushing congratulated him on Nashua. From Billy's table, Martha Frost watched Ann and Billy walking together arm in arm. Cushing thought that they seemed comfortable together after dinner, talking by the fireplace in the wood-paneled living room. Martha Frost thought the same thing.

"How is Lady Astor?" Ann asked Phipps, who was a grandson of Nancy, Lady Astor, the mother of Bill Astor.

Before Tommy could reply, Ann became alarmed. She noticed that Billy was striding toward the little telephone alcove. She walked quickly to him: "What's going on?"

"I'm calling about the boys," he said, hanging up. "Nobody answers. That cook is lazy."

Ann Gorney, the new cook and maid, heard the telephone ring but refused to get out of bed.**

---

*Years later, Butler was the principal producer of the theatrical and film versions of the rock opera *Hair*. Fern Tailer Gimbel also appeared briefly as an actress in the film *Hair*.

**Three days after the shooting, *The New York Times* devoted half a column to an unsubstantiated report that Billy had received a phone call during the dinner party which precipitated a bad fight with Ann. The North Shore gossip was that Billy received a call from Marina Torlonia. Eventually, the phone call became a kind of mythic "fact," by which Ann's accusers, including Truman Capote, established a motive for her killing Billy Woodward.

But butlers report that Billy received no calls. Sidney Mutum, who watched Billy and his

In the dining room, the other party guests remained seated, but Harry Evans wanted to ask the Duchess to dance. "Do it first, old sport," he said to Billy.

Ann stood to observe her husband bowing to the Duchess. Billy's long legs moved gracefully toward and away from the Duchess's swollen ankles. The horse country of Maryland was a good topic to discuss with her. The Duchess was descended from two Baltimore families, the Warfields and the Montagues. She listened to Billy's plans to breed Tuylar, the Irish stallion.

The Duchess asked, "How is the health of your wonderful horse?"

"Excellent."

"And that of your wonderful mother?"

"Even better." Billy paused. "What is the news of Princess Margaret?" he asked boldly.

Wallis pulled away. Billy had broken protocol; she would lead the conversation, if not the fox-trot. Then she forgave him by telling about her new pug litter. One pup, she said, was named Group Captain Peter Townsend.

Afterward, Ann rushed to his side, eager for a report of his conversation. But Billy feigned indifference and drifted away. Ann had a pang as Billy approached Brenda Frazier Kelly, seated at a nearby table. Brenda took a cigarette from Billy's gold cigarette case. Seventeen years before, in 1938, the delicate brunette had been debutante of the year. Billy had admired Brenda when she was a national figure, but she had had too many beaux to notice him on any stag line. Now Billy was in the news and she was fading.

Parties forced temperamental people like Ann, Billy, and Brenda to abide by strict social rules—no shouting or petulance. These gatherings were enforced moments of seeming sanity.

Ann turned to Brenda's escort, Robert Chatfield-Taylor, descendant of one of the founders of the Marshall Field department store, who talked primarily of guns and hunting. As she described the plan for shooting the prowler, Chatfield-Taylor, a gun salesman for the Olin Company, told her to use something stronger than her shotgun. "You can't kill a person with birdshot. It's too light."

---

wine goblet like a hawk, saw no fight. Mutum observed Billy get up again to try to call his children's nurse. "He was calling his house," said Mutum. Butler Douglas Griffin does not remember a fight. Nobody, including the police, the Woodward family detectives, and the eight surviving party guests interviewed by the author, was ever able to get anybody who was present to verify a spat.

After the dance, the two couples strolled to the paneled drawing room for coffee and brandy. Mary Phipps joined them. Ann was still going on about how frightened she was. The prowler gave her a spotlight; it was the evening's most interesting topic. "My dear, you're obsessed," said Mary.

The parlormaids set up bridge tables. Griffin coaxed the fire as Ann stood by the fireplace, her gold hair lit from behind. She still drank only sparkling water. Titi and John Schiff joined the conversation. They lived next door to Billy and Ann, separated by six acres of thick woods. Nervous about the prowler, Titi Schiff asked the Woodwards, "What are you going to do?"

"I will sit in the kitchen all night with my gun," said Billy.

"No, that's crazy," said Titi. "Aren't you worried you'll shoot a child or a governess? Why not leave shooting him up to the police?"

"We're just protecting ourselves," Ann added.

"Let's change the subject," Titi said. "For all we know, the prowler is sleeping right now in one of our garages or pantries. I usually don't lock up my place. I'm going to have nightmares about the prowler sleeping in your pool house." Ann, sounding excited and nervous, replied, "But that's all we've been thinking about the whole day."

Mrs. Schiff felt frightened. It felt as if they were telling ghost stories. She was prepared for something terrible to happen then and there. Fern Tailer Gimbel suggested that Billy dissolve ten sleeping pills in a glass of milk and leave it on the kitchen table all night long. Since the prowler was known to steal food, the milk would knock him out.

More guests arrived after dinner. "You live near us," said Ann to Mrs. John Winslow. "Helen, has that prowler been around your home?"*

Helen Winslow joined the circle: "Yes, I had to lock him out forcibly." She said that two days earlier she had looked out her front window and seen a big man running off Route 25A toward her door. Her children had just come home from school. She screamed to the children, "I'm locking the front door, get Anna [the maid] to lock the back." Then Mrs. Winslow closed it against his bulk. He tried to push his way inside her home. "I called the police. I was absolutely petrified," she told the horrified group.

As midnight approached, the Duchess climbed the stairs, a grand, solitary figure.

"Billy," whispered Ann, watching the Duchess's back, "let's go before the rain gets worse."

*John Grenville Winslow was a childhood friend of Billy's, Bean's first cousin, and one of many members of the Baker family at the party.

Billy disappeared to ask Mary Sanford for a last dance. She felt, as he guided her around the dance floor, that despite his good fortune with Nashua, Billy had no buoyancy that night. He was young, he was handsome, he was rich, he had everything, but he did not have the aura of a happy man.

As the Woodwards said good night to Mr. and Mrs. George Leib just before midnight, Billy said he and Ann planned to fly his Helio to Brazil during the winter. Two parlormaids brought wraps from the coatroom.

Michael Butler stood in the doorway waiting for the butler to bring his Bentley, as Billy and Ann climbed into the Studillac. He chatted with Joe Thomas, who was dismayed by the fog and rain. Helen and John Winslow, who lived a mile from the Woodwards, pulled their car up to the Studillac. Ann rolled down the window. Billy said, "It's too foggy to drive home."

"Two sets of lights are better than one," said Winslow. "We'll follow you."

The Winslows turned their headlights high and followed the dim red glow of the Woodwards' taillights as they drove toward 25A.* The Studillac's tires skidded as Billy almost missed the Remson Lane turnoff.

---

*Later, there was a rumor that Billy and Ann stopped the car to fight. *The New York Times* printed the "unconfirmed" report. It was one of a score of titillating stories that did not prove to be true.

19

THE SHOOTING

12:00 Saturday night.

As Ann and Billy were driving home, a black police car cruised the fogged, wet grounds of the Pine Hollow Country Club adjoining the Woodward estate. The night watchman had reported a man running away from a snack stand. Patrolman Thomas Costello turned on his wipers at the tenth hole. He rolled down his window, turning his flashlight on the snack stand. The awkward burglar had alerted the Cove operator when he knocked the telephone off the counter.

Now the watchman appeared under an umbrella and led Costello to a bottle of milk, a half-eaten sandwich, and discarded food wrappings about a hundred feet away on a bench. Costello had missed the thief by only an hour.

"Nobody here," Costello said. He did not envy the prowler. It was a rotten night.*

---

*The following interrogation took place on Tuesday, three days after the shooting, in Ann Woodward's room in New York Hospital:

EDWARD ROBINSON: What did you do when you got home from the Baker dinner party?

ANN WOODWARD: Well, I was frightened to go in the house, you know. And we had left all the lights on, because my husband said, "Well, nobody will be around when it is light."

EDWARD ROBINSON: And when you got home did your husband go in the house first, or did you go in with him, or what?

ANN WOODWARD: Well, we got home and we talked about the thing all the way home. And so when we got out—and I had misplaced my jewel case at that point. It isn't a case, it is a flat folding thing, and I had put it underneath my coat and it had slipped, so I looked for it. And I didn't see where it was. I was looking around for it. And then he crawled in the window. He said, "Oh, this is how the man might get right in," which was even more terrifying.

287

*   *   *

Inside the Playhouse, Ann followed Billy as he searched the house for new signs of the prowler. Holding his revolver, Billy opened every closet door. Ann checked the refrigerator. She whispered, "I think he's been in here."

Billy decided they should both go to sleep armed and shoot if the prowler came inside their home. Billy tied the old miniature poodle Sloppy up in the kitchen to stand watch.

EDWARD ROBINSON: Did you take a gun out yourself from the gun case?

ANN WOODWARD: Yes, I took a gun out and put it on the chair in my bedroom.

EDWARD ROBINSON: Did you load the gun down there?

ANN WOODWARD: I don't remember if I loaded it—yes, I think I did. I don't remember, to tell you the truth.

EDWARD ROBINSON: What gauge gun was it?

ANN WOODWARD: My gun is a specially made gun that was made for me, that my husband gave me. It is a very light gun, for women.

EDWARD ROBINSON: Do you know what gauge it is?

ANN WOODWARD: It is a .12, I think.

EDWARD ROBINSON: Well, your husband didn't take any out, then, at that time?

ANN WOODWARD: He didn't take anything out then.

EDWARD ROBINSON: Did he go down to the gun case with you?

ANN WOODWARD: Yes.

EDWARD ROBINSON: Where did you put the gun?

EDWARD ROBINSON: Your husband climbed in?

ANN WOODWARD: Yes, he climbed in the bedroom window right there, which is my room.

EDWARD ROBINSON: Into your room?

ANN WOODWARD: Yes. So then I unlocked the door and went in. And he said, "You see how easy the man could get in the house? We thought we had locked everything, but it is so easy to just crawl right in the window."

ANN WOODWARD: I put the gun on a chair that was used for the telephone—to sit on when you are at the telephone.

EDWARD ROBINSON: Well, do you know whether you loaded it before
you went to sleep, before you got into bed to go to sleep?

ANN WOODWARD: The gun? Yes, it definitely was loaded when I put it
by the chair.

EDWARD ROBINSON: What nightclothes did you wear to go to bed?

ANN WOODWARD: A nightgown, and I always wear a bed jacket because
I am cold, you know. I get cold around my shoulders and I usually
sleep in a bed jacket.

EDWARD ROBINSON: Did you have a bra on?

ANN WOODWARD: Yes, I always wear a bra because I have always had
the idea that it is good for your bust to wear a bra, and I always
sleep in a bra.

In her bathroom, Ann brushed her teeth, took a sleeping pill, and
lay in the large bed in her bedroom. In his bathroom, Billy took a shower
and got into a narrow bed in his room. He did not put on his long pajama
top; he preferred to sleep in the nude.

EDWARD ROBINSON: Did you put a sleeping mask on at that time when
you went to bed? I ask that because you had one on when I was
there.

ANN WOODWARD: I don't think—I don't remember whether I had one
on or not. I put one on a lot in the daytime, and I also put ear plugs
in if I want to rest in the daytime.

EDWARD ROBINSON: What is the next thing you remember after getting
off to sleep?

Ann heard footsteps on the roof of her bedroom. Then she heard a
crash upstairs in the hall. Ann took off her sleep mask and grabbed the
gun beside the bed. The dog was barking, as it did at strangers. The butt
fit snugly into her armpit. The rush of adrenaline did not clear the effects
of the sleeping pill. She walked directly toward the noise she had heard.
Opening her bedroom door, she saw a shadow.

ANN WOODWARD: Oh, you don't know. (Witness sobs and becomes incoherent before continuing.) I moved quickly to open the door and stepped back in and then I fired the gun at a shadow.

EDWARD ROBINSON: This gun was a double-barrel, was it not?

ANN WOODWARD: Yes.

She aimed the gun through the half-opened door and pulled the trigger twice. Birdshot slammed across the eighteen-foot hall that led to Billy's room and to the staircase. The acrid gunpowder stung her nose. A second after she fired the gun an awful thought cut into her brain. "No, God, no!" The pale form on the floor in the dark hallway was her naked husband. She had shot Billy.

EDWARD ROBINSON: Yes, I understand. You didn't see any light coming from your husband's room when you opened that door and fired, did you?

ANN WOODWARD: I don't remember a light. There might have been a light. I don't remember it.

EDWARD ROBINSON: When you opened the door approximately how far inside of your door were you standing when you fired?

ANN WOODWARD: It was all done in one movement, practically. It was so quick. I heard the noise, opened the door and fired.

Ann stood in her bedroom doorway trying to think. But her mind would not focus. She did not recall looking into the dark hallway. Had something rustled out there? Had she seen Billy's shadow? She knew her husband in the light, she knew him in the dark. She always knew if Billy was asleep by her side without even opening her eyes.

She ran across the hallway in her bare feet and fell to her knees beside his naked body. She sobbed. Although he was lying on his stomach, she saw that his cheek was a bloody pulp. She ran downstairs to the basement and threw a handful of ammunition back into the gun cabinet, fearing that if she had any ammunition at all she would shoot herself.

She returned to Billy and dropped the gun. Perhaps Billy was not shot, he had just fallen down. Any minute now, he would say something to her. She grabbed his shoulders with both hands. There was not much blood on the carpet. It was only a face wound. Birdshot was not heavy ammunition.

Ann Woodward shot her husband at 2:07 a.m. No one has ever known with complete certainty what happened. Ann and Billy had stood at opposite ends of the eighteen-foot dark hall. The second shot from his wife's custom-made shotgun ricocheted off his bedroom door and hit Billy, making superficial flesh wounds on the right side of his face and neck. Billy had turned his head, perhaps having heard a noise upstairs. A small pellet entered his brain. From the impact of the shots, Billy fell back into his room on his stomach. He was dead within ten minutes.

The prowler had been on Ann's mind before she fell asleep; she had felt his presence around her. When she raised her shotgun and fired two shots, she had told herself that she was helping Billy.*

---

*Dr. Jane Oldden, a psychiatrist, treated Ann Woodward when her husband, Dr. John Prutting, was unavailable. She believes the shooting was an accident based on Ann's unconscious impulse. Dr. Oldden had been disturbed by Ann's lack of emotional stability when examining her: "Ann had no center. She only lived to please Billy, she was desperate to keep him and her position as Mrs. William Woodward. Her marriage was her career, and he stabilized her. I don't buy her shooting him as a conscious decision. Once he was gone, she was destroyed. Still, subconsciously she had to hate his hold over her. Studies of battered wives show that fatal accidents do occur after fights."

Ann had one goal. She had gone to enormous lengths to make herself into someone who would be accepted by Billy as Mrs. William Woodward, Jr. In fact, Billy's death would not release her. It fueled her determination to live up to the Woodward standards.

20

THE COLLAPSE

The lamp inside Billy's bedroom cast little light. Ann kissed the bleeding neck and hair of her dying mate. Around them were bits of brown paper from the shotgun cartridges. The framed prints of fashionable nineteenth-century ladies remained untouched against the wall. But the trellised wallpaper and open door to Billy's bedroom were riddled with buckshot.

Nearby, she heard Sloppy bark in the kitchen. Billy's right cheek was still bleeding. His right ear had been torn, his eye crushed. There was a dark little puddle under his head. But birdshot was not supposed to be fatal to people from such a distance. She patted his warm body, feeling the little acne scars on the skin on his back.

Talking to herself and to Billy, she looked around his bedroom, searching for something she had lost—she could not say what it was. He did not like her in here, but she had liked to sneak in and look at his things. Everything looked the same; there was his black briefcase that had been moved by the prowler from the Studillac. On the unused bed were two crumpled pillowcases and two bare pillows.

Ann wished she had spent more time decorating his room. She stared hopelessly at Billy's shotgun, lying near his bed.*

Ann saw night watchman Steve Smith, peering into the front door, framed by its yellow grillwork. "Help, please help me," she shouted.**

---

*The presence of the shotgun in the room inevitably became controversial. Why was Billy unarmed when he came to the door? Had he heard a noise? Was he coming to see Ann?

**Ten minutes after hearing the two loud explosions, Smith had stepped outside in back of the Playhouse. He was 300 feet from Ann's and Billy's bedrooms. He felt the light rain. He was

Smith banged on the windowpane and shouted, "Are you in there, Mrs. Woodward?"

"Oh, God, help me, help me," she said. She stumbled toward him. He would help her get Billy to a doctor. "Something terrible happened," she said. "Help me."

The heavy door was locked. In shock, she did not realize she could have unlocked the door from the inside.

Smith ran back to his room to telephone for help.

Ann listened. The watchman had gone away. She needed to get somebody to help her. She groped her way slowly into the library and dialed Lee Principe in nearby Bayville.*

She mumbled something to Principe's sleepy wife, and then told him: "Lee, come quick, there's been an accident."

"Yes, ma'am, it's not the boys, is it? You sound bad." Mrs. Woodward unnerved him the way she could laugh and cry in ten minutes. He figured it was because she had been a showgirl.**

At 2:07 a.m. Ann telephoned the local operator. "Help me, help me quick," Ann shouted, sobbing. Gladys Gallagher listened without comprehension, distressed. "Who's calling, please?" she asked.

Somebody else was calling the operator. Gladys Gallagher put Ann on hold. "Something bad happened at the Woodward Playhouse," Steve Smith said back in the Cinerama office. "Something's going on in there."

"Look, I'm talking to somebody in Woodwards', at Oyster Bay 6-1333," the operator said, noting that the time was 2:08 a.m. "The woman is hysterical. I'm calling the police now."***

Ann hung up the telephone, still moaning to herself.

The telephone felt wet. She wiped it on her arm. It was Billy's blood

_____

confused about the time. He could not remember whether he was supposed to move his watch an hour forward or an hour back at midnight for Eastern Standard Time.

He suddenly heard a woman screaming for help from inside the living quarters of the Playhouse.

(Before daybreak, when speaking with the Nassau County Police, Smith at first confused the length of time that had passed between the sounds of the two shots and the cries for help. He did not realize at first that he could not hear Ann Woodward shouting until he opened his bedroom door.)

*She did not have to use the operator except for long-distance calls—therefore, the police had no record of her calls that night.

**After speaking to a reporter and being chastised by Billy's oldest sister, Libby Pratt, Principe would refuse to speak of his part in the evening to anybody except his wife. He was forty-five, the father of two girls, a dutiful husband, a simple man. He was a second-generation servant who stood by the Woodwards, expecting that in return they would take care of him.

***The operator, Mrs. Gladys Gallagher, called the Oyster Bay Cove police station, a little booth on Northern Boulevard, a half mile away. Then she put in a call to the second precinct of the Nassau County Police in Hicksville, some ten miles to the south.

from her hand, and she shrieked. Then she stopped at the sound of her voice. She must not wake the children. The boys must not see what she had done to their father.*

Ann dialed the telephone, talking to herself. A woman answered and took her name. Mr. Rosenblatt was not available. He was not at Sands Point tonight. Ann hung up and called back again, "Please help me, please find him." Ann rushed to her bedroom to pull a nightgown over her body, smeared with Billy's blood.

Ann threw herself on her husband, as if that could stop the life from draining from his body. But then something happened. It was nothing she could describe except as a loosening of his flesh. Bill Woodward died beneath her. She rolled away on her back. She wanted to retch. It was all finished now.

2:15 a.m.

Oyster Bay Cove police chief Russ Haff thought of himself as a glorified night watchman. He enjoyed patrolling the woods, formal gardens, and tennis courts of these quiet estates, which were largely unoccupied every winter.

Haff usually rode by the Woodwards' near the Cove on his night rounds. He had seen that good-looking Ann Woodward just that afternoon, buying cosmetics at Snouders drugstore.

Haff sent out a radio bulletin to Cove patrolman Henry Cormier** to meet him at the Woodward estate. Cormier had ridden by the estate at about 1:30 a.m. and noticed the bright spotlights flooding the main driveway as well as the light in Billy's bedroom.

2:20 a.m.

Russ Haff was carrying two guns. The prowler had been spotted running across Route 25A, and Haff knew the man was armed. As Haff sped down the tree-lined lane past the dark Leffingwell mansion, he passed a produce truck filled with apples.

2:26 a.m.

---

*On the second floor in the front of the Playhouse, several hundred feet closer to the gunshots, Jimmy, who was eight, and Woody, eleven, did not stir in their two small bedrooms. They later said that they had heard nothing. Ann Gorney heard what she assumed were noises of a car backfiring. But in a second, she fell back to sleep.

**By day, Cormier was the popular assistant postal clerk. An identical twin, Cormier was an amateur policeman, but he was diligent. In the line of duty, he had recently helped Russ Haff rescue duck hunters overturned in a pond. When Brenda Frazier Kelly had a party, Cormier met guests' cars at the township line and escorted them to her house.

A half mile away at the Pine Hollow Country Club in Laurel Hollow, Costello received a "signal 13" from the Nassau County second-squad station on his police radio, signifying a disturbance. Then came a "signal 12": an emergency. Costello was told to drive over to the tennis courts of the Woodward estate. A woman had been screaming into the telephone for the police.

A minute or two later, Costello turned off Berry Hill Road into the entrance to the Woodward estate. Henry Cormier had just arrived. In the corridor between the two bedrooms, Ann shouted to them to help her. Behind Costello were two more second-squad detectives, John Moylan and Kenneth Boyd. Steve Smith called them to the Woodward front door.

Ann was shouting to them to help her. She saw the flashlights jumping through the small bedroom window. The officers said, "We are police, let us in."*

Ann ran to the front door, but she could not open it. She heard the sound of glass shattering. Russell Haff had broken Ann's bedroom window with the butt of his shotgun and climbed into the Playhouse. Suddenly, Ann heard footsteps and saw him in the dim light from Billy's bedroom.** Her hands shook, and her fingers were slippery with Billy's blood. She turned and ran back to Billy. Then she heard someone turn the key in the lock of the front door, but they were too late to help her and Billy. She clung to Billy's naked body. Lee Principe pushed open the door and shouted her name. Haff knelt by Ann. The police rushed in.

The police shouted to each other to fan out, with guns cocked, to search the grounds for whoever had shot Billy Woodward. Haff and the Nassau County police assumed the prowler had shot Woodward. Haff tried to pull Ann off Billy. At first she would not let go. Her knees buckled when Haff stood her up. She wept convulsively as he carried her to her bed.

Behind them, another policeman picked up Billy's wrist. There was no pulse.

"It's going to be okay," Haff told Ann. "What happened?"

---

*Police always vie for the status of "first man at the scene." Russ Haff claimed that he was first. Cormier's version in the police report places Haff as arriving at 2:35 a.m., a few minutes after he and the three Nassau County detectives arrived. The 400-page report, filled with interviews, photographs, descriptions, autopsy reports, and official classifications, was compiled by members of the Nassau County Second Precinct. According to this record, their man Thomas Costello was the first policeman to reach the actual scene of the crime. Cormier was probably first by a few seconds to arrive outside the Playhouse.

**The matter of the amount of light in the hallway would be much discussed in the press. Marina Torlonia's husband, Edward Slater, commented recently, "Isn't it impossible not to recognize your own husband's bandy legs in the shadows?"

She did not know how to say what had happened.

"Can I get you a glass of water?" Haff believed the intruder must have shot Mr. Woodward right before poor Mrs. Woodward's eyes. "Did you see the man who shot your husband?" he asked her.

"No, no," she screamed, weeping.

He was glancing all around. He could not help it. The dressing table was littered with little jars. On the night table was a lamp, a radio, a water bottle, and a cigarette box. There were at least ten more bottles of prescription pills on the bureau. A satin bed bolster was crumpled in a corner. Ann closed her eyes as Haff walked over to a little table and bent down to see a framed picture of Billy and the two boys.

The children must be told. Ann moaned and tried to stand up. But the policeman gently pushed her back onto her bed, where she lay crying in a fetal position.

She saw that her hands were smeared with blood, as was the front of her nightgown. There was blood on her pillows. "Did you see the man who did it?" he asked a second time. Her sobs deepened.

He picked up the telephone and called his family doctor, Dr. James Trousdell, who lived close by on Main Street. When Ann found her voice, she told Haff in a normal tone, "I did it. I thought it was that man who has been around here."

Haff looked frightened. He searched his pockets and came up with a scrap of napkin. He wrote down her words and put the napkin next to the telephone. Then he told the other policemen to stop searching, since the prowler had not shot Woodward.

At 2:50 a.m., Dr. Francis Moore, from the coroner's office, knelt over Billy, who was lying facedown on the floor with a pool of blood under his head. The shots had peppered the right side of his face and head. Dr. Moore touched Billy's naked back and found it was still warm. But there was no pulse. He pronounced him dead.

2:55 a.m.

Ann said, "I want to speak to someone of my family." Ann was calling the Woodwards her "family." Dr. Moore asked the second-squad detective now standing guard to leave while he examined her. She refused to take off her bra and nightgown. Ann may have been afraid he would see the bruises from her recent fights with Billy. Dr. Moore did not insist.

The second-squad detective guarding her was criticized later when it was learned that Dr. Moore had given Ann a strong sedative injection to calm her. Sedating a suspect so that she could not tell her story was against standard practice.

At 3:20 a.m., the telephone rang, and Ann grabbed it. She said "Hello," then hung up.

At this point there was a mysterious breach in police protocol that seemed to give Ann special privilege. Assistant Chief Inspector Jim Farrell—dapper, six feet one, and controversial—was an unexpectedly early visitor. Farrell arrived at the Playhouse before District Attorney Frank Gulotta, Chief Assistant District Attorney Eddie Robinson, and Chief of Detectives Stuyvesant Pinnell.

A man of few words, "Gentleman Jim" Farrell played golf with members of the powerful Pratt family, including Billy's sister Libby. He attended Libby Pratt's parties in black tie, but although he drank with the guests he was actually working as a security guard. The Pratts and other society people liked him—and often asked for him when they had police business. Unlike his boss, Chief Pinnell, Farrell took pride in doing favors for the wealthy. (The favors could be as small as a request for a red light instead of a "yield" sign in front of an estate, because screeching tires on a curve kept people awake.) The county detectives assumed he was given gifts and gratuities for these favors.

The Woodward case was right for Farrell. He was the kind of man who could talk easily to Ann. If necessary, he would be able to talk to Elsie Woodward. Farrell may well have been summoned by Frank Gulotta or Eddie Robinson, which would have been an example of their treating Ann with utmost respect.

Ann kept hearing her front door slam. The local press, who routinely monitored the police radio channel, had come running. At 3 a.m., Jim O'Neill of *Newsday* elbowed his way past the police inside the house. "What do you have? Murder one?" he asked a tired policeman. "We don't have the foggiest," replied the police officer, who ordered him out of the house. Press was forbidden on the murder site.

At 3:30 a.m., the detectives guarding the front door of the Playhouse were shocked to see the District Attorney himself drive up. Frank Gulotta*

---

*Gulotta was born in Brooklyn of poor Italian parents and educated at Columbia and St. John's Law School. Possessed of a thoughtful, gentlemanly manner, he liked to quote Schopenhauer on the futility of life: "We're born into this world crying and we leave it vainly gasping for air." In 1949, he was appointed district attorney by Governor Thomas Dewey to fill a sudden vacancy, and he proceeded to be reelected. After ten years Gulotta was nominated by his party and elected to the New York State Supreme Court. His son, Thomas, was elected the chief executive—in effect the mayor—of Nassau County in 1987.

In a 1985 interview, Gulotta said, "Mrs. Woodward got no preferential treatment from the Nassau County detectives or D.A.'s office. Since Eddie Robinson was the assistant D.A. who lived nearest Ann, I assigned him to the case."

When asked, he made the astonishing claim that the sedatives administered to Ann, a

was of higher rank than Farrell. The several reporters who had gathered in the courtyard instantly surrounded the forty-seven-year-old Gulotta. He had a small mustache and a melancholy air and was famous for his harassment of local mobsters whom he claimed to "protect" by stationing police cars outside their houses.

Reporters rarely saw him at the scene of a crime. A reporter yanked at Gulotta's suit coat: "Are you making an arrest tonight?" Gulotta refused to comment as he entered the Playhouse.

Under Gulotta's eye, the detectives ran a two-inch fluorescent yellow tape from tree to tree around the front door of the Playhouse. A small sign hung from it: CRIME SCENE, POLICE DEPARTMENT.

Inside, the district attorney asked the ballistics detectives to measure the position of every birdshot pellet lodged in the wall of Billy's bedroom and bedroom door. The physical evidence of the angle of shot and the powder burns would either back Ann up or tell another story.* Gulotta suspected the worst of Ann. He instructed police to tear the house apart and look for "anything, physical evidence, anything that might indicate there was bad blood between the Woodwards, or any reason for her to kill him."

Dr. Theodore Curphey and his assistant, Dr. Leslie Lukash, from the Nassau County Medical Examiner's office, along with the ballistics men, scrupulously examined Billy's bedroom. They determined that Billy's wounds did not have powder burns; they were inflicted from a distance of at least fifteen feet. The medical examiner poked into every corner of the house. The men found stains on the ironing board downstairs by the gun rack that looked like old blood. (The stains did not test as blood.)

They photographed and measured the scattered shot pattern on the wall of Billy's bedroom just behind his body and found it to be about two feet wide.

As Dr. Lukash noted recently, Billy was about six feet two inches tall and weighed approximately 180 pounds. It would have been impossible for Ann to move him. Dr. Lukash found no traces of blood anywhere

---

murder suspect who had not yet been questioned, were not unusual. He had not ordered them. "We gave her sedatives like we would give anybody," said Gulotta.

He insisted his own presence was in the line of duty. "In those days, the District Attorney moved on every major crime. These things never did happen at convenient hours."

*The pattern on the wall negated the rumor that the body was deliberately moved. Truman Capote and others whispered that Ann shot Billy in the shower and dragged him to the bedroom door.

else, including the bathroom or on the floor between Billy's body and the bathroom.

The investigators checked the pistol on the edge of Billy's desk and the shotgun on the floor for fingerprints. They found irregular dust patterns on Billy's evening jacket, lying across the chair with his dress shirt and undershorts. Lukash was amazed that the single pellet had killed Billy. All the other wounds were surface wounds, but one fluke pellet had penetrated his brain.

3:35 a.m.

Gulotta and Eddie Robinson stood above Ann, who could not speak, but when the sedatives took hold, her sobs became whimpers. Gulotta agreed to wait to interrogate her. At least they had her confession to Russ Haff.

Homicide detective Dan Stark arrived at the Playhouse, but was told to wait in the living room before he questioned the suspect. The brass was keeping the case under wraps. Stark sent out to the Greenvale Diner for coffee. He walked around the house and decided the furniture was "too old-fashioned" and in need of cleaning.

After a while Stark and the other detectives sprawling in the living room began to grumble. Ordinarily, they would oversee things. Even Squad Commander George Erdoty complained, as did Deputy Squad Commander Ferdinand Wendt. Why were they there at all? When was the brass going to clear out?

The work was getting done—photographs, checking the house thoroughly for information and fingerprints. But because of the social prominence of the Woodwards and the Pratts, the investigation was being directed by Chief of Detectives Stuyvesant Pinnell, rather than by the local second squad and the homicide squad. Stark had never seen Chief Pinnell stay so involved in a crime scene. He was going over every detail.

Stark wondered what ballistics would come up with. There were two big questions so far: Would she be booked? What about bail?

At 4:15 a.m., Claire Moore, a registered nurse, entered Ann's closed bedroom without knocking.

It was unusually generous for the county to hire a registered nurse to tend a murder suspect, and Eddie Robinson may well have acted beyond his authority. Ordinarily, the police would relentlessly question their suspect. There is no point in waiting until the subject gets his wits about him. It is when he is weak and vulnerable that he will tell his full story. If a suspect was ill, there was always Meadowbrook Hospital—complete with its own prison wing. There was also a jail for questioning and booking.

Detective Richard Ebright stood to leave. Ann raised her head to watch him. "Who is it? What is it? What's going on?" She sank back onto the pillow, while Nurse Moore told Ann that she had been hired to look after her. Ann asked if her children were awake.

Moore read the labels of the barbiturates, tranquilizers, and anti-depressants. Worried that Ann might try to commit suicide, she went to the kitchen, ignoring the ragged half-blind dog and Lee Principe, and brought back three paper bags. She filled them with the pill bottles, the majority prescribed by Dr. Prutting. Ann raised her head and said clearly, "No, please, don't take the pills."

Moore did not say why she was taking them. She silently handed the bags to a detective; they became evidence.

Moore washed the blood off Ann's hands and face. Ann tossed her head from side to side, telling Billy how sorry she was, pleading with him to make up with her. She turned to Moore, seated on a chair beside her bed: "What should I do?" "Don't worry, Mrs. Woodward. Things aren't as bad as all that," Moore said, patting her hand.

4:26 a.m.

Young Billy Bancroft of Hastings Lane in Old Westbury arrived at the Playhouse to identify his uncle's body. Chief Farrell had called Libby Woodward Pratt, who had sent Bancroft, unable to force herself to go. She had been like a second mother to Billy. It was she who made the decision not to wake Elsie with the news.

Bancroft walked by the body of his uncle on the floor. He tapped on Ann's bedroom door: her shame and wretched grief touched him. It is a curious fact that nearly everyone present that morning believed Ann was innocent. In years to come, the Woodward family would be split. Bancroft believed Ann innocent, while his grandmother Elsie did not.

5:00 a.m.

Ann heard the man from the police department enter her room. He told her that he was a medical examiner. Dr. Lukash inspected every surface of her bedroom. Nurse Moore and Dr. Lukash had the same reaction to the house: they were shocked by its state of disrepair. Dr. Lukash was particularly surprised that Billy slept in such a tiny bedroom.

By the time Assistant District Attorney William Kahn arrived, at about five-thirty, Frank Gulotta had gone. Kahn stopped short at the sight of Billy Woodward's corpse. A detective remarked, "Separate bedrooms? Don't these rich people have sex?" "Don't ask me," Kahn replied.

The ballistics people needed help unscrewing the hinge on Billy's door. The surface, imbedded with birdshot pellets, was important evidence.

The detectives were turning the light in Billy's room off and on to see how much it illuminated the hallway.

Ann heard a scuffle in the yard in front of her bedroom. Somebody shouted, "Hey! Hold it!" Reporter Jim O'Neill had pushed his way inside past Cove patrolman Cormier. O'Neill was thrown out again.

The police photographer took his last picture of Billy's naked body. He also photographed several wads of brown paper from the shotgun cartridges near Billy's head and the little Duchess of Windsor cushion: "Never explain, never complain." Because of the position of Billy's body on the floor, the detectives hypothesized that seconds before he had been shot he had turned to the left, toward the small staircase leading upstairs. He took the shot on the right side of his face.

But what made him turn? Had he heard a noise upstairs? Or had he seen the glint of Ann's gun?

At 5:45 they were photographing the little alcove from which Ann had telephoned the police. Nurse Moore told Ann she was leaving to go to Mass. Taking her chair, Detective Ebright asked Ann what had happened. She began to answer him weakly, saying that she had put the loaded shotgun by her bedside. She had heard footsteps, Sloppy barked, and then she had jumped out of bed.

Ann was dreaming intermittently under heavy sedation that she was in the midst of the FBI raid on her house back in Kansas on the day of the shooting at Union Station. She implored the detective by her bed to help her. "Get my mother," she said. "She's working around the corner."

7:50 a.m.

A kind of order had finally been imposed at the Playhouse. Dr. Theodore Curphey sat in the wood-paneled living room and dictated his report to a stenographer. He began, "Body found nude in northeast bedroom in the small entrance passageway leading from the lobby of the main entrance . . . with a large amount of smeared blood on the back, face downward, lying on left side of face. There is a pool of blood surrounding the head. Left arm flexed at right angles to elbow. Left forearm under body at about level of iliac crest. There are two beds, one obviously occupied recently."

The police photographers had opened the gun cabinet in the basement and maneuvered around the stacked cartons of English ammunition.

The forensic evidence seemed to confirm Ann's story. Little by little the detectives began to believe her. Only Detectives Fred Catapano and Andy Heberer seemed to have doubts.

But outside, the reporters muttered their suspicions about Ann. What about the light? Had it been off or on in the hallway? How dim was it? If it had been on, how much had Ann seen? Had she recognized her husband or not?

7:52 a.m.

Billy's body was wrapped in a sheet and carried out of the Playhouse. Two policeman held the ends of the stretcher. The press photographers moved to take pictures of Billy's naked feet dangling from the blanket.

8:00 a.m.

Sol Rosenblatt, the short, swarthy lawyer Ann had tried to reach the night before, waited outside the Playhouse behind the yellow police line with the reporters. Chief Pinnell was against having a private attorney present at the scene of a crime. But Rosenblatt insisted he had the right to talk to his client.*

He was soon sitting on Ann's bed, with his face close to hers to hear her. It calmed her to see Rosenblatt taking care of things. "Do I have blood on my face?" she asked him in a bleak whisper. Then, between sobs, she described in a sketchy way what had happened. It took her less than a minute. Rosenblatt did not press. He quoted the common-law rule that if a homeowner legitimately fears for his own safety or that of his home, he may shoot an intruder to kill. The lawyer said that she was innocent and that she had had a terrible accident.

Rosenblatt added, "Tell them as little as possible." He repeated her story back to her the way she should tell it.

Rosenblatt asked if she had anything of value in the house. He claimed he was worried about theft, since there were so many people around. Ann

---

*Rosenblatt was part of the privileged series of relationships that distinguished the Woodwards from ordinary people. He cultivated a reputation for skulduggery and for going out of his way for clients such as Clare Boothe Luce, Marlene Dietrich (his wife's best friend), Elsa Maxwell, Bishop Fulton Sheen, Alfred Gwynne Vanderbilt, C.Z. and Winston Guest, and Joe DiMaggio. He was said to use his influence with his friends Governor Averell Harriman and Tammany Hall boss Carmine DeSapio to keep cases out of court. "He knew everybody who was anybody in the whole Southampton set," said his son Richard Russell.

Upon his second marriage to Estrella Boissevain, a tiny, svelte international socialite, Rosenblatt moved from middle-class Great Neck, New York, to a beach cottage at exclusive Sands Point, where he played golf with Harriman at the Sands Point Golf Club.

Rosenblatt's presence at the Playhouse was not recorded in the police report, although *Life* magazine named him as the first nongovernment lawyer at the scene of the shooting.

None of the police or members of the district attorney's office whom I interviewed remember he was there.

Rosenblatt's lifelong legal secretary, Mrs. Margaret Soper ("Sopie"), knew he was working around the clock for Ann Woodward that weekend. His name appeared several months later in Billy's probated will. Ann would submit his $25,000 bill with her expenses for October and November. "Sol worked in mysterious and silent ways," said his former associate Mitchell Booth, confirming that Rosenblatt was at the Playhouse.

said her jewelry was not in the safe. "Don't let them take you out of here without it. Or you will never see it again," he whispered. He was particularly worried that the family was not going to make things easy for her.

If ever a legal situation seemed tailored for a particular attorney, the Woodward shooting fit Sol Rosenblatt. He could protect a grieving woman, surround himself with society figures, and move behind the scenes. By saying little he implied that his task had been enormous. Most of the rumors about Ann's "murder" of Billy can be traced to Sol Rosenblatt and his desire to place himself at the pivotal center of a major scandal. Rosenblatt would later claim that he danced circles around Frank Gulotta.*

"Sol fixed the Woodward murder," said photographer Jerome Zerbe. According to the myth as told by Joan Fontaine, Zerbe, and countless others, Rosenblatt first woke Elsie Woodward in New York and insisted she sign an enormous number of blank checks. He then drove out to Oyster Bay Cove and ("with the butler's help") moved Billy's body out of the shower. "He also removed the bathroom door because it was full of bullet holes. He helped Ann drag the body out of the shower," said Zerbe.

The rumor was that Ann shot Billy while he was taking a shower. Some, like Liz Whitney Tippett, would add that Billy raped Ann first and that Ann then invented the prowler out of whole cloth. Ann supposedly washed Billy's blood down the drain and, with Rosenblatt's help, covered the traces.

Zerbe said, "Sol had to calm her down. She was going nuts. Then he had to get the caretaker to put another door on the bathroom before the police came."

The story continues that Rosenblatt then bribed policemen, maids, district attorneys, butlers—with Elsie's checks. "Four hundred thousand in blank checks," said Joan Fontaine.**

8:50 a.m.

Sol Rosenblatt left the Playhouse. From a nearby diner, he made several calls. Among other things, Rosenblatt had decided that Ann should retain local counsel.

As usual in Oyster Bay Cove, Rosenblatt went behind the scenes and

---

*The truth was that Rosenblatt would have been too cautious to gossip maliciously about his venerable clients like Alfred Gwynne Vanderbilt. If he did, valued dinner invitations would stop. It came down to the fact that Rosenblatt or anybody else who spoke against Ann was speaking in favor of the heroism of Elsie Woodward.
**Patrick O'Higgins, as told to Frank Zachary, editor of *Town & Country*, said the same.

right to the top. He awakened the single most powerful person in Nassau County, the local Republican political boss, J. Russell Sprague. Rosenblatt retained Sprague's law firm, Sprague and Stern, whenever he needed Nassau County counsel.*

Sprague ran the North Shore like a feudal lord, doling out favors, but he was a gentleman, not a big-city political boss. He was also bigger than elections and more important than any governor—Republican or Democrat. Even his party rival, Leonard Hall, the former chairman of the Republican National Committee, who lived in Nassau County, had no muscle against him.

Rosenblatt told Sprague he had to work fast. He had to make sure the district attorney did not charge Ann with murder or place her in jail. Since Rosenblatt was not a criminal lawyer, he enlisted Sprague to help find a highly respected criminal lawyer for Ann.**

The criminal lawyer had to be of the highest moral reputation. Rosenblatt asked if the former governor, Thomas E. Dewey, would handle the case. Sprague agreed to ask him. In the meantime, Sprague designated his young associate Henry Root Stern, Jr.,*** as his firm's liaison to Ann and Rosenblatt. Stern Jr. was a good choice as liaison: his connections to the district attorney's office would provide the Woodwards with an insider's grasp of Eddie Robinson's investigation.

Rosenblatt next called John Hay Whitney, the owner of the New York *Herald-Tribune*, at Greentree. Rosenblatt had been to parties with him and had handled divorces for his family. Whitney was known as the godfather of the North Shore. Not only was he highly respected and believed to have all the answers, he also liked to help people. He was approachable, unlike his friend the late William Woodward, Sr.

"Jock" Whitney was crucial to Rosenblatt's plan. Whitney had donated the money used to build Doctors Hospital in Manhattan, known as

---

*Rosenblatt made it a rule never to appear in court out of town without a local lawyer at his side. He made sure the judge noticed him, bowing his head from time to time to confer with the local attorney, showing respect. Rosenblatt's question would be along the lines of "How long will this wonderful weather last?" But he knew these whispered conferences ingratiated him to both the judge and the jury.

**Rosenblatt's office had only once handled a minor criminal proceeding, and that was for Long Island socialite and island owner Robert Gardiner.

***Stern would be left a $25,000 bequest in Ann Woodward's will. Stern's father was also a member of Sprague's law firm. Henry Root Stern, Jr., had been employed as an assistant district attorney under Frank Gulotta until recently. If he had stayed in Gulotta's office, he, not Eddie Robinson, would probably have been assigned to the Woodward case, chiefly because of his ability to "talk to rich people."

Stern Sr. had been an early confidant of neighbor Teddy Roosevelt. Years earlier, Stern Sr. had introduced Sprague to Governor Dewey at Stern's home.

a hospital for the privileged (it was even rumored to serve patients cocktails). Rosenblatt hoped to get Ann admitted to move her outside the jurisdiction of the Nassau County district attorneys and police.

One problem was that Ann was suggestible. Her remorse might lead her to confess God knows what. She might say things about her marriage that would further alienate the Woodwards. Rosenblatt knew that if Elsie could be persuaded by the facts of the investigation that Ann was not guilty, the district attorney would take her attitude most seriously.

The telephone at Greentree was answered by Edward Moss, the English butler. Moss refused to wake his master. Rosenblatt became more persuasive, threatening and cajoling at the same time. Finally, the servant relented. Jock Whitney was awakened.

When the head butler returned to the extension telephone, he overhead the terse report: "Ann killed Billy Woodward and we've got to take care of it."

The caller explained that he would appreciate it if Whitney would get the wheels rolling at Doctors Hospital. "We have to get her out of here before some hothead detective tries to put her in jail." Jock Whitney agreed.

The district attorney agreed to allow Ann to be taken to a private hospital outside their jurisdiction. Through Rosenblatt's skillful manipulation, the district attorney would lose a full day before speaking to her again. Nassau County detectives guarded her room.

At nine o'clock, Elsie's grandson Tommy Bancroft arrived at her stone mansion on East Eighty-sixth Street. Like Billy Bancroft, his brother, Tommy, at twenty-six, was one of the best-trained athletes on the North Shore, and had won amateur tennis tournaments around the world. A Princeton graduate, he was working in his father's textile company.

Her family had decided to let Elsie sleep until about nine o'clock. Elsie was known for her fortitude and great spirit, but she was seventy-two years old, and still in mourning for her sister. Moreover, although Elsie often called Billy "impossible," he was her only son, and the Woodward sisters saw Billy's fights with his mother as proof of their closeness.

Putz, the butler and perhaps the closest person to her, and Tommy Bancroft woke Elsie. According to friends, Tommy never forgot his grandmother's initial unguarded shock and pain as she was told about her son's death. Tommy always believed—as did Elsie—that Ann had killed Billy in cold blood.

Elsie's long-standing fears had been realized. All her class instincts had been against Ann. When Billy married Ann, he had jeopardized the family name and all it had stood for.

After saying that she could not believe her son was gone, Elsie said, "Thank God, Bill's father isn't around to see this."

The physical evidence of the shooting had been recorded by the police six hours before Elsie learned of her son's death, and without tampering or bribing from Elsie or her representatives. And although Elsie believed Ann was covering up a murder, she had no proof.

Society people speak of a murder cover-up; they believe that Elsie Woodward had more power than an "out of town" district attorney's office, court of law, and police force. Enlarging Elsie Woodward's power makes her social peers feel more powerful.

At 9:30 Elsie called Walter Gray Dunnington, the Woodward family trusts and estates lawyer. Dunnington had a hauteur not unlike Billy's late father's. He was also a director of Colgate-Palmolive and, like Billy and his dad, a trustee of the Hanover Bank. Dunnington's hobby was not racing, but art. He was a vice president of the Whitney Museum of American Art. He also had enough sense of his own importance to start his own private club.

Elsie told Dunnington that Ann had murdered Billy and was claiming it was an accident.

"What do you want to do?" asked Dunnington in his Virginian's drawl.

"I want to protect my grandsons."

Elsie did not want to leave the fate of the Woodward name in Ann's hands. Dunnington told Elsie he would make sure that her grandsons would live with her and added that he would go to Oyster Bay at once.

As a rule, the estate lawyer would not become involved with criminal law. He usually handled assessments of property for taxes for such families as the Phippses and for the estate of Gertrude Vanderbilt Whitney. However, if Elsie Woodward was in trouble, he would do anything to help.

He believed Elsie's assertion that Ann had murdered Billy. As the family lawyer, he had drawn up Billy's separation agreement six years earlier. In supervising the Woodward family's private investigation, Dunnington would help Elsie decide Ann's fate—should the family press for an indictment?

Dunnington explained to Elsie how important it was to find out

exactly what had actually happened in Oyster Bay. He told Elsie that the
police would try to establish a motive. They would probably try to dig up
a great deal about the marriage. Elsie did not want any surprises about
Billy's marriage. She said, "Let's get the facts."

Dunnington promised to hire the best private investigator.

Dr. John Prutting insisted on attending Ann as soon as Sol Rosenblatt had
awakened him with the news. By going to Oyster Bay, Dr. Prutting would
miss his wife's speech at church service. Her feelings were hurt, but she
knew her husband would do anything to keep his society clients happy.
Like Rosenblatt, he had listened for hours to Ann's insecurities about losing
her husband. He had soothed her and played into her desire for self-
improvement by teaching her new medical words and psychiatric ideas. As
a physician herself, Dr. Oldden respected Prutting's dedication. A doctor's
family becomes accustomed to medical emergencies. But in Dr. Oldden's
mind, this was no medical emergency. Ann's problems were emotional
and legal.

In the next three weeks Dr. Prutting's gaunt face, balding crown, and
small mustache would become a familiar sight to television viewers and
newspaper readers. A born showman, he would describe Ann's mental state
to reporters. This was, in fact, a clever idea of Rosenblatt's. Bulletins from
a lawyer would have made Ann look like a criminal. This way, she was
presented as "the patient."

At 9:30 a.m. the next morning Nurse Moore and a group of men in
business suits sat around Ann's bed. Bill Kahn had never seen anybody so
racked with shame and grief. "Mrs. Woodward?" asked Edward Robinson.
He was making a note on a pad. It was time to ask Ann official questions.
Next to him stood Dan Stark, the homicide detective.

In the group was Nathan Birchall, age fifty-three, the court stenographer. Nate was a fixture at all local criminal investigations. He had begun
his career when he was in his teens, and nothing ever seemed to shock
him. But now he was shaken. Robinson* cleared his throat and asked Ann
to state her name.

*Robinson, then a young lawyer, had been summoned by the district attorney to interrogate
Ann. He was the skilled law partner of the former Republican National Committee Chairman
Leonard Hall and up-and-coming in the local Republican party, which ran Nassau County. Rob-
inson was a superb trial lawyer and a much-sought-after public speaker. Recalls a peer, "Eddie was

Nate Birchall leaned over the bed. Nurse Moore prayed for Ann.

Robinson had waited more than five hours to question his suspect. The Woodward case would be a big newspaper story, and Robinson could not afford any enemies among the rich families in the county.

Ann sobbed, "I just hope my children are all right." Robinson answered her. "Yes, they're all right, Mrs. Woodward. Do you want to turn around this way a minute? As I told you, my name is Robinson, I am an assistant district attorney, and it becomes necessary to find out what happened today. Would you give me your name, please?"

As Nate Birchall lay on the bed in order to hear Ann's words, she made her preliminary statement.

Ann Woodward: "Yes. There was a man—"

Edward Robinson: "Well, I want you to tell me that, will you?"

Ann sobbed. "There was somebody around the property," she said. "What else can I say? We were all scared. We were so terrified. My husband got a gun out and told me I should get one because we didn't know what might happen."

Robinson asked, "Well, did you have the gun out yesterday afternoon or last night?"

"Last night, because he said it was dangerous. The man might come at night. He never moved in the daytime."

"Did he get the gun or did you?"

"He told me to get it."

"Where did you get it?"

"Downstairs in the basement. In the closet."

"When you came home from dinner?"

"Yes, because he said it was dangerous."

"He had a gun in his bedroom?" Robinson asked.

Ann squeezed her eyes closed and slurred her words. "He had a gun that he had gotten out earlier in the day, and he took it out when we went to dinner because he was so afraid that the man was on the property and, you know, he might do something to us. We stopped on our way out to turn on the lights so that the man might be scared away."

She burst into a scream.

Robinson took her hand. "What time did you get home from dinner?"

"I don't know exactly."

---

honest, but he was so political I wouldn't turn my back on him." Robinson was eager to become district attorney. His boss, District Attorney Frank Gulotta, had often wondered aloud how much Robinson's ambition, like Napoléon's, was a compensation for his being short. The two men were in competing factions of the Republican party.

"Well, did you go down the stairs right away to get the gun?"

"Well, he said he would go around to look and check all the rooms and see for sure that the man wasn't anywhere, you know."

"And did he do that? Or did you go with him?"

"No, he did because he said he didn't want me to go, you know. I started to go and he said, 'No, go back to your room, leave the door open if anything happens,' you know."

"Yes. Well, did you go down then yourself and get the gun?"

"That was before."

"Oh, before you went out to dinner?"

"No, before, before. Oh, it's too horrible, it's terrible."

But Robinson persisted. "Was the light on in the hall when you shot the gun, Mrs. Woodward?"

After a moment, she answered him. "I don't think there were any lights on—"

"Had you been in bed?"

"Yes."

"What did you do, hear a noise or something?"

Ann whispered, "I heard a noise and I heard the dog bark. The dog was in the sitting room. The dog was barking and it scared me so terribly."

"And what did you do? Do you remember what you did?"

"I picked the gun up and walked with it toward the noise. I shot at a shadowy figure."

Robinson had what he wanted. "You are doing wonderfully now."

Ann burst out with a scream, remembering Billy's hurt eye, "Oh, you don't know." Nate Birchall recorded: "Witness sobs and becomes incoherent. Statement concluded at 9:40 A.M."*

Dr. Prutting arrived at the Playhouse and knelt with one knee on Ann's bed. He told her that Jock Whitney had worked his magic and a private room had been reserved for her at Doctors Hospital.

---

*In the police report, the first interrogation ended before Ann described a controversial detail of the shooting. *The New York Times*, however, reported that on first questioning Ann went on to say that she had shot at "a figure in the shadows." At her next questioning, Ann apparently changed her statement to say, "I shot at a noise," implying that she had seen nothing.

When the police report was filed, the facts were put neatly into order. Police reports are made by human beings—and those human beings—and a grand jury—had decided Ann Woodward was not guilty by the time the report was typed up several months later. Therefore, the police probably omitted Ann's first comment about shooting at a figure in the shadows and included her statement that she had shot at a noise.

Dr. Prutting spoke sharply to Nurse Moore for having gone to Mass: "How dare you leave Mrs. Woodward alone?" When Ann told Prutting that she wanted to die, he gave her more sedatives.

At 10:30 a.m. the ambulance attendants wheeled in a stretcher and wrapped Ann in a plaid blanket. She clutched her jewelry case to her bare stomach under her nightgown. When she heard someone mention the reporters outside, she asked the nurse to put a towel over her face.

Outside, Nurse Moore was pushed aside by a reporter who tried to pull the towel off Ann's face. Ann barely heard the clamor. The stretcher was jolted by the shoving photographers. Dr. Prutting climbed into the ambulance next to her. When he took the towel off Ann's face, she clasped his hand and held it. Dr. Prutting believed Ann's story. Being Mrs. William Woodward was her whole life. He thought she would not consciously destroy her identity, although he also knew she had built up a lot of resentment against her husband. Dr. Prutting had seen the bruises.

After the Shooting

Left: Billy Woodward's bedroom. *Below*: Ann Woodward's bedroom, October 31, 1955.

Billy's bedroom, where he fell after he was shot. Note the coroner's outline of the body on the rug.

Dr. John Prutting, Ann Woodward's physician, became known nationally as a result of giving daily reports about Ann's collapse to the press.

Reporters with detectives from the Nassau County Police Department. The Woodwards' chauffeur and gardener, Lee Principe, leans against the family's Thunderbird.

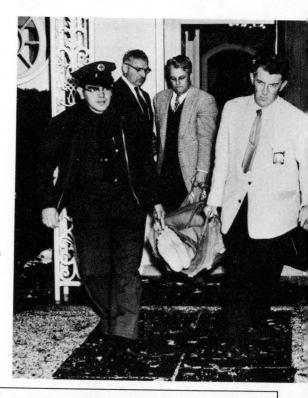

The body of Billy Woodward.

The New York Times.

LATE CITY EDI

Partly cloudy with showers
Partly cloudy, cool tom
Temperature Range Today—Max., 6

VOL. CV..No. 35,709.

NEW YORK, MONDAY, O

Wife Kills Woodward, Owner of Nashua; Says She Shot Thinking He Was a Prowler

Widow Taken to Hospital After Tragedy in Dark Oyster Bay Home

By MILTON BRACKER
Special to The New York Times.

OYSTER BAY, L. I., Oct. 30 — A shotgun blast early this morning took the life of William Woodward Jr., 35-year-old financier, sportsman and owner of the great racehorse Nashua.

District Attorney Frank A. Gulotta of Nassau County said the gun was fired by the victim's wife, Ann Eden Crowell Woodward, 32, who told investigators she thought she had aimed it at a prowler.

After preliminary questioning, which is to be resumed, she was taken to Doctors Hospital, Manhattan. She arrived there on a stretcher in a private ambulance early this evening.

Mr. Gulotta said that, pending further inquiry, the death would be considered accidental. Inspector Stuyvesant Pinnell, chief of the Nassau County detectives, described the case as "more likely to be accidental than homicide."

The pellets, from a 12-gauge, double-barreled British model gun, were fired across a ten-foot hall between the door of Mrs. Woodward's bedroom and that of her husband. Mrs. Woodward told the police she had been awakened by the barking of a

William Woodward Jr. and his wife at Hialeah last year

poodle called Sloppy, which slept in the kitchen.

The crack of the shot did not disturb the couple's two sons, who were sleeping upstairs.

According to the story assembled by Mr. Gulotta and Inspector Pinnell, the Woodwards

had attended a party last night in honor of the Duchess of Windsor at near by Locust Valley. Their hostess was Mrs. George F. Baker, widow of the chairman of the First National Bank of New York. There were

Continued on Page 19, Column 2

TY'S REVENUES OP PREDICTIONS, AS DO THE STATE'S

69,097,383 in First Fiscal Quarter Compares With $462,941,874 Year Ago

LES TAX BIG FACTOR

Yields Most of $5,000,000 eneral Fund Rise—More Albany Aid Is Expected

By PAUL CROWELL

The city's revenues for the first fiscal year are, like most of the state, running ahead of expectations.

Figures made public by City Treasurer Joseph A. Sarafite yesterday showed a trend in support of Mayor Wagner's confidence that municipal services can be reasonably expanded in 1956-57 without the need for new taxes to assure a balanced budget.

Mr. Sarafite's statistics, covering the first quarter of the fiscal year 1955-56, showed receipts of $469,097,383, compared with $462,941,874 in the same three months of 1954-55. The city's fiscal year begins on July 1.

The city's fiscal experts said yesterday that the unexpected in-

LIFE

Vol. 39, No. 20
Nov. 14, 1955

RED AND WHITE FLOWERS—HIS RACING COLORS: ADORN WOODWARD'S GRAVE. THEY WERE SENT BY WIDOW, "DUNK," "MONK" WERE COUPLE'S NICKNAMES

FAME, BEAUTY, WEALTH, SENTIMENT AND MYSTERY—ELEMENTS OF THE SHOOTING OF THE CENTURY

In a grave marked by chrysanthemums and carnations the body of William Woodward Jr. at last immensely wealthy young sportsman who had moved in the glittering international social set, was buried in New York last week. The flowers had come from his widow who four days earlier had fired the shotgun blast that all but tore open his back.

Not in this century had circumstances combined to produce so entrancing a shooting: a tragedy involving people of great wealth, the meteoric career of a poor girl raised to heights of fame and elements of mystery that would puzzle novel a grand jury weighed all explanations. The

death occurred after midnight in the Woodwards home on Long Island's North Shore gold coast. Woodward, 35, was world famous as the owner of the great racing thoroughbred Nashua. His wife Ann, 32, a onetime model and chorus girl, was renowned for her beauty and vivacity. Even Woodward's death was set against a backdrop in keeping with the couple's society life: they had just returned from a party at the home of a wealthy neighbor in honor of the Duchess of Windsor. To ascertain how it happened, the police sought the answer in the couple's folded life together, right up to the moment of the shot (scene on following pages).

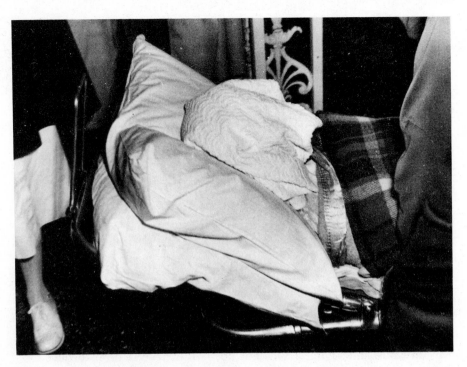

Ann Woodward being taken to Doctors Hospital.

The family dog, Sloppy, who was barking when Ann awoke and shot her husband.

21

AFTERMATH

I was dressing to come down to breakfast when I heard my husband saying, "Oh, no, no, it isn't true. I don't believe it." "What?" I asked, leaning down the banister. "Billy Woodward is dead, Ann shot him." I mean we wondered, naturally we discussed it with the Frosts, our hosts for the weekend—was Ann guilty of murder or not. Either all that talking she did [to us] about getting ready to shoot a prowler meant that she was setting up an alibi or that she was perfectly innocent. I mean, but I don't know. I just did feel myself, under certain circumstances I would have been terribly frightened. But I think if you—what was funny, is to go off—I myself wouldn't have gone off and left my children.

—Mary Phipps, police report, 1955, and interview, 1988

There he was the scion of a wealthy and aristocratic family, a popular figure in the sports world and international society, a man with a splendid war record and the head of a charming family with a beautiful wife and two growing children. Today Bill is lying in his casket, his handsome face torn away by a shotgun blast fired at close range by his wife Ann. . . . Everyone who knows Ann is familiar with her meteoric temperament. Her fits of temper were enough to put the fear of God in a platoon of British Grenadiers.

—CHOLLY KNICKERBOCKER, "A Great American Tragedy,"
New York *Journal-American*, November 1, 1955

Homicide police Dan Stark and Henry Koehl began at once to track down party guests, whose names were supplied by Charles Cushing;* Cushing told the police that the Woodwards seemed "quite happy and in extremely good spirits throughout the party."** Guests from the night before began calling the Baker estate. Cushing spoke for Mrs. Baker, saying that Elsie would not want dirty linen aired about Ann and Billy's marriage. This was the basis of the much-mentioned cover-up, "the great hush," that anybody who aspired to be anybody pretended to have heard at first hand from Elsie Woodward over the years.

Florynce Baker Martinau heard the news on the radio and called her sister, Titi Schiff. Bean Baker's sisters were stunned. They agreed that Ann could not have done it on purpose. Titi Baker Schiff dismissed the idea that it was a murder: "Ann is a shrewd woman, and he was worth much more to her alive than dead."*** The two City Bank heiresses were talking

---

*What remains today are repetitive summaries of these interviews in the typed 50,000-word police report.

**While speaking to Cushing the detectives wrote that "the Woodwards spent most of the evening in each other's company and during the evening the main topic of conversation of the Woodwards seemed to center around their being frightened of a prowler that was known to be in the vicinity of thier [sic] house. They also made mention of the fact that they were planning a trap to catch this prowler that evening when they went home, but to the best of his knowledge did not discuss the details of this plan. Stated that they left together at about 0100 hours, Sunday, October 30, 1955."

***Titi Schiff also spoke to the homicide police. "Present at this address [Berry Hill Road, Oyster Bay Cove] and there interviewed Mrs. John Schiff . . . and that during the evening of the Baker party on October 29, 1955, she spent considerable time with the Woodwards. She stated that the main topic of conversation of the Woodwards had been the 'prowler' that has been known to be operating in the neighborhood of their house. She stated that during the evening, the Woodwards had formed a plan to catch this prowler and thought they might be able to do so when they returned home from the party. She stated that they seemed in very good spirits and spent most of the evening in each other's company. She also stated that as far as she knew their married life together had been quite normal."

Over the years, some society people told each other that socialites such as Edith Schiff lied to protect the Woodwards. Rumors have her covering up a bad fight at the party the night before. Her sister, Florynce Martinau, said recently that she did nothing of the kind. Their sister-in-law, the late Dorothy Schiff, agreed with her. Florynce Martinau seemed to be a thoughtful, independent, and factual woman. She was a good source because she takes a grim satisfaction in finding her own truths—important and trivial. She speaks freely of matters that it would be in her own interest to cover up, such as alcoholism in the Baker family. Mrs. Martinau alluded to her dislike of her mother's parties. "I got sick of those parties. Either you can do it, or you can't. You can't live your whole life making the same superficial conversation to the same people year after year."

Mrs. Martinau is candid about the Duchess of Windsor's lack of real affection for her

in terms of dollars and cents. Neither mentioned how strange it was that both Bean and Billy had died in accidental gun deaths.

Wednesday.

At 11:45, Libby Woodward Pratt stepped over the yellow tape blocking the front door to her slain brother's home. She was accompanied by her second husband, John T. "Jack" Pratt, and her mother-in-law, Ruth Pratt, a congresswoman who had fought Tammany Hall and endowed Lincoln Center. The Pratts lived in one of six splendid Georgian mansions on the 800-acre Pratt family compound in nearby Lattingtown, Long Island.

Jack Pratt politely urged Libby to turn back, but she wanted to see her nephews, Woody and Jimmy. Libby had drifted away from her brother in recent years, in part because Billy had been flying all over the world. The main reason was that she shared her mother's dislike of Ann.

When Billy was away on his own, Libby had made her preferences clear by entertaining the family without Ann, whom she saw as a vulgar person with uncontrolled appetites. What Libby could not acknowledge was that Ann's passions had attracted Billy. At the Playhouse, Libby gave the impression that she was in control of herself, nodding to the policeman on guard. She had already spoken to Inspector Jim Farrell, her special friend on the force. He had told her every detail he knew. She asked him to keep her posted. No matter what anybody said, Libby would always believe it was murder. Libby had timed her arrival to miss facing Ann and would be Elsie Woodward's deputy throughout the ordeal. Handsome, wiry, five feet ten inches tall, with an even haughtier accent than those of the other Woodward daughters, she was the reigning queen of Newport society. Diana Vreeland described her as "a very normal, not-that-smart upper-class American woman." Her hair was coiffed by Kenneth, but Libby had inherited her mother's lack of real style. She wore bright Pucci print pajamas,

---

mother, Edith Baker. "I mean, the Duchess arranged her life around what she wanted. If we had not had a plantation for the Duke to go shooting at, the Duchess would have cultivated whoever did. She was a sponge. And my mother liked having her because that whole generation was brought up to be Anglophiles."

Mrs. Martinau denied that Elsie Woodward covered up a murder. "There was nothing to hide," she said recently, "except the fact that Billy and Ann were not happily married.

"I can assure you Bill and Ann had no public fight at Mother's party. Truman Capote and Nick Dunne tried to establish a fictional motive for a murder. But that fight never happened. The servants would have mentioned it to me. Of course, they fought every day, but there was no big public fight at Mother's house that night."

but awkwardly. Her lipstick often caked. Her parties seemed to go on until people felt they were falling asleep.

Her first husband, Robert Stevens, had gone on to marry a Vanderbilt. Now Libby's life was complicated by her second husband's alcoholism. It was a source of great pain to her—but she felt it her duty to pretend not to notice it in public.

In Oyster Bay Cove that morning, Libby Pratt told Lee Principe that they must not contradict Ann or say anything that might cause scandal. She told him that he would be taken care of for his efforts.* Unfortunately Lee had already told at least one reporter that the Woodward marriage was full of fights.

A. C. Bostwick soon joined the Pratts for a public display of support. Bostwick, another pillar of North Shore society, was a familiar sight in his Rolls-Royce with his golden Labrador retriever in the front seat. In a few minutes, C. Z. Guest would appear to offer her condolences.

Bill Kahn could not get over Libby Pratt's answers to Stuyvesant Pinnell. Chief Pinnell had a poker face, but his eyes flashed Kahn an I-don't-believe-this-is-for-real look. Libby shrugged off one of Billy's books of pornographic photographs as "normal reading." Kahn recalled recently, "Sty Pinnell tried to establish if Ann was a good shot. The chief asked Mrs. Pratt, 'Didn't Ann and Billy hunt tigers?' "

"Doesn't everybody?" said Libby.

Kahn almost said, "Of course, I hunted tigers all along the Grand Concourse in the Bronx until it became a bore."

The boys were brought downstairs by Ann Gorney. Libby instructed them to answer the detectives' questions. They solemnly assured the police that they had not been playing games and breaking into the pool cabana themselves.

The little boys were then packed up by Lee Principe and taken by their aunt to stay in her old nursery on East Eighty-sixth Street. Elsie Woodward wanted her grandsons—the only inheritors of the Woodward name—under her roof. She hired a nurse named Ingeborg Sorenson, recently fired by Ann, to look after them.

---

*Such promises were confusing to servants, who thought perhaps they were being offered money. But Libby was implying that, to her class, servants were like children—who would perish without the goodwill of their masters.

22

NEVER AGAIN

Over now,
The dream is over now . . .

—Noël Coward, "Never Again,"
from *Set to Music,* 1939

"In my opinion, they were an ideal couple," said the
Duchess of Windsor.

—Police report interview, Jim Farrell,
November 3, 1955, Manhattan

The medical examiners started the autopsy at 11:15 in the morning on October 30 and finished three hours later. Their final report was the most grotesque description ever written of Billy Woodward. Scott Fitzgerald's dictum notwithstanding, in death, the rich are not very different.

Dr. Theodore Curphey read a simple statement to the press: "The autopsy shows William Woodward Jr. dying from a shotgun wound which involved a vital part of the brain (pons).

"On the strength of the autopsy findings only, the Medical Examiner's office at this stage of the investigation has no opinion to express as to whether the nature of the wound was accidental or not."

In a penciled note that did not appear in the police report, Dr. Lukash noted the presence of attorney Walter Gray Dunnington: "Comes at request of Mrs. Woodward Sr."

Shortly after six o'clock on Sunday evening, Billy's body was removed from Meadowbrook Hospital. The press was told it would be taken to the Willis Scott funeral home at 2 East Ninetieth Street, but Elsie brought Billy back home to Eighty-sixth Street.

The Nassau County Police still suspected Ann of murder. The presence of the prowler was the critical question. Second Precinct detective Frank Steiner was consulted. He remembered the German boy who had been arrested for burglary and then jumped parole. Steiner sent out another all-points bulletin with a photograph and a description of Paul Wirths.

While Billy's body lay in his mother's house, Ann Woodward tried to sleep in Room 1005, on the tenth floor at Doctors Hospital. There was no reason to go on living without Billy. The boys would never forgive her. She kept thinking she heard Sloppy barking. Ann hated the furniture—reproductions of Victorian English. It was one of the largest rooms at the hospital, about twelve by fourteen feet, according to one reporter, who managed to get inside dressed as a nurse.

Ann wore a sleep mask and a plain white hospital gown. Dr. Prutting had ordered another massive dose of sedatives when she told him she wanted to take her life. The policeman from Nassau County kept staring at her from the doorway.

When Sol Rosenblatt arrived, she told him the policeman upset her. Rosenblatt told Dr. Prutting to ask Ebright to leave: "She feels as if she is in jail," he explained. "Ann cannot sleep."

Dr. Prutting wrote a note to Chief Pinnell: "Mrs. Wm. Woodward will not need police protection while at the hospital. Since she is instantly hysterical it would be best if she were not disturbed or interviewed by the police for the next 24–48 hours."

Instead Dr. Prutting hired a private nurse and obtained a whole day for Ann to reflect before she submitted to full questioning. This was an extraordinary privilege. Dr. Prutting told Nassau County Police that they must come to her, since Ann was too fragile to leave her hospital bed.

Guided by Rosenblatt, Dr. Prutting described Ann's and Billy's jittery natures to reporters: "Separately they were able to keep themselves under control. But when they were together they infected one another with the sort of tension each might be feeling at the moment, and built it up tremendously. It was like that with everything, and that obviously was what happened in the case of the prowler. Between them, they built up their fear and determination to catch the prowler into an obsession. When Mrs.

Woodward was startled by the noise, grabbing the shotgun and shooting was a conditioned reflex."

Within hours of her arrival at the hospital Ann Woodward was awakened by a formal visitor. Al Monacelli was a lawyer in Walter Dunnington's firm, who offered to help Ann find a good criminal lawyer. He hinted that it did not matter to the family if Ann had done it on purpose or not. The implied condemnation stung Ann. She said, "No thank you. I already have my own lawyer, J. Russell Sprague."

After Monacelli left, Ann picked up the telephone to call Rosenblatt. She did not want the nurse who sat on a nearby folding chair to hear. The nurse stared as Ann padded to the bathroom. When Dr. Prutting came, Ann seemed worse: "It's that nurse."

"What has she done?" asked Dr. Prutting.

"She keeps staring at me like I'm a freak."

Prutting told Ann that she must get better for her sons. "They will hate me," she said, in tears.

The nurse was dismissed.

A few blocks away, Elsie Woodward's butler refused reporters' calls. Libby Pratt and Elsie's triplet sister Ethel were staying at the house. Grief-stricken, Elsie did not take a public position for or against her daughter-in-law. She did call Dr. Prutting daily to ask about Ann's health. Ann wept when she heard of "Mother's" call. Elsie was stunned to hear from Dunnington that Ann had declined the family's offer of legal help. It made Ann too dangerously independent. When she was told that the powerful J. Russell Sprague's firm had already been retained, Elsie became more convinced than ever that Ann was a cold-blooded murderess. She assumed the powerful party boss had been retained even before the shooting. It did not occur to her that the Sprague firm had been retained in the small hours of the night. Rosenblatt's moves may have been too clever. Fast footwork can imply guilt.* Although Sprague's presence in the case distressed Elsie, she remained determined to keep control of the situation. She wanted vengeance—but no further public scandal. Elsie decided to fight Ann, in private, for custody of Woody and Jimmy. Clearly a woman who killed the boys' father was an unfit mother.

Libby Pratt visited Ann at the hospital to keep up appearances. Ann

---

*Charles Wacker recalled recently, "Here was this distraught lady who wasn't able to leave the hospital for at least a week because she was so saddened and Al Monacelli got there early in the morning to offer all the backing and help of the firm and Ann announces, 'No thanks, I got my own lawyer already.'"

wept with relief at the sight of Billy's sister. Perhaps the Woodwards would forgive her. Ann asked if her sons could be brought to see her. Libby soon explained to Ann that the lawyers thought Elsie should assume custody of Ann's boys. The truth was, said Libby, that Ann had taken a terrible beating. She was in no shape to act as a mother. Billy had been her only friend in the world; her life was in pieces. "It will help your case," said Libby. "Mother will tell the police that you are not a strong person."

The Woodwards sometimes made Ann feel that she was still working the taxi telephones. But Libby Pratt's unhappy face only served to revive Ann's fighting spirit, and she refused to say she would surrender her sons. She needed an adversary to remind her that she wanted anything at all. Ann did not eat her afternoon snack. An hour later, she pushed the dinner tray off her lap. Dr. Prutting brought Ann a steak from outside the hospital, but she did not eat it. "I will eat when I see my boys," she said. He put her on intravenous feeding. He described her problem to the press with the then unfamiliar word: anorexia.

Dr. Prutting kept the suicide watch. The new nurse sat three feet away from the door, blocking hallway traffic. But no one dared complain; Mrs. Woodward was a special case.

When Elsie Woodward called Dr. Prutting the next morning to ask about Ann's condition, he told her Ann had refused to eat until she saw her little boys. But Elsie would not send Woody and Jimmy to the hospital.

Walter Dunnington hired a private investigator named Harold Danforth. It was decided that Elsie would maintain her public silence on Ann's guilt until Danforth made his report. Elsie needed to learn exactly how much Ann knew about Billy. Dunnington and Elsie knew that the Torlonia episode would not sit well. What other scandals would a police investigation uncover?

More than the answers about her son, Elsie wanted to know two things: Was there any proof of Ann's guilt? And if Ann were brought to trial, would she be convicted?

The next morning at Mrs. Lyon Slater's home, Wyoming, in Locust Valley, Fern Tailer Gimbel and Michael Butler were the first houseguests to appear on the porch for breakfast. Denny Slater and another ten guests had also slept in the barn, which was decorated with the mounted heads of rhinoceros and buffalo shot by Mrs. Slater. "I got bad news for you," Sidney Mutum announced abruptly at about nine-fifteen.

Denny Slater looked surprised.

"You been listening to the radio, sir?" asked Sidney.

"No."

"Well, Bill Woodward got shot. He's dead."*

"They didn't cry. Rich people don't," recalled Sidney, implying his and other servants' belief that money is compensation for life's sadness.

The shooting produced the most thrilling Sunday luncheon party that Mrs. Lyon Slater ever gave. She served a six-course meal for thirty-six.** The Duke of Windsor's ennui of the previous evening had vanished. "Nothing like a murder in the country to cure what ails you," said the Duchess.

By noon, the tables had been set with the crystal candelabra used only for the Windsors. Elsie Woodward was the only invited guest who did not attend. The party went flawlessly despite the homicide detectives on the front lawn.

Although negative comments flew about Ann, the guests at the party barely knew her. It was not that they all believed she had shot Billy in cold blood. But she clearly had been Billy's youthful mistake. "Elsie and Bill did everything in their power to stop the marriage from taking place," said Mrs. Nelson Doubleday. Ann had been a "bad wife." "She should have stayed home with those lovely boys instead of gallivanting around the world with men," said Mrs. Slater. Since Ann had crashed the upper class with "sex appeal," her sexuality was condemned the most. She was said to have been loose before she met Billy. Listening to these people, it might have appeared to an outsider that they were upright and prudish.

A steak-and-kidney pie was served in honor of the Duke. As the luncheon wore on, one guest joked, "There's only one worse thing Ann could have done. She could have murdered the horse."

The Schiffs spoke of their fears of the prowler. "He was nowhere near their house, was he?" asked the Duke. "I bet he was," said Titi Schiff. "He has been on our estate."

---

*Denny jumped up to tell his mother, Mrs. Slater, who was still asleep upstairs. The butler said, "Leave her alone, she's still sleeping. You'll get hell." Like Elsie Woodward's butler, Mrs. Slater's butler was closer to his employer in many ways than were her own children.

When she finally awoke, Sidney put a frozen daiquiri and a brief note on her silver breakfast tray: "Sorry to put this on our breakfast table. Bill Woodward was shot by his wife."

Mrs. Slater disappeared for three hours to prepare her bath and proper clothing. She gave no thought to canceling her luncheon party. Mrs. David Mellon Bruce, wife of the English ambassador, was driving up from Manhattan to see the Windsors.

**Other guests were Mrs. Nelson Doubleday, George Baker, Jr. (Bean's brother, who would be a pallbearer at Billy's funeral), Mr. A. C. Bostwick (who had just been over to the Playhouse with Libby Pratt), Mr. and Mrs. George Leib, John and Titi Schiff, Polly Howe, and Mrs. Mellon Bruce, whose husband was Ambassador to the Court of St. James's.

*   *   *

At the hospital, Ann was still not eating. Her racking sobs became familiar to nurses and patients who passed by her open door. She told Dr. Prutting she deserved to die. "How did I do it?" she asked. "What did I do?" He increased her doses of Thorazine and sleeping pills.

Sol Rosenblatt spent Sunday eating salted nuts and talking on the phone in the library at his beach cottage at Sands Point. Since Ann had not been arrested, he had decided that no lawyer would be visible at the district attorney's next interrogation. When Rosenblatt called Ann in the hospital, she was grateful to hear from him. Rosenblatt knew the terms of Billy's will. Ann fastened her sense of loss on money, insisting she did not have enough to live on.

True, she was only "poor" by Woodward standards, but Titi Schiff was right: Billy was worth more to her alive than dead. Instead of his $10 million fortune, she would have the interest only on $3 million. Billy had not yet inherited his full share of Elsie's $22 million estate. But the two houses were in Ann's name—and she had her jewelry.

Weeping, Ann asked Rosenblatt if she could visit her Aunt Lydia. She figured nobody in western Kansas would know about the incident. Rosenblatt did not say that nearly every newspaper in the country had been carrying her name in front page, wire service headlines. Perhaps, he said, Ann should invite Lydia Smiley to New York. He did not tell her that although the Nassau County Police had let her leave the county, she would not be allowed to travel halfway across the country. Rosenblatt assured her and said, "Those boys need you more than ever now." Near the end of the phone conversation, Ann worried about the hospital bill. Rosenblatt said he would petition Billy Woodward's estate to pay her legal and medical expenses during this period.

Ann slept fitfully until Rosenblatt knocked on her open door. He had come with good news. He and J. Russell Sprague had hired a great lawyer for Ann. The man was waiting in the hospital corridor. He had been recommended by ex-governor Dewey. Rosenblatt probably did not say that Dewey had declined to take the case himself. The lawyer had to be their secret for now, he told Ann, because his presence might make people think Ann was guilty.

Ann felt deserted by Rosenblatt: "I don't want another lawyer." Rosenblatt did not say the harsh truth: Ann needed a criminal lawyer. He told Ann that Governor Dewey had said Murray Gurfein was "the best trial lawyer I know." Dewey said that if he had not lost the 1948 presiden-

tial election he would have nominated Gurfein to the Supreme Court.*
Gurfein had made headlines as a crime-busting prosecutor for Governor
Dewey. He had nailed mobster Lucky Luciano. Gurfein was a family man,
a solid citizen who ran HIAS, an organization that rescued Jewish refugees
from places like Tunisia. He would make a good impression on members
of a Long Island jury.

Plump and mustached, at forty-eight Gurfein dressed in conservative
suits. He wore his Phi Beta Kappa key on a chain at his waist. (He had
been second in the Harvard Law School class of 1930.) He rose before
dawn to read his law books. Gurfein's father had been an upper-middle-
income Brooklyn businessman who traveled often to Europe to trade in
jewelry. Gurfein had been a hero during World War II, when he had
supervised an intelligence operation that used convicted Italian-American
mobsters to help invade Italy. Afterward he had assisted the chief American
counsel at the Nuremberg trials. (He received citations from foreign gov-
ernments, including the Croix de Guerre.)

After listening to her halting story by her hospital bed, Gurfein told
Ann, "I believe you. I will help you." He would replace Sol Rosenblatt
for the rest of Ann's life as her lawyer. His family believes that Gurfein
took Ann's case because he thought her innocent of murder.**

He told Ann that he would help her shape responses to questions he
knew Eddie Robinson would ask and explained the procedure for the interrogation. When she said she did not care what happened to her, he
urged her to clear herself for the sake of her two sons. They must not
grow up thinking the shooting was anything but an accident.

Meanwhile, on Long Island, Chief Pinnell summoned detectives to his
office that morning to push the investigation. The homicide chief and the
second-squad commanders usually supervised. But this was a problem case.

---

*In June 1971, as a judge, Gurfein would write a defense for freedom of the press, saying
that the government could not stop *The New York Times* from publishing the Pentagon Papers.
The United States Supreme Court upheld his ruling, making it one of the most important First
Amendment cases in our history. Ann wired him congratulations. Gurfein's opinion is framed in
many law professor's offices: "A cantankerous press, an obstinate press, a ubiquitous press must be
suffered by those in authority in order to preserve an even greater freedom of expression and the
right of people to know.

"These are troubled times. There is no greater safety valve for discontent and cynicism
about the affairs of the government than freedom of expression in any form."

**Some socialites, like Mary Sanford, believe Elsie hired Murray Gurfein after consulting
with Governor Averell Harriman. She also believes Elsie put Ann into Doctors Hospital: "She
couldn't let poor Ann go to jail. How would it look? So she got that lovely man, who became a
grand judge, to be her lawyer."

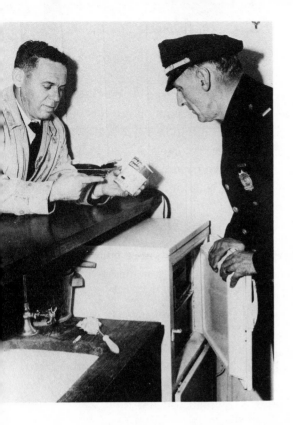

The Woodward chauffeur, Lee Principe, and the Oyster Bay Cove police chief, Russell Haff, examine traces left by the prowler in the kitchen of the Woodward pool cabana.

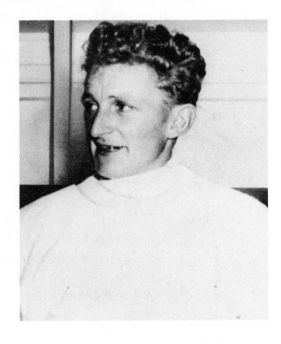

Paul Wirths, the prowler who broke into a number of North Shore houses and was on the roof of Ann Woodward's bedroom, climbing into a hallway window on the second floor, when he heard the gunshots.

The police department was already being attacked by the press for giving Ann "kid gloves" treatment.

Stuyvesant Pinnell had received his college degree late in life and had come up through the ranks. He was known for coming into his office and reading all division reports on Saturdays and Sundays. He had great compassion for his detectives. His retired detectives explain it: "He had integrity." "He was a stand-up guy." "A man you can trust." "He was a man's man." "He'd never hedge things." "He'd back up his men and admit that a decision was his—right or wrong."

Second Precinct detective Frank Steiner sent out another bulletin on Paul Wirths. The young German burglary suspect had not reported to his parole officer for months. Steiner cited Wirths's suspended sentence for the burglary of food, a gun, and small amounts of money.

That Monday the police got a break. At noon, two patrolmen spotted Paul Wirths eating a hamburger at the Suffolk Grill counter in nearby Huntington. They waited until he left. Shouting for him to stop, they fired a warning shot. He was arrested getting into a 1952 Ford convertible with a .20-gauge shotgun, stolen from a clergyman, on the front seat. Wirths was jocular. "You have me," he told the Huntington police.

In the stolen car, they found stolen jewelry, knives, and more shotguns. Paul Wirths was relieved that the nightmare was over. "Thank God," he said, in German-accented English.

At the Huntington police station, Wirths was glad to see a familiar person, Frank Steiner. Steiner was of German descent, and the other detectives kidded him for his hard-nosed police work, but he was respected for it. Steiner felt sorry for Paul Wirths. "You're in a bit of trouble," he said in German. Steiner and Wirths had a mutual friend from Wirths's home in Germany, Föhr Island, who ran a delicatessen near Mineola. Speaking German soothed Wirths until the policeman said he had been the cause of a woman shooting her husband. Wirths was shocked to be "accused of murder." *Nein, nein,* not my fault. I was not there."

Something, however, told Steiner that Paul Wirths was lying. Steiner got permission to tell Wirths that he would not be prosecuted for burglary in the Woodward case.*

By two that afternoon, Wirths admitted only that he had burgled the Woodward estate on Friday night—twenty-four hours before the shooting.

---

*This exemption was not delivered. Wirths would be convicted of burglary in several counts, including the Woodward case, and serve six years in prison.

He said he had peered in on Billy Woodward. He did not mention that he had also watched Ann. He told police how on Saturday morning at daybreak, he had broken into the Woodward garage. Wirths continued to deny being at the Playhouse at the time of the shooting. His admission gave credibility to Ann Woodward's story.

The police fed Wirths, cut his hair, gave him clean clothes, and locked him in a seven-foot-square gray holding cell that was part of three tiers of cells. But he did not mind jail. He had a cot to sleep on, even if it was chained to the wall.

On Monday, November 1, when the police showed up at 6:30 p.m. to interview Ann, there was no lawyer in sight. Forty hours had elapsed since the shooting, and the circumstances surrounding her questioning had changed dramatically. Her fears of an intruder had an apparent basis in fact. Ann's questioning would be much milder. The pressure was off. Eddie Robinson sat by Ann's bed and began to ask her questions designed to show her he was on her side. This time she had a clear answer for what she thought she had fired at.

"Do you know whether or not you had been having some dreams with reference to this prowler? If you don't know, tell me."

Ann answered: "I don't know. I couldn't say that I had. It was very much in my mind."

EDWARD ROBINSON: What is the next thing that you remember after getting off to sleep?

ANN WOODWARD: Well, I remember hearing the dog bark. I picked up the gun which was by me and I don't know whether I walked or ran, but I moved quickly to open the door and stepped back in and then I fired the gun in the direction of the noise.

EDWARD ROBINSON: Was the light on in the hall?

ANN WOODWARD: There weren't any lights in the house.

EDWARD ROBINSON: No light in your room, either?

ANN WOODWARD: No light.

EDWARD ROBINSON: There was a light in Mr. Woodward's bedroom over near his bed. Do you know whether that was lighted at the time that you fired the gun?

ANN WOODWARD: I don't know. I don't remember any lights.

EDWARD ROBINSON: Did you see your husband at all as you fired?

ANN WOODWARD: I didn't see anything. I just heard the noise and fired in the direction of the noise. I really didn't intend to even hit anybody. I just intended that they would know that, you know, we were protected. And whatever it was would go away.

EDWARD ROBINSON: This gun was a double barrel, was it not?

ANN WOODWARD: Yes.

EDWARD ROBINSON: With separate triggers for each barrel?

ANN WOODWARD: Yes.

EDWARD ROBINSON: Do you recall whether you fired one at a time, or did you pull both triggers simultaneously?

ANN WOODWARD: I am so accustomed to shooting a gun that I think I probably pulled as quickly as I could, one after the other.

EDWARD ROBINSON: One after the other?

ANN WOODWARD: Because I am accustomed to guns.

EDWARD ROBINSON: You have done quite a lot of hunting, I understand?

ANN WOODWARD: Yes.

EDWARD ROBINSON: Was this movement of opening the door to your room and the firing of the gun one that took place in quick succession, if I can convey my thought to you?

ANN WOODWARD: Yes, very quick.

EDWARD ROBINSON: In other words, you threw the door open—

ANN WOODWARD: Yes, very quick.

EDWARD ROBINSON: I'm sorry. Stay with me just a few minutes more now and I think I can get finished. It was very quick, is that right?

(Witness sobs.)

DR. PRUTTING: You are doing a wonderful job. Now, just pull yourself together for a minute. Try to help them a little bit. So far you have done wonderfully, so just go in for the last pull. It is going to be tough now, and just, you know, try to pull yourself together a little bit.

EDWARD ROBINSON: Take all the time you want, Mrs. Woodward.

DR. PRUTTING: Do you think you could talk just a little bit more now?

ANN WOODWARD: I was trying.

EDWARD ROBINSON: You are doing wonderfully. Just tell me if I am asking too many questions. Besides the barking of the dog did you hear any other noises?

ANN WOODWARD: Well, I heard a noise and that's why I fired the gun.

EDWARD ROBINSON: And you fired in the direction of that noise?

ANN WOODWARD: Yes.

EDWARD ROBINSON: Could you tell me what the noise sounded like? Did it sound like someone walking, or a dog?

ANN WOODWARD: Like a person moving.

EDWARD ROBINSON: A person moving? Do you remember whether or not after firing—did you put the light on?

ANN WOODWARD: I put the light on, yes.

EDWARD ROBINSON: The hall light?

ANN WOODWARD: No, I put the light on in my room.

EDWARD ROBINSON: Did you see the dog at all when you opened the door?

ANN WOODWARD: No, it was dark in the hall.

EDWARD ROBINSON: Did you see any shadows or anything in the hall that you can remember?

ANN WOODWARD: I just heard—I mean, it was all so fast.

EDWARD ROBINSON: A quick reaction, in other words.

ANN WOODWARD: Yes.

EDWARD ROBINSON: Did you give any thought to the fact that the door to your husband's room was across from yours?

ANN WOODWARD: I didn't fire that way.

EDWARD ROBINSON: Which way do you think you were firing?

ANN WOODWARD: I thought there was someone coming from the stairs.

EDWARD ROBINSON: Toward the living room, do you mean?

ANN WOODWARD: Yes.

EDWARD ROBINSON: Is that the way you thought you had fired?

ANN WOODWARD: Yes.

EDWARD ROBINSON: How long had the poodle barked? Was it a constant barking as if somebody were approaching, or what? Do you remember?

ANN WOODWARD: I don't remember because I was in bed. But I just remember hearing the dog bark and I jumped out of bed.

EDWARD ROBINSON: Very quickly?

ANN WOODWARD: Yes.

EDWARD ROBINSON: Thank you very, very much, Mrs. Woodward.

Max Lerner of the New York *Post* published a rare column defending Ann. He wondered why people are surprised if rich people have uncharmed lives. He pitied people who slept in separate bedrooms with shotguns at their sides. He said nobody would be writing about the shooting if Ann were a suburban Levittown wife.

At dusk, ten reporters followed a showered Wirths around the Playhouse. His wrists were handcuffed to uniformed policemen. Music rode the evening breezes. In the indoor tennis courts, the eighty-piece Cinerama orchestra was recording the sound track to the film *Seven Wonders of the World.* "Take these off"—Paul raised his fists—"and see how fast I disappear." When he grinned, he exposed empty spaces where his front teeth had been. Despite thefts of food, the young German immigrant looked emaciated, his skin splotchy, his long chin jutted.

It was the first police reenactment of Wirths's visit to the Woodward estate. Frank Gulotta walked beside him as he pointed out places he had broken into—the pool house, a window of the Cinerama office, the six-car garage. Afterward, Chief Pinnell announced to the reporters that he still wanted to find out everything he could about the Woodward marriage.

Pinnell was astonished at the piles of letters he received describing the Woodwards' sex lives and fights. Some letters accused Billy of being a drag queen. Crank calls blocked Elsie Woodward's telephone. Hundreds of letters filled her mailbox. Lieutenants Sims and Drum of the New York City Police packed them in huge wood boxes for the Nassau County Police. One letter stated that Ann had taken a shot at Billy at the Golden Sands Hotel in Miami Beach. The police flew down to find Crawford Adams, who said only that he "might have said that he heard Mr. and Mrs. Woodward argued a lot while drinking in Miami Beach." A Miami prostitute was said to have clothing that belonged to Billy Woodward. But nobody could find her. The fashion designer Charles James told intimates that while fitting Ann in a pumpkin-colored dress a week earlier, he had seen a workman replacing woodwork peppered with buckshot from another of Ann's attempts to kill Billy.

Pinnell summed up for reporters: "On Saturday night, the night of the shooting, Wirths was not on the Woodward property—if his story is true. He says that on Saturday night he broke into the snack bar of the Pine Hollow Country Club, which is about a half mile from the Woodward place. He stole a bottle of milk, two hamburgers, and four sandwiches from the refrigerator and went outside on to a bench and ate them.

"He says he left there and went to Roslyn about 10 p.m. because he saw a police car coming."

Meanwhile Dan Stark interviewed Alfred Gwynne Vanderbilt, whose guests were just leaving an all-night party. Later, Michael Butler offered Stark the run of his apartment and the services of his Japanese houseboy. Brenda Frazier Kelly told the detective that the Woodwards seemed too excited about the prowler. She also told a reporter that an investigation into her own marital life or those of any of her friends would produce dozens of reasons for murder.

Jim Farrell achieved the pinnacle of his police career: he interviewed the Duchess of Windsor. Her remarks were printed in nearly all American newspapers. The Duchess told Farrell that she had known the Woodwards for twelve years and had seen them twice yearly at parties attended by a large number of people. "In my opinion," the Duchess of Windsor said, "they were an ideal couple. I knew of no marital difficulties." The Duchess undoubtedly meant that they made great entrances together.

Elsa Maxwell, the public relations woman, was feuding with the Duchess. Miss Maxwell told reporters that the Duchess's observations were "very odd indeed. Since everybody who is anybody knows that Ann and Bill Woodward have both had private detectives spying on each other for months."

Police detective Tom Martin was recruited for an "unofficial" inquiry by Farrell, since Martin moonlighted weekends selling in the golf shop at Piping Rock Club. Martin was told not to write anything down. He was to fill out several "to-from" memorandums and just write "Woodward." Farrell debriefed him in person. Martin engaged Piping Rock members in conversation to learn what he could about the Woodwards' sex lives. On the way out at night, if a member asked, "What's going on with the investigation?" Martin mentioned the rumor that Billy was homosexual. One club member responded, "No, he had plenty of effete gestures, and he might have had a picture taken once when he tried dressing like a woman, at a costume party, but that was it."

Another ploy was the mention of adultery. Martin reported that Ann seemed as pure as the driven snow. Billy had had a serious flame named Princess Torlonia several years before, but that was history. These reports never showed up in the official police documents, and the possibility remains that Gentleman Jim was investigating on behalf of the family—and protecting them.

That Tuesday night Michael Butler gave another dinner party for the Duchess of Windsor. The main course was Ann Woodward. Had Ann bribed the prowler? Perhaps Elsie had bribed him; she had more money. Was the prowler telling the truth about not being around when Billy was shot? Did Elsie think Ann was guilty of murder? The Duchess had expressed her condolences to Elsie—who was very shaken. This was the third day of Elsie's public silence, and it was logical that she would communicate with the Duchess. Caste was crucial, even in times of grief.

The party guests laughed over Russell Havenstrite's views—quoted at length in the New York *Post*—of Ann's unstable shooting based on their tiger hunts in India. He concluded, "I believe that Ann would have had a much better chance of hitting Bill Woodward if she was not aiming at him." The socialites ignored the fact that Havenstrite's remarks implied Ann's innocence.

They eagerly discussed more damaging newspaper controversy. Ann was accused of deliberate murder by the press. Headlined articles asked why, if Billy had heard the noise, too, he hadn't brought a gun to the door of his bedroom. His presence in his doorway, unarmed, seemed suspect if he had planned, as Ann said, to hunt the prowler. Some of his friends wondered if Billy had been on his way to visit his wife on an amorous mission. A wire service story had asked why Ann left her bedroom window unlocked if she was so afraid of a prowler. After interviewing Steve Smith, the Cinerama night watchman, the *Post* postulated a suspicious "twenty-minute interval between the shots and Ann Woodward's screams." The article was picked up by the Associated Press and reprinted on scores of front pages: "Reported Lapse Between Shots, Mrs. Woodward Cries Denial."

Newsday reporter Bob Greene did an excellent summary of the conflicting stories about the marriage. The Baker party guests had described "a happy couple"; the Helio airplane pilot in Kansas insisted Billy was a happy husband. Eddie Arcaro enjoyed dining with "the happy couple." On the other hand, Cholly Knickerbocker described quarrels, long separations, and divorce threats in an article called "A Mystery of Contradictions." (What seems obvious in retrospect, however, was that the cover-up was of a scandalous marriage—not of a murder.)

The Woodward shooting was fodder for a newspaper war. *Newsday* felt proprietary—Long Island was its bailiwick. Bob Greene, who later won a Pulitzer Prize for another story, cleared up the problem of the twenty-minute interval before Ann's scream. He had Steven Smith wait inside the Cinerama offices. After firing a gun inside the front of the house, Greene had somebody near him scream. From his room Smith heard the shots, but not the screams, proving the *Post* wrong. The point was that Smith could not have heard Ann's cries for help until he walked outside and toward the front of the house. *Post* headlines, however, continued to accuse Ann of scheming for twenty minutes while Billy's blood flowed.

One night, soon after the shooting, Ned Patterson sat with guests talking sadly about his Buckley days with Billy. Somebody brought up Ann's age. At first the newspapers had reported she was thirty-two, but the *Times* had said she was thirty-nine. Ned tried to be fair: "Ann isn't tough or strong enough to have killed Billy on purpose. I feel so terrible about the children. Will they ever recover?" said Ned.

The telephone rang, and Joan Patterson answered. When she hung up, she told her guests in a tight voice that it had been Ann Woodward. Later, she told her husband that she had agreed "for Billy's sake" to visit Ann in the hospital.

Ned thought that Ann called Joan because he and his wife would be polite and not ask a lot of questions: "There was no secret agreement between Joan and Elsie. No one urged Joan to stand by Ann. She knew her duty. She undoubtedly realized that Ann was using her, but it did not matter. Joan was known as a good wife and mother. She was not a café society type. She was also E. F. Hutton's stepdaughter. A week of visits from her certified that Ann was still accepted by a certain group."

*   *   *

That night, after he finished his paperwork, Frank Steiner brought Paul Wirths back to the holding cell. He said, "Paul, be a man, there's a woman with two small children involved."

Wirths did not answer. He was looking at a copy of the *Journal-American* with his picture smiling toothlessly under the headline "Woodward Prowler Miles Away at Time of Shooting."

Wirths changed his story the following morning. In fact, he went so far as to offer that he had broken into the second floor of the Playhouse moments before Ann shot Billy. The jailhouse log reveals that Wirths had no visitors to help him change his mind on Tuesday evening.

Early the next morning, Frank Steiner was notified that Wirths wanted to talk to him. Steiner called his supervisor, Sergeant Edward Curran, the future chief of police:

"Wirths wants to talk."

"Go yourself," said Curran.

"Nope. It's too hot for me," said Steiner. "I think I know what he's got in mind."

Steiner had a court stenographer and another detective on hand when Wirths made another statement. Curran joined them in Wirths's cell. Wirths told the two policemen that on Saturday night, he left the Pine Hollow Country Club and went back to the Woodward house carrying a rifle. He had been living on the Woodward grounds for several days. It felt like home. The fog reminded him of wet mornings on Föhr Island, Germany.

Paul was always hungry, it had seemed, living on the run. Opening the refrigerator in the shack next to the Woodward swimming pool, he ate four frozen hot dog rolls. The lights of the big house were shining through the fog. The garage was still empty. The pretty woman was not home. He had been watching Ann for two days. The first time he saw her open the door and get out of her car, he inhaled hard. In his entire twenty-four years, he had never seen such a fine woman. He had peeked in the little round window and watched her in her bedroom, naked. In his mind, she had become his girlfriend.

When her light went out, he crept to another window and watched the man in his bathroom. Paul decided that the woman did not belong to the man since he was not sleeping in the same bed with her. He must be the woman's brother, not her husband.

The night of the shooting the woman walked under Paul as he sat in an elm tree. She wore a beautiful gown. After she and her "brother" drove away in the little car, the lights went on around the house, like magic. Paul walked inside her house as if it were a game. He saw her bed, bigger than any bed in Germany. He smelled perfume. He decided to go outside and wait for her to come home.

Paul Wirths was confused and sad in this strange country. He missed the old brick church, St. Johannes, the windmill, and the cows on the green grass. He had learned some English by reading Donald Duck comic books. But he talked to himself in German, like his mother in her thatched farmhouse. He had been so excited to come to America two years ago. He found work as a bricklayer. His landlady in Floral Park had teased him for buying new shirts instead of washing his dirty ones. But a shovel fell on his shoulder just before Christmas, and he could not work.

Then his girlfriend's father told him not to come to the Lutheran Valley Stream Church with him and his family because he had no place to live.

He slept in cars. He took food and money from cash registers and refrigerators. He stole a turkey from the icebox at the Golden Arrow Diner, and four nights later, on the last day in January, he had stolen a roll of stamps to write home for help. He broke into a lumber office and took a bag of eight dollars in quarters—and there a policeman had shot at him. He ran away and bought himself two beers. The policemen came into the bar and grabbed him hard by his sore shoulder. In jail, they yelled at him. He did not understand everything they said. He felt ashamed. "I never took anything I did not need," he said.

Finally, a policeman named Frank Steiner spoke to him in German. Paul promised Steiner he would never steal again.

Then his father spent all his money to come from Germany to take charge of him. Steiner told the judge to let him out of jail on probation. Paul's father found a job as a janitor at a private school for boys in Denton Farms, New Jersey. The school gave them rooms. Then his father got a job on Long Island as a chauffeur. He and Paul slept in the same double bed in a rooming house. His father beat him for not working. After four weeks, Paul hit him back and ran away.

At least it was spring, and Paul could live outdoors. He started stealing the milk bottles delivered to people's front doors. He washed himself with garden hoses. His gums hurt a lot after he fell and lost his front teeth. He never called his probation officer. He kept moving north on Long Island. The houses kept getting bigger.

That night, outside the pretty woman's big house, he heard the Woodward car returning. He knew what he would do to the pretty woman on that bed of hers. It was after midnight. Wirths climbed the elm tree again and watched his pretty lady step out of the car. Her brother was talking in a very loud voice, as if he was drunk. The man climbed in the woman's window.

Ten minutes later, Paul Wirths tried to peek inside her window. It was raining. He decided to go inside to be with her. He began to climb up the tree again to the low roof over the ceiling of her bedroom. The shotgun was under his arm. He walked across the roof to a long window, broke a pane of glass with the butt of his shotgun, and reached inside to unlock the window. As he was climbing through the window, his foot got tangled in the curtains. He lost his balance, his shotgun fell, and he heard shots. He smelled gunpowder and heard screams. He thought he had been shot. He rushed out the window, slid down the tree trunk, and hit the ground.*

After hearing his confession, Steiner asked Wirths, "How come you told us yesterday that you weren't at the Woodward house?"

"I was afraid," said Wirths. "I was afraid they might say I shot the man. I decided to say the truth because of the two children of the poor dead man and I did not want their mother hurt anymore."

A few years ago, Steiner angrily recalled *Newsday* headlines that implied he had induced Wirths to change his story for a fee: "I never took a penny from anybody, nor did I give Paul Wirths any money."

Wirths swore that neither Sergeant Curran nor Detective Steiner or anybody else had threatened him or promised him money to induce him to change his story.

With no legal case against Ann, Elsie sent Woody and Jimmy to the hospital to visit their mother. Elsie was still planning to fight for their custody. She warned the boys not to ask questions of their mother. "She's feeling too sick," she told them.

Woody and Jimmy weathered an assault by photographers on their way to Ann's tenth-floor room with their aunt Edie Bancroft. Jimmy dragged a bouquet of flowers along the corridor floor. "Don't cry, Mommy," said Jimmy, bursting into tears himself as he buried his head in Ann's lap.

Afterward, Dr. Prutting told reporters: "Mrs. Woodward and the

*The police found a deep footprint at the base of the tree after this confession.

children had displayed great, warm affection." When the boys left, "there was sadness all around," and "Mrs. Woodward had a good cry."

Each day brought a new twist. The wire services had a field day when they learned that Ann Woodward's father, sixty-four-year-old Jesse Claude Crowell, lived in a trailer on Lake Otsego in Michigan and was a retired streetcar conductor who had yearned to speak to his only daughter for the last thirty years. He told reporters that his ex-wife "poisoned Angeline's mind against me. That's why I never felt like pressing the search for her."

The press was fascinated, too, by Crowell's mistaken notion that Angeline had grown up to be Eve Arden. As the wire services reported, "Last Sunday, Crowell received a long-distance call from the Detroit *News* and was questioned at length about his family and his past. 'I didn't know what was going on,' he said. 'This reporter kept asking all kinds of questions and kept mentioning Mrs. Ann Woodward, but he never seemed to get to the point.

" 'I always thought my little Ann went to Hollywood and became Eve Arden.' " He liked Eve Arden because she had spirit like his first wife, Ethel Crowell.

"He remembers Ann as a 'very lovable child and very bright. She was good-looking and quick to learn things.

" 'After all these years, it's a little difficult to remember too much about her. But I'll never forget how much she loved horses. I taught her to sit on a horse and later she became a good rider. I'm sure that was a great help to her when she began to associate with high society.' "

Crowell told reporters that he would love to see his daughter but that the first move would have to be hers. He felt very sorry for her and wanted to comfort her.

The gulf between father and daughter seemed further evidence of Ann's ruthless climb from her working-class past. Diana Vreeland remembered a conversation in which Elsie said, "I wish Billy had just married one of our attractive housemaids. At least we would have known where she came from."

Elsie still refused to speak to the press about the shooting. But when she learned that Ann was planning to attend the funeral, she put her foot down. Ann's presence would turn a religious ceremony into a circus. It would be advisable for Elsie to represent the family. The press was told that Ann had been ordered by her doctor not to attend. Early on the morning of the funeral Dr. Prutting visited Ann for a half hour. She begged him for a sedative that would make it possible for her to go to the funeral. He told her it was not possible.

For appearance's sake, Elsie permitted Ann to order the flowers covering the casket. Prutting told the press, "She [Ann] had a bad reaction of intense grief when she asked me to have my secretary send flowers for her. She ordered a blanket of white chrysanthemums and red carnations. She said they were his favorite colors, and his racing colors.

"She also ordered their nicknames [Monk and Dunk] to be put on a small ribbon with the flowers, discreetly written so that people wouldn't see them."

Flags flew at half-mast at the Hanover Bank and at the Creek, Brook, Knickerbocker, Piping Rock, and Racquet & Tennis clubs. For some, such as C. Z. Guest, it felt like the end of an era. At 10:30, C.Z. came with her car and driver to pick up Mary Sanford. She did not take off her black gloves when she poured herself a straight double brandy. C.Z. had little sympathy for Ann, and believed that Ann had killed Billy deliberately.

One policeman called it the biggest funeral in New York since Babe Ruth's. More than a thousand spectators jammed the several blocks around St. James Episcopal Church at Seventy-first Street and Madison Avenue, tying up traffic. Twenty black limousines were parked in front of the church. Promptly at 11:30, the Reverend Arthur Lee Kinsolving mounted the pulpit in front of the 900 society mourners. To the right of the flower-draped casket, three pews were reserved for Billy's family. The Woodward servants sat behind them.

Nearby were the familiar hunched shoulders of old Jim Fitzsimmons. Mary Sanford caught her breath as Elsie appeared—an angular figure draped in swaying black organza veils. Elsie was holding Billy's little boys' hands. Wearing black suits and starched white shirts, they blinked at the hushed crowd. Their pale hair had been cut short. Seven-year-old Jimmy's black tie looked too tight. Woody's jaw was clenched. They sat next to their grandmother.

Kinsolving opened the funeral service with Psalm 130, "Out of the depths have I cried unto thee, O Lord," following it with Psalm 23. Then he announced the hymn "Ten Thousand Times Ten Thousand," one of Billy's favorites. The coffin was placed in the center aisle of the church. The honorary pallbearers were all-powerful figures in American society.

Ann and Billy Woodward's sons—Woody, age eleven, and Jimmy, age nine—with Dr. Prutting at Doctors Hospital, where they had come to visit their mother.

Jack Pratt with two of Billy Woodward's sisters, Ethel Woodward de Croisset (center) and Elizabeth "Libby" Woodward Pratt, outside the Woodward house on East Eighty-sixth Street.

Elsie with her grandson Woody, leaving St. James Episcopal Church after Billy's funeral.

Billy Woodward's casket. An Associated Press photograph captioned: "A blanket of white chrysanthemums and red carnations, the color scheme of the late sportsman's racing stable . . ."

Billy Woodward commissioned this painting of Nashua by W. Smithson Broadhead. Sunny Jim Fitzsimmons, the horse's trainer, sits on the bench; Eddie Arcaro stands facing him. On the far left Broadhead had originally painted Ann and Billy Woodward. A year after her son's death, Elsie had the artist remove the couple; Broadhead was so annoyed, he painted himself and his wife in Ann and Billy's place.

Elsie had known the older men for the last half century—and their sons for all of their young lives. They included white-haired George D. Widener, the new president and successor to Billy's father at the Jockey Club; Jock Whitney; A. B. "Bull" Hancock, the salty southerner whose Claiborne Farm housed the Belair stud horses; and Walter Dunnington, the family lawyer.

Five of Billy's childhood friends stood guard while servants lifted his coffin. There was George F. Baker, Jr., Bean's brother (who would commit suicide years later); Eustice Paine, Jr., with whom Billy had recently dined at the Brook Club; Gordon Lyle; Anthony Villa; and William Steele Gray. Later that day, Billy was buried near his father's two-year-old grave at Woodlawn Cemetery, not far from the Whitneys and the Vanderbilts. Racing fans stole roses from the flower cars as souvenirs.

Cleveland Amory wrote an editorial in *Life* magazine damning Ann. Amory announced that Ann was not at the funeral, adding, "In a way this was as it should have been." Amory wrote that Ann had lived a modern life of adultery and sleeping pills. He condemned Ann as a social climber, a parvenue, a member of "Publi-ciety." In contrast, Elsie lived in a world of order, duty, and fair play. Elsie Woodward was described as belonging to the elite late-nineteenth-century Four Hundred and as someone who believed a woman had her name in the newspapers only when she was born, married, and died. (Amory undoubtedly knew that Elsie had not been in the Four Hundred: he'd reprinted the list on the inside cover of *Who Killed Society?*) Amory dismissed the social climbing, snobbery, stupidity, and anti-Semitism of Elsie's world—and said that at least it was conducted in private.

Paul Wirths's story was embarrassing to the German consulate. A decade after the end of World War II, a young armed German man running through Long Island stealing cars and food made them wince. On November 8, they dispatched Alvin Corngold, the lawyer who had represented Paul in his first trial. Corngold brought a newspaper reporter to Paul's cell. Paul told them the same story he had told Frank Steiner. Afterward, Wirths joked to Steiner that the reporter had given him a bribe. According to Wirths, the reporter had pulled a roll of bills out of his lapel pocket and thrown ten dollars on the table.

"What is that for?" Paul asked.

"Cigarettes. I'm lending it to you."

"But I have no money, I can't pay you back."

"Don't worry about it," said the reporter.

Wirths had picked up the money and handed it to Corngold, asking him to give it to the officer at the desk who would give Wirths credit for it.

The New York *Post* had a field day quoting Corngold: Wirths had been coerced into the new confession. Corngold said Wirths was impressionable, a poor German boy who did not understand English and who had not been treated fairly.

Wirths fired Corngold. He said he did not need him or any lawyer and that his story was true.

On Friday night, Joan Patterson called her husband, Ned, and told him that Ann wanted him to visit the hospital. A plainclothes Nassau County detective escorted him on the service elevator. His wife had been there all day.

The hospital room was dark.

Ann asked bright questions about nothing at all. A nurse placed a food tray in front of each of them: "Now, Mrs. Woodward, you've got to eat something today."

Ann did not touch her soup. The nurse switched on the light. Ann put her hands over her eyes and cried in an anguished voice, "Oh, Neddy looks just like him. Make him leave. He reminds me of Billy. I can't stand the sight of him. Please, get him out."

"I think you'd better go," Joan said to her husband.

Not only the tragedy itself but the gossip surrounding it was destroying the family name. It was turning out to be far more devastating than the Cryder banking scandal that had driven Elsie Cryder Woodward's father to exile in France at the end of the previous century. The image of Ann behind bars was satisfying to Elsie, but it would further stain the Woodward family.

Elsie's investigators had provided her with the names of the women her son had been dating, but neither Libby Pratt nor her mother was disturbed by Billy's philandering. During the marriage, Billy had been a good enough husband as far as the Woodward women were concerned, although it did not prevent the gossip. The new information made it imperative that Elsie act to protect Ann, even though Elsie was certain the shooting hadn't been an accident.

Elsie was working through intermediaries—her P.R. man, her law-yers—but she left the hardest job of all to Libby Pratt, who masked her feelings and made daily visits to Doctors Hospital.*

Elsie firmly believed that lies were necessary—although she called it "protecting those poor little boys."

The day after the funeral, the Woodward family took direct action against the press scandal. Elsie had her genial and deft P.R. man, Drew Dudley, telephone Millicent Hearst, wife of the owner of the *Journal-American,* to ask a favor: columnist Igor Cassini must be asked to stop his salacious columns.

Dudley also contacted *Time* magazine. A reporter was admitted to the first-floor reception area of the Woodward home. Footsteps clattered on the black-and-white marble floor. Libby and her husband, Jack, ap-peared. Her clipped voice had a dismissive authority. At first she defended Ann and denied that there had been problems: "Their [Ann's and Billy's] differences have been blown up out of proportion. The newspapers like to print unattractive stories about public figures, and, because of Nashua, Bill and Ann were public figures. What is duller than the story of a happy home? Bill and Ann had as happy a home as anyone leading their sort of life can have."

The speech she gave became the family's public stand. The shooting was an accident. Billy had loved Ann. Libby had no qualms about lying to the press: "Ann has had a hard time all her life. And she has her faults—who doesn't? But she's done the best she could, and it's been pretty good. She's done a wonderful job with her two boys."

Libby played down Ann's pill taking. "Oh, she did keep a mild bottle on her shelf, but who doesn't? I've taken a sleeping pill every night since my brother was shot."

When pressed about Billy's hyperactive temperament, she confirmed he was high-strung. She blamed Ann for her brother's restless circling of the globe. It was Ann who loved parties, not he: "They were both high-strung, high-spirited, nervous people. We're a nervous family. And they had their squabbles—who doesn't?"

Libby remarked on the "talk of divorce seven or eight years ago" and

---

*Newsday's Bob Greene saw through Libby's visits. He quoted a family friend: "This is merely a family device to prevent gossip about Ann."

Greene reported, "As for the shooting, the family would like the investigation over with as quickly as possible. Even if the shooting was in doubt, the family would want to see Ann cleared because of the possible scandal involved."

"sporadic separations before and since." Jack explained, "Every once in a while Bill would get fed up, have all he could take." But he claimed that the senior Woodwards had urged them to make up their differences for the sake of their two sons. Pratt said he believed that Billy and Ann had been getting along better in recent years.

It was hard for Libby to avoid digs at Ann. She added, "And Ann— not only did she love him, but it was as Mrs. William Woodward, Jr., that she was able to live the life she loved."

Libby admitted that Ann was accepted by her mother "with reserve." She described Elsie as "disappointed" in Billy's choice of a wife from outside their set. Finally, Libby defended the love of Ann and Billy: "Despite everything, they were in love. Bill didn't have to stay with her, you know. He stayed because he loved her and liked her. She was fun to be with."

Libby broke down as she repeated her mother's thought about how her father would have taken the scandal and tragedy: "I'm glad he's not here to see it. He always stood for the best. So did Bill." Then Libby remembered the point of the interview: "And so, I think, does Ann."

In spite of these maneuverings, Elsie noted with dismay that Ann and Billy's relationship was still under scrutiny. The press was still checking rumors of a fight on the night of the shooting. A report was published by *The New York Times* that Ann might have made a "mysterious phone call" from her home after she killed her husband.

On November 4, Chief Pinnell announced that the district attorney had decided to present the evidence to a grand jury. In such matters it is customary for the prosecutor to look to the position of the injured party— in this case, the Woodward family—for some guidance. Since the Woodward family had hardly been pressing for Ann's head on a platter, under ordinary circumstances the case might have been dismissed at this point for lack of evidence to indict.

Allegations in the press were still selling newspapers, however. The press indicted not only Ann but the Nassau County Police. Reporters accused the district attorney of going soft on her. He needed the grand jury hearing to protect himself and the police.

Often, a district attorney will seek to have a grand jury rubber-stamp a police investigation. He hopes to convey the appearance that a group of objective observers have made the important decision to clear the suspect or to recommend a trial. Naturally the district attorney presents evidence that supports his own view. In this case, for example, the district attorney would present evidence to the jury that showed Ann's innocence.* Pinnell told reporters, "If the grand jury dismisses the shooting as an accident, we won't press charges."

Ten days after Billy died, Elsie paid Ann a one-hour visit. Ann combed her hair and sat in a chair. Elsie did not lift the veils from her face as she greeted the woman who killed her son. Elsie, however, had underestimated the effects of her rage; speaking politely cost her a lot, despite more than half a century of practice at presenting a calm appearance.**

At Doctors Hospital, Elsie told Ann that her hunger strike was not important to Elsie, and that, as usual, Ann was only hurting herself. She also said that Ann would probably be shunned in the best homes. Newspapers still suspected her—despite Paul Wirths's story. But Elsie declared that she might have the power to neutralize the scandal. In return, Ann must let the boys go.

The two women had been fighting for control of Billy Woodward's life for thirteen years. Now Billy's sons were the issue. The irony, of course, was that neither woman wanted the total responsibility of rearing the two children. (The little boys had been underfoot in East Eighty-sixth Street for only a matter of weeks and already Elsie realized that she did not want to play full-time grandmother.) Elsie had contacted the international Swiss boarding school Le Rosey Institute in Gstaad, whose students were sons of kings and millionaires. The boys must be removed at once from Ann and the gossip about the shooting.

Her desire to fight Elsie revived Ann. She insisted that she would never give up her sons. In fact, Ann was impressed with Le Rosey. She promised to consider it, though she repeated that she wanted to be near

---

*As William Kahn put it, "We were convinced after a thorough and detailed investigation that the prowler had been on that roof and the killing was accidental. The case was brought before a grand jury to protect Frank Gulotta and the district attorney's office from expected public criticism."

**Many rumors about the "murder" took on a validity because of Elsie's failure to muffle her rage. During the first twenty years after the shooting, Elsie's accusations took the form of raised eyebrows. Her sighs announced her view of Ann to extra men Robert Leylan, Serge Obolensky, and Herschel Williams. Elsie's power and hauteur were such that a sigh was rigid condemnation. Later on, she made direct accusations of guilt. (She denounced Ann on separate occasions in the mid-seventies to socialite and New York *Post* owner Dorothy Schiff and to Herschel Williams. "She shot him on purpose, of course she did," Elsie said at lunch with Dorothy at the French restaurant Le Madrigal.)

the boys. After Elsie left, Ann wept, saying that Billy's mother's disapproving facial expressions reminded her of Billy. Dr. Prutting reported to the press that Ann's appetite improved, although she had "a little cold." He predicted that she might leave the hospital "before a week—maybe in a few days."

The balance tipped slightly in Ann's favor when Elsie learned that a reporter was tracking Billy's visits to a West End Avenue brothel in Manhattan. Elsie reasoned that if she supported Ann, the press would be less interested in the dirt. After five days of silence, Elsie made her public statement: "I feel as sorry for Ann as I do for my own son."

On November 4, Elsie and Assistant Chief Inspector Jim Farrell sat in the ground floor of her home. "I am the mother of William Woodward, Jr.," she said, "whom I last saw alive two weeks ago. However, he did call me frequently on the telephone." Elsie explained that her son was a busy person with his business and racing interests. She admitted that he and Ann had had a "little difference" some ten years earlier, "but since then they have been very happy." Elsie blamed Billy for the foolish shooting game. "I blame my son," said Mrs. Woodward, "for giving his wife a shotgun to keep in her bedroom, knowing how nervous she was. I know Ann loved Bill very much and the shooting could be nothing but an accident."

She ended the five-minute interview, "I have never felt more sorry for anyone in my life than I do for Ann knowing she shot her husband whom she loved so much."

Even twenty years later, retired New York State Supreme Court Justice Frank Gulotta, the district attorney at the time of the shooting, said that Elsie's backing of Ann was important: "That's one of the things that impressed me. Here was this dowager, her son dead, and she goes to the defense of this woman. Other members of her husband's family vouched for the marriage."

Gulotta noted, however, that ultimately it was not Elsie's statements but rather Paul Wirths' confession that settled the legal question of Ann's guilt. "Let's assume they had the greatest dislike for each other. Still, the confession of the burglar shows that it was his presence that triggered the shooting—and proves it was an accident."

*   *   *

In the hospital, Ann was distraught to learn that Elsie had installed investigator Harold Danforth in the dining room of Ann's house. He was interviewing her social friends from address books labeled by country. Elsie still wanted to prove Ann was an unfit mother. After all, had she not fired without thinking of her children's presence?

Ann reached out for help to her aunt Lydia Smiley. The spinster schoolteacher was the only person actively in Ann's corner who was not being paid to be there. Lydia did her duty by "sister Ethel's girl." She asked her sister, Mrs. Edna Smiley Cobb, in Kinsley, Kansas, to accompany her to Manhattan. The two sisters withdrew virtually all their savings to make the trip, although Ann later reimbursed them for their travel expenses.

The sisters took the train through Dodge City. Edna and Lydia wore their Sunday hats with veils, their wire-rim eyeglasses, and their hair in buns covered with hair nets. They spoke of the humiliation over *Life* magazine photographs of the unkempt back entrance of Jesse Claude Crowell's farm. Memories of their late sister weighed on them. They were eager to see Ann and set up a place for the boys. But Harold Danforth turned them away from the door of the East Seventy-third Street house—on orders from Elsie—and they spent the night at an inexpensive Hotel.

Early the next morning, Ann wept upon hearing that her aunts had not been invited into her house. Ann called Elsie and was quietly told by Ethel Fowler, Elsie's triplet sister, to have her aunts call Dunnington. Ann told her aunts to take rooms at the Barbizon Hotel.

The following day, Tuesday, November 8, Lydia and Edna came to the hospital. It made Lydia cry to see Ann so low. It took another full day for the aunts to be allowed to enter Ann's house. Even so, Danforth and Ann's secretary, Miss Buffum, were under instructions from Walter Dunnington to scrutinize their every move. By Wednesday, Ann's aunts had moved into the boys' rooms on East Seventy-third Street. They introduced themselves to Ann's secretary, who was pasting news clips about Nashua and the shooting in scrapbooks on a bed upstairs. *Newsday* printed a report that the secretary was reporting to the Woodward family as an agent against Ann. The aunts were not permitted to talk to or see their nephews.

Meanwhile, a *Journal-American* reporter broke the story that a top private investigator had been hired by Elsie to dig up dirt on Ann. Headlines soon announced more conflict between Elsie and her daughter-in-law. Dunnington denied hiring the detective. He said that Harold Danforth had been hired merely to guard Ann's aunts. But Danforth's associates assured the press that he would never take a lowly guard job.*

Their third day in New York, the aunts again visited their niece in the hospital. Mrs. Cobb recalls, "She looked pretty shaken but she was pretty glad to see us. She was upset at the mean columns and the things people were saying. She was a beautiful girl, and that's why he married her, but he married outside."

On November 11, the two little Woodward boys were photographed entering the hospital on their way to visit Ann for the third consecutive day. The visits were part of Elsie's campaign to demonstrate that she meant Ann no harm.

Back home that afternoon, on East Eighty-sixth Street, Jimmy was clamoring to go to a movie. Elsie inspected his combed cowlick and starched white shirt collar. Then she and her daughter Ethel de Croisset, visiting her mother from Paris, sneaked the boys out the back door of the house and into a taxi. At the cinema on Forty-second Street, the boys begged to sit through the film a second time. Elsie reluctantly agreed.

Afterward, the boys dragged their grandmother and aunt next door into a penny arcade. The Woodward heirs took turns firing a rifle at moving targets. Suddenly, Elsie looked around in horror at the other children in the arcade. Suppose someone recognized them. The last thing Elsie needed was a newspaper picture of the Woodward boys shooting rifles. She rushed home.

On Monday, November 14, as usual, Elsie Woodward called Dr. Prutting for Ann's health bulletin. He told her, "She is still suffering from shock and grief." Dr. Prutting had showed Ann the ten-page *Life* magazine article on Billy's death to prepare her for the intense public interest in the shooting. Ann wept, saying she wanted to run far away. Dr. Prutting delayed the grand jury interrogation.

Sol Rosenblatt knew that any delay would gall Elsie. To buttress Ann's child custody battle, however, he needed time to give her respectable Kansan aunts press exposure. That afternoon, a reporter noted that "in a mysterious unexplained move," after staying at Ann's house for six days and visiting her almost daily at the hospital, "Lydia Smiley and Edna Cobb drove out on a fact-finding trip to Oyster Bay Cove." They were picked up by Lee Principe in a black Triumph sedan.

---

*A college graduate in philosophy, Danforth was famous for having posed as a thug, pimp, longshoreman, homosexual, gun for hire, and loan shark.

On November 16, Dr. Prutting reported "Ann's best day so far." But he would not commit himself to a release date from Doctors Hospital. The custody fight was heating up. Walter Dunnington asked that Ann formally grant Elsie control of the boys' education and upbringing. When told that Ann had refused, Elsie cried. Finally, Dr. Prutting announced that Ann could go home and added, "I have had long talks recently with the Nassau County detectives. Mrs. Woodward is also eager to talk with them, and get this entire situation cleared up. The way things look now, she may leave here Monday—early Monday."

Cruel questions from other children would tell little Jimmy Woodward more about the shooting than his own family ever did. Neither Elsie nor Ann understood Jimmy's need for reassurance at this critical time in his life. Exiling him and his brother to Switzerland would confirm his fears that he was being punished for having done something very wrong. Since Jimmy was chastised for asking questions, he assumed the worst. He believed that he had caused his father's death.

The problem was that Ann could barely speak about what had happened. Elsie had decided the mess had originated with Ann's mysterious family. She told Jimmy clearly—once—that there had been a terrible accident. It was a matter of a gun going off in his mother's hands and killing his father by mistake.

On November 21, Dr. Prutting announced that Ann would leave Doctors Hospital for special questioning in Nassau County. He said that it was Ann's wish not to dodge the press. She put on a black dress with the help of two nurses. When Sol Rosenblatt called, she begged him to let her stay in the hospital.

At four o'clock, she sat on the side of her bed, crying, wearing a long black broadtail coat, black hat and veil, and black gloves. A moment later thirty-five photographers and reporters pressed forward in the hospital corridor to witness her first public appearance since the shooting. The elevator door opened. Television lights beamed.

Nobody said a word as Ann advanced, supported by Dr. Prutting and Murray Gurfein. Neither Rosenblatt nor any member of the Woodward family was present. Reporters had heard that Ann had been spirited out of the hospital to go to the hairdresser, but her appearance belied this rumor.

Ann's hair was white, her cheeks looked hollow. A sympathetic frown knit Gurfein's brow as she wept. She was oblivious to the reporters' awed silence.

Two sergeants and four patrolmen tried to clear a path. She was pushed by the crowd of photographers to the front door. Ann crossed East End Avenue and disappeared into the black Triumph sedan. The gathering crowd was hushed. Outside, Gurfein stopped reporters' questions with a raised hand. He read a statement saying that he had been hired by the Woodward family to advise Ann. Then came the bombshell: "Mrs. Woodward desires to speak in her own defense before the grand jury later this week." Gurfein had advised Ann to waive her constitutional immunity against self-incrimination. Her grief and her description of the shooting would be the most eloquent defense.

Four days before the grand jury hearing, the *Journal-American* had all but convicted Ann of murder. It also accused the Nassau County Police of calculated negligence. A series of articles purported to be an attempt to clear up "the mystery, confusion, rumor, and innuendo" that still surrounded the shooting of William Woodward, Jr. The newspaper attacks pushed Ann to the breaking point. Despite Rosenblatt's assurances, she began to believe that the grand jury would indict her for murder. The articles appeared under the byline of Harold Fox, identified as "a famous detective." He had been hired by Billy's friends Denny Slater and Laddie Sanford, who wanted "better answers to a lot of questions." They released Fox's findings to the *Journal-American*, hoping the information would influence the grand jury to indict Ann. (This is another indication that the crowd was not acting in unison according to a "cover-up" plan of Elsie Woodward's.)

Fox's series assumed that readers had intimate knowledge of the Woodward case. He accused the police of lying or covering up for Ann. Otherwise, he claimed, they would have discovered Paul Wirths's outdoor footprint and a broken tree bough long before he confessed. Fox dismissed Wirths's confession: "The belated and controversial confession of Paul Wirths, the prowler, only lends more confusion to the case because no physical evidence except a broken tree limb can be produced to support his version outside of his own contradictory statements." (Fox ignored the broken window on the second floor for the sake of his argument.)

"Why was the first officer on the scene, previously revealed to me to be Patrolman Henry Cormier, not questioned by detectives as to what he saw and what he heard and what he knew?" (Fox was wrong—the police report has a full statement from Cormier.)

Fox demanded to know why the police did not release physical evidence to the press, such as a ballistics test of powder burns on Ann's hand and arm. (Since Ann had confessed to the shooting, such powder burn tests were not crucial.) He accused the police of failing to prove they had done a complete autopsy report. He demanded they reveal the full extent of the wound and the number of pellets extracted from the body. As Fox probably knew, however, by law the autopsy could not be released to the press until the grand jury hearing. Fox claimed, erroneously, that there were no shotgun pellets on the wallpaper, only on the door itself.

Fox pointed to the dripping shower as a suspicious clue. He also cited the "conflicting" press reports that Billy's body was both in the hall and in his room. He ignored the obvious: the body was half in the room and half in the hall.

That afternoon, Ann was exhausted by three hours of questioning, the final interrogation before the grand jury hearing. The *Herald-Tribune* reported that Ann broke down and wept three times. Still smarting from criticism for having let her leave Nassau County, Chief Pinnell told reporters, "We do not want to question her in a hospital room with nurses and other people around." Afterward, Gulotta and Pinnell told the press that in their opinion the shooting was an accident.

Ann left Mineola and was driven to Elsie's house, where she and Elsie met with Walter Dunnington, Murray Gurfein, and Billy's secretary, John Ludevig. Elsie had called this meeting to announce the plans of the Woodward family. She made it crystal clear that in the past three years she had remained in the background for Billy's sake, but now she was taking charge of the family and its finances.

First, the Belair stables would be closed; Elsie was retiring the colors. Elsie had been shocked by a newspaper report that Ann might race a new filly. For the sake of squelching the scandal and for her own peace of mind, she was also selling the family's bank shares and the homes in Manhattan, Long Island, and Maryland, worth more than $40 million. Elsie's personal fortune, in excess of $25 million, could have supported the houses and the horses, but she did not want them.

Ann felt humiliated by the terms of Billy's eleven-page will, drawn up on December 14, 1948—at the height of his romance with Marina Torlonia. Since then, Billy had made three revisions in it to punish Ann. Ann was to receive income from the minimum statutory one-third "widow's share," while the income from the remaining two thirds of his estate went to the boys. When each boy turned twenty-one he would receive his entire inheritance.

Elsie told Ann that, in her opinion, Billy had been generous to her. She owned the houses in Oyster Bay Cove and on East Seventy-third Street. The Woodward family would also forgive a promissory note in which Ann promised to pay Billy $100,000 for some of the Oyster Bay acreage. As an added incentive to cooperate with Elsie's plans to send the boys to Switzerland, Elsie made Ann an offer. "Since my son's will did not leave you any personal property," said Elsie, "the estate will look kindly upon a petition for any household furnishings." Ann would later ask for one-third of the Spode dinner plates with the Woodward horses pictured on them.

Murray Gurfein put his arm around Ann's shoulders and suggested that Ann's and the boys' expenses in the difficult two months following her husband's death be paid out of Billy's estate. Walter Dunnington repeated Elsie's first rule: If Ann cooperated with family plans, then of course reasonable requests would be granted. (He did not have to say that otherwise the estate would fight her for every penny.)

Elsie announced that the boys would begin immediately at Le Rosey. Her philosophy was a little chilling: they would sink or swim there. (It would turn out that Woody swam, Jimmy did not.) Most important, Elsie made it clear that Ann would be better off for at least four years if she made her home abroad.

The myth that most society people tell is that Elsie paid Ann to disappear. Ann's income from Billy's estate would be over $500,000 a year. The travel money from the boys' funds was slightly more than $50,000 a year. But to Ann it represented Elsie's support.

Ann wept as the Triumph carried her down to the East Seventy-third street house. In the past, she would smile as the car crossed Park Avenue at Seventy-third Street. Her plain grand house was exactly 150 footsteps from the corner. She and Jimmy had counted them together. Sometimes the plain façade and the ground-floor archways had looked inviting to Ann; other times she found the house intimidating.

In the past, her shoulders had relaxed as the door swung open. But tonight she tensed as Lee Principe fumbled for the key.

The house had contained her life with Billy.

Lydia Smiley was standing behind the maid, Ann Gorney. Without a word, Ann led her aunt to the elevator.

*   *   *

At 10 a.m. on Friday, November 25, the grand jury began its inquiry into the death of William Woodward, Jr., in the courthouse in Mineola. The first witness was Fern Tailer Gimbel, who entered wearing a fur coat.

Ten other witnesses assembled in a small room near the echoing rotunda. Some sat on benches. Stan Freeman, the piano player, would testify about Billy's talk at the party of gunning for the prowler. Lee Principe and Ann Gorney stood together. Harry Evans winked at the ladies. It was starting to feel like a party until Libby Pratt arrived, hatless, with pearls in place over her black suit. Libby sat next to her nephew, young Billy Bancroft, who had identified his uncle's body. Among them, only Titi Baker Schiff actually liked Ann, but many witnesses would swear that Ann and Billy had had a wonderful marriage.

Assistant District Attorney Eddie Robinson supervised the proceedings, although District Attorney Frank Gulotta was present. The grand jury voted against visiting the scene of the shooting. Homicide Detective Dan Stark escorted each witness to the closed doors. Fern Gimbel told Stark as they walked through the empty courthouse rotunda that he looked like Robert Mitchum. A long line of county police experts presented ballistics reports, targets, photographs, the Churchill shotgun, and the broken tree branch Paul Wirths had said he snapped off.* Steve Smith, the Cinerama night watchman, told of Ann's cries for help. Dr. Theodore Curphey and Dr. Leslie Lukash testified about the autopsy and the patterns of the bullet holes. Second-squad detectives Edward Curran and Frank Steiner described Paul Wirths's confession.

Harry Evans was a voluntary character witness, who told the jurors of Ann's "sunny disposition." (His help would ensure his welcome at the Meadowbrook Club until he died.) He testified, "That night [of the Baker party] you could not find two better suited people. They were in splendid spirits. Bill discussed the prowler with me, and preparations. He may have said armed preparations, but you couldn't take Woodward seriously about a thing like that."

Libby Pratt testified on behalf of her sister-in-law, impressing the grand jurors with both her generous spirit and her "upper-class" accent.

That afternoon, accompanied by Gurfein and Dr. Prutting, Ann had been driven by Principe in her black Triumph to the Garden City Hotel, where her presence created a small riot in the lobby. She wore black mourning clothes and no makeup on her pale, puffy face. Her hair was tucked

---

*Police witnesses included detectives Stark, John Moylan, Kenneth Boyd, and Kenneth Soper, Chief Russ Haff, Lieutenant Edward Barry, and Patrolman Tom Costello.

into a small black cap. She waited in a hotel suite for the telephone call that would summon her to the courthouse.

At 4:45, eight policemen pushed the mob away from Ann as she made her way into the courthouse. Her eyes were squeezed closed as she sobbed into her handkerchief. Looking alarmed, Gurfein grasped her shoulders. Ann sometimes believed it would make no difference if she were indicted for murder. She was alone. A woman without a man to love her was not a real woman. A woman who had killed her husband did not deserve to live. As she entered the courthouse, twenty-two more policeman held back the press. Her lips moved. She was talking to Billy, asking him to tell people to leave her alone.

Ann sat in a small room near the grand jury room. A court clerk handed Gurfein a waiver of immunity. Gurfein handed it to Ann with his gold-trimmed fountain pen. It stated that anything she might say to the grand jury could be used against her in any potential prosecution. She stood and clung to Dr. Prutting, but he was not permitted to attend Ann during her cross-examination. Gurfein waited outside the grand jury room. Inside, Lee Principe guided Ann to a little chair. Ann put her left hand on a Bible held by a senior court clerk. Twenty-two grand jurors, five of whom were women, watched her.

The thirty-one-minute cross-examination by Eddie Robinson was halted when Ann broke down. A grand juror named Mrs. Lillian Bucken, a nurse in Rockville Centre, held her shoulder and helped her drink cold water. The New York Times described Ann's appearance for the grand jury. She was, after all, still a fashion symbol: "Mrs. Woodward wore no makeup. Her face was blanched and her long eyelashes were blonder than her hair. These contrasted to the jet black of her Chinese-coolie-type hat, her karakul coat, and her square handbag and her unadorned black shoes." An editorial in the Times later that week would plead for her privacy.

Ann turned out to be an impressive witness in her own defense. Her voice was so weak that her remarks had to be repeated by Robinson for the grand jurors. However, the autopsy and forensic information also confirmed her story. The grand jurors were not told of Ann's jealous rages or of Billy's affairs.

Afterward, Ann waited, head bowed, in the huge rotunda. She was moving her lips, praying and talking to Billy. Later, Nurse Moore saw a newspaper picture of Ann waiting for the verdict and was shocked to see how much she had aged. As she waited, the final witness, Paul Wirths, told his latest version of the events of the night of the shooting. Wirths's ankles and wrists were bound in chains that dragged on the floor. He left the stand at 6:55. He was not permitted near Ann Woodward; authorities feared for her fragile mental state. Wirths brandished his manacled fists to the waiting press. "If I didn't have these on, you'd see what I can do with my hands," he shouted.

After listening to nine and a half hours of testimony by thirty-one witnesses, the grand jurors deliberated. Thirty minutes later, they voted unanimously not to indict Ann. Paul Wirths did not fare as well. Despite Detective Steiner's promises of immunity, Wirths was indicted for several counts of burglary.

The acting foreman of the grand jury, Alfred T. Allin of Lynbrook, cited the letter of the law: "She shot thinking she was defending herself and her family." Another juror, Mrs. Ann Warner of Mineola, said, "We were annoyed that there was any question that this was anything but an accident. She's miserable. Being free still leaves her with an awful lot of fear in her." Mrs. Warner said that the testimony by Gladys Gallagher, the local telephone operator, about Ann's emotional state after the shooting helped convince the grand jurors.

The nurse who had comforted Ann during her testimony, Mrs. Bucken, told reporters, "It was quite an ordeal for her. Many times she was unable to continue with her testimony. We tried conscientiously to reach a proper verdict. It was an objective decision and not an emotional one. Nobody seemed to know positively if the light was on or off. Mrs. Woodward certainly didn't know. In a situation such as this, people can't really be expected to remember every detail. As far as the jury was concerned, her being wealthy meant nothing to us. It was strictly a case of listening to the facts and coming to an objective conclusion."

At 7:48, Frank Gulotta told Ann, "You can go home now." Ann murmured that she had nothing to look forward to. Gurfein and Dr. Prutting guided her to the car as flashbulbs popped. Gulotta told reporters, "The grand jury has found no evidence of culpability in the Woodward homicide."

The grand jury, however, did not accomplish what the district attorney and the Woodward family had hoped. It failed to remove all doubt. The Woodward family, for example, believed Ann had escaped prison only through their efforts. Her social friends took a cue from Elsie Woodward and continued to resent Ann for having killed Billy. They strongly suspected her of murder.

The following day, Newsday ran an unflattering picture of Ann on the front page next to a beautiful photograph of Fern Tailer Gimbel. The four-inch headline read: "Ann Absolved by Grand Jury." The story splashed over the entire page and onto another page and a half. It was major news around the country.

The next day, Sunday, Ann's two aunts, Edna Cobb and Lydia Smiley, were finally invited to Elsie's house to see their nephews. Ann, however, was not invited. Edna was going home the next day, while her sister Lydia was to stay a few more days. Elsie showed them through her house, and the sisters thanked her for helping their niece. The following day, Jimmy and Woody were sent to their mother for a few days before leaving for their new life at Le Rosey.

On November 28, Ann was described in *Newsday* as having spent a quiet weekend in her town house. The press was unaware that Ann had unofficially lost her custody fight. Murray Gurfein declared she was near exhaustion: "Her only desire is for quiet and to be with her children. Her physician advises her to leave the city as soon as she is able."

Libby Pratt was quoted as saying, "Ann's taken an awful beating. If she can go away and just forget it all, she'll be so much better off."

A month later, Ann Woodward took her first walk alone, hidden in long mourning veils and black fur. Ann Slater, Denny's wife, waved at her on Madison Avenue and asked, "How are you?"

Ann replied, "I will never recover."

23

EXILE

Jimmy and Woody had been sent to Le Rosey just before Christmas, 1955. They were now "Roseens," among the 100 extremely privileged boys taking the English course. Jimmy roomed with Jay Sicre, scion of one of the wealthiest merchant banking families of Spain. The European royal families were familiar names on the roll call. Alumni included Prince Rainier of Monaco, the Duke of Kent, the King of Belgium, the Shah of Iran, Karim Khan (the future Aga Khan), the King of Belgium, and the sons of the major Greek shipping magnates. In France the school was known as *"l'école des rois."*

At first, the Woodward boys sat stunned in classes on rock climbing, Latin, and European football. They learned to kiss the hand of Madame Juanot, the headmistress, upon entering the dining room. They skied every day from one-thirty to four-thirty. The other boys remember the notorious American newcomers as pale and frightened. The news spread quickly about why the two American students arrived at the school midyear.

Unfortunately, Elsie had misgauged the proportions of the scandal. The Cryder banking scandal was less interesting and had taken place in another century, when television, radio, and wire service press communications did not exist.

Nine months after the shooting, on July 3, 1956, 300 wealthy passengers, including old John Jacob Astor, Long Island hostess Mrs. Lyon Slater, and Mrs. Slater's escort, Harry King, boarded the Cunard Line's luxury cruiser, the R.M.S. *Caronia*. They were about to set sail for the North Pole.

As the gangplank was about to be withdrawn, a family arrived to board, led by an erect old woman. She was dressed in black gloves and a black hat with a veil. Over her suit, she wore an animal fur, the head and tail of which lay on her chest.

The younger woman in the group had puffy eyelids and deep circles under her eyes. She was not attractive, partly because of the sullen set to her jaw. She wore her dark blond hair pulled back under a hat and veil. Her tailored navy suit did not hide the curves of her body. The two women did not speak. By their side were two yellow-haired boys in navy blazers.

A few passengers wondered why the boys and the younger woman were boarding the ship at the last possible minute. Then Martha Slater recognized them and whispered to Harry King, "Oh, my, good lord, that's dear Elsie saying good-bye to Ann and those poor boys. I think they're boarding." She searched the passenger list. "They must be traveling under an assumed name."

In fact, Ann would be traveling to the North Pole under no name at all. Although the cruise had been sold-out for a year, they had been booked anonymously at the last minute by Elsie through Robert Livingston Clarkson, the chairman of the board of American Express, which owned the Cunard Line. Ann, Woody, and Jimmy would share a little stateroom with three bunks, usually occupied by members of the ship's staff. Jimmy's dreams were troubled by his mother's White Shoulders perfume and bath powder.

School was out, but Elsie did not want the family vacationing in the United States. Ann was still too unhinged. Besides, the scandal was still fresh in many minds.

At first Ann had resisted the idea of the boat trip. She had made up her mind to continue her life in Manhattan as Mrs. William Woodward, Jr. But then she was denied membership at the Southampton Beach Club because of the objections of Angier Biddle Duke and some of Billy's other friends. She couldn't take the boys to Southampton for the summer; they would feel left out. But Ann had also turned down Elsie's invitation to Newport. A summer under Elsie's disapproving eye would be an ordeal. The worst of it was: Cholly Knickerbocker had reported the whole thing.

They compromised on the leisurely and exclusive North Cape cruise to Reykjavik, Iceland. Clarkson himself was aboard for the 3,000-mile trip. A crew of 700 attended the 500 mostly elderly passengers. The only staff person on the *Caronia* who was officially told the identity of the woman in the cramped stateroom was the handsome cruise manager, William Sudduth, who had been instructed to look after Ann by Robert Clarkson.

"Please help me protect Ann. I promised Elsie Woodward," Clarkson had told Sudduth.

Clarkson had made a brilliant choice in Bill Sudduth as Ann's care-taker. For the next twenty years, as Ann became more dependent on the fleeting kindness of lotharios, gigolos, Good Samaritans, oddballs, and con men, Bill Sudduth's support would be the one constant. It was not a sexual match. Sudduth was homosexual, but, nevertheless, he would be available to her night and day. Sudduth was drawn to lost souls. Out of his own pocket, and with funds he had raised, Sudduth had rescued 450 orphaned and displaced European children after World War II. He found families and jobs for each one of them in the United States and then persuaded colleges such as Dartmouth (which pledged eight scholarships) to sponsor them.*

He lived in a large, empty apartment at 56 East Eighty-seventh Street, a three-minute walk from Ann's house. In years to come, as soon as she would land in New York, she'd call and say, "Bill, come quick, I need you." Some people thought he was her butler. In fact, he did coordinate her household when she was away, hiring his refugee students to sort her mail and polish her crystal and silver.

During the first three days at sea, Ann hid in the small stateroom, terrified. Sudduth reported that she never complained about the tight quarters. Three people in that space did, however, feel to Ann like jail—or as though they were very poor.

Curious elderly passengers whispered at the sight of Jimmy and Woody Woodward. The crew taught Jimmy to fish off the back of the boat. Woody made friends with a teenage girl, a granddaughter of a pas-senger who was a member of the Candler family, which originated Coca-Cola. But nobody on board caught so much as a glimpse of Ann. Other children had learned she was aboard from Jimmy and Woody. They told their grandparents. Word of her presence swept the *Caronia*.

Sudduth brought her lunch tray himself on the fourth day and on impulse said, "Oh, Ann, it's so dark and crowded in here, let's go up on deck. It's so beautiful to see the sun on the water." At that moment they looked at each other and knew they did not have to be afraid of each other. Sudduth, however, had the impression she was waiting for him to leave her stateroom so she could continue weeping. It was not only Ann's Balenciaga dresses and her manners. It was the almost physical pain she

---

*Sudduth also regularly housed and fed homeless people. In 1988, one such person killed him with a running shoe that had a steel arch and stole a few dollars.

had to live with that gave her an incandescent beauty for him. He decided she was a superior person, a tragic figure on the order of Marie Antoinette.

By the sixth day, Sudduth had convinced Ann to come up on deck to play shuffleboard while the other passengers were occupied at the ship's cinema. He ordered two trays for dinner. He hoped the fresh salt air would tempt her appetite. But she sat with him without eating, watching the stars from the rear deck, which was used only by the crew. It became clear to Sudduth that all she thought about was her husband.

The rear deck became their place. Bill started inviting her there for luncheon. They watched the ship's wake in silence. Ann did not sunbathe. Every now and then she would say her husband's name, hesitate, and then confide a single fact, such as how much he liked to dance. She kept a pair of his cuff links in her purse.

It took Ann a week before she agreed to go into the dining room. Knowing how frightened she was of the other passengers, Sudduth did not tell her she would have to walk through the whole room to reach her table. He explained to Ann, "We'll just go down late and walk in."

Around the dining room, conversations were left hanging. Everyone had seen pictures of Ann's bedroom and her nightwear. They had been debating her sex life and her shooting ability. "That's her, I'd know her anywhere," said one elderly woman.

She ate alone at a small table. Sudduth could not sit with her since he was a member of the crew. A crew member stood behind her throughout the meal. The boys had eaten with some new friends at any earlier seating.

In Reykjavik, fearing that local reporters had learned of her presence, Sudduth persuaded Ann to leave the ship for a private tour of a Viking museum. She walked stiffly down the gangplank like an invalid, wearing a scarf over her hair, a sensible skirt, and canvas espadrilles. She was fascinated by a hot geyser that spurted soothing thermal waters.

In Trondheim, Norway, on July 16, while the tour went in one direction to see a waterfall, Sudduth guided Ann in another. The tourists had upset her. "Why do they look at me like that?" she asked.

"Dear Ann," he said, "hold up your head. It doesn't matter."

On the north coast of a desolate island in Norway, Ann agreed to climb to a rock plateau, the last point of land before the North Pole. She loved the silent expanse of rocks, sky, and Arctic Sea. Picking daisies on the way down, she found a four-leaf clover. Out here, thousands of miles from Oyster Bay Cove, it almost seemed possible that her luck might change.

* * *

After the cruise, Sudduth visited Ann and the boys in Oyster Bay Cove. The hedges needed pruning, but the Playhouse still looked like a grand palazzo. As he arrived, however, a maid stepped out the front door, shouting at Ann. The maid had been sent that morning by an agency and had been fired by Ann for not cleaning properly. Jimmy stood behind his mother in the front hall. "What did I expect?" shouted the maid. "You didn't pay me right and you murdered your own husband."

Jimmy started to cry. Ann swayed; she did not collapse. Nor did she tend to her son. Sudduth hugged Jimmy. "Jimmy, the woman is upset. Your mother loves you very much, and she loved your father. It was a terrible accident that happened, and it made your mother very sad. You'll understand better when you get older." Bill Sudduth was one of the few people with whom Ann discussed the shooting. He tried to ease her mind, but only rarely succeeded.

In the fall of 1956, Ann took the boys back to Le Rosey. Then she flew to Paris, where she was introduced to Nelson Iriniz Casas, a diplomat and playboy from Uruguay who was visiting from his embassy in Vienna. He was a very handsome man, blond, several years younger and an inch shorter than Ann. She suddenly believed she could find happiness with another man. Casas loved taking her to the Parisian night spots. He was soon told by acquaintances that he was keeping company with the "famous American murderess." But that did not bother him so much as the fact that he never felt alone with Ann. She was always talking about Billy. A man with a serious side, Casas would later take a doctorate in philosophy in Vienna. It was thanks to him that Ann read Proust and Maupassant.

In Paris she was still in hiding, avoiding the haunts of international society. When she visited Billy's youngest sister, Ethel de Croisset, on Rue Weber, she made sure they would be alone.*

Ann forced herself to take care of her appearance. In the early mornings, when she would not risk seeing old acquaintances, she went around to the houses of Givenchy and Balenciaga to order gowns. She also stopped in at Dior's boutique, where she bought a dark necktie for Casas. Elsie wrote her a reproving letter when an item about her relationship with Casas appeared in American newspapers.

---

*Ethel was perhaps attracted to violent situations. Besides her sister-in-law, she was friends with Barbara Baekeland and her son, Tony, who would wind up killing his mother.

Ann's relationship with Nelson Casas lasted three and a half years; it would be the longest one she was able to sustain after Billy's death.

In October 1957, Ann was in Vienna with Casas when William Levitt, the real estate developer who had built Levittown, bought the Belair estate. It was sad for Ann to learn that the thousands of acres of Woodward pasture would be broken up into plots for 5,000 ranch houses.* She wrote politely to Jimmy that she was pleased the Woodward house would be preserved.

The symbols of the Woodward dynasty were disappearing. Elsie had sold the grand house on East Eighty-sixth Street and had bought a seven-room apartment in the Waldorf Towers, near the Duchess of Windsor's and the Presidential Suite.

When Ann was in Vienna in 1957, a Sunday night television movie called *People Kill People, Sometimes* was broadcast. Directed by John Frankenheimer and starring Jason Robards, George C. Scott, and Geraldine Page, the movie was about a couple concerned over a prowler coming in and out of their house. The hysterical wife winds up killing her husband. The society columns noted the similarity to Ann's story and reported that Ann was careful to stay out of the country at the time.

The following year Casas broke up with Ann. Her moods had been too much for him. She provoked fights, challenging his affection because he would not propose marriage. She kept trying to make him into Billy.

Alone again at forty-three, she returned from Europe and rented the Seventy-third Street town house to the government of Albania to use as its consulate. She began looking for a new place to live. She fell in love with a duplex maisonette being sold by the estate of New York couturiere Hattie Carnegie; it occupied the first two floors of a stately old apartment building at 1133 Fifth Avenue, at Ninety-fourth Street. The unusual main sitting room of the maisonette had high ceilings and was paneled in French beech. The maisonette's private wrought iron entrance on Fifth Avenue opened onto a marble foyer and a circular staircase.

To her dismay, when Ann petitioned in surrogate court for two thirds

---

*Another realty firm, Webb and Knapp, was initially awarded the farm (the enterprising deal maker was a vice president named William Zeckendorf) for a lower bid of $1,187,000, but the Prince Georges County court of appraisals nullified the sale on the grounds that the Woodward trustees had not been diligent enough in trying to get the highest price. They had refused to sell to Levitt because they did not want a Levittown at Belair. On July 21, 1957, the sale was readvertised by a legal order. Levitt paid $1,750,000, his opening bid in the auction in Prince Georges County.

of the $150,000 purchase price of the apartment from the principal from her sons' estates to help buy the duplex, her photograph appeared in newspapers. Her sons, who were each worth well over $4 million, had more money than she did. The court granted Ann's petition and she bought the maisonette.

Although she enjoyed the income of Billy's bequest, without him Ann felt like a child who might have to flee in the night because there were too many bills to pay.

Ann liked the sunny garden in the maisonette courtyard. She added several carved cherubs from Oyster Bay. She did not use a decorator, but made careful diagrams and went alone to auctions, neatly marking Sotheby's and Parke-Bernet catalogues with prices and her opinions of paintings and furniture. Over the next three years, Ann filled the apartment with antique French furniture, including a beige silk Aubusson carpet that she sent out to be rewoven after cocktail parties, when the heels of her guests tore it. She bought a Renoir drawing and a Modigliani that reminded her of her son Jimmy. A Picasso that may have been a forgery hung in her bedroom. The controversial Dalí portrait of her was hung in an upstairs guest room.

She decided she wanted to become an interior designer. She enrolled in several courses and was told she had a good eye. Unfortunately, Billy was still her obsession. She made up her mind to "marry a man just like him."

The invitation came by telephone. "Join us for the 'April in Paris' thing," said Elsie Woodward in her deep voice.

"My dear, how perfect," said Herschel Williams.

"Ann's coming. Do be a lamb and escort her."

"I am thrilled by your invitation," said Herschel. "I'll be at the Plaza with bells on."

It was March 1958, and this was to be Ann's first public appearance since the shooting two and a half years earlier. It would be a famous evening. "You are a brave lady," he told Elsie before they hung up. Herschel Williams* pondered the honor. He would outshine the chairman of

---

*Herschel Williams was the handsome extra man who had arrived in New York just after World War I with a letter of introduction from Elsie's triplet sister, the Washington hostess Mrs. Ethel Fowler. He had enjoyed shocking Elsie at an early dinner party with the story of Mrs. Fowler's policy of "personal relief." A great friend of Alice Longworth's, Ethel Fowler was less imperious than Elsie. Since she had no guest bathroom on the ground floor of her Georgetown house, after dinner and before brandy at parties there she instructed the gentlemen to step into the garden to relieve themselves.

Herschel prided himself on knowing everybody. George Burns had once called him "comthe ball, President Eisenhower's wife, Mamie, and the co-chairman, C. Z. Guest, who—along with Tommy Bancroft's wife, Missy—had replaced Ann Woodward as the photographers' favorite at such events.

The night of the April in Paris Ball, Herschel gave Ann a wrist corsage of white orchids. She thanked him, twisting the wire stem over and over. Ann's mascara did not hide her puffy eyes.

He guided her by her bare elbow into Elsie Woodward's new apartment at the Waldorf Towers. The room seemed to shift as they entered. Nobody was comfortable. Herschel nodded at the head of the Jockey Club, George Widener. Ann stared at the birdlike head of her mother-in-law. Elsie wore a dress that covered her chest bones with black gauze. Ann had changed her mind about her own low-cut black gown at least six times. She touched her cheek to Elsie's and felt the other woman move away. "Ma?" said Ann. Elsie greeted someone else. Ann sighed.

Herschel Williams remembered that at Cap d'Antibes everyone was calling her "Annie-get-your-gun." He had heard rumors that Ann was looking for another rich husband. Count Rudi Crespi had told him that in Venice she had asked Salvador Dalí's wife about an Italian industrialist. "Is Gianni Agnelli really engaged?" she asked.

Señora Dalí had kicked Crespi's leg. "What man would have her?" whispered Señora Dalí loud enough for Ann to hear. "A self-made widow."

At Elsie's party, Eleanor Whitney kissed Ann's cheek. "I love you, Ann. I'm sorry. I've been praying for you." Ann dabbed at her eyes with a handkerchief. Eleanor sounded sincere. She was the divorced wife of Cornelius "Sonny" Whitney and a devout born-again Christian. She patted Herschel Williams's arm, as if to say "Good for you" for helping Ann.

An hour later photographers swarmed the Woodward party in the Grand Ballroom, transformed into a French sidewalk café by tall chestnut trees. Ann kept her eyes on the ground, her chin high.

"Stand still together," said Jerome Zerbe to Elsie and Ann. He was dying to take a picture of the two Mrs. William Woodwards.

_____

mercial Herschel" because he made hobnobbing with important people his job. Elsie commended him, saying, "Good stags are rare gems in New York. Men with dinner coats and good manners are always in short supply."

He knew Elsie liked like his good looks, his Yale degree, and his love of the theater. In fact, he worked hard at Elsie's dinner parties. He entertained the ladies on either side of him with great diligence. Although he had rarely glimpsed Elsie's husband, he had met Prince Juan Carlos of Spain and the Duke of Windsor.

"Absolutely not," said Elsie Woodward.

When the Duchess of Windsor paid her respects to Elsie, Ann looked up, but the Duchess only glanced at her with her clever eyes. Herschel ate and told Ann about his conversations with the Duke of Windsor: "Hitler meant the English no harm. We were Roosevelt's dupes. We never should have entered the war. The Duke told me so."

During the fashion show, Ann played with her food and barely noted the entrance of the Dior mannequins between streams of a "dancing fountain."

Elsie Woodward failed with Ann that evening. She did not have the requisite sangfroid to pull off a social relationship with Ann. Although Elsie pretended otherwise, she hated the idea that Ann had not been convicted of murder. Her friends assumed that Elsie's dislike was proof of Ann's guilt.

Ann flew to Rio de Janeiro the next week, where heads turned at the Hotel Copa Palace. A friend soon showed Ann a picture of her and Herschel Williams in *Time*. Ann saved it. The magazine sold out at the hotel newsstand. The shooting was news again. Ann resolved to remain abroad. Sunning by the Copa Palace pool, she struck up a conversation with a Brazilian man. He told her one could make millions of dollars by investing in the new planned city of Brasília. Today it was jungle; in five years it would be the proud capital of Brazil. The possibility of a new start in a new place thrilled Ann.

She discussed Brasília with her dinner companion, a tall twenty-nine-year-old Swiss banker from Lugano who worked for an American investment company. She confided to M. Casellini that she liked the idea of a building with her name on it. All the buildings in Brasília would be named for the owners. A five-foot metal sign bearing her name would hang over the entrance. Ann said, "I want people to see it and remember me when I am dead." The next morning she and Casellini flew three hours to Brasília's only hotel, which was almost completely booked because of the presence of Fidel Castro and his staff.

Ann never made the investment; after four hours of meetings Casellini told her he thought the project was a swindle. He thought the five Brazilians were lying to her. He also told her she was too eager to believe whatever people told her.

A week later, despite her determination to stay away from the United States, Ann flew back to Manhattan to join the boys, home from Le Rosey. Tensions between Ann and Elsie were growing. Ann shouted into the telephone. Her mother-in-law ordered her to send the boys to Newport. Ann finally consented.

That summer Ann shuttled between Oyster Bay and her silent apartment. She felt suicidal and soon began visiting Eleanor Whitney at her home, Serendipity, on the edge of an arboretum on Feeks Lane in Locust Valley. Eleanor was a friend and follower of Billy Graham's. Ann's suffering touched her. The two women sat on Eleanor's patio, shaded by a green awning, surrounded by brilliant pink flowers. Behind them, a steep hill and gardens led down to a swimming pool and tennis courts. After a swim, Eleanor gave Ann some self-help books and talked to her about God's ability to love people through all kinds of difficulties. Ann impulsively put her head on Eleanor's shoulder and said, "Oh, Eleanor, you talk just like my mother."

Eleanor was recovering from a rough divorce. Her husband had ordered her out of the North Shore house she had shared with him. Since she no longer had her River House apartment, she drove in to the city to shop every Monday afternoon. Then she would go to Ann's duplex to change into her evening gown before she and Ann went to Eleanor's box at the Metropolitan Opera. Sometimes she stayed overnight at Ann's.

Ann fled to Brazil twice, once taking her sons with her in August. In the fall, the boys returned to Le Rosey and Ann told friends she was frightened of losing them to Elsie. Early the following year, in 1959, she broke her back while driving a car in Brazil. She wore a body cast for several months.

When Ann could travel again, she turned next to Madrid. "Billy liked it so much," she told Bill Sudduth. It was more provincial than Paris, but there were fewer foreign magazines on the newsstands, and she hoped that publicity about the shooting had not reached here. But C. Z. Guest and Sol Rosenblatt were just a few of the Americans who had already discovered Madrid, and Ann soon realized that the Americans—particularly wives—had spread the word. Waiters, salesgirls, and society people at the Hotel Ritz in Madrid whispered, *"La Matadora"* (the one who kills).

She developed a mask of placidity, but when she met people's stares, it often broke. Her eyes narrowed, and her expression seemed to say, "I know what you think you know about me, so just stare at me and be done with it."

She rented the top floor of a five-story nineteenth-century mansion near the Prado. The house, at 33 Méndez Núñez, faced the tall windows of the stone armory, filled with thousands of guns. It was a neighborhood where Americans usually did not live.

Ann imposed rituals on her household. There was her late-morning breakfast tray with fresh flowers and fruit juice, social telephone calls to be made, notes written in Spanish thanking hosts for dinner. The maid tended her clothing and took her shoes to be reheeled. In the afternoon, despite the heat, Ann took the elevator down to the old marble entrance and walked out the wrought iron gate.

Often she strolled through the Prado, where for hours she took notes on paintings.

She started accepting invitations to dinner from a married minister in the Spanish government. "He won't marry you. It's your divorce," said Baroness Terry von Pantz, the Avon heiress. She knew not to mention the murder.

Betty Sicre, the mother of Jimmy's roommate at Le Rosey, said, "Ann, dating a married man isn't the way to have people accept you. The women are just going to crucify you when they find out about this. And they control the dinner parties."

Ann sighed. American society women had never respected her marriage to Billy. It seemed unfair to make her give up the Spaniard's attentions. He made her feel almost human.

Ann sat on the veranda of the men's shooting club Tiro de Pigeon, near Madrid. She wore a khaki pantsuit. Packed around her were a hundred laughing European sportsmen drinking warm Scotch. There was sudden silence as Generalissimo Francisco Franco drove up, his silver Rolls-Royce flanked by ten black Cadillacs.

Ann quietly walked into the gaming room. She asked for a local bottled water. Leonard Puccinelli was betting on the shooting skills of his friend Vizcounde Pepe Alcimira. Puccinelli was an international champion from San Francisco who had been giving Ann shooting lessons. She had recently cooked him dinner.

Ann heard the loudspeaker blare: "Señora Ann Woodward." She ran to get her polished Purdey shotgun from the armory.

Ann's hands shook as she faced the five little pigeon boxes on the lawn. She was listening to the gamblers behind her placing bets on the performance of *"la Matadora Americana"* in English, Portuguese, Spanish, and Italian. They waved money at each other. "A thousand pesetas." "Six to one." *"Tres."* *"Cinq."* *"Douze."* As she took aim, jokes were made. "If she kills the bird, it's proof she killed her husband in cold blood." "No, no, if she misses, she feels guilty and cannot shoot straight."

The odds on skilled international shooters like Puccinelli were seven to one in his favor. But the odds on Ann were even money. These gamblers knew that if Ann became rattled, she could miss a buffalo a foot in front of her. Trying to steady her nerves, Ann raised the shotgun. *"Listo,"* she said. Behind her, the attendant in a red beret and scarf stuck a long microphone under her chin. Ann said, "Pull."

One box opened—nobody ever knew which one it would be—and a little brown pigeon, Zurigo, flew out in a zigzag. His tail feathers had been pulled out. Golden retrievers waited to pick up the wounded or dead birds. Ann missed both shots. Afterward, she went inside. She approached several wives eating caviar and gazpacho in the dining room. "I shot poorly," said Ann.

A single woman was unwelcome. "We're having a private conversation," said Mrs. Stafford Sands.

"May I join you?"

"Mrs. Woodward, please excuse us." The blood rushed to Ann's face as she backed away.

Elsie invited Ann to her Christmas party in 1959. This time she was allowed to have Bill Sudduth escort her. When he arrived to pick her up, she frowned at the sight of his blue ruffled tuxedo shirt. "Please change it, Bill," Ann said, explaining, "My mother-in-law won't like it, and I want her to like you, because I do."

It was March on the Costa del Sol, and in 1960, Marbella was still an unspoiled fishing village. The women were whitewashing houses for spring. Soon twisted olive trees, cactus, and scarlet bougainvillea would bloom against the turquoise Mediterranean. Above the town loomed a twelfth-century Moorish castle. The slow-paced little Spanish settlement was surrounded by the purple Sierra Blanca Mountains. Thirty fishermen and their families tolerated the twenty wealthy Spanish and English young people seeking refuge from their families.

One night, the young people went to a party where five Sevillanas in flounced red skirts danced the flamenco. The host, Howard Herrerra, a wealthy homosexual Venezuelan, had hired two guitarists and the dancing girls. The girls flapped their skirts outrageously at the drunken young guests.

At 1 a.m., Ann Woodward arrived at the party alone. At a dinner party in Madrid two days earlier, she had asked Herrerra to find her a place in the remote fishing settlement. Herrerra offered to drive her down and to rent her one of his two palatial villas. The idea of a seaside village where no one knew about the shooting filled her with anticipation.

Although most of the barefoot, carousing group ignored her arrival, one boy stared at Ann. He looked like Billy Woodward had when Ann had first met him, but he had a more sensuous mouth. His curling black hair made him look Spanish. He was unusually fine-featured. At twenty-four, Peter Townend, a British aristocrat, was on an extended romantic lark in Marbella. He spent his days accepting the attentions of women and playing on the beach. Peter had been an actor in Rome, and now he was writing a thriller set in the south of France.

Tonight he was drinking the local red wine he loved, Marqués de Riscal, and wondering where he would sleep that night. He was having a difficult time with his girlfriend, a young Spanish woman named Carmen Torrez. Fortunately, the older woman was staring back at him. He liked her style. She was wearing a tailored blue dress, matching gloves, stockings, and pumps.

"What are you doing here?" he asked.

He seemed kind, and she thought she recognized a certain pain in his handsome face. She wanted to photograph him—in bright light. "I came down with Howard. I have taken La Maryana," she said.

Peter was impressed. La Maryana was one of the best villas in Marbella. It had polished red tile floors and a tall A-frame living room, and it loomed above a long overgrown hill of olive, jacaranda, and jasmine trees. It had its own swimming pool of hand-painted local tiles surrounded by fragrant oleanders. The six bedrooms in separate wings overlooked the woods behind the house.

Peter asked Ann to leave the party with him two hours later. "Let's go down to the beach and look at the moon," said Ann. She drove a black Cadillac convertible, whose tires got stuck in the sand. They put a blanket on the sand and kissed until sunrise. She told him she adored him; she was telling the truth. Finally, some fishermen gave the Cadillac a push. They drove up to La Maryana at about six, tires crunching the gravel road. Whispering to avoid waking the maid, Ann cooked Peter scrambled eggs and fish. Her two sons were sleeping far in the back of the house. In the bedroom, Peter admired framed photographs of her sons. She wore her wedding ring. Ann knew Peter did not know who she was. Ann wanted to be cuddled, but Peter wanted sex. They made love.

Later that morning she introduced him to her sons; he was impressed by their European manners. Peter took the boys swimming and gave them tennis lessons. Ann offered him a salary to stay on and tutor the boys. "Oh, come on, Ann," he said, "that's too much money for teaching."

One afternoon, her sister-in-law Ethel de Croisset stopped by unexpectedly on her way to nearby Málaga. Ann was embarrassed by Peter's presence, realizing that Ethel did not believe he was only the tutor.

A few days later, Peter moved back to Carmen's apartment, where friends showed him the *Life* spread on the shooting. Ann Woodward seemed a hell of a lot more interesting. Peter would still have drifted away, but Ann pursued him. She walked into the crowd of young people at his girlfriend's clothing shop, browsing among the embroidered dresses. Peter tried to be kind, but Carmen and the other Spaniards laughed at the way Ann kept smiling at Peter. Ann invited him to ride in her new motorboat in the town's little harbor. He accepted. She drove too fast, as Billy might have, in the placid sea. The boat pitched at a dangerous angle. Peter swore he would never get into a boat with her again.

Peter began to like dallying with Ann in the afternoon. It was a welcome change from his beach existence. She was voluptuous and reminded him of a woman in a Rubens painting. Things did not go smoothly. Ann bought him a ticket to a bullfight in Málaga on August 14, but Carmen had already bought tickets. He smiled at Ann over a sardine lunch in a hotel in nearby Torremolinos. Ann saw the crowd of young people looking her way. She sensed they were tittering about the shooting. She tried to keep her mind on fifteen-year-old Woody, who wanted a camera for his birthday.

Afterwards Peter tried to joke with her about the bullfight. He thought she was slow to get a joke because she was sad. Ann decided to have a housewarming party and bought quarts and quarts of caviar and champagne. But when she found out that Peter was planning to bring his vivacious Spanish girlfriend, she canceled the entire party.

One afternoon while Peter and Carmen were lying in Carmen's bedroom, Ann came by in her Cadillac. "The door's open," said Carmen. "Come on in and have a drink." It was a civilized visit. The three went downstairs to Carmen's shop, where Ann bought a ruffled blouse. She felt silly, but watching Peter smile made it worth the embarrassment.

Two or three days later Peter asked Carmen if she had seen his espadrilles. They were nowhere to be found and were his only pair of shoes. Later that week, after a fight with Carmen, he slept with Ann during the siesta and peeked into her closet, filled with neatly arranged, expensive dresses. There on the floor of her closet were his own brown shoes. Ann said, "Yes, I took them. I want your shoes in my closet. I miss a man's shoes in my closet." She proposed marriage, but Peter did not take her seriously.

One hot afternoon at cocktails, Ann ordered the living room curtains drawn. The maid was too short to reach them, so Peter helped her. Ann thought she saw a glint in Peter's eye, and said, "You only love me for my money. You're not attracted to me." This insult to both of them stunned him. Unlike Billy, he did not like fights. He shouted back, however, and they made love.

Ann and her boys took a quick tour of the south of France with Howard Herrerra. In Cannes, they were on the Boulevard de la Croisette, the main road by the sea, when Ann refused Jimmy's request for ice cream. Jimmy blew up, crying. "Well, how come you won't let me have it when you killed my father?"

Ann could not stop weeping. Jimmy looked stricken.

Herrerra told him, "Now you get down on your knees and apologize to your mother for saying that."

"No, no," said Ann.

Jimmy apologized and bowed a stiff little bow.

When fall came, Ann put the boys on a train to Le Rosey. She packed to go back to Madrid for the winter, asking Peter to join her. He declined her offer. Knowing that he was broke, she offered to pay his expenses. He reminded her that she had on several occasions worried that he just wanted her for her money.

Sadly, Ann returned to Madrid alone, back to her house across from the armory. She bought a book of European titles and set out to learn the best names. She was taking Spanish lessons from her maid. Traveling and sleeping alone brought up memories of Billy; she was still determined to find another man as handsome and aristocratic as he. She would show Elsie Woodward and her crowd.

After another major fight with Carmen, Peter called Ann and moved into the maid's small living room that overlooked a cobbled courtyard with pots of geraniums.

Ann refused to spend the night with him, saying she did not want the maid to know about them. Ann's sleep was interrupted by nightmares.

When Peter left her bed after making love, she put cream on her face, did her Powers stomach exercises, and put on her bra.

During the siesta, Ann would put on a negligee, give Peter long looks, and ask if he loved her. He decided she was dead boring in bed. She was only interested in being loved and felt the sex was proof of that.

Peter went to the Prado afternoons to write. Ann would go to the library reading room looking her best and sit next to him: "Let's go to the cafeteria. Take a break."

"Ssshh," Peter said, and made silly faces at her.

"Come on."

"No, I'm doing my work. I like you very much, Ann. But you must go shopping or get on with your life. I'll see you in the evening."

One night, C. Z. and Winston Guest saw her in Madrid on Peter's arm, and it was not long before an article appeared in the New York *Mirror*, in early December, a few days before Ann's forty-fifth birthday:

"Ann's feeling no pain in Spain. Ann Woodward, the socialite who accidentally shot to death her husband Bill Woodward on Long Island several years ago, is content to live in Spain—primarily because the rain there falls mainly on her and a Spanish lad who is her close and constant companion. This Iberian broth of a boy is no grandee, let's face it, he isn't even a hidalgo. But he makes Ann happy and at the moment, that's what counts."

After Ann received Elsie Woodward's reproachful note about the item, she and Peter began to eat dinners at Ann's apartment. But after four months, Peter left Ann, exhausted by her demands for proof of his love. That summer Ann returned to her villa in Marbella. She chased Peter and saw him sporadically, but in the fall he decided to return to London.

Meanwhile, the Spanish government threatened to confiscate Ann's big black Cadillac unless she paid a heavy fine for parking tickets. Ann decided instead to take the car to Gstaad to be near the boys. She persuaded Peter to come with her. They quarreled on the three-day drive to Switzerland. First, Peter insisted she stop speeding. Then, sixty miles outside Marseilles, Peter discovered he had left his old camel hair coat at a restaurant. He wanted to forget the coat and keep going toward Gstaad.

"No, let's turn back," said Ann. "You love that coat." He refused.

Ann slept with a sleep mask, and Peter noticed she was taking an enormous number of pills. She rarely exposed her body in daylight. She spent an hour making up her face in the bathroom each morning while Peter searched for breakfast. They slept in separate rooms once they got to Alsace. He suspected she was more afraid of being recognized in France.

They stopped one night in Lausanne and then drove up to Gstaad on a winding, snow-covered road. Ann had rented a Swiss chalet a hundred feet from the main street, near the Palace Hotel. It was surrounded by pine trees and overlooked a little valley.

One afternoon, the boys showed up unexpectedly after classes while Ann and Peter were making love. Peter hid under the eiderdown comforter. Ann wept with embarrassment.

Ann took Peter to expensive restaurants because she thought it pleased him. She would pause before they entered a restaurant and take his arm, smiling. She coaxed him out of bed for lunchtime appearances at the Iggle Club by the ski lift, where she fed him croques monsieurs and white sausage.

Peter felt embarrassed by his financial dependence on Ann. The thrill of her celebrity was wearing thin. She was too old, bossy, and she quarreled too often. Finally, he said, "Look, Ann, I must go. Will you drive me to the station?"

"Of course not," she said.

"Will you call me a taxi?"

"No. You don't have the money for train fares."

Peter had hidden his passport and his money, afraid she would take them to keep him there.

"I'm not a prisoner here. I've got to get back," he said.

"No, please," she said. "Wait. I'll go to London with you. We'll have a better time. I'll make sure of it."

She followed him around as he packed his small grip.

"Good-bye," she said, standing outside the door to catch a last glimpse of him. But after a few minutes, she ran to her room to dress, and ran, crying, all the way to the train station. She felt redeemed when he smiled slightly to see her turn up on the platform.

Ann hugged him. "Stay with me."

Other people began arriving after skiing. "Come on, behave," said Peter. He hated the way she made loud scenes in public over him. "Look, I can't take it anymore. I've got my own life, and you've got yours. And I'm not going to traipse all over Europe while you pick up the bills."

A few days later, Peter called, asking noncommittal questions. Ann waited for another call, rushing home from ski lessons and polite lunches on the slopes with passing social Europeans.*

---

*On one such outing, they met Claus Von Bülow, who taught Jimmy how to use the toboggan. In a letter, Von Bülow denied having had an affair with Ann Woodward, although his

She collected the boys on Saturdays at noon. They always ate enormous meals of roast beef and chicken and then went to the ski slopes.

Ann, who became known as a good cook, invited parents of the other pupils to American dinners she cooked herself or to the fashionable Palace Hotel. Her cheer seemed artificial; she made guests uncomfortable.

Ann started calling Peter's mother's house, confiding her desire to marry Peter. Mrs. Townend believed Ann to be one of the poor unfortunates of the earth and finally told her where Peter was living with an old British girlfriend.

Ann pursued Peter to London. She checked into Brown's Hotel and took a cab to his flat, where she invited him and his girlfriend to lunch. "Let's sail down the Amazon," she whispered to Peter. "I'll buy the tickets."

Ann was too famous in London. She was followed by the Fleet Street press. A photograph of Peter appeared in a newspaper, with a quote: "I'm just a good friend of Ann Woodward's." Ann was worried that Elsie would chastise her again. She warned Peter to be more careful because of the "family."

When Ann realized Peter was not interested in the Amazon, she said, "Oh, look, I know the movie director John Huston. Come to Ireland, and we'll show him your novel. Maybe he'll hire you as an assistant director."

"Why the hell not," Peter said.

Ann said, "I'll call you when it's fixed."

She soon wrote Peter a letter telling him to join her in western Ireland at Huston's Georgian manor. A week later Peter's flight was grounded in London for hours because of fog. He was bringing fifty pages of his novel about a young man stranded in the south of France. Peter arrived late in Dublin and missed his train connection. He sat drinking in the Gresham Hotel bar, waiting for the next train.

As the hours passed, Ann told herself sadly that Peter was not coming and did not love her after all. She went to her room, but could not sleep. At midnight, Peter's cab pulled up to the manor house. He had had too much to drink and was exhausted. He saw Huston in the hall with a cast on his leg. "How-de-do," said Peter.

"I'm going off to bed," said Huston. "See you in the morning. Help yourself to sandwiches and wine."

Peter wanted only to sleep. He was shown to the Napoleon Room,

---

friends claim it happened. He wrote, "The only time I was in a horizontal position with a member of the family was when I was skiing on the slopes with little Jimmy."

which had a huge four-poster canopy bed with a giant *N* on it. A bathroom and dressing room connected to Ann's suite. Ann heard him run his bath. Finally, after an hour passed, she rushed into his room in a whirl of a long negligee. She leapt on him, in his bed. "Let's just cuddle," she said.

"I'm too tired," Peter replied.

Fighting exhaustion, Peter tried to make love. But she stood up in a flood of tears, saying, "You don't mean it. You don't love me."

"All right, Ann!" Peter shouted. "For God's sake, let me get some sleep!"

She ran back to her own bedroom.

Peter settled down to sleep, but she returned to his bed again. "Peter, I didn't mean it," she said. Peter was tired of Ann. He had come here only because John Huston was one of his heroes. Ann began kissing him again. He picked up the oversized room key and brandished it. "Oh, Ann, go away. Stop it."

She ducked as he almost slugged her with the key. She wrestled the key from him and thumped him with it. He hit her back. "Peter, please," she said, "let's make love."

Peter said, "Now I see how you could have murdered your husband."

The butler awoke Peter at dawn, asking, "Would you like some tea?"

The butler added, "Mrs. Woodward said you are leaving us. The car will be here in an hour's time." Peter stared around the disheveled bedroom. Bits of paper were scattered on the floor: the fifty pages of his novel torn to shreds. He thanked his lucky stars that he had a copy in London, and he told the butler that he preferred to walk to the train station. He would not see Ann again for twelve years.

By January 1963, Ann was still attempting to make her life a fashionable exile, much like that of the Windsors, giving herself over to high seasons and parties. She traveled relentlessly to find "a man" and to escape "the incident," but the story of her life traveled with her. Since Ann was determined to stay a Woodward, Billy's tastes had become her bible. He had enjoyed visiting beaches and ski slopes around the world.

She felt loved when she was having sex and often imagined marriage to a relative stranger. That would, she thought, solve her problems. She went to bed with men soon after meeting them, behavior that had, after all, captured Billy Woodward's heart. It had little effect on playboys in an era of casual sex. Her affairs were numerous and disorderly.

Her sons gave her a reason to exist. She tried to be a dignified and organized mother. Fifteen-year-old Jimmy was her favorite. Woody was freezing her out. She wrote bitterly to her aunt Lydia that he preferred his grandmother.

Winters, she hovered around Switzerland to be near Woody and Jimmy. Her pattern when she arrived in a new city was always the same. She would check into her hotel and begin telephoning people: "This is Ann Woodward. I have just arrived. How is your family?" She recorded whole families' first names in her many loose-leaf notebooks, each one labeled by city. "I am in town for a week. Is your family?"

Ann's calls were answered with a flurry of invitations to luncheons and dinners. People who entertained her thought of themselves as adventurous.

She skied and watched races at the Cresta Run in St. Moritz. Jimmy was skiing the run, and she was proud of him. In the evenings she gave dancing parties and dinners for which she cooked Southern fried chicken.

That year she also began keeping another careful journal of her thoughts, the boys' school holidays, her land investment ideas, and her social calendar. According to her journal, she spent the first days of 1963 in St. Moritz, lunching at the Corviglia Club with Jimmy and her new Viennese friend, a man named Wigi Piatnik. She also made a note to herself to find out what was the best party season in Vienna.

Now she began to have moments, infrequent though they were, of contentment. She jotted schoolgirl notes to herself in a slanted, orderly hand: "Climbed to the top, looked out over the circle of mountains. I went into the chapel to pray many times over and over during the day. I pray for God's guidance for those I love."

On January 14, she printed in big letters: "JTW birthday, 16 years old." Money always worried her. "Looked at all hotels in Kitzbuhel," she wrote. "Postkurcher most attractive, Fruenhaf the least expensive." She took ski lessons at 9:30 every morning. She had lunch with Prince Ferdinand of Liechtenstein and dinner with Prinz Touy Croy, a member of the Belgian royal family. She was also following the travels of a man named Lars, who would be in Caracas by the seventeenth.

Ann was still suffering from a chest cold at the Hahnenkammrennen ski races on January 19. She was pleased enough with her life again to start pasting programs from the race and her purple ticket into her album. Her schedule included getting her ski pants fitted, having massages, and taking dance lessons. She listed the important people she spoke to on the afternoon she had lunch at the Corviglia Club with Stavros Niarchos. Afterward, she sat with "Baby" Montero, a Brazilian who agreed to help Woody get a place at a Brazilian newspaper, "although eventually," she wrote, "I feel the best future for Woody in Brazil is in industry. I asked his wife and Baby Montero to be Woody's godparents in Brazil. They both said they would."

The journal continued to note the travels of Lars, who was on his way to Rome and then would see her in St. Mortiz.

That summer, Murray Gurfein was sitting on the beach of the Lido off the mainland of Venice with his wife, his daughter, and his grandchildren. Suddenly, he stood up, waving. Ann's arrival was a strange surprise. Mrs. Gurfein, the daughter of a Columbia University scholar, thanked Ann Woodward for her gifts over the years, including a fur lap rug. It turned out Ann was alone, on her way to Sardinia, and also staying at the Danieli. Gurfein invited her to dinner. His family found Ann a bit stiff, but they pitied her.

Ann looked as though she did not belong in the tourist section of the small plane alighting at Lod airport in Tel Aviv. She was wearing a sable coat over a tailored suit. The other travelers wore khaki shorts, T-shirts, and sneakers. After landing, she waved a gloved hand. "Steward."

The Arab flight attendant appeared at her side. "Please give me a hand with this," she said. He walked away. "I need help," said Ann Woodward woefully. The other tourists looked away. It was October 28, 1965, and Ann, at fifty, had developed an organized life on a road to nowhere. That summer her eighteen-year-old son, Jimmy, had written to her in Marbella, "I know you are moving around a lot. I hope you find what you want at the end of it all."

Ann had been glad to leave Morocco, where she had spent three days at the Villa Taylor and had invested several hundred thousand dollars in a mining operation headed by King Hassan's brother. At the airport, she had changed her ticket from Switzerland to Israel. She wanted to pray in the Holy Land.

As she descended the stairway in Tel Aviv holding one suitcase handle under her chin, David Carlson, a twenty-nine-year-old former Mormon minister, reached for her other four bags. Although she had struck him as a pain in the neck when she had spoken to the steward, he always tried to look for the best in people. Ann sat next to him in the packed hotel van heading into Tel Aviv. Accustomed to depending on strangers, she had already made up her mind about Carlson. "What are you doing in Israel?" she asked.

"Nothing in particular. I'm taking a trip around the world," he said, not mentioning his recent and painful divorce. It turned out they had both been raised in the Midwest. He told her he was planning to rent a car and visit Masada and Hagad, a riding stable and ranch in the north. Ann was reading James Michener's book *The Source*, about the Middle East.

She asked, "Can I tour with you for the next week?" He had not reacted at all to her name. She was pleased that he had not heard of her.

Carlson did not want a spoiled, older woman trailing along. "Let me think about it," he said. "I kind of have my own itinerary, and I don't want to be constrained."

Ann pressed him. "I'll do anything that you want me to do. I'll share car expenses. I'll pay my own food and hotel." She explained that her accountant told her that if she stayed out of the United States for another month, she would avoid New York State taxes. She did not mention that there was nothing in New York to go home to.

David Carlson had been on the road for four months and was grateful to speak English again. Ann struck him as someone he might otherwise never have met. The next day he rented a gray Fiat and carried her luggage to the car.

Ann had only one disagreement with Carlson. It took place on the dangerous West Bank. They were working their way toward Jericho and he wanted to take a very narrow, precarious road. Ann thought it was the wrong way, but Carlson pulled rank, saying, "I'm the driver."

The road wound through a desolate, rocky desert landscape and tiny Arab villages. It was exciting, but they were both frightened that they might drive the little car off a cliff. Carlson later decided he had made a mistake taking the road, but for another reason. Three weeks later an Israeli bus carrying soldiers would be blown to bits on it.

To Ann, the week with Carlson was more than a vacation. He seemed to believe she was an entirely different person. A load lifted from her shoulders. She told Carlson that her husband had been a wealthy business-man who had left her a fortune.

Carlson began to talk to Ann more freely than he had talked with anyone in his life. He confided his concern about the effect of his divorce on his two-year-old daughter. Ann did not mention her children, but she did discuss the problems of her love life. Carlson and she talked about whether she should bring a Moroccan man she adored to Switzerland. The man was like a puppy, full of affection. "He makes me feel young," she told a shocked Carlson. "We have great sex. We have sex in the house, we have sex on the patio, we have sex in the car, we have sex on the beach." Ann interrupted herself. "I know I should find a man my own age."

Although Carlson did not condemn Ann, he had never met a woman her age who took such an avid interest in sex. He had no way of knowing that Ann was trying to behave like Billy and his male friends. She did not seem to understand that in a woman this behavior appeared pathetic to most people. David was amazed that a woman over forty would permit the whims of a young sexual partner to affect the course of her life. But he believed that, to Ann, there was something very real and attractive about the Moroccan.

As they drove, Carlson would not book a hotel in advance, but always found one by sunset. After they checked in, he took her luggage to her room. They met at a restaurant the next morning at eight for croissants and coffee. She paid a great deal of attention to her appearance and wore low-heeled shoes, khaki pants, light lipstick and rouge, nail polish, and a scarf at her neck.

On another impulse, Ann followed Carlson to the war-torn city of Nicosia in Cyprus. By now it was clear to Carlson how very lonely she was. They walked for hours in the desolate no-man's-land filled with barricades and barbed wire.

They cried when they said good-bye. Ann had not made a sexual overture toward him. He kept a list of his gasoline expenses, and at the end of the trip Ann paid $130 for car and gas. Ann saved Carlson's postcards, which came every five days for the next several months.

24

ELSIE WOODWARD TRIUMPHANT

I n New York, Elsie, at eighty-three, was now the reigning Mrs. William Woodward. Her triplet sisters were both dead. Six years earlier, however, in 1959, she had hired the genial public relations man Drew Dudley to help her create a salon of people who did interesting things. He had invited Joan Fontaine and the Shah of Iran to parties at the Waldorf that—at first—had a stiff quality.

Famous guests flocked to the yellow drawing room to meet the grande dame from the Gilded Age who had covered up a murder. She was declared the bravest and most wrinkled woman anyone had ever seen by Norman Mailer, Dinah Shore, Gore Vidal, Bill Blass, and Kenneth Jay Lane, the jewelry designer.

She whirled around New York wearing bright Pucci gowns and big fake jewelry. Ironically, her life was becoming similar to the one her daughter-in-law had led. Elsie's Sunday soirees in her large Waldorf Towers apartment started at five in the afternoon and included nearly everybody from the worlds of politics and the lively arts. The Windsors met Andy Warhol, who sent Elsie yellow roses every Christmas, and Adlai Stevenson met Joan Fontaine. Rosalind Russell played the piano and sang. Elsie read her guests' palms and never let the conversation get gloomy. "I believe money is more important than good health, don't you?" Elsie liked to ask over the soup course.

To Arlene Francis, Kenneth Lane, and Bill Blass, she complained, "I'm tired of stuffy people." When Merle Oberon married a very young man, Elsie pointedly made no judgments. She accepted movie people if they "had table manners and did not hit children in public."

The shooting was on all her guests' minds. One evening, Elaine Lorillard admonished her husband, Pierre, "Whatever you do, don't mention guns."

Elsie said to them, "Oh, I admire so much what you did in Newport with the Jazz Festival." Elaine gasped as her husband said, "But our neighbors nearly shot us for it."

As she had when she was younger, Elsie preferred big names and great conversation to family members. She ignored her grandson Woody and a friend of his who stopped in for lunch when Gore Vidal was dining with her. Kenneth Lane simply called her "a starfucker."

After a trip to California in 1966, at the age of eighty-five, Elsie struck up a friendship with Frank Sinatra, and they flirted on the telephone. He sent her weekly flowers and what she called "love notes." He seemed fascinated by her Edwardian manner and her mythic role in covering up Billy's murder. Elsie hid his letters among her underwear. "Let my daughter Libby find them after I'm gone and suspect the worst," she told a friend.

In 1973, Elsie Woodward invited Gore Vidal to lunch at La Grenouille. Vidal appreciated Elsie's spirit, which he believed was like that of an Englishwoman of her generation. She chided him for *Myron*, a camp sequel to his novel *Myra Breckenridge:* "You've gone too far." As they were leaving, she told him, "Today is my ninetieth birthday, and there's going to be a party tonight which I dread. Thank you. I wanted to have lunch with somebody who did not know it was my birthday."

Seated with author Norman Mailer, who was drinking heavily, she scolded him for his intemperance. "It's water, madam," he said finally. "Don't be silly," she said, sipping it.

At her dinners for thirty at Le Madrigal, she toasted Bill Blass by reminiscing that she used to toast dukes and earls. She also said she had no money before she married her husband. Few believed her.

At the age of eighty-six, she danced by Kenneth Jay Lane at a party and said, "Kenneth, I can't keep your rhinestone earrings on. They're too heavy." "Elsie, they're too big for you and you're too old and too rich to be wearing them." "Nonsense." The next time they met she was wearing another pair of his enormous rhinestone earrings. "Elsie, I thought they were too heavy." "My dear, I have found the solution," she told him. "Spirit gum" (false hair glue).

One night before a party, she fell. Instead of missing the fun, she went to the ladies' room and calmly applied makeup to the long gash on her forehead. She became infatuated with a six-feet-four-inches-tall, very handsome, ginger-haired former Irish guardsman, a society journalist named

Herschel Williams, a friend of Elsie Woodward's, with Ann at the April in Paris
ball, 1959.

The two Woodward boys, Jimmy (foreground) and Woody, with Ann and Elsie, about to embark on the *Queen Elizabeth*, April 1, 1958.

The two Mrs. Woodwards, 1958.

Elsie Woodward at El Morocco.

Patrick O'Higgins with Helena Rubinstein. O'Higgins grew up in Paris and served in the Irish Guard. He came to America after attending Le Rosey, was a society writer for *Town & Country*, and went to work for Madame Rubinstein as her personal secretary. He became close friends with Elsie Woodward and traveled with her to Paris, Morocco, and Cap d'Antibes.

Patrick O'Higgins. O'Higgins had been the paid companion of Helena Rubinstein, founder of the cosmetics firm. He had suffered torment at her hands and a *crise de nerfs* in Paris, but he survived to write *Madame*, a lively book describing Rubinstein as a woman of greed and base style. Patrick's principal problem in life was his lack of funds. Elsie began paying some of his bills, but he still had to work at *Town & Country* magazine for a living.

Whenever Patrick called, Elsie ran to the phone and was soon in peals of laughter like a young girl. Elsie had the time of her life attending parties with Patrick, whose father had been a merchant in China like Duncan Cryder. She liked to flirt and sit close to him on a loveseat. It was done in good humor and with great style.

Patrick spoke like a person in a drawing room comedy. Educated at Le Rosey, he wore fitted hacking jackets, had a fine calligraphic handwriting, and his friends adored him. When *Town & Country* researched a story on a European city, he would prepare a memorandum on who was of social importance.

Patrick was the one exception to Elsie's dislike of people without money. When a nurse told her she was going to Morocco on an American Express tour, Elsie said, "Oh, dear, you'll meet all those awful people." "Does that mean only rich people should go abroad?" "Oh, yes, I suspect so," said Elsie.

But Patrick compensated brilliantly for his lack of funds. Elsie's beloved young companion was eager to please: he wore lemon cologne so he would not clash with Elsie's perfume. He also dined out on fantastical stories of Billy's murder. He told appreciative dinner guests who believed they were in the presence of "history" that his friend Elsie had signed $400,000 worth of blank checks and distributed them to the local Oyster Bay Cove police and politicians.

Elsie invited Patrick to travel with her. She would pay the bills. "South America? China? Africa?" he asked. "Africa," she said.

Elsie and Patrick planned their trip to Marrakech over Elsie's silver tea service. "Perhaps I can defray costs by writing a little sally about the trip for *Town and Country*," said Patrick. "Rather a good idea," said Elsie, pleased to save the expense of tickets.

Elsie believed Patrick to be a person of style, but she would also approve the article before it was submitted. Elsie had changed her view of publicity. She had lived the first eight decades of her life by the nineteenth-century gentlewoman's rule "A lady's name appears in the newspapers three times: when she is born, when she marries, and when she dies." But it was now the middle of the twentieth century, and Elsie liked being a star; she sent flattering little thank-you notes to society columnist Aileen Mehle, who wrote about her in "Suzy."

On the day of their departure, Elsie picked up Patrick O'Higgins ten minutes early in her Rolls. The trip was an example of Elsie's spirit. She ignored dizzy spells and constipation and went off with Patrick. Elsie was thin and now carried a mallaca cane. She dressed in a crisp new Givenchy raincoat with lots of pockets, a set of Kenneth Lane's fake heirloom pearls under a Lanvin scarf, and one of four pairs of slacks that she had brought. When she told Patrick the cane was for support, he teased her: "Rubbish, it's a divining rod. You'll be striking oil with it." She smiled. "Perhaps."

Boarding the airplane to Casablanca, Elsie informed Patrick that they would be sitting separately. He did not question her. Later, she explained why he must never see her sleeping: "What would be left for us to share?"

The airplane from Casablanca to Marrakech was old and the flight bumpy—and just above the tops of palm trees. Elsie liked their taxi driver, a pleasant man in a huge burnoose: "He has nice hands. Capable. We'll get there on time." She was right.

The moment she checked in, Elsie ordered a massage and a pedicure. Her maid, Pauline, removed the hotel sheets and towels and made up the bed with Elsie's own ironed and monogrammed linen. In Morocco, sitting by the hotel swimming pool, Elsie lost her appetite. "I don't think naked flesh and shrimp cocktail go together," she said tartly to Patrick, "particularly if followed by rare roast beef."

"You should try eating sheep's eyes," said Patrick. "I hate crunchy food," said Elsie Woodward.

"*C'est la reine de New York*," whispered one restaurant owner after seating them. A procession of international society figures came by and kissed Elsie's hand, a ritual she adored. Elsie delighted Patrick with her flawless French enhanced by a nineteenth-century lilt. She wrote down names of trees, flowers, people encountered, and places visited.

She and Patrick dined in the massive Art Deco dining room of the Villa Taylor, a residence converted into an exclusive hotel. Paying respects to Elsie at dinner were Sean Connery and John Huston, who were filming *The Man Who Would Be King*. Elsie captivated Connery by flirtatiously reading his palm and declaring him strong and independent. (Huston had the discretion not to mention to Elsie that he had hosted the tempestuous reunion between Ann Woodward and the English writer Peter Townend.)

When they returned to America, Patrick wrote about the trip as a sparkling romantic tale.

*   *   *

In the fall of 1963, Elsie had invited her daughter-in-law to a large dinner party. "Ann's materialized," Elsie sighed to only a few guests. Ann had just returned home for a visit after a bird-shooting party near Madrid. The day before Elsie's party, President Kennedy was assassinated. Elsie loved the Kennedys, referring to them as "our royal family." When she called her friend Eleanor Lambert, asking whether to cancel the party, Eleanor advised the great hostess to carry on. Out of the seventy-five invited guests, seventy-three came.

The guests stared at Ann, who said nothing as they discussed how an assassin could have shot Kennedy in a moving car. "Well, have you ever shot at a moving target?" Ann asked. No one could believe she had asked such a question. There was a startled hush. "Well, I have," Ann said, aware of the shock she had created. "It's a lot easier than you think."

Not long after Elsie's party, Ann was on a gondola in Venice. She had wandered into an open-air nightclub and had been invited along for the ride. She came to life talking alone with a titled Italian at one end of the boat. His wife appeared and said in a loud voice, "It's one thing to flirt, darling, but must you flirt with a murderess?"

25

A DEATH IN THE FAMILY

I n the summer of 1964 Ann wrote Jimmy letters from Sardinia begging
him to visit her. She was spending a few weeks in the Aga Khan's
new resort. Her house was a replica of a local shepherd's cottage,
above a small rocky cove. Ann had come to see her life as "a disaster a
minute," as she told friends, and she now drank wine to wash down
antidepressants and sleeping pills. Ann had believed that Sardinia held the
promise of a fresh start. That implied a romance—and the turmoil she had
with Billy. But no home could provide roots. It was only when Ann was
falling in love that she felt less at loose ends. It took a man's desire for her
to make her feel beautiful.

Although she had just made a substantial down payment on her cottage, she was already in conflict about whether she should build a bigger
house. Jimmy urged her to stop worrying about her investments and to
try to enjoy her life. He arrived in Sardinia on a summer break from
Le Rosey. Ann had painted the walls of the cottage with a pale green
wash to give them the patina of age. Jimmy opened the green shutters to
inhale the fragrant maquis: shrub grass of juniper, wild sunroses, heather,
myrtle, and rosemary that grew on the sandy patches between windswept
rocks.

During the previous summer Ann had come home to the Playhouse
crying after having been to Piping Rock on her own, so Jimmy volunteered
to be her "escort." The two made a dignified couple on the golf course.
To avoid snubs, they drove right up to the first hole in Ann's black Triumph. First, Jimmy would take a lesson with the club pro while Ann sat
near him on a small blanket, reading a book. Afterward, they walked

quickly back to the car, Jimmy urging Ann to hold her chin up, despite staring members.

With his clumpy blond hair and powerful shoulders, Jimmy looked like the Crowell side of the family. He had Ann's seductive charm and a thin Woodward mouth. There were a lot of fights at Le Rosey, but Jimmy, big for his age, dominated the other kids in fistfights.

Jimmy was still *moyens*, middle school, in the ninth grade, and lived in a long narrow room with two beds against the wall. A fat Frenchwoman named Mademoiselle Finche monitored the "lights out." Her boyfriend, Herr Poison, who was head of athletics, would sometimes sneak in and spend the night in her room. Jimmy seemed to get a little crazy at these times. For example, one night when Poison reached to turn out Jimmy's light, Jimmy lunged at him. "Don't you touch my light," shouted Jimmy. "I'm not taking any shit from you."

He pushed Poison and then started throwing punches. The other boys gathered around in their pajamas to watch as Jimmy, who did a lot of boxing in the gym, held his own. The fight ended when Poison retreated.

Jimmy roomed with Jay Sicre and Egon von Furstenberg, the German count (whose future wife, Diane, would become a fashion designer). Another roommate was Paul Porhino, an introverted half-black Venezuelan. Many, including Ann, believed Jimmy and Paul were lovers. Elsie was confused about Paul because of his race and said, "Jimmy is having an affair with his butler." Together, Paul and Jimmy were obsessed with going to Vietnam. "The battlefield is good because it is the most democratic place on earth," Jimmy said, defying his grandmother's belief in the innate superiority of the Woodward family. "Fighting to the death makes everybody equal."

It was in Switzerland that Jimmy met Dana Osborne, a beautiful American girl from Center Island in Oyster Bay. After graduation, Dana became the "prettiest" model for Chanel in Paris, and she would leave her husband, Count François de Nerciat, to be with Jimmy until his death.

In Sardinia, Jimmy walked barefoot across the terrace and down a sandy hill to the beach. He would suck a blood orange and stare at the treacherous Strait of Bonifacio and the distant hills of Corsica on the horizon. Jimmy thought that Ann's Costa Smeralda view matched her personality. The strait could be calm and beckoning one minute, but the next, the skies and sea could darken to black and a storm would dash ships into what was called "the ship's graveyard."

During the afternoons, Jimmy and Ann sat on the beach in front of the Pitrizza Hotel and Ann's villa. The Pitrizza Hotel had bright flowers cascading from the roof and attracted guests such as Princess Margaret and Princess Alexandra of Kent. The hotel was on a protected little bay of its own. The nearby roads were left unpaved to discourage tourists.

One night Ann and Jimmy went to an early emeralds and blue jeans party given by her neighbor Count Henri de Beaumont. At the party, Ann greeted another neighbor, the middle-aged Bettina Grazziani, who was with a young lover. Bettina, a former Dior model, had been the longtime mistress of Ann's brief flame, Aly Khan. Bettina's property in Sardinia had been a gift from Aly's son. Ann and Bettina were still rivals. When Bettina bought a local fishing boat (a Gozza) with an outboard motor, Ann bought one, too.

Ann and Jimmy would stroll out for a late dinner at a bar named Pedro's, which was crowded with Italian tourists. Bright crepe-paper flowers were stuck in bamboo fishermen's traps. Ann would look around for her current flame, a big, handsome dark-skinned Sard boy of twenty-two named Flavio, who dreamed of a career as an actor. She adored him, even wondering aloud—smiling—if she could marry him. He, too, reminded her of Billy. It did not matter to her that Flavio was homosexual.

Ann lent Flavio her new red Alfa Romeo convertible and paid him 2,000 lire a week (about six dollars) to run errands for her. He would drive hundreds of miles over the sandy countryside. One night at Pedro's bar with Jimmy, Ann spotted Flavio dancing with Count Kasimir, a Pole, on the terrace. Ann walked out and asked Flavio to dance with her. "No," said the count, continuing to dance.

"*Sono Flavio,*" shouted the proud Flavio, flattered by the battle. Everybody in the restaurant smiled at the sound of his voice. He tossed back his long black hair. "Dance with me," said Ann, smiling. "Bitch," shouted the Pole at Ann. He pulled Flavio's arm.

Inside the bar, Jimmy cringed. Kasimir's voice had carried. Ann pulled Flavio's other arm. Disentangling himself, Flavio jumped up on a small tile table, his arms outstretched to the night sky. "Murderess," shouted the Pole.

"I can't take this," Jimmy said as Ann walked back inside. No one in the restaurant spoke.

Jimmy did kitchen chores at Pedro's bar with the owner Peter Kent's children. He seemed to court danger, once forcing the owner's son Travis to drive at ninety miles an hour to the edge of a road overlooking a drop.

One night, Jimmy appeared at a neighbor's and asked if he could spend the night, adding that his mother had taken his passport. The next morning, Ann stormed to her neighbor's house, accusing the woman of sleeping with Jimmy and looking for proof. An hour later Jimmy told the neighbor, smiling, "I got my passport back. I'm leaving now." That night Ann appeared at Pedro's with a black eye. "That's how he got his passport," said the neighbor.

It was during this tempestuous summer that Jimmy resolved to fight in Vietnam. In a letter to his mother from New York, he tried to explain his decision, saying just that his life seemed very different from their time on the Costa Smeralda. He would soon go into the army, although the Woodwards objected, "and everybody is screaming. I suppose you don't like the idea either, but then you also know that life just is not working out for me the way it should."

He told Ann to stop worrying about Elsie Woodward's influence over him. "I'm staying independent like always." He inquired after her life in Sardinia. "I hope the situation with Flavio is coming along alright for you and that you are getting some amount of happiness out of your life there."

He concluded by telling her, "Keep your chin up Mom, and if there are any problems etc. which I can help you with or advise you on write me. Love, Jimmy."

No one in Jimmy's family understood why he joined the army. Elsie was horrified: her friends' grandchildren easily avoided the war in Vietnam. She ordered Jimmy's aunt Libby to take him out to lunch at the Colony Club to talk him out of it. Jimmy's trust fund provided more money each month than he ever needed. He gave a drug dealer named Johnny Moonshine $100,000 to buy a house. He kept money in paper bags in his closets and urged guests to take it. One night at dinner at the Palace Hotel in Switzerland, he lit a cigar with a hundred-franc note. "It doesn't matter," he said. "It's just money."

He and his best friend, Paul Porhino, hoped the war would make them heroes. Jimmy was ashamed of the side of his nature that was like his mother's, sensitive and easily hurt. He was bisexual, and sought to prove his manhood. And killing was an important part of his fantasy life. He often dreamed of his dying, bleeding father.

26

BLACKMAIL

At Clinton Correctional Facility in Dannemora, New York, inmate Paul Wirths fantasized for six years about Ann Woodward. She was bound to send him money. He spent his time learning boxing and the saxophone from a fellow prisoner. In 1961, Wirths was deported back home to Föhr Island.

The North Sea winds were bitter cold on February 3, 1964, as Wirths sat down to a late dinner. His infant daughter, Rautrout, cried under her blankets in a chilly bedroom near the kitchen. Wirths lived with his wife, Hannelore, and child in a crumbling brick farmhouse with a full second-floor hayloft. They had seven small bedrooms and no indoor bathroom. The house had been built by a sea captain in 1810.

Wirths drank three Flensburger beers. He was in the middle of his seven-day, sixteen-hour-a-day workweek. He worked outdoors at the rate of twenty-five cents an hour and had no time to play the blues on his saxophone. He and his wife worried about losing their farmhouse. They had moved in before the financing was settled. "Call the bank manager," said his wife, "and make him give us a mortgage." Wirths shook his head. "No good."

Perhaps the bank manager had decided Wirths was a bad risk because he had been in jail. Wirths had heard the local island talk. Some still thought it was he who had killed Billy. "Forget the rich woman in America," said Hannelore, clearing the table. "She will only put you back in jail."

"Leave me alone," he said.

Wirths began to write the date on a blank aerogram. "You wrote bad letters to her before, and you received nothing," said Hannelore.

"I know what I'm doing," said Wirths. His only hope was Ann Woodward. She was his secret love and had made him famous. Nobody else on Föhr had ever had his picture in so many newspapers. He would make her pay him big money.

"Aaach." Wirths threw the pen on the floor. Outside, the snow was thickening on the pine trees surrounding the farmhouse. "When we lose this house, tell me, where do we go?" Wirths asked, his forehead in his hands.

Wirths addressed the envelope: "An [*sic*] Woodward Oyster Bay Long Island New York, N.Y." He was too proud to use a dictionary; the English he had learned in jail would be good enough.

Feb. 3, 1964

Dear Ann,

At this time I would like to write you this letter and hope for the best of everything. I will come in right to the point. I like for asc you some moeny. I would like you to borrow me 10,000 dollar from you. I don't ecspect to give it to me for nothing. . . . For you should be 10,000 D. so much as for me 1 cent. . . . Since I have done you the biggest favor of your life, I think you could help me get a new start in life. . . . I hope to God you don't make a bigger mistake by not answering me.

Till then,

Very yours truly.
Paul Wirths

He told himself that he was put in prison for six years for "borrowing" cars, and sandwiches and soup. Ann Woodward had shot her husband and had left the Mineola Courthouse a free woman. Three weeks passed, and each day he checked the mail. If she sent him the money, he would drink beer and play the saxophone at parties and never work again.

His next letter was more threatening:

. . . Now since I have done you a big very big favor, I think you could let me have the 10,000 to get a new start in life. . . . Hir has also bem a book writer, he wants me to tell my whole story ron wat has happened. The money is the same amount and I don't even have to pay him back. But I would rather

borrow it ron you. So tot the publik don't have to now everything. . . . Please answer me right away.

> Very thruly yours.
> Paul

"I am a damn good liar," said Wirths when he finished the letter.
He had invented the book writer; it was a clever story. Every morning for
weeks, his first thought was of the money she would send him.

In late February 1964, Ann brought Paul Wirths's first letters to Murray
Gurfein in his office overlooking Park Avenue and Sixtieth Street. He
advised her to ignore them: "Don't worry. There's no book writer. You
would have heard from him by now, too."

But Gurfein's words did not give Ann peace of mind. She woke up
at night with visions of new trials. When the neat little notes with the big
spaces between each line had arrived, she would crawl into bed, her chest
wracked with pain. After many tests, the cardiologist dismissed the pains
as anxiety attacks. Ann had read that there was no statute of limitations
on murder and feared that her case could be reopened at any time—if new
evidence were to come to light.

"No, Ann," said Murray Gurfein, "Paul Wirths will not be able to
get you in trouble. He cannot say 'I saw her pull the trigger,' now, can
he? It will not happen. Be strong. Go to church. Take a trip. Don't torture
yourself. Ignore him."

"I can't sleep," said Ann. "It will never go away, will it?"

"Paul Wirths is breaking the law, Ann," said Gurfein, adding, "Don't
send him money."

Ann called Bill Sudduth, who now had his own travel business. "I want
to go away," she said. "Where to, Ann?" he asked.

Ann made plans to go to Paris. But at the airport, she changed her
mind. She called Sudduth back, weeping: "I want to go to Marbella now."
But instead she decided to return to the Playhouse and try to sell it. She
hated rattling around in its dusty rooms. The glass roof of the tennis court
had open cracks. Snowdrifts had eaten holes in the floor, where dead star-
lings rotted. She usually had to cancel her dinner parties there because

guests were "busy." At the last one, the women had seemed appalled by the Chanel No. 5 she'd sprinkled on the light bulbs.

She slept upstairs in the small bedroom, using the roof as a terrace. She spent her days on the roof, sunbathing nude on a padded white wrought iron reclining chair. Her secretary, Marie Byrd, did not know where to look as Ann sat, naked, dictating her letters. They would eat lunch from separate trays overlooking Ann's hedges and rose gardens. Ann had made one change in the house: she had had the door to Billy's small bedroom closed up. A nearby closet was made into an entrance door. Thus, the hallway was no longer a direct passageway between the two bedrooms.

Coco Chanel came to lunch in Manhattan, curious to meet the rich American woman who had gotten away with murder.

When Ann Woodward's expensive emerald engagement ring did not suit Chanel, Ann disappeared to bring another piece for Chanel's approval. Chanel's philosophy was that fake jewelry was better; she designed and sold it. She was fond of proclaiming, "Jewelry is not meant to make you look rich but to adorn you, and that's not the same thing at all."

At the sight of Ann's opal-and-diamond necklace, Chanel said, in French, "It's not a particularly good example of anything." Ann stubbornly brought out six or seven pieces, all gifts from Billy. Chanel dismissed each of them.

Ann told Marie Byrd, who had a business school background, to familiarize Woody with his trust funds, his hundreds and hundreds of stocks and bonds; in a year, he would be twenty-one. The money would no longer be at Ann's disposal. As they went over the accounts, Woody noticed that Ann had bought fur coats on three consecutive Christmases and charged them to her sons' estates. They were called "Christmas and birthday gifts from Woody and Jimmy." "I didn't know about that," said Woody.

One night Jimmy invited a friend named Larry Kaiser to dinner. Eating roast chicken and salad on the terrace, Ann announced, "The cost of our guest's food will be divided among us three ways."

In November 1966, just before he shipped out to Vietnam, Jimmy wrote his mother a polite letter from Fort Gordon, Georgia, where he would be training for the next eight weeks. He said that he'd been marching and shining boots. After writing that he would be home for Christmas, Jimmy warned her that his hair was shaved off, "and I look pretty funny. I'll be that way at Christmas too." He requested that she send him one hundred dollars in cash. He concluded that he had a new uniform to wear back home, "very well tailored indeed. You'll like it—it's good looking as *hell* [underlined]. Only thing wrong is that my head will be shaven. Love from Private Jimmy, Co. B. 5th Tng. Bn., 2nd Tng, Brd. USATC, Fort Gordon Georgia 30905"

From Vietnam, Jimmy wrote asking his brother Woody for books on the people of South America because he was thinking of starting his "own little empire," making himself a sort of "grand padrone." He confided that this was his current dream "instead of becoming a junior president of this or that company. But I don't like to think I was cut out for that kind of shit—wife and kids in Southhampton [*sic*], cocktails with Suzy Knicker-bocker 'divine' etc. etc." He also wrote to his friends explaining that on guard patrol, he carried broken and bleeding bodies off the battlefield.

But in Vietnam, Jimmy was not able to escape himself. When his best friend Paul Porhino was killed, Jimmy snapped. He wrote letters to Ann from Saigon asking how she had dared to murder his father in cold blood. He called her a "bitch."

In New York, Ann collected Jimmy's airmail letters in her night-table drawer next to her bottles of antidepressants. One evening she sat on the rug in front of the fireplace, her skirt spread around her in a graceful circle, and showed them to Bill Sudduth.

Sudduth told her, "These letters are not from your son's heart. They are from a troubled mind. It is better to burn them so they do not haunt him when he recovers." Ann drew aside the fireplace grate, and she and Sudduth tossed in the letters one by one.

When Jimmy returned to New York in the early 1970s, Ann was in Marbella. Jimmy raved to friends about killing himself and his mother. He was sent to a private psychiatric hospital in upstate New York called Bloomingdale's. But even inside the hospital, Jimmy was buying cocaine and heroin and giving away handfuls of cash. Ann returned from Spain and drove up to visit him. Jimmy pointed a trembling hand at his mother and shouted, "Why did you shoot my father? Leave me in peace." Sobbing, she ran outside to the parking lot.

In February 1970, Ann escaped to Gstaad, but was laid up for a month with bronchitis. She flew to Paris for Easter, spending hours at the Cathedral of Notre Dame and strolling to afternoon movies and to the Louvre with a Russian friend, Princess Adelaide Scherbatow. Late one afternoon, Ann sat in her room at the Bristol on the Rue du Faubourg St.-Honoré and wrote sympathy letters about the death of Jack Pratt to Libby Pratt and Tommy Bancroft as well as to her mother-in-law.

To Elsie Woodward she wrote, in her never-ending effort at courtship:

> Pâques, 1970
> Paris March 29.
>
> Dear Ma,
>
> Today is Easter, and I think of you and all of the family which I miss very much. So sad about Jack Pratt's death and Tom Bancroft Sr.

Ann then described a lunch with her sister-in-law Ethel, and asked Elsie to write and tell her the latest news.

Jimmy was more difficult. Out of the hospital and still delusional, he seemed to hate her. She tried several versions of the letter she sent to him, but she had little strength to address his accusations.

> Pâques, 1970
> Paris March 29.
>
> Dear Jim,
>
> I had started another letter to you, but now it is out of date. I have been to church nearly all day at the Cathedral of Notre-Dame. I prayed for you, your happiness and your success. I want only the best always—

She suggested he mount his safari trophies on the dining-room walls above his army uniform. Ann drew a little diagram labeled "trophy, wood, metal plaque Uganda nineteen—James Woodward."

> . . . Perhaps you could [also] get copies of your cups etc. from Le Rosey days, racing cups of Grandpa's—and some photographs of you and Woody giving the Woodward cup.
>
> MAYBE a photo of ME [underlined]. I would like that.

Ann then wrote to Woody warning him against being "taken over" by New York, meaning his grandmother. Ann's handwriting slanted in all directions as she told Woody she had gotten him a job on the most interesting newspaper in Portugal. "You speak perfect Portuguese," she wrote. Elsie had used her friendship with Dorothy Schiff to get Woody a job on the New York *Post,* and he would soon go to Vietnam too, as a reporter for that newspaper.

Ann continued, "Somehow I feel you have let other people influence you too much. Get away, think things over *alone* [underlined three times] then proceed forward. I LOVE YOU VERY MUCH MOTHER [underlined two times]"

By 1972, Jimmy was living in New York in an expensive cooperative apartment on Fifth Avenue and taking recreational drugs as well as medication for paranoia. He furnished his apartment with steel Italian furniture and had the windowpanes painted black. His mother suspected he was having affairs with men and that a former classmate from Le Rosey was taking him to bisexual orgies. She took Betty Sicre out to lunch and asked, "What are we going to do with our homosexual sons?" Betty's jaw dropped open: none of her four sons was homosexual.

Ann was frantic about Jimmy's wild spending. He would withdraw $25,000 from his bank account in cash, buy drugs, and hand money out to casual friends. Jimmy was bending the handles of nineteenth-century silver spoons from Belair to heat up heroin. Ann wrote distraught notes to herself about not wishing to stigmatize him further by having him committed to a psychiatric hospital.

Ann also made notes of lines to use when speaking to her mother-in-law: "I have no illusions about your grandson." After a shouting match over Jimmy, Elsie refused to take Ann's calls. Elsie did not want to impose limits on Jimmy and tried to deny his illness.

Afraid to be alone, Jimmy often stayed with friends at a four-story brick town house on Carmine Street in Greenwich Village. His doctors thought Jimmy's condition stemmed from childhood trauma, the stress of drugs, and Vietnam. Not true, said Elsie. She declared that Jimmy's problems dated only from Vietnam.

Jimmy began to hallucinate that people on television were spying on him. One night in late 1972, he rushed over to his friend Jacques Gelardin's apartment above the Venezuelan embassy. He said he was afraid to be alone with the eleven o'clock news. While watching the news with Jacques, Jimmy took off all his clothes and talked wildly about his sexual fantasies about men. He ran to the open window and, naked, jumped out. He ricocheted off a ledge, hit an awning, and landed in the street. He broke at least ten bones, but survived. Elsie had her own view of the episode. "Jimmy was very brave," she told friends. "He jumped from four stories."

At New York Hospital's Payne Whitney Psychiatric Clinic, Jimmy was treated for mental and physical problems. He had long casts on his arms and legs. He received electroshock therapy and continued to use heroin.

In Spain, when Ann learned of Jimmy's jump, she believed it was part of her continued punishment for the shooting. She told acquaintances all over the world that Jimmy would never be right again.

Shortly after his first suicide attempt, Jimmy began to see the woman who calls herself Xaviera Hollander, the author of the "Happy Hooker" books. Still in casts, Jimmy brought Xaviera and some of her girls down to the Carmine Street crash pad for parties best remembered for young women running around in their underpants.

In Hollander's book *Xaviera: Her Continuing Adventures* there is a chapter entitled "Jimmy, Don't Jump Again." The author writes that of all the men she'd met in the past year, only a few had elicited her sympathy, "and perhaps the most remarkable of all was Jimmy."

Jimmy told friends, "The stories the bitch wrote about me are true." Xaviera claimed she was given Jimmy's number by an Italian count named Fabrizio. According to her account, Xaviera first saw "Jimmy" in his posh apartment soon after his suicide attempt. He had lost sixty pounds: "He most resembled a walking skeleton hanging in between two wooden crutches . . . He had shoulder-length blonde hair and haunting blue eyes, kind of sad and melancholic, yet something wild and cynical, perhaps, there as well."

Later, Jimmy apparently told her he was the victim of too much breeding: "Well, it's a long boring story, but here goes. . . . I'm twenty-six and I've lived an absolutely worthless life. I was born with a silver spoon in my mouth—you know the expression—because my granddaddy was the founder of a large banking and trust company here in the city. I never have to lift a finger to take care of my material needs. It's all there, all the loot I'll ever need for the rest of my life."

Jimmy sounded his theme about ambitious girls who had nothing on their minds except weekends in Southampton, evenings at Le Club and Raffles and P. J. Clarke's, and black-tie dinner parties: "The eternal small-talk, the eternal drivel—all the bullshit and intrigue and behind their small minds, one thought: to get the right catch and live at the right address and then to buy the right house in the right suburb—

"Look I have no right to complain . . . but you've got to be pretty stupid not to know when you're leading a meaningless existence, that there's a real world out there and you've got no part in it." That was why he went to Vietnam.

Xaviera waxes philosophical about Jimmy's disappearances from her life: "Jimmy's world had no timetable. You saw him when you saw him."

After his release from the hospital, Jimmy decided to be a carpenter. Two blocks east of the Carmine Street house, he rented an industrial loft and slept in a bare, windowless room in the back. He crafted miniature coffins to serve as cigarette boxes, and gave them as gifts to his grandmother, his mother, and his friends on Carmine Street. One Le Rosey classmate who was studying to be a psychiatrist at the time was worried about Jimmy, telling Woody, "The coffins are an obvious cry for help." The friend, Dr. Brian Muldoon, suggested it had started with Jimmy's tempestuous family life. "He always seemed perfectly fine to me," said Woody.

In Marbella in 1973, Ann suddenly spent $250,000 for three apartments in a new beachfront development called "The Oasis." No longer a tiny fishing village, Marbella had seen its land increase 5,000 times in value since she first rented the villa La Maryana.

Her main apartment was a magnificent glass-walled penthouse with views of open sky and the Mediterranean. But every afternoon, the scorching sun heated the apartment to 100 degrees, and Ann was told to install expensive air conditioning.

For lunch, she would ask her part-time secretary, a local girl, to buy a cooked chicken leg and leave it out on the kitchen table. Ann was still a lovely woman, groomed and dressed in the rich American manner with good designer clothing. When she met a man, she radiated charm. She soon began pushing him away, however, by fighting and making demands.

Upon arriving in Marbella, she still dialed scores of people listed in her "Marbella" book, but they were beginning to instruct their servants to tell her they were not at home. Ann was too strange. Her small talk was interrupted by abrupt complaints. The napkin did not match the tablecloth. The butter was melting. She knew Elsie Woodward would not approve. In restaurants, she further embarrassed acquaintances by counting pennies.

Ann's boyfriends were becoming increasingly less suitable. Her latest escort in Marbella was an Englishman, a former boxer who had been convicted of burglary. He was a tough character and as young as Woody. She took a Hungarian garage mechanic with her to visit her sister-in-law Ethel de Croisset in nearby Málaga. She seemed to ignore the difficulty these escorts presented to incredulous hostesses.

In the summer of 1974, Ann was in Paris for a month. At three every afternoon, she went to the couturier collections with Princess Adelaide Scherbatow, a woman who seemed determined to heal the wounded people she met. The Princess lived in a small apartment in the same mansion as Bobo Rockefeller (who had married Winthrop Rockefeller) opposite the palace of the President of France. Ann stayed at the Bristol two blocks away.

One day, Princess Scherbatow accompanied Ann to Givenchy to help with the fittings of a floor-length dress. She had once worked at Chanel, and Ann questioned her on every detail.

At about one-thirty that night, Ann was wide awake, weeping. Another letter had arrived from Paul Wirths. She swallowed more sleeping pills, noting them in her journal. She believed she was going to lose all her money, some $1.5 million, in a matter of two or three years and be put out of her New York apartment by her sons' attorneys.

Frightened, she put a coat on over her nightgown and tied a red Hermès scarf over her head. Then she fled into the Rue du Faubourg St.-Honoré, past the British embassy, to Princess Scherbatow's home. Ann said, "I cannot be alone. Just let me sleep on the floor. I am afraid of what I will do to myself."

Princess Scherbatow calmed Ann, thinking she had never met such a lonely soul. Ann showed her friend a picture of "her new boyfriend," a young Pole in a dinner jacket. He was Count Jan R. Rostrowski, and he wore a big ribbon on his chest. The Princess realized that he was a fraud, since only a few Russian families, such as the Scherbatows, had been given the Order of Saint Andrew. But she said nothing.

She dressed and took Ann back to the Bristol, where she sat with her. Princess Scherbatow told her neighbor Bobo Rockefeller afterward, "I know she will commit suicide someday."

In New York, Truman Capote was appearing on "The Tonight Show" and at society dinner parties. He was a superb extra man, spinning tales spiced with malice and wit about movie stars and society people. He had been amazed to learn that C. Z. Guest had known Billy Woodward since girlhood and had visited Ann at the Playhouse after his death.

From a friend at the *The New York Times*, Capote collected clippings about the shooting. A Nassau County policeman copied the microfilmed police report on the burglaries and shooting that had been gathering dust in a metal file drawer in Mineola. Capote relished the private detective reports on Billy's second cousin, Princess Marina Torlonia.

Capote liked to tell about his "shoot-out" with Ann. He claimed he and Ann had once been sitting at separate tables at a bar at Biarritz, when someone pointed over Ann's shoulder and said, "There's Truman Capote." Ann asked, "Where's that faggot?" Unfortunately, Capote said, he was only two feet from Ann, but hidden from view by a pillar. Ann made a gesture of apology to him, but Capote just stared.

The next evening he toasted her silently from the bar. Then, he claimed, he'd cocked his thumb and pointed his forefinger at her, saying "Bang-bang, bang-bang."

Capote became fascinated with Ann. A friend would simply need to say "Ann Woodward" to him and it would be like dropping a coin in a slot machine. He could tell an hour of tales about her whose details he embellished over the years. He described Ann as a prostitute who landed Billy with sexual tricks, then plotted to murder him when he wanted to leave her.

Some of Capote's early writing about Ann was submitted in 1973 to Lenore Hershey, editor in chief of the *Ladies' Home Journal*. The anecdotes formed part of a group of gossip stories called "Blind Items" and were not as polished or as long as the version that later appeared in *Esquire* under the title "Answered Prayers" in 1975.

For many years, Hershey had had lunch with Capote and listened in shock and delight to his stories. She thought he was the best and nastiest gossip in New York.

"Truman, I have an idea for something that would be so easy for you to write," Hershey said to him one day in East Hampton, as he drank vodka. "It's such fun that you can't say no. It's a chance to convert your gossip into something else."

A month later Capote produced the little manuscript. On the advice of the *Journal*'s attorneys, however, Hershey refused to consider publishing it until Capote revealed the real names of the people upon whom the stories were based. Capote submitted a handwritten note identifying the people in the five separate stories. He mentioned Mrs. William Woodward, Sr., Mrs. William Woodward, Jr.,* Edgar Bronfman, and Averell Harriman, but avoided identifying Bill Paley "because he liked him." The *Journal* ultimately decided not to publish.

---

*The story about Ann was called "Mrs. Willow's Dinner Party." In it a woman murders her husband because she is afraid to lose him to his dull second cousin. Her mother-in-law protects her from the electric chair to protect the family name. The piece describes Mrs. Willow's annual Christmas party to which she invites her daughter-in-law. The guests wonder what the two women say when they are alone before the party.

27

WANDERINGS

And with tears of blood he cleansed the hand,
The hand that held the steel:
For only blood can wipe out blood,
And only tears can heal . . .

—OSCAR WILDE, *The Ballad of Reading Gaol* (1898),
  written in prison near the end of his life

The end of that January, Ann was "boat-sitting" a sixty-foot teak trawler in tranquil Papeete Harbor in Tahiti.*

Ann's notebooks were now a series of disjointed lists of sales-ladies at Chez Ninon ("a very fashionable store"), "literary extra men" for her parties, a store in Paris that sold custom-made umbrellas, vitamin pills, and regimens for the antidepressants and sleeping pills in her night-table drawer.

Ann strolled tropical beaches, collecting seashells in silence with her friend Joyce Coit, and wondered if peace of mind lay in buying her own island, as Marlon Brando had done.

Unlike, Joyce, Ann dreaded going home; Jimmy was still taking drugs and denouncing her. Instead, she moved into a thatch-roofed Club Med camp where she hoped the English and Australian young people had not heard of her. She would sunbathe for hours in the shallow blue lagoon. Her bathing suit was fishnet over beige and from a distance could give the impression that she was naked.

One morning, as she was thinking about how to write a letter to Jimmy and mulling over a rejection from an Australian Army colonel, a

*The owner of the boat, whom she had met briefly with socialite Ellen Vanderhook, would sue her for "piracy on the high seas" because she had fired a sailor on his boat, installed curtains, and moved in—he claimed—without his permission.

young man waded toward Ann. He was as tall as Billy, but had a mustache. He was Dennis Ran, a writer from San Francisco. "Hi, I'm Ann from New York."

Dennis Rano liked her fishnet bathing suit and her big smile. They strolled to the open-air bar. They wandered along the beach, watched the sunset together, and listened to island music. The next morning, they awoke to the sound of Tahitian maids singing as they cleaned. Ann watched as people took Dennis aside. At lunch, she and he sat by the espresso bar. "You know, don't you?" Ann asked heavily. He blurted out, "So many people went out of their way to tell me—" Ann put on her sunglasses with a resigned expression. The subject was closed.

Ann reeled from one romantic disappointment to another. In Milan, at an international shooting meet, she donned a team hat and a koala bear pin and became the unofficial mascot of the Australian rifle team. It did not occur to her that it might be unseemly for a notorious fifty-eight-year-old woman to be waving a banner for a team of boisterous young shooters. Brian Mark was her new Australian friend. Afterward, Ann cried when he turned down her suggestion that he stay in Europe to be her shooting teacher. He said, "Annie, I must return to my family."

In Madrid, Ann bought a new condominium, a large apartment, high up and filled with light, in a beautiful residential area near a park called Puerto Hierro. She often appeared at expensive nightclubs catering to American expatriates, such as the Jockey Club. She knew all the head-waiters. Her lament about her young escorts was always the same: "They only want my money."

She asked Teresa Van Dyke, a wealthy acquaintance from Texas, "Should I get another face-lift?" "Your appearance is fine," Teresa said. "It's your unhappiness that's in your way."

Ann would pay as much as $15,000 to attend "exclusive" private shooting parties on thousand-acre estates in Spain. The galas were black tie for dinner, and in the fields, lunches were served in huge striped tents.

She was invited to shoot at Valdepeñas, 250 kilometers south of Madrid, by Julio Noyes, of the New York brokerage family. She brought a new friend, Sam Taylor of New Orleans. He was a geophysicist, six feet tall, startlingly handsome, and forty years old. He had sold his oil company for several million dollars and was learning to relax in Spain.

Taylor saw Ann as an icon. She held herself in her sequined gowns as though she had once been a great beauty. She always got the best tables in restaurants. They drove to the shoot in her sand-colored Alfa Romeo. Taylor was impressed with the car; it looked to him like a Rolls-Royce. When they stopped at a café for lunch on a tiled patio surrounded by palmettos, Ann reached across the table and put her hand on his. Rattled, he removed his hand and frowned, unable to tell Ann he thought she was too old.

In Valdepeñas, they were shown to a cottage with two large connecting bedrooms. Taylor locked his door. Ann summoned up her courage and knocked. "I'm not dressed," Taylor responded. "Well, we're invited for cocktails before dinner over at the main lodge," she said.

Through the door Taylor called, "Ann, I just feel like hell. You go on over there. I'll take a shower and shave, and maybe I'll feel better." After Ann left disappointed, he hid in his room, reading, and ordered a steak sandwich and a glass of milk.

The next morning Taylor and Ann went out on the shoot. He felt left out among the Manhattan society men, who seemed to talk about the same parties. He was glad to see his old friend John Buckley, brother of William. Between drives, John said, "I didn't see you at dinner last night." Then he asked, "Oh, Sam, do you mind if I drive Ann back to Madrid?" Surprised, Taylor agreed.

For the next several days Ann and John Buckley were shooting partners. Ann made plans to see a lot of him in Madrid.

However, when Buckley told Ann that Sam would be accompanying them back to Madrid, she felt rejected by them both. She sat in the back-seat as Taylor drove her car. They had a packed lunch of sandwiches and cold beer. Neither man knew what to say to Ann, who spent the entire drive muttering to herself that she was incapable of finding a love like Billy's. Taylor trained his eyes on the road. The two men did not speak for fifty miles.

In Madrid, Sam drove into the garage under Ann's building, where he prayed no one would hear or see them. He did not know what Ann might do.

A month later, Ann rushed back to New York from Marbella. Her pills were no longer working. She would awaken in the middle of the night with heart murmurs and bad digestion. She was worn out from pretending she was still the glittering young Mrs. William Woodward, Jr.

In February, she went to an opening at the Metropolitan Museum, hired another secretary, listed the Marbella properties for sale in *The New York Times* classified section, and saw six doctors in New York, including a plastic surgeon. She was given a smallpox inoculation and an Australian visa. On February 28, she flew to Reno, where she met Joyce Coit, and they returned together to Tahiti.

In Tahiti, Ann sobbed as Joyce consoled her about growing older and less attractive to men. She adopted a lost kitten, which she carried around in a canvas bag. Whenever they saw a church, Ann would say, "Excuse me for a moment," and slip inside to pray. Joyce would wait for her outside.

A month later, Ann left for Australia to visit Brian Mark, the young shooting champion, and Lord Percy Spender, a former Australian ambassador to the United States who had met Ann on an elephant hunt in Kenya.

A recent widower, Lord Spender seemed captivated by Ann. By the time she had arrived in Sydney at the end of May 1975, she was hoping to become his second wife. On June 18, he wrote to Ann in New York from Washington. He wrote with some intimacy that "perspiration is pouring out of every pore of my body." Soon he was himself, staying at the Plaza in New York, and paying his respects to Ann every night for a week. Thrilled by his attention, she asked Bill Sudduth, "I should marry him, shouldn't I?" "Ann, he's a diplomat with a career," Sudduth said to her, "It would be fine for a couple of months, but even in Australia the women would find out about your past and say the worst things." She suspected that Sudduth was right.

Ann was also having money woes, and waking up nights worrying about finances. She had been following the Bolivian political situation since a friend had told her Bolivian gold mines were good investments. She invited art dealers to bid on her paintings, including the Dalí portrait and the Modigliani that reminded her of Jimmy. But when she was given low estimates, she decided not to sell. Henry Geldzahler, the curator of twentieth-century art at New York's Metropolitan Museum, came to tea, examined her Picasso, and told Ann it was "dubious." She called the Wildenstein gallery to get it X-rayed.

Ann had established a modest charitable foundation. The Ann Eden Woodward (Mrs. William Woodward, Jr.) Foundation was worth about $40,000 during her lifetime, and on her death nearly doubled. She donated sums of $2,000 and $5,000 a year to such causes as the World Wildlife Fund; WNET, New York's public television station; and the Vivian Beaumont Theater. After her death, her accountant Joseph Lapatin, acting as trustee, gave money to the Burden Center for the Aging and to the city to build a park near Macy's.

On July 20, Bill Sudduth packed Ann, who was still complaining of heart pains, on a kind of stretcher and drove her to Woodstock, Vermont, for a restful visit with his daughter. During the ride, the fumes from the exhaust pipe leaked into the back of the van, but Ann was too drugged to realize she was inhaling them.

A few weeks later, Sudduth and Ann drove to the Mishomac Hunt Club on Shelter Island. Ann was eager to get away to nature, where there would be no gossip. She liked walking through the forest of white dogwood trees that would be in bloom. No sign marked the rustic club, of which Ann and her sons were members. It consisted of a bird-shooting range, eight New England–style frame houses, and a clubhouse—which was a dark wood farmhouse filled with Gothic furniture, twig art, and hunting prints.

One afternoon Ann and Sudduth drove four miles through the dogwood forests to an empty beach where Ann had recently bought two lots. Ann cocked her head at the crashing of the waves and announced to Sudduth, "This beach will be a good home." She planned to build two houses, decorate them, then sell one. Her leather notebook was filled with neat floor plans and sums. Ann was still seeking a way to put down roots, and she was preparing herself for another difficult task. She wanted to explain the shooting to Jimmy.

At sunset, Ann attempted to drive back to the club. Sudduth took over, turning the car several times on the loose sand until the tires sank.

A yacht was anchored four hundred yards out. Ann whistled and yelled and wept. With the car flashlight, she blinked the code signal for "help," but she could not get the sailors' attention.

It was dark as they hiked back over jagged rock. Ann was wearing a wide wraparound skirt, a kerchief, stockings, and canvas espadrilles. They walked in circles for an hour, the wild underbrush tearing at Ann's legs. Deerflies bit her arms. Ann had visions of having to sleep in the woods, but Sudduth tried to bolster her spirits, reminding her, "You have a wonderful sense of direction."

She soon led them to the edge of a pond, which they crossed, teetering on fallen tree trunks. Ann said, "We'll die out here."

Sudduth congratulated her as they stumbled into the dining room at eleven-thirty. When they got back from the doctor, Ann had a cognac, one of the rare times Sudduth saw her drink hard liquor.

*   *   *

The month of September 1975 was a disaster. Ann's penthouse in Marbella
was burglarized. She flew there to change the locks and to hire an exter-
minator to get rid of hundreds of moths. While she was there, a friend
called from New York to tell her about a short piece of fiction by Truman
Capote that seemed to be about her. It accused her of murder. The story
was scheduled to appear in the November issue of *Esquire*.

Ann returned to New York in the care of a registered nurse. At
Kennedy Airport, she tried to dismiss the woman and called Bill Sudduth.
Ann was inconsolable: "I must go far away." At the maisonette, Sudduth took one look at Ann's anguished face and called Woody, telling
him, "Your mother needs my help. I'm going to stay over here for a few
days."

Ann told Sudduth about the *Esquire* article. In a few weeks, everybody would be talking about the thinly disguised Capote story in which
someone very like Ann Woodward turns out to be a bigamist and the
former girlfriend of a gangster who trapped her rich society husband into
marrying her by becoming pregnant.

"I never met Truman Capote, and he never met me," Ann told
Sudduth. There had been only the unpleasant episode between them in
the bar at Biarritz. Sudduth started to open the curtains, but she stopped
him. "I want it dark," she said, adding, "I must go far away. The boys
will be relieved if I go."

In her pocket diary, she noted the date—October 25—that the Capote
article would be on newsstands. "I must be far away," she wrote. She
called her part-time secretary, a Korean student named Chayan Kim. "Let's
go to Africa."

As the publication date approached, Ann's anxiety consumed her.
Sudduth did not tell her that a year earlier he had dined at a friend's house
with Capote. Throughout dinner, the writer held forth with his fantasies
about Ann's life. Sudduth thought Capote was mad, as he told the fascinated group that he alone knew the motive for the deliberate murder.
Ann had never been divorced from her first husband, a policeman in
Oakland, California. Ann was a tramp, Capote declared, and her children
illegitimate.

Three days after her return from Marbella, Sudduth accompanied Ann to
Jimmy's psychiatrist, Dr. Wheaton. Then she went to Dr. Prutting, who

suggested that if her mood did not improve, she should enter a psychiatric hospital.

Ann was irrational; she believed she was a pauper. She had been digging into her capital and was down to $750,000. Hundreds of thousands of dollars had gone into airplane tickets, investments, and dinners with young men in Gucci shoes.

Now that the boys were grown, she had lost access to their trust fund money. She was, however, still getting the interest on her inheritance from Billy. The $2 million was yielding an income of $100,000 after taxes. The maisonette at 1133 Fifth had not been home for Woody and Jimmy for some time. The house was becoming a symbol of loss, and she begged for help with her money problems both in New York and in Marbella. "I'm going to end up in the poorhouse," she sobbed.

The morning of October 9, 1975, Ann and Miss Kim walked down Fifth Avenue.

Ann asked her to visit a Catholic church for ten minutes. Their second stop was Temple Emanu-El on Fifth Avenue at Sixty-fifth Street. Ann opened the doors to the main sanctuary, approached the altar, and bowed her head. Her high forehead creased with tension. Miss Kim stayed far away to give her privacy. They stopped at a third church for a half hour.

At St. James Episcopal Church, Ann stayed in the back. She looked it over as though trying to visualize something. It was where Billy's funeral had been held. By that afternoon, Ann had visited every church or synagogue directly south of her apartment within two miles.

Ann sadly told the young Korean woman that she was carrying a cyanide pill with her. Back at the maisonette, Ann invited Miss Kim to dinner. She agreed to go inside for only a few minutes. The duplex seemed empty. A few minutes later, Ann paged her son Jimmy at the Mishomac Hunt Club, where he was with his girlfriend. Ann asked him to come to see her. That evening, she could not eat, but asked her maid Reever Paige to hold her close and pray with her.

She telephoned Kim to plead with her to return. Kim refused. Jimmy arrived at the maisonette looking as though he had been awakened from sleep. His teeth were yellow, his eyes red. His long hair was greasy. When Ann chided him on his appearance, he called her a "bitch." "Your father used to hit me," she said. "He was no saint—" Jimmy jumped up. "You murdered him on purpose," he shouted and fled her apartment.

When Sudduth returned to the maisonette at ten-thirty, Ann was lying in bed in a flowing blue nightgown. He sat by her side, trying to convince her she had much to live for. Jimmy was ill, but underneath it all he loved her. Ann asked, "Bill, promise me you'll look after Jimmy." "Of course, Ann," he replied. "Woody can take care of himself. He'll be president," she said, "but Jimmy needs a lot of help." By eleven, she was under the covers. Sudduth told her, "Now, Ann, take the medicine and go to sleep." Fumbling among the twenty pill bottles in her night-table drawer, she swallowed a single pill with water and then took Bill Sudduth's hand, saying, "Bill, I am at peace with God."

Sudduth kissed her on the forehead and left.

Ann found a notepad with DON'T FORGET stamped in red block letters. She wrote her name in uneven script: ANN WOODWARD. Then she placed the single sheet on the dial of her beige telephone.

At nine-thirty the next morning, Bill Sudduth asked Reever to go in and awaken Ann.

Ann Woodward lay on her side, both hands clasped under her head. Ordinarily she slept with cream on her face. This morning, she wore a makeup base, lipstick, green mascara, and eyeshadow. Like the actress she once was, she seemed posed for a lovely death scene. Sudduth put his palm on Ann's forehead. "Ann has gone to sleep for good," he said. He and Reever knelt and prayed. He suddenly remembered her request that he hold something for her and became convinced it had been a cyanide pill that she had brought back from Spain.

In the next two hours, policemen, detectives, the medical examiner, representatives of Walter Dunnington's law firm, and New York City health officials inspected Ann's bedroom, looking for signs of foul play. Sudduth told the police that her weak heart had given way. But he took Woody aside to say he believed Ann had decided to end it all.

The night before the funeral, Lydia Smiley flew alone to New York from Kansas. "You look so like Ann," said Sudduth, kissing her at the airport. Woody had given him the money for a cab. Sudduth took Lydia to the Frank E. Campbell Funeral Chapel to pray over the open coffin. Ann was dressed in beige, surrounded by flowers.

Few mourners attended Ann's funeral on Tuesday, October 14. Billy's childhood friend Ned Patterson paid his respects. Lee Principe, his wife, and other Oyster Bay servants drove in. Drew Dudley, Elsie's public relations friend, escorted her and her daughter, Libby Pratt. Bobo Rockefeller attended with Barbara Rosenwald, a Sears Roebuck heiress. Woody put pictures of his mother from her Broadway and radio days around the small mourners' room at Campbell's. A family group sat thinking of the whirlwind events of Ann's life. "I had no idea Mother was that beautiful," Woody whispered to her Aunt Lydia, pointing to the photographs.

Jimmy seemed on the verge of collapse and went off to be sick. After the brief ceremony in the nearly empty St. James Church, Sudduth helped Elsie into her limousine. Jimmy and his girlfriend, Dana Osborne, rode out to the cemetery with Sudduth, Woody, and Woody's girlfriend.

At the Woodward family plot (near the Vanderbilts') at Woodlawn Cemetery, Dana seemed to be holding Jimmy upright by the elbow. He stumbled along in a trench coat, his shoelaces untied. Elsie and her daughter Libby paused by the fresh grave. Ninety-three-year-old Elsie Woodward was in a lively mood; her daughter-in-law, Ann, was one person she did not mind outliving. Like most things, death did not frighten her. She took the occasion to walk over to her own final resting place. "It's just fine, over here," she told Libby.

Six weeks later, Elsie summed up her reaction to Ann's death: "Well, that's that; she shot my son, and Truman just murdered her, and so now I suppose we don't have to worry about that anymore."

Ann's will made one thing clear: she was determined to lie beside Billy in the Woodward plot. She requested that she be buried next to "my late husband William Woodward Jr. if [it is] possible and if agreeable to those having an interest in his plot."

Ann left bequests of $25,000 each to the two lawyers who had helped her through the shooting crisis—Henry Root Stern, Jr., and Murray Gurfein, by now a judge in Manhattan. She left $5,000 to each of her aunts. Sudduth had been given paintings and small sums of money while she was alive.

To the Metropolitan Museum of Art, she left her paintings and her collection of ancient Chinese objects with the provision that the museum gifts be marked by a plaque that read: "Bequest of Mrs. William Woodward, Jr.''*

A week after Ann's death, Chayan Kim was at the maisonette index-

---

*There were twenty-four ancient Chinese statues, vases, and boxes—ceramic, bronze, and glass—left to the Metropolitan Museum, including a sixth-century tomb ornament of a lady in green glazed pottery, a fifteenth-century bright blue glazed bottle, and a Ming Dynasty black glazed horse. A few pieces had been bought under the guidance of Sue Valenstein, Curator of Far Eastern Art. The museum turned the rest down.

Ann's paintings were rejected by the Met, and most of them were eventually sold at Parke-Bernet, including a small Manet depicting prunes, a painting of Pandora and her box by Redon, a Bonnard oil painting showing a woman in a sea of flowers, and a sensual oil painting of white roses by Fantin-Latour. A head of a boy done in chalk was pronounced a fake Watteau.

ing Ann's belongings for the Parke-Bernet auction when the telephone rang. It was Truman Capote. He was trying to turn his *Esquire* story into a novel, and was looking for additional information. "How long did you know her?" he asked Kim.

"Only three or four years."

"What was Ann Woodward really like?" he asked.

"She was a sad person, very sad person."

"She was more than that. She came from a rural slum," he said, as though he had known Ann forever. "Honey, was it suicide or just an overdose?"

At first, Capote found Kim a willing subject. She had always been a little too talkative. "Poor Ann. People were always mean to her. She didn't want to live anymore."

"Right, but I bet she killed herself over a man."

"No, not one man," Kim said, feeling pushed. "She was too sad."

Capote asked, "More than one?"

"No, but men just were after her for money," said Kim.

"She was taking drugs, wasn't she?"

Kim admitted hearing Ann mention cyanide.

"Where did she hide it?" he asked.

"I just don't know."

Capote persisted. "When was the last time you saw her?" Kim rattled off the slow pilgrimage from church to church. "Tell me everything about her last day," Capote said.

Kim was silent. He did not ask her if Ann had read his *Esquire* story.

EPILOGUE

Woody called his mother's acquaintances, saying, "I know Mother would have liked you to have something of hers." Bill Sudduth and Reever Paige had laid out Ann's handbags, shoes, twenty-seven fur coats, and costume jewelry around her bedroom. Ann Slater picked a Hermès scarf, Bobo Rockefeller an embroidered pillow. Princess Scherbatow asked for a silk scarf, Paige received a sable coat. In Marbella, Woody arranged a similar ceremony, during which Baroness Terry von Pantz chose crates of Ann's African sculpture. She was not sentimental about Ann, but considered the trophies beautiful.

On October 25, Kim bought the November issue of *Esquire*. It was hard for her to recognize Ann in Capote's fiction. There was little sadness in the New York social community over Ann's suicide. They recognized some of Capote's facts and assumed he had uncovered the rest with research. As Elsie's friends saw it, Capote had accused Ann in print and she had responded like a guilty person by committing suicide. Capote, however, was condemned for dragging poor old Elsie Woodward's family name through the mud once more.

On the twentieth anniversary of his father's death, two weeks after his mother's funeral, Jimmy let himself into the maisonette. He was carrying a small bundle of newspapers. He did not turn on any lights. He was having agonizing stomachaches from alcohol, heroin, and cocaine. To Jimmy, Ann's maisonette smelled of evil, and he was going to exorcise it once and for all. He had learned voodoo incantations from a black Puerto Rican priest.

Jimmy began in the guest bathroom with the gold faucet by tearing strips of newspaper and making nests in the corners of the room. Then he knelt, lighting the little piles. He inhaled the smoke, mumbling Spanish chants. He was determined to banish the evil spirit of his mother from the maisonette. He repeated the ritual in each corner of the large sitting room.

The rows of Ann's shoes in the closet, each with its own stretcher plunged inside it, made him feel her presence. He sat in the dark, hunched over on the satin bed. Within hours, Jimmy called his psychiatrist, asking to be taken to a hospital.

Elsie Woodward exacted a promise from her favorite grandson. "Yes, ma'am," said Jimmy, "I promise I will never jump out a window again." For Elsie, this closed the matter. Nervous breakdowns were simply not part of her world. She defended him: "It's not his fault. No matter where he goes, those pushers find him, and make him take drugs."

Despite Jimmy's problems, the two Woodwards—sixty-four years apart—dined together every six weeks at the Waldorf. They would inch their way down the hotel corridor, a nurse holding one of Elsie's sticklike arms, Jimmy holding the other. One afternoon a month after his mother's death, Jimmy brought a beautiful black-haired Brazilian girl and announced to Elsie that he was going to marry her.

In December 1975, after his mother's birthday, Jimmy failed to appear for pre-Christmas dinner with his grandmother. Elsie telephoned his permanent suite at a hotel on Park Avenue. Jimmy sounded strange. He complained of stomach pains. There seemed to be two different Jimmys—one who was high on drugs and one who was the charming boy Elsie loved. Elsie sent a doctor to see him. The doctor called her back in less than an hour, reporting, "Jimmy's high on something."

Elsie called for her old Rolls limousine and driver. When she entered his suite, Jimmy stood uncertainly and then sat down. He was almost a hundred pounds overweight from tranquilizers. Elsie found a huge dog, a cat, a short, muscular man who introduced himself as "Johnny Moonshine," Moonshine's wife, and a baby in a crib.

Johnny Moonshine told Elsie, "Jim doesn't need to go to the hospital. I will take him to the beach in Nassau. Don't worry. I can handle it. I have a medical background. I was an orderly in a hospital."

As Elsie left, she said to her nurse, "How nice that Jimmy has a family for the Christmas season."

When the doctor was ushered in to see his patient the following day, Jimmy was standing alone in front of an open window. Cold winds were twisting the satin curtains. His houseguests were out looking at the Christmas displays in department store windows on Fifth Avenue. Jimmy was returned to Payne Whitney.

The problems continued. The hotel manager called Elsie Woodward the next afternoon and said, "That young man is still in your grandson's room, and he is a pusher. If he's not out of there, I'm calling the police."

"I'll handle it," said Elsie.

First, she asked her nurse the meaning of the word the hotel manager had used. Her nurse told her the contemporary definition of "pusher." Elsie dialed Jimmy's hotel room. "Young man, you must leave at once," the ninety-four-year-old dowager said.

"But Jim gave me permission to stay," Johnny Moonshine told Elsie.

"I am Mrs. William Woodward, and my grandson is ill. You must leave at once." He did.

Nine months later, Jimmy Woodward jumped out a window of the Hotel Navarro on Central Park South. He died instantly. His brother, Woody, went to the Waldorf Towers to tell his grandmother. Woody, who was then a Democratic party candidate for the House of Representatives from Manhattan, had had dinner with Jimmy only the night before. He had seemed fine. When Elsie's nurse, Monica Davis, began to weep at the news, Woody told her, "Don't cry. You'll upset my grandmother. I just don't want her to cry."

Elsie managed to keep the suicide out of the newspapers for nearly a week. Her attitude was the same as it had been during the shooting scandal twenty-two years earlier: the Woodwards were not news unless they wanted to be.

Elsie attended Jimmy's funeral at St. James Episcopal Church with her daughter Libby. She had buried too many people. Afterward, a girlfriend of Jimmy's who had been in Europe during the funeral telephoned Elsie. "He was destined to commit suicide," she said. "He lived with tragedy."

Elsie said the girl was crazy and instructed her maid to refer calls about Jimmy to his brother. "Jimmy was a good person," she said. That night she suffered a mild heart attack in her sleep and was admitted to

Jimmy, Ann, and Woody,
circa 1965.

Merry Christmas

and a

Happy New Year

Ann, Woody and Jim Woodward

1133 Fifth Avenue
New York 28
Atwater 9-7210

William (Woody) Woodward campaigning for the at-large Democratic seat on the New York City Council, August 27, 1981.

Jimmy Woodward, age nineteen, 1965.

Elsie Woodward in front of La Côte Basque restaurant, Manhattan, 1975.

New York Hospital. To a few friends who telephoned, she replied, "I am very fine, thank you. I am waiting to die." But she recovered and was soon released from the hospital.

At ninety-five, Elsie was in remarkable health. She had all her teeth and ate whatever she liked. She was hard of hearing, however, and it was difficult for her to read. "That's the bane of old age," she said. "I miss books the most."

The following year, when her beloved Patrick O'Higgins began to cough, Elsie sent him to her doctor. It was cancer of the lung, and Elsie paid the bills. She spent at least $400,000 in 1978 and 1979 caring for him. When Patrick worsened, she moved him into her library in a hospital bed with a screen around it. (Twenty-four years earlier she had similarly nursed her dying husband.)

Patrick's death finally broke Elsie's resilient heart. She refused to attend his funeral. She revised her will to bestow Patrick's $25,000 stipend to his sister, Odette Hinton.

Elsie was still herself. When a new nurse did not leave the bathroom quickly enough to give her privacy, she said, "Don't you know who I am? I am Mrs. William Woodward."

But a year after Patrick's death, ninety-seven-year-old Elsie gave up. She had lost two of her favorite young men in the world—her grandson Jimmy and Patrick O'Higgins. She suffered another small heart attack and was briefly hospitalized. Too proud to use a wheelchair, she rarely went out. She went to the Woodward stakes race at Belmont with Mary Sanford and afterward spilled food on her bodice. Her eyes filled with tears. "I am too old," she said. "Too old to keep living."

When Patrick's sister told her she was bringing her a bouquet of flowers, Elsie said, "Very well, leave them downstairs at the front desk. I don't want people to see me." Elsie had high standards for infrequent guests such as Arlene Francis. Her maid, Pauline, put old pink silk sheets bordered in handmade French lace on her bed. Elsie spoke of Billy's death to her nurses when she heard a relative was going to wed his secretary: "Oh, what a dreadful idea."

"Why?" asked the nurse.

"It's the money, she hasn't any."

The nurse resisted saying that Elsie herself had been a poor clever girl who married a man who owned a bank.

Elsie continued, "Look at what happened to Billy. I knew he should not have married Ann. I had an extrasensory perception that things would go very wrong because she had no money."

One key to Elsie Woodward's longevity was her remarkable temperament. She had few strong emotions—and no fears. In Elsie's final years, Arlene Francis, her daughter Libby, and her grandson Woody seemed to be the people she cared about. She shuddered when a nurse recommended a reunion of her grandchildren and great-grandchildren. When her daughter Ethel came from France with a grandchild, Elsie was polite. But afterward, she said, "Well, that was not very amusing. Imagine, a sixty-year-old woman who still must ask her mother for money."

Occasionally, Elsie became confused. She telephoned a friend who knew full well that she was bedridden to say, "Well, dearie, I've just had a lovely weekend in the country. The ride in was a bit slow." She continued to send her friends books and notes. To her friend Eleanor Howard, whose family owns a chain of newspapers, she said, "I'm just going down like a sailing ship. All my sails are up, but I'm just sinking." Elsie told her nurses, "I am waiting to die. I do not believe in suicide. It hurts other people too much."

The day before she died, Elsie had buttered toast for breakfast, soup for lunch, and canned hash and potatoes with an egg for dinner. Her night nurse dressed her in a long, mended silk nightgown.

At 1 a.m. on July 14, 1981, Elsie Woodward's strong heart stopped in her sleep. She was not particularly sick: she had mild Parkinson's disease and her gall bladder had been removed. She had suffered a few falls, two minor heart attacks, and several small strokes.

She was surrounded by framed photographs of people she had outlived: on her night table were pictures of her husband and her son, on a bureau was one of her daughter Edie, who had died of premature Alzheimer's disease, and nearby on a small table was a portrait of Rosalind Russell. Hidden in her underwear drawer was the glossy photograph of Frank Sinatra, inscribed, "I love you, Elsie, Frank."

NOTES

INTRODUCTION

xi "THE SHOOTING OF THE CENTURY": *Life*, November 14, 1955.

xi–xii WIRE SERVICE INTERVIEW: Interview with Jesse Claude Crowell, October 31, 1955.

xiii–xv "CÔTE BASQUE": From *Answered Prayers*, by Truman Capote, *Esquire*, November 1975.

xvii "WASP ASCENDANCY": Joseph Alsop, *New York Review of Books*, November 9, 1989.

xvii–xviii THE WEEK OF THE SHOOTING: *New York Times*, October 20–30, 1955.

I KANSAS POOR

3 EARLY SETTLER: *Our Heritage, 150 Years of Progress* (Christian Church of Lawrence, Kansas, 1957), 12.

NOR WERE HER HANDS: Interview with Eugene Condon, 1983.

ANGELINE AND JESSE JR.: Interviews with Lydia Smiley Wasson, Edna Smiley Cobb, and Mary C. Cuthbertson, sister of Jesse Claude Crowell, 1981, 1982, 1983, 1984.

STATE MANUAL TRAINING NORMAL SCHOOL: Normal-school records of Ethel Crowell.

3–4 BACKGROUND ON FAMILY AND FRONTENAC: Interviews with Lydia Smiley Wasson, 1981, 1982.

4 MINISTERS AND CHURCH ELDERS: Interviews with Lydia Smiley Wasson, 1983, 1984.

HAROLD BELL WRIGHT: Interview with Eugene DeGruson, 1987.

RINGLEADER: Interview with Lydia Smiley Wasson, 1982.

TENNYSON'S POEMS: Interview with Lydia Smiley Wasson, 1982.

5 HER PROVISIONAL CERTIFICATE: Normal-school records of Ethel Crowell.

COPENHAGEN BLUE BROCADE: Pittsburg *Headlight*, December 27, 1913; interview with Lydia Smiley Wasson, 1982.

FIRST CEREMONY: Interview with Eugene Condon, 1981.

"KANSAS IS JUST A DESERT": Interview with Eugene Condon, 1981.

6 BIRTH OF ANGELINE: Kansas State Department of Records, birth certificate.

   SHE HAD BEEN BORN: Interview with Lydia Smiley Wasson, 1982.

   CROWELL FAMILY HISTORY: Interview with Mary C. Cuthbertson, 1981.

   "WHERE'S DADDY?": Interview with Eugene Condon, 1985.

   SQUARE DEAL: Interview with Lydia Smiley Wasson, 1982.

   "HIS OWN FLUIDS": Interview with Lydia Smiley Wasson, 1982.

7 "STAYING WITH US": Interview with Lydia Smiley Wasson, 1983.

   "THAT BOX WON'T KEEP OUT THE RAIN": Interviews with Lydia Smiley Wasson, 1982, and Eugene Condon, 1984, 1985.

   RETURN TO THE NORMAL SCHOOL: Interview with Eugene Condon, 1984.

   IQ TESTS: School records, released upon request by Little Union, Kansas.

   BOX TO BOX: Interview with Lydia Smiley Wasson, 1983.

   MOST VIVIDLY: Interview with Eugene Condon, 1983.

8 GONE BROKE: Divorce petition, Pittsburg, Kansas: Ethel Crowell v. Jesse Claude Crowell, 1926.

   EARLY PERIOD IN HUGOTON: Interview with Lydia Smiley Wasson, 1983.

9 QUIET WATCHFULNESS: Interview with Eugene Condon, 1985.

   MASTER'S DEGREE: School records, history compiled by Eugene DeGruson, Pittsburg State University; interview with Eugene Condon, 1983.

   ROUGH FRONTIER TOWN: Interview with Thelma Keating Stevens of Liberal, Kansas, 1984.

   WHILE ETHEL WAS AT LIBERAL: Interview with Lydia Smiley Wasson, 1983.

   ETHEL LEFT HER HUSBAND: Interviews with Eugene Condon, 1983, 1984.

10 IMAGINARY CONVERSATIONS: Interview with Eugene Condon, 1983.

   WOMEN'S SUFFRAGISM: Interviews with a student and with Eugene Condon, 1982.

   ANGIE'S BIRTHDAYS: Interview with Eugene Condon, 1983.

   ETHEL STRIKING HER DAUGHTER: Interview with Eugene Condon, 1981.

11 EMOTIONAL CENTER: Interviews with Eugene Condon, 1981, 1984.

   HOMESTEADING PARCEL: Divorce papers, Crowell v. Crowell, November 10, 1923, Crawford County, Kansas.

   ANGIE'S GRADES: Lakeside School report cards.

   LILLIAN GISH AND CLARA BOW: Interview with Eugene Condon, 1984.

   SHE DISAPPROVED: *Time* internal reporting file, November 1955.

12 "JEALOUS WOMEN": Interview with Eugene Condon, 1984.

   ANGIE FELT BETRAYED: Interview with Eugene Condon, 1981.

   NATURAL GAS: Interview with Lydia Smiley Wasson, 1983.

   "THAT LAND": Interview with Eugene Condon, 1985.

   NOT BEING ABLE TO SUPPORT: Interview with Mary C. Cuthbertson, 1981.

   INTERCEPTED LETTERS: Interview with Eugene Condon, 1984.

   "P.V.": Interview with his sister, Mary Jordan, 1986.

13 EGGSHELLS: Interview with Eugene Condon, 1985.

   GESTURES AND SHIVERING IN BED: Interview with Eugene Condon, 1981.

UNCONSCIOUS MOTIVATIONS: Interview with Eugene Condon, 1984.

"HELLCAT WIFE": Interview with Ken Simons of Pittsburg, Kansas, 1984.

14 ETHEL'S TRUE ALLY: Interview with Eugene Condon, 1983.

SELLING ENCYCLOPEDIAS: Interview with Lydia Smiley Wasson, 1982.

PACKING: Interview with Eugene Condon, 1981.

CALAMITOUS RELATIONSHIP: Interview with Beulah Boulware of Pittsburg, Kansas, 1982.

PEN AND PENCIL SET: Interview with Lydia Smiley Wasson, 1982.

THESIS: "The Status of Social Sciences in Kansas High Schools," by Ethel Smiley Crowell, June 4, 1928, University of Kansas Library.

15 EDUCATION COURSES: Kansas State transcripts, 1919–26.

CIVIL SUMMONS: Newspaper clipping in chronology assembled by Eugene DeGruson, Pittsburg State University.

VENEREAL DISEASE: Interview with Eugene Condon, 1984.

MARY ELIZABETH JORDAN: Interview with Eugene Condon; and *Time* internal reporting file, November 1955.

PROPERTY SETTLEMENT: Kansas divorce petition, Jordan v. Jordan, March 21, 1929.

AMBITIOUS EXIT: Interview with Eugene Condon, 1981.

16 LECTURES: Interview with Eugene Condon, 1984.

FASHIONABLE NEIGHBORHOOD OF WESTPORT: Interview with Lydia Smiley Wasson, 1982.

SEPTEMBER 1928: Interview with Eugene Condon, 1985.

2 ANN IN KANSAS CITY

17 WESTPORT TAXI: Interview with Eugene Condon, 1983.

17–18 "HIT AND RUN": Interview with Eugene Condon, 1981.

19 ETHEL AND TRABON: Interview with Eugene Condon, 1982.

20 WESTPORT TAXI STAFF: Interviews with Eugene Condon, 1981, 1982.

20–21 ANGIE'S ARTICLE: Interviews with Eugene Condon, 1981, 1982, 1983.

21 JOAN CRAWFORD: Interviews with Eugene Condon, 1981, 1982, 1983.

22 HER MOTHER'S CARETAKER: Interviews with Eugene Condon, 1981, 1982, 1983.

23 ANGIE'S SECRET LETTER: Interviews with Eugene Condon, 1981, 1982, 1983.

24 THE CHARGES AGAINST ETHEL: Interviews with Eugene Condon, 1981, 1982, 1983.

25 NOT KNOWING WHO WOULD SHOW UP: Interview with Bill Sudduth, 1984.

HARDING'S MONOPLANE: Interviews with Eugene Condon, 1981, 1982, 1983.

26 JOHNNY'S BACKGROUND: Interview with John Elston, 1987.

ANGIE'S MOVIE ASPIRATIONS: Westport *Crier*, February–June 1932; interviews with Eugene Condon, 1981, 1982, 1983.

A LIVING IN KANSAS CITY: Interviews with Eugene Condon, 1981, 1982, 1983.

DID NOT BOSS HER: Interview with Eugene Condon, 1982.

27 TO RESCUE A DRIVER: Interviews with Eugene Condon, 1981, 1982, 1983.

SHE BURST INTO TEARS: Interviews with Eugene Condon, 1981, 1982, 1983.

END OF PROHIBITION: Interview with retired police captain John Mullin, 1983.

28 FRANK "JELLY" NASH: Merle Clayton, *Union Station Massacre: The Shootout That Started the FBI's War on Crime* (Indianapolis and New York: Bobbs Merrill Company, 1978).

31 NIGHTMARES OF FBI AGENTS: Interviews with Eugene Condon, 1981, 1982, 1983.

32 "I NEVER WORE IT": Interviews with Eugene Condon, 1981, 1982, 1983.

33 STREETS OF DENVER: Interview with Edna Smiley Cobb, 1981.

34 MODEL IN THE MILLINERY DEPARTMENT: Interviews with Eugene Condon, 1981, 1982, 1983.

35 THE DAY ANN LEFT: Interviews with Eugene Condon, 1981, 1982, 1983.

3   SCANDAL

36 EPIGRAPH: Cleveland Amory, *"Who Killed Society?"* (New York: Harper and Row, 1960), 12.

37 OGDEN FAMILY TREE: Lawrence Van Alstyne, Charts of Ogden English and American Ancestry. New York Genealogical Society.

W. WETMORE CRYDER BANKING SCANDAL: New York *Daily Tribune*, February 22, 1893; *New York Times*, November 17, 1893; *New York Times*, December 2, 1893.

ROBBERY: *New York Times*, February 16, 1905.

"FAMILY CREST": Interviews with Herschel Williams, 1980, 1981.

PRESIDENTIAL ADAMSES: Interviews with Herschel Williams, 1980, 1981.

"CLUBROOM GOSSIP": *New York Times*, December 5, 1893.

38 CORSET PINCHED: Interviews with Robert Leylan, 1984, Herschel Williams, 1980, 1981, and Mrs. Frederick Prince, 1981.

"EQUIPAGE": Elizabeth Wharton Decies, *"King Lehr" and the Gilded Age* (Philadelphia and London: J. B. Lippincott Company, 1935), 28.

SCOTLAND TO AMERICA: Dixon Wector, *The Saga of American Society: A Record of Social Aspiration, 1607–1937* (New York: Charles Scribner's Sons, 1937).

SHINNECOCK GOLF CLUB: Cleveland Amory, *The Last Resorts* (New York: Harper & Brothers, 1952), 54.

39 TOGETHER IN PUBLIC: Felicia Warburg Roosevelt, *Doers and Dowagers* (New York: Doubleday, 1975), 25.

QUOTATIONS FROM DUNCAN CRYDER: Interviews with Robert Leylan, 1980, 1981, 1983.

ELSIE'S FATHER'S BANKRUPTCY: *New York Times*, September 4, 1966.

40 FRENCH AND ENGLISH: Interview with Herschel Williams, 1980.

LITTLE OF SEX: Interview with Herschel Williams, 1980.

REAL YELLOW ROSE: Interview with Herschel Williams, 1980.

ELSIE FROM HER SISTERS: Roosevelt, *Doers and Dowagers*, 25.

41 CONSUELO'S UNHAPPY MARRIAGE: Consuelo Vanderbilt Balsan, *The Glitter and the Gold* (New York: Harper & Brothers, 1952), 17–18.

SISTERS SMOKED: Interview with Lily Auchincloss, 1980.

CASINO: Interview with Herschel Williams, 1981.

NOT UP TO HER STANDARDS: Interviews with Herschel Williams, 1980, 1981, 1982.

SEA WIND: Interview with Herschel Williams, 1980; Roosevelt, *Doers and Dowagers*, 25–26; and Christopher Matthew, *A Different World: Stories of the Great Hotels* (London: Paddington Press, 1975), passim.

GIRLHOOD MEMORIES: Interview with Herschel Williams, 1980.

42–43 STORY OF THE EMPRESS: Interviews with Herschel Williams, 1982, and Robert Leyland, 1983.

43 BILLY LOVED THE STORY: Interview with Bill Sudduth, 1983.

UNTIL THE 1920S: *Flora Whitney Miller: Her Life, Her World* (New York: Whitney Museum of Art, 1987).

HOMEGROWN IMITATIONS: Max Weber, *The Protestant Ethic and the Spirit of Capitalism* (New York: Charles Scribner's Sons, 1958); Werner Sollors, *Beyond Ethnicity: Consent and Descent in American Culture* (New York: Oxford University Press, 1986).

"ANY MORE AT HOME LIKE YOU?": Interviews with Herschel Williams, 1981, 1982.

44 "ORIGINAL MEMBER": Cleveland Amory, *Life*, November 1955.

FRONT-PAGE ARTICLE: *Town Topics*, May 1900.

45 DIAMOND JIM BRADY: Amory, *The Last Resorts*, 430.

FIRST DAY: Interview with Herschel Williams, 1981.

SARATOGA: Interview with Herschel Williams; Amory, *The Last Resorts*, 431; George Waller, *Saratoga: Saga of an Impious Era* (Englewood Cliffs, N.J.: Prentice-Hall, 1966), 244.

46 *LIFE*, THE ELEGANT SOCIETY HUMOR MAGAZINE: Not related to Henry Luce's later magazine; interview with William Draper, 1982.

47 "LOVE AT FIRST SIGHT": Roosevelt, *Doers and Dowagers*, 27.

EDWARD VII AND MARY GOELET: Cornelius Vanderbilt, Jr., *Queen of the Golden Age: The Fabulous Grace Vanderbilt* (New York: McGraw-Hill, 1956), 194.

MORE IMPRESSIVE SOCIAL BACKGROUND: Paul Porzelt, *The Metropolitan Club of New York* (New York: Rizzoli, 1982), 15.

SARAH OGDEN: Amory, *The Last Resorts*, 243.

48 IN HIS THIRTIES IN 1841: Thomas W. Hall, *History of Severn Parrish* (Unpublished manuscript).

FADS AND FANCIES: Denys Sutton, *Fads and Fancies*, introduction by Kenneth Clark (New York: Witenborn, 1979).

"BOUQUETS FROM THE AUDIENCE": *The Grotonian*, February 1893, March 1893, June 1893, October 1893, February 1894, March 1894.

49 REMARK ABOUT HIM: Interview with Herschel Williams, 1982.

"MY COMPREHENSION": Edward Sanford Martin, *Ambassador Choate: The Life of Joseph Hodges Choate, as gathered chiefly from his letters including his own story of his boyhood* (New York: Charles Scribner's Sons, 1920), 199, 202, 213, 219, 220.

DISAPPROVAL OF HIS ASSOCIATES: *New York Times*, June 10, 1901.

50 $2 MILLION: *New York Times*, October 16–18, 1902.

700 CORRECT INVITATIONS: New York *Herald*, March 1902.

NEGOTIATING TO BUILD: Bill Curling, *The Captain: A Biography of Captain Sir Cecil Boyd-Rochfort, Royal Trainer* (London: Barrie & Jenkins, 1970), 60–65.

THE OUTING: Interviews with Herschel Williams, 1980, 1981; Balsan, *The Glitter and the Gold*, 18.

TO WIN THE DERBY RACE: Interviews with Herschel Williams, 1980, 1981.

51 ELSIE DREAMED: Interviews with Herschel Williams, 1980, 1981.

FOOTNOTE SOURCE: *New York Times,* October 12, 1904.

52 "AND THAT SET": *Town Topics, the Journal of Society,* October 27, 1904; Newport *News,* October 25, 1904. See also, Porzelt, *The Metropolitan Club of New York.*

OPPORTUNE MARRIAGE: Interview with Herschel Williams, 1980.

EXHAUSTED LISTENER: Interviews with Herschel Williams, 1980, 1981.

55 ILL WITH PNEUMONIA: Roosevelt, *Doers and Dowagers,* 26.

WELL IN SOCIETY: Interview with Valentine Lawford, 1983; Balsan, *The Glitter and the Gold,* 207; interview with Phillip Benkard, 1982.

WOODWARD WAS HOME: Roosevelt, *Doers and Dowagers,* 28–29.

SKYSCRAPER: History Gallery, pamphlet describing the ninth-floor historical displays at Hanover Bank.

"RESTRICTED": Roosevelt, *Doers and Dowagers,* 27.

NAPS GREW LONGER: Interviews with Mary Sanford, 1980, 1982.

YOUNG LADIES: Interview with Herschel Williams, 1984.

56 BEYOND REPROACH: Roosevelt, *Doers and Dowagers,* 28.

DIRECT PERSONAL QUESTIONS: Interviews with Herschel Williams, 1980, 1981, 1982; Billy Baldwin, *Billy Baldwin Remembers* (New York: Harcourt Brace Jovanovich, 1974).

REFUSING TO COMPLAIN: Interviews with Herschel Williams, 1985, and Joan Fontaine, 1982.

OPEN HORSE AND CARRIAGE: Amory, *The Last Resorts,* 198.

SOCIAL IMPORTANCE: Roosevelt, *Doers and Dowagers,* 27.

57 "TOO CRUDE FOR WORDS": Vanderbilt, *Queen of the Golden Age,* 233.

HALF-MAST: *Wall Street Journal,* April 14, 1910.

THE GROWTH OF THE BANK: *Wall Street Journal,* April 14, 1910.

"CIGARS": William Woodward, *Gallant Fox: A Memoir* (New York: Derrydale Press, 1931).

58 "THEATER OR THE ARTS": Roosevelt, *Doers and Dowagers,* 28; *Time* internal reporting file, November 1955.

TRAGEDY ON BELAIR ESTATE: Shirley Vlasak Baltz, *A Chronicle of Belair* (Bowie, Md.: The Bowie Heritage Committee, 1984), 77.

59 ELSIE BOUGHT HIM A RESTAURANT: Interview with Joseph Chaprionière, 1986.

SILVER HOLDERS ON THE TABLE: Interview with Lady Sarah Churchill, 1984.

60 BAILEY'S BEACH: Interview with Gavin Young, 1983.

GENEROUS BONUSES: Interview with Monica Davis, 1989.

RUINED BY ALCOHOL: Interviews with Phillip Benkard and Rudolph Schirmer, 1985.

63 JUST UNDER THIRTY: Interviews with Mary Sanford, 1981, and Phillip Benkard and Rudolph Schirmer, 1985.

SOLDIERS, SAILORS, AND AIRMEN: Interviews with Mary Sanford, 1980, 1981, 1982, 1983.

4 WILLIAM WOODWARD, JR., ARRIVES

64 SARA WAS NINE: Interviews with Herschel Williams, 1980, 1981.

BOTH SIDES OF THE ATLANTIC: Interview with Dorothy Davison, 1985.

65 SLEEPING AT THE BROOK: Interview with Herschel Williams, 1981.

SHOULDERS WERE NARROW: Interviews with Herschel Williams, 1981, and Robert Leylan, 1983.

66 LETTER TO PRESIDENT: Belair Museum, Bowie, Md.

TRAVELING TO BELAIR: Baltz, *A Chronicle of Belair*, 77.

WOODWARD'S PREFERENCES: Interviews with Herschel Williams, 1981, and Robert Leylan, 1983.

TREES: Interview with Herschel Williams, 1981.

67 ELABORATE FRENCH PRAM: Interview with Herschel Williams, 1982.

MORE THAN WADE: Interview with Herschel Williams, 1982.

HIS LAUGH: Interview with Edward Patterson, 1983.

MORTIFIED: Interview with Herschel Williams, 1980.

NEVER CARED FOR BEING A MOTHER: Roosevelt, *Doers and Dowagers*, 28.

FOOTNOTE SOURCE: Interview with Kenneth Jay Lane, 1980.

68 "WHEN YOU FEEL BETTER": Interviews with Herschel Williams, 1981, Kenneth Jay Lane, 1982, and Odette Hinton, 1981.

RACING MONOGRAPHS: Interview with Ina Claire, 1980.

GOSSIP: Interview with Rudolph Schirmer, 1982.

PRINCE FERDINAND OF LIECHTENSTEIN: Interview with Robert Leylan, 1983.

"BAWDY HOUSE IN CHINA": Interview with Mary Sanford, 1980.

FORBIDDEN TOPIC: Interview with Joan Fontaine, 1981.

69 "ORDINARY WAY OF THINKING": Interviews with Bill Sudduth, 1983, and Herschel Williams, 1981.

CHILDREN'S PLAY: Interview with Herschel Williams, 1980.

LONG, MIRRORED CENTERPIECE: Interview with Eleanor Lambert, 1982.

HE BOWED: Interview with Ina Claire, 1980.

UNEASY SENSE OF POWER: Interview with Robert Leylan, 1983.

70 GAMEKEEPERS: Interview with Robert Leylan, 1983.

BRANDY IN THE LIBRARY: Interview with Robert Leylan, 1983.

71 VANDERBILT FORTUNE: Interview with Robert Leylan, 1982.

SARAH AND THE TRIPLETS: Interview with Lady Sarah Churchill, 1986.

"GOOD BEAN": Interview with Florynce Baker Martinau, 1984.

72 HUNTERS: Interview with Robert Leylan, 1981.

73 HIDDEN GUNS: Interview with Florynce Baker Martinau, 1984.

NEWPORT HOUSE: Interview with Senator Claiborne Pell, 1982.

74 FLOURISHING MUSTACHES: Interview with Henry Mortimer, 1981.

NOT THEIR CODE: Interviews with Edward Patterson, 1983, 1984, 1985.

CLASSMATES: Interviews with Edward Patterson and Harry Monroe, 1989.

75 PLAY BASEBALL THEMSELVES: Interviews with Edward Patterson and Harry Monroe, 1989.

76 BUSINESS MANAGER: *The Grotonian*, 1893.

CHIP OFF THE OLD BLOCK: Interviews with Robert Leylan, 1981, 1982, 1983.

GROTON STUDENT NEWSPAPER: *The Grotonian*, 1928.

YOUNG WOMEN: Interviews with Robert Leylan, 1981, 1982.

81 PROVINCE OF WIVES: Interviews with Mary Sanford, 1981, 1982.

FOOTNOTE SOURCE: F. Scott Fitzgerald, *Babylon Revisited and Other Stories* (New York: Charles Scribner's Sons, 1971), 152.

82 A BEAUTIFUL WOMAN WHO REALLY LOVED HIM: Interview with Ted Peckham, 1982.

VIRTUOUS AND DOWDY: Interview with Mrs. Charles S. Bird, 1985.

AT FEFE'S MONTE CARLO: Interview with Ted Peckham, 19

UNLICENSED GUNS: Interviews with Florynce Baker Martinau, 1982, 1985, and Ted Peckham, 1984.

DINNER JACKETS: Interviews with Jean Vanderbilt, 1982, and Dorothy Davis, 1984.

83 NOBODY TOLD THEIR PARENTS: Interview with Ann Hoffman Cutler, 1985.

FIFTY DOLLARS A NIGHT: Interview with Ted Peckham, 1982; also, Ted Peckham, *Gentleman for Hire* (Hollywood, Fla.: Frederick Fell, 1954), 136–37.

DEFLOWERING WOODWARD: Interview with Ted Peckham, 1982.

SPANISH WOMEN: Interview with Florynce Baker Martinau, 1985.

PRIVATE CEMETERY: Interviews with Ellen Violet and Cassie Sands Weeks, 1983.

LITTLE SEXUAL INTENSITY: Interviews with Ellen Violet, 1983, and Ann Cutler, 1985.

PIPING ROCK: Interview with Ellen Violet, 1983.

84 PREFERRED BENNY GOODMAN: Interview with Bill Sudduth, 1982.

NAVAL RESERVE: Interview with Ted Peckham, 1985.

CUSTOM-MADE AT DUNHILL: Interviews with Edward Patterson and Jack James, 1982.

FOLLOWING ORDERS: Interview with Ted Peckham, 1983.

TOWING A TARGET: Telephone interview with Oliver Ames, 1986.

TROUSERS AND BLUE BLAZER: Interview with Ted Peckham, 1983.

85 EDWARD M. KENNEDY: Interview with Edward Bemberg, 1986.

86 IN PANAMA CITY: Interview with Floyd "Shorty" Whiddon, 1988.

TO DANCE CHEEK TO CHEEK: Interview with Bill Sudduth, 1981.

5   NEW YORK

87 MOTHER'S BOARDERS: Interview with Eugene Condon, 1982.

88 NEW YORK SHOWROOMS: Interview with Eugene Condon, 1983.

GLOVES AND COSTUME JEWELRY: Interview with Telde Getz, 1981.

EQUIPMENT AND CLOTHING: John Robert Powers, *The Powers Girls* (New York: E.P. Dutton, 1941), 92.

90 60 PERCENT OF MODELING: Powers, *The Powers Girls*, 61.

"SALESMAN'S JOB": Powers, *The Powers Girls*, 111–12.

BARBARA STANWYCK, ET AL.: Powers, *The Powers Girls*, 191.

91 DWINDLED FOR A TIME: Interview with Herschel Williams, 1981.

CAMAY AND TANGEE: Interviews with Telde Getz and Herschel Williams, 1981, Eric Brotherson, 1983, and Bill Sudduth, 1985.

MODELING FUR COATS: Powers, *The Powers Girls*, 116.

92 PROMOTION FOR PHILIP MORRIS: Interview with Alvira Milligan, 1986.

93 REALIZE HER AMBITIONS: Interview with Bill Sudduth, 1985.

AFTER LOSING CRAWFORD: Interview with Noel Behn, 1986.

94 HONORED BY HIS PRESENCE: Interviews with Bill Sudduth, 1985.

"LOW BORN" GIRLS: Interviews with Bill Sudduth, 1985, and John Kobal, 1981.

SHE EXPECTED LOVE: Interviews with Bill Sudduth, 1982, and Herschel Williams, 1983.

STANISLAVSKY: Interview with Mrs. Jules Buck, 1991.

UNATTRACTIVE WITHOUT IT: Interview with Herschel Williams, 1983.

6 THE TEN MOST BEAUTIFUL GIRLS

96 "FOR MY MOTHER": Interview with Herschel Williams, 1983.

97 MUSIC BOX THEATRE: Interviews with Telde Getz and Eric Brotherson, 1984.

EVERY MUSICAL COMEDY: Powers, *The Powers Girls*, 192–93.

HER HIGH SCHOOL: Interview with Telde Getz, 1984.

98 FRENCH RIVIERA: Interview with Bill Sudduth, 1981.

"GREEK" CHANT: Interview with Eric Brotherson, 1982.

NOËL COWARD'S FURY: Interview with Telde Getz, 1981.

COWARD AND MRS. EDEN: Lesley Cole, *Remembered Laughter: The Life of Noël Coward* (New York: Alfred A. Knopf, 1977), 201.

ANN'S NEW NAME: Interview with Eric Brotherson, 1982.

AMERICAN GIRLS SHIVERED: Interview with Telde Getz, 1981.

103 "MISS AMBITION": Interview with Telde Getz, 1984; Cole, *Remembered Laughter*, 200; also Beatrice Lillie, written with James Brough, *Every Other Inch a Lady* (Garden City, N.Y.: Doubleday, 1972).

INTO HER NOTEBOOK: "High Jinx at the Music Box," *Theater Arts Monthly*, 23:2 (February 1939): 120–23.

ETHEL AND ANGELINE: Interview with Eugene Condon, 1985.

104 COWARD AT HIS BEST: Interview with Alfred de Liagre, 1986.

FUSS OVER MRS. WOODWARD: Interview with Angelo, at El Morocco, 1981; see also New York *Herald Tribune*, January 8, 1939.

SIX STANDING OVATIONS: Brooks Atkinson, *New York Times*, January 19, 1939.

HEMINGWAY: See Ernest Hemingway, *The Fifth Column and Four Stories of the Spanish Civil War* (New York: Charles Scribner's Sons, 1969).

105 BURNING UP WITH FEVER: Robert Sherwood, *Abe Lincoln in Illinois* (Dramatists' Play Service, 1937), 55.

ELMER RICE: Interview with Eugene Condon, 1985.

HOLD HER HAND: Interview with Telde Getz, 1984.

AFFAIR WITH RICE: Interview with David Clarke, 1982.

106 EXPERIMENTING ON THEM: Interview with David Clarke, 1982.

    MILLIGAN: Interview with Eugene Condon, 1985.

    "PLACES": Interview with Alvira Milligan, 1984.

    MILLIGAN AND ANN: Interviews with David Clarke, 1982, 1984.

7 SUCCESS

107 HUGGING MILLIGAN: Interview with Allen Shaw, 1981; *Abe Lincoln in Illinois* road shows, courtesy of Lincoln Center Library.

    MORAL QUANDARY: Interview with Victor Samrock, 1982.

    MILLIGAN'S FURY: Interview with Victor Samrock, 1982.

    COPY OF PLAY: Interview with Eugene Condon, 1981.

108 MOTHER LIVED PERMANENTLY: Kansas City *Star*, March 20, 1940.

    SOCIETY GIRL: Interview with Augusta Dabney, 1984.

    DAUGHTER'S PERFORMANCE: Interview with Eugene Condon, 1980.

    MADE HER FEEL GOOD: Interview with Eugene Condon, 1981.

    PERFORMANCE ON MONDAY NIGHT: Wichita *Eagle*, Thursday, March 28, 1940, p. 7; Friday morning, April 5, 1940, p. 9.

108–109 THE AUNTS: Interviews with Lydia Smiley Wasson, 1985, and Edna Smiley Cobb, 1983.

110 EDNA KNEW HER DUTY: Interview with Edna Smiley Cobb, 1985.

    MORE ALOOF THAN EVER: Interviews with Eugene Condon and Bill Sudduth, 1985.

    MILLIGAN DROPPED OFF: Interview with David Clarke, 1982.

    UNCONDITIONAL LOVE: Interview with Eugene Condon, 1984.

111 HER RESISTANCE: Interview with Lydia Smiley Wasson, 1983.

112 STANDING-ROOM-ONLY: Interview with Eugene Condon, 1984.

    GUILTY LEAVING HER MOTHER: Interview with Eugene Condon, 1984.

    EXPLAINING AWAY LANNY ROSS: Interview with Telde Getz, 1985.

    FILLED WITH MAGIC: Interview with Eugene Condon, 1984.

    FEFE'S CLUB: Interview with Telde Getz, 1985.

    FOOTNOTE SOURCE: Interview with Alvira Milligan, 1984.

113 THE DANCE FLOOR: Interviews with Telde Getz, 1985, Adele Jurgens (Monte Carlo dancer), 1982, and Dolly Davis (former Monte Carlo publicist), 1985.

    "NO THANK YOU": Interview with Telde Getz, 1985.

    FRANK COSTELLO: Interviews with Telde Getz, 1985, and Bill Sudduth, 1984.

    DOGWOOD: Interview with Telde Getz, 1985.

    RADIO: Erik Barnouw, *The Golden Web: A History of Broadcasting in the United States, 1933–1953* (New York: Oxford University Press, 1968), 94–100.

114 A MATTER OF PULL: Interviews with Bill Sudduth, 1983, and Telde Getz, 1984.

    THE SHOW: Interviews with Dorothy Davis, 1982, and Adele Jurgens, 1983.

115 ALICIA'S POLITICAL SYMPATHIES: FBI records, and interview with Bill Sudduth, 1984.

    WOODWARD SR.: Interview Florynce Baker Martinau, 1984.

    LECTURING: Interviews with Jo Hartford Bryce, 1986, and Mary Sanford, 1983.

SILENT BILLY: Interview with Bill Sudduth, 1983.

INVITED ANN: Interview with Bill Sudduth, 1983; Curlino, *The Captain*, 90.

OLD MAN'S GIRLFRIEND: Interview with Liz Whitney Tippet, 1983.

NOT A CALL GIRL: Interview with Bill Sudduth, 1981.

BEAN AND ANN: Interview with Bill Sudduth, 1983.

116 BILLY AND ANN: Interview with Bill Sudduth, 1983.

COPA GIRLS: Interview with Ted Peckham, 1985.

SUBTERRANEAN: Interview with Bill Sudduth, 1983.

4 a.m.: Interview with Bill Sudduth, 1983.

116–117 ETHEL'S DEATH: Interview with Lydia Smiley Wasson, 1983.

117 UNION STATION: Interview with Bill Sudduth, 1983.

HEARSE: Interviews with Lydia Smiley Wasson, 1983, and Edna Smiley Cobb, 1986.

ANN IN KANSAS: Interviews with Bill Sudduth, 1982, 1983.

118 MOTHER'S EXAMPLE: Interviews with Lydia Smiley Wasson, 1983, and Edna Cobb, 1986.

MANHATTAN MORTICIAN: Interview with Lydia Smiley Wasson, 1983.

119 FOOTNOTE SOURCE: Anthony Slide, *Great Radio Personalities in Historic Photographs* (New York: Dover Publications, 1982).

120 BRIEF NOTICE: *New York Times*, July 27, 1941.

ANN'S APARTMENT: Interviews with Telde Getz, 1983, and Bill Sudduth, 1981.

121 GIRL NEXT DOOR: Interview with Augusta Dabney, 1986.

AUDIENCE OF 8 MILLION: *Variety*, March 20, 1940.

122 CATASTROPHES: Interview with Augusta Dabney, 1986.

RADIO PARTS: Museum of Broadcasting, New York.

WOODWARD SR. TO BILLY: Interview with Ted Peckham, 1984.

MISTRESS: Interview with Liz Whitney Tippet, 1985.

FIVE YEARS OLDER: Interview with Bill Sudduth, 1984.

123 SMOKED A LOT: Interview with Bill Sudduth, 1986.

MALE LOVER: Interviews with Ann Cutler, 1985, and Ellen Violet, 1983.

WISHED TO ESCAPE: Interviews with Ted Peckham, 1985, and Liz Whitney Tippet, 1984.

"MONK" AND "DUNK": Interview with Bill Sudduth, 1984.

124 RACING WEEKEND: Interview with Bill Sudduth, 1981.

NATIONAL ESCAPES: *Saratogan*, July 25, 1942.

BRILLIANT AFFAIRS: *Saratogan*, July 26, 1942.

COCKTAIL PARTIES: Interview with Liz Whitney Tippet, 1985.

BILLY'S TARDINESS: Interview with Bill Sudduth, 1984.

RAILROADS AND BANKS: Interview with Bill Sudduth, 1983.

WILLIAMS: Interview with Edward Patterson, 1990; *Saratogan*, August 1, 1942.

125 ANN AND WOODWARD SR.: Interview with Bill Sudduth, 1984.

ESP: Interview with Herschel Williams, 1981.

POWERS OF SEX: Interview with Reynaldo Herrera, 1986.

"SHOPGIRL'S BONNET": Interview with Ann Cutler, 1986.

WELL-WISHERS: *Saratogan*, July 25, 1942.

FOOTNOTE SOURCE: John Galsworthy, *The Man of Property* (New York: Charles Scribner's Sons, 1918), 3–6.

126 ANN'S TRANSGRESSIONS: Interview with Bill Sudduth, 1983.

GIRL FROM BROOKVILLE: Interview with Bill Sudduth, 1984.

ANN'S HAT: Interview with Ann Cutler, 1986.

129 WORD "BEST": Interview with Bill Sudduth, 1984.

AUCTION: Waller, *Saratoga: Saga of an Impious Era*, 366–67; 370–71.

ANN IN LOVE: Interview with Bill Sudduth, 1984.

ELSIE AND MARY: Interviews with Mary Sanford, 1981, 1983, 1984.

129–130 DETECTIVE: Interview with Bill Sudduth, 1983.

130–131 ELSIE, WOODWARD SR., AND BILLY: Interviews with Bill Sudduth, 1980–1985, and Robert Leylan, 1980–83.

131 BILLY AND BEAN: Interview with Bill Sudduth, 1984.

SACRIFICE: Interview with Robert Leylan, 1982.

8 WAR BRIDE

132 REMOTE DESERT ISLAND: Interview with Bill Sudduth, 1984.

"ONLY GIRL": *Newsweek*, November 10, 1955; interview with Ted Peckham, 1985.

133 UNDERWATER: Interview with Bill Sudduth, 1984.

MADE LOVE: Interview with Ted Peckham, 1985.

"GO AWAY FOREVER": Interview with Bill Sudduth, 1984.

"ROUND THE BEND": Interview with Ted Peckham, 1985.

WARTIME MARRIAGES: Interview with John James, 1985.

134 STREETCAR CONDUCTOR: Interview with Ted Peckham, 1985.

PORCELLIAN: Interview with Edward Bemberg, 1984.

134–136 BILLY AND WILLIAM SR.: Interview with Ted Peckham, 1985.

136 HAD TRAINED HER WELL: Interview with Herschel Williams from Mary Borneau Taylor, 1983.

THE WOODWARD WOMEN AND ANN: Interview with Herschel Williams, 1983.

MAKE THEM PROUD: Interview with Ted Peckham, 1985.

137 MIGHT SUDDENLY SHIP OUT: Interview with Herschel Williams, 1983.

CHEERLEADER: Interview with Herschel Williams, 1983.

BEST MAN: Interview with John James, 1985.

BOEING FAMILY: Letter to Ann Woodward from Elsie Woodward, 1943.

WOODWARD GENEALOGY: Interview with Herschel Williams, 1984.

LINEAGE OF HORSES: Interviews with Herschel Williams, 1982, 1983.

HER EXUBERANCE: Interview with Herschel Williams, 1984.

138 ONE WEEK AFTER HER WEDDING: *Time* internal reporting file, November 1955.

"DEAR GRANDMOTHER": Letter dated March 20, 1943, *Life*, November 14, 1955, 35–39.

Notes

"CLOSED MY APARTMENT": Letter dated March 20, 1943, *Life*, Nov
35–39.

BILLY FELT HUMILIATED: Interview with Ted Peckham, 1985.

"TO MAKE IT WORK": *Life*, November 14, 1955.

139 DIVANS AND CHAIRS: Interviews with Herschel Williams, 1981, 1982.

AEW: Interview with Herschel Williams, 1983; also, Ann Woodward's household books.

140 "OUR HOSPITALITY": Interview with Bill Sudduth, 1982.

IMPROVE HER ACCENT: Interview with Elaine Lorillard, 1987.

DRUNK TO THEM: Interview with John James, 1985.

141 CHILDHOOD DEPRIVATION: Interview with Bill Sudduth, 1980.

142 TWENTY YEARS LATER: Will of William Woodward, Jr., Schedule G.

HER ROLLEIFLEX: Interview with Bill Sudduth, 1985.

MUST COME HOME NOW: Interview with Bill Sudduth, 1985.

TO KEEP HER DISTANCE: Interview with Lady Sarah Churchill, 1984.

143 WITHOUT ENTHUSIASM: Interview with Bill Sudduth, 1983.

EIGHT-HOUR WORKING SHIFTS: Interview with Ted Peckham, 1985.

FIFTEEN KNOTS: Declassified navy records on the sinking of the carrier *Liscome Bay*.

CRESCENT MOON ON THE HORIZON: Chronological log, destruction of the *Liscome Bay*.

144 ORDERING THE SHIP AROUND: Interview with Ted Peckham, 1985.

TO BEGIN TO REPAIR IT: Report of William Woodward, Jr., on *Liscome Bay* disaster.

145 DECKS OF THE *NEW MEXICO:* Henry H. Adams, *Years of Expectation: Guadalcanal to Normandy* (New York: David McKay, Inc., 1973).

NOT BEEN A HIT AT ALL: Interview with Ted Peckham, 1985.

FOOTNOTE SOURCE: Statement of William Woodward, Jr., Ens. D-V (G), USNR, USS *Liscome Bay*, November 25, 1943.

145–146 ACCOUNT OF THE SINKING: Samuel Eliot Morison, *History of the United States Naval Operations in World War II*, Vol. 2: *Aleutians, Gilberts, and Marshalls, June 1942–April 1944* (Boston: Little, Brown and Company, 1963); Secret: "Rough Log, US Navy Report, Sinking of the *Liscome Bay*"; "Chronological Sequence of Events 1600–1847 Oct. 24" (November 1943), File number AI6-3; Classified: "Report of War Operations in Rescue of USS *Liscome Bay*" (December 8, 1943, USS *Saratoga*).

146 AFRAID TO JUMP: *New York Times*, December 15, 1943, p. 1.

TRANSFERRED TO A HOSPITAL SHIP: Interview with Ted Peckham, 1985.

147 MADE A MAN OF HIM: Interview with Liz Whitney Tippet, 1984.

LIKE A TRUE HERO: Interview with Ted Peckham, 1985, and Bill Sudduth, 1982.

WHITE HOUSE FOR INFORMATION: Interview with Ted Peckham, 1985.

DIE AT WAR: Interview with Bill Sudduth, 1982.

9 AFTER THE HONEYMOON

148 HER VICTORY GARDEN: Interview with Jo Hartford Douglas Bryce, 1986.

149 SATISFYING PART OF BILLY AND ANN'S LIFE: Interview with Bill Sudduth, 1983.

150 RITZ BAR: Interview with Edward Patterson, 1986.

Notes

PE GIRARDEAU: FBI file #100–4714.

FOREIGN AGENT: FBI file #100–4714.

CLOSE CALLS WITH DEATH: Interview with Edward Patterson, 1986.

FLOATING FIRES: Interviews with Ted Peckham, 1983, 1984.

LABRADOR: Interview with Florynce Baker Martinau, 1984.

CHECKBOOK: Interview with John Richardson, 1982; probated will of Grenville Baker, 1949.

BERNARD M. BARUCH: Interview with Prince Kyril Scherbatow, 1988.

"CAN'T LIVE WITHOUT HER": Interview with Florynce Baker Martinau, 1984.

OUT ON DATES: Interview with John James, 1984.

BEFORE REWARDING HIM: Probated will of William Woodward, Sr.

NEW YORK OFFICES: Interview with Dana Woodward, former president of American Shoe Machinery, 1988.

AND INDUSTRIAL BELTING: *Wall Street Journal*, October 8, 1946.

PLAID PATTERNS: Interview with Elaine Lorillard, 1985.

152 TRANSVESTITE WAITERS: Interview with Elaine Lorillard, 1983.

RACING OBSESSIONS HAD: Interview with Alfred Gelardin, 1985.

FATHERHOOD: Interview with Alfred Gelardin, 1985.

153 AFTER-DINNER MUSICIANS: Ann Woodward's notebooks.

LATE NINETEENTH CENTURY: *The Genius of Charles James* (New York: Brooklyn Museum, 1984), 11.

BROKEN WITH THE FAMILY: Interview with Lady Sarah Churchill, 1984.

ANY OTHER CLIENT: Interviews with Homer Layne and Richard Zoerink, 1985.

HIGHLIGHTS OF ANN'S HAIR: Ann Woodward's notebooks.

154 CONSERVATIVE: Interview with Edward Bemberg, 1984.

ASKING QUESTIONS: Interview with Peter Pels, 1983.

"ALL CHIC THINGS": Ann Woodward's notebooks; interview with Peter Pels, 1983.

10 PRINCESS MARINA TORLONIA

156 "A LAWYER LIKE SOL": Interview with Irene Selznick, 1981.

BEAUTIFUL WIFE: Interview with Edward Bemberg, 1985.

157 "TERRIBLY HEALTHY": Interview with Leda Redmond, 1984.

RUSSIAN WOLFHOUND: Interview with William Draper, 1982.

EMPHATIC MANNER: Interview with Irene Selznick, 1981.

FRANK SHIELDS: Interview with John James, 1985.

BLACK EYEBROWS: Interview with Leda Redmond, 1984.

FOOTNOTE SOURCE: William X. Shields, *Bigger Than Life: A Biography of Francis X. Shields* (New York: Freundlich Books, 1986), 70–72.

158 NONPLUSSED GUESTS: Interview with Mrs. Walter Pidgeon, 1987.

CALLS FROM BILLY: Interview with Mrs. Walter Pidgeon, 1987.

159 PLAYING WITH HIM: Interview with Mrs. I. Townsend Burden, 1986.

AND PUSHED HER: Interviews with Bill Sudduth, 1984, 1985.

160 SARAH DID NOT SAY A WORD: Interview with Lady Sarah Churchill, 1983.

AGE OF TWENTY-SEVEN: Interview with Lady Sarah Churchill, 1985.

"BLUE AND RED BLOOD": Conversation with the author, New York, circa 1971.

"AFTER MY MONEY": Letters of James Woodward.

SPEAKING TOO LOUDLY: Interview with Elaine Lorillard, 1986.

IN LOS ANGELES: Interview with Robert Leylan, 1982.

161 A SEPARATE ENTRANCE: Interview with Robert Leylan, 1982.

FREQUENT ESCAPES: Interview with Bill Sudduth, 1985.

HAPPIEST IN HER LIFE: Interview with Chayan Kim, 1982.

PREFERRED THE ENGLISH STYLE: Interview with Robert Leylan, 1982.

CEMENTING: Interview with Mrs. John James, 1987.

ENGLISH BUTLERS: Interview with Maurice Page, 1988.

SMOKED-GLASS MIRROR: Author's visit to the home of Dominique DeMenil (the former Woodward home), 1988.

INTIMATE PARTS: Interview with Bill Sudduth, 1983.

BRANDY WITH GUESTS: Interview with Natalie Sherman, 1985.

162 "SCREWS ITSELF": Interview with John James, 1985.

KEEP BILLY: Interview with Bill Sudduth, 1983.

SILVERWARE SETTINGS: Ann Woodward's notebooks, 1944–46.

SOUTH OF FRANCE: Interviews with Sidney Mutum, 1985, and Leda Redmond, 1986.

STROLLING VIOLINIST: Interview with Henry Rosner, 1985.

CALL ME MADAM: Interview with Sidney Mutum, 1984.

AT THE COOK: Interview with Frederick Eberstadt, 1985.

TOUCHED HIM: Interview with Edward Patterson, 1982.

163 "THE CHARGES": Interview with Teddy Bemberg, 1987.

TWO WOMEN: Interview with Bill Sudduth, 1980.

INTO THE NIGHT: Police report, November 1955, and interview with Bill Sudduth, 1984.

HUGGING BILLY: Interview with Sidney Mutum, 1982.

"THAT'S NOT NICE": Interview with Natalie Sherman, 1985.

164 "WHEN IT COUNTS": Interview with John James, 1983.

"BUSINESS REASONS": Interview with Leda Redmond, 1984.

AND MARILYN MONROE: Shields, *Bigger Than Life*, 125.

LOVE LETTERS: Interviews with Mrs. Walter Pidgeon, 1985, and Bill Sudduth, 1984.

THREW THEM OUT: Interview with John Chapin, 1985.

MARINA TELEPHONED: Interview with John Chapin, 1985.

167 QUEEN ELIZABETH: Interview with Bill Sudduth, 1985; Curling, *The Captain*, 140–41, 144.

PRINCE TORLONIA: Interview with Francis X. Shields, 1986.

CLOUDS AND CHERUBS: Interview with Francis X. Shields, 1988.

DIRECTLY FROM ENGLAND: Interview with John Chapin, 1985.

REUPHOLSTERED: Interview with Francis X. Shields, 1985.

STEAMY SEDUCTION: Interview with Bill Sudduth, 1984.

168 HANDBAG: Police report, November 1955; and interview with Bill Sudduth, 1984.

SNAPSHOT: Police report, November 1955; interview with Bill Sudduth, 1981.

"LET YOU GO": Interview with Bill Sudduth, 1984.

169 OR MOVE IN: Interviews with Bill Sudduth, 1985, and Charles Pfeiffer, 1988.

LET HIM COME IN: Author's conversation with James Woodward, circa 1971.

AMPHETAMINES: Interviews with Bill Sudduth, 1984, and Katherine Hourigan, 1989.

CONCUSSION: Interview with Bill Sudduth, 1985.

BOYS WERE FINE: Interview with Maurice Page, 1988.

170 INVOLVING UNIONS: Interview with Irene Selznick, 1981.

CARMINE DESAPIO: Interviews with Richard Russell, 1984, Carmine DeSapio, 1986, Irene Selznick, 1986, Cynthia Boissevain, 1984, and Eleanor Whitney McCullom, 1985.

ELSA MAXWELL: Interview with Richard Russell, 1983.

TRAVEL PLANS: Interview with Roy Cohn, 1983.

DRIVE AND SPARKLE: Interview with Herschel Williams, 1982.

OBOLENSKY: Interview with Ivan Obolensky, 1985; newspaper photographs and clippings, 1955–65.

POOR BILLY: Interview with Herschel Williams, 1981.

SUM TO ANN: Will, William Woodward, Jr., December 14, 1948.

171 RARE OCCASIONS: Police report; interview with Bill Sudduth, 1985.

DIOR LABELS: Interview with Maurice Page, 1988.

HOUSE BUGGED: Interview with Mr. and Mrs. John James, 1986.

WALKS IN THE WOODS: Interviews with Harry Monroe, 1982, Prince Kyril Scherbatow, 1987, and Jerome Zerbe, 1982.

171–72 MOSLEMS: Interview with Charles Wacker, 1988.

172 GOLD THREAD: Interview with Joyce Coit, 1988.

LIVING WITH HIM: Interview with Charles Wacker, 1988.

"LIKE THE AGA KHAN:" *Vanity Fair,* 1988.

ICE-COLD WATER: Interview with Bill Sudduth, 1986; see also Igor Cassini, with Jeanne Molli, *I'd Do It All Over Again* (New York: G.P. Putnam's Sons, 1977).

EXTRACTING THESE CONFIDENCES: Interview with Bill Sudduth, 1985.

11 BILLY COMES BACK

173 A DIVORCE: Interview with Florynce Baker Martinau, 1985; *New York Times,* January 19, 1949, p. 1, and January 24, 1949, p. 1.

DRINKING AND CAROUSING: Interview with Floyd Whiddon, 1986.

174 SHOT HIMSELF IN THE HEAD: Interview with Floyd Whiddon, 1988.

THE COVER-UP: Interview with Floyd Whiddon, 1988.

GRACIOUSLY ACCEPTED: Newsclips.

CHOLLY KNICKERBOCKER: New York *Journal-American,* January 20, 1949, 16.

CRIMINAL JUSTICE SYSTEM: Interviews with Edward Patterson, 1988, and Eleanor Whitney McCullom, 1988.

"HONORARY PALLBEARER": Interview with Florynce Baker Martinau, 1987.

179 HER EMBRACE: Interview with Herschel Williams, 1981.

MONEY TO BUILD: Interview with Florynce Baker Martinau, 1986.

HORSESHOE: Interview with Bill Sudduth, 1986.

TELLING THE TRUTH: Interview with Bill Sudduth, 1986.

HAWAII: Interview with John James, 1986.

180 BROOK CLUB: Interview with Bill Sudduth, 1984.

WINTER HONEYMOON: Interviews with Jerome Zerbe and Maurice Page, 1984.

MAKEUP EN ROUTE: Interview and photograph, Jerome Zerbe, 1984.

GALA INTERNATIONAL PARTY: Interviews with Jerome Zerbe, 1982, and Constantine Alajalov, 1983.

BILLY GLARED: Interview with Jerome Zerbe, 1984.

GOLDEN CIRCLE: Interview and photographs, Jerome Zerbe, 1983; interview with Bill Sudduth, 1985.

BEST POLO: Interview with Devereau Millburn, 1984.

THORAZINE: Interview with Bill Sudduth, 1986.

181 CRYING AND HITTING: Interviews with Bill Sudduth, 1986, and Edward Patterson, 1988.

MARINA'S LIFE: Interviews with John Chapin and Leda Redmond, 1986.

HUSBAND'S SIDE: Interviews with Ed Slater and Bill Sudduth, 1984.

FLAWLESS WOODWARD CARRIAGE: Interview with Lydia Smiley Wasson, 1982.

REASON GIVEN: Interviews with Herschel Williams, 1981, and Jimmy Darrow, 1985.

MORTALLY FRIGHTENED: Interview with Elaine Lorillard, 1985.

EVERY NIGHT: Interview with Elaine Lorillard, 1987.

182 HOUSES: Monica Randall, *The Mansions of Long Island's Gold Coast* (New York: Hastings House, 1979), 219.

$200 A MONTH: Randall, *The Mansions of Long Island's Gold Coast*, 223; also, interview with Frank Vargata, estate caretaker, 1985.

MUSICIANS TRAIPSED: Interview with Frank Vargata, 1985.

185 CINERAMA FOR TAX PURPOSES: Legal documents, Nassau County leases; interview with Bill Sudduth, 1984.

FOTHERINGHAY CASTLE: Interviews with Father Kelly, 1985, and Bill Sudduth, 1986; Randall, *The Mansions of Long Island's Gold Coast*, 83.

BOYS' LESSONS: Interviews with Livio Principe, Mrs. Principe, and Jody O'Neill, 1985.

BIRTHDAY PARTY: Interview with Mrs. Joseph Thomas, 1986.

186 NEWSDAY: Interview with Edward Patterson, 1988.

EXPERTISE OF HER COMPANION: Interview with Edward Patterson, 1984.

"OVERBRED": Interviews with Elaine Lorillard and Robert Leylan, 1982.

"THAT'S MY WIFE": Interview with Edward Patterson, 1984.

12 THE BEST TIMES

187 BELMONT BALL: Interviews with Mrs. John James, 1986, and Bill Sudduth, 1988.

IMPORTANT PERSON: Interviews with Bill Sudduth, 1988, and Maria Estaban, 1989.

DEXEDRINE: Interview with Bill Sudduth, 1988.

AFTERNOON "DATES": Interview with Sally Parsons Oriel, 1985.

CARRYING HERSELF: Interview with Bill Sudduth, 1985.

188 "STRONGEST WOMAN ON EARTH": Interview with Bill Sudduth, 1983.

MOST EXPENSIVE WEDDING: Interview with Bill Sudduth, 1985.

OYSTER BAY BEDROOM: Interview with Bill Sudduth, 1985.

"WONDER GIRL": Gayatri Devi, Maharani of Jaipur, with Santha Rama Rau, *A Princess Remembers: The Memoirs of the Maharani of Jaipur* (Philadelphia: Lippincott, 1976), 135.

PEACOCKS: Interview with Bill Sudduth, 1985.

SHE PHOTOGRAPHED THE LAKE: Photographs in Jaipur province by Ann Woodward.

191 TINKLING ANKLET: Interview with Bill Sudduth, 1984.

POLO AGAINST THE SUNSET: Photographs by Ann Woodward.

HIMALAYAS: Interview with Mrs. Phyllis Havenstrite Hall, 1984.

CEREMONIAL VISITS: Interview with Bill Sudduth, 1985; Devi, *A Princess Remembers,* 176–79.

FERNANDA MONTEL: Police report, Woodward case, November 22, 1953.

192 KNOWN LESBIAN: Interview with Marianne Strong.

RITZ HOTEL: Police report, November 22, 1955.

AT THE BROOK: Interview with Ted Peckham, 1984.

RULES BENT: Interview with Ted Peckham, 1984.

193 SUCH A FEAT: Interview with Bill Sudduth, 1983.

DALÍ COMMISSION: Interview with Bill Sudduth, 1986.

SALVADOR DALÍ: See Meryle Secrest, *Salvador Dalí: A Biography* (New York: E.P. Dutton, 1987), especially pages 185 and 189.

LIZARDS: Winthrop Sargeant, *Life,* September 10, 1945, 24–25.

194 "I UNMASK YOU": Interview with Bill Sudduth, 1984.

SPECTRE OF SEX APPEAL: Secrest, *Salvador Dalí: A Biography,* 130.

UNPAID FEE: Interviews with Bill Sudduth, 1983, and Eugene Condon, 1981.

DALÍ SUED: Cleveland *Plain Dealer,* August 26, 1954.

195 "GRAY GRIM COLORS": *Time,* "People" section, September 6, 1954.

INHERITED BY WOODY: Interview with Lydia Smiley Wasson, 1981.

196 HUNTER COLLEGE: Interview with Bill Sudduth, 1984.

CLIVEDEN: Interview with Bill Sudduth, 1986.

BILL ASTOR: *Times* (London), March 17, 1966.

NANCY ASTOR: *Times* (London), clippings 1950–55.

FOOTNOTE SOURCE: Burton J. Hendrick, "The Astor Fortune," *McClure's Magazine* (April 1905).

197 CALL GIRL'S LONDON FLAT: Anthony Summers and Stephen Dorril, *Honeytrap* (London: Weidenfeld & Nicolson, 1987), 65.

NAKED GIRLS: Interview with Bill Sudduth, 1986; see also Summers and Dorril, *Honeytrap*.

LUXURY OF ASTOR'S ENTERTAINING: Summers and Dorril, *Honeytrap*, 65–66.

FOOTNOTE SOURCE: Interviews with Bill Sudduth, 1986, and Charles Wacker, 1987. On the Profumo affair, see Phillip Knightley and Caroline Kennedy, *An Affair of State: The Profumo Case and the Framing of Stephen Ward* (New York: Atheneum, 1987), 31; and David Mure, *The Last Temptation* (London: Buchan and Enright, 1984). See also Summers and Dorril *Honeytrap*, 72ff, and the London *Times* of the period. For Ward's suicide see *Honeytrap*, 19.

198 FREE SESSION: Summers and Dorril, *Honeytrap*, 66; interview with Bill Sudduth, 1986.

WARD AND ANN: Interview with Bill Sudduth, 1986.

STUNNING CONQUEST: Interview with Bill Sudduth, 1984.

HE NEEDED HER: Interview with Bill Sudduth, 1984.

201 ETHEL DE CROISSET: Interview with Kenneth Jay Lane, 1981.

ELSIE'S DISFAVOR: Interview with Renee Link, 1989.

ETHEL REBELLIOUS: Interview with Constantin Alajalov, 1984.

PROUST: Interview with John Richardson, 1981.

DE CROISSET A JEW: Interview with Robert Leylan, 1982.

FOOTNOTE SOURCE: Lonfranco Rasponi, *The International Nomads* (New York: G.P. Putnam, 1966), 66. Also interviews with Hurley Papock, 1987, Michelle Porges, 1988, Jeanne Vanderbilt, 1984, Ruth Dubonnet, 1982, Rod Coupe, 1983, and Michael Butler 1986.

202 TRAIN DE VIE: Interview with Rod Coupe, 1982.

UPSTAIRS FOR A ROMP: Interviews with Ruth Dubonnet, 1987, and Bill Sudduth, 1984.

ENDED IN SEX: Interviews with Bill Sudduth, 1982, 1984.

202–204 DE CUEVAS MASQUERADE PARTY: *Time* internal reporting file, November 5, 1955.

204 WRONGED BUT CHERISHED MAN: Interview with Albert Gelardin, 1986.

CIRCLES OF HUSH: Interview with Bill Sudduth, 1985; also *Time* internal reporting file, November 5, 1955.

13 MATCH RACE

208 FULLY EQUIPPED HOSPITAL ROOM: Interview with Dr. Ben Keane, 1986.

CECIL BOYD-ROCHFORT: Curling, *The Captain*, 149–50.

FOOTNOTE SOURCE: *New York Times*, November 25, 1931.

209 TEN DAYS BEFORE: Curling, *The Captain*, 151–52.

ANN NOT INVITED: Interview with Bill Sudduth, 1984.

BEYOND HIS GRASP: Interview with Bill Sudduth, 1984.

ANN CRIED FOR BOTH: Interview with Bill Sudduth, 1984.

210 NEW YORK HOSPITAL AND GROTON: Last will and testament of William Woodward, Sr., March 5, 1952.

BARELY COMPATIBLE: Baldwin, *Billy Baldwin Remembers*.

DUTIFUL WIFE: Roosevelt, *Doers and Dowagers*.

212 "BREEDING HORSES": Jimmy Breslin, *Sunny Jim* (Garden City, N.Y.: Doubleday, 1962), 20–21.

"LOOKS FINE": Breslin, *Sunny Jim*, 18

STEP INTO HIS SHOES: Jimmy Canno, New York *Post*, 1955.

213 "ANN WOULD HAVE LEFT YOU": Interview with Mary Sanford, 1982.

215 "LUCKY" TIE: *Sports Illustrated*, September 1955.

FLORIDA DERBY: *New York Times*, March 27, 1954.

"LOWER PROFILE": Interviews with Bill Sudduth, 1984 and Mary Sanford, 1982.

HYSTERIA: Interview with Mary Sanford, 1981.

216 "YOUR MOTHER'S LESSONS": Interview with Bill Sudduth, 1982.

OVERHEARD THE FIGHT: Police Report; interview with Bill Sudduth, 1982.

MAKE UP IN BED: Interview with Bill Sudduth, 1983.

217 DRUGS: Interviews with Diana Vreeland, 1981, Bill Sudduth, 1986, and Dr. Jane Oldden, 1982–1986.

DRUG REGIMEN: Interview with Bill Sudduth, 1984.

218 "PERFECT WIFE": Interviews with Bill Sudduth and Sally Parsons Oriel, 1985.

YOUNGER WOMAN: Interview with Jean Vanderbilt, 1985.

SEEING ENEMIES EVERYWHERE: Interviews with Bill Sudduth, 1984, and Sally Parsons Oriel, 1985.

CLUBHOUSE ROOF: Interview with Charles Wacker, 1987.

219 HE DID NOT SEEM TO NOTICE: Interview with Bill Sudduth, 1984; *New York Times*, May 8, 1955.

AGAINST SUMMER TAN: Breslin, *Sunny Jim*, 27.

220 INHERITED HORSES: Interview with Bill Sudduth, 1984.

RISKING THE REPUTATION: Interview with Bill Sudduth, 1981.

14 INDIA

221 "I LOVE MY HUSBAND": Police report, November 10, 1955.

TO STAND NEAR HER: Interview with Sally Parsons Oriel, 1984.

ELECTRIFYING ENTRANCES: Interview with Sam Wagstaff, 1980.

222 "FANTASTIC DANCER": Interview with Sam Wagstaff, 1980.

SILVER PIN: Interview with Sally Parsons Oriel, 1984.

223 JAI ESCAPED: Devi, *A Princess Remembers*, 215.

LACK OF EXPERTISE: Interview with Phyllis Havenstrite Hall, 1986; Police report, Homicide 894 (1955), 283–91.

FELL IN LOVE: Interview with Phyllis Havenstrite Hall, 1986.

224 BILLY'S DATE: Interview with Robert Leylan, 1983.

HALF CIRCLE OF THE HIMALAYAS: Devi, *A Princess Remembers*, 69.

ENORMOUS PARASOL: Interview with Phyllis Havenstrite Hall, 1986.

FATAL STAMPEDE: Interview with Phyllis Havenstrite Hall, 1986.

227 "STABLE PERSON": Police report, November 1955.

SALLY WAS CONVINCED: Interview with Sally Parsons Oriel, 1984.

"YOU'RE LUCKY": Interview with Diana Vreeland, 1983.

RED-AND-WHITE COLORS: *New York Times*, May 29, 1955.

228 BILLY BLAMED ANN: Interview with Herschel Williams, 1982.

"PREPUNCTUAL": Interview with Robert Leylan, 1982.

TINY PERFUME BURNER: Author's conversation with Ann Woodward and Jimmy Woodward, 1973.

WITH MATCHING BRACELET: Author's conversation with Ann Woodward and Jimmy Woodward, 1973; interview with Bill Sudduth, 1986; *Time* internal reporting file, February 1979. See also Suzy Menkes, *The Windsor Style* (Boston: Salem House Publishers, 1988).

DUCHESS'S FRANK HOSTILITY: Author's conversation with Ann Woodward and Jimmy Woodward, 1973.

229 FULL-BODY ELASTIC CORSET: Author's conversation with Ann Woodward and Jimmy Woodward, 1973.

HUSBANDS' ATTITUDES: Interview with Bill Sudduth, 1984.

SETS OF DISHES: Author's conversation with Ann Woodward and Jimmy Woodward, 1973.

CHINESE WALL PANELS: Author's observation, conversation with Ann Woodward and Jimmy Woodward, 1973.

EYES SEEMED TO GLEAM: Interview with Bill Sudduth, 1981.

230 FRENCH INTONATIONS: Author's conversation with Ann Woodward, 1973.

HOT BREAD CRUMBS: Menkes, *The Windsor Style*, 31.

ANN HAD TRIUMPHED: Author's conversation with Ann Woodward and Jimmy Woodward, 1973; interviews with Bill Sudduth, 1980, Sam White, 1986, Hurley Papock, 1987. See also Charles Higham, *The Duchess of Windsor: The Secret Life* (New York: McGraw-Hill, 1988).

"DANCE WITH HER": Author's conversation with Ann Woodward and Jimmy Woodward, 1973.

15   HOME IS WHERE THE HEART IS

232 "ALL THOSE STAIRS": Interview with Sally Parsons Oriel, 1985.

STATEMENTS ABOUT NASHUA: Interview with Robert Leylan, 1981.

233 DON AMECHE: Interview with Charles Wacker, 1988.

234 "AS GOOD A BRED HORSE": *New York Times Magazine*, 1955.

BOISTEROUS SPORTSWRITERS: Breslin, *Sunny Jim*, 29.

JUMP INTO SECOND PLACE: Red Smith, New York *Herald Tribune*, May 7, 1955.

235 "PAINT MYSELF BLACK": Interview with Special UN Ambassador for Refugees Francis Kellog, 1987.

BILLY'S BACK: Interview with Jerome Zerbe, 1984.

CHOLLY KNICKERBOCKER REPORTED: Interviews with Jerome Zerbe, 1981, 1983.

236 BAR AND SUN LOUNGE: Interview with Jo Hartford Bryce, 1984; also John Pearson, *The Life of Ian Fleming* (New York: McGraw-Hill, 1966), 180.

FORMER WIFE: *The New Yorker*, April 21, 1962, 34.

CAME ON TOO STRONG: Interview with Edward Patterson, 1989.

BEST AMERICANS: Interview with Jo Hartford Bryce, 1986.

239 GRADED CURVES: Ian Fleming, *Diamonds Are Forever* (London: Gildrose Productions Inc., 1956), 75–76.

LEITER EXPLAINS: Fleming, *Diamonds Are Forever*, 87.

PREFERENCE OF BILLY'S: Interview with Robert Leylan, 1981.

GANGLAND CRIMINALS: Fleming, *Diamonds Are Forever*, 173.

240 SHOOTING A FOX: Interview with Herschel Williams, 1981.

CUSTOM-MADE SHOTGUN: Police report, November 10, 1955, p. 108.

"YES, DIVORCE": Interview with Herschel Williams, 1982.

FLEMING'S ARREST: Interview with Jo Hartford Bryce, 1984.

VERMONT BRIDGE: Interview with Charles Wacker, 1988.

IN A FOLDING CHAIR: Breslin, *Sunny Jim*, 27–28.

241 NASHUA'S LEGS: Breslin, *Sunny Jim*, 30–31.

16   BOAR HUNT

242 HEADY THOUGHT: Interview with Bill Sudduth, 1981.

WILD BOAR AND CHAMOIS: Interview with Princess Honeychile Hohenlohe, 1986.

"HONEYCHILE": Interviews with Princess Honeychile Hohenlohe, 1987, Charles Allen, Jr., 1985, and Baroness Terry von Pantz, 1983.

SOCIALIZE HERE: Interview with Princess Honeychile Hohenlohe, 1987.

243 DINNER PARTNER: Interview with Princess Honeychile Hohenlohe, 1987.

ANCIENT ROYAL CASTLE: Ann Woodward's notebooks, 1955.

244 BILLY AND MARILYN PEEK: Interview with Baroness Terry von Pantz, 1984.

245 "DAMN YOU, WOODWARD": Interview with Princess Honeychile Hohenlohe, 1987.

"WAIT A DAY": Interviews with Princess Honeychile Hohenlohe, 1987, and Baroness Terry von Pantz, 1984.

ON THEIR WAY HOME: Interview with Herschel Williams, 1981.

OSTENTATIOUS CLOTHESHORSE: Interviews with Whitney Tower, 1984, and Charles Wacker, 1987.

"BEST-DRESSED WOMAN": Interview with Robert Leylan, 1981; *Sports Illustrated*, July 4, 1955.

246 ANN TOLD THE PRESS: Interview with Bill Sudduth, 1984.

247 REFUSED TO COME TO CHICAGO: Interview with Robert Leylan, 1983.

248 LEFT HER SOBBING: Interview with William Sudduth, 1986.

POOR BILLY: Interview with Charles Wacker, 1987.

HIS PRIVATE GAME: Interview with Bill Sudduth, 1986.

"OH, WEAR THAT": Interviews with Bill Sudduth, 1982, 1986.

249 ARCARO STILL WHIPPING HIM: Breslin, *Sunny Jim*, 36.

250 THE BETTER HORSE: Interviews with Charles Wacker, 1987, and Whitney Tower, 1984.

TOASTED ONE ANOTHER: Interviews with Sally Iselin, 1983, and Mary Sanford, 1982.

251 A CLOSE SECOND: Interview with Robert Leylan, 1983.

NEW SILENCE: Interview with Robert Leylan, 1983.

A LOSING FIGHT: Interview with Edward Bemberg, 1988.

MANHATTAN'S WEST SIDE: Interview with Joan Fontaine, 1981.

NEVER FOUND THE EARRING: Interview with Lydia Smiley Wasson, 1982.

JEWELRY WAS MISSING: *New York Times*, November 24, 1955.

17 WINNER TAKE ALL

252 ENGLISH STYLE: Interview with Robert Leylan, 1981.

GANGPLANK: Breslin, *Sunny Jim*.

MALE PORNOGRAPHIC FILMS: Interview with Monica Randall, 1982.

253 BARNEY BALDING: Police report, October–November 1955.

"VAGRANT" QUALITY: Interviews with Sally Parsons Oriel, 1985, and Bill Sudduth, 1984.

ELSIE TOLD BILLY: Interview with Mary Sanford, 1981. Also interviews with Joyce Coit, Bill Sudduth, Sally Parsons Oriel, and Sarah Churchill.

SALLY PARSONS ORIEL TO AQUEDUCT: Police report, November 1955.

"MAN IN BED": Interviews with Bill Sudduth, 1982, 1985.

WIND GONE: Interviews with Bill Sudduth, 1982, 1985.

"TAKING A NAP": Interviews with Herschel Williams, 1987, and Bill Sudduth, 1982, 1985.

PRESERVE HER FIGURE: Interview with Robert Ellsworth, 1988; also Ann Woodward's notebooks, 1949.

254 FORMAL FALL BASH: Barbara Goldsmith, *Little Gloria . . . Happy at Last* (New York: Alfred A. Knopf, 1980), 219–20.

GRACE KELLY: Interview with Bill Sudduth, 1983.

BEST-DRESSED WOMAN: *Sports Illustrated*, September 6, 1955.

ANN, PULLING HIS ARM: Interview with Bill Sudduth, 1983.

BEST TABLES: Interview with Betty Jane Henry, 1988.

255 BILLY TORMENTED HER: Interview with Bill Sudduth, 1984.

BRICK ENTRANCE PILLARS: Interview with Father Kelly, a current resident, 1983.

ANN IN LATE MORNING: Police report, November 1955.

257 "I'LL BE YOUR FRIEND": Interview with Edward Patterson, 1989.

COST $10,257: Interviews with Stewart Clement, 1983, and Clarence Brent, retired chief engineer, Mid-State Aviation, 1988.

258 "TENNIS-COURT AIRPLANE": Interviews with Stewart Clement, 1983, Herschel Williams, 1981, and Merle Markley, 1983.

"I'LL GO WITH YOU": Interview with Bill Sudduth, 1983.

PURSUING WOMEN: Interview with Stewart Clement, 1985.

259 ATKINSON MUNICIPAL AIRPORT: Pittsburg *Headlight*, October 21, 1955.

SOCIAL STUDIES TEACHER: Interview with Bill Sudduth, 1985; *Time* internal reporting file, 1955.

TREELESS PITTSBURG: Interview with Bill Sudduth, 1985.

NEVER GET A SCRATCH: Interview with Merle Markley, 1983.

260 ANN'S COUSIN: Interview with Bill Sudduth, 1984.

OWING FOLKS MONEY: Interviews with Bill Sudduth, 1983, and Eugene Condon, 1981.

ANN'S FATHER: Interview with Bill Sudduth, 1983.

"CEMETERY LOOKS NICE": Quotation from William Carpenter, Long Island *Newsday*, November 1, 1955; *Time* internal reporting file, November 1955; interview with Mrs. William (Mary) Carpenter, 1989.

"BANKING": Interview with Mary Carpenter, 1989.

261 THREE IN THE MORNING: Interview with Mary Carpenter, 1989.

BILLY TOLD THE CARPENTERS: Long Island *Newsday*, November 1, 1955.

262 BELAIR: Baltz, *Chronicle of Belair*, 85–86.

FOOTNOTE SOURCE: Gerald Clarke, *Capote* (New York: Simon & Schuster, 1988), 463. Interviews with Charles Wacker, 1986, Herschel Williams, 1980, Robert Leylan, 1984, Ann Cutler, 1985, Princess Honeychile Hohenlohe, 1986. On earlier marriage: author's research, and interviews with Herbert Bayard Swope, 1988, John Richardson, 1982, and Ann Cutler, 1987.

263 IRISH STALLION: Probated will and testament of William Woodward, Jr., itemized the unused ticket to Ireland, 1955.

SLEEPING OFF HIS TRIP: New York *Daily News*, November 4, 1955; interview with Herschel Williams, 1981.

AIMING HER GUN: Interview with Harriet Aldrich Bering, 1984.

264 MARIBOU-EDGED BALL GOWN: Interview with Mrs. Charles Schwartz, 1982.

DOUBLE SILK LINING: Interview with Peter Pels, Maximilian Furs, 1987.

ROTHMANN'S: Interview with Herschel Williams, 1981; District Attorney's Investigation into the death of William Woodward, Jr., New York City, October 31, 1955, at Doctors Hospital, 6:37 p.m., in the presence of Frank A. Gulatto, District Attorney, Inspector Stuyvesant A. Pinnell, Dr. John Prutting, Nathan Birchall, stenographer: pp. 433–454.

265 STEPPED ON HIS HAND: Interview with Jackie Gebhardt, 1985.

"WHO SUSTAINED THE LOSS": Police report, November 10, 1955; interview with retired detective Ray Soper, 1984.

OUT-OF-WORK GERMAN: Police report, November 10, 1955; interviews with Lee Principe and Russell Haff, 1982.

266 FOOTNOTE SOURCE: Interview with Russell Haff, 1981.

18   THE DINNER PARTY

273 "MILLIONAIRE SPORTSMAN": Interview with Edward Patterson, 1986.

ANN'S ACCENT: Police report, November 1955.

274 SKUNK'S MISERY: Police report, November 1955; interviews with Retired Detective Tom Martin, 1983, 1984.

"IT'S A COMPLIMENT": Interview with Bill Sudduth, 1983.

BROADTAIL SUIT: Interview with Peter Pels, 1984.

"NEVER COMPLAIN": Interview with Bill Sudduth, 1983.

AFTER THE DOGS: Interview with Florynce Baker Martinau, 1987.

DULL SUBURBAN DINNER: Interview with Bill Sudduth, 1983.

LITTLE RAG DOLL: Menkes, *The Windsor Style*.

277 BUTLER'S RENDEZVOUS: Interview with Michael Butler, 1986.

FRESH FRUIT, AND CUT FLOWERS: Interview with Douglas Griffin, the Baker butler, 1985.

"BIT EARLY": Interview with Sidney Mutum, 1982.

PREVIOUS AUTUMNS: Interview with Bill Sudduth, 1985.

FOOTNOTE SOURCE: Stephen Birmingham, *Duchess: The Story of Wallis Warfield Windsor* (Boston: Little, Brown, 1981), 260.

278 RIDDEN TRICYCLES: Interview with Florynce Baker Martinau, 1987.

"FLOWERS OF DEATH": Interview with Sam Wagstaff, 1983.

CHINESE CARPET: Police report interview with Stan Freeman, November 23, 1955, p. 279; also, author's interview with Douglas Griffin, 1986.

EYELIDS LOOKED PUFFY: Interviews with Mary Sanford, 1981, 1983; photographs from the period.

DI VERDURA: Interview with Bill Sudduth, 1985; Menkes, *The Windsor Style*, 170–72.

POWDERED HER CHEST: Interview with Bill Sudduth, 1982.

279 "WE HAVE A PLAN": Police report interview with Mary Sanford, November 2, 1955.

THE AMUSING SANFORDS: Interviews with Edward Patterson, 1983, and Michael Butler, 1986.

ONION DIP: Interview with Sidney Mutum, 1982.

PRINCESS MARGARET: Long Island *Daily Press*, October 28, 1955.

"FUNNILY ENOUGH": Interview with Odette O'Higgins Hinton, 1982; see also J. Bryan III and Charles J. V. Murphy, *The Windsor Story* (New York: William Morrow and Company, 1979), 490–93.

A JOLLY GUEST: Interviews with Stan Freeman and Harry Evans; Police report, November 1955.

"PRINCESS PAPULA": Interviews with Herschel Williams, 1981, Charles Sibre and Marcia Kaufman, 1982, and Tom Hanley, 1983.

280 "I HAVE A PISTOL": Long Island *Newsday*, November 25, 1955.

CUSHING: Interview with Florynce Baker Martinau, 1987.

THE DUKE: Interview with Sam Wagstaff, 1985.

THE DUCHESS'S TOILETTE: Interview with Florynce Baker Martinau, 1987.

DARED NOT BE LATE: Interview with Florynce Baker Martinau, 1987.

281 READY TO BE KISSED: Birmingham, *Duchess*, 258; interview with Michael Butler, 1986.

SECRET DRAWERS: Interview with Bill Sudduth, 1983.

ETHEL MERMAN: Interview with Telde Getz, 1983.

ROARING FIRE: Interview with Mary Phipps, 1988.

CARDS AT THE TABLES: Interview with Sidney Mutum, 1985.

HOUSEGUESTS: Interview with Florynce Baker Martinau, 1983.

LOBSTER PULLMAN: Interview with Douglas Griffin, 1981.

282 "EX-CHORUS GIRL": Interview with Oleg Cassini, 1986.

FERN TAILER GIMBEL: Police report, November, 1955.

TITI: Interview with Cassie Sands Weeks, 1984.

INTERNATIONAL RACES: Interview with Bill Sudduth, 1984.

CHINESE HORSES: Randall, *The Mansions of Long Island's Gold Coast;* interview with Douglas Griffin, 1981.

FOOTMAN WAS DIZZY: Interview with Sidney Mutum, 1983.

FOOTNOTE SOURCE: Police report interview with Mrs. Winston Frost, November 5, 1955.

283 BILLY AND MISS MONTEL: Police report interview with Michael Butler, November 10, 1955.

"WANTS TO SHOOT HIM": Police report interview with Denny Slater, November 3, 1955.

CLEVELAND AMORY: *Life,* November 1955.

AFTER THEIR DANCE: Interview with Martha Frost, 1985.

ANN GORNEY: Police report, November 10, 1955.

FOOTNOTE SOURCE: Police report; interview with Sidney Mutum, 1983. Also, interviews with Paul Chase, 1986, Fern Tailer Gimbel (quoted by her mother, Florynce Baker Martinau), 1983, Edith Baker Schiff (quoted by her sister-in-law, Dorothy Schiff), 1985, Mary Sanford, 1981, 1982, 1983, Mrs. John Winslow, 1986, Michael Butler, 1985, Mary Phipps, 1986, Mrs. Charles Schwartz, 1986, and Mr. and Mrs. Winston Frost, 1985.

284 FEIGNED INDIFFERENCE: Interview with Bill Sudduth, 1984.

SHE WAS FADING: Gioia Diliberto, *Debutante: The Story of Brenda Frazier* (New York: Alfred A. Knopf, 1987).

"BIRDSHOT": Interview with Bill Sudduth, 1983.

"YOU'RE OBSESSED": Interview with Mary Phipps, 1988.

BRIDGE TABLES: Interview with Sidney Mutum, 1983.

285 SCHIFF CONVERSATION: Interviews with Florynce Baker Martinau, 1983, and Sam Wagstaff, 1985.

SOMETHING TERRIBLE: Interview with Sam Wagstaff, 1985.

GLASS OF MILK: Police report interview with Fern Tailer Gimbel; author's interview with her mother, Florynce Baker Martinau, 1986.

MRS. WINSLOW: Police report, November 1955; interview with Mrs. John Winslow, 1988.

HORRIFIED GROUP: Interview with Mrs. John Winslow, 1988.

"RAIN GETS WORSE": New York *Post,* October 30, 1955.

286 HAPPY MAN: Interview with Mary Sanford, 1987.

HELIO TO BRAZIL: Police report, Detective Supplementary Report, p. 37.

FOG AND RAIN: Interviews with Mrs. Joseph Thomas, 1987, Michael Butler, 1986, and Mrs. John Winslow, 1986.

WINSLOWS FOLLOWED: Interview with Mrs. John Winslow, 1986.

19   THE SHOOTING

287 FOOTNOTE SOURCE: Police report, Ann Woodward interrogation, 1955.

288 SLEEP ARMED: Police report; interview with Bill Sudduth, 1983.

289 A CRASH UPSTAIRS: Police report; author's interview with Paul Wirths, 1984.

290 OPENING HER EYES: Interview with Bill Sudduth, 1983.

SHOOT HERSELF: Interview with Bill Sudduth, 1983.

20   THE COLLAPSE

292 FATAL TO PEOPLE: Police report, Coroner's report.

293 TELEPHONE FOR HELP: Interview with Steve Smith by Assistant D.A. Edward Robinson, Oyster Bay Cove, 9:12 a.m., October 30, 1955.

"WHO'S CALLING": Interview with Gladys Gallagher, 1985.

FOOTNOTE SOURCE: Interview with Jody O'Neill, 1983; telephone conversations with Mr. and Mrs. Livio Principe, 1985.

294 "PLEASE FIND HIM": Interview with Cynthia Boissevain and daughter, 1986.

ALL FINISHED NOW: Interview with Bill Sudduth, 1983.

BRIGHT SPOTLIGHTS: Letter to Russell Haff from Henry Cormier, October 31, 1955.

CORMIER: Interview with Russell Haff, 1981.

FILLED WITH APPLES: Interview with Russell Haff, 1981.

295 RAN BACK TO BILLY: Statement of Henry Cormier; patrolman's report from midnight to night tour, October 30, 1955.

HAFF KNELT BY ANN: Interview with Russell Haff, 1983, and Claire Moore, 1981.

WEPT CONVULSIVELY: Interview with Russell Haff, 1983.

FOOTNOTE SOURCE: Police report; interview with Bob Greene of *Newsday*, 1983.

296 PRONOUNCED HIM DEAD: Interview with Dr. Francis Moore, 1986.

RECENT FIGHTS: Interview with Joyce Coit, 1983.

297 FARRELL ARRIVED: Interview with Bob Greene, 1983.

PRESS WAS FORBIDDEN: Interview with Jim O'Neill, 1985.

298 HARASSMENT OF LOCAL MOBSTERS: Interview with Bob Greene, 1983.

GULOTTA'S INSTRUCTIONS: Police report, November 10, 1955; interview with Frank Gulotta, 1983.

IMPOSSIBLE FOR ANN TO MOVE HIM: Interview with Dr. Leslie Lukash, 1983.

FOOTNOTE SOURCE: Interview with Liz Whitney Tippet (the former Mrs. John Hay Whitney), 1985.

299 THE BRASS: Interviews with retired Nassau County detective George Erdoty, 1986, and Ferdinand Wendt, 1986.

AT 4:15 a.m.: Interview with Claire Moore, 1987.

300 ANN TOSSED HER HEAD: Interview with Bill Sudduth, 1983.

ELSIE AND BILLY BANCROFT: Interviews with Mary Grant, 1986, and Dorothy Schiff, 1985.

"SEPARATE BEDROOMS": William Kahn (unpublished manuscript).

301 THROWN OUT AGAIN: Interview with Jim O'Neill, 1985.

JUMPED OUT OF BED: Police report, November 10, 1955.

ANN'S DREAM: Interview with Bill Sudduth, 1983.

FORENSIC EVIDENCE: Interview with Tom Martin, 1987.

303 MAKE THINGS EASY FOR HER: Interview with Bill Sudduth, 1983.

FOOTNOTE SOURCE: Interviews with Morris Wirths and Mitchell Booth, 1986.

304 POLITICAL BOSS: Interview with Morris Wirths, 1986.

FIRM'S LIAISON: Interview with George Milligan, 1986.

WILLIAM WOODWARD, SR.: Interviews with retired detectives Andy Hebrerer and Tom Martin, 1986, 1987.

FOOTNOTE SOURCE: Oral history document, Henry Root Stern, Sr., Columbia University.

305 MOSS REFUSED: Interview with Andy Hebrerer, 1986.

WHITNEY AGREED: Interview with Andy Hebrerer, 1986.

BANCROFT ARRIVED: Interview with Mary Grant, 1985.

TEXTILE COMPANY: Interviews with Edward Patterson, 1986, 1987, 1988.

LET ELSIE SLEEP: Interview with Mrs. Walter Dunnington, 1983.

THEIR CLOSENESS: Interview with Robert Leylan, 1982.

IN COLD BLOOD: Interview with Mary Grant, 1985.

306 ANN MURDERED BILLY: Interview with Mrs. Walter Dunnington, 1984.

307 BUSINESS SUITS: Interview with Bill Sudduth, 1987.

NATE: William Kahn (unpublished manuscript).

FOOTNOTE SOURCE: Police report, November 10, 1955; interviews with William Kahn, 1983, and Frank Gulotta, 1983.

310 BRUISES: Interviews with Dr. Jane Oldden, 1982, 1983, 1984.

21 AFTERMATH

317 FIRST HAND FROM ELSIE: Interviews with Douglas Griffin, 1982, Ann Cutler, 1984, and Liz Fondaras, 1986.

CUSHING FOOTNOTE SOURCE: Detective Division Supplementary Report, p. 41.

SCHIFF FOOTNOTE SOURCE: Detective Division Supplementary Report (interview by Lieutenant Koehl), November 20, 1955, p. 36; also, interview with Florynce Baker Martinau, 1986.

318 GUN DEATHS: Interviews with Florynce Baker Martinau, 1986, and Dorothy Schiff, 1985.

DISLIKE OF ANN: Interview with Robert Leylan, 1985.

LIBBY'S PREFERENCES: Interview with Bill Sudduth, 1984.

319 FALLING ASLEEP: Author's attendance at a party in the Newport home of Elizabeth Woodward Pratt, 1972.

LIBBY PRATT AND LEE PRINCIPE: Interview with Jody O'Neill, Lee Principe's grandson, 1985.

C. Z. GUEST'S CONDOLENCES: Newspaper accounts; interview with Mary Sanford, 1982.

"NORMAL READING": Interview with William Kahn, 1986.

"GRAND CONCOURSE": Interview with William Kahn, 1986, and his unpublished manuscript.

POOL CABANA: Police report, November 10, 1955.

22 NEVER AGAIN

321 DESCRIPTION OF PAUL WIRTHS: Interview with Detective Frank Steiner, 1984.

DRESSED AS A NURSE: Interview with Bill Sudduth, 1986; *Time* internal reporting file (Dave Murray reporting), November 1955.

POLICEMAN FROM NASSAU COUNTY: Interview with retired detective Richard Ebright, 1983.

"ANN CANNOT SLEEP": Interview with Richard Ebright, 1983.

"24–48 HOURS": *Newsday*, November 1, 1955.

322 "CONDITIONED REFLEX": *Time* internal reporting file, November 10, 1955.

"MY OWN LAWYER": Interview with Charles Wacker, 1987.

NURSE DISMISSED: Interview with Bill Sudduth, 1983.

ANN'S HEALTH: Interview with Dr. Jane Oldden, 1982.

"MOTHER'S" CALL: Interview with Bill Sudduth, 1984.

BEFORE THE SHOOTING: Interview with Charles Wacker, 1986.

323 HER SONS: Newspaper clippings, November 3, 1955.

"NOT A STRONG PERSON": Interview with Herschel Williams, 1981.

324 "WHAT AILS YOU": Interview with Sidney Mutum, 1982.

"MURDERED THE HORSE": Interview with Natalie Ittleson, 1987.

GUESTS FOOTNOTE SOURCE: Interview with Sidney Mutum, 1982.

325 SLEEPING PILLS: Interview with Bill Sudduth, 1984.

DEWEY HAD DECLINED: Interview with Jerry Finklestein, 1983.

325–26 GURFEIN: Interview with Saul Shames, 1984.

326 INNOCENT OF MURDER: Interview with Abby Gurfein Hellworth, 1984.

ANYTHING BUT AN ACCIDENT: Interview with Bill Sudduth, 1983.

COMMANDERS USUALLY SUPERVISED: Interview with Ferdinand Wendt, 1983.

SANFORD FOOTNOTE SOURCE: Interview with Mary Sanford, 1980.

328 "RIGHT OR WRONG": Interviews with detectives Tom Martin, Dan Stark, Andy Hebrerer, Ferdinand Wendt, and former district attorney William Kahn.

"YOU HAVE ME": Interviews with Paul Wirths, 1985, and Detective Frank Steiner, 1983, 1984; also, police report.

GERMAN-ACCENTED ENGLISH: Interview with Paul Wirths, 1985; Police and probation reports, 1954, 1955.

"NEIN, NEIN": Interview with Paul Wirths, 1985.

329 GAVE CREDIBILITY: Police report, November 15, 1955; interview with Frank Steiner, 1983.

333 ATTEMPTS TO KILL BILLY: Interview with Richard Zoerink, 1982.

EXCITED ABOUT THE PROWLER: Police report, November 5, 1955.

REASONS FOR MURDER: Cleveland Amory, *Life*, November 14, 1955.

"DETECTIVES SPYING": Birmingham, *Duchess*, 287.

334 BILLY WAS HOMOSEXUAL: Interviews with Tom Martin, 1985, 1986.

CASTE WAS CRUCIAL: Interview with Herschel Williams, 1981.

338 PAUL PROMISED STEINER: Interviews with Paul Wirths, 1985, and Frank Steiner, 1983, 1984.

KEPT GETTING BIGGER: Interviews with Frank Steiner and Paul Wirths, probation report, case #8149, individual #13553, March 1955; also, author's interview with Paul Wirths, 1986.

WOMAN'S WINDOW: Interviews with Paul Wirths, 1986, 1988.

LONG WINDOW: Police report, November 5, 1955.

"FEELING TOO SICK": Author's conversation with Jimmy Woodward, circa 1973.

ANN'S LAP: Interview with Lydia Smiley Wasson, 1982.

339 "GOOD CRY": New York *Herald-Tribune*, November 4, 1955.

"WHERE SHE CAME FROM": Interview with Diana Vreeland, 1985.

340 COVERING THE CASKET: Interview with Robert Leylan, 1982, 1983.

KILLED BILLY DELIBERATELY: Interview with Mary Sanford, 1981.

345 GIVE WIRTHS CREDIT: Interview with Frank Steiner, 1983.

HADN'T BEEN AN ACCIDENT: Interview with Robert Leylan, 1984.

346 DAILY VISITS: Interviews with Robert Leylan, 1983, 1984.

"POOR LITTLE BOYS": Interview with Robert Leylan, 1984.

SALACIOUS COLUMNS: Interview with Robert Leylan, 1983.

RECEPTION AREA: *Time* internal reporting file.

347 EVIDENCE TO INDICT: Interview with Harold Edgar, Columbia Law School, 1985.

348 CALM APPEARANCE: Interview with Robert Leylan, 1983.

LET THE BOYS GO: Interview with Robert Leylan, 1983.

GOSSIP ABOUT THE SHOOTING: Interviews with Robert Leylan, 1983, 1984.

RUMORS FOOTNOTE SOURCE: Interviews with Dorothy Schiff, 1984.

349 NEAR THE BOYS: Interview with Robert Leylan, 1984.

351 SCRAPBOOKS: Interview with Edna Cobb, 1987.

ELSIE'S CAMPAIGN: Interview with Robert Leylan, 1982.

SHE RUSHED HOME: Interview with John Richardson, 1982.

FOOTNOTE SOURCE: See Harold Danforth and James D. Moran, *The D.A.'s Man* (New York: Crown, 1957).

352 ELSIE CRIED: Interview with Robert Leylan, 1981.

HIS FATHER'S DEATH: Author's conversation with Jimmy Woodward, 1973.

KILLING HIS FATHER: Interview with Robert Leylan, 1983; author's conversation with Jimmy Woodward, 1973.

353 CHEEKS LOOKED HOLLOW: Interview with Jerome Zerbe, 1981.

ELOQUENT DEFENSE: New York *Herald-Tribune*, November 1955.

355 ELSIE MADE IT CLEAR: Interviews with Odette O'Higgins Hinton, 1981, 1984.

SHE AND JIMMY HAD COUNTED: Author's conversation with Jimmy Woodward, 1973.

356 WONDERFUL MARRIAGE: Interview with Dorothy Schiff, 1983.

357 SMALL BLACK CAP: Interview with Jacqueline Gebhard, 1982; *Newsday*, November 26, 1955.

TALKING TO BILLY: Interview with Bill Sudduth, 1986; *New York Times*, November 26, 1955.

TWENTY-TWO GRAND JURORS: Interviews with Tom Martin, 1987, 1988.

358 COUNTS OF BURGLARY: Interview with Paul Wirths, 1984.

ANN MURMURED: Interview with Bill Sudduth, 1986.

359 SISTERS THANKED HER: Interviews with Lydia Smiley Wasson and Edna Smiley Cobb, 1982, 1983.

23 EXILE

360 NOTORIOUS AMERICAN NEWCOMERS: Interview with Allen Tarwater West, 1985.

361 "ASSUMED NAME": Interviews with Herschel Williams, 1981, and Bill Sudduth, 1983.

PERFUME AND BATH POWDER: Author's conversation with Jimmy Woodward, 1973.

ELDERLY PASSENGERS: Howard Johnson, *The Cunard Story* (New York: Whitter Books, 1987).

363 BOYS HAD EATEN: Interview with Bill Sudduth, 1983.

364 TALKING ABOUT BILLY: Interview with Bill Sudduth, 1983.

PROUST AND MAUPASSANT: Interview with Umberto Goyen, 1986.

FOOTNOTE SOURCE: Natalie Robins and Steven M. Aronson, *Savage Grace* (New York: William Morrow and Company, 1985).

365 RELATIONSHIP WITH CASAS: New York *Daily News*, November, 9, 1956.

KILLING HER HUSBAND: Interview with Noel Behn, 1987.

366 DALÍ PORTRAIT: Interviews with Bill Sudduth, 1985, and Maria Esteban, 1989.

A GOOD EYE: Eden House incorporation papers and checkbooks, 1966–73.

HER OBSESSION: Interview with Bill Sudduth, 1983.

FOOTNOTE SOURCE: Interview with Robert Ellsworth, 1988.

367 "SELF-MADE WIDOW": Interview with Count Rudy Crespi, 1985.

PATTED HERSCHEL: Interviews with Eleanor Whitney McCullom, 1984, 1985, and Bill Sudduth, 1985.

368 "ABSOLUTELY NOT": Cholly Knickerbocker, *Journal-American*, April 1958; also, interview with Jerome Zerbe, 1984.

CONVICTED OF MURDER: Interview with Robert Leylan, 1985.

WHATEVER PEOPLE TOLD HER: Interview with M. Casellini, 1982.

369 FINALLY CONSENTED: Interview with Bill Sudduth, 1986.

BODY CAST: Interview with Bill Sudduth, 1985.

"BE DONE WITH IT": Interview with John Richardson, 1989.

370 33 MÉNDEZ NÚÑEZ: Interviews with Peter Townend, 1984, 1985.

NOTES ON PAINTINGS: Interview with Peter Townend, 1984.

ALMOST HUMAN: Interview with Bill Sudduth, 1985.

PURDEY SHOTGUN: Interview with George Neary, 1986.

371 "SHOOT STRAIGHT": Interviews with Len Puccinelli, 1983–87.

MISSED BOTH SHOTS: Interview with Joyce Coit, 1985.

SHE BACKED AWAY: Interview with Mrs. Stafford Sands, 1984.

372 "TAKEN LA MARYANA": Interview with Bill Sudduth, 1985.

373 CANCELED THE ENTIRE PARTY: Interviews with Robert Mosher, 1985, and Bill Sudduth, 1986.

374 JIMMY APOLOGIZED: Interview with Peter Townend, 1984.

376 CROQUES MONSIEURS AND WHITE SAUSAGES: Interview with Betty Sicre, 1985.

FOOTNOTE SOURCE: Letter from Claus Von Bülow, 1986; interview with John Richardson, 1985.

378 NUMEROUS AND DISORDERLY: Interview with Peter Townend, 1984.

379 FIFTEEN-YEAR-OLD JIMMY: Interview with Dorothy Gary, 1987.

PREFERRED HIS GRANDMOTHER: Interview with Lydia Smiley Wasson, 1984.

"IN TOWN FOR A WEEK": Interview with Dorothy Gary, 1987.

380 THEY PITIED HER: Interview with Abby Gurfein Hellworth, 1987.

24   ELSIE WOODWARD TRIUMPHANT

383 STIFF QUALITY: Interview with Irene Selznick, 1982.

LIVELY ARTS: Interview with Diana Vreeland, 1983.

GET GLOOMY: Interview with Mrs. Serge Obolensky, 1987.

SOUP COURSE: Interview with Diana Vreeland, 1981.

NO JUDGMENTS: Interview with Kenneth Jay Lane, 1982.

"HIT CHILDREN IN PUBLIC": Interview with Arlene Francis, 1988.

384 GORE VIDAL WAS DINING: Interviews with Richard Pollak and Kenneth Jay Lane, 1983.

FLIRTED ON THE TELEPHONE: Interview with Robert Leylan, 1982.

"SUSPECT THE WORST": Interview with Renee Link, 1986.

"MY BIRTHDAY": Interview with Gore Vidal, 1986.

"DON'T BE SILLY": Interview with Norman Mailer, 1989.

BEFORE SHE MARRIED: Interview with Bill Blass, 1987.

388 PEALS OF LAUGHTER: Interview with Diana Vreeland, 1984.

GREAT STYLE: Interviews with John Richardson, 1981, 1982.

EUROPEAN CITY: Interviews with Alison Aarons and Frank Zachary, 1982.

"I SUSPECT SO": Interview with Renee Link, 1986.

POLICE AND POLITICIANS: Interview with Norton Rosenbaum, 1986.

389 IN "SUZY": Interview with Aileen Mehle, 1982.

WENT OFF WITH PATRICK: Patrick O'Higgins, "Share the Sensuous Pleasures of Marrakesh with a Dear Friend," *Town & Country*, November, 1975.

390 SEVENTY-THREE CAME: Interview with Eleanor Lambert, 1988.

"EASIER THAN YOU THINK": Interview with Eleanor Lambert, 1988.

"A MURDERESS": Interview with Bill Sudduth, 1983.

25   A DEATH IN THE FAMILY

391 SLEEPING PILLS: Interview with Bill Sudduth, 1985.

WINDSWEPT ROCKS: Interview with Dorothy Gary, 1987.

392 STARING MEMBERS: Interviews with Tom Niepot, 1982, and Dorothy Gary, 1987.

IN FISTFIGHTS: Interview with Brian Muldoon, 1987.

POISON RETREATED: Interviews with Prince Egon von Furtstenberg, 1986, Brian Muldoon, 1984, and Betty Sicre, 1982.

"AFFAIR WITH HIS BUTLER": Interview with Bill Sudduth, 1985.

"EVERYBODY EQUAL": Letter from Jimmy Woodward.

UNTIL HIS DEATH: Interview with Anna de Nerciat and Count François de Nerciat, 1989.

"SHIP'S GRAVEYARD": Conversation with Jimmy Woodward, 1973; also, interview with Mr. and Mrs. Peter Kent, 1987.

393 OUTBOARD MOTOR: Interview with Henri de Beaumont, 1984.

FLAVIO WAS HOMOSEXUAL: Interviews with Peter Townend, 1986, and Peter Kent, 1987.

KASIMIR'S VOICE: Interview with Peter Kent, 1987.

TAKEN HIS PASSPORT: Interview with Brigite Desausseure, 1984.

394 "THAT'S HOW": Interview with Oscar Streuber, 1984.

COLONY CLUB: Letter from Jimmy Woodward.

URGED GUESTS: Interview with Brian Muldoon, 1987.

EASILY HURT: Interview with Prince Egon von Furstenberg, 1986.

BLEEDING FATHER: Conversation with Jimmy Woodward, circa 1973.

26 BLACKMAIL

395 FÖHR ISLAND: Interview with Paul Wirths, 1985.

397 "DON'T SEND HIM MONEY": Interview with Bill Sudduth, 1985.

398 LIGHT BULBS: Interview with Mrs. Geraldyn Redmond, 1984.

TWO BEDROOMS: Interview with Bill Sudduth, 1984.

"TO ADORN YOU": Interview with Valentine Lawford, 1984; see also Pierre Galante, *Mademoiselle Chanel* (Chicago: H. Regnery, 1973), 166.

CHANEL DISMISSED: Interview with Valentine Lawford, 1984.

"I DIDN'T KNOW": Interview with Marie Byrd, 1986.

"THREE WAYS": Interview with Larry Kaiser, 1988.

399 SOBBING: Interview with Bill Sudduth, 1984.

BRONCHITIS: Ann Woodward's notebooks, 1950–1955.

RUSSIAN FRIEND: Interview with Princess Adelaide Scherbatow, 1985.

400 SYMPATHY LETTERS: First drafts of letters.

400–401 REPORTER FOR THAT NEWSPAPER: Interview with Dorothy Schiff, 1985.

401 WILD SPENDING: Ann Woodward's notebooks, 1951–1953.

SPOONS FROM BELAIR: Interview with Bill Sudduth, 1986.

"ILLUSIONS ABOUT YOUR GRANDSON": Ann Woodward's notebooks, 1950–1955.

HIS ILLNESS: Interview with Robert Leylan, 1983.

ONLY FROM VIETNAM: Interview with Robert Leylan, 1983.

FANTASIES ABOUT MEN: Interview with Willard Morgan, 1986.

TEN BONES: Interview with Bill Sudduth, 1984.

402 NEVER BE RIGHT: Interview with Bill Sudduth, 1985.

UNDERPANTS: Interview with Brian Muldoon, 1985.

"MOST REMARKABLE OF ALL": Xaviera Hollander, *Xaviera: Her Continuing Adventures* (New York: Warner Books, 1973), 102.

"THE STORIES": Interview with Bill Sudduth, 1985.

403 TO BE A CARPENTER: Interviews with ex-girlfriend (name withheld by request), 1982, 1983, 1984.

"SEEMED PERFECTLY FINE": Interview with Brian Muldoon, 1985.

COUNTING PENNIES: Interview with Princess Giacci, 1984.

IN NEARBY MÁLAGA: Interview with Gavin Young, 1983.

404 ORDER OF SAINT ANDREW: John McAward Associates private detective report, 1974; and interview with Princess Adelaide Scherbatow, 1985.

405 "THERE'S TRUMAN CAPOTE": Interview with Joseph Lapatin, 1982.

"BANG-BANG": Interview with Joseph Lapatin, 1982.

PLOTTED TO MURDER HIM: Interview with John Richardson, 1982.

27   WANDERINGS

406 SHE WAS NAKED: Interview with Jo Zimmerman, 1984.

FOOTNOTE SOURCE: Interview with Joseph Lapatin, 1982.

407 SUBJECT WAS CLOSED: Dennis Rano (unpublished manuscript, copyright 1987); also, interview with Rano, 1987.

"RETURN TO MY FAMILY": Interview with and letter from Brian Mark, 1988.

ALL THE HEADWAITERS: Interview with Sam Taylor, 1984.

"ONLY WANT MY MONEY": Interviews with Sam Taylor, 1984, Bill Sudduth, 1986, Joyce Coit, 1983, and Len Puccinelli, 1983–87.

408 A LOT OF HIM IN MADRID: Interviews with Len Puccinelli, 1983–87.

WHAT ANN MIGHT DO: Interview with Sam Taylor, 1987.

BAD DIGESTION: Ann Woodward's notebooks, 1975.

409 PLASTIC SURGEON: Interview with Dr. Mary Markham, 1987.

RETURNED TOGETHER TO TAHITI: Ann Woodward's notebooks, 1953–1955.

JOYCE WOULD WAIT: Interviews with Joyce Coit, 1984, and Brian Mark, 1986.

DECIDED NOT TO SELL: Ann Woodward's notebooks, 1953, 1954.

VERY "DUBIOUS": Interview with Henry Geldzahler, 1986.

X-RAYED: Ann Woodward's notebooks, 1975.

410 PARK NEAR MACY'S: Interview with Joseph Lapatin, 1982.

INHALING THEM: Interview with Linda Karin, 1987.

HUNTING PRINTS: Interview with Monica Randall, 1983.

411 NOVEMBER ISSUE OF ESQUIRE: Interviews with Bill Sudduth, 1984, Gordon Lish, 1983, and Don Ericson, 1981.

412 "THE POORHOUSE": Interview with Chayan Kim, 1984.

DUPLEX SEEMED EMPTY: Interviews with Pam Stevens, secretary to Ann Woodward, 1984, and Chayan Kim, 1986.

FLED HER APARTMENT: Interviews with Bill Sudduth, 1984, and Jimmy Darrow, 1985.

413 SURROUNDED BY FLOWERS: Interview with Lydia Smiley Wasson, 1981.

414 POINTING TO THE PHOTOGRAPHS: Interview with Lydia Smiley Wasson, 1981.

FINAL RESTING PLACE: Interview with Joseph Lapatin, 1982.

"WORRY ABOUT THAT": Interview with Robert Ellsworth, 1988.

FOOTNOTE SOURCE: Interview with Bill Sudduth, 1984.

415 TOO TALKATIVE: Interview with Bill Sudduth, 1984.

EPILOGUE

416 A SABLE COAT: Interviews with Bill Sudduth, 1984, Ann Slater, 1983, Princess Adelaide Scherbatow, 1983, Barbara Rockefeller, 1984, and Chayan Kim, 1984.

LIKE A GUILTY PERSON: Interview with Robert Leylan, 1983.

ALCOHOL, HEROIN, AND COCAINE: Interview with Larry Kaiser, 1987.

417 TAKEN TO A HOSPITAL: Interview with Larry Kaiser, 1987.

CLOSED THE MATTER: Interviews with Renee Link and Monica Davis, 1989.

STICKLIKE ARMS: Interview with Monica Davis, 1989.

418 "MY GRANDSON IS ILL": Interview with Monica Davis, 1989.

SUFFERED A MILD HEART ATTACK: Interviews with Monica Davis and Renee Link, 1989.

422 "WAITING TO DIE": Interviews with Odette Hinton, 1981, and Irene Selznick, 1980.

O'HIGGINS BEGAN TO COUGH: Interview with Roz Cole, 1980.

NURSED HER DYING HUSBAND: Interviews with John Richardson, 1980, 1981, and Renee Link, 1989.

"LEAVE THEM DOWNSTAIRS": Interview with Odette O'Higgins Hinton, 1981.

423 "THE RIDE IN": Interview with Robert Leylan, 1983.

"JUST SINKING": Interview with Eleanor Howard, 1988.

"HURTS OTHER PEOPLE": Interview with Renee Link, 1989.

BIBLIOGRAPHY

Adams, Henry. *The Education of Henry Adams: An Autobiography.* Boston: Massachusetts Historical Society, 1918.

Adams, Henry H. *Years of Expectation: Guadalcanal to Normandy.* New York: David McKay Company, 1973.

Ainslie, Tom. *Ainslie's Complete Guide to Thoroughbred Racing: Revised and Updated.* New York: Simon & Schuster, 1979.

Amory, Cleveland. *The Last Resorts.* New York: Harper & Brothers, 1952.

——. *Who Killed Society?* New York: Harper & Brothers, 1960.

Auchincloss, Louis. *The Rector of Justin.* Boston: Houghton Mifflin Company, 1964.

——. *A Writer's Capital.* Boston: Houghton Mifflin Company, 1979.

Baker, Grenville. *Last Will and Testament.* Probated 1949.

Baldwin, Billy. *Billy Baldwin Remembers.* New York: Harcourt Brace Jovanovich, 1974.

Baldwin, Billy, and Michael Gardine. *Billy Baldwin: An Autobiography.* Boston: Little, Brown and Company, 1985.

Baldwin, Hanson W. *The Crucial Years 1939–1941.* New York: Harper & Row, 1976.

Balsan, Consuelo Vanderbilt. *The Glitter and the Gold.* New York: Harper & Brothers, 1952.

Baltz, Shirley Vlasak. *A Chronicle of Belair.* Bowie, Md.: Bowie Heritage Committee, 1984.

Barnouw, Erik. *The Golden Web: A History of Broadcasting in the United States, 1933–1953.* New York: Oxford University Press, 1968.

Barrymore, Ethel. *Memories: An Autobiography.* London: Hulton Press, 1956.

Beaverbrook, Lord. *The Abdication of King Edward VIII.* New York: Atheneum, 1966.

Birmingham, Stephen. *Duchess: The Story of Wallis Warfield Windsor.* Boston: Little, Brown and Company, 1981.

——. *The Right People.* Boston: Little, Brown and Company, 1968.

——. *The Right Places (For the Right People).* Boston: Little, Brown and Company, 1973.

Black, David. *The King of Fifth Avenue*. New York: Dial Press, 1981.

Bloch, Michael, ed. *The Intimate Correspondence of the Duke and Duchess of Windsor*. New York: Avon Books, 1988.

Bosburg, W. S. *Cherished Portraits of Thoroughbred Horses*. New York: Derrydale Press, 1929.

Breslin, Jimmy. *Sunny Jim*. Garden City, N.Y.: Doubleday & Company, 1962.

Brody, Iles. *Gone with the Windsors*. Philadelphia: John C. Winston Company, 1953.

Browder, Clifford. *The Money Game in Old New York*. Lexington: University Press of Kentucky, 1986.

Brown, Angela. *When Battered Women Kill*. New York: Free Press, 1987.

Bryan, J., III, and Charles J. V. Murphy. *The Windsor Story*. New York: William Morrow and Company, 1979.

Buchanan, Mariel. *Ann of Austria: The Infanta Queen*. London: Hutchinson & Company, 1937.

Byron, Joseph. *Photographs of New York Interiors at the Turn of the Century*. Text by Clay Lancaster. New York: Dover Publications, 1976.

Caffrey, Nancy. *Hanover's Wishing Star*. New York: E. P. Dutton & Company, 1956.

Cameron, Deborah, and Elizabeth Frazer. *The Lust to Kill*. New York: New York University Press, 1987.

Capote, Truman. *Answered Prayers: The Unfinished Novel*. New York: Random House, 1987.

——. *In Cold Blood*. New York: Random House, 1965.

Carosso, Vincent P. *Investment Banking in America*. Cambridge: Harvard University Press, 1970.

Carr, Harry. *Queen's Jockey*. London: Stanley Paul, 1966.

Carr, Virginia Spenser. *The Lonely Hunter: A Biography of Carson McCullers*. New York: Carroll & Graf Publishers, 1985.

Cassini, Igor, with Jeanne Molli. *I'd Do It All Over Again*. New York: G. P. Putnam's Sons, 1977.

Charlton, Warwick, and Judge Gerald Sparrow. "The Profumo Affair," *Today Magazine*, 1963.

Choate, Joseph Hodges. *Arguments and Addresses*. Ed. Frederick C. Hicks. With a memorial by Elihu Root. St. Paul, Minn.: West Publishing Company, 1926.

Churchill, Winston S. *The Second World War: The Grand Alliance*. Cambridge: Riverside Press, 1950.

——. *The Second World War: The Hinge of Fate*. Cambridge: Riverside Press, 1950.

——. *The Second World War: Triumph and Tragedy*. Cambridge: Riverside Press, 1950.

Clarke, Gerald. *Capote*. New York: Simon & Schuster, 1988.

Clayton, Merle. *Union Station Massacre: The Shootout That Started the FBI's War on Crime*. Indianapolis: Bobbs Merrill Company, 1978.

Cole, Lesley. *Remembered Laughter: The Life of Noël Coward*. New York: Alfred A. Knopf, 1977.

Coleman, Elizabeth Ann. *The Genius of Charles James*. New York: Brooklyn Museum, 1982.

Collis, Maurice. *Nancy Astor: An Informal Biography.* New York: E. P. Dutton & Company, 1960.

Corry, John. *Golden Clan: The Murrays, the McDonnells, and the Irish American Aristocracy.* Boston: Houghton Mifflin Company, 1977.

Cowles, Virginia. *Edward VII and His Circle.* London: Hamish Hamilton, 1956.

Curling, Bill. *The Captain: A Biography of Captain Sir Cecil Boyd-Rochfort, Royal Trainer.* London: Barrie & Jenkins, 1970.

Danforth, Harold, and James D. Moran. *The D.A.'s Man.* New York: Crown Publishers, 1957.

Davis, Richard Harding. *About Paris.* New York: Harper & Brothers Publishers, 1895.

Decies, Elizabeth Wharton. *"King Lehr" and the Gilded Age.* Philadelphia: J. B. Lippincott Company, 1935.

Devi, Gayatri, Maharani of Jaipur, with Santha Rama Rau. *A Princess Remembers: The Memoirs of the Maharani of Jaipur.* Philadelphia: J. B. Lippincott Company, 1976.

Diliberto, Gioia. *Debutante: The Story of Brenda Frazier.* New York: Alfred A. Knopf, 1987.

Donaldson, Frances. *Edward VIII.* Philadelphia: J. B. Lippincott Company, 1975.

Dorset, Lyle W. *The Pendergast Machine.* Lincoln: University of Nebraska Press, 1968.

Drutman, Irving, ed. *Janet Flanner's World: Uncollected Writings, 1932–1975.* New York: Harcourt Brace Jovanovich, 1979.

Dumas, Alexandre. *The Three Musketeers.* New York: Penguin Books, 1952.

Dunne, Dominick. *The Two Mrs. Grenvilles.* New York: Crown Publishers, 1985.

Farrell, Frank. *The Greatest of Them All.* New York: K. S. Giniger Company, 1982.

Federal Bureau of Investigation File #100–4714. Investigation into the activities of Alicia and Grenville Baker.

Finder, Joseph. *Red Carpet.* New York: Rinehart Winston, 1983.

Fitzgerald, F. Scott. *The Great Gatsby.* New York: Charles Scribner's Sons, 1925.

———. "The Little Rich Boy." *Babylon Revisited and Other Stories.* New York: Charles Scribner's Sons, 1971.

Galante, Pierre. *Mademoiselle Chanel.* Translated by Eileen and Jessie Wood. Chicago: H. Regnery, 1973.

Galbraith, John Kenneth. *Money: Whence It Came, Where It Went.* Boston: Houghton Mifflin Company, 1975.

Galsworthy, John. *The Forsyte Saga.* New York: Charles Scribner's Sons, 1928.

———. *The Man of Property.* New York: Charles Scribner's Sons, 1918.

Goldsmith, Barbara. *Little Gloria . . . Happy at Last.* New York: Alfred A. Knopf, 1980.

Hall, Thomas W. *History of Severn Parrish.* Unpublished manuscript.

Higham, Charles. *The Duchess of Windsor: The Secret Life.* New York: McGraw-Hill, 1988.

The History of Stevens County and Its People. Stevens County History Association. Hugoton, Kans.: Lowell Press, 1979.

Hollander, Xaviera. *Xaviera: Her Continuing Adventures.* New York: Warner Books, 1973.

Houston, David. *Jazz Baby.* New York: St. Martin's Press, 1983.

Huvos, Eva C. *No Risk, No Fun: The Reminiscences of Baron Hubert von Pantz as Told to Eva C. Huvos.* New York: Vantage Press, 1986.

James, Henry. *The American*. New York: Viking Penguin, 1981.

Johnson, Howard. *The Cunard Story*. New York: Whitter Books, 1987.

Kahn, William. Unpublished manuscript, 1983.

Kelly, Liz. *Surviving Sexual Violence*. Minneapolis: University of Minnesota Press, 1988.

Kleinman, Ruth. *Anne of Austria: Queen of France*. Columbus: Ohio State University Press, 1986.

Knightley, Phillip, and Caroline Kennedy. *An Affair of State: The Profumo Case and the Framing of Stephen Ward*. New York: Atheneum, 1987.

Lapham, Lewis H. *Money and Class in America: Notes and Observations on Our Civil Religion*. New York: Weidenfeld & Nicolson, 1988.

Landes, David S. *Bankers and Pashas*. Cambridge: Harvard University Press, 1958.

Langhorne, Elizabeth. *Nancy Astor and Her Friends*. New York: Praeger Publishers, 1974.

Lefevre, Edwin. *Reminiscences of a Stock Operator*. Burlington, Vt.: Books of Wall Street, 1980.

Leslie, Anita. *Edwardians in Love*. London: Hutchinson, 1972.

——. *Lady Randolph Churchill: The Story of Jennie Jerome*. New York: Charles Scribner's Sons, 1969.

Lillie, Beatrice, written with James Brough. *Every Other Inch a Lady*. Aided and abetted by John Philip. Garden City, N.Y.: Doubleday, 1972.

Loewy, Raymond. *The Designs of Raymond Loewy*. Published for the Renwick Gallery of the National Collection of Fine Arts. Washington, D.C.: Smithsonian Institution Press, 1975.

Marlowe, Derek. *Nancy Astor*. New York: Dell Publishing Company, 1984.

Marquand, John P. *H. M. Pulham, Esquire*. Chicago: Academy Chicago Publishers, 1986.

Martin, Edward Sanford. *Ambassador Choate: The Life of Joseph Hodges Choate, as gathered chiefly from his letters including his own story of his boyhood*. New York: Charles Scribner's Sons, 1920.

Matthew, Christopher. *A Different World: Stories of the Great Hotels*. London: Paddington Press, 1975.

Maxwell, Elsa. *The Celebrity Circus*. New York: Appleton-Century, 1963.

——. *How To Do It, or The Lively Art of Entertaining*. Boston: Little, Brown and Company, 1957.

——. *R.S.V.P. Elsa Maxwell's Own Story*. Boston: Little, Brown and Company, 1954.

Menkes, Suzy. *The Windsor Style*. Boston: Salem House Publishers, 1988.

Meyer, Anton. *The Last Convertible*. New York: G. P. Putnam's Sons, 1978.

Flora Whitney Miller: Her Life, Her World. Ed. Whitney Museum of Art. New York: Whitney Museum of Art, 1987.

Morison, Samuel Eliot. *History of the United States Naval Operations in World War II*. Boston: Little, Brown and Company, 1968.

——. *The Two-Ocean War: A Short History of the United States Navy in the Second World War*. Boston: Little, Brown and Company, 1963.

Mure, David. *The Last Temptation*. London: Buchan and Enright, 1984.

Myers, Gustavus. *History of the Great American Fortunes*. New York: Random House, 1947.

Nassau County Department of Records. Leases to the Playhouse, Sunken Orchard, and Ann Woodward's property in the vicinity of the McCann estate.

Nassau County District Attorney's Office. Investigation into the Death of William Woodward, Jr., October 31, 1955.

Nassau County Police Department. Probation report, Paul Wirths, case #8149, individual #13553, March 1955.

O'Higgins, Patrick. *Madame: An Intimate Biography of Helena Rubinstein.* New York: Viking Press, 1971.

Pearson, John. *The Life of Ian Fleming.* New York: McGraw-Hill, 1966.

Peckham, Ted. *Gentleman for Hire.* Hollywood, Fla.: Frederick Fell, 1954.

Peters, Margot. *Mrs. Pat.* New York: Alfred A. Knopf, 1984.

Pier, Arthur Stanwood. *The Story of Harvard.* Boston: Little, Brown and Company, 1913.

Ponsonby, F. *Recollections of Three Reigns.* London, 1951.

Porzelt, Paul. *The Metropolitan Club of New York.* New York: Rizzoli, 1982.

Powers, John Robert. *The Powers Girls.* New York: E. P. Dutton, 1941.

Randall, Monica. *The Mansions of Long Island's Gold Coast.* New York: Hastings House, 1979.

Rasponi, Lanfranco. *The International Nomads.* New York: G. P. Putnam's Sons, 1966.

Reddig, William M. *Tom's Town: Kansas City and the Pendergast Legend.* Philadelphia: J. B. Lippincott Company, 1947.

"The Residence of William Woodward, Esq. New York City, Delano & Aldrich Architects, New York." *The Architectural Record,* April 1919.

Rhodes, Dr. Sonya, and Dr. Martin S. Potash. *Cold Feet: Why Men Don't Commit.* New York: E. P. Dutton, 1988.

Robins, Natalie, and Steven M. Aronson. *Savage Grace.* New York: William Morrow and Company, 1985.

Roosevelt, Felicia Warburg. *Doers and Dowagers.* New York: Doubleday, 1975.

Rostron, Phil, additional material by Richard Onslow. *Henry Cecil: On the Level.* London: Harrap, 1983.

Sampson, Anthony. *The Money Lenders.* New York: Viking Press, 1982.

Saroyan, Aram. *Trio: Portrait of an Intimate Friendship, Oona Chaplin, Carol Matthau, Gloria Vanderbilt.* New York: Simon & Schuster, 1985.

Secrest, Meryle. *Salvador Dalí: A Biography.* New York: E. P. Dutton, 1987.

"A Selection from the Works of Delano & Aldrich, New York." *The Architectural Record,* July 1923.

Sherwood, Robert E. *Abe Lincoln in Illinois.* New York: Dramatists' Play Service, 1937.

Shields, William X. *Bigger Than Life: A Biography of Francis X. Shields.* New York: Freundlich Books, 1986.

Slide, Anthony. *Great Radio Personalities in Historic Photographs.* New York: Dover Publications, 1982.

Social Register 1985. New York: Social Register Association, 1984.

Sollors, Werner. *Beyond Ethnicity: Consent and Descent in American Culture.* New York: Oxford University Press, 1986.

Spender, Percy. *Politics and a Man.* Sydney, Australia: William Collins, 1972.

Steel, Ronald. *Walter Lippmann and the American Century.* Boston: Atlantic Monthly Press, 1980.

Stratton, Joanna L. *Pioneer Women: Voices from the Kansas Frontier.* New York: Simon & Schuster, 1982.

Summers, Anthony, and Stephen Dorril. *Honeytrap.* London: Weidenfeld & Nicolson, 1987.

Sutton, Denys. *Fads and Fancies.* New York: Wittenborn, 1979.

Thomas, Bob. *Joan Crawford.* New York: Simon & Schuster, 1978.

Thompson, Jacqueline. *The Very Rich Book.* New York: William Morrow and Company, 1981.

Townend, Peter. *Out of Focus.* London: Macmillan and Company, 1971.

Townsend, Reginald T. *God Packed My Picnic Basket: Reminiscences of the Golden Age of Newport and New York.* New York: Hastings House, 1970.

United States Navy Report. "Sinking of USS *Liscome Bay,* Rough Log" (Secret), 1943.

——. USS *Saratoga,* "Report of War Operations in Rescue of USS *Liscome Bay*" (Classified), December 8, 1943.

——. "Chronological Sequence of Events 1600–1847," File #A16–3, November 24, 1943.

——. USS *Liscome Bay,* Statement of William Woodward, Jr., Ens. D-V (G), November 25, 1943.

Vanderbilt, Cornelius, Jr. *Queen of the Golden Age: The Fabulous Grace Wilson Vanderbilt.* New York: McGraw-Hill, 1956.

Vanderbilt, Gloria. *Once Upon a Time: A True Story.* New York: Alfred A. Knopf, 1985.

Waller, George. *Saratoga: Saga of an Impious Era.* Englewood Cliffs, N.J.: Prentice-Hall, 1966.

Warfield, J. D. *The Founders of Anne Arundel and Howard Counties, Maryland: A Genealogical and Biographical Review From Wills, Deeds and Church Records.* Baltimore: Regional Printing Company, 1967.

Weber, Max. *The Protestant Ethic and the Spirit of Capitalism.* New York: Charles Scribner's Sons, 1930.

Wector, Dixon. *The Saga of American Society: A Record of Social Aspiration, 1607–1937.* New York: Charles Scribner's Sons, 1937.

Welch, Ned. *Who's Who in Thoroughbred Racing.* New York: Vantage Press, 1962.

West, Robert Craig. *Banking Reform and the Federal Reserve, 1863–1923.* Ithaca, N.Y.: Cornell University Press, 1977.

Wetmore, Judge William. *The Wetmore Memorial, A Genealogical Record of the Wetmore Family.* Boston, 1792.

Wharton, Edith. *The Age of Innocence.* New York: Macmillan Publishing Company, 1920.

——. *A Backward Glance.* New York: Charles Scribner's Sons, 1934.

——. *The Custom of the Country.* New York: Charles Scribner's Sons, 1913.

Wheeler, William Ogden. Edited by Lawrence and Ogden Van Alstyne and the Reverend Charles Burr. *John Ogden, The Pilgrim and His Descendants, Their History, Biography, and Genealogy.* Philadelphia: J. B. Lippincott Company, 1907.

Wilde, Oscar. *The Picture of Dorian Gray and Other Writings.* Ed. Richard Ellmann. New York: Bantam Books, 1982.

——. *Plays of Oscar Wilde,* vol. 2. Boston: John W. Luce & Company, 1905.

Wilder, Laura Ingalls. *These Happy Golden Years.* New York: Harper & Brothers, 1943.

Wining, Dining, and Dancing in New York. United States Armed Services, 1944.

Whitney, Marylou. *Cornelia Vanderbilt Whitney's Dollhouse.* New York: Farrar, Straus & Giroux, 1976.

Wodehouse, P. G. *Carry On, Jeeves.* New York: George H. Doran, 1916.

——. *The Ice in the Bedroom.* New York: Simon & Schuster, 1961.

——. *Meet Mr. Mulliner.* New York: Penguin Books, 1962.

——. *The Small Bachelor.* New York: Penguin Books, 1987.

Woodward, Ann. Last Will and Testament. Probated 1976.

——. Notebooks and Journals, 1965–75.

Woodward, Elsie. Last Will and Testament. Probated 1982.

Woodward, James T. Last Will and Testament. Probated 1910.

Woodward, James T. Last Will and Testament. Probated 1977.

Woodward, William. *Gallant Fox: A Memoir.* New York: Derrydale Press, 1931.

——. *Andrew Jackson, Africanus: A Memoir.* New York: Derrydale Press, 1938.

Woodward, William, Sr. Last Will and Testament. Probated 1953.

Woodward, William, Jr. Last Will and Testament. Probated 1955.

Wright, Harold Bell. *The Printer of Udells.* Pittsburg, Kans., 1902.

NEWSPAPERS AND MAGAZINES

Cincinnati *Enquirer*, *The Grotonian*, Kansas City *Star*, *Life*, *McClure's Magazine*, New York *Herald*, *The New York Review of Books*, *The New York Times*, *The New York Times Magazine*, *Outing*, *Theater Arts Monthly*, *Time*, *Town Topics*, *Variety*, *The Wall Street Journal*, Westport *Crier* (Newspaper of Westport High School, Kansas City), Wichita *Eagle*

INDEX

PERMISSIONS
ACKNOWLEDGMENTS

PHOTOGRAPHIC CREDITS

page 29, top: Courtesy Kansas State Manual Training Normal School

page 29, bottom: Courtesy William Sudduth

page 30, top and bottom: Courtesy Westport (Kansas) High School Yearbook

page 53, top: Courtesy Manufacturers Hanover Bank

page 53, middle and bottom: Courtesy the Belair Museum

page 54, top: Courtesy Robert Leylan

page 54, bottom: Courtesy Manufacturers Hanover Bank

page 61, top: Courtesy Rudolph Schirmer

page 61, bottom, and page 62, top and bottom: Courtesy Jerome Zerbe

page 77: Courtesy Edward Patterson

page 78: The Bettmann Archive

page 79, top: Courtesy Jerome Zerbe

page 79, bottom: Courtesy Turf Pictures

page 80, top: Courtesy Jerome Zerbe

page 80, bottom: The Bettmann Archive

page 99: The Billy Rose Collection, The New York Public Library at Lincoln Center

page 100, top: The Kobal Collection

page 100, bottom: Performing Arts Research Center, The New York Public Library at Lincoln Center

page 101: Performing Arts Research Center, The New York Public Library at Lincoln Center

page 102, top: Courtesy Telde Getz

page 103, bottom: Courtesy the Estate of Malcolm Milligan

page 127, top: The Kobal Collection

page 127, bottom, and page 128, top: Courtesy the Museum of Thoroughbred Racing

page 128, bottom: Courtesy *The Bloodborse Magazine*

page 134: The Bettmann Archive

page 165: Courtesy Fashion Institute of Technology

page 166, top: Courtesy Jerome Zerbe

page 166, bottom: Courtesy Lydia Smiley Wasson

page 175, top: Courtesy Jerome Zerbe

page 175, bottom: The Bettmann Archive

pages 176 and 177: Courtesy Jerome Zerbe

page 178: The Bettmann Archive

page 183: Nassau County Police Archives

page 189: Courtesy Jerome Zerbe

page 190: Courtesy William Sudduth

page 200: The Bettmann Archive

page 205: Courtesy Jerome Zerbe

page 206, top, left, and right: Courtesy Jerome Zerbe

page 206, bottom: Courtesy Sally Parsons Oriel

page 207, bottom: Courtesy the Museum of Thoroughbred Racing

page 225: Courtesy Russell Havenstrite

page 226: Courtesy Sally Parsons Oriel

pages 237, 238, 275, and 276: Courtesy Jerome Zerbe

pages 311, 312, and 313 (top): Nassau County Police Archives

page 313, bottom: The New York Times

pages 314 and 315 (top): The Bettmann Archive

page 315, bottom: The New York Times

page 327: Nassau County Police Archives

page 341: Associated Press

page 342: The Bettmann Archive

page 343, top: Associated Press

page 343, bottom: Courtesy the Museum of Thoroughbred Racing

pages 385 and 386: The Bettmann Archive

page 387: Courtesy Jerome Zerbe

page 419: Courtesy Retired Oyster Bay Cove Police Officer Russell Haff

page 420, top: The New York Times

page 420, bottom: Courtesy Willard Morgan

page 421: Courtesy Jerome Zerbe

A NOTE ON THE TYPE

This book was set in Janson, a recutting made direct from type cast from matrices long thought to have been made by the Dutchman Anton Janson, who was a practicing type founder in Leipzig during the years 1668–1687. However, it has been conclusively demonstrated that these types are actually the work of Nicholas Kis (1650–1702), a Hungarian, who most probably learned his trade from the master Dutch type founder Dirk Voskens. The type is an excellent example of the influential and sturdy Dutch types that prevailed in England up to the time William Caslon (1692–1766) developed his own incomparable designs from them.

Composed by Creative Graphics, Inc.,
Allentown, Pennsylvania

Printed and bound by Halliday Lithographers,
West Hanover, Massachusetts

Designed by Cassandra J. Pappas